CW01238543

HANDBOOK OF RESEARCH ON IPOS

Handbook of Research on IPOs

Edited by

Mario Levis

Emeritus Professor of Finance, Cass Business School, City University London, UK

Silvio Vismara

Associate Professor, University of Bergamo, Italy

Edward Elgar
Cheltenham, UK • Northampton, MA, USA

© Mario Levis and Silvio Vismara 2013

All rights reserved. No part of this publication may be reproduced, stored in a retrieval system or transmitted in any form or by any means, electronic, mechanical or photocopying, recording, or otherwise without the prior permission of the publisher.

Published by
Edward Elgar Publishing Limited
The Lypiatts
15 Lansdown Road
Cheltenham
Glos GL50 2JA
UK

Edward Elgar Publishing, Inc.
William Pratt House
9 Dewey Court
Northampton
Massachusetts 01060
USA

A catalogue record for this book
is available from the British Library

Library of Congress Control Number: 2013938070

This book is available electronically in the ElgarOnline.com
Economics Subject Collection, E-ISBN 978 1 78195 537 6

ISBN 978 1 78195 536 9 (cased)

Typeset by Servis Filmsetting Ltd, Stockport, Cheshire
Printed and bound in Great Britain by T.J. International Ltd, Padstow

Contents

List of contributors	ix
Preface	xix

Introduction	1
Mario Levis and Silvio Vismara	

PART I   WHY AND WHEN FIRMS GO PUBLIC

1	Economies of scope and IPO activity in Europe *Jay R. Ritter, Andrea Signori and Silvio Vismara*	11
2	The decline in venture-backed IPOs: implications for capital recovery *Susan Chaplinsky and Swasti Gupta-Mukherjee*	35
3	Survey evidence: what do we know about European and US firms' motivations for going public? *Franck Bancel and Usha R. Mittoo*	57
4	IPO waves and hot markets in the UK *Shantanu Banerjee, Ufuk Güçbilmez and Grzegorz Pawlina*	76

PART II   PREPARATION FOR THE IPO

5	IPO offer price selection, institutional subscription, and the value of the firm: theory and evidence *Chitru S. Fernando, Vladimir A. Gatchev and Paul A. Spindt*	101
6	The Canadian junior IPO market and the Capital Pool Company program *J. Ari Pandes and Michael J. Robinson*	124
7	Investor protection and IPO survival in the Italian stock market *Mattia Cattaneo and Michele Meoli*	141
8	Underwriter reputation, bookbuilding and IPO duration *Hugh M.J. Colaco and Shantaram P. Hegde*	159

PART III   TRANSACTION STRUCTURE AND GOVERNANCE AT THE IPO

9	Corporate governance in newly listed companies *David B. Audretsch and Erik E. Lehmann*	179

vi *Contents*

10 The allotment of IPO shares: placing strategies between retail versus institutional investors 207
Fabio Bertoni, Matteo Bonaventura and Giancarlo Giudici

11 VC investment timing and IPO pricing 219
Jean-Sébastien Michel

12 The underwriters of IPOs in Europe's second markets 237
Katrin Migliorati and Stefano Paleari

PART IV   TRADING IN THE AFTERMARKET

13 Orphan versus non-orphan IPOs: the difference analyst coverage makes 257
Romain Boissin

14 Do directors trade after IPO lockup expiry? 275
Susanne Espenlaub, Marc Goergen, Arif Khurshed and Marko Remenar

15 Venture capital and IPO waves in Europe: an analysis of firm and performance characteristics 295
Wolfgang Bessler and Martin Seim

16 IPO pricing and ownership structure: the business-group effect 327
Aharon Cohen Mohliver, Gitit Gur-Gershgorn and Shinjinee Chattopadhyay

PART V   THE AFTERMARKET PERFORMANCE OF IPOS

17 Acquisitions, SEOs, divestitures and IPO performance 347
Naaguesh Appadu, Anna Faelten and Mario Levis

18 Private equity, RLBOs and IPO performance 375
Jerry Cao

19 The impact of venture capital/private equity investment on the performance of IPOs in Australia 400
Sian Owen and Jo-Ann Suchard

20 Development in financial markets and the performance of German IPOs 421
Dimitrios Gounopoulos and Johannes Hoebelt

PART VI   SPECIAL TYPES OF IPOS

21 The IPO as an exit strategy for venture capitalists: regional lessons from Canada with international comparisons 465
Douglas Cumming and Sofia Johan

22 Choice between alternative routes to go public: backdoor listing versus IPO 503
Philip Brown, Andrew Ferguson and Peter Lam

23 An empirical analysis of cross-listing decisions in share-issue privatizations: evidence from developed and developing countries 531
Juliet D'Souza, William L. Megginson and Robert Nash

24 How bank health affects the capital structure and performance of IPO firms: evidence from the Japanese financial crisis in the 1990s 552
Kazuo Yamada

Index 569

Contributors

Naaguesh Appadu is a Research Fellow of the M&A Research Centre and a member of the Faculty of Finance at Cass Business School. His research focus relates to general corporate finance more specifically to merger and acquisition (M&A), IPO, capital structure and corporate governance. He has previously taught finance courses at Middlesex University Business School. Naaguesh was Research Analyst at Mergermarket, responsible for forecasting new M&A deals and also worked at the State Bank of Mauritius as an analyst in the Value-Based Performance Management team and was also a freelance advisor for small firms in Mauritius.

David B. Audretsch is a Distinguished Professor and Ameritech Chair of Economic Development at Indiana University, where he also serves as Director of the Institute for Development Strategies. He is an Honorary Professor of Industrial Economics and Entrepreneurship at the WHU-Otto Beisheim School of Management in Germany. In addition, he serves as a Visiting Professor at the King Saud University in Saudi Arabia, Honorary Professor at the Friedrich Schiller University of Jena in Germany, and is a Research Fellow of the Centre for Economic Policy Research in London. Audretsch's research has focused on the links between entrepreneurship, government policy, innovation, economic development and global competitiveness. His research has been published in over 100 scholarly articles in leading academic journals. He is co-founder and co-editor of *Small Business Economics*. In 2008, he received an honorary doctorate degree from the University of Augsburg, and in September, 2010 he received an honorary doctorate degree from Jönköping University.

Franck Bancel is Professor at ESCP Europe (France). He received a PhD (Grenoble II) and is Habilité à Diriger des Recherches (Paris IX Dauphine). Professor Bancel has published several books including *Fusions d'Entreprises* (Eyrolles, 2008), *Choix des Investissements* (Economica, 2002), and articles in academic journals such as *Journal of Applied Corporate Finance*, *Financial Management* and *European Financial Management*. He has published several articles with Professor Mittoo comparing European firm financial practices with their US peers and measuring distances between theories and practices. Professor Bancel was Associate Dean for research from 2002 to 2006 and Director of the ESCP Europe PhD program of the Paris campus from 2003 to 2006.

Shantanu Banerjee joined Lancaster University as a faculty member in 2005 after completing his doctoral degree in finance from Hong Kong University of Science and Technology. His research is mainly empirical and focuses on capital structure, equity issuance, investment decisions of firms, cash holding and the role of stakeholders. He has published in well-respected journals including the *Journal of Finance*. He has designed and taught a wide range of undergraduate and postgraduate courses over the years. Before starting his doctoral studies, he has completed a master's degree in economics in Jawaharlal Nehru University, India.

Fabio Bertoni, PhD, CFA®, is Associate Professor of Corporate Finance at EMLYON Business School. His research activity focuses on the relationship between financing and firm performance, new listings, venture capital and entrepreneurship. Recently he has also studied sovereign wealth fund investments. He visited the Copenhagen Business School, Universidad Computense de Madrid, Centre for European Economic Research (ZEW) in Mannheim and the University of Oxford – Said Business School. He acted as project manager in the project funded by the EU: VICO – Financing Entrepreneurial Ventures in Europe: Impact on Innovation, Employment Growth, and Competitiveness.

Wolfgang Bessler is Professor of Finance and Banking at Justus-Liebig-University in Giessen. Previously, he was a faculty member at Syracuse University, at Rensselaer Polytechnic Institute, and Hamburg University. His research interests are in corporate finance, financial markets and institutions, and asset management. In corporate finance he focuses on venture capital, IPOs, capital structure and M&As. His research has been published in the *Journal of Banking and Finance*, *European Financial Management*, *European Journal of Operational Research* and *Journal of International Financial Markets, Institutions & Money*. He serves on the editorial board of various international finance journals including the *European Journal of Finance*, *Journal of Multinational Financial Management* and *Financial Markets and Portfolio Management*.

Romain Boissin is an Associate Professor of Finance at Ecole Superieure de Gestion (ESG) Management School, Paris, France. His recent research focuses on IPOs, analyst coverage and securities laws in an international context. Romain Boissin received his PhD in finance from the University of Montpellier, France in 2011. He is a member of the French Finance Association.

Matteo Bonaventura is a research assistant and PhD student at Politecnico di Milano, Department of Management, Economic and Industrial Engineering. His main research area is the financing of small technology companies.

Philip Brown is a commerce graduate of the University of New South Wales, where he received a University Medal. He completed his graduate work in the Graduate School of Business at the University of Chicago. In 1991 Philip Brown was the American Accounting Association's Distinguished International Visiting Lecturer; and in 1991/92 he was the inaugural Coopers and Lybrand-Accounting Association of Australia and New Zealand Visiting Research Professor in Australasia. In 2000 he was made a life member of the Accounting and Finance Association of Australia and New Zealand. In accounting circles Philip is known for his research into the role accounting reports play in informing financial markets.

Jerry Cao is an Assistant Professor of Finance at Singapore Management University and Co-director of Asia Private Equity Institute. His research interests span empirical corporate finance, venture capital and private equity. In his work, one of the key research questions he has addressed is the role of private equity firms in leveraged buyouts (LBOs) and reverse leveraged buyouts (RLBOs). His research has been published in top finance journals such as *Journal of Financial Economics* and *Journal of Financial and Quantitative Analysis*. His studies on private equity have been widely cited by the *Wall Street Journal*, *Business Week*, *Forbes* and other financial journals.

Mattia Cattaneo is a PhD student in economics and technology management at the Department of Engineering, University of Bergamo, and at the CISAlpino Institute for Comparative Studies in Europe (CCSE), University of Bergamo and University of Augsburg. His research interests include corporate finance, academic entrepreneurship and higher education.

Susan Chaplinsky is Tipton R. Snavely Professor of Business Administration at the University of Virginia, Darden School of Business. Her research interests are primarily in capital raising and corporate finance with specialized interests in private equity, security issuance, capital structure, private investment in public equity (PIPEs) and employee stock ownership plans (ESO-Ps). She is the author of numerous articles that have appeared in the *Journal of Finance*, *Journal of Financial Economics*, *Journal of Business* and *Financial Management*. Before coming to Darden in 1994, she was a Visiting Associate Professor at Northwestern University, where she was also named the Kellogg Outstanding Professor, and was an Assistant Professor at the University of Michigan's Ross School of Business.

Shinjinee Chattopadhyay graduated from Columbia Business School in May 2013 with a PhD in finance and economics. Her dissertation is titled 'Essays in the economics of entrepreneurship'. She is at present an Adjunct Lecturer in the College of Business at University of Illinois at Urbana-Champaign.

Hugh M.J. Colaco is a Lecturer in Finance at Aston Business School in Birmingham, UK and a CFA® charterholder. He has taught at the undergraduate, MBA, and MSc levels at University of Connecticut, Simmons College, Merrimack College (all USA) and Aston Business School. His research interests are primarily focused in corporate finance with a special emphasis on initial public offerings.

Douglas Cumming, JD, PhD, CFA®, is a Professor of Finance and Entrepreneurship and the Ontario Research Chair at the Schulich School of Business, York University. He is a co-editor of *Entrepreneurship Theory and Practice*, and has been a guest editor for nine special issues of top journals. He has published 96 articles in leading refereed academic journals, such as *Journal of Financial Economics*, *Review of Financial Studies* and *Journal of International Business Studies*. He is the co-author of *Venture Capital and Private Equity Contracting* (Elsevier Academic Press, 2009, and Second Edition, 2013) and *Hedge Fund Structure, Regulation and Performance around the World* (Oxford University Press, 2013).

Juliet D'Souza teaches courses in corporate finance, intermediate finances, investments, international finance, financial markets and financial planning. Her research has been in the area of privatization and she has been published in journals such as *Journal of Finance* and *Journal of Corporate Finance*. She has led study abroad programmes to China and Chile. She was also awarded the Fulbright Hayes Scholarship to Russia, Lithuania and Latvia.

Susanne Espenlaub holds a DPhil in economics from the University of Oxford. She is a Senior Lecturer in Finance at the Manchester Business School, University of Manchester. Her research interests are in the areas of initial public offerings, corporate governance, share repurchase programmes, closed end funds and venture capital. She has published her research in finance and accounting journals including the *Journal of Corporate Finance*, *Journal of Banking and Finance*, *Journal of Business Finance and Accounting*, *European Financial Management* and *European Journal of Finance*. Susanne has been an external consultant to the UK Financial Services Authority (FSA).

Anna Faelten is Deputy Director of the M&A Research Centre at Cass Business School, City University London, where she also teaches mergers and acquisitions on the MSc programme. Her research focuses on M&A but also encompasses related areas such as general corporate finance, corporate governance, corporate distress and restructuring and investment in emerging markets. She consulted the UK Government's Department for Business, Innovation and Skills (BIS) on the economic impact of M&A in the UK and regularly carries out research on global M&A for the business community. She was previously editor of the corporate finance publication *Deal Monitor*.

Andrew Ferguson is a Professor of Financial Accounting at the University of Technology, Sydney (UTS). Prior to joining UTS in 2009, Andrew was a Senior Lecturer and an Associate Professor of Accounting at the University of New South Wales (UNSW). His research interests are in capital markets-based accounting research.

Chitru S. Fernando is the John and Donnie Brock Chair and Professor of Finance at the University of Oklahoma Price College, and Research Fellow at the Wharton Financial Institutions Center. He is published in major refereed journals including the *Journal of Finance* and *Journal of Financial Economics*. He has served as a consultant to major institutions and corporations worldwide. He received the PhD (Finance) from Wharton; MA (Applied Economics) from the University of Pennsylvania; MS (Management) from the MIT Sloan School; MS (Technology and Policy) from MIT; and BSc (Mechanical Engineering) with First Class Honours from the University of Sri Lanka.

Vladimir A. Gatchev is an Associate Professor of Finance at the College of Business, University of Central Florida. He has published in major refereed journals including the *Journal of Finance* and the *Journal of Financial and Quantitative Analysis*. He received his PhD in finance from the A.B. Freeman School of Business, Tulane University and his MS and BSc degrees in international economic relations from the University of National and World Economy, Sofia, Bulgaria.

Giancarlo Giudici, PhD, is Associate Professor of Corporate Finance at Politecnico di Milano – School of Management. He has written several articles and books on initial public offerings (among others *The Rise and Fall of Europe's New Stock Markets*, Elsevier, co-authored with Peter Roosenboom). He served as referee for *Small Business Economics*, *Journal of Empirical Finance*, *Journal of Small Business Management* and *Accounting & Finance*. He is director of the start-up incubator of Politecnico di Milano in the campus of Lecco. He is also a board member in two spin-off companies of Politecnico. He leads several research and consulting projects funded by the Italian government and by private companies.

Marc Goergen holds a DPhil in economics from the University of Oxford. He has held appointments at the University of Manchester, UMIST, the University of Reading and the University of Sheffield. He currently holds a Chair in Finance at Cardiff Business School, Cardiff University. His main research interests are in corporate governance and corporate control, initial public offerings, corporate investment models, mergers and acquisitions, insider trading, human capital issues across corporate governance systems and dividend policy. He has papers published in a number of academic journals, including *Journal of Finance*, *Journal of Corporate Finance*, *Journal of Financial Intermediation*, *Journal of Law* and *Economics & Organization and European Financial Management*.

Dimitrios Gounopoulos is a Senior Lecturer in Accounting and Finance and Director of the BSc in accounting and finance in the Surrey Business School, University of Surrey (UK). He holds a BSc in electrical and electronic engineering with management and an MSc in radio communication and high frequency engineering from the University of Leeds, and an MBA from Leeds University Business School. His desire to carry out research work led him to proceed with a PhD in initial public offerings at the University of Manchester (Manchester Business School). Since 2008, he has published research papers in well-known international finance academic journals (*European Financial Management*, *International Review of Financial Analysis* and *Applied Financial Economics*) and top international journals in other disciplines (*Annals of Tourism Research*, *Transportation Research Part E* and *Maritime Policy and Management*). He is Senior Research Advisor at PriceWaterhouseCoopers and Visiting Professor at the University of Southampton and the Vrije University of Amsterdam.

Ufuk Güçbilmez is a Lecturer in Finance at the University of Edinburgh Business School. He obtained his PhD degree in finance at the Lancaster University, where he completed an MSc course on finance as well. Ufuk's main research area is initial public offerings. He is particularly interested in the cyclical nature of IPO activity and hot issue markets. His teaching experience lies in the areas of corporate finance and investments. He has taught courses at both undergraduate and postgraduate levels.

Swasti Gupta-Mukherjee is Assistant Professor of Finance at Loyola University Chicago's Quinlan School of Business. She completed her doctoral degree in finance from Georgia Institute of Technology, and her bachelor's degree in engineering from the Indian Institute of Technology Kharagpur. Her research interests are mutual funds, private equity and venture capital, IPOs, mergers and acquisitions, behavioural finance, and information economics. She has published in well-respected academic journals including the *Journal of Financial and Quantitative Analysis*, *Journal of Banking and Finance*, *Financial Management*, *Journal of International Business Studies*, and *Journal of Economic Behavior and Organization*.

Gitit Gur-Gershgorn has been the Head of the Economic Research Department and Chief Economist of the Israel Securities Authority since 2008. She received her BA in economics and international relations from the Hebrew University, Jerusalem, an MBA from the School of Business at the Hebrew University and a PhD in finance from the University of Colorado at Boulder in 2007. She completed a post-doctoral programme at Yale University, where she served as the advisory editor of the *Review of Financial Studies*. She taught finance theory, portfolio management, international finance and Israel's financial markets at the University of Colorado at Boulder, the University of New Mexico (Albuquerque), Ben Gurion University (Israel) and Ono Academic College (Israel).

Shantaram P. Hegde is a Professor of Finance at the School of Business, University of Connecticut, USA. He has taught in programmes at undergraduate, MBA, executive MBA and PhD levels, worked as Coordinator of the Finance PhD programme, and served as Associate Dean of Graduate Studies and Director of Executive Education. His prior work experience covers undergraduate colleges in Bangalore, India, Indian Institute of Management, Bangalore, University of Massachusetts, Amherst, Wayne State University, University of Michigan, University of Notre Dame and Yale School of Management (Visiting Faculty Fellow). His research interests include hedge funds and private equity, financial risk management, corporate finance and market microstructure.

Johannes Hoebelt works in the financial services industry assurance department at Deloitte & Touche in Hanover. After completing his vocational training in banking at Sparkasse Krefeld savings bank, he studied business studies (BA) at the University of Applied Sciences in Bremen, Germany. His special interest in accounting and finance led him to continue his studies with an MSc in international financial management at the University of Surrey. Due to his high degree of enthusiasm for research, Johannes graduated with an Outstanding Distinction as one of the best students at his universities.

Sofia Johan, LLB (Liverpool), LLM (Warwick), PhD (Tilburg), is the AFM Senior Research Fellow at the Tilburg Law and Economics Centre (TILEC) and Adjunct Professor of Law and Finance at the Schulich School of Business, York University. Her recent publications have appeared in numerous leading journals including the *Journal of Financial Economics*, *American Law and Economics Review*, *International Review of Law and Economics*, *Journal of Banking and Finance* and *Journal of International Business Studies*, among others. She is the co-author of *Venture Capital and Private Equity Contracting* (Elsevier Academic Press, 2009, and Second Edition, 2013) and *Hedge Fund Structure, Regulation and Performance around the World* (Oxford University Press, 2013).

Arif Khurshed is a Senior Lecturer in Finance at the Manchester Business School, University of Manchester. His research interests are in the areas of IPOs, venture capital, institutional investments, share repurchase programmes, and corporate governance. His research has been published in *Journal of Corporate Finance*, *Journal of Banking and Finance*, *Journal of Financial Intermediation* and *Journal of Business Finance and Accounting*. He is the author of *Initial Public Offerings: The Mechanics and Performance of IPOs* (Harriman House) and has contributed several book chapters. Arif has been an external consultant to the UK Financial Services Authority (FSA) and the British Venture Capital Association (BVCA). He holds a PhD in finance from the University of Reading.

Peter Lam is a Senior Lecturer of Accounting at the University of Technology Sydney (UTS) Business School, Australia. Before joining UTS, he has held academic positions with several other universities in Hong Kong and Australia. Peter has also held senior management positions with conglomerates and corporations in the Asia-Pacific region prior to becoming an academic. His research interests are in capital markets-based accounting research and empirical corporate finance.

Erik E. Lehmann is a Full Professor of Management and Organization at Augsburg University, Germany and Director of the Program Global Business Management (GBM).

Together with Silvio Vismara he directs the CISAlpino Institute for Comparative Studies in Europe (CCSE). He serves as an associate editor of *Small Business Economics: An Entrepreneurial Journal*. His research has been published in leading academic journals such as *European Finance Review (Review of Finance)*, *Research Policy*, *Entrepreneurship Theory and Practice*, *Journal of Economic Behavior and Organization*, *Small Business Economics*, *Journal of Small Business Management*, *Review of Accounting and Finance* and *Journal of Technology Transfer*. His most recent books include *Entrepreneurship and Economic Growth* by Oxford University Press in 2006, *Technology Transfer in a Global Economy* by Springer in 2013 and *Corporate Governance in Small and Medium-Sized Firms* with Edward Elgar in 2011.

Mario Levis is an Emeritus Professor of Finance at Cass Business School, City University London. He graduated from the Hebrew University of Jerusalem in economics and received his PhD from Bath University, UK. He is known for his academic and professional work on initial public offerings (IPOs), private equity and equity trading strategies. He has published in these areas in academic and professional journals. His first book, *Empirical Issues in Raising Equity Capital*, was published in 1996 by Elsevier, North-Holland. He has worked as an advisor in investment banking, a number of leading asset management firms and various professional and government bodies. He has served as President of the European Financial Management Association and was a member of the editorial boards of various academic journals, including *Journal of Banking and Finance*, *European Financial Management* and *Omega*.

William L. Megginson is Professor and Rainbolt Chair in Finance at the University of Oklahoma's Michael F. Price College of Business. Professor Megginson's research interest has focused in recent years on the privatization of state-owned enterprises, especially those privatizations executed through public share offerings. He has published refereed articles in several top academic journals, including *Journal of Economic Literature*, *Journal of Finance*, *Journal of Financial Economics*, *Journal of Financial and Quantitative Analysis* and *Foreign Policy*. He is author or co-author of eight textbooks.

Michele Meoli (PhD) is Assistant Professor of Corporate Finance at the Department of Engineering, University of Bergamo, and member of the CISAlpino Institute for Comparative Studies in Europe (CCSE), University of Bergamo and University of Augsburg. He was Marie Curie Research Fellow at the Centre for Econometrics Analysis, Cass Business School (City University London). His research interests include corporate governance, IPO valuation, academic entrepreneurship and governance in higher education systems.

Jean-Sébastien Michel, PhD, is Assistant Professor at the Department of Finance of HEC Montréal. His current research focuses on behavioural finance issues related to venture capital, initial public offerings and analyst coverage. He is also interested in how managerial biases are formed as well as how they affect firm financing and investing decisions. His publications have appeared in academic journals such as *Financial Management* and *Entrepreneurship Theory and Practice*.

Katrin Migliorati holds a PhD in the 2012 Economics and Management of Technology Programme at the University of Bergamo, Italy. She graduated with distinction in management engineering at the University of Bergamo in 2008. Before joining the PhD programme, she worked for an engineering firm and joined the financial service industry in the global transaction banking sector. Recently, she was a Visiting Scholar at Cass Business School, City University of London. Her research interests include initial public offerings, seasoned equity offerings and technology transfer.

Usha R. Mittoo is the Stuart Clark Professor of Financial Management at the Asper School of Business, University of Manitoba, Canada. She received her PhD in finance from the University of British Columbia. Her main research is in international capital markets and corporate finance areas. She has published papers in several top academic and practitioner journals including *Journal of Finance*, *Journal of Banking and Finance*, *Journal of Corporate Finance* and *Journal of Applied Corporate Finance*. She serves on the editorial boards of several academic journals and has won several awards for her teaching, research, and service.

Aharon Cohen Mohliver is an Assistant Professor of Strategy and Entrepreneurship at London Business School. Aharon studies antecedents for the diffusion and adoption of practices that violate legal and ethical codes in financial markets, such as stock option backdating and manipulation of financial statements. Among these he studies the relationship between ownership structure and conflicts of interests in fund managing companies around the world. Aharon has worked extensively with regulators and policymakers in Israel on issues of ownership structure and market competitiveness, among which are the Ministry of Finance, the Israeli Securities Authority and the Parliament's Economics Committee. Aharon was a senior economic policy adviser to the Israeli Former Prime Minister, Mr Benjamin Netanyahu.

Robert Nash holds the Orr Fellowship in Finance. He has been teaching corporate finance at Wake Forest University since 1997. Prior to joining Wake Forest, he taught at the University of Baltimore and at the University of Georgia (where he received his PhD in 1994). Rob also holds CCM (Certified Cash Manager) and CMA (Certified Management Accountant) designations. Rob's research focuses on international capital markets and financial contracting. He has published in the *Journal of Finance*, *Journal of Financial Economics*, *Journal of Banking and Finance*, *Financial Management*, *Journal of Corporate Finance* and *Journal of Financial Services Research*, among others.

Sian Owen (PhD) is a Senior Lecturer in the School of Banking and Finance at the University of New South Wales, Sydney, Australia. She was born and studied in the UK, receiving a BSc (Hons) in mathematics from the University of Leicester and a MSc and PhD, both in finance, from Brunel University. Her research interests are in corporate finance, corporate governance and equity issuance with particular emphasis on issues of firm performance.

Stefano Paleari is Professor of Finance of the University of Bergamo. His research interests include IPOs, corporate governance, competitiveness studies in the aviation industry and governance of higher education institutions. He is author of numerous books and articles in journals such as *European Financial Management*, *Entrepreneurship Theory and Practice*, *Small Business Economics*, *Transportation Research* and *Tourism Management*. He has also conducted professional work for governmental departments and international institutions. Rector of the University of Bergamo, he is a member of the Council and the General Secretary of the CRUI (Italian Council of the Rectors of Italian Universities).

J. Ari Pandes, BComm, MA, PhD, is an Assistant Professor of Finance at the Haskayne School of Business at the University of Calgary. His research focuses primarily on issues in empirical corporate finance, with specific focus on securities issuance, raising financing, investment banking, analyst forecasts, and the going public decision. Ari's publications have appeared in a number of leading refereed academic journals, such as *Financial Management*, *Journal of Banking and Finance* and *European Financial Management*, and his research into the Canadian capital markets has twice won the Bank of Canada best paper award. Ari's research has also been cited in the press, and he frequently provides financial and economic insight to various news outlets.

Grzegorz Pawlina holds an Associate Professor in Finance position at the Lancaster University Management School. He earned his PhD and MSc in finance from Tilburg University, the Netherlands, and MSc in economics from Warsaw School of Economics. He has taught various courses related to financial management and capital markets at both undergraduate and postgraduate levels. Grzegorz has published in such journals as *Review of Finance*, *Journal of Corporate Finance* and *Journal of Economics & Management Strategy* as well as in a number of practitioners' outlets. His main research interests include interactions between corporate financing and investment decisions, real options and the valuation of corporate debt.

Marko Remenar is a Management Board Member of Zagrebacka Banka, Croatia, and is in charge of the markets and investment banking. Marko holds an MSc in finance and accounting from the University of Manchester.

Jay R. Ritter is Cordell Professor of Finance at the Warrington College of Business Administration, University of Florida. He is widely recognized as a leading academic expert on IPOs and has won several best paper awards from top academic journals in finance. A recent study listed him as the ninth most-cited author in the world in the major academic finance journals. He serves on the boards of seven different academic journals, has been a visiting professor at several universities around the world, and has won several teaching awards. He has testified before the US Senate Banking Committee, and is frequently quoted in the financial press.

Michael J. Robinson, BMath, MBA, PhD, CFA®, ICDD is an Associate Professor of Finance at the Haskayne School of Business at the University of Calgary. His publications have appeared in a number of leading journals including the *Journal of Banking and Finance*, *Journal of Small Business Management*, *Journal of Business Ethics* and *Journal of Business Finance and Accounting*. He is the sole author of a chapter in *Innovation and Transformation in the Oil Industry: Global Experiences and Financing Growth in Canada*, and is the co-author of several books including *Canadian Capital Markets*.

Martin Seim works for the financial services transaction advisory division at Ernst & Young. He holds a PhD in finance and graduated with a degree in business administration from Justus-Liebig-University in Giessen, Germany. He focuses in his research on corporate finance, IPOs and venture capital, and has published in books and international finance journals including the *European Journal of Finance* and *Venture Capital*.

Andrea Signori has been a PhD candidate in finance at the University of Bergamo since October 2010. Prior to entering the PhD programme, he received his MS degree in management engineering in December 2009, with a dissertation on the trading activity of newly listed firms. His primary research interests are in the field of corporate finance, with a particular focus on initial public offerings. He has been a visiting academic at Manchester Business School in 2012.

Paul A. Spindt is the Keehn Berry Chair of Banking and Finance at the Freeman School of Business at Tulane University. He was previously a Chair of the Federal Reserve System and taught at the University of North Carolina at Chapel Hill and Arizona State University before coming to Tulane. In addition to teaching and researching, he also works as a consultant. He has published a multitude of influential finance articles, and has contributed to the economic understanding of the analysis of monetary transactions. Additionally, he regularly publishes research on IPO analysis and dividend versus stock repurchase decisions. He is an award recipient of the *Journal of Finance*.

Jo-Ann Suchard (PhD) is an Associate Professor in the School of Banking and Finance at the University of New South Wales, Sydney, Australia. Her research focuses on how firms raise capital. Her research interests include venture capital and private equity, capital raising in debt and equity markets and corporate governance. Jo-Ann is a director on the board of the Asian Finance association and organizes and hosts an annual online workshop on venture capital and private equity in Asia.

Silvio Vismara (PhD) is an Associate Professor of Corporate Finance at the University of Bergamo, Italy. Together with Erik Lehmann, he directs the CISAlpino Institute for Comparative Studies in Europe (CCSE), a joint initiative with the University of Augsburg, in Germany. Silvio is associate editor of *Small Business Economics* and is author of articles in journals such as *Entrepreneurship Theory and Practice*, *European Financial Management* and *Journal of Technology Transfer*. His most recent book, *Newcits – Investing in UCITS Compliant Hedge Funds*, was published by Wiley. He is scientific consultant for the Italian Stock Exchange and founder of Universoft, a spin-off from the University of Bergamo.

Kazuo Yamada is a Lecturer at the College of Business Administration of Ritsumeikan University. His research focuses on equity issuance including initial public offerings (IPOs) and seasoned equity offerings (SEOs), entrepreneurial finance, and the financial aspects of the Japanese economy. Yamada received his PhD from Kobe University.

Preface

The rapid growth of emerging markets, the need to fund new technological developments and the pursuit of worthy investment opportunities by institutional and individual investors has led to a remarkable increase of new companies seeking a public listing. During the past two decades more than 30 000 firms went public across 89 countries. The volume and complexity of such activity attracted considerable academic interest. Research on this subject has expanded rapidly and scholars in a wider range of disciplines now regularly investigate topics pertaining to initial public offerings. More than 1000 research papers in scholarly journals investigated a wide range of IPO-related issues and offered valuable insights into the functioning and developments of these markets. Some of the issues addressed in the literature relate to the initial valuation of IPOs and their long-term performance, the timing and waves of IPOs, the choice and implications of alternative issuing mechanisms, the transaction structure, the institutional framework and the choice of the listing location. This handbook offers some important new insights into issues that would be of interest not only to the academic community but also to the professionals involved in the preparation, structure and execution of such transactions, market regulators and private and institutional investors.

We would like to take this opportunity to thank Matthew Pitman, Edward Elgar's commissioning editor, for proposing the development of this handbook and consistently encouraging us to complete this project. Our greatest debt is to the 52 (excluding ourselves) contributing authors from 11 countries, who have entrusted us with their original and previously unpublished work. In a hugely competitive academic environment dominated by numerous research and journal ratings the value of such contributions are just immeasurable. We are immensely grateful to them all!

To
Melina and Beatriz Marina

Introduction
Mario Levis and Silvio Vismara

The purpose of this handbook is to provide an updated source of reference based on recent empirical research on some of the key issues related to IPO trends that should be relevant to a wide audience including company directors, investment bankers, financial analysts, regulators and institutional investors. The book is organized into six parts each addressing different stages and issues of the IPO process. A brief synopsis of the handbook's contents follows.

PART I WHY AND WHEN FIRMS GO PUBLIC

Chapters 1–4 provide an insightful view on the recent trends in IPO activity across Europe and the long trend in the decline of IPOs in recent years, the emerging patterns in the structure of venture capital (VC) exits, the motivation for going public, and the timing of such decisions. The European evidence on these issues, although broadly consistent with the USA, nevertheless highlights some subtle differences related to the institutional frameworks and the overall structure of the markets.

Jay R. Ritter, Andrea Signori and Silvio Vismara investigate the IPO volume in European markets, and report a decline in the number of IPOs similar to the USA. Controlling for the impact of market valuations, their evidence suggests a downward trend in European IPOs over time. Although Europe is characterized by more fragmented regulation and by the existence of second markets with lower compliance costs, they argue that the decline in the number of IPOs is consistent with the economies of scope explanation. The 'Panic' of 2008 and the 'Eurozone crisis' of 2011 have also temporarily depressed IPO volume, consistent with the market conditions hypothesis. They also present evidence of increased difficulty for small firms to remain profitable, underperformance and their higher propensity to be acquired soon after the IPO, with respect to large firms. They show that these patterns persist even among second market IPOs, where the regulatory overreach hypothesis does not apply.

Susan Chaplinsky and Swasti Gupta-Mukherjee show that in line with the overall decline in the volume of IPOs there has also been a gradual shift of venture capital exits from IPOs to M&As. They find that the average return to IPO exits is significantly higher than the average return to M&A exits; this has raised concerns about how the lower returns from M&A exits can sustain the industry. In fact they find that 40 per cent of exits fail to recover the full amount of capital invested in the portfolio company, with M&A exits accounting for a disproportionately larger share of these. High M&A returns require VCs to have more discipline in capital allocation, while achieving good exit market valuations, which in turn requires VCs to have greater skill in managing all stages of their investments. By contrast, high IPO returns are more a function of market timing and having companies ready when the 'window is open'. In short, the evidence raises questions about the viability of the venture capital industry and suggests that, if IPOs continue to be scarce and M&A exits are the predominant form of exit, VCs will face a large challenge adapting to this new market reality.

The decline of IPOs, however, may have wider implications for the growth of some firms as going public offers multiple benefits to the issuing company. On the basis of a comparison on the evidence of managers' surveys in Europe and USA, Franck Bancel and Usha R. Mittoo report that most European chief financial officers (CFOs) identify enhanced visibility and access to financing as the major benefits of going public. Managers also value the role of IPO in creating a currency for mergers and acquisitions and to facilitate an exit strategy but view cost of capital considerations as less important. They also attempt to time the initial public offering based on hot market and industry conditions. The European CFOs' views about major benefits are largely similar to those of their US peers but differ significantly regarding the IPO costs. The European CFOs are less concerned about the IPO costs than their US peers and view outside monitoring as a major benefit, whereas their US peers consider it as a major cost.

Shantanu Banerjee, Ufuk Güçbilmez and Grzegorz Pawlina, on the basis of their investigation of the cyclical nature of IPO activity in the UK, provide further support to the importance of timing an IPO in the best interests of the issuer. Their results indicate a lead–lag relationship between IPO initial returns and volume. Initial public offering volume is sensitive to recent changes in market conditions. There is evidence of industry concentration in hot markets, and firms raise more equity during these periods. Overall, IPO waves in the UK share similar characteristics with those in the USA. The findings are consistent with rational explanations of IPO waves. However, explanations based on investor sentiment and market timing cannot be ruled out, since there is a strong positive relationship between IPO volume and the market's price-to-book ratio.

PART II PREPARATION FOR THE IPO

Chapters 5–8 discuss some aspects of the regulatory framework and its implications for the functioning of the markets, the underlying quality of the admitted firms as well as some critical decisions in terms of pricing and type of listing.

Chitru S. Fernando, Vladimir A. Gatchev and Paul A. Spindt show how the role of institutional investors in monitoring and information gathering can substitute for the benefits derived from a broad-based ownership of the firm, including more information generation by analysts. Firms that can benefit more from institutional ownership selecting higher IPO offer price levels. Furthermore, they argue that the IPO offer price level provides investors a robust measure of a firm's quality, with higher-quality firms selecting higher offer prices and lower share floats than equal-sized lower-quality firms. The empirical tests confirm that the positive association between IPO offer prices and institutional ownership persists after controlling for liquidity and size differences.

J. Ari Pandes and Michael J. Robinson investigate the implications of the regulatory framework on the development of an IPO market by focusing on the junior equity market in Canada, the Toronto Venture Stock Exchange (TSX-V), which has evolved over the past 100 years to become one of the world's largest markets for development-oriented, early-stage firms to go public. While the average IPO size of TSX-V firms is small compared with IPOs in other international junior markets, the absolute number of firms going public on the TSX-V is substantially higher than the number of IPOs in these other junior markets. One key aspect of Canada's junior market has been the development of its Capital Pool Company (CPC) programme, which is a highly regulated blind pool programme. Unlike the blind pool experience in the USA, the Canadian experience with blind pools illustrates how effective regulation and the presence of high-quality underwriters can balance the capital needs of early stage, entrepreneurial firms, while still serving to protect the interests of investors.

Mattia Cattaneo and Michele Meoli address another important aspect of the institutional framework by examining the impact of investor protection on the survival of all the IPOs in the Italian capital markets, from the birth of the Reign of Italy, in 1861, until 2011. Their results suggest that the improvement in the level of investor protection that occurred in Italy increased the IPO survival over time. In particular, the punctual evaluation of the level of investors' rights with respect to some of the regulatory innovations implemented in the Italian context, like the establishment of Commissione Nazionale per le Società e la Borsa (CONSOB) and the Draghi Reform, highlight that the level of shareholders and creditors' protection contributes to explain the improvement of the IPO survival, and therefore the development of the Italian capital market.

Hugh M.J. Colaco and Shantaram P. Hegde study the role of underwriters during the book-building process, primarily their impact on the duration of initial public offering (IPOD), defined as the waiting time firms spend from the filing of the preliminary prospectus to the final public offering of shares. High-reputation underwriters are more efficient than their low-reputation counterparts during the book-building process and generate greater incremental value both in terms of price and proceeds for their clients, while taking them public quicker. They also find that short-IPOD firms are more likely to have buy analyst recommendations than long-IPOD firms, which adds further evidence to the claim that short-IPOD firms are intrinsically stronger.

PART III   TRANSACTION STRUCTURE AND GOVERNANCE AT THE IPO

Chapters 9–12 explore some of the key characteristics of IPOs' structure at the time of their public listings and their potential implications on investors' perceptions.

David B. Audretsch and Erik E. Lehmann offer a reflective survey of corporate governance mechanisms in entrepreneurial and newly listed companies and of why and how governance mechanisms differ from those in large and publicly traded corporations. They focus on a set of corporate governance mechanisms more prevalent in newly listed companies, such as the product and capital market, the market for corporate control, boards of directors and the capital structures. They conclude that academic research is still far away from providing sufficient solutions about the pros and cons of the different mechanisms in corporate governance, and how these differ across newly listed companies and large and established firms. They provide a number of important suggestions for future research, including the role of universities and research institutes as large shareholders of entrepreneurial firms.

Fabio Bertoni, Matteo Bonaventura and Giancarlo Giudici discuss an additional intriguing dimension of the role of information collection during the book-building process on the decision about the final allocation and pricing when both small retail investors and professional institutions are invited to join the offer (hybrid IPOs). They show that underwriters preserve their discretion also when demand from institutions is poor. Optimistic information collected during book-building is reflected in a preferential treatment for institutional investors. The data suggest that underwriters are more likely to increase the number of shares allotted to institutions when the overallotment option is exercised and when retail investors undersubscribe the offering. On the contrary, underwriters are more likely to increase the IPO price when the demand from retail investors is strong. This maximizes their bargaining power over professional investors.

Jean-Sébastien Michel examines the role of VC investment timing on short-run IPO pricing. Lower file delay is associated with higher short-run IPO performance. Furthermore, lower file delay is associated with VCs that are younger and book-building periods which are longer. Overall, this evidence is consistent with the grandstanding hypothesis, but it is also consistent with a modified 'market' grandstanding hypothesis where grandstanding is associated with IPO overvaluation instead of information asymmetry. Research about the impact of venture capitalists on IPO pricing is important given venture capitalists have first contact with the firms they bring public, and so are arguably the most informed investors in the company.

Katrin Migliorati and Stefano Paleari compare the role of investment banks taking companies public on the Alternative Investment Market (AIM) unique market model relative to those on second-tier regulated markets in continental Europe. The AIM regulatory structure entails the outsourcing of substantial part of regulations on the Nominated Advisors (that is, Nomads) who are not just underwriters but act as 'regulators'; they are in fact required to advise and guide AIM-companies at all time. As a result they find that Nomads that are smaller and with higher expertise in IPOs (that is, higher IPO relevance) reduce underpricing. In sharp contrast, underwriters in Paris, Frankfurt and Milan, increase significantly their number of IPO mandates by being established banks. They also find Nomads that are smaller and with higher expertise in IPOs (that is, higher IPO relevance) reduce underpricing.

PART IV   TRADING IN THE AFTERMARKET

Chapters 13–16 investigate four different aspects of post-IPO activities, that is, analyst coverage, directors' trades at lock-up expiration, VC strategies and implications of ownership structure.

Romain Boissin compares the long-run performance of firms that do not receive analyst coverage (orphans) to those that do (non-orphans). This abnormal long-run performance is considerably more severe for orphan IPOs than for non-orphan IPOs given a three- to five-year horizon. The evidence suggests that analyst coverage is indeed important to the issuing firm but the market does not fully incorporate the perceived value of this coverage. Once they control for other characteristics that have been shown to influence the long-run performance of IPOs, we find that investors and market participants pay attention to analyst coverage when IPOs have large underwriting syndicates and are highly underpriced.

Susanne Espenlaub, Marc Goergen, Arif Khurshed and Marko Remenar use a sample of UK IPOs, to examine the stock price behaviour and the volume and pattern of directors' trades around the expiry of lock-up agreements. In contrast to the US evidence, they find that the average cumulative abnormal return around the lock-up expiry is not significantly different from zero. As is to be expected, there is a substantial increase in share sales by 'unlocked' directors in the weeks immediately after the lock-up expiry. Surprisingly, the stock price reaction to share sales by unlocked directors around the expiry of lock-up agreements is not unfavourable. The subsample of companies that report directors' sales around the expiry date has positive average cumulative abnormal returns, albeit not statistically significant. By contrast, the subsample of companies without directors' sales shows negative average cumulative abnormal returns.

Wolfgang Bessler and Martin Seim show that exit strategies of venture capitalists in the USA and Europe underwent dramatic changes in recent years. They analyse venture capital-backed IPOs in Europe for the last two VC and IPO waves. During the 'new economy' period (1996–2003) IPOs were more underpriced, had higher valuation multiples and a superior financial performance. Second period IPOs (2003–10) reveal a superior operating performance, suggesting that venture capitalists only took the most profitable firms public. These findings differ from the US evidence. Since the last IPO waves ended in the USA in 2001 and in Europe in 2007, interesting questions about the future of VC and IPO activities remain.

Aharon Cohen Mohliver, Gitit Gur-Gershgoren and Shinjinee Chattopadhyay explore the potential links between firm ownership structure and the average IPO underpricing. They highlight some new avenues of exploring the effects of market competition, information asymmetry, power and conflicts of interest on IPO pricing. Using a cross-country analysis based on two independent data-sets, they show that the amount of money 'left on the table' for investors decreases with the degree of concentration of ownership within the economy. They also report that the greater the degree of separation between power and equity ownership, the smaller the average IPO underpricing.

PART V   THE AFTERMARKET PERFORMANCE OF IPOS

Chapters 17–20 focus on long-term aftermarket underperformance that remains one of the most debated and puzzling issues in the IPO literature.

Naaguesh Appadu, Anna Faelten and Mario Levis investigate the implications of the type and pattern of follow-on activities like acquisitions, seasoned equity offerings (SEOs) and divestitures during the three-year period of going public on long-run performance. They find that such corporate events follow periods of significant stock price movements and positive market sentiment, suggesting that the timing of such events is important either in terms of taking advantage of temporary overvaluations or responding to feedback received from market participants at certain points in time. Their evidence suggests that post-IPO corporate activity is directly related to long-term aftermarket performance. Controlling for firm specific characteristics, IPO firms pursuing future growth opportunities through a series of corporate events of the same or different types during the first three years of going public, outperform their passive counterparts by the end of the three-year period after flotation.

6   *Handbook of research on IPOs*

Jerry Cao examines the impact of IPO timing of buyout sponsors in listing leveraged buyouts (LBOs) publicly on firm performance and exit strategy post IPO. Although the evidence indicates that reverse leveraged buyouts (RLBO) companies experience no significant deterioration in operating performance in post-IPO years, there is evidence that buyout sponsor's LBO restructuring duration is affected by IPO timing; RLBOs with shorter duration experience more deterioration in operating performance following their IPOs. Furthermore, buyout sponsors (quickly) flip LBOs to time both operating performance and market conditions. Hence, compared with other RLBOs, quick flips experience worse operating performance and greater probability of bankruptcy. Initial public offering timing drives RLBO decisions but does not affect sponsor's exit post-IPO, while lock-up provisions and concern for reputation help align buyout sponsor incentives to public investors. In short, buyout sponsor's IPO timing has important value implications for investors: listing immature LBOs destroys value and leads to financial distress, while sponsor's reputation partially mitigates this problem.

Sian Owen and Jo-Ann Suchard investigate the long-term performance of Australian venture capital and private equity (PE) backed initial public offerings. They find that on average, Australian IPOs underperform the market index over two years post listing but have similar performance after three years. However, there is no significant difference in the market adjusted stock performance of VC/PE backed and non-VC/PE backed IPOs, except in the first year of listing where VC backed IPOs perform worse than non-VC/PE backed IPOs. The operating performance is similar for non-VC/PE backed IPOs and VC/PE backed IPOs. Thus, although most VC/PE investors retain some ownership in the firm post listing, VC/PE backing does not have a sustained impact on the long-term stock or operating performance of Australian IPOs. These results are in contrast to US and UK markets and may be driven by less experienced managers operating in a relatively smaller and earlier-stage VC/PE market.

Dimitrios Gounopoulos and Johannes Hoebelt use an expanded sample of German IPOs listed between 1992 and 2012 covering two major amendments on the financial market, IFRS adoption and the recent financial crisis. Their results indicate that International Financial Reporting Standards (IFRS) adoption has reduced underpricing in Germany and has significantly affected their long-term performance. This clearly suggests the advantanges of preparing IFRS accounts which might be an incentive for private companies to use IFRS voluntarily. Similarly' firms that have gone public during the recent financial crisis offered significantly less initial returns to their aftermarket investors.

PART VI   SPECIAL TYPES OF IPOS

Chapters 21–24 address four different issues related to VC IPOs, reverse takeovers, cross listing of previously stated-owned enterprises and the implications of the recent financial crisis on the capital structure and performance of IPOs.

Douglas Cumming and Sofia Johan investigate the pattern of VC investments and IPO exits in Canada, in comparison to other countries. They report that during the period 2000 to 2008 the amount of capital commitments to newly established funds focused on investment in seed, early and expansion stage entrepreneurial ventures in

Ontario was considerably lower than in some parts of the USA. Moreover, a significant part of the VC activity in Canada is dominated by US funds while there are problems with the quality of VC investment in Canada. Such apparent deficiencies raise questions about government's initiatives to encourage VC investment, the complementary roles of local and foreign investors in stimulating local innovation and entrepreneurship, and targeted measures to address the apparent shortage of skilled VCs.

Philip Brown, Andrew Ferguson and Peter Lam investigate the pattern and characteristics of reverse takeovers (RTOs), one of the less researched topics in the IPO research in spite of the considerable increase in the volume and public attention of such transactions in recent years. Reverse takeovers, or backdoor-listings (BDL) as they are sometimes referred to, are private firms that choose to go public by backing their assets into the shell of listed companies. They find that, compared with a matched sample of IPOs, such firms are more likely to be start-up endeavours, concentrated in industries with high information asymmetry, less liquid and less profitable. Contrary to common belief, BDL transactions generally take a longer time to complete and are associated with more sell-down by private firm owners. Backdoor listings firms also raise less equity capital when going public and are less likely to use an underwriter.

Juliet D'Souza, William L. Megginson and Robert Nash, provide evidence on another important group of relatively under-researched IPOs, that is, cross-listings of privatizations of state-owned enterprises. Using a unique sample comprising 822 privatizations from 78 countries during 1985–2007, they find that the protection of shareholder rights, commonly recognized as an important factor in cross-listing by private firms, generally plays no significant role in governments' decisions to cross-list. This suggests that the effect of private benefits of control on cross-listing choices may differ when the state, rather than a private investor, is the controlling shareholder. Also, factors determining cross-listings vary significantly between developed and developing economies. In developed nations, firm-level factors most significantly affect cross-listing privatizations, while in developing nations, institutional factors are the primary determinants of such cross-listings.

Kazuo Yamada, in the final chapter of this handbook, highlights an intriguing dimension of the recent banking crisis on the decision-making process of firms planning to go public. He shows that poor-health banks in Japan lend more money to their client firms that are planning to go public. To resolve such over-lending, firms issue more shares than they need at the time of the IPO or at a later point through SEOs. Such practices, however, appear to have a negative impact on long-term performance.

PART I

WHY AND WHEN FIRMS GO PUBLIC

1. Economies of scope and IPO activity in Europe
Jay R. Ritter, Andrea Signori and Silvio Vismara

1 INTRODUCTION

Initial public offering (IPO) activity in Europe has recently come to a near halt, due to the 'Panic' of 2008 and the Eurozone crisis of 2011. The 280 companies going public on the London, Euronext, Frankfurt, and Milan stock exchanges from 2008 to 2011 is fewer than the 353 companies going public in 2007 alone. An analogous dearth of IPOs has occurred in the US, as documented in Gao et al. (2012). Gao et al. discuss three hypotheses that have been proposed to explain the low volume of IPOs in the US during 2001–11.

First, the Sarbanes–Oxley Act (hereafter, SOX) of 2002 made going and staying public more costly, owing to additional compliance requirements, and the reduction in bid–ask spreads from 1994 to 2001 and Regulation FD in 2000 led to a reduction in analyst coverage for smaller firms that decreased the attractiveness of going public. Supporters of the 'regulatory overreach' hypothesis argue that the combination of these effects significantly lowered the market valuation of small publicly traded firms, discouraging other IPOs.

Second, lower stock market valuations after the collapse of the technology bubble starting in March 2000 have reduced the attractiveness of going public. Supporters of the 'market conditions' hypothesis argue that the drop in IPO activity is just temporary.

Third, the 'economies of scope' hypothesis states that due to an ongoing change in the economy, small firms are worth more as part of a larger organization that can realize economies of scope and scale. Thus, they find it more convenient to get big fast by selling out in a trade sale (merging) rather than going public and remaining independent. The economies of scope hypothesis is based on the evidence that the decline in IPOs has been most pronounced among small firms, and that small firms have been increasingly unable to be profitable. The economies of scope hypothesis views the decline in IPO activity as a consequence of a change in the attractiveness of being big rather than small, instead of the attractiveness of being private rather than public.

This chapter sheds light on the decline of European IPO activity and tests the different hypotheses laid out in Gao et al. (2012). Similar to the US, we find that the decline in IPO activity has been mainly driven by small firms. In the main markets of the four largest European economies, the percentage of IPOs by small firms, where small firms are defined as those with less than €30 million in pre-IPO annual sales using 2011 purchasing power, has dropped to an annual average of 25.4 percent in 2001–11 from an annual average of 38.2 percent in the six years 1995–2000 preceding the bursting of the technology bubble. Small firms may have suffered more than others from higher compliance costs, as argued by the regulatory overreach hypothesis. On the other hand, the IPO drought may be due to an ongoing change in the economy whereby small firms receive higher valuations in trade sales (acquisitions by strategic buyers) than in public markets, because they can create greater profits as part of larger organizations rather than as small independent firms. Europe is a privileged setting in which to examine the economies of scope hypothesis. We take advantage of the presence of second markets for small companies, exempt from regulatory changes, to test whether the predictions of the regulatory overreach, market conditions, and economies of scope hypotheses hold in an environment where regulatory overreach is not as important.

We find that the decline in the number of small firm IPOs in Europe is only partly attributable to general market conditions. The decline in the number of IPOs during 2001–03 and 2008–11 occurred in conjunction with unfavorable market conditions. However, our evidence suggests that the economies of scope motivation is also important. First, the profitability of small firm IPOs has declined over time, and has been persistently lower than for large firm IPOs. Among small firm IPOs, the percentage that are profitable in the three years after going public has declined from 67.1 percent in 1995–2000 to 44.4 percent in 2001–11, while the downtrend has been less pronounced for large firm IPOs (from 91.3 percent to 80.1 percent). The pattern of low profitability for small firms also persists among seasoned listed companies. Second, the long-run performance of small company IPOs has been poor for public-market investors. The average three-year buy-and-hold return for investors buying at the closing market price following the first 21 days of trading, has been −2.9 percent for small company IPOs from 1995 to 2008, in contrast to +14.6 percent for large company IPOs. European IPOs from 1995 to 2008 have given investors an equally weighted average three-year buy-and-hold return of only 2.5 percent, less than 1 percent per year on an annualized basis.

This evidence is consistent with that in Vismara et al. (2012), who examine European IPOs from 1995 to 2006. They report a negative abnormal performance for IPOs on European second markets: the average three-year buy-and-hold abnormal return for main market IPOs has been +12.3 percent, whereas the average for second market IPOs has been −19.0 percent.[1] Third, while European IPO activity has fallen, the number of merger and acquisition (M&A) deals has risen, suggesting an increased preference for external growth by means of trade sales rather than internal growth financed by equity issues. The propensity to be acquired soon after the IPO has increased among small companies over the past decade. This is consistent with the desire to get big fast, posited by the economies of scope hypothesis. Moreover, inconsistent with the regulatory overreach explanation, we find that the fraction of non-European companies listed in Europe has not been affected by regulatory changes, and listed companies are not going private more frequently in an attempt to avoid the higher compliance costs of staying public.

Finally, we test our explanation in a multiple regression with the quarterly volume of IPOs scaled by real gross domestic product (GDP) as the dependent variable. Our results support the market conditions hypothesis, as the level of general stock market valuations is found to be a primary determinant of IPO activity. However, we also find a negative time trend affecting IPO activity that is not attributable to poor market valuations. Consistent with the economies of scope hypothesis, this trend is driven by small firms. That is, the negative time trend that is unrelated to market conditions is stronger for small firm IPOs than large firm IPOs. Evidence in support of the economies of scope hypothesis persists also in second markets. Although facing considerably looser regulation, the number of companies going public on these markets has significantly declined over time. This downtrend on the lightly regulated second markets confirms that increased compliance costs due to SOX-like regulatory changes are not the primary cause of the drop in IPO activity since 2000.

This chapter can be viewed as a companion of the Gao et al. (2012) study, which focuses exclusively on US IPOs for its empirical evidence. Their theoretical analysis predicts a decline in the number of small company IPOs in all countries with high levels of economic development. Both the present analysis and the Gao et al. (2012) analysis attempt to explain long-term trends, while controlling for the shorter-term fluctuations in IPO volume associated with bull and bear markets. Despite substantial differences with the US environment, such as European regulatory fragmentation and the existence of second markets for small companies, we find evidence in support of the economies of scope hypothesis. The decline in the number of companies going public in the US has raised concerns about its effect on GDP and employment growth. Many public companies are indeed leaders in innovation and job creation, and the drop in IPOs may be detrimental for economic growth. The number of companies going public has also fallen in Europe, although until recently not as severely.

The remainder of this chapter is organized as follows. Section 2 describes securities regulation in Europe. Section 3 defines the testable hypotheses, and section 4 presents the sample and the results. Section 5 focuses on the second markets for small companies. In section 6, we report the results of time series regressions with the quarterly volume of IPOs scaled by real GDP as the dependent variable. Section 7 concludes.

2 SECURITIES REGULATION IN EUROPE

The introduction of the Sarbanes–Oxley Act in 2002 by US authorities served as a paradigm that influenced analogous regulatory changes in Europe. In the same year, the *Report of the High Level Group of Company Law Experts on a Modern Regulatory Framework for Company Law in Europe*,[2] issued by the European Commission, recommended corporate governance practices that are similar to the SOX provisions. A number of member states responded by either issuing national corporate governance codes or revising the existing ones. Although the contents vary across countries, the codes are highly aligned with EU guidelines in recommending a balance of independent directors and non-independent directors, the separation of the chief executive officer (CEO) and chairman-of-the-board positions, formal and transparent procedures for the appointment of directors to the board, and effective internal control systems (Akyol et al., 2012).

Analogous regulatory changes have been implemented across EU member states at different points in time. The four countries that we focus on have put into force changes in their governance codes between 2002 and 2004. First, German authorities introduced the German Corporate Governance Code on 26 February 2002; in the UK, the Combined Code was passed on 23 July 2003; French authorities approved the Law on Financial Securities of 2003 on 1 August 2003; finally, the Legislative Decree no. 310/2004 was enacted in Italy on 1 January 2004. Such staggered implementation offers better identification of the regulatory effects than a single regulatory event such as SOX (Christensen et al., 2012).

However, 'SOX-equivalent' regulations do not apply to all the companies going public in Europe, where stock exchanges are organized in segments, with a main market and one or more second markets that are typically designed to meet the needs of small and young companies (Vismara et al., 2012). These second markets are present in all of the four countries we consider, and have been used instead of the main markets by the majority of companies going public over the past decade in these four countries. From 1995 to 2011, 3055 IPOs took place on second markets and 893 on main markets. These 'exchange-regulated markets' are characterized by looser regulation, as defined by the European Financial Services Directive, and are not affected by regulatory changes at a national level.[3]

3 TESTABLE HYPOTHESES

A private firm in the US was much more likely to have been acquired than to go public over the past decade (Bayar and Chemmanur, 2011). The regulatory overreach hypothesis explains this pattern as a consequence of post-SOX compliance costs, which are posited to have been detrimental to the market value of small publicly traded firms, and a lack of analyst coverage, owing to the 2003 Global Settlement and the effects of decimalization. Conversely, the economies of scope hypothesis ascribes the drop in small-firm IPOs to the higher earnings that can be realized as part of a larger organization rather than as a small independent company, whether the company is public or private. In this section, we present a number of testable hypotheses that emanate from the economies of scope explanation.

3.1 Profitability

The economies of scope hypothesis asserts that, in a dynamic setting where profitable growth opportunities may be lost if they are not quickly seized, a larger organization is able to earn higher profits because it can realize economies of scope and bring new technologies to market faster. Consistent with this perspective, we expect small firms to be less profitable after the IPO than is the case for large firms.

Hypothesis 1: Over the last decade, the percentage of firms that are profitable in the years following the IPO decreases more among small than large companies.

3.2 Long-run Performance

There is no direct implication of the economies of scope hypothesis on the relative long-run performance of small-firm IPOs with respect to large-firm IPOs. Low returns owing to an unanticipated decrease in earnings of small companies could be caused either by increased compliance costs or by an unanticipated deterioration in profitability relative to large firms. However, if the costs brought by stricter regulation were unanticipated, companies that were already public when these changes occurred would see low returns, regardless of their size, as investors incorporated the effects into market prices. If the unanticipated increase in costs was greater for small firms on a percentage basis, as has been documented in the US (Iliev, 2010), then small firms would have lower returns. In contrast, an unanticipated decline in the profitability of small firms due to a technological change, as argued by the economies of scope hypothesis, would result in low returns only for small firms.

Hypothesis 2:   Over the past decade, the long-run returns for small firms are lower than the long-run returns for large firms.

3.3   Foreign Listings

If higher compliance costs due to stricter regulation had been detrimental for European public markets' attractiveness, as argued by the regulatory overreach hypothesis, we would expect a drop in the number of foreign companies going public once European countries began to implement regulatory changes.

Hypothesis 3:   Over the past decade, there is no significant decrease in the market share of foreign IPOs in European markets.

3.4   Survival Rates and M&A Activity

A decline in the value of small independent firms relative to large firms, according to the economies of scope hypothesis, should have two effects. First, M&A activity should rise, since small private firms would get better valuations in trade sales, in which they become part of a larger organization, than in IPOs; second, small companies that do go public should exhibit an increased propensity to take part in M&A deals, either being acquired or making acquisitions. Conversely, if high compliance costs brought by SOX-like regulatory changes are the main reason for why being a small publicly traded firm has become less attractive, we would expect an increase in the fraction of recent IPOs that subsequently leave the market and go private in an attempt to avoid such costs. The economies of scope hypothesis thus produces the following testable hypotheses:

Hypothesis 4:   Over the past decade, while the number of IPOs decreases, small firm M&A activity does not.

Hypothesis 5:   Over the past decade, the percentage of small firms that are acquired after their IPO increases.

Hypothesis 6:   Over the past decade, the percentage of small firms that go public and make acquisitions after their IPO increases.

Hypothesis 7:   Over the past decade, there is no significant increase in the fraction of IPOs that subsequently go private as an independent firm.

4   SAMPLE AND RESULTS

Our sample is composed of 3948 European IPOs that took place on the London, Euronext,[4] Frankfurt and Milan stock exchanges from 1995 to 2011. We identify the

Table 1.1 Number of European IPOs

	All markets						Main markets			
	No. IPOs	No. IPOs missing sales	Small-firm IPOs No.	Small-firm IPOs %	Large-firm IPOs No.	Large-firm IPOs %	Proceeds (2011 €bn)	No. IPOs	No. IPOs missing sales	Small-firm IPOs No.	Small-firm IPOs %
1995	87	0	49	56.3	38	43.7	8.0	58	0	29	50.0
1996	230	15	147	68.4	68	31.6	13.4	83	8	31	41.3
1997	219	0	146	66.7	73	33.3	10.7	76	0	32	42.1
1998	275	0	159	57.8	116	42.2	24.6	71	0	22	31.0
1999	373	2	252	67.9	119	32.1	55.1	78	0	23	29.5
2000	572	4	391	68.8	177	31.2	60.8	108	3	40	38.1
2001	191	0	149	78.0	42	22.0	33.5	32	0	4	12.5
2002	120	2	94	79.7	24	20.3	10.0	25	2	6	26.1
2003	89	0	66	74.2	23	25.8	7.7	13	0	2	15.4
2004	309	0	238	77.0	71	23.0	18.0	40	0	4	10.0
2005	429	0	309	72.0	120	28.0	39.9	69	0	15	21.7
2006	421	0	294	69.8	127	30.2	48.0	98	0	34	34.7
2007	353	2	232	66.1	119	33.9	28.4	79	0	25	31.6
2008	60	1	46	78.0	13	22.0	10.1	12	0	6	50.0
2009	27	13	9	64.3	5	35.7	1.2	3	0	1	33.3
2010	102	1	64	63.4	37	36.6	49.4	25	0	4	16.0
2011	91	2	64	71.9	25	28.1	5.4	23	0	5	21.7
Annual											
1995–2000	293	4	191	65.9	99	34.1	28.8	79	2	30	38.2
2001–11	199	2	142	72.1	55	27.9	22.9	38	0	10	25.4
Total	3 948	42	2 709	69.4	1 197	30.6	424.0	893	13	283	32.2

Notes:
Sample of IPOs in Europe (London, Euronext, Frankfurt, and Milan) from 1995 to 2011.
Small-firm IPOs are defined as initial public offerings conducted by companies with less than €30 million in pre-IPO annual sales, in 2011 purchasing power (Eurostat).
Proceeds are the aggregate amount raised in all of the IPOs, excluding overallotment options that get exercised.
Statistics are computed for all markets and for main markets IPOs.
Main markets are Official List (London), Eurolist (Euronext), Amtlicher Markt (Frankfurt), and MTA (Milan).
'Annual' rows show the mean values of IPO volume and aggregate proceeds per year, and the percentage of small and large firms, for the pre- and post-bubble periods.

Source: EurIPO.

IPOs and collect the data from the EurIPO database.[5] We focus on the stock exchanges of the UK, France, Germany and Italy, since these countries are the four largest European economies. The sample includes IPOs on both the main and second markets.[6] In this section, we test the seven testable hypotheses of the economies of scope explanation developed above, in order to shed light on the causes of the drop in European IPOs.

Initial public offering activity in Europe has recently shown a sharp decline. Table 1.1 reveals that, while an average of 293 companies went public each year from 1995 to 2000, this number has fallen by approximately one-third after 2000, to 199 IPOs per year. Small firms, defined as those with an inflation-adjusted pre-IPO annual sales of less than €30 million using 2011 purchasing power,[7] are responsible for the largest fraction of the IPO activity, in contrast to the US pattern after 2000 (see Gao et al., 2012). Since 1995, the percentage of offerings by small firms, averaging 69.4 percent, has been persistently higher than the percentage of IPOs by large firms. Indeed, the market share of small firm IPOs increased slightly, from 65.9 percent in 1995–2000 to 72.1 percent in 2001–11. This is inconsistent with an increased inability or unwillingness of small private firms to access the public market, as documented by Gao et al. (2012) for the US context. However, if we exclude second markets, the story is different.

In main markets, only one-third of the IPOs since 1995 were conducted by small firms, and this fraction is decreasing over time. The share of small firm IPOs dropped from 38.4 percent to 25.5 percent after the technology bubble burst in 2000, with a decrease of 20 small-firm IPOs each year, on average, between 1995–2000 and 2001–11. Such a decline in small-firm IPOs could be either driven by increased compliance costs, consistent with the regulatory overreach hypothesis, or by a structural disadvantage of small firms with respect to large firms, as argued by the economies of scope explanation. We now shed light on which of the two hypotheses is able to explain this pattern.

4.1 Profitability

Table 1.2 reports the percentage of publicly traded firms with non-negative earnings each year from 1995 to 2011. Initial public offerings are from the prior three years, while listed firms have been publicly traded for at least three years. We define small and large firms using a cutoff of €30 million in inflation-adjusted pre-IPO annual sales, and €250 million in fiscal year annual sales (both using 2011 purchasing power) for our IPOs and seasoned listed firms, respectively. Note that if a company grows its sales from less than €30 million before the IPO to more than €30 million during the three years after the IPO, it is still classified as a small firm. Thus, there is no look-ahead bias.

Panel A of Table 1.2 shows that there is a considerable decline in the post-issue profitability of small-firm IPOs over time, with an approximately 20 percent drop in the annual fraction of profitable firms after the bubble (from 67.1 percent to 44.4 percent). In comparison, the decline in the percentage of large-firm IPOs reporting positive earnings is less pronounced (from 91.3 percent to 80.1 percent). This is consistent with our first hypothesis. In general, large firms seem to make profits more easily than their smaller counterparts. The percentage of large firm IPOs with non-negative earnings indeed averages 85.4 percent, compared to 50.7 percent for small firm IPOs, and is higher in every year of our sample period.

Panel B of Table 1.2 shows that among seasoned listed firms, the same pattern is present. The percentage of small firms that are profitable falls from 77.7 percent during 1995–2000 to 59.4 percent after the bubble, while the decrease is modest among large firms (from 90.4 percent to 84.8 percent). Across the entire 1995–2011 period, on average 87 percent of large firms have been profitable, while only 65.5 percent of small firms have reported positive profits in a given year. Therefore, the evidence in Table 1.2 is consistent with our hypothesis 1 that the percentage of firms that are profitable in the years following the IPO decreases more among small than large companies.

18   Handbook of research on IPOs

Table 1.2   Profitability of recent IPOs and listed firms by year

	Panel A: IPOs from the prior 3 years				Panel B: Firms listed by more than 3 years			
	Small-firm IPOs		Large-firm IPOs		Sales < €250 m		Sales > €250 m	
	No. with EPS	% EPS ≥ 0	No. with EPS	% EPS ≥ 0	No. with EPS	% EPS ≥ 0	No. with EPS	% EPS ≥ 0
1995	46	67.4	298	92.5	1 508	79.8	1 871	89.0
1996	70	64.3	347	91.6	1 527	79.0	1 915	89.1
1997	168	76.7	121	93.4	1 664	79.5	2 184	89.5
1998	338	74.6	210	94.8	1 587	78.4	2 102	91.2
1999	421	73.4	249	94.0	1 536	75.4	2 031	91.6
2000	569	55.4	281	84.0	1 471	73.8	1 947	91.8
2001	633	44.1	261	75.1	1 506	70.3	1 890	88.6
2002	519	35.8	184	62.5	1 583	59.3	1 834	77.4
2003	217	42.9	66	69.7	1 804	51.4	1 759	78.0
2004	252	43.3	85	88.2	1 757	57.1	1 739	83.8
2005	384	43.0	142	85.2	1 693	61.3	1 689	89.6
2006	624	44.6	228	85.5	1 613	65.8	1 653	90.4
2007	653	48.2	278	88.1	1 638	66.5	1 599	91.6
2008	464	52.2	207	88.9	1 671	60.7	1 546	90.4
2009	227	47.1	113	69.0	1 792	46.8	1 494	70.2
2010	80	41.3	43	72.1	1 845	56.6	1 493	83.5
2011	93	36.6	53	81.1	1 699	61.2	1 465	89.6
Annual								
1995–2000	269	67.1	251	91.3	1 549	77.7	2 008	90.4
2001–11	377	44.4	151	80.1	1 691	59.4	1 651	84.8
Total	5 758	50.7	3 166	85.4	27 894	65.5	30 211	87.0

Notes:
The table reports the percentage of recent IPOs and seasoned listed firms with non-negative earnings per share (EPS) each year, from 1995 to 2011. EPS is after extraordinary items.
'IPOs from the prior 3 years' are IPOs taking place in Europe (London, Euronext, Frankfurt, and Milan) for which year t is one of the first three post-IPO fiscal years.
Small- and large-firm IPOs are defined on the basis of pre-IPO annual sales of €30 million, in 2011 purchasing power (*source*: Eurostat).
'Firms listed by more than 3 years' are firms listed in Europe (London, Euronext, Frankfurt, and Milan) with at least three years of trading history.
This sample of listed firms is from Datastream and it is selected each year t (from 1995 to 2011) considering all the firms 'alive' in that year t with a Datastream 'base date' before year $t - 3$.
Listed firms are classified in two categories with €250 million in 2011 purchasing power being the cutoff number.
'Annual' rows show the mean values of IPO volume and proceeds per year, and the percentage of small and large firms, for the pre- and post-bubble periods.

Figure 1.1 shows the evolution over time in the number of listed firms with positive earnings, distinguishing between small and large firms using the data from Table 1.2. For each year, the number of small (large) firms is computed as the sum of small (large) firm IPOs from the prior three years and small (large) firms listed by more than three years, with earnings per share available from Datastream. An inspection of the graph clearly reveals that the fraction of unprofitable firms, represented by the dark shaded area, is

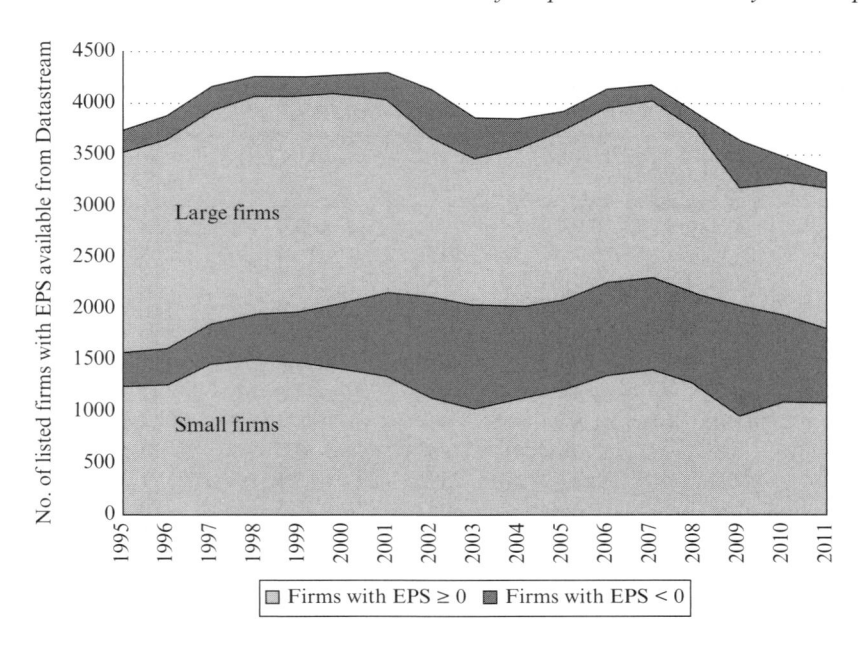

Notes:
The graph reports the number of firms with earnings per share available from Datastream each year from 1995 to 2011, categorized by firm size and profitability.
The black line divides small firms from large firms.
The light shaded area represents the fraction of firms with non-negative earnings per share, while the dark shaded area represents the fraction of firms with negative earnings per share.
For each year, the number of small firms is the sum of small firm IPOs from the prior three years (pre-IPO annual sales < €30 million, 2011 purchasing power) and small firms listed more than three years (annual sales < €250 million, 2011 purchasing power).
Analogously, the number of large firms is the sum of large firm IPOs from the prior three years and large firms listed more than three years.

Figure 1.1 Profitability of small and large listed firms

larger among small companies and is widening over time. Conversely, the fraction of unprofitable large firms is smaller and remains quite stable across the sample years. This evidence is consistent with the predictions of the economies of scope hypothesis.

4.2 Long-run Performance

We measure stock price performance as three-year buy-and-hold returns (BHR), measured from the closing market price after the first 21 days of trading until the three-year anniversary (35 months) or the closing market price on the delisting day, if this occurs earlier. Table 1.3 shows that mean three-year BHR returns decreased from 4.9 percent for companies listing during 1995–2000 to 0 percent for those listing during 2001–08. Over the entire sample period, the equally weighted three-year BHR averaged 2.5 percent, less than 1 percent per year. Most importantly, large firm IPOs outperform small firm IPOs: on average, the three-year BHR is 14.6 percent for large and −2.9 percent for small companies. Average returns associated with the two subperiods,

Table 1.3 Long-run performance of IPOs by firm size

	All IPOs		Small-firm IPOs		Large-firm IPOs	
	No. with sales	3y BHR (%)	No. with sales	3y BHR (%)	No. with sales	3y BHR (%)
1995	87	110.0	49	103.0	38	119.1
1996	215	26.7	147	16.4	68	48.1
1997	219	188.9	146	214.3	73	140.4
1998	275	12.0	159	9.8	116	14.8
1999	371	−39.9	252	−52.8	119	−12.6
2000	569	−63.9	392	−71.0	177	−45.7
2001	191	−21.8	149	−23.6	42	−15.4
2002	118	41.8	94	38.4	24	53.0
2003	89	42.2	66	28.7	23	88.5
2004	309	30.2	238	13.6	71	79.4
2005	429	13.8	309	7.5	120	27.5
2006	421	−9.0	294	−2.2	127	−23.7
2007	351	−37.2	231	−38.0	120	−35.6
2008	58	−4.0	46	−5.0	12	−0.2
Annual						
1995–2000	289	4.9	191	−2.5	99	19.7
2001–08	246	0.0	178	−3.3	67	8.3
Total	3702	2.5	2572	−2.9	1130	14.6

Notes:
Average three-year buy-and-hold returns (in percentage) of IPOs in Europe (London, Euronext, Frankfurt, and Milan) from 1995 to 2008.
The sample includes all the IPOs from the EurIPO database for which we have information on pre-IPO sales. Small-firm IPOs are defined as those from companies with less than €30 million in pre-IPO annual sales, in 2011 purchasing power.
The first 21 trading days after the IPO are excluded, as underwriters are often still stabilizing prices during this period.
Returns are thus over the 35 months starting one month after the IPO, or a shorter time if a stock is delisted before its third year anniversary.
'Annual' rows show the mean values of IPO volume and proceeds per year, and the percentage of small and large firms, for the pre- and post-bubble periods.

before and after the technology bubble burst in 2000, are positive for large firm IPOs (19.7 percent and 8.3 percent), while they are negative for small firm IPOs (−2.5 percent and −3.3 percent). With a few exceptions (1997 and 2006), the poorer long-run performance of small-firm IPOs exists across all of the sample years. Regardless of the cause, the low realized returns on small-company IPOs would inevitably dampen investor enthusiasm towards them, resulting in lower volume. One possible motivation is, as argued by Gao et al. (2012), that the declining profitability of small firms, if unanticipated, results in low returns. Although we do not find evidence that the long-run returns for small firms decreased more than the long-run returns for large firms, as predicted in our hypothesis 2, we show that the underperformance of IPOs is concentrated among small firms, consistent with the evidence for the US in Ritter (2011) and Gao et al. (2012).

Table 1.4 IPOs by foreign companies in European and US markets

	European exchanges					US exchanges		Other exchanges	
	No. IPOs	Non-EU firm IPOs		US firm IPOs		No. EU firm IPOs	% EU firm IPOs	No. EU firm IPOs	% EU firm IPOs
		No.	%	No.	%				
1995	87	1	1.1	0	0.0	2	0.4	0	0.0
1996	230	5	2.2	1	0.4	1	0.1	1	0.2
1997	219	3	1.4	2	0.9	0	0.0	0	0.0
1998	275	3	1.1	1	0.4	2	0.7	1	0.4
1999	373	11	2.9	6	1.6	0	0.0	0	0.0
2000	572	19	3.3	4	0.7	1	0.3	0	0.0
2001	191	3	1.6	1	0.5	2	2.5	0	0.0
2002	120	5	4.2	3	2.5	2	3.0	0	0.0
2003	89	4	4.5	0	0.0	1	1.6	0	0.0
2004	309	30	9.7	5	1.6	0	0.0	0	0.0
2005	429	53	12.4	9	2.1	1	0.6	1	0.2
2006	421	49	11.6	14	3.3	1	0.6	0	0.0
2007	353	49	13.9	11	3.1	1	0.6	3	0.5
2008	60	9	15.0	3	5.0	2	9.5	1	0.6
2009	27	5	18.5	3	11.1	0	0.0	1	0.8
2010	102	15	14.7	6	5.9	3	3.2	2	0.6
2011	91	7	7.7	4	4.4	6	7.4	2	0.5
Annual									
1995–2000	293	7	2.4	2	0.8	1	0.2	0	0.1
2001–11	199	21	10.4	5	2.7	2	1.7	1	0.9
Total	3948	271	6.9	73	1.8	25	0.7	12	0.2

Notes:
The table shows the number and percentage of IPOs conducted by foreign companies from 1995 to 2011 on the following stock exchanges: 'European exchanges' are London, Euronext, Frankfurt, and Milan stock exchanges; 'US exchanges' are NYSE and NASDAQ; 'Other exchanges' include Australia, India, Singapore, Hong Kong and Toronto stock exchanges. Non-European IPOs are those conducted by firms registered in a country outside the EU27 area.
Firms domiciled in tax-haven countries are included as non-European, irrespective of the main country of operations.
The 'European exchanges' column shows both the fraction of non-European and US firm IPOs.

Source: EurIPO, Datastream.

4.3 Foreign Listings

The fraction of IPOs from foreign companies on our four European markets did not decrease over the last decade. As reported in Table 1.4, non-European firms are not a large percentage of European IPOs (6.9 percent of the overall sample, with 1.8 percent being US companies). This percentage was particularly low (2.4 percent) in the period 1995–2000, and increased afterward (10.4 percent in the period 2001–11), when the level of regulation in Europe increased. The same pattern has been followed by US firms listing in Europe, increasing from 0.8 percent during 1995–2000 to 2.7 percent from 2001 onwards. Therefore, the decision to list on European stock exchanges from overseas has not been negatively affected by changes in regulation. This is consistent with our hypothesis 3, which states that there was no significant decrease in the market share of foreign IPOs in European markets over the past decade.

Although most capital raising occurs predominantly in domestic markets, the decreasing transaction costs resulting from ongoing financial globalization have pushed more companies to turn to global markets as a source of funds (Kim and Weisbach, 2008). Hence, an impact of the overreach of regulation may be hidden by the higher mobility of IPOs. To this extent, Table 1.4 reports the fraction of European firms going public abroad, namely the US and other countries that have received an increasing interest by European issuers over the past decade ('other exchanges' includes those of Australia, Hong Kong, Singapore, India, and Canada). Results show that the flow of European companies going public abroad, either in the US or in other countries, is minimal. The annual average fraction is 0.7 percent for US exchanges, and 0.2 percent for other exchanges. This reveals that European companies have not started emigrating to other countries after the regulatory tightening, while European IPO markets have become more attractive.

4.4 Post-IPO M&A Activity and Delistings

Figure 1.2 compares the trends of IPO and M&A activities in Europe. The IPO volume refers to companies going public on the four stock exchanges included in our sample, while M&A volume includes all deals completed each year and involving a target based in Western Europe (the source is Zephyr Annual Report). After a common peak around 2006, IPO volume suffers a dramatic decline, as already documented in Table 1.1. The low volume of IPOs in 2008–11 is at least partly attributable to the lower valuations following the 'panic' of 2008 and the subsequent Eurozone crisis. For France, Germany, Italy, and the UK, the total real return on equities was negative during 2007–11. However, the volume of mergers and acquisitions does not show the decline that IPO volume does, remaining stable at a high level. This is consistent with an increased preference of private firms to sell to another company instead of raising public equity capital, as implied by the economies of scope hypothesis. Therefore, inspection of Figure 1.2 offers support to our hypothesis 4 that, while the number of IPOs decreases, M&A activity does not.

Table 1.5 shows the fraction of European companies that delist, either voluntarily or for bankruptcy, and those that are acquired or acquire another firm, within three years after their IPO. After the technology bubble burst, there is an increased propensity to be targeted shortly after going public. Of the IPOs listed before 2001, 7.1 percent were acquired within three years; this percentage increases slightly to 7.7 percent from 2001 onwards. Conversely, the propensity to acquire after going public has decreased. The fraction of newly listed firms making at least one acquisition has dropped from 42.3 percent to 28.7 percent. By splitting the analysis according to firm size, evidence shows that the upward trend in being targeted is driven by small firms. Before the bubble, 7.4 percent of small and 6.8 percent of large firms were acquired in the three years following the IPO; after the bubble, these percentages change to 8.5 percent and 5.4 percent respectively. The fraction of firms completing at least one

Economies of scope and IPO activity in Europe 23

Yearly deals/total 1995–2011 deals

Notes:
The black solid line refers to the number of IPOs in Europe (London, Euronext, Frankfurt and Milan; *source:* EurIPO), while the dashed line refers to the number of M&As involving a target based in Western Europe, both public and private (*source:* Zephyr).
Values are computed as the ratio between the number of IPOs (M&As) in the corresponding year on the X-axis and the overall number of IPOs (M&As) completed during 1995–2011.

Figure 1.2 IPO vs M&A activity in Europe

M&A as an acquirer is instead decreasing regardless of firm size: from 40.4 percent to 26.6 percent among small-firm IPOs, and from 47.5 percent to 34.5 percent among large-firm IPOs.[8] Overall, the evidence in Table 1.5 is consistent with our hypothesis 5, that the percentage of small firms that go public and are acquired soon after their IPO has increased over the past decade. Our hypothesis 6, predicting an increase in the percentage of small firms that go public and make acquisitions after their IPO, does not find support.

The fraction of companies that decide to delist fluctuates across the years, with no striking evidence of an increased propensity to leave the public market in the last decade, consistent with our seventh hypothesis. The percentages of 2006 (1.7 percent) and 2007 (0.3 percent) are far below the average value of the sample period (3.3 percent), while the result of 2008 (3.3 percent) may be influenced by the advent of the financial crisis. Also the mean delisting rate in the pre-bubble period is slightly higher than the post-bubble value. Hence, there is apparently no support for arguing that the IPO drought among small firms is primarily caused by increased costs of going (and staying) public. At least, there is no significant increase over the last decade in the fraction of IPOs that subsequently go private as an independent firm, consistent with hypothesis 7.

Table 1.5 M&A activity and delistings of IPOs within three years

	All IPOs							Small firm IPOs							Large firm IPOs				
	No. IPOs	Target		Acquirer		Delisting		No. IPOs	Target		Acquirer		No. IPOs	Target		Acquirer	
		No.	%	No.	%	No.	%		No.	%	No.	%		No.	%	No.	%
1995	87	9	10.3	31	35.6	1	1.1	49	3	6.1	20	40.8	38	6	15.8	11	28.9
1996	230	18	7.8	89	38.7	7	3	147	11	7.5	53	36.1	68	7	10.3	36	52.9
1997	219	17	7.8	95	43.4	11	5	146	9	6.2	63	43.2	73	8	11	32	43.8
1998	275	17	6.2	123	44.7	5	1.8	159	10	6.3	71	44.7	116	7	6	52	44.8
1999	373	13	3.5	163	43.7	10	2.7	252	11	4.4	100	39.7	119	2	1.7	63	52.9
2000	572	51	8.9	245	42.8	31	5.4	391	41	10.5	157	40.2	177	10	5.6	88	49.7
2001	191	24	12.6	66	34.6	5	2.6	149	21	14.1	48	32.2	42	3	7.1	18	42.9
2002	120	8	6.7	34	28.3	5	4.2	94	7	7.4	25	26.6	24	1	4.2	9	37.5
2003	89	8	9	38	42.7	4	4.5	66	7	10.6	27	40.9	23	1	4.3	11	47.8
2004	309	44	14.2	120	38.8	26	8.4	238	36	15.1	85	35.7	71	8	11.3	35	49.3
2005	429	44	10.3	132	30.8	15	3.5	309	35	11.3	93	30.1	120	9	7.5	39	32.5
2006	421	18	4.3	92	21.9	7	1.7	294	12	4.1	55	18.7	127	6	4.7	37	29.1
2007	353	4	1.1	73	20.7	1	0.3	232	4	1.7	37	15.9	119	0	0	36	30.3
2008	60	1	1.7	11	18.3	2	3.3	46	0	0	10	21.7	13	1	7.7	1	7.7
Annual																	
1995–2000	293	21	7.1	124	42.3	11	3.7	191	14	7.4	77	40.4	99	7	6.8	47	47.5
2001–08	247	19	7.7	71	28.7	8	3.3	179	15	8.5	48	26.6	67	4	5.4	23	34.5
Total	3728	276	7.4	1312	35.2	130	3.5	2572	207	8	844	32.8	1130	69	6.1	468	41.4

Notes:
The sample is composed of 3 728 IPOs in Europe (London, Euronext, Frankfurt, and Milan) from 1995 to 2008.
'Target' includes IPOs that are taken over within three years from the IPO.
'Acquirer' includes IPOs that completed at least one merger or acquisition (M&A) deal as acquirer within three years from the IPO.
'Delisting' includes IPOs that delist due to bankruptcy or at direct request of the company within three years from the IPO.
Small-firm IPOs are defined as companies with less than €30 million in pre-IPO annual sales, in 2011 purchasing power.

Source: EurIPO, Thomson OneBanker for the number of acquisitions.

5 SECOND MARKETS

The existence of second-tier markets is a peculiarity of European stock exchanges that should not be neglected.[9] The role of second markets, characterized by considerably looser regulation, has been relevant in Europe. The most popular second market in Europe, London's Alternative Investment Market (AIM), accounts for 79 percent of the IPOs taking place in London from 1995 to 2011. As documented by Vismara et al. (2012), these markets are dominated by small firms. In particular, they provide small firms that do not succeed in meeting main markets' requirements with an easier opportunity to go public. Since second markets have not been affected by the post-SOX regulatory tightening, the motivations behind the regulatory overreach hypothesis do not apply. Thus, second markets represent an ideal setting in which to test whether the predictions of the economies of scope hypothesis persist even in the absence of regulatory concerns.

Our previous analysis of the profitability of recent IPOs revealed that large firms seem to be able to remain profitable more easily than small firms. If the decrease in profitability was primarily caused by increased compliance costs, we would expect a higher level of profitability among second market IPOs, which are exempt from strict regulatory requirements. Table 1.6 documents that this is not the case. First, the percentage of recently listed firms that remain profitable is persistently higher among main market IPOs, both for small and large firms. On main markets, 80.3 percent of recent IPOs are profitable on average each year, while on second markets this percentage is only 58.9 percent. Second, the profitability rate among second market IPOs is worse for small than for large companies. This suggests that, even in the absence of regulatory burdens, small firms still face a higher difficulty to remain profitable than their large counterparts, as argued by the economies of scope hypothesis. On average, 82.3 percent of large-firm IPOs from the prior three years on second markets are profitable, while this occurs for only 52.8 percent of small-firm IPOs.

Table 1.7 provides a picture of the long-run performance of European IPOs, distinguishing between main and second markets. At an aggregate level, in Table 1.3 we previously documented the persistently poorer long-run performance of small-firm IPOs in comparison to large-firm IPOs. Again, if low returns were caused by an unexpected decrease in earnings due to higher compliance costs, this pattern should not be present among second market IPOs. However, results show that second market IPOs perform worse than main market IPOs, and this is true for both small and large firms. The average three-year buy-and-hold return across the entire 1995–2008 sample period for main market IPOs is 27.5 percent, considerably higher than the −5.1 percent return associated with second market IPOs. Further, the lower returns on small firm IPOs compared to large firm IPOs are confirmed even in second markets, consistent with the economies of scope explanation. Here, large firm IPOs outperform their small counterparts by an average 12.5 percent over three years, with a mean three-year buy-and-hold return on large firm IPOs of 4.9 percent compared to −7.6 percent on small firm IPOs.

The increase in the fraction of foreign companies going public in European markets, documented in the previous section and inconsistent with the regulatory overreach hypothesis, needs to be clarified by considering the two market categories separately. Only main markets are indeed affected by regulatory changes. Thus, the aggregate result may by driven by second markets, characterized by a substantially larger number of companies going public each year. An increasingly large number of non-European

Table 1.6 Profitability of recent IPOs by market type

	Main market IPOs from the prior 3 years				Second market IPOs from the prior 3 years			
	No. with EPS	EPS ≥ 0 (%)	Small with EPS ≥ 0 (%)	Large with EPS ≥ 0 (%)	No. with EPS	EPS ≥ 0 (%)	Small with EPS ≥ 0 (%)	Large with EPS ≥ 0 (%)
1995	89	87.6	77.2	95.2	58	81.5	76.6	96.3
1996	102	88.2	74.9	93.0	143	81.1	75.8	97.0
1997	121	81.0	68.6	92.6	168	77.0	71.4	95.7
1998	185	87.0	78.4	93.6	363	80.2	73.5	96.0
1999	173	90.2	79.0	96.4	497	77.9	72.4	92.0
2000	174	74.7	53.2	86.6	676	62.3	55.6	82.2
2001	173	67.1	42.6	80.4	721	49.8	44.2	71.1
2002	131	53.4	28.3	67.1	572	40.4	36.6	58.6
2003	57	66.7	40.0	72.3	226	44.7	43.0	63.2
2004	65	86.2	72.7	88.9	272	47.1	41.9	87.1
2005	105	78.1	42.1	86.0	421	48.5	43.0	83.9
2006	184	81.0	54.0	91.0	668	48.5	43.7	77.7
2007	225	83.6	62.3	92.9	706	52.7	46.6	82.0
2008	177	84.2	69.8	92.1	494	56.1	49.4	84.9
2009	89	69.7	51.6	78.0	251	49.4	46.4	59.3
2010	34	76.5	60.0	80.0	89	43.8	38.6	61.1
2011	40	77.5	37.5	84.8	106	44.3	36.5	75.0
Annual								
1995–2000	141	84.7	72.6	92.8	318	74.0	68.0	90.7
2001–11	155	76.8	55.9	85.8	411	49.1	43.9	75.5
Total	2124	80.3	65.2	88.5	6431	58.9	52.8	82.3

Notes:
The table reports the percentage of recent IPOs with non-negative EPS each year, distinguishing between main and second markets.
The 'No. with EPS' columns refer to IPO firms with EPS available in Datastream.
'Main market IPOs from the prior three years' are IPOs taking place on Official List (London), Eurolist (Euronext), Amtlicher Markt (Frankfurt), and MTA (Milan), for which year t is one of the first three post-IPO fiscal years.
'Second market IPOs from the prior three years' are IPOs taking place on AIM (UK), Second Marché, Nouveau Marché, Marché Libre and Alternext (France), Neuer Markt and Freiverkehr Markt (Germany) and Expandi, Nuovo Mercato and AIM Italia (Italy), for which year t is one of the first three post-IPO fiscal years. Small and large firm IPOs are defined on the basis of pre-IPO annual sales of €30 million, in 2011 purchasing power (Eurostat).
'Annual' rows show the mean values of IPO volume and proceeds per year, and the percentage of small and large firms, for the pre- and post-bubble periods.

companies going public on second markets to avoid higher compliance costs may hide a negative trend on main markets, which would instead be consistent with the regulatory overreach hypothesis. However, Table 1.8 reveals that this is not the case. The market share of foreign IPOs is increasing both in main and second markets. Before the technology bubble burst in 2000, the percentage of IPOs by non-European firms averages 1.5 percent on main markets and 2.7 percent on second markets; from 2001 onwards, these percentages increase to 4.8 percent and 11.8 percent, respectively. Thus, the upward trend

Table 1.7 Long-run performance of IPOs by market type

	Main market IPOs				Second market IPOs			
	No. with sales	All IPOs	Small-firm IPOs	Large-firm IPOs	No. with sales	All IPOs	Small-firm IPOs	Large-firm IPOs
1995	58	115.9	121.1	110.2	29	98.4	74.4	143.9
1996	75	47.8	16.4	53.2	140	15.2	10.7	37.8
1997	76	141.1	214.3	114.6	143	217.1	228.5	177.5
1998	71	39.8	9.8	24.1	204	2.8	−0.6	9.0
1999	78	−35.8	−52.8	−28.1	293	−40.9	−52.9	−2.3
2000	105	−51.7	−70.9	−37.9	463	−66.5	−71.0	−50.3
2001	32	0.2	−23.6	−9.2	159	−26.6	−26.4	−29.6
2002	23	73.7	38.4	80.2	95	32.3	36.8	−19.5
2003	13	113.5	28.7	120.4	76	27.7	26.8	35.4
2004	40	81.3	13.6	92.4	269	21.5	14.5	64.7
2005	69	36.5	7.5	41.6	360	9.3	7.2	16.9
2006	98	−12.5	−2.2	−17.8	323	−7.7	−2.5	−32.9
2007	79	−34.3	−38.2	−41.1	272	−38.0	−40.5	−30.5
2008	12	17.6	−5.0	20.5	47	−10.6	−8.3	−22.7
Annual								
1995–2000	77	36.6	46.0	30.2	212	−6.4	−11.8	10.5
2001–08	46	15.1	5.1	18.3	200	−3.8	−4.0	−2.9
Total	829	27.5	33.5	24.5	2873	−5.1	−7.6	4.9

Notes:
Average three-year percentage buy-and-hold returns of IPOs in Europe (London, Euronext, Frankfurt, and Milan) from 1995 to 2008, distinguishing between main and second markets.
The sample includes all the IPOs from the EurIPO database for which we have information on pre-IPO sales. Main markets are Official List (London), Eurolist (Euronext), Amtlicher Markt (Frankfurt), and MTA (Milan); second markets are AIM (UK), Second Marché, Nouveau Marché, Marché Libre and Alternext (France), Neuer Markt and Freiverkehr Markt (Germany) and Expandi, Nuovo Mercato and AIM Italia (Italy).
Small-firm IPOs are defined as those from companies with less than €30 million in pre-IPO annual sales, in 2011 purchasing power.
The first 21 trading days after the IPO are excluded, as underwriters are often still stabilizing prices during this period.
If a stock is delisted before the 36-month anniversary of the IPO, the buy-and-hold return is less than 35 months.
'Annual' rows show the mean values of IPO volume and proceeds per year, and the percentage of small and large firms, for the pre- and post-bubble periods.

in non-European IPOs is confirmed also on main markets, despite increased compliance costs. This is in contrast to the predictions of the regulatory overreach hypothesis.

Our previous analysis on post-listing activity documented that the percentage of small firms that are acquired soon after their IPO has increased, and that regulatory changes have apparently not pushed publicly traded firms to go private more frequently. We now test the implications of the economies of scope hypothesis at the market level. Specifically, a sharper increase in the propensity to be acquired should be observed among second market IPOs, where the presence of small firms is predominant. At the same time, the regulatory overreach hypothesis would predict a higher propensity to delist only for main market IPOs, in an attempt to avoid compliance costs. Results are shown in Table 1.9.

28   Handbook of research on IPOs

Table 1.8   The market share of non-European companies by market type

	Main market IPOs			Second market IPOs		
	No. IPOs	Non-EU	% non-EU	No. IPOs	Non-EU	% non-EU
1995	58	0	0.0	29	1	3.4
1996	83	0	0.0	147	5	3.4
1997	76	0	0.0	143	3	2.1
1998	71	1	1.4	204	2	1.0
1999	78	1	1.3	295	10	3.4
2000	108	5	4.6	464	14	3.0
2001	32	0	0.0	159	3	1.9
2002	25	0	0.0	95	5	5.3
2003	13	3	23.1	76	1	1.3
2004	40	3	7.5	269	27	10.0
2005	69	0	0.0	360	53	14.7
2006	98	2	2.0	323	47	14.6
2007	79	3	3.8	274	46	16.8
2008	12	0	0.0	48	9	18.8
2009	3	0	0.0	24	5	20.8
2010	25	6	24.0	77	9	11.7
2011	23	3	13.0	68	4	5.9
Annual						
1995–2000	79	1	1.5	214	6	2.7
2001–11	38	2	4.8	161	19	11.8
Total	893	27	3.0	3055	244	8.0

Notes:
IPOs in Europe (London, Euronext, Frankfurt, and Milan) from 1995 to 2011, distinguishing between main vs second markets.
Main markets are Official List (London), Eurolist (Euronext), Amtlicher Markt (Frankfurt), and MTA (Milan); second markets are AIM (UK), Second Marché, Nouveau Marché, Marché Libre and Alternext (France), Neuer Markt and Freiverkehr Markt (Germany) and Expandi, Nuovo Mercato and AIM Italia (Italy).
Non-European IPOs are considered as IPOs conducted by firms registered in a country outside the EU27 area. Firms domiciled in tax-haven countries are included as non-European, irrespective of the main country of operations.

Source: EurIPO.

Inconsistent with the regulatory overreach hypothesis, only second market IPOs experience an increase in their propensity to be targeted. While the average fraction of IPOs acquired in the following three years decreases from 11.4 percent in 1995–2000 to 2.4 percent in 2001–08 on main markets, it increases from 5.5 percent to 8.9 percent among second market IPOs. These patterns suggest that the desire to get big fast by becoming part of a larger organization predominantly concerns small firms, as posited by the economies of scope explanation. The propensity to acquire is instead decreasing in both markets. The fraction of firms making at least one acquisition decreases from 45.8 percent to 36.4 percent after the bubble burst among main market IPOs, and from 41.0 percent to 26.9 percent among second market IPOs. Inconsistent with the regulatory overreach hypothesis, the average propensity to delist is lower for main market IPOs (1.4

Table 1.9 M&A activity and delistings of IPOs within three years, by market type

	Main market IPOs							Second market IPOs					
	No. IPOs	Target No.	%	Acquirer No.	%	Delisting No.	%	No. IPOs	Target No.	%	Acquirer No.	%	Delisting No.	%
1995	58	8	13.8	22	37.9	0	0.0	29	1	3.4	9	31.0	1	3.4
1996	83	10	12.0	37	44.6	1	1.2	147	8	5.4	52	35.4	6	4.1
1997	76	11	14.5	36	47.4	1	1.3	143	6	4.2	59	41.3	10	7.0
1998	71	11	15.5	34	47.9	1	1.4	204	6	2.9	89	43.6	4	2.0
1999	78	1	1.3	34	43.6	1	1.3	295	12	4.1	129	43.7	9	3.1
2000	108	13	12.0	54	50.0	5	4.6	464	38	8.2	191	41.2	26	5.6
2001	32	2	6.3	12	37.5	2	6.3	159	22	13.8	54	34.0	3	1.9
2002	25	1	4.0	9	36.0	1	4.0	95	7	7.4	25	26.3	4	4.2
2003	13	1	7.7	6	46.2	0	0.0	76	7	9.2	32	42.1	4	5.3
2004	40	3	7.5	17	42.5	0	0.0	269	41	15.2	103	38.3	26	9.7
2005	69	1	1.4	31	44.9	0	0.0	360	43	11.9	101	28.1	15	4.2
2006	98	1	1.0	31	31.6	0	0.0	323	17	5.3	61	18.9	7	2.2
2007	79	0	0.0	25	31.6	0	0.0	274	4	1.5	48	17.5	1	0.4
2008	12	0	0.0	3	25.0	0	0.0	48	1	2.1	8	16.7	2	4.2
Annual														
1995–2000	79	9	11.4	36	45.8	2	1.9	214	12	5.5	88	41.0	9	4.4
2001–08	46	1	2.4	17	36.4	0	0.8	201	18	8.9	54	26.9	8	3.9
Total	842	63	7.5	351	41.7	12	1.4	2886	213	7.4	961	33.3	118	4.1

Notes:
Sample of IPOs in Europe (London, Euronext, Frankfurt, and Milan) from 1995 to 2008, distinguishing between main and second markets.
Main markets are Official List (London), Eurolist (Euronext), Amtlicher Markt (Frankfurt), and MTA (Milan); second markets are AIM (UK), Second Marché, Nouveau Marché, Marché Libre and Alternext (France), Neuer Markt and Freiverkehr Markt (Germany) and Expandi, Nuovo Mercato and AIM Italia (Italy).
Target includes IPOs that are taken over within three years from the IPO.
Acquirer includes IPOs that completed at least one merger or acquisition (M&A) deal as acquirer within three years from the IPO.
Delisting includes IPOs that delist due to bankruptcy or at direct request of the company within three years from the IPO.

Source: EurIPO, Thomson OneBanker for the number of acquisitions.

percent on average) than for second market IPOs (4.1 percent). Additionally, while this percentage increases among second market IPOs, which are exempt from most regulatory requirements, it decreases among main market IPOs, where companies instead face the increased regulatory costs of staying public.

6 TIME-SERIES REGRESSIONS EXPLAINING IPO ACTIVITY

Market conditions have been widely documented to play a substantial role in a firm's decision to go public. Figure 1.3 reports the number of IPOs taking place each year on the London, Euronext, Frankfurt, and Milan stock exchanges from 1995 to 2011, both

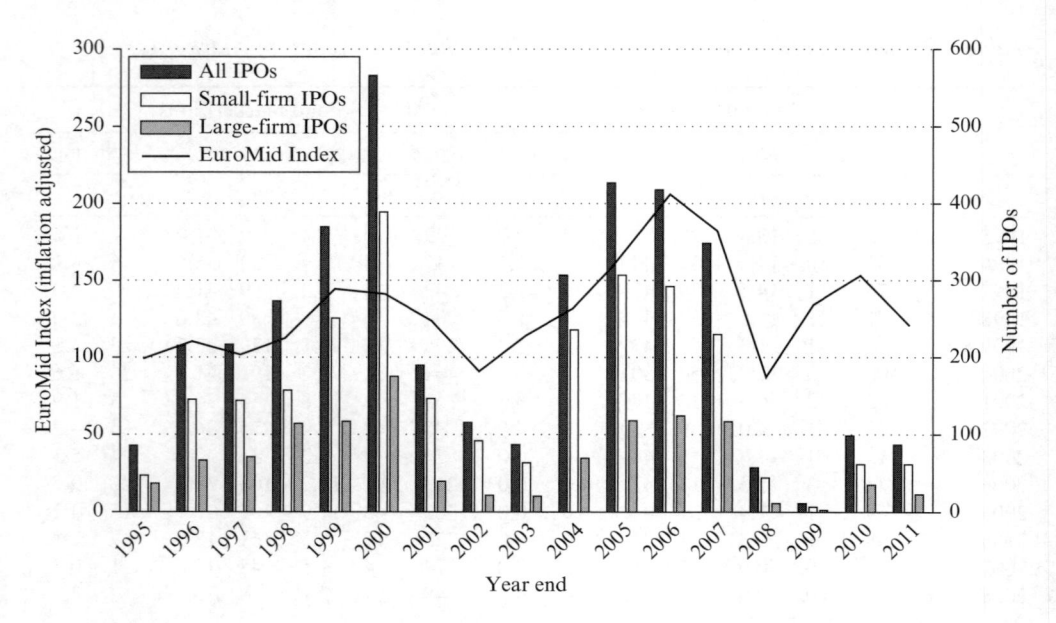

30 *Handbook of research on IPOs*

Notes:
The bars show the number of IPOs taking place each year in Europe (London, Euronext, Frankfurt and Milan; *source:* EurIPO) from 1995 to 2011, categorized by firm size. The aggregate number of IPOs is represented by the black bar, while the light (dark) grey bar shows the number of small (large) firm IPOs. Small-firm IPOs are defined as with less than €30 million in pre-IPO annual sales, in 2011 purchasing power. The black line shows the inflation-adjusted year-end value of the EuroMid index excluding dividends (*source:* Datastream) in 2011 purchasing power (Eurostat), scaled at 100 for the 1995 year end value.

Figure 1.3 IPO activity and market valuation in Europe

at an aggregate level (black bars) and by firm size (light grey for small firm IPOs, and dark grey for large firm IPOs). The black line shows the FTSE EuroMid index, excluding dividends, adjusted for inflation using 2011 purchasing power and scaled at 100 for the 1995 year end value. The correlation between IPO activity and the equity index stands out immediately. Specifically, the 2008–11 and the 2001–03 volume declines appear to be largely due to depressed market valuations. This evidence supports the market conditions hypothesis. In addition to cyclical fluctuations, however, there is a negative trend in IPO activity, which could be due to either increased compliance costs and/or structural changes penalizing small firms.

To discriminate among the alternative explanations for changing IPO volume, we examine the volume of European IPOs in a time-series setting, and test whether a downward trend in the number of companies going public is present after controlling for market conditions. The economies of scope hypothesis predicts a more pronounced decline among small-firm IPOs. Table 1.10 shows the results of the quarterly time series regression estimated using maximum likelihood with a first-order autoregressive error term. The dependent variable in model (1) is the number of IPOs in each quarter divided by quarterly real GDP (measured in € trillions) in the same quarter. In model (2) and model (3), the dependent variable is respectively the scaled number of small-and large-firm IPOs, using a

Table 1.10 Quarterly time-series maximum likelihood regressions of scaled IPO volume

	Mean value (std deviation)	(1) No. of IPOs	(2) No. small-firm IPOs	(3) No. large-firm IPOs	(4) No. IPOs on second markets
Mean value of the dependent variable		29.76	20.35	9.09	22.88
Standard deviation of the dependent variable		(21.66)	(14.97)	(7.71)	(17.62)
Time trend	34.00	−0.71**	−0.34*	−0.26	−0.39*
	(19.49)	(−2.10)	(−1.93)	(−1.52)	(−1.88)
EU SOX-equivalent	0.57	−11.91	−2.90	−5.76	−8.90
	0.50	(−1.32)	(−0.52)	(−1.43)	(−0.98)
EuroMid Index	1.70	29.96***	13.46***	12.57***	17.51***
	(0.50)	(2.83)	(2.67)	(3.76)	(2.65)
M/B small firms $(t-2)$	6.17	0.47	0.27	0.20	0.05
	(5.21)	(0.73)	(0.99)	(1.12)	(0.38)
EuroMid return $[t-2, t-1]$	1.46	−0.13	−0.08	−0.04	−0.09
	(10.93)	(−0.79)	(−1.07)	(−0.53)	(−0.86)
Initial IPO return $(t-1)$	15.98	0.19**	0.08*	0.12***	0.10*
	(23.66)	(2.18)	(1.83)	(3.71)	(1.94)
EuroMid future return $[t+1, t+4]$	4.84	0.10	0.05	0.05	0.07
	(21.56)	(1.14)	(1.01)	(0.83)	(1.02)
Real GDP growth $[t, t+3]$	1.16	0.85	0.20	0.43	0.42
	(2.59)	(1.33)	(0.49)	(0.84)	(0.94)
Percentage of small firms with EPS ≥ 0 $(t-1)$	67.05	−0.46	−0.04	−0.20	−0.34
	(10.15)	(−0.89)	(−0.11)	(−0.79)	(−0.79)
Quarter 1 dummy	0.25	−12.55***	−7.85***	−3.97*	−8.33***
	(0.44)	(−5.21)	(−5.32)	(−1.89)	(−4.58)
AR(1) coefficient		0.57***	0.78***	0.02	0.74***
		(2.67)	(7.45)	(0.10)	(5.31)
Constant		36.64	11.53	10.22	30.92
		(1.00)	(0.38)	(0.54)	(0.97)
Observations		67	67	67	67
R-squared		0.77	0.76	0.64	0.77
Durbin-Watson statistics		1.27	1.05	1.97	1.16

Notes:
Time-series regressions using maximum likelihood estimation with residuals following an AR(1) process on the sample of 3948 European IPOs (London, Euronext, Frankfurt and Milan) from 1995 to 2011.
The dependent variable is the number of IPOs (model 1), the number of small firm IPOs (model 2), the number of large firm IPOs (model 3), and the number of second market IPOs (model 4) in each quarter, all scaled by quarterly real GDP, measured in €trillions of 2011 purchasing power.
Small and large IPO firms are distinguished using a cutoff of €30 million in inflation-adjusted pre-IPO annual sales.
GDP is the sum of the quarterly GDPs of the UK, France, Germany and Italy, plus Belgium, Netherlands and Portugal since the establishment of Euronext in 2005, and is measured in trillions of euros.
Time Trend equals 1 for the first quarter of 1995 and increases by 1 for each quarter onwards until the third quarter of 2011.
EU SOX-equivalent dummy equals 1 from the second quarter of 2002, when the implementation of SOX-like regulatory changes began in Europe with the introduction of The German Corporate Governance Code by German authorities.
EuroMid Index is the value of the FTSE EuroMid equity index adjusted for inflation using 2011 purchasing power and scaled at 1 for the first quarter of 1995.

Table 1.10 (continued)

Notes:
M/B for small firms is the market-to-book ratio for small firms (defined as less than €250 million in annual sales using €2011), calculated as the sum of market value of small firms divided by the sum of book value of small firms.
Both the market value and the book value are measured at quarter $t - 2$.
EuroMid return $[t - 2, t - 1]$ is the FTSE EuroMid Index percentage return in quarter $t - 1$.
Initial IPO return $(t - 1)$ is the average first day percentage return for IPOs in quarter $t - 1$, defined as the difference between the first day closing price and the offer price divided by the offer price.
EuroMid future return $[t + 1, t + 4]$ is the FTSE EuroMid Index percentage return in quarter $(t + 1)$ to $(t + 4)$.
Real GDP growth $[t, t+3]$ is the percentage growth in real GDP from quarter t to quarter $t + 3$, downloaded from Eurostat.
Percentage of small firms with EPS ≥ 0 $(t - 1)$ is the percentage of firms with at least three years of trading history that have non-negative EPS in quarter $t - 1$ (small firms are with less than €250 million in annual sales using €2011).
Quarter 1 dummy is a first quarter dummy that equals one in the first quarter of each year and zero otherwise.
AR(1) is the lagged error term.
The Durbin-Watson statistics and the *R*-squareds are also reported.
The 67 quarters are from the first quarter of 1995 to the third quarter of 2011 (the EuroMid future return $[t + 1, t + 4]$ variable is not available for observations of the fourth quarter of 2011).
T-statistics are in parentheses below the coefficients.
***, **, and * indicate significance at the 1%, 5%, and 10% level respectively.

cutoff of €30 million in inflation-adjusted pre-IPO annual sales. In model (4), the dependent variable is the scaled number of second market IPOs. The aim is to test whether, in the absence of compliance costs, the decline in the number of IPOs persists.

There are three explanatory variables of interest. First, a time-trend variable is aimed at capturing the hypothesized gradual impact of economies of scope and speed to product market on scaled IPO volume. Second, a dummy variable that equals one for quarters beginning with the passage of the first European SOX-equivalent code, introduced in February 2002 by German authorities, should clarify whether excessive regulatory costs are a valid motivation for the low IPO volume of the past decade. Third, the inflation-adjusted FTSE EuroMid index value controls for the influence of market valuations.

Results in Table 1.10 show that the coefficient of the time trend variable is negative and significant at the 5 percent level in model (1), and at the 10 percent level in model (2), while insignificant in model (3). Consistent with the economies of scope hypothesis, this implies that a negative trend is affecting the IPO activity in Europe, and this trend is driven by small firms. This evidence is robust to the effects of market conditions which, predictably, are found to significantly influence IPO volumes in all model specifications, as posited by the market conditions hypothesis. At the same time, the insignificant coefficients on the European SOX-equivalent dummy variable indicate that regulatory changes have no reliable impact when considering the gradual downtrend in IPOs together with other control variables. This is inconsistent with the predictions of the regulatory overreach hypothesis.

The coefficient of the time-trend variable is negative and significant also in model (4), where the dependent variable is the scaled number of IPOs on second markets. This is inconsistent with the regulatory overreach hypothesis: in an environment where the compliance costs of being a publicly traded firm are minimal and do not change over time, there is no regulatory-based reason for a decrease in the number of companies going public. Instead, the results unveil a downward trend in the number of companies going public on second markets, where small firms predominate. This significantly negative trend provides further support to the economies of scope hypothesis, since even in the absence of regulatory constraints the decline in IPO activity is present. Predictably, the coefficient on the European SOX-equivalent dummy variable is insignificant.

The average number of IPOs per quarter is approximately 60, and with real GDP averaging approximately €2 trillion per quarter, the dependent variable in model (1) has an average value of approximately 30. The coefficient on the time trend of −0.71 (in model 1) implies that scaled IPO volume is falling at −2.84 per year (−0.71 × 4 quarters) over our 17-year sample period. This is an economically large amount relative to the mean of approximately 30 scaled IPOs per quarter.

7 CONCLUSIONS

Three alternative explanations have been proposed for the recent drop in the number of firms going public in Europe. First, the 'economies of scope' hypothesis (Gao et al., 2012), which states that getting big fast has become more important, resulting in small firms being acquired; second, the 'regulatory overreach' hypothesis, which states that small firms are remaining private due to an increase in the regulatory costs borne by publicly traded firms; and third, the market conditions hypothesis, which points to depressed stock market levels as the primary cause for the low IPO volume. Although the patterns are not quite as strong as those documented by Gao et al. (2012) for US IPOs, our European evidence for 1995–2011 suggests that small-firm IPO activity is experiencing a long-term secular decline. Consistent with the market conditions hypothesis, European IPO volume has been depressed by lower market valuations following the collapse of the technology bubble, the 'Panic' of 2008, and the Eurozone crisis. However, we find a negative trend in IPO volume that persists even after controlling for the influence of market conditions on IPO volumes, and is largely consistent with the economies of scope hypothesis.

The drop in the number of IPOs has been less dramatic in Europe than in the US prior to the Eurozone crisis, thanks to the presence of second, loosely regulated, markets. Even in these markets, however, we find a negative trend in the yearly number of IPOs. This is inconsistent with the regulatory overreach hypothesis: in an environment where the compliance costs of being a publicly traded firm are minimal and did not change over time, there is no regulatory-based reason for such a decrease in the number of companies going public.

As in the US, small publicly traded companies are increasingly finding it difficult to earn positive profits. Furthermore, M&A activity has been on an uptrend. After going public, small firms are increasingly being acquired, suggesting that small firms prefer to get big fast by becoming part of a larger organization rather than to remain independent and rely on internal growth as either a private or public firm. As in the US, public market investors have earned low returns on small company IPOs. European small company IPOs from 1995 to 2008 have given public market investors an average three-year buy-and-hold return of −2.9 percent, markedly lower than the average three-year BHR of 14.6 percent for large company IPOs, consistent with the empirical results of Vismara et al. (2012). The average three-year BHR on all IPOs has been only 2.5 percent, giving investors an average return of less than 1 percent per year. Our analysis suggests that the 2004–07 boom in second market IPOs, primarily on London's AIM, is unlikely to be repeated.

NOTES

1. In their table 1.5, Vismara et al. (2012) report mean three-year buy-and-hold returns of 35.2 percent for main market IPOs and −0.7 percent for second market IPOs, before adjusting for the returns on the FTSE EuroMid index to compute abnormal returns.
2. http://ec.europa.eu/internal_market/company/docs/modern/report_en.pdf (accessed December 2012).
3. All the second markets of the four stock exchanges that we study here are now categorized as 'exchange-regulated'. The main effect is that the national listing authorities (equivalent to the US Securities and Exchange Commission) are not required to approve a firm's prospectus when its listing does not involve a public offer. In practice, shares are issued exclusively to qualified institutional buyers (QIBs), but there are no restrictions on the ability of the QIBs to resell the shares to individual investors. This model is typically associated with London's popular AIM, and was emulated by the other stock markets in continental Europe when trying to (re)launch second-tier markets such as the Alternext by Euronext, the Freiverkehr in Germany (Frankfurt), and the MAC in Italy (Milan).
4. We use the French Paris Bourse until the creation of Euronext with the merger of the four stock exchanges of Belgium, France, the Netherlands and Portugal, where the first listing took place on 27 January 2005. Afterwards, we consider Euronext in its entirety.
5. See Vismara et al. (2012) for a description of the database.
6. Main markets include: Official List (UK), Premier Marché and Eurolist in 2005 (France) Amtlicher Markt (Germany) and MTA (Italy); second markets include: AIM (UK), Second Marché, Nouveau Marché, Marché Libre and Alternext (France), Neuer Markt and Freiverkehr Markt (Germany) and Expandi, Nuovo Mercato and AIM Italia (Italy). Only a few of these markets are still active. See Vismara et al. (2012), table 1.1 for details.
7. Price level adjustments use data from Eurostat.
8. The number of acquisitions is from Thomson OneBanker and considers all completed deals within three years from the IPO. We do not test whether these changes are statistically significant or not. There is industry clustering, so the number of independent observations is less than the total number of observations.
9. Second-tier markets exist elsewhere, such as Hong Kong's GEM and Shenzhen's ChiNext, but the difference in regulation with their respective main markets is not as extreme. In the US, the Amex had a short-lived Emerging Company Marketplace from 1992 to 1995, described by Aggarwal and Angel (1999).

REFERENCES

Aggarwal, R. and Angel, J.J. (1999), 'The rise and fall of the Amex Emerging Company Marketplace', *Journal of Financial Economics*, **52** (2), 257–89.
Akyol, A.C., Cooper, T., Meoli, M. and Vismara, S. (2012), 'Do regulatory changes affect the underpricing of European IPOs?', working paper, University of Bergamo.
Bayar, O. and Chemmanur, T.J. (2011), 'IPOs versus acquisitions and the valuation premium puzzle: a theory of exit choice by entrepreneurs and venture capitalists', *Journal of Financial and Quantitative Analysis*, **46** (6), 1755–93.
Christensen, H.B., Hail, L. and Leuz, C. (2012), 'Capital-market effects of securities regulation: the role of implementation and enforcement', working paper National Bureau of Economic Research.
Gao, X., J.R. Ritter and Z. Zhu (2012), 'Where have all the IPOs gone?', working paper, University of Florida.
Iliev, P. (2010), 'The effect of SOX Section 404: costs, earnings quality, and stock prices', *Journal of Finance*, **65** (3), 1163–96.
Kim, W. and M.S. Weisbach (2008), 'Motivations for public equity offers: an international perspective', *Journal of Financial Economics*, **87** (2), 281–307.
Ritter, J.R. (2011), 'Equilibrium in the initial public offerings market', *Annual Review of Financial Economics*, **3** (1), 347–74.
Vismara, S., S. Paleari and J.R. Ritter (2012), 'Europe's second markets for small companies', *European Financial Management*, **18** (3), 352–88.

2. The decline in venture-backed IPOs: implications for capital recovery
Susan Chaplinsky and Swasti Gupta-Mukherjee

1 INTRODUCTION

The performance of venture capitalists (VCs) depends critically on the capital recovered from exits of portfolio companies, which occur primarily through initial public offerings (IPOs), or sales or acquisitions (hereafter referred to as 'M&A exits').[1] Over the period 1985 to 2008, the number of M&A exits has exceeded the number of IPO exits in 21 of 24 years – with the gap widening markedly since 2001. The lack of IPO exits has become a source of growing concern, leading many observers to openly ask whether the VC model is broken and question the viability of the venture industry – at least at its present scale.[2] Others have suggested these concerns are exaggerated in an industry prone to ups and downs. The vitality of the VC industry, which has traditionally been an important source of growth and innovation, has broad implications for the overall health of the economy. At the center of this debate is the belief that the returns from M&A exits are decidedly inferior to the returns from IPO exits, and that they fail to produce sufficient capital recovery to justify the highly risky nature of investments in this industry. The main goal of this chapter is to inform this debate by estimating and analyzing the returns to M&A and IPO exits, paying particular attention to the role M&A exits play in capital recovery.

Several recent studies analyze the returns to private equity investments (for example, Ljungdqvist and Richardson, 2003; Cochrane, 2005; Kaplan and Schoar, 2005; Phalippou and Gottschalg, 2009; Korteweg and Sorensen, 2010; Robinson and Sensoy, 2011; and Harris et al., 2012). These studies primarily focus on the overall risk and return characteristics of venture investments relative to public equity markets and typically do not differentiate between the returns earned from IPO and M&A exits. Other studies that analyze M&A exits either use the number of such exits as an indicator of successful performance or treat the exit as an 'event'. Although this approach provides insight into the frequency and nature of M&A exits compared to IPOs, it does not yield an estimate of the capital recovered from exits.[3] In general, academics and practitioners alike have placed more emphasis on the wealth creation of IPOs with a limited understanding of the role that M&A exits have. As IPO exits have decreased in frequency as the primary avenue of exit, however, it raises the question of to what degree M&A exits can substitute in terms of capital recovery.

In contrast to previous studies, we focus on the differences in returns between M&A and IPO exits to directly address the concerns surrounding the form of exit. We calculate portfolio company returns for 1401 IPO exits and 1215 M&A exits from US venture-backed companies that occur over 1985 to 2008, primarily using post-money valuation data from Venture Economics. Using these exit returns, we provide insight on several important questions relevant to the issue of capital recovery in the VC industry:

1. How do the distributional properties of returns differ between IPO and M&A exits?
2. How do the fundamental components of exit returns, the amount of money invested, VC equity stakes, and the amount of money received from exits, differentially affect the returns to IPO and M&A exits?
3. What does the decreased incidence of IPO exits over time imply for industry-wide capital recovery?

With respect to the first question, we find for the overall sample, that the mean company-level return from IPO exits is 209.5 percent and the median return is 108.8 percent. By comparison, the mean return for M&A exits is 99.5 percent and the median return is −32.1 percent. The substantially lower returns for M&A exits are consistent with the concerns expressed by industry observers and prior academic work which has viewed IPOs as the primary vehicle of VC wealth creation. Consistent with Cochrane (2005), there is also a wide dispersion in the returns. For the lowest quintile of returns, both IPO and M&A exits have mean and median returns on the order of −90 percent. The lowest two quintiles of exit returns (40 percent of the sample) result in average losses of around 40 percent to 90 percent of the capital invested by VCs. Contrary to previous research that treats an exit as a sign of success, these results show that an exit itself is not necessarily a reliable indicator of success. Within the highest quintile of returns, M&A exits have mean returns of 719.4 percent (median = 764.6 percent) while IPO exits have a mean return of 633.2 percent (median = 601.1 percent). Therefore, contrary to general perceptions, the best M&A exits compare favorably to the best IPO exits. In the parlance of baseball analogies often used to describe exits, both M&A and IPO exits are capable of producing 'home runs' and both can result in 'strike outs'.

Although both forms of exit exhibit wide return dispersion, it is the frequency of returns in the lowest and highest return quintiles that differs most markedly by type of exit. Only 8 percent of the IPO returns fall in the lowest return quintile compared to 25 percent that fall in the highest return quintile. Therefore, as IPOs decline, it substantially diminishes the cushion that VCs have to cover the losses on investments that do not pay off. The upshot is that this reduces VCs' margin for error – they cannot afford to make as many mistakes in their investment decisions – compared to periods where IPOs were more plentiful.

When returns are decomposed into their fundamental components, we find, in circumstances where both exits achieve similarly high exit valuations, that the highest M&A returns are generated with approximately half the capital invested on average compared to the highest IPO returns. Consistent with this, regression analysis indicates that the returns to both M&A and IPO exits are five times more sensitive to money-in than money-out, with the magnitude of the effect being larger for M&A returns. These findings highlight the importance of discipline in capital allocation as a driver of higher returns, especially for M&A exits. Therefore, as IPO exits become less frequent, an implication is that VCs must become more disciplined in their allocation of capital, which likely affects the kind of investments they choose to undertake.

Finally, we examine the capital recovery of the VC industry as a whole. For investments in portfolio companies made prior to and including 1998, investments which should be largely exited by 2008, the industry total cumulative value to paid-in capital (TVPI) multiple averages 3.2.[4] For the investments made in the years from 1999 to 2008, assuming unrealized investments are exited at cost, TVPI averages 1.6. To put the results in perspective, assuming five years between entry and exit (and no interim cash flows), a TVPI of 3.0 (1.5) equates to a gross return on investment of 24.6 percent (8.4 percent) per annum, suggesting a marked fall-off in latter period industry returns. Moreover, in all years, roughly 50 percent of the total dollars recovered in the industry arise from M&A exits but, prior to 1999, M&A exits represented 44 percent of total exits and in the years thereafter this percentage increases to 71 percent. Hence, the dollars realized from M&A exits have not kept pace with their rise as a proportion of total exits, suggesting that VCs must produce increasingly greater numbers of exits to return the total dollars allocated to portfolio companies.

Taken together, the picture that emerges from our findings is one in which it is more difficult to achieve outsized returns from M&A exits than IPO exits. High M&A returns, which occur with less frequency, require VCs to exercise greater discipline in capital allocation while achieving superior exit valuations.[5] The recovery rates from M&A exits have not kept pace with their growth in occurrence in recent years, necessitating increasing numbers of exits to recover the total capital at risk. While this poses an obvious threat to financial returns, it understates the burden VCs face by ignoring the costs of finding, monitoring, and otherwise managing these investments. In sum, our findings support the concerns for capital recovery following from the decline in IPO exits, and if M&A exits continue as the principal form of exit, VCs will face a large challenge adapting to this new market reality.

2 SAMPLE CHARACTERISTICS

The primary source of data on venture capital investments is Thomson Financial's Venture Economics (VE) database. We identify the US-based portfolio companies with reported investments from venture capital firms and that had exits during the period 1985 to 2008. Our sample consists of all US companies with VC investments having exits either via (1) mergers or acquisitions or (2) initial public offerings. In addition, in order to calculate returns, we require that the deals have a reported deal value and exit date. The deal values for M&A exits are collected from VE when available. The M&A exits which are missing deal values in VE may either be transactions where the deal value was not disclosed or was disclosed but missing from the database. To fill in values for the latter case, we search Thomson Financial's SDC Platinum Mergers and Acquisitions (M&A) database for companies identified as having M&A exits but missing deal values in VE. We are able to fill in approximately 400 M&A missing deal values from SDC's M&A database.[6]

The resulting sample is shown in Table 2.1. There are 1447 VC-backed companies that had an IPO exit and 3171 VC-backed companies that had an M&A exit over the period 1985 to 2008. One observes in Table 2.1 an increased incidence of M&A exits over the sample period. Focusing on the number of exits, one observes that the number of M&A exits is greater than the number of IPO exits in 21 of the 24 years, and M&A exits as a proportion of total exits have increased over time. In Table 2.1, the mean M&A deal

38 Handbook of research on IPOs

Table 2.1 Venture capital exits via M&A and IPO (1985–2008)

Year	Total exits	Total M&A exits	Total IPO exits	% of exits as M&A	Mean M&A deal value ($MM)	Median M&A deal value ($MM)	Mean IPO offer size ($MM)	Median IPO offer size ($MM)
1985	6	4	2	66.7	70.5	85.0	21.3	21.3
1986	8	4	4	50.0	53.7	54.3	44.5	27.0
1987	13	8	5	61.5	106.8	22.0	81.2	50.4
1988	20	16	4	80.0	98.7	59.5	67.8	81.8
1989	23	20	3	87.0	103.6	36.9	105.5	123.2
1990	21	13	8	61.9	49.6	13.8	75.4	77.3
1991	33	14	19	42.4	83.9	54.5	79.9	63.7
1992	99	71	28	71.7	76.5	16.9	80.9	69.6
1993	133	86	47	64.7	98.8	35.0	87.9	53.8
1994	123	92	31	74.8	99.4	34.6	81.2	60.0
1995	222	116	106	52.3	148.4	63.9	100.5	80.6
1996	315	149	166	47.3	205.1	65.0	128.0	79.2
1997	330	220	110	66.7	309.0	70.7	149.2	83.4
1998	313	239	74	76.4	394.1	73.1	246.1	148.1
1999	517	275	242	53.2	758.0	109.9	424.8	278.8
2000	540	327	213	60.6	438.1	136.1	433.2	177.3
2001	284	249	35	87.7	147.0	33.5	356.3	253.3
2002	226	198	28	87.6	136.8	35.5	254.7	167.0
2003	166	136	30	81.9	126.8	50.0	233.6	187.0
2004	286	194	92	67.8	143.6	50.0	515.5	197.3
2005	269	214	55	79.6	185.5	81.3	283.0	194.6
2006	271	212	59	78.2	233.3	75.0	345.6	209.9
2007	279	201	78	72.0	337.0	135.0	485.4	276.8
2008	121	113	8	93.4	201.8	86.1	386.8	204.0
Total	4618	3171	1447	68.7	274.4	70.0	292.3	147.9

Notes:
This table reports statistics for exits from US venture-backed companies via (1) mergers, acquisitions, or leveraged buyouts (LBO), reported broadly as M&A, and (2) initial public offerings (IPOs) with exit dates during 1985 to 2005.
M&A exits included are those with disclosed deal values.
The effective date of M&A deals and IPO offer date are used as exit dates. The primary data source is Thomson Financial's Venture Economics.

value of $274 million, is comparable to the mean IPO offer size of $292 million, although the median M&A deal value is less than half the median IPO offer size. While IPOs were the focus of most commentary in the 'hot' 1999–2000 period, the mean M&A deal values in that period, like IPO offer sizes, are among the highest in our sample. The mean M&A deal value of $758 million in 1999 is by far the highest in a given year, with $438 million in 2000 a distant second.

Several reasons have been advanced for the decrease in IPO exits. Since 2002, analysts have attributed part of the increase in M&A exits to a greater reluctance of companies to go public following the passage of the Sarbanes–Oxley Act. Since Sarbanes–Oxley was prompted by some of the excesses of the 'dotcom' era IPOs, investors appear to have

The decline in venture-backed IPOs 39

become less willing to invest in riskier, negative cash flow companies, and the minimum size necessary to bring a firm public may have increased, seemingly making IPO exits harder to achieve. Alan Patricof, managing director of Greycroft Partners elaborates on these changes:

> The bubble finally burst in 2001 and virtually overnight the IPO market dried up as the public realized that in many cases 'the emperor had no clothes.' The collapse of the Internet bubble only served to compound the problem as public interest in IPOs dwindled to a trickle as their losses increased. Then, in 2002, in the wake of the Enron, WorldCom and Tyco debacles, the government intervened with the passage of the Sarbanes–Oxley Act, which imposed tougher rules on corporations. This only added further to the cost of an IPO in terms of legal and accounting requirements for both the issuer and underwriter. The sum and substance of all of these developments is that the minimum economic level to bring a company public today is at least a $50 million offering at a $250 million market value. (Patricof, 2009)

Related to this, entrepreneurs may have less desire to head public companies or may be willing to settle for lower returns (McGee, 2007). Recognizing the concern posed by the decline in IPOs to the vitality of the US economy, the Jumpstart Our Business Startup (JOBS) Act was signed into law in the US in April 2012 allowing for a more gradual phase-in of certain disclosure and independent audit requirements mandated by Sarbanes–Oxley. The intent of the act was to promote more young companies to go public.

Others point to more macro factors and suggest that many of the industries that were in their infancy in the mid-1990s have matured and that continued investment in these sectors has lower growth potential. Some of the earlier VC-backed companies (for example, Cisco, Intel) have grown to become frequent acquirers of portfolio companies themselves and more large public companies have looked to acquire VC-backed companies to build their research and development (R&D) portfolios. Finally, there has been a sharp rise in the total dollars allocated to private equity, such that there may be more companies funded with less potential to go public.

2.1 Estimation of Exit Returns

The sample used to estimate returns is a subset of the overall sample shown in Table 2.1. To estimate returns we require that the companies have post-money round valuations for consecutive rounds of financing. A total of 1401 IPO exits and 1215 M&A exits have sufficient post-money valuation data to calculate returns.[7] We first calculate VC equity stakes for a portfolio company using the post-money round values. The VC method of valuation posits a simple relationship between the pre-money (PRE) and post-money values ($POST$) of a portfolio company for each round of investment (I) by VCs. We assume before the first round investment that founders of the firm hold 100 percent of the equity ownership. For each round 'j', the fraction of ownership sold to VCs (F) is measured as $F_j = I_j \div POST_j$.[8] Each round of subsequent investment to the first round results in a larger cumulative share of the company being sold to VCs, as the first round investors' stakes are diluted by additional equity sold to the subsequent round investors. To capture this effect, we calculate the total percentage ownership stake sold to VCs

($VC\%_T$) for each portfolio company that exits at time T after N financing rounds in the following manner:

$$VC\%_T = \sum_{j=1}^{N} [F_j \times (1 - F_{j+1}) \times \ldots \times (1 - F_N)]$$

Using the VE data, we then estimate the equity stake at exit held by VC firm 'i', $VC\%_i$, based on the proportional capital invested in a company as follows:

$$VC\%_i = (Total\ amount\ invested\ in\ company\ by\ VC\ firm\ i \div Total\ amount\ invested\ in\ company\ by\ all\ VC\ firms) \times (VC\%_T)$$

where $VC\%_T$ is the aggregate equity stake held by all VCs at exit.

While this method can underestimate the stake of an individual VC firm that continues to invest in subsequent rounds, it provides a reasonable estimate of the total ownership accumulated by all VCs in a portfolio company. The total VC stake accumulated through the last round of investment is then multiplied by the disclosed transaction value for M&A exits or the pre-IPO market value of equity for IPO exits to estimate the capital received by VCs upon exit. The returns VCs realize on investment in a given portfolio company is calculated by the form of exit as follows:

$$Return(M\&A) = [(VC\%_T \times Disclosed\ transaction\ value) \div Total\ amount\ invested] - 1$$

$$Return(IPO) = [(VC\%_T \times IPO\ offer\ price \times Pre\text{-}IPO\ shares\ outstanding) \div Total\ amount\ invested] - 1$$

Our return construct is similar to the widely used investment multiple (TVPI), in which a zero percent return indicates break even in terms of capital recovery (that is, the exit returns the capital invested in the portfolio company). These returns are more representative of gross returns in that they are not net of fees and carried interest (carry), although invested capital is after fees in early years. Following Cochrane (2005), we use the offer price in calculating IPO returns to abstract from the issue of underpricing, which has been the subject of extensive discussion elsewhere in the literature. Several empirical studies document that VCs typically sell their stakes following the end of lock-up period at positive returns on average, suggesting our estimates of IPO returns are conservative.[9]

Our empirical analyses differ from prior studies in that we do not examine aggregate VC fund returns but focus the returns to individual investments that have had an M&A or IPO exit. Owing to our focus on exits, the selection bias created by VCs being more likely to disclose good news is likely mitigated in our study. However, selection bias can still arise from the fact that investors are required by law to disclose the exit value of all IPOs but are only required to report the transaction values for a subset of M&A exits. Transaction values must be disclosed to the US Securities and Exchange Commission (SEC) if a private company is purchased by a publicly listed firm and, depending on the form of payment and year of sale, it represents more than 10 percent to 20 percent of its assets (Rodrigues and Stegemoller, 2007). Since this

Table 2.2 Equity stakes in venture-backed portfolio companies

Round number	Overall		M&A		IPO	
	N	% VC stakes	N	% VC stakes	N	% VC stakes
1	2615	27.0	1215	29.5	1401	24.9
2	1817	43.3	789	47.2	1029	40.2
3	1260	58.0	481	60.8	779	56.3
4	782	67.2	255	68.8	527	66.4
5	429	73.7	121	75.1	308	73.2
6	219	76.0	58	76.4	161	75.9
7	91	81.4	22	86.1	69	79.9
>7	71	81.7	15	96.7	56	77.7
Total rounds	7284		2956		4330	
Years to exit	2615	4.5	1215	4.9	1401	4.2

Notes:
The table reports the equity stakes in US venture-backed portfolio companies that have an M&A or IPO exit over the period 1985 to 2008.
The equity stakes are computed using the postmoney round valuations from Venture Economics.
The average percentage of equity held by VCs is reported following each round of investment.
Years to exit is reported as the average years between the first date of VC investment and exit date.

threshold is not met by all sales, and we also include sales to private acquirers who are not subject to mandatory disclosure requirements, it is likely that our sample of M&A exits is biased toward those with higher disclosed transaction values. Since the concern with M&A exits is that they have lower returns on average than IPO exits, the exclusion of M&A with disclosed transaction values likely biases the returns to M&A exits upward.

In Table 2.2, we report the equity stakes that VCs accumulate by round of investment as derived from the post-money round valuations data. A first-round investor in a portfolio company that eventually exits via an M&A has a 29.5 percent equity stake on average compared to a 24.9 percent equity stake for a first round investor in an IPO exit. As expected, as the number of rounds increases, the total percentage of equity sold to VCs increases, so that after five rounds of investment VCs hold approximately 75.1 percent of the equity in M&A exits and 73.2 percent of the equity in IPO exits.[10]

In Table 2.3, we provide descriptive statistics on VC investments for the overall sample and by industry groups, with the portfolio companies classified into the six broad industry major groups used by VE. For the overall sample, a typical exit occurs after approximately five rounds of investment in which 7.4 VC firms participate. The round amount averages close to $14 million and the average total dollars invested per company is $56.5 million. There is a good representation of exits in all industry groups with the largest number of exits (1100) occurring in the computer-related industry. Due to long lead times for development, the biotech and medical/health/life sciences have the highest number of rounds and also the highest average VC equity stakes at exit.

42   Handbook of research on IPOs

Table 2.3   Descriptive statistics: portfolio companies with exits via IPO or M&A

	Overall	Biotech	Communications/ media	Computer related	Medical/ health/life sciences	Non-high tech	Semi-conductors/ Other electrical
No. of rounds	4.8	5.8	4.9	4.5	5.4	3.9	5.0
No. of firms invested in company	7.4	9.1	8.4	7.1	7.9	4.6	8.3
Round amt ($MM)	13.7	11.4	17.5	10.5	11.5	24.3	13.8
Total amt invested ($MM)	56.5	63.0	78.9	42.5	53.2	74.5	50.4
VC stakes at exit (%)	54.2	62.3	55.3	52.4	61.4	45.5	52.9
No. of companies	2616	226	477	1100	337	295	181

Notes:
The table reports descriptive statistics for US venture-backed portfolio companies that had M&A or IPO exits during 1985–2008. Mean values are reported for the overall sample along with means across the six industry major classifications used by Venture Economics.
No. of rounds is the number of rounds of financing received by the company.
No. of firms invested in company is the number of venture capital firms that invested in the company.
Round amt ($MM) is the average amount invested per round.
Total amt invested ($MM) is the total known amount invested in the company.
VC stakes at exit (%) is the total equity stake held by venture capitalists calculated using disclosed postmoney valuations, accounting for dilution of stakes after each round of financing.

3   HOW DO THE DISTRIBUTIONAL PROPERTIES OF RETURNS DIFFER BETWEEN IPO AND M&A EXITS?

In Table 2.4, we report portfolio company returns for the sample of 1401 IPO exits and 1215 M&A exits. In panel A, for equally weighted returns in the overall sample, the mean return for IPO exits is 209.5 percent and the median return is 108.8 percent. By comparison, the mean return for M&A exits is 99.5 percent and the median return is −32.1 percent. The large differences observed between the mean and median returns are consistent with Cochrane's (2005) finding that venture capital returns exhibit a high degree of positive skewness. The mean company-level return to IPO exits is significantly higher than the mean return to M&A exits, with the difference significant at the 1 percent level, supporting the view that M&A exits have inferior returns to IPOs. Exit returns do not account for the time value of money when, in principle, a 50 percent return achieved in five years is superior to a 50 percent return achieved in 10 years.[11] To account for the time to exit, we also compute an annualized return (r) derived from the relationship $(1 + Ret) = (1 + r)^t$, where Ret is the company-level exit return and t is the number of years to exit. The average annual return for IPO exits of 61.8 percent is significantly higher than the average annual return of 26.9 percent for M&A exits. Hence, the results for annualized returns that adjust for the time to exit are consistent with exit returns.

In unreported results, we also compute an adjusted return that measures performance

Table 2.4 *Returns from venture-backed portfolio companies (1985–2008)*

			Panel A: Portfolio company returns (equally weighted)					
			Overall	(Lowest return) Pooled Q1	Pooled Q2	Pooled Q3	Pooled Q4	(Highest return) Pooled Q5
Company-level return								
% returns M&A	Mean		99.5	−87.7	−42.0	45.8	204.5	719.4
	Median		−32.1	−89.6	−43.0	40.6	188.9	764.6
% returns IPO	Mean		209.5	−85.8	−35.1	53.5	205.8	633.2
	Median		108.8	−86.7	−35.9	51.6	195.9	601.1
Difference in mean (IPO-M&A) (*p*-value)			110.0*** (0.00)					
Difference in median (IPO-M&A) (*p*-value)			140.9*** (0.00)					
Annualized return								
% returns M&A	Mean		26.9	−47.8	−11.4	8.3	37.8	282.2
	Median		−7.2	−41.5	−11.2	7.8	35.6	181.9
% returns IPO	Mean		61.8	−47.3	−10.4	9.3	39.4	237.1
	Median		21.6	−40.8	−9.7	8.7	36.7	159.3
Difference in mean (IPO-M&A) (*p*-value)			34.9*** (0.00)					
Difference in median (IPO-M&A) (*p*-value)			28.8*** (0.00)					

			Panel B: Portfolio company returns (value-weighted)					
			Overall	(Lowest return) Pooled Q1	Pooled Q2	Pooled Q3	Pooled Q4	(Highest return) Pooled Q5
Company-level return								
% returns M&A	Mean		168.0	−88.7	−41.8	42.1	199.0	729.4
% returns IPO	Mean		148.7	−89.6	−36.0	51.8	203.1	613.9
Difference in mean (IPO-M&A) (*p*-value)			−19.3* (0.06)					
Annualized return								
% returns M&A	Mean		33.3	−46.2	−10.4	12.4	27.7	182.9
% returns IPO	Mean		33.6	−56.5	−7.8	11.0	40.2	181.2
Difference in mean (IPO-M&A) (*p*-value)			0.3 (0.41)					

Table 2.4 (continued)

		Panel B: Portfolio company returns (value-weighted)				
	Overall	(Lowest return) Pooled Q1	Pooled Q2	Pooled Q3	Pooled Q4	(Highest return) Pooled Q5
Annualized return						
No. exits	2616	524	523	523	523	523
% M&A	46.4	78.2	55.6	32.7	31.7	33.8
No. M&A	1215	410	291	171	166	177
No. IPO	1401	114	232	352	357	346

Notes:
The table reports mean and median returns and returns sorted into quintiles for the sample of venture-backed M&A and IPO exits.
Statistics reported are for the sample of M&A and IPO exits and for exits that fall within each quintile group.
In panel A, equally-weighted exit portfolio returns are computed as the mean return from each type of exit. Annualized return (r) is derived from $(1+Ret) = (1+r)t$, where Ret is the company-level exit return and t is the number of years to exit.
In panel B, value-weighted exit portfolio returns are reported where weights are computed using the total amount invested in the company with the weights for each portfolio reported scaled to add up to one.
The data are winsorized by excluding the top and bottom 5% of the returns for each type of exit.
***, **, * indicates statistical significance at the 1%, 5%, and 10% level respectively.

relative to other VC exits (M&A and IPO) that occur in the same industry and in the same calendar quarter as the company return. Because portfolio companies that exit in the same industry and under similar market conditions could have similar risk exposures, this adjusted return could be viewed as a risk-adjusted comparison of returns. We do not, however, attempt to explicitly measure the systematic risk of an investment (that is, calculate betas) due to the illiquid nature of VC investments and inability to observe interim market valuations of the investments. The mean adjusted returns for IPO exits is 30 percent, and the mean adjusted return for M&A exits is −34.5 percent, a difference which is significant at the 1 percent level.[12] Having shown that the main findings hold after accounting for the time to exit and risk, in our subsequent analyses we rely on exit returns because they provide the most intuitive interpretation of capital recovery.[13]

To examine the dispersion of returns, we pool the overall sample of company-level returns and sort them into quintiles. Quintile 1 (Q1) contains the companies with lowest exit returns and Quintile 5 (Q5) contains the companies with the highest exit returns. There is a wide dispersion of returns observed for both types of exits. Both M&A and IPOs ranked in the lowest quintile of pooled returns have mean and median returns on the order of −90 percent. Given that VCs lose 40 percent to 90 percent of the capital invested on average in the bottom 40 percent of our sample of exits, it suggests that using the occurrence of an exit as an indication of success potentially leads to significant overstatement of VC performance. For the highest quintile of returns, M&A exits have mean returns of 719.4 percent (median = 764.6 percent) while IPO exits have a mean return of 633.2 percent (median = 601.1 percent). The distribution of returns illustrates that the best M&A exits compare favorably to the best IPO exits and the worst IPO and M&A

exits fail (by a wide margin) to return the full amount of capital invested. The frequency of returns in the lowest and highest return quintiles however differs markedly by type of exit. Merger and acquisition exits account for 78.2 percent of exits in the lowest return quintile compared to only 33.8 percent in the highest return quintile. Thus, the evidence so far lends support to the concerns surrounding the decline in IPOs owing to the lower capital recovery from M&A exits.

In panel B of Table 2.4, we repeat the analyses in panel A but factor in the size of investments by computing the returns on a value-weighted basis. For the value-weighted exit portfolio returns, the weights are computed using the total amount invested in the company with weights for each quintile portfolio scaled to sum to one. Ideally, *ex ante* measures of weights should be used to compute future value-weighted performance of investments but such weights are not possible given data limitations. Information about an investment is likely to be revealed during intermediate rounds before the final exit, leading VCs observing better intermediate performance to increase their stakes or capital invested in the company. Although exit valuations which are also a driver of returns likely still remain uncertain, this may lead to an *ex post* overweighting of the higher returns in our value-weighting framework. However, there is no reason to believe this effect differs between M&A and IPO exits.

On a value-weighted basis, the mean company-level return for M&A exits is 168.0 percent compared to 148.6 percent for IPO exits, a difference in returns that is significant at the 10 percent level. For M&A exits, the increase in the value-weighted mean return relative to its equally weighted mean return (99.5 percent) suggests that VCs invest more in companies that achieve relatively higher returns. By contrast, the lower value-weighted mean return for IPOs relative to its equally weighted mean return suggests VCs invest more in portfolio companies with the relatively lower returns. This implies that VCs earn higher returns on their bigger 'bets' on M&A. These results underscore an important finding – higher M&A returns occur in circumstances where VCs have made more judicious use of capital compared to IPOs and made relatively larger bets among the companies with M&A exits that pay off in relatively higher returns. The wide disparity between the value-weighted returns and equally weighted returns from M&A exits suggests certain conditions (perhaps more disciplined capital allocation or selectivity) are associated with achieving outsized returns from M&A. Additionally, the disparity suggests that healthy capital recovery in M&A may be concentrated in relatively fewer (albeit larger) investments.

4   HOW DO THE FUNDAMENTAL COMPONENTS OF RETURNS DIFFER BETWEEN IPO AND M&A EXITS?

In an attempt to understand the factors that drive returns – especially extreme returns where substantial capital is lost or gained – in Table 2.5 we decompose the pooled quintile returns reported in Table 2.4 into the three fundamental components of returns: the VC stakes, the capital allocated to portfolio companies (money-in), and the money received from exits from portfolio companies (money-out). Money-out for M&A exits is measured by the disclosed transaction value and for IPO exits it is the IPO offer price × pre-IPO shares outstanding. Each of these components reflects, to varying degrees, a

46 Handbook of research on IPOs

Table 2.5 Decomposition of returns into fundamental factors

	(Lowest return) Pooled Q1	Pooled Q2	Pooled Q3	Pooled Q4	(Highest return) Pooled Q5	Q5 avg/ Q1 avg
VC stakes (%)						
M&A	46.2	50.5	53.3	55.2	57.7	1.2
IPO	28.4	52.8	55.4	61.6	65.6	2.3
IPO avg/M&A avg	0.6	1.0	1.1	1.1	1.1	
Money-in ($MM)						
M&A	54.5	48.5	47.3	38.2	19.9	0.4
IPO	153.8	88.4	58.9	53.6	44.4	0.3
IPO avg/M&A avg	2.8	1.8	1.2	1.4	2.2	
Money-out ($MM)						
M&A	22.6	78.2	139.8	207.0	532.6	23.6
IPO	100.8	138.3	169.6	267.8	616.7	6.1
IPO avg/M&A avg	4.5	1.8	1.2	1.3	1.2	
N	524	523	523	523	523	
No. M&A	410	291	171	166	177	
No. IPO	114	232	352	357	346	
% M&A (in quintile group)	78.2	55.6	32.7	31.7	33.8	

Notes:
This table reports the averages for the three fundamental factors used to compute exits returns.
Observations include portfolio companies with M&A or IPO exits.
The pool of company-level returns in the panel dataset is sorted into quintiles.
Averages of the fundamentals are reported for the M&A and IPO exits within each quintile group.
Q5 avg/Q1 avg is the ratio of average values in the highest return quintile (Q5) and the lowest return quintile (Q1).
IPO avg/M&A avg is the ratio of averages values for IPOs and for M&A within each quintile group.

choice that VCs make with respect to their management of investments in portfolio companies. All else equal, it is expected that higher returns should be associated with larger VC stakes, less money-in, and more money-out.

Across the quintiles of returns in Table 2.5, money-in falls and VC stakes and money-out increases from Quintile 1 (Q1 = lowest returns) to Quintile 5 (Q5 = highest returns) for both M&A and IPO exits. We measure the change in these fundamentals for extreme quintiles with the Q5 avg/Q1 avg variable reported in the last column, which is the ratio of the average values of the fundamentals in the highest and lowest return quintiles. Of the three fundamentals, money-out exhibits the largest variation between Q1 and Q5, and the differences in exit value are much more pronounced for M&A exits than IPO exits. In Q1, M&A exits have a $22.6 million exit value on average compared to $532.6 million in Q5, a 23.6 times increase from Q1 to Q5, versus IPOs which have an $100.8 million exit value in Q1 and $616.7 million in Q5, a 6.1 times increase from Q1 to Q5. With respect to money-in, in every quintile M&A exits have less capital allocated on average than IPOs exits, perhaps reflecting the fact that VCs do not have to develop a company to the same point to achieve an M&A exit compared to an IPO exit (see Bayar and Chemmanur, 2009). However, within the Q1 and Q5 quintiles there are important differences in money-in between M&A and IPO exits. In the lowest return quintile, M&A exits have 2.8 times fewer dollars in capital allocated than IPO exits but the lower capital allocation is not sufficient to offset their 4.5 times lower exit value. In other words, even though VCs have allocated far less capital to M&A exits in Q1, it still results in poor returns because of the inability to deliver good exit valuation.[14] In the highest return quintile, M&A exits have an average $19.9 million in capital allocated, 2.2 times fewer dollars than IPO exits and the fewest dollars of all categories, and these investments achieve roughly the same exit value as IPOs in Q5. This suggests that outsized M&A returns which provide the greatest capital recovery to VCs are associated with both more disciplined capital allocation and excellent exit valuation. This is an important finding because it suggests that VCs must couple strong selection ability at the outset of an investment with strong valuation at the end to duplicate the type of capital recovery more frequently associated with IPOs. As M&A exits become more prevalent, unless VCs can adapt to these conditions, it suggests that the breathing room that IPO exits provide for failed investments will increasingly constrain VCs ability to recover from mistakes (that is, investments that do not pay off).

The evidence in Table 2.5 suggests that the fundamentals may have a differential impact on the returns to M&A and IPO exits. To examine this issue further, in Table 2.6 we estimate separate ordinary least squares (OLS) regressions of the M&A and IPO exit returns using the return fundamentals as independent variables.[15] The regressions include year and industry fixed effects to control for potential differences in the fundamentals across time and industries.[16] As returns are calculated from the fundamentals, it is a mathematical artefact that the coefficients of the fundamentals will be significant. Our focus is on the relative magnitude of the coefficients between M&A and IPO exits in the regression setting which allows for an analysis of the marginal effects of variables holding all others

Table 2.6 Regressions examining sensitivity of returns on fundamental factors

Fundamental factors	(1) M&A	(1) IPO	(2) M&A	(2) IPO	(3) M&A	(3) IPO	(4) M&A	(4) IPO
VC stakes (%)	1.74*** (6.09)	1.99*** (7.93)					2.14*** (7.98)	2.18*** (8.36)
Money-in ($MM)			−0.73*** (−4.46)	−0.39*** (−3.34)			−1.27*** (−6.26)	−0.50** (−2.54)
Money-out ($MM)					0.24*** (5.50)	0.09*** (2.61)	0.27*** (5.30)	0.11** (2.45)
Year fixed effects	Yes	Yes	Yes	Yes	Yes	Yes	Yes	Yes
Industry fixed effects	Yes	Yes	Yes	Yes	Yes	Yes	Yes	Yes
Adj. R-squared	0.159	0.229	0.154	0.198	0.276	0.229	0.359	0.314
N	1215	1401	1215	1401	1215	1401	1215	1401

Notes:
This table reports OLS regression estimates with exit returns as the dependent variable and the estimates are based on robust standard errors including year and industry fixed effects.
t-statistics are reported in parentheses.
Returns are winsorized by excluding the top and bottom 5% of the returns for each type of exit.
***, **, * denote significance at the 1%, 5% and 10% level, respectively.
VC stakes (%) are the total stakes held by VCs at exit.
Money-in ($MM) is the total amount invested in the company.
Money-out ($MM) for M&As is the deal value or for IPOs the IPO offer price × pre-IPO shares outstanding.

48 *Handbook of research on IPOs*

constant. In model (4), the most inclusive specification, there is relatively little variation in the magnitude of the respective coefficients of VC stakes between the two forms of exits. Exit returns exhibit nearly five times greater sensitivity to money-in than money-out for both M&A and IPO exits. That is, for M&A exits, the coefficient of money-in (−1.27) is approximately five times the size of the coefficient of money-out (0.27) and a similar pattern holds for IPOs. On a relative basis, the large magnitude of the coefficient for money-in for M&A exits suggest that more disciplined capital allocation has a more pronounced impact on returns than for IPOs. That is, a 1 percent decrease in money-in will increase M&A (IPO) returns by 1.27 percent (0.5 percent) and 1 percent increase in money-out will increase M&A (IPO) returns by 0.27 percent (0.11 percent). Therefore, while the capital allocated to portfolio companies is an important driver of returns for both forms of exit, M&A returns are especially sensitive to it.

4.1 Components of Exit Returns in Calendar Time

To provide a sense of the flows of money in calendar time, in Figures 2.1 and 2.2 we plot the annual money-in and money-out from M&A and IPO exits in relation to the year-end value of the NASDAQ market index. Both figures show a high degree of sensitivity to aggregate stock market performance. In Figure 2.1, companies that eventually had M&A exits receive the greatest inflows of money in 1999 and 2000, and those that had IPO exits received the greatest inflows of money in 2000 and 2001. In Figure 2.2, the largest amounts of money-out for both M&A and IPO exits occur in 1999 and 2000, which coincides with the peak of the NASDAQ market valuation.

One observes in Figures 2.1 and 2.2 the pronounced influence of the dotcom years (that is, 1998–2000) on capital recovery in the industry. If we aggregate the money-in and money-out across all quintiles in Table 2.5 and calculate realization ratios (unreported), we find for the overall sample, the realization ratio for M&A exits is 3.39× and for IPO exits it is 4.42×. If we exclude the exits from the dotcom years the realization ratio for M&A exits drops to 2.21×, a 35 percent decline, and for IPOs it drops to 3.54×, a 20 percent decline. Much of the concern about the viability of the VC industry stems from the fall-off in IPOs since the dotcom collapse. However, in actuality the loss of those years has resulted in a larger drop off in the capital recovered from M&A exits than IPOs. Because M&A exits have increased in frequency since that time, it underscores why highly disciplined capital allocation is essential to the achievement of high returns.

5 WHAT DOES THE DECREASED INCIDENCE OF IPO EXITS OVER TIME IMPLY FOR INDUSTRY-WIDE CAPITAL RECOVERY?

Up to this point our study has focused on the returns to IPO and M&A exits and some of the factors that affect these returns. We now turn to the important question of what the pattern of returns implies for the industry as a whole. Increasingly, the lack of exits and the prospect of lower returns have led many market observers to question the viability of the venture industry, an issue with broad implications for economic growth. This issue

The decline in venture-backed IPOs 49

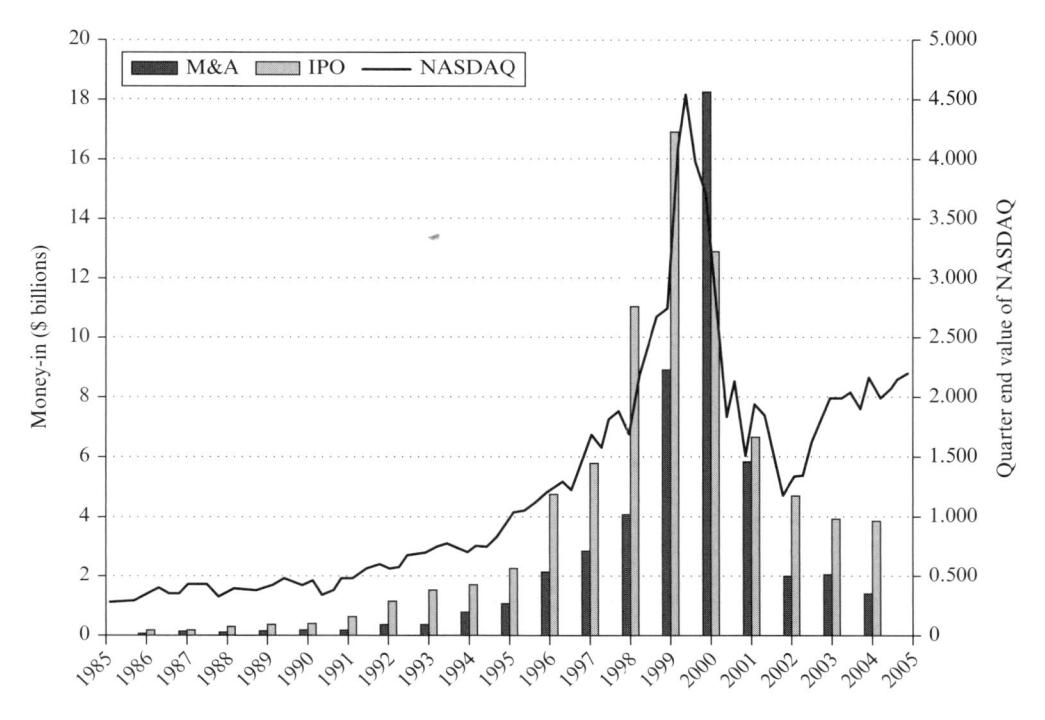

Notes:
The figure plots the money invested in portfolio companies that eventually result in M&A or IPO exits against the quarter-end level of the NASDAQ market index.
Investment in a portfolio company begins in the year of the first round of VC investment; follow-up rounds are placed in the year they occur.
The years after 2005 are not shown because of the small number of exits per year.

Figure 2.1   Total money invested (US$ billions) in companies with M&A or IPO exits versus NASDAQ

can be informed by an analysis of the capital recovery associated with M&A and IPO exits and how these recovery rates have varied over time.

In Table 2.7, we assess the total capital recovered by the venture industry using an approach based on portfolio company start years. Start year is defined as the year in which the first round of VC investment is made in a portfolio company.[17] For all companies started in a particular year (regardless of whether they were exited or not), we accumulate the total paid-in capital from the first round of investment through exit.[18] Capital is subsequently recovered from M&A or IPO exits (realized investments) and potentially from investments that have yet to be exited (unrealized investments). In the VE database, unrealized investments are designated as 'active' investments. In this analysis we assume that active investments have the potential to be recovered at cost (that is, the capital recovered is equal to the capital allocated). To be considered an active investment, a portfolio company must have received at least one round of investment within the last five years as of December 2008. Unrealized investments therefore exclude investments referred to in the industry as the 'living dead' or active investments

50   *Handbook of research on IPOs*

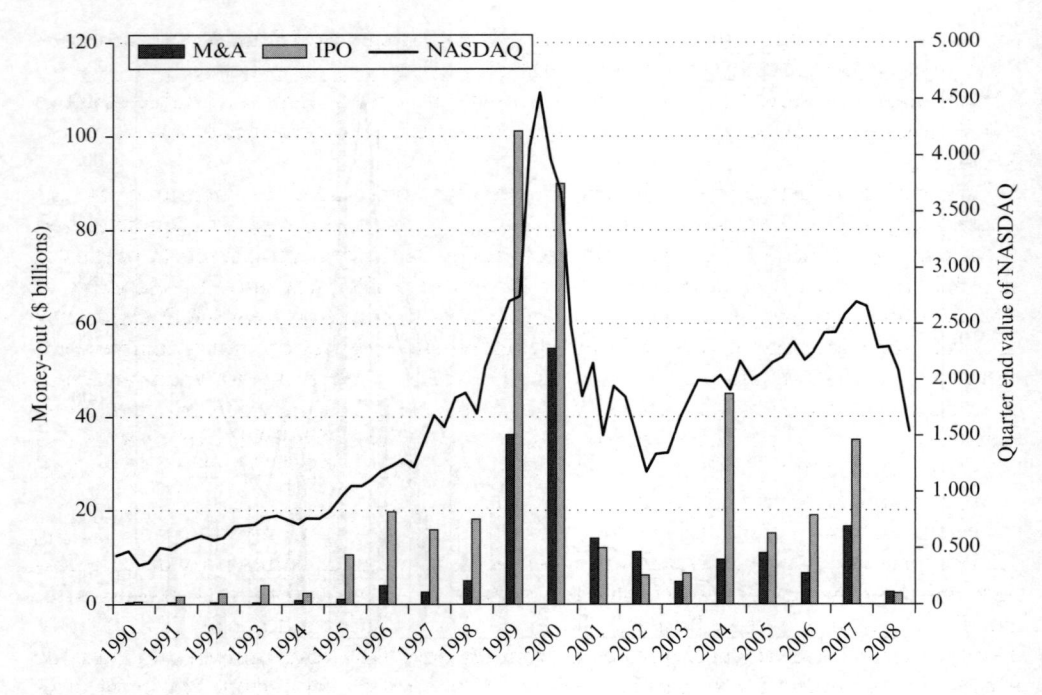

Note:
The figure plots the disclosed deal value for M&A exits and the pre-IPO market value of equity for IPO exits against the quarter-end level of the NASDAQ market index. The years before 1990 are not plotted because of the small number of exits per year.

Figure 2.2   Total money received (US$ billions) from M&A and IPO exits versus NASDAQ

deemed in reality to have little chance of exit. Because of the prior five-year investment requirement, this adjustment only affects companies started before 2003. Our analysis includes the paid-in capital for these investments and assumes zero recovery for them. This adjustment is reasonable in light of VCs' reluctance to write-down or write-off investments.[19]

In Table 2.7, we report two summary numbers of the industry's capital recovery over 1985–2008. In column (5), we compute the ratio of the value of realized exits (or cumulative distributed capital) to paid-in capital, referred to as the DPI Multiple. Since this multiple is based on actual realizations, the DPI provides a lower bound on industry performance. In column (6), we report the TVPI Multiple which is the ratio of the value of realized exits and unrealized investments at cost to paid-in capital. To the extent that the unrealized investments are exited at less (more) than cost, our numbers will be biased upwards (downwards) in terms of capital recovery. Since the bulk of unrealized investment falls in the post-2003 period, barring a near term rebound from the precipitous market declines of 2007 and 2008, our estimates could represent an upper bound on capital recovery.

Given the long horizon of venture investments, with fund lives typically in the order of

Table 2.7 Industry recovery of capital through M&A and IPO exits

Start year	Paid-in capital (1)	Unrealized investments at cost (2)	Realized exits (3)	Total capital recovery (4) = (2) + (3)	DPI multiple (5) = (3) ÷ (1)	TVPI multiple (6) = (4) ÷ (1)	Realized M&A exits (7)	M&A DPI multiple (8) = (7) ÷ (1)	%(M&A/M&A + IPO) (9)	%M&A recovery (10) = (7) ÷ (3)
1985	$4.1	$0.0	$9.9	$9.9	2.39	2.40	$0.8	0.19	19.4	7.8
1986	$5.0	$0.1	$12.5	$12.5	2.50	2.51	$5.3	1.06	27.4	42.3
1987	$10.0	$1.3	$34.2	$35.5	3.40	3.54	$25.5	2.54	25.3	74.5
1988	$7.0	$0.1	$17.6	$17.7	2.52	2.54	$6.9	0.99	35.4	39.4
1989	$10.0	$0.1	$48.8	$48.9	4.87	4.88	$33.2	3.31	41.4	68.0
1990	$6.0	$0.1	$15.8	$15.9	2.65	2.67	$6.0	1.01	41.0	38.1
1991	$4.6	$0.1	$23.5	$23.6	5.13	5.14	$12.6	2.75	43.9	53.7
1992	$8.3	$0.3	$27.9	$28.2	3.36	3.40	$16.0	1.92	40.9	57.1
1993	$8.3	$1.5	$25.4	$26.9	3.05	3.23	$10.4	1.24	42.9	40.8
1994	$13.4	$0.8	$38.5	$39.3	2.87	2.93	$13.7	1.02	51.5	35.5
1995	$19.8	$1.3	$48.2	$49.5	2.43	2.50	$19.7	1.00	50.9	41.0
1996	$37.2	$6.1	$113.9	$120.0	3.06	3.23	$52.4	1.41	60.3	46.1
1997	$35.9	$5.9	$97.2	$103.1	2.70	2.87	$44.7	1.24	67.2	46.0
1998	$57.8	$11.3	$153.7	$164.9	2.66	2.85	$90.2	1.56	68.5	58.7
1999	$75.5	$16.7	$111.5	$128.2	1.48	1.70	$48.0	0.64	74.4	43.1
2000	$72.5	$22.4	$65.5	$87.9	0.90	1.21	$37.7	0.52	83.0	57.5
2001	$27.8	$12.9	$31.2	$44.1	1.12	1.59	$19.5	0.70	74.4	62.4
2002	$32.4	$13.6	$35.5	$49.1	1.09	1.51	$12.2	0.38	58.1	34.5
2003	$31.4	$17.1	$31.4	$48.6	1.00	1.55	$13.6	0.43	65.7	43.2
2004	$31.5	$22.4	$42.1	$64.5	1.34	2.04	$24.6	0.78	56.5	58.4
2005	$26.8	$21.7	$14.6	$36.3	0.54	1.35	$6.8	0.25	69.2	46.4
2006	$39.6	$36.0	$11.2	$47.2	0.28	1.19	$4.6	0.12	76.3	41.5
2007	$28.2	$23.0	$10.2	$33.2	0.36	1.18	$7.1	0.25	73.3	69.6
2008	$19.4	$18.5	$1.3	$19.8	0.06	1.02	$0.7	0.03	75.0	53.9

Notes:
This table reports the total industry capital recovery (in $US billions) from investments by start year, defined as the year of the first round of VC investment in the portfolio company.
Paid-in capital is the total capital allocated to all portfolio companies started in a given year from start to exit, or through 2008 if unexited.
Realized exits are the total dollars recovered via M&A or IPO exits for companies started each year.
Unrealized investments at cost is the carrying cost of active investments. To be active, a company must have had at least one round of investment within the last five years as of the end of the sample period.
Realized M&A exits are the total dollars recovered via M&A exits only.

10 years, the most accurate performance assessments from TVPI and DPI can be made for investments in companies which by 2008 should be fully exited, that is, those with start years before 1999 (1998 and before), as seen by the closeness of the totals in column (3) and column (4). As VCs would hope to begin exiting after the end of the investment period (typically five years), some qualified judgment can be formed for the investments in companies started before 2005. We report the multiples for 2005 to 2008, but with the caution that 87 percent of the paid-in capital invested in those years is still unrealized, leaving the ultimate judgment of the performance in those years to the future.

In general, the results for the DPI and TVPI do little to alleviate the concerns about industry returns. For the start years before 1999, the TVPI averages 3.2 (DPI = 3.1) compared to an average TVPI of 1.6 (DPI = 1.2) for the start years 1999 to 2004. To offer a more intuitive perspective on the performance embedded in the multiple, we convert the TVPI into an annual return based on the average years from entry to exit. Assuming five years between entry and exit and no interim cash flows, a TVPI of 3.2 (1.6) translates into a 26.2 percent (9.9 percent) return per annum. Because we have not excluded the fees (typically 2–3 percent) or carried interest (typically 20 percent) paid to VCs, these estimates represent the gross returns on venture investment. Given the greater risk associated with the development of young companies and estimated betas reported in previous studies that range from 2 to 3, gross returns on the order of 10 percent in the post-1998 period do not suggest a high degree of outperformance for the industry on a risk adjusted basis.[20]

Prior studies have shown there is a strong consistency of returns among the top VCs (Kaplan and Schoar, 2005) and it is generally believed that they generate the lion's share of returns. To see if the trend observed for the entire industry applies to top performing VCs, we rank the VCs into quartiles based on their number of rounds in the five years before a start year (not reported). We then recalculate the TVPI and DPI for investments made in portfolio companies in which at least one upper quartile VC participated. For the years 1985 to 1998, the average TVPI for portfolio companies of upper quartile VCs is 3.9 (DPI = 3.8) and the TVPI declines to 2.0 (DPI = 1.5) for the years 1999 to 2004. Similar to the pattern observed for the universe of VC investments, exits by more reputable VCs also experience a substantial decline in performance after 1998.

In the final four columns of Table 2.7, we examine the recovery of capital from M&A exits. For the years 1985 to 1998, on average 50.6 percent of realizations come through M&A exits and the recovery rates are little changed if the start years through 2004 are included (49.0 percent). In all years, roughly 50 percent of capital is recovered through M&A exits, and consequently, they are an important mechanism by which capital is recovered in the industry.

While the recovery from M&A exits is substantial, the chief issue of concern is whether the recovery rates are sufficient to recoup the investment in the industry. To judge the adequacy of the recovery rates from M&A exits, we must have a benchmark for expected recovery rates. Under the assumption of random occurrence of the forms of exits, the null hypothesis is that the recovery rates from M&A exits should be proportional to their percentage occurrence in a given year. In column (9), the percentage occurrence of M&A exits (number of M&A exits divided by total number of exits in a given start year) generally increases over the course of the sample period, which is consistent with the earlier evidence shown in Table 2.1. The recovery rates from M&A exits in column (10) typically lag the percentage occurrence of M&A exits in column (9). For example, for start years 1985 to 1998, on average 44.0 percent of exits are M&A exits and their recovery rate in this period is 50.3 percent, exceeding proportional expectations. For the start years 1999 to 2004, on average 68.7 percent of exits are M&A exits, but the recovery rate in this period of 49.0 percent falls below proportional expectations. As this lag in M&A recovery rates has grown, a greater number of exits are required to recoup the total investment in portfolio companies. While this has negative consequences for industry returns, our calculations also do not factor in the greater costs of due diligence, monitoring, and other effort that go into producing a greater number of exits that realize proportionally fewer dollars in return. Thus the overall evidence in Table 2.7 validates concerns about low capital recovery rates from M&A exits and the decline in IPO exits.

6 CONCLUSION

The decline in IPO exits from venture capital has raised concerns about how the lower returns from M&A exits can sustain the industry. To date, although the returns from exits can shed light on how the form of exit affects the recovery of capital, no study has examined returns from IPO and M&A exits in venture capital investments. We examine the returns from 1401 IPO exits and 1215 M&A exits of US venture-backed companies over the period 1985 to 2008. The use of exit returns is an important departure from earlier studies which have mainly focused on the overall performance of private equity and VC funds relative to public equity markets, and have not addressed the issue of capital recovery by type of VC exit.

Overall, the average return to IPO exits is significantly higher than the average return to M&A exits. This finding is robust to alternative measures of returns that account for the time to exit and the risk of the investments. The properties of returns reveal substantial variation in the distribution of both M&A and IPO exit returns. The highest M&A returns are comparable to the highest IPO returns but 40 percent of exits fail to recover the full amount of capital invested in the portfolio company, with M&A exits accounting for a disproportionately larger share of these. The large number of investments with negative returns questions the reliability of the number of exits as a gauge of successful VC performance used in previous studies.

When we examine the industry recovery rates by portfolio company start years, we find that the realization rates from M&A exits are below their occurrence as a proportion of total exits. Because the frequency of M&A exits has increased since 1999, it suggests that greater numbers of M&A exits are required to recover the total dollars invested in portfolio companies. While this has an overall effect of dampening industry returns, it is worrisome also because greater numbers of exits requires additional costs of due diligence, monitoring, and other effort that are not factored into our return calculations.

The venture industry is often described as a 'hit driven' business. High returns are the means by which substantial amounts of capital are returned to investors and this capital provides a margin for error that enables VCs to take risks, knowing that while a number of companies may fail, a few may achieve great success. When we consider the totality of the evidence, outsized returns for M&A exits are simply harder to achieve in sufficient numbers to produce the kind of returns investors seek from this asset class. High M&A returns require VCs to have more discipline in capital allocation, while achieving good exit market valuations, which in turn requires VCs to have greater skill in managing all stages of their investments. By contrast, high IPO returns are more a function of market timing and having companies ready when the 'window is open'. Consequently, our evidence supports concerns about the viability of the venture capital industry and suggests that, if IPOs continue to be scare and M&A exits are the predominant form of exit, VCs will face a large challenge adapting to this new market reality.

NOTES

1. For a general reference on venture capital, see Gompers and Lerner (1999).
2. See, for example, Kedrosky (2009), Kaplan and Lerner (2010): http://venturebeat.com/2008/11/12/the-vc-model-is-broken/ and http://blogs.wsj.com/venturecapital/2009/02/06/the-slow-quiet-death-of-venture-firms/ (accessed 16 May 2012).
3. Studies that treat exits as an event frequently examine the choice of an IPO or M&A exit. Brau et al. (2003), Poulsen and Stegemoller (2008), and Ball et al. (2011) examine the exit choice and find that, relative to acquisitions, IPOs are more likely to occur under favorable market conditions, when firms have strong growth opportunities, or when firms are capital constrained.
4. Total cumulative value to paid-in capital (TVPI), also known as the investment ratio, is the sum of the value of realized investments (or cumulative distributed capital) and the value of unrealized investments at cost divided by paid-in capital.
5. The findings broadly support Bayar and Chemmanur's (2009) theoretical model of the M&A versus IPO exit decision, which predicts that the average valuation of firms going public will be greater than the average valuation of firms being acquired because the firms going public consist of a mix of firms with and without sustainable businesses (that is, firm with an ability to survive against product market competition), whereas only firms with unsustainable businesses are acquired.
6. For further information on the sample construction and additional steps taken to ensure its completeness and accuracy, see Chaplinsky and Gupta-Mukherjee (2012).
7. The number of M&A and IPO exits is comparable to Korteweg and Sorenson (2010) which computes round-to-round returns using post-money data from Sand Hill Econometrics.
8. For example, consider a company which exited after two rounds of financing. Assume that the fraction of equity stakes acquired by VCs in the first round is 30 percent and in the second round is 20 percent. The aggregate VC stakes at exit (accounting for dilution) will be calculated as $VC\%_T = 30\% \times (1 - 20\%) + 20\% = 44\%$. The venture capital method of valuation is a widely used method of valuation by practitioners. See Smith and Smith (2004) for a discussion of the method.
9. Bradley et al. (2001) find for VC backed IPOs that the average stock price increases 27.34 percent 90 days after the offer date, and increases 29.40 percent 180 days after the offer date, the most frequently employed lock-up period.
10. A key question is the accuracy of the equity stakes estimated from VE data. We have no means to check the accuracy of M&A equity stakes but we check the IPO equity stakes against the stakes reported in IPO S-1 filings for sample firms from 1995, where the data on EDGAR become more generally available. For the matched sample of 4194 VC firm-company level stakes, the average VC equity stake from S-1 filings is 15 percent (median = 12 percent) compared to an average equity stake of 12 percent (median = 9 percent) computed from the post-money valuation data. There is no statistically significant difference in the stakes estimated from the S-1 filings and post-money valuations. Consequently, the additional steps taken to check the accuracy of the VC equity stakes strengthen the use of the post-money valuation data as a means to estimate equity stakes.
11. We do not compute an internal rate of return (IRR) because of missing interim round data and because it does not provide as intuitive a measure of capital recovery.
12. As an additional approach to risk adjustment, we calculated the Sharpe ratios for M&A and IPO exits. This is equivalent to comparing a portfolio containing the universe of venture-backed M&A exits in our sample with the portfolio of IPO exits based on the risk-return trade-off reflected in each form of exit. The Sharpe ratio is defined as the expected return of an asset minus the risk-free rate, divided by the standard

deviation of returns. Using realized returns and their standard deviations, the M&A and IPO exit portfolios have Sharpe ratios of 0.33 and 0.71, respectively. This is consistent with our findings of inferior capital recovery from M&A relative to IPO exits.
13. The subsequent results are not sensitive to whether returns are measured using company-level returns, annualized returns, or adjusted returns.
14. Venture capital stakes are also lower in each quintile for M&A exits and show less variation across quintiles than IPO exits. The lowest IPO returns are associated with an average 28.4 percent stake compared to a 46.2 percent stake for M&A returns. The lower stakes might suggest that VCs exert better selectivity in these IPOs by limiting their exposure through smaller stakes but an alternative explanation is that the VCs end up with lower stakes while investing relatively large amounts of capital because these investments were made in circumstances where entrepreneurs had greater bargaining power.
15. This regression framework is a case of a 'composite dependent variable' (that is, exit return) regressed on its components (that is, VC stakes, money-in, and money-out).
16. The qualitative regression results remain unchanged if time and industry fixed effects are excluded.
17. We use the term 'start year' to distinguish it from birth or founding year. Firms can have a birth or founding date which falls before their first round of VC funding.
18. Paid-in capital includes investments in portfolio companies that are classified as defunct or bankrupt as reported in VE.
19. See for example 'Private equity valuation survey results', Foster Center for Entrepreneurship and Private Equity, Tuck School of Business, Dartmouth College, May 2003.
20. For example, Cochrane (2005) estimates an average beta on venture capital investments of 1.7 and Korteweg and Sorensen (2010) estimate betas that range from 2.6 to 3.2.

REFERENCES

Ball, E., C. Hsin Hui and R. Smith (2011), 'Can VCs time the market? An analysis of exit choice for venture-backed firms', *Review of Financial Studies*, **24**, 3105–38.
Bayar, O. and T. Chemmanur (2009), 'IPOs or acquisitions? A theory of the choice of exit strategy by entrepreneurs and venture capitalists', working paper, Boston College.
Bradley, D., J. Bradford, I. Roten and H. Yi (2001), 'Venture capital and IPO lock-up expiration: an empirical analysis', *Journal of Financial Research*, **24**, 465–93.
Brau, J., F. Francis and N. Kohers (2003), 'The choice of IPO versus takeover: empirical evidence', *Journal of Business*, **76**, 583–612.
Chaplinsky, S. and S. Gupta-Mukherjee (2012), 'Investment risk allocation and the venture capital exit market', working paper, University of Virginia, Darden Graduate School of Business.
Cochrane, J., (2005), 'The risk and return of venture capital', *Journal of Financial Economics*, **75**, 3–52.
Gompers, P. and J. Lerner (1999), *The Venture Capital Cycle*, Cambridge, MA: MIT Press.
Harris, R., T. Jenkinson and S. Kaplan (2012), Private equity performance: what do we know?, NBER Working Paper 17874, available at: http://www.nber.org/papers/w17874 (accessed 14 May 2012).
Kaplan, S. and J. Lerner (2010), 'It ain't broke: the past, present, and future of venture capital', *Journal of Applied Corporate Finance*, **22**, 36–47.
Kaplan, S. and A. Schoar (2005), 'Private equity performance: returns, persistence, and capital flows', *Journal of Finance*, **60**, 1791–823.
Kedrosky, P. (2009), 'Right-sizing the U.S. venture capital industry', working paper, 10 June, Ewing Marion Kauffman Foundation.
Korteweg, A. and M. Sorenson (2010), 'Risk and return characteristics of venture capital-backed entrepreneurial companies', *Review of Financial Studies*, **10**, 3738–72.
Ljungqvist, A. and M. Richardson (2003), 'The cash flow, return and risk characteristics of private equity', working paper, New York University.
McGee, S. (2007), 'No exit', *Institutional Investor*, January, 21–4.
Patricof, A. (2009), 'Another view: V.C. investing not dead, just different', DealBook blogs, *New York Times*, 9 February.
Phalippou, L. and O. Gottschalg (2009), 'The performance of private equity funds', *Review of Financial Studies*, **22**, 1747–76.
Poulsen, A. and M. Stegemoller (2008), 'Moving from private to public ownership: selling out to public firms vs. initial public offerings', *Financial Management*, **37**, 81–101.
Robinson, D. and B. Sensoy (2011), 'Private equity in the 21st century: cash flows, performance, and contract terms from 1984–2010', Working Paper No. 2010-021, Ohio State University, Charles A. Dice Center.

Rodrigues, U. and M. Stegemoller (2007), 'An inconsistency in SEC disclosure requirements? The case of the "insignificant" private target', *Journal of Corporate Finance*, **13**, 251–69.
Smith, R. and J. Smith (2004), *Entrepreneurial Finance*, New York: John Wiley & Sons.

3 Survey evidence: what do we know about European and US firms' motivations for going public?
Franck Bancel and Usha R. Mittoo

1 INTRODUCTION

Most of the chapters in this book provide evidence from traditional empirical studies that employ large financial data and conduct powerful statistical analysis. This chapter, instead, focuses on studies based on surveys of managers that are less common in finance but provide unique information that cannot be easily collected through traditional empirical methods.

The survey method has several unique advantages as well as limitations. First, surveys allow researchers to ask direct questions on both the assumptions and implications of different financial theories. Second, traditional empirical studies are limited in their ability to deal with qualitative issues whereas surveys can facilitate such analysis. Third, survey information can also help in developing new theories or modifying existing views. For example, Lintner's (1956) field study of US managers' dividend policies and Pilcher's (1955) survey on why firms issue convertible debt have led to new theoretical and empirical studies in these areas. Finally, managers also find surveys useful in learning about the practices of their peers. The survey method is particularly useful in learning about cross-country practices since differences in reporting and accounting requirements could make it difficult to compare financial data across countries. The survey studies can partly overcome this problem by asking similar questions to managers around the world and comparing responses from multiple countries simultaneously. The survey method also has several limitations. A major drawback is that surveys measure beliefs – and not necessarily actions – of managers. Non-response could also be a problem since the respondents might not be representative of the population. Another limitation is that managers may not understand some questions or may give a 'politically correct' answer. Despite these limitations, survey studies complement empirical studies, and their use in finance is growing.

The survey technique is particularly useful in gaining insights into firms' motivations for going public. While a large number of theories have been proposed for why firms go public, testing these theories has been challenging primarily because of a lack of data availability. Pagano et al. (1998) is the only study that directly tests different initial public offering (IPO) theories using a proprietary database to compare both *ex ante* and *ex post* characteristics of 69 Italian firms that went public between 1982 and 1992. Such data are neither easily available nor comparable across countries. Consequently, while IPO research is one of the most researched areas in finance, there is little empirical evidence on why firms go public. Survey method allows researchers to overcome this constraint by directly asking chief financial officers (CFOs) about the major motivations, and costs and benefits of going public.

This chapter is not a comprehensive review of survey research on IPOs. Instead, it focuses on the findings of a few survey studies with the goal of providing a clear understanding of the major determinants of European and US managers' going public decisions. Specifically, we draw survey evidence mostly from one European IPO survey (Bancel and Mittoo, 2009) and two US survey studies (Brau and Fawcett, 2006; Brau et al. 2006). Readers interested in a more in-depth analysis or evidence related to other countries will find several useful references in this chapter. In addition, for those who are more interested in survey research, some useful references are presented by Bancel and Mittoo (2011) who summarize the survey research in cost of capital and capital structure financing, and by Baker et al. (2010) who provide a synthesis of survey research in corporate finance.

The remainder of the chapter is organized as follows. Section 1 summarizes different theories about why firms go public. The next two sections present the European and US survey evidence respectively, and the following section compares and discusses cross-country survey findings. The final section summarizes and concludes the chapter.

2 THEORETICAL LITERATURE: MOTIVATIONS FOR GOING PUBLIC

The firm's going public decision has important consequences for the firm. While a public listing on stock exchanges brings several benefits for the firm, such as increased recognition and stock liquidity, it also subjects the firm to additional costs, such as higher level of disclosures and intense public scrutiny. Most IPO theories model the decision to go public as a trade-off between costs and benefits of going public. However, all theories focus on one major motivation, such as funding for growth or cost of capital. Firms, on the other hand, might seek multiple benefits that could vary across firms, industry, and countries. Firms are also likely to choose their IPO timing to maximize their net benefits. In this section, we discuss IPO theories grouped by a benefit, cost, or market timing decision. These groupings are not mutually exclusive because two IPO theories might propose the same motivation but with different assumptions or costs of going public. We present a summary of testable predictions for different IPO theories and the survey findings in the appendix to this chapter.

2.1 Major Benefits

Funding for growth strategy
Maksimovic and Pichler (2001) and Chemmanur and Fulghieri (1999) model the firm's IPO decision as a strategic choice to raise funds for growth, but the former models it as a trade-off between enhanced credibility and disclosure of sensitive information, and the latter between widening the firm's ownership base and its information production costs.

Maksimovic and Pichler (2001) assert that the firm conducts an IPO to gain first-mover advantage in the product market relative to their industry peers by raising funds for growth. A public listing enhances the firm's visibility and credibility because of higher disclosure levels and public scrutiny which facilitates financing but may also require the firm to disclose sensitive information that may be valuable to its competitors.

Chemmanur and Fulghieri (1999) argue that an IPO allows the firm to raise cheap financing by broadening its ownership base. They model the going-public decision in an asymmetric information framework as a trade-off between raising equity in public markets by widening the investor base and issuing private equity to a small group of large investors. The major cost for the firm is the cost of production of information to minimize the asymmetric information between managers and investors for obtaining cheaper financing. Their model predicts that firms tend to go public when they are older, well established, and have a track record so that there is a sufficient amount of public information available. However, firms in industries with a greater need for public financing, such as high-technology industry, might go public early.

Several theoretical and empirical studies support the notion that firms go public to raise funding, to widen their investor base, and to enhance investor recognition. Ritter and Welch (2002) show that most firms go public primarily to raise new capital for growth. Merton (1987) argues that enhanced investor recognition helps in broadening the firm's investor base and lowers its cost of capital. Bancel and Mittoo (2001) report that European managers cite enhanced visibility as the most important benefit of listing on foreign exchanges, and Bradley et al. (2003) show that analyst recommendations tend to be biased upward after an IPO. Kim and Weisbach (2005) study IPOs from 38 countries and find that almost all IPO firms raise a substantial amount of new capital in the IPO but they use the new funds for several purposes including financing growth, rebalancing leverage, and increasing cash balances.

Mergers and acquisitions strategy
Lyandres, Zhdanov and Hsieh (2008) argue that firms go public primarily to pursue an efficient merger and acquisition (M&A) strategy. They assert that an IPO removes the uncertainty about the precise value of a firm or its assets and allows the firm to exercise its restructuring options for merger and acquisitions optimally with cash or stock financing. Brau et al. (2003) argue that an IPO facilitates the creation of publicly traded shares that can be used as a currency in either acquiring other companies or in being acquired in a stock deal. This merger and acquisition motivation may also play an important and previously unrecognized role in the long-run underperformance of IPOs (Brau et al., 2012). As shown by Loughran and Vijh (1997) and Rau and Vermaelen (1998), acquirers significantly underperform in the long run. The fact that newly public firms are active acquirers may be a potential explanation for the IPO underperformance puzzle.

Exit strategy
Several studies propose that an IPO is a vehicle to facilitate owners to exit the firm and sell their shares. Zingales (1995) argues that an IPO is a first step in the owner's exit strategy. By selling part of the cash flow rights in the IPO, and the ownership control rights at a later stage, the owner designs a strategy that maximizes the total proceeds from the firm's eventual sale. Mello and Parsons (1998) argue that IPO enhances stock liquidity and firm value, enabling the owners to sell shares in several stages, whereas Black and Gilson (1998) assert that an IPO provides an attractive harvest strategy for venture capitalists by allowing them to cash out their investments. Ang and Brau (2003) demonstrate that insiders opportunistically sell shares in the IPO for personal gain. The empirical

evidence, however, suggests that in several countries for which data are available, most major pre-IPO owners continue to maintain their control after the IPO (see for example, Holmén and Högfeldt, 2003, for Sweden, and Goergen and Renneboog, 2003, for Germany).

Cost of capital
The cost of capital literature argues that firms conduct a public offering when external equity will minimize their cost of capital (Modigliani and Miller, 1963; for example, Scott, 1976). Myers and Majluf (1984) and Myers (1984) argue that firms use a pecking order of financing based on the degree of asymmetric information and raise financing in the following order: internal equity, debt financing, and then external equity as a last resort.

Financial flexibility and bargaining power strategy
Managers around the world identify the need for financial flexibility as the main driver of their financing decisions (see Graham and Harvey (2001) and Bancel and Mittoo (2004)). DeAngelo and DeAngelo (2007) argue that financial flexibility is the critical missing link for an empirically viable theory of capital structure and Gamba and Triantis (2008) develop a dynamic model for the value of financial flexibility that focuses on the strategic management of corporate liquidity, financing and investment policies. Huyghebaert and Hulle (2005) argue that an IPO generates new financing options and allows the firm to enhance its financial flexibility by facilitating many sources of financing for its growth and expansion, and Denis and Sibilkov (2010) provide empirical evidence supporting the notion that the need for financial flexibility is an important factor in firms' debt decisions. Rajan (1992) argues that an IPO enhances the firm's bargaining power with bankers and financial creditors, and consequently, reduces its cost of borrowing. Pagano et al. (1998) report that Italian firms experienced a reduction of about 0.30 percentage points in cost of credit after going public – consistent with Rajan (1992).

Enhancing stock liquidity
Amihud and Mendelson (1986) suggest that a stock exchange listing enhances stock liquidity, which in turn increases firm value. Several models hypothesize that stock liquidity is closely related to several other IPO benefits. For example, enhanced liquidity allows stock to be used as a currency to raise cheap financing, to facilitate mergers and acquisitions, to design an exit strategy, and to allow management to increase effective control while diversifying ownership (for example, Booth and Chua, 1996; Brennan and Franks, 1997; Chemmanur and Fulghieri, 1999; Brau et al., 2003). Maug (1998) argues that stock liquidity is valuable for managerial incentive schemes, and predicts a positive correlation between liquidity and external monitoring.

2.2 Major Costs

The IPO involves both direct and indirect costs. The major direct costs are underwriting fees and commissions which are considered as costs in all IPO models. The indirect costs which include enhanced increased disclosure requirements of the stock exchanges and the public scrutiny, on the other hand, are treated as cost in some IPO models but as a benefit in others. For example, Jensen and Meckling (1976) argue that the firm's commitment to meet the regulatory and reporting requirements of stock exchanges lowers the agency costs between managers and shareholders. In addition, the intense scrutiny of analysts and market participants limits the private benefits of control and imposes pressure on managers for performance. A public listing also allows the firm to devise incentive plans to align managers' interest with those of shareholders. By contrast, Maksimovic and Pichler (2001) consider enhanced transparency as a major cost since it forces the firm to disclose crucial information that may be advantageous to competitors. Pagano and Röell (1998), on the other hand, argue that monitoring of managers is higher at the pre-IPO stage because a small group of investors can monitor the firm more closely than can dispersed investors.

2.3 IPO Market Timing Decision

The asymmetric information literature argues that managers use their superior information opportunistically to take advantage of temporarily favorable market conditions and attractive stock prices in making stock offerings. Survey of managers also support that managers use windows of opportunities to raise debt and equity financing (Bancel and Mittoo, 2001, 2004, 2011; Graham and Harvey, 2001).

Several empirical studies document that IPOs come in waves and are clustered during strong industry and market conditions in both the US and European countries (Ibbotson and Jaffe, 1975; Lucas and McDonald, 1990; Pagano et al., 1998; Lowry and Schwert, 2002; Ritter and Welch, 2002). A large number of empirical studies also document that IPO firms have abnormal returns on the first day of the offering but underperform their peers during three to five years following initial public offerings. Such evidence is available in both the US and European countries and supports the notion that firms take advantage of windows of opportunities to capture favourable offering prices (Ibbotson and Jaffe, 1975; Loughran and Ritter, 1995; Ritter, 1991, 2003).

Some studies also examine when a firm decides to go public within a hot IPO market. Lowry and Schwert (2002) argue that the recent first-day stock performance of firms going public leads other firms to decide to go public. Choe et al. (1993) argue that firms prefer to go public when other good firms are currently issuing and when they reach a certain point in the business growth cycle and need external equity capital to continue to grow. Colak and Günay (2011) develop a model about the IPO timing decision in a game theory framework. They assume that managers have private information about the quality of their firms, and firms update their learning about the status of the market through a Bayesian process. When one of the private firms goes public successfully or unsuccessfully, the other agents in the economy obtain new information about the aggregate economic conditions. In such a game, the informational advantages of delayed issuance (that is, information externalities) cause the private firms to engage in strategic waiting. They predict that both low- and high-quality firms tend to delay their IPOs until a favorable market condition is confirmed, but a separating equilibrium exists in which lower quality firms will issue ahead of higher quality firms in the expanding IPO cycle. They test and find supporting evidence for these predictions in a US sample.

3 EUROPEAN SURVEY EVIDENCE

In this section, we summarize and discuss the European evidence which is based primarily on Bancel and Mittoo (2009). Bancel and Mittoo survey 78 European firms that went public between 1994 and 2004. The UK firms form the largest component (23 percent), followed by the French (22 percent) and German (13 percent) firms. Three countries – Greece, Italy, and Austria – comprise about 19 percent of the sample, and six other countries (Switzerland, Portugal, the Netherlands, Spain, Ireland and Belgium) make up the remaining 23 percent of the sample.

The survey questionnaire (see appendix; Bancel and Mittoo, 2009) included over 100 questions and was mailed to European CFOs in 2005 with an accompanying letter presenting the objectives of the study and promising a summary of findings. Bancel and Mittoo ask questions on the costs and benefits of both exchange listings and going public, and collect data on several pre-IPO and post-IPO characteristics, including ownership structure and the types of dominant shareholders.

To discriminate between different IPO theories, Bancel and Mittoo conduct univariate analysis conditional on several firm characteristics, such as firm size, age, ownership structure, and capital raising and non-capital raising in the IPO, and examine cross-correlations among responses on different questions. To address the concern that respondents may not have been closely involved with the IPO decision, they also interview six CFOs who had first-hand knowledge of their firms' IPO decisions. Table 3.1 presents the main findings about European CFOs' views on IPO motivations. The first column reports the questions asked in the survey, and the second reports the percentage of respondents that view the motivation as important or very important.

The European CFOs cite 'to enhance the company's prestige and visibility' as the most important benefit of going public. Over 80 percent of CFOs agree that the IPO acts as an advertisement for the company and increases its reputation/image (Table 3.1). The CFOs also highlight these benefits as important, with written comments in open-ended questions, such as: 'reputation among businesses, awareness of the company by stakeholders, good reputation as an employer and international visibility'. They find support for the Merton model since the CFOs who value enhanced visibility are also more likely to agree that the IPO has lowered the cost of financing. Bancel and Mittoo (2009) also report that high-technology firms assign significantly higher ranking to the enhanced visibility and prestige, and firms that tend to agree that an IPO enhances the firm's reputation also tend to place a higher value on external monitoring.

Most CFOs agree that funding for growth is a major benefit of an IPO, consistent with the Maksimovic and Pichler (2001) and Chemmanur and Fulghieri (1999) models. Three-quarters of firms in their sample raised new capital in the IPO, and over 70 percent of the CFOs agree that financing investment opportunities is one of the most important benefits of the IPO. About 75 percent of CFOs agree that an IPO increases the firm's financial flexibility by generating new financing alternatives. In line with Kim and Weisbach (2005), they find that the cash raised in the IPO is used for several purposes, including a reduction in leverage and enhancing financial flexibility. Consistent with the Chemmanur–Fulghieri model, typical firms in their sample go public when they are older (average (median) age of 24 (12) years) whereas high-technology firms go public at a younger age, and value the financing benefit and the enhanced balance of

Table 3.1 European managers' views on IPOs

Motivations for IPOs	Important and very important (%)
To enhance the company's prestige, image and visibility	77.78
To facilitate raising capital	76.39
To implement a 'natural path' of growth for our firm	70.83
To increase shareholder base	69.86
To increase the liquidity of the company's securities	62.50
To appeal to institutional investors	60.56
To be recognized by the relevant financial community as a major player	59.72
To facilitate mergers and acquisitions	55.56
To facilitate business operations	52.11
To provide stock ownership plans for employees	50.68

The IPO has allowed the firm to:	Important and very important (%)
To make the firm's share more liquid and to increase the firm value	75.32
To increase financial flexibility (generating new financing alternatives)	75.32
To finance investment opportunities	73.33
To be monitored by outsiders (analysts, investors, etc.) in order to increase the firm value	69.74
To compensate employees and managers (ability to provide stock options, etc.)	59.74
To reduce the cost of financing (debt and equity)	57.89
To sell the company to external shareholders	56.58
To estimate the market value of the firm	56.58
To reinforce the firm's balance of power with bankers and other financial creditors	56,00
To pay for future acquisitions with the firm's shares	53.33

Do these statements agree with your company's IPO decisions?	Important and very important (%)
The IPO acts as advertising for the company and increases its reputation/image	83.12
Making the IPO, we believed it was the best time to do it	72.73
The IPO is a normal 'stage' in the growth of a company	68.83
Making an IPO, we had a clear vision of our capacity to give an acceptable return to shareholders	58.11

Notes:
This table is based on the main findings of Bancel and Mittoo (2009).
The first column reports the question and the second the percentage of respondents who find it 'important' or 'very important' on a Likert scale of −2 (not important) to +2 (very important).

power with creditors more than their peers do. However, they find little support for the Chemmanur–Fulghieri model's implication that access to better financing stems from broadening the shareholder base, since the correlation between the responses for the two benefits is low.

Bancel and Mittoo find medium support for the models that highlight IPOs' role as a vehicle to facilitate merger and acquisition currency. About 56 percent of the CFOs agree that facilitating mergers and acquisitions is an important benefit. Over half of the CFOs also agree that the IPO has allowed them to estimate the market value of the company and to use stock currency for future acquisitions. Two CFOs mentioned in their interviews that growth through M&A was a primary objective in their firm's IPO decision, and they completed a major acquisition within three years of their IPO.

Bancel and Mittoo also find some support for the theories that highlight IPO's role in facilitating exit strategy and in enhancing their balance of power with banks or creditors. Over half of the CFOs agree that the IPO has reinforced the firm's balance of power with bankers and creditors but this support is strong mainly among family-controlled firms. Over half of the CFOS identify the sale of the company as a major motivation but the support is stronger among firms that do not reduce leverage after the IPO.

Bancel and Mittoo find little support for cost of capital theories. Only 45 percent of the CFOs agree that cost of capital is important in their listing decision. The support for pecking-order theory is even weaker because few CFOs agree with the statement that asymmetric information was a problem at the time of the IPO. Moreover, capital-raising firms agree even less with this statement. Although about 58 percent of the CFOs agree that going public has reduced their firms' cost of financing, this support appears to be due to the enhanced balance of power with creditors. There is also some support for Holmstrom and Tirole's (1993) argument that firms can reduce their cost of capital by obtaining cheap financing from capital markets since most capital-raising firms agree that the IPO has reduced the cost of capital whereas non-capital raising firms do not.

The European managers also view the timing of the IPO as a major factor. About 73 percent of European CFOs believe that it was the best time to execute an IPO, and about 40 percent agree that the IPO has allowed them 'to benefit from favorable market conditions (such as, bullish stock exchange/industry valuation)'. Although most managers support market timing theories, the support is stronger among high-technology firms that list on foreign exchanges.

The European managers also support the notion that external monitoring increases firm value but the support is stronger among larger firms, and among firms that went public primarily to allow founding owners to disengage from the business. About 60 percent of CFOs also agree that an IPO enables the firm to design compensation schemes for managers and employees. The capital-raising firms and high-technology firms value external monitoring less than their peers, suggesting that the value of external monitoring varies across firms by size and industry.

The IPO literature mentions both direct costs, such as underwriting costs, and indirect costs of going public, such as higher disclosure and listing requirements and loss of confidentiality. The European CFOs are less concerned with the costs of going public, and 42 percent of CFOs agree that the cost of IPO is not a real issue. In an open-ended question, the CFOs mention the professional fees, such as banking, lawyers and accountants fees, as the major direct costs of an IPO. Other IPO costs mentioned by respondents include public relations costs, management time, the frequency of reporting, and the need to change accounting systems. A few CFOs also mention opportunity costs, such as the short-term focus of the market but they find little support for asymmetric information, or loss of confidentiality costs mentioned in several models.

Table 3.2   US managers' views on IPOs

Major motivations for conducting an IPO (Brau and Fawcett, 2006)	Important and very important (%)
To create public shares for use in future acquisitions	59.41
To establish a market price/value for our firm	51.17
To enhance the reputation of our company	49.11
To broaden the base of ownership	45.89
To allow one or more principals to diversify personal holdings	44.11
To minimize our cost of capital	42.51
Major factors influencing IPO timing (Brau and Fawcett, 2006)	**Important and very important (%)**
Overall stock market conditions	82.94
Industry conditions	69.82
We will need the capital to continue to grow	66.47
Major benefits/costs for conducting an IPO (Brau, et al., 2006)	**Stongly and mildly agree (%)**
A benefit of the IPO was that it allowed the company to gain additional financing for long term growth	86.8
A benefit of the IPO was that it allowed the company to gain additional financing for immediate growth	82.6
A benefit of the IPO was that it increased liquidity	82.5
A benefit of the IPO was that the market was strong at the time of IPO.	59.2
A benefit of the IPO was that it improved market perception of stock.	48.7
A benefit of the IPO was that it allowed original owners to diversify their interests	46.0
A benefit of the IPO was that it allowed the company to reduce its debt	44.4
A benefit of the IPO was prestige of being on an exchange	39.6
A benefit of the IPO was to decrease the total cost of capital	38.2
A disadvantage of the IPO was that it made the company suddenly open to public scrutiny	68.9

Notes:
This table is based on the main findings of Brau and Fawcett (2006) and Brau et al. (2006).
The first column reports the question and the second the percentage of respondents who find it 'important/midly agree' or 'very important/strongly agree' on a Likert scale of +1 (not important/strongly disagree) to +5 (very important/strongly agree).

4 US SURVEY EVIDENCE

The US evidence is based on Brau and Fawcett (2006) and Brau et al. (2006) survey studies. Their main findings are presented in Table 3.2.

Brau and Fawcett (2006) conduct a survey of 336 CFOs of US firms. Their sample includes 87 US firms that went public in the post-Internet bubble period (January 2000 to December 2002). The remaining sample comprises private firms and includes firms that began the IPO process but chose to withdraw the issue as well as those that are large enough to go public but did not attempt an IPO. They also conduct univariate analysis based on firm characteristics and test robustness of their main findings using financial data and empirical analysis.

They examine seven issues related to IPOs: motivations for going public, timing of the IPO, underwriter selection, underpricing, signaling, IPO process issues, and the decision to stay private. In this section, we focus mainly on the motivations and market timing issues.

Brau and Fawcett find that the primary motivations for going public are to facilitate acquisitions, and ascertaining the value of the firm. The US CFOs identify the ability to create public shares for use in future acquisitions, and the establishment of market price or value for the firm as the first and the second most important motivation respectively for going public (Table 3.2). Since the establishment of a market price could also be interpreted as the first step in the acquisition process, the authors conclude that the US firms conduct an IPO primarily to facilitate acquisitions. They also analyze merger and acquisition activity for their sample of IPOs and find support for their main findings, that IPOs facilitate acquisition activity by forming a currency of stock for mergers and takeovers.

Brau and Fawcett find that cost of capital motivations are less important. Fewer than half the CFOs agree that minimizing the cost of capital is an important rationale for going public. The questions pertaining to financing operations – our company has run out of equity, and debt is becoming too expensive – were cited as least important factors. They also find that IPOs have an influence on the firm's reputation, and about half of the respondents consider this criterion as important or very important. They also find some support for an IPO as a strategic decision, especially among high-technology firms who view an IPO more as a strategic reputation-enhancing move than as a financing decision. They also find that enhancing firm reputation is more important among smaller, younger, high-technology, and venture capital (VC)-backed firms, whereas firms that sell large insider holdings in the IPO are less concerned about enhancing the reputation of the firm or establishing a market price.

Brau and Fawcett also ask questions about IPO underpricing since the literature shows that, on average, IPOs are priced lower than their first-day market closing price. They find that CFOs are well informed regarding expected underpricing, and attribute most underpricing to market uncertainty and the need to reward investors for taking the risk of the IPO. Other important sources of underpricing cited in their survey include a desire on the part of underwriters to incur the favor of institutional investors, a desire to achieve a wide base of owners, and a desire to increase post-issue trading volume. The CFOs also view past historical earnings as an important signal, and select underwriters based on reputation.

Brau and Fawcett find that the timing of the IPO plays a major role in going public decision. Stock market conditions and industry conditions are important or very important for 83 percent and 70 percent of respondents respectively (Table 3.2). Venture capital backed firms and firms with small insider ownership decreases in the IPO tend to view market timing issues as more important than their counterparts. They also report that some firms that are desirous to go public are deterred by poor market conditions and by factors that increase the cost of an IPO, such as low demand (measured by an offer price less than the original mid-filing price).

Brau and Fawcett also examine factors that influence the decision to withdraw or not conduct an IPO and find that maintenance of decision-making control and ownership appear to be the primary reasons for remaining private, especially among firms that are larger, and older. High-technology firms are less concerned about control and dilution but are more concerned about market timing and pricing issues.

Based on their survey findings, Brau and Fawcett conclude that the academic theory regarding the IPO process is generally well grounded but suggest that several ideas that are commonly held in the IPO literature need to be revisited and refined.

Brau et al. (2006) survey 438 CFOs about their motivations and concerns about going public. Their sample consists of IPOs in both pre-Internet bubble (1996–98) and post-Internet bubble (2000–2002) periods. They also examine whether CFO sentiments are stationarity across the bull and bear market periods, and test CFO perspectives on aftermarket IPO returns.

Brau et al. (2006) report that to finance investment opportunities, and to increase stock liquidity and firm value are the two most important benefits, and over 80 percent of CFOs consider these important or very important (Table 3.2). A majority of respondents (59.2 percent) agree that conducting an IPO in a strong market is a benefit to the IPO firm. They find less support for other criteria, such as the exit strategy, enhancing prestige, and cost of capital considerations.

Based on their survey evidence, Brau, Ryan and DeGraw conclude that US firms' IPO decisions are motivated by three interrelated strategic considerations: growth, ownership control, and liquidity. First, firms go public primarily to fund both immediate and long-term growth since many CFOs report their plans for seasoned equity offerings (SEOs) after the IPO. They also find support for implications of Maksimovic and Pichler (2001) model that firms try to take the first-mover advantage, and view the increased public scrutiny as a major cost. Second, an IPO is not a vehicle for changing control or facilitating owners' exit since most CFOs indicate a strong motivation to retain ownership control. Third, IPOs are motivated by a desire for liquidity to gain a currency for future growth through generic investments and M&A activity. They also find support for market timing theory. A majority of CFOs report increased benefits if offerings coincide with strong market conditions and the degree of perceived IPO benefits is considerably higher during bull periods.

While the results of both US surveys are largely similar, there are some differences. For example, Brau and Fawcett find that US firms go public primarily to facilitate merger and acquisition activity whereas Brau, Ryan, and DeGraw find that they go public primarily to raise funds for growth. This divergence could reflect differences in survey questionnaires, or in respondents – indicating some of the limitations of the surveys. These differences could also reflect the effects of different market conditions since Brau and Fawcett's sample comprised firms that went public in the post-Internet bubble period whereas Brau et al.'s sample included firms that went public in both pre- and post-Internet bubble periods. Despite these differences, both studies share several common findings. For example, both surveys find that managers try to time the IPOs to benefit from strong market conditions and that CFOs define windows-of-opportunities in terms of overall stock market and industry conditions rather than the IPO market conditions. Both surveys also find little support for exit strategy, and cost of capital considerations.

5 CROSS-COUNTRY COMPARISONS

Several studies suggest that a country's legal and institutional environment is an important determinant of the firm's external financing choices and its ownership structure, which in turn could influence its motivations for going public. La Porta et al. (1997, 1998) stress that the legal system is the primary determinant of the availability of external financing, the size of capital markets and the proportion of firms that go public in a country. They argue that a common-law system provides better quality of investor protection than a civil-law system, and show that the size and breadth of capital markets vary systematically and positively with the quality of legal systems across countries. Demirgüç-Kunt and Maksimovic (2002) argue that the legal system in a country can generate comparative advantage for firms in supporting the quality of the banking system or the quality of securities markets. Demirgüç-Kunt and Maksimovic (1999) study debt policies across 30 countries and find that debt maturity is affected by both financial and legal institutions. Rajan and Zingales (2003) examine the evolution of the European financial system over time and conclude that it reflects a complex interaction of global economic and political factors.

Corporate ownership structure also varies widely across countries. While widespread ownership is observed in the US and the UK, concentrated ownership is the norm in most European countries where large holdings are held by family members or by other individuals, corporations, or financial institutions. La Porta et al. (1998) document a strong negative correlation between ownership concentration and the strength of investor protection at the country level.

In this section, we compare managers' views about going public across countries with different legal systems and ownership structure. We first compare views of European and US managers. Next, we compare managers' views between the English and civil legal system European countries, and among Continental European countries.

5.1 European and US CFOs' Views

Both US and European CFOs broadly share similar views but there are some noticeable differences. Both groups view financing for growth opportunity, stock currency for mergers and acquisitions as major benefits, and find little support for the cost of capital theories. Both also support the notion that managers use windows-of-opportunities when conducting IPOs. However, US managers view stock liquidity as more important and exit strategy benefit as less important compared to their European peers. The European CFOs, on the other hand, consider enhanced investor recognition, and reputation as a major benefit of an IPO, whereas few US CFOs consider it important. Second, the European CFOs are less concerned about the IPO costs compared to US managers. Brau et al. (2006) report that about 60 percent of the CFOs consider the underwriting costs and auditing fees as significant whereas Bancel and Mittoo (2009) find that less than 15 percent of European CFOs view these costs as important. More striking is the difference in their views about the public scrutiny. Over two-thirds of the European CFOs say that the increased transparency and external monitoring is a benefit, whereas about two-thirds of the US CFOs consider the public scrutiny as a major disadvantage of the IPO.

These differences could reflect institutional and capital markets as well as ownership differences between the US and European countries. For example, the gross underwriting spread that makes up the largest explicit IPO costs clusters around 7 percent in the US, but between 3 and 4 percent in Europe (for example, Chen and Ritter, 2000; Torstila, 2001). Further, the IPO costs are likely to be disproportionately smaller and less onerous for European firms since they go public when they are much larger and older compared to US firms. European IPO samples also include many recently privatized firms who might find enhanced market scrutiny useful in motivating managers and improving firm performance. Consistent with this reasoning, small and high-growth European firms tend to view external monitoring as a cost – similar to their US peers. Several European managers of large firms, interviewed by Bancel and Mittoo (2009), also support the notion that the disclosure requirements of stock exchanges helped them in designing better accounting systems and internal controls that improved managerial performance. Bancel and Mittoo (2001) find similar evidence in their survey of European firms that cross-list on the US stock exchanges.

5.2 Comparison of CFOs' Views across European Countries

In this section, we discuss the cross-country results from Bancel and Mittoo (2009), and the survey findings of Burton et al. (2006) and Marchisio and Ravisi (2003) in the UK and Italy respectively. The main results are summarized in Table 3.3.

English-versus civil-law system countries
Bancel and Mittoo (2009) find several striking differences between the English-system countries (the UK and Ireland) and civil-law system countries that comprise several continental European countries, including France, Germany, and Italy. English-system firms go public primarily to sell the company and to enhance stock liquidity, and are significantly less concerned with IPO costs and investor recognition than their European peers (Table 3.3). English-system firms are also significantly smaller and younger than their civil system peers when they go public. The ownership and control structures also differ between the two groups; family-controlled firms comprise about 42 percent of the civil-system firms but only 5 percent of English-system firms. Prior to the IPO, English-system firms are typically controlled by five or more large shareholders, whereas the largest shareholder in a pre-IPO civil-system firm owns an average of 80 percent of shares and continues to hold a majority stake after the IPO.

Burton et al. (2006) survey managers and interview financial intermediaries who were associated with the IPOs conducted in the UK between 1999 and 2001 about the determinants of their decisions regarding the IPO timing, the amount to raise, and the choice

Table 3.3 Managers' views about IPOs across European countries

Bancel and Mittoo (2009)		
Comparison English law versus civil law	UK & Ire	Civil-law countries
To sell the company to external shareholders	***	
To make the firm's share more liquid and to increase the firm value	**	
To be recognized by the relevant financial community as a major player	**	
The IPO is a normal 'stage' in the growth of a company	*	
Comparison Italian law versus other civil-law countries	Italy	Other civil
To reduce the cost of financing (debt and equity)	***	
To allow founding shareholder(s) to disengage as major shareholder	***	
We analyze the IPO as a trade-off between diversification gains and private benefits of control	**	
To list an entity/business separately and to achieve a better firm valuation	*	

Burton, Helliar and Power (2006): The UK	
Influence on the timing of a company's decision to float	Mean (1–3 Likert scale)
Need for funds for growth	1.20
Views of the firm's major investors	1.39

Marchisio and Ravasi (2003): Italy	
Reasons for going public	Mean (1–7 Likert scale)
To finance internal growth	5.75
To facilitate external growth	5.59
To improve the image and the prestige of the company	5.46
To increase the visibility of the company	5.25

Notes:
This table is based on the main findings of Bancel and Mittoo (2009), Burton et al. (2006) and Marchisio and Ravasi (2003).
In Bancel and Mittoo (2009), statistical differences between major 'UK & Ire, Civil law, Italy and Other civil law systems' are reported.
***, **, *, denote significance at the 1%, 5% and 10% respectively.
'Mean' in Burton et al. (2006) is based on a three-point Likert scale where 1 indicates a strong influence and 3 suggests no influence.
'Mean' in Marchisio and Ravasi (2003) is based on a 1–7 point Likert scale where 1 indicates 'irrelevant' and 7 'very important'.

of an exchange. Their evidence indicates that a company's need for funds for growth, to overhaul the capital structure, and diversification of the investor base are important influences for IPO timing. The views of the firm's major investors are also important (Table 3.3). The investors generally wanted to realize some of their investment (especially in the smaller companies) and strengthen the management team. Facilitating an exit route for major shareholders was also vital, particularly for venture capitalists who often did not like to hold shares in any company for too long. They report that the dominant reasons for the decision to go public are: (1) to increase the visibility of the company, thereby getting its name known among investors and the potential customer base, and (2) to raise the status of the company to assist with future growth in terms of sales and business contacts. Raising the firm's profile was viewed as very important since it could lower the cost of credit and allow the firm to take full advantage of its reputational and social capital.

Burton et al. (2006) find that the choice of an exchange is mainly dependent upon the size of company, with larger companies in the UK listing on the Official List, and smaller companies joining the Alternative Investment Market (AIM). The costs of listing also influenced the decision about where to list, especially for smaller companies. The costs of the issue were also seen as being significant but the perception of costs differed depending upon the circumstances of the company. For example, underwriters' fees were significant for those whose IPO was underwritten. There was an economy of scale with regard to costs, where the relative costs for smaller companies were higher than for larger ones.

In sum, both Burton et al. (2006) and Bancel and Mittoo (2009) find that enhancing stock liquidity, obtaining funds for growth, facilitating sale of the company and exit strategy are the primary motivations for the UK firms' going-public decision. However, while funding for growth is also a major motivation for US firms in going-public, pre-IPO owners in the US tend to retain their control after going public – contrary to that in the UK. Since both the US and the UK are English-system countries, these differences suggest that the local institutional factors might play a role in firms' going-public decisions even across countries with similar legal systems.

Italian versus other civil-law system countries
Bancel and Mittoo (2009) find that the managerial views are largely similar across most civil-law countries, except Italy (Table 3.3). The Italian CFOs agree more strongly that an IPO reduces the cost of financing, and value visibility and prestige more than their European peers do. They are also more likely to agree that an IPO is a trade-off between diversification gains and private benefits of control, and less likely to agree that an IPO allows owners to disengage from the business compared to their European peers.

Several managerial surveys and empirical studies have also examined why Italian firms go public. Marchisio and Ravasi (2003) survey Italian IPO firms and conduct case studies of companies who went public between 1995 and 1999. They conclude that besides providing an important inflow of capital, going public may actually improve the reputational and social capital of a company, by increasing its visibility, prestige and perceived trustworthiness (Table 3.3). Therefore, going public may be an important way to support entrepreneurial activity, as it may expand and reinforce the network of relationships that offer access to external resources, complementary skills and investment opportunities. Further, IPOs enabled the appointment of professional managers by facilitating managerial incentive schemes to reward the managers.

Pagano et al. (1998) find that Italian firms go public primarily to rebalance their accounts and to lower their cost of credit. They also find that the need to take advantage of a window of opportunity and to issue shares when profits were relatively high was an important factor in the IPO timing.

In sum, the evidence in this section supports the notion that while major motivations for IPOs are largely similar across different legal system countries, there are also some differences even across countries with similar legal systems.

6 SUMMARY AND CONCLUSIONS

In this chapter, we discuss major theories of why firms go public and discuss survey evidence on their implications about the costs and benefits of going public in the US and in European countries.

The appendix summarizes the main IPO theories and survey findings in the US and Europe. In the first column, we present the theory and its implications. In the second column, we summarize our survey evidence and conclusions for each theory with a rating of strong support, moderate support, and low support based on the European and US survey studies.

The CFOs' views are largely similar across legal systems and countries but differ on some dimensions. European CFOs identify enhanced visibility and prestige, funding for growth, and financial flexibility as the most important benefits of going public, but the English-system firms also consider the ability of the pre-IPO investors to exit as a major benefit of going public. The European and US CFOs agree on several major benefits of going public but disagree strongly on external monitoring which is considered as a major benefit by European CFOs but an onerous cost by their US peers. Motivations for an IPO also differ significantly across firms based on ownership structure, size, and age. Large European firms consider external monitoring to be the most important benefit, whereas small firms highly value the ability to raise capital for growth, and care less about monitoring. Family-controlled firms view an IPO as a vehicle to strengthen their bargaining power with creditors without relinquishing control, and care less about growth through mergers and acquisitions, and stock liquidity compared to their peers. Old firms and non-family controlled firms value stock liquidity more than their peers.

In sum, the survey evidence suggests that the decision to go public depends on both financial and strategic considerations. The evidence suggests that the decision to go public cannot be explained by any single IPO theory since most focus on one motivation, whereas firms seek multiple benefits that vary based on different firm and industry characteristics. The views of managers are largely similar on major benefits but are influenced by the legal system and institutional environment in some dimensions.

REFERENCES

Amihud, Y. and H. Mendelson (1986), 'Asset pricing and the bid–ask spread', *Journal of Financial Economics*, **17**, 223–49.

Ang J. and J. Brau (2003), 'Concealing and confounding adverse signals: insider wealth-maximizing behavior in the IPO process', *Journal of Financial Economics*, **67** (1), 149–72.

Baker, H.K., J. Singleton and T. Veit (2010), *Survey Research in Corporate Finance: Bridging the Gap between Theory and Practice*, Oxford: Oxford University Press.

Bancel, F. and U.R. Mittoo (2001), 'European managerial perceptions of the net benefits of foreign stock listings', *European Financial Management*, **7** (2), 213–36.
Bancel, F. and U.R. Mittoo (2004), 'Cross-country determinants of capital structure choice: a survey of European firms', *Financial Management*, **33** (4), 103–32.
Bancel, F. and U.R. Mittoo (2009), 'Why do European firms go public?', *European Financial Management*, **15** (4), 844–84.
Bancel, F. and U.R. Mittoo (2011), 'Survey evidence on financing decisions and cost of capital', in M. Kent Baker and S. Maria (eds), *Capital Structure and Corporate Financing Decisions: Theory, Evidence, and Practice*, Hoboken, NJ: John Wiley & Sons, pp. 229–48.
Black, B.S. and R.J. Gilson (1998), 'Venture capital and the structure of capital markets; banks versus stock markets', *Journal of Financial Economics*, **47**, 243–77.
Booth, J.R. and L. Chua. (1996), 'Ownership dispersion, costly information, and IPO underpricing', *Journal of Financial Economics*, **41**, 291–310.
Bradley, D., B. Jordan and J.R. Ritter (2003), 'The quiet period goes out with a bang', *Journal of Finance*, **58**, 1–36.
Brau, J. and S.E. Fawcett (2006), 'Initial public offerings: an analysis of theory and practice', *Journal of Finance*, 399–436.
Brau J., R.B. Couch and N.K. Sutton (2012), 'The desire to acquire and IPO long-run underperformance', *Journal of Financial and Quantitative Analysis*, **47** (3), 493–510.
Brau. J., B. Francis and N. Kohers (2003), 'The choice of IPO versus takeover: empirical evidence', *Journal of Business*, **76** (4), 583–612.
Brau, J., P. Ryan and I. Degraw (2006), 'Initial public offerings: CFO perceptions', *Financial Review*, **41**, 483–511.
Brennan, M. and J. Franks (1997), 'Underpricing, ownership and control in initial public offerings of equity securities in the UK', *Journal of Financial Economics*, **45**, 391–413.
Burton B., C. Helliar and D. Power (2006), 'Practitioners' perspectives on the IPO process and the perils of flotation', *The European Journal of Finance*, **12** (8), 671–92.
Chemmanur, T.J. and P. Fulghieri (1999), 'A theory of the going public decision', *Review of Financial Studies*, **12**, 249–79.
Chen, H.C. and J.R. Ritter (2000), 'The seven percent solution', *Journal of Finance*, **55**, 1105–31.
Choe, H., R. Masulis and V. Nanda (1993), 'Common stock offerings across the business cycle', *Journal of Empirical Finance*, **1**, 3–31.
Colak, G. and H. Günay (2011), 'Strategic waiting in the IPO markets', *Journal of Corporate Finance*, **17**, 555–83.
DeAngelo, H. and L. DeAngelo (2007), 'Capital structure, payout policy and financial flexibility, USC Marshall School of Business, Working Paper No. FBE 02-06, available at: http://ssrn.com/abstract=916093 (accessed after October 2007).
Demirgüç-Kunt, A. and V. Maksimovic (2002), 'Funding growth in bank-based and market-based financial systems: evidence from firm-level data', *Journal of Financial Economics*, **65**, 337–63.
Demirgüç-Kunt, A. and V. Maksimovic (1999), 'Institutions, financial markets, and firms debt maturity', *Journal of Financial Economics*, **54**, 295–336.
Denis, D.J. and V. Sibilkov (2010), 'Financial constraints, investment, and the value of cash holdings', *Review of Financial Studies*, **23**, 247–69.
Gamba, A. and A. Triantis (2008), 'The value of financial flexibility', *Journal of Finance*, **63**, 2263–96.
Goergen, M. and L. Renneboog (2003), 'Why are the levels of control (so) different in German and U.K. companies? Evidence from initial public offerings', *Journal of Law, Economics, and Organization*, **19**, 141–75.
Graham, J.R. and C.R. Harvey (2001), 'The theory and practice of corporate finance: evidence from the field', *Journal of Financial Economics*, **60** (2/3), 187–243.
Holmén, M. and P. Högfeldt (2003), 'A law and finance analysis of initial public offerings', Stockholm University working paper, available at: http://papers.ssrn.com/sol3/papers.cfm?abstract_id=236042 (accessed after 2009).
Holmstrom B. and J. Tirol (1993), 'Market liquidity and performance monitoring', *Journal of Political Economy*, **101** (4), 678–709.
Huyghebaert, N. and C. Hulle (2005), 'Structuring the IPO: empirical evidence on the portions of primary and secondary shares', *Journal of Corporate Finance*, **12** (2), 296–320.
Ibbotson, R.G. and J.F. Jaffe (1975), '"Hot issue" markets', *Journal of Finance*, **30**, 1027–42.
Jensen, M.C. and W.H. Meckling (1976), 'Theory of the firm: managerial behaviour, agency costs and ownership structure', *Journal of Financial Economics*, **3** (4), 305–60.
Kim, W. and M.S. Weisbach (2005), 'Do firms go public to raise capital?', NBER Working Paper, February.
La Porta, R., F. Lopez-de-Silanes, A. Shleifer and R.W. Vishny (1997), 'Legal determinants of external finance', *Journal of Finance*, **52**, 1131–52.

La Porta, R., F. Lopez-de-Silanes, A. Shleifer and R.W. Vishny (1998), 'Law and finance', *Journal of Political Economy*, **106**, 1113–55.
Lintner, J. (1956), 'Distribution of incomes of corporations among dividends, retained earnings and taxes', *American Economic Review*, **46** (2), 97–113.
Loughran T. and J.R. Ritter (1995), 'The new issue puzzle', *Journal of Finance*, **50**, 21–51.
Loughran, T. and A.M. Vijh (1997), 'Do long-term shareholders benefit from corporate acquisitions?', *Journal of Finance*, **52**, 1765–90.
Lowry, M. and G.W. Schwert (2002), 'IPO market cycles: bubbles or sequential learning?', *Journal of Finance*, **57**, 1171–200.
Lucas, D.J. and R.L. McDonald (1990), 'Equity issues and stock price dynamics', *Journal of Finance*, **45**, 1019–43.
Lyandres, E., A. Zhdanov and J. Hsieh (2008), 'A theory of merger-driven IPOs', EFA 2008 Athens Meetings Paper.
Maksimovic, V. and P. Pichler (2001), 'Technological innovation and initial public offerings', *Review of Financial Studies*, **14**, 459–94.
Marchisio G. and D. Ravasi (2003), 'Going public and the enrichment of a supportive network: some evidence from Italian initial public offerings', *Small Business Economics*, **21**, 381–95.
Maug, E. (1998), 'Large shareholders as monitors: is there a tradeoff between liquidity and control?', *Journal of Finance*, **53** (1), 65–98.
Mello, A.S. and J.E. Parsons (1998), 'Going public and the ownership structure of the firm', *Journal of Financial Economics*, **49**, 79–109.
Merton, R. (1987), 'A simple model of capital market equilibrium with incomplete information', *Journal of Finance*, **42**, 483–510.
Modigliani F. and M. Miller (1963), 'Taxes and the cost of capital: a correction', *American Economic Review*, **53**, 433–43.
Myers, S. (1984), 'The capital structure puzzle', *Journal of Finance*, **39**, 575–92.
Myers, S. and N. Majluf (1984), 'Corporate financing and investment decisions when firms have information that investors do not have', *Journal of Financial Economics*, **13**, 187–221.
Pagano, M. and A. Röell (1998), 'The choice of stock ownership structure: agency costs, monitoring, and the decision to go public', *Quarterly Journal of Economics*, **113**, 187–225.
Pagano, M., F. Panetta and L. Zingales (1998), 'Why do companies go public? An empirical analysis', *Journal of Finance*, **53**, 27–64.
Pilcher, J.C. (1955), *Raising Capital With Convertible Securities*, Ann Arbor, MI: University of Michigan Press.
Rajan R.G. (1992) 'Insiders and outsiders: the choice between informed and arm's-length debt', *Journal of Finance*, **47**, 1367–400.
Rajan, R. and L. Zingales (2003), 'Banks and markets: the changing character of European finance', University of Chicago Working Paper.
Rau, P.R. and T. Vermaelen (1998), 'Glamour, value and the post-acquisition performance of acquiring firms', *Journal of Financial Economics*, **49**, 223–53.
Ritter, J.R. (1991), 'The long-run performance of initial public offerings', *Journal of Finance*, **46**, 3–27.
Ritter, J.R. (2003), 'Differences between European and American IPO markets', *European Financial Management*, **9** (4), 421–34.
Ritter, J.R. and I. Welch (2002), 'A review of IPO activity, pricing, and allocations', *Journal of Finance*, **57** (4), 1795–828.
Scott, J. (1976), 'A theory of optimal capital structure', *Journal of Economics*, **7**, 33–54.
Torstila, S. (2001), 'What determines IPO gross spreads in Europe?', *European Financial Management*, **7**, 523–41.
Zingales, L. (1995), 'Insider ownership and the decision to go public', *Review of Economic Studies*, **62**, 425–48.

APPENDIX: SUMMARY OF THEORIES AND SURVEY FINDINGS

A theoretical concept or a factor is listed in the first column followed by the direct survey evidence (column 2).

Theory or concept	Survey evidence (Strong support; moderate support; low support)
a. Investor recognition, reputation and credibility	Strong support in Europe (especially in civil law countries)
	Moderate support in the US
b. Funding for growth	Strong support in Europe and the US
c. Mergers and acquisitions (M&A)	Moderate support in Europe
	Strong support in the US
d. Exit strategy	Moderate support in Europe and the US
	Strong support in the UK
e. Lower cost of capital	Moderate support in Europe and the US
f. Greater bargaining power with banks and financial flexibility	Strong support in Europe
	Low support in the US
g. External monitoring and better corporate governance	Strong support in Europe
	Low support in the US
h. Windows-of-opportunity	Strong support in Europe and the US
i. Stock liquidity	Moderate support in Europe and the US

4 IPO waves and hot markets in the UK
Shantanu Banerjee, Ufuk Güçbilmez and Grzegorz Pawlina

1 INTRODUCTION

A stream of literature tries to explain the cyclical nature of the initial public offering (IPO) market, which is well documented using US data. Some papers argue that IPO waves emerge as a result of improving market conditions (Pástor and Veronesi, 2005), whereas others favor a market timing explanation such that hot IPO markets (that is, the peaks of IPO waves) coincide with windows of opportunity when the cost of equity is temporarily low (Alti, 2006).

There are also a few stylized facts documented about US IPO cycles. Lowry and Schwert (2002) show that periods of high initial returns lead to periods of high volume in the IPO market. Pástor and Veronesi (2005) find that IPO volume responds to changes in market conditions. Alti (2006) provides evidence that hot market IPOs issue substantially more equity. Helwege and Liang (2004, p. 543) find that hot and cold market IPOs are driven from similar industries, such that 'IPOs in hot (high volume) markets are not more concentrated in particular industries than IPOs in cold markets'.

While the cyclical nature of the IPO activity in the US is well established, and the stylized facts of US IPO cycles are identified, the same cannot be said for the UK IPO market. The UK evidence on IPO waves is rather sparse. For instance, Chambers and Dimson (2009) use long time-series data on IPO volume and initial returns in the UK, but they focus on long-run changes in IPO underpricing, rather than IPO cycles. Other papers on IPO underpricing in the UK tend to focus on determinants of underpricing rather than its cyclical nature (see, for example, Levis, 1990; Brennan and Franks, 1997). Rees (1997) documents a positive relationship between the level of stock market index and IPO volume. However, he does not examine IPO initial returns and his sample ends in 1994 before the launch of the Alternative Investment Market (AIM), which has caused a significant shift in the IPO activity in the UK.

The purpose of this chapter is to fill a gap in the literature by investigating the IPO waves and hot markets in the UK. The UK is the most important IPO market in an environment relatively similar to the US. We test whether the cyclical nature of IPO activities identified in the US are present in the UK as well. We also report stylized facts about the UK IPO market and compare them with those of the US.

Our main findings are as follows. The lead–lag relationship between IPO initial returns and volume documented by Lowry and Schwert (2002) in the US is present in the UK as well. Moreover, consistent with Pástor and Veronesi (2005), the UK IPO volume increases following periods of positive market returns and low market volatility. On the other hand, while Pástor and Veronesi (2005) find no relationship between the level of aggregate market-to-book ratio and IPO volume in the US, we document a strong positive relationship in the UK. While this relationship can be explained in a rational framework, it is also consistent with the investor sentiment explanation and the results of Pagano et al. (1998).

In terms of hot markets, we find that they tend to emerge when IPOs in the same or similar sectors cluster in time. For instance, while the UK hot market in 2000 is mainly driven by technology and telecommunications firms, the market between 2004 and 2006 is fuelled by oil and mining firms. These results accord with the theoretical findings of Benveniste et al. (2002), and contradict with the empirical findings of Helwege and Liang (2004), who do not find evidence of industry clustering in the US hot markets. We also find that hot market IPOs raise substantially higher equity. This is consistent with the US evidence provided by Alti (2006).

Overall, our results suggest that the UK IPO market shares similarities with the US IPO market in the sense that IPO activity is cyclical in both of these markets. Hot markets in the UK emerge following improvements in market conditions and high market valuations. Firms raise more equity in hot markets and there is evidence of industry clustering in hot markets. While these pieces of evidence are consistent with a rational explanation in which hot markets are periods when growth opportunities are abundant and firms go public in order to raise the capital needed to invest in their projects, they do not rule out a behavioral explanation in which IPOs cluster in times when stock are overvalued and cost of equity is temporarily low.

The rest of this chapter is organized as follows. In section 2, we describe our data. In sections 3 and 4 IPO waves and hot markets in the UK are investigated, respectively. Section 5 concludes.

2 DATA

We use market- and firm-level data provided by the London Stock Exchange (LSE). The market-level data includes annual time series of the number of listed firms and their total market value, and quarterly time series of the new lists and money raised by them. The annual and quarterly time series go back to 1966 and 1970 respectively. The firm-level data includes a list of new issues on AIM since its launch in 1995 and on the Main Market since 1998. It also includes variables on industry, nation, issue type, price, proceeds and market value. Our sample period ends in May 2012.

2.1 Market-level Data

The number of listed firms and their total market values are presented in panels A and B of Figure 4.1 respectively. Panel A reveals a decreasing trend in the number of listed firms on the Main Market between 1966 and 1992. This trend reverses between 1993 and 1996, but has been back since then. The increase in the number of listed firms on AIM since its launch in 1995 compensates the decreasing numbers on the Main Market.[1] Consequently, the total number of listed firms has been more stable between 1995 and 2012 compared to the prior period between 1966 and 1994. Panel B documents a steady increase in the market value of listed firms starting around 1980 and reaching a peak around 1999 and 2000, before the burst of the dotcom bubble. During the post-bubble period, the market value remains relatively stable until 2006, and then

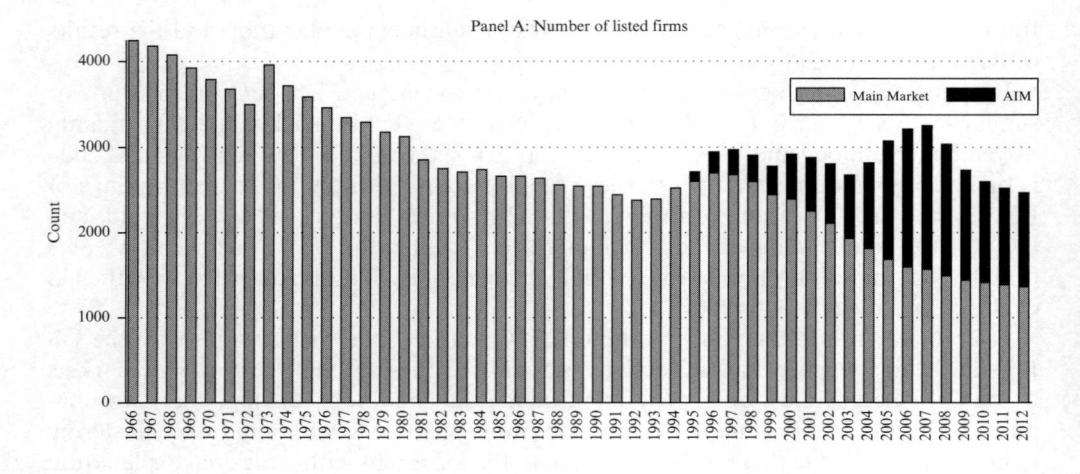

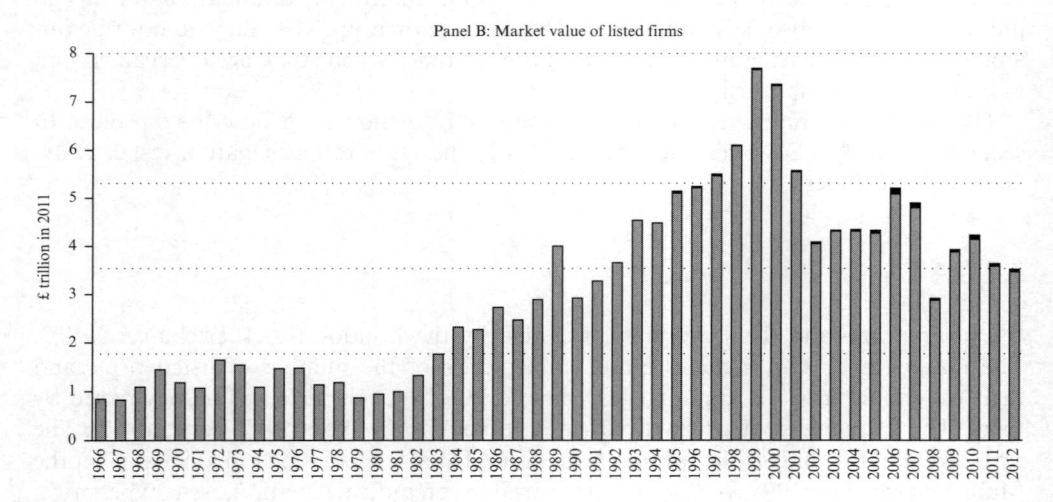

78 *Handbook of research on IPOs*

Panel A: Number of listed firms

Panel B: Market value of listed firms

Notes:
The main market data includes UK and international firms.
The market value figures are reported in 2011 £ trillions.

Figure 4.1 Market-level annual data on listed firms

it starts to increase again, but only to fall substantially in 2008 when the financial crisis hit. A comparison of panels A and B suggests that while AIM-listed firms contribute substantially to the number of listed firms after 1995, their contribution to the market value is tiny. For instance, at the end of 2011, there were about 1400 UK firms listed in the Main Market and 1100 firms listed in the AIM (56 percent versus 44 percent of listed firms). The market value of the former group was about £3.6 trillion, while that of the latter group was only £0.6 trillion (86 percent versus. 14 percent of market value).

IPO waves and hot markets in the UK 79

Notes:
The number of new lists includes IPOs, introductions, and readmissions, but excludes transfers between the Main Market and AIM.
The main market data includes UK and international firms.
For UK and international firms, the data on money raised is available from 1972 and 1979 respectively.
The money raised figures are reported in 2011 £ billions.

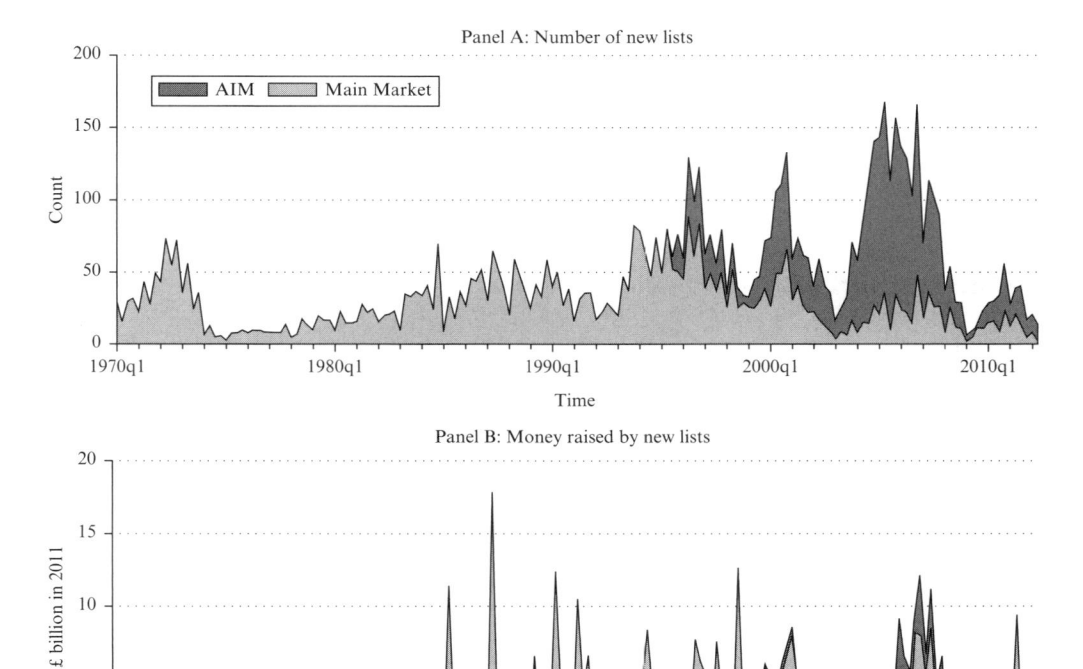

Figure 4.2   Market-level quarterly data on new lists

The number of new lists and the total money raised by them are presented in panels A and B of Figure 4.2 respectively. The number of new lists includes IPOs, introductions, and readmissions, but excludes transfers between the Main Market and AIM. Panel A shows that, since its launch in 1995, AIM has grown rapidly to account for an increasing proportion of the total number of new lists. Panel B shows that, while the number of new lists has been large on AIM, most of the money raised is due to the new lists on the Main Market, except the period between 2004 and 2008 when AIM has been most active in its history both in terms of the number of new lists and the amount of money raised. As a final note, some of the spikes in panel B are partially due to giant IPOs, such as the £6 billion IPO of Glencore International Plc in the second quarter of 2011.

2.2 Firm-level Data

The firm-level data includes 2761 IPOs on the LSE. Of these, 1043 are conducted by financial firms and the remaining 1718 by non-financial firms.[2] In our analysis, we use the 1718 non-financial IPOs. The majority of these IPOs are by UK firms (1306), which are followed by the US (54), Republic of Ireland (43), Australian (34), and Canadian (30) firms. Descriptive statistics on the sample are provided in Table 4.1. While there were many more IPOs on AIM than on the Main Market, the firms that go public on AIM are much smaller and raise on average a significantly less amount of proceeds (see also Figures 4.1 and 4.2).

While the firm-level data includes offer prices, it does not provide first trading day closing prices, which are necessary to calculate initial returns. Consequently, we search for each non-financial IPO firm manually on Datastream and find 1539 out of 1718 firms. The price data from Datastream is used to calculate initial returns for these 1539 firms. An IPO's initial return is defined as the percentage change between the offer price and the first trading day closing price.

Table 4.1 Firm-level data on IPOs

Year	AIM Count	AIM Pro	AIM Mv	Main Market Count	Main Market Pro	Main Market Mv	All Count	All Pro	All Mv
1995	16	3.10	7.81				16	3.10	7.81
1996	94	3.55	12.94				94	3.55	12.94
1997	70	2.50	7.98				70	2.50	7.98
1998	37	2.96	10.91	66	38.07	68.71	103	13.00	34.21
1999	38	3.26	11.70	34	73.20	141.91	72	6.60	24.56
2000	124	5.39	20.91	76	51.70	164.02	200	11.95	46.98
2001	72	2.94	10.10	12	42.42	92.91	84	3.36	13.44
2002	47	3.00	9.13	13	173.77	570.40	60	4.50	13.41
2003	48	2.22	14.83	5	27.00	213.69	53	4.00	15.51
2004	176	5.03	18.07	24	78.97	130.88	200	6.20	21.13
2005	221	6.02	20.35	29	148.80	353.29	250	8.00	23.21
2006	172	6.97	24.94	36	139.30	272.20	208	9.67	35.41
2007	113	8.80	30.75	38	184.37	328.82	151	15.27	55.00
2008	25	7.49	35.50	9	152.82	227.32	34	18.29	53.72
2009	3	5.26	20.28	2	45.98	111.02	5	9.75	23.51
2010	39	10.00	24.78	16	215.92	345.45	55	28.00	78.74
2011	38	4.09	16.55	10	283.45	1166.15	48	11.00	27.57
2012	12	6.20	32.23	3	117.00	390.00	15	7.01	33.20
Total	1345	4.91	18.18	373	82.50	196.96	1718	7.33	24.48

Notes:
Descriptive statistics on non-financial IPOs in the London Stock Exchange.
The sample period is June 1995 to May 2012.
The data on IPOs in the Main Market is available from 1998.
Pro is the median primary proceeds in £ million and *Mv* is the post-IPO market value based on the offer price.

3 IPO WAVES IN THE UK

3.1 Lead–Lag Relationship between Initial Returns and Volume

The literature that documents time variation and serial correlation in IPO activity goes back to Ibbotson and Jaffe (1975). Ibbotson and Jaffe find that initial returns of IPOs in the US are highly autocorrelated, such that the first order autocorrelation coefficient is 0.744. They find that the autocorrelation of monthly number of IPOs (that is, IPO volume) is even stronger with a first order autocorrelation coefficient of 0.83. They also investigate the relationship between initial returns and volume, but their results show that the relationship is not strong. Lowry and Schwert (2002) re-examine this relationship using longer time series and vector autoregressive (VAR) models. They find that higher initial returns lead to higher future volume, whereas there is no strong relationship between volume and future initial returns. They explain that the positive relationship between initial returns and future volume can be due to the partial adjustment of issue prices to the positive information revealed during the registration period (see Hanley, 1993, and Loughran and Ritter, 2002, for the partial adjustment phenomenon). The idea is that, positive information increases initial returns due to the partial adjustment, and at the same time it causes more firms to go public, but since going public takes time the increase in IPO volume is only observed with a delay, hence the lead–lag relationship between initial returns and volume.[3]

We investigate the relationship between initial returns and volume in the UK using VAR models with monthly lags as in Lowry and Schwert. We use the firm-level data, since the market-level data does not include initial returns. The firm-level data gives us a time series of 204 months between June 1995 and May 2012. The mean and median monthly volume of nonfinancial IPOs over this period are 8.42 and 5 respectively. The corresponding statistics for monthly initial returns are 16.46 percent and 12.23 percent respectively. Like in the US, both time series (especially the volume series) are highly autocorrelated. The autocorrelations of volume are above 0.40 up to 7 lags; and the first and second lag autocorrelations of initial returns are 0.42 and 0.35 respectively. There are 17 months with no non-financial IPOs. Eleven of these months are between October 2008 and October 2009, when the effects of the financial crisis were felt strongly in the UK.

Our findings are reported in Table 4.2. In models (1)–(4), monthly volume is the dependent variable. Model (1) is an ordinary least squares (OLS) regression. It shows that the first three lags of volume explain 41 percent of the time variation in this variable. Model (2) is a Cochrane-Orcutt regression.[4] The second and third lags of initial returns are significant at 1 percent in this model. Model (3) is a third-order VAR model. The second and third lags of initial returns remain significant at 5 percent, and the first lag becomes significant at 5 percent. The Granger F test shows that the three lags of initial returns are together significant at 1 percent in forecasting volume. Finally, in model (4) we add dummies to account for the seasonality of IPO activity (see, for example, Helwege and Liang, 2004). The second and third lags of initial returns still remain significant, whereas the first lag turns back to being insignificant. The lags of initial returns are together significant at 5 percent.

In models (5)–(8), monthly average initial return is the dependent variable. Model (5)

Table 4.2 Lead–lag relationship between initial returns and volume

	Volume (V)				Initial returns (I)			
	(1)	(2)	(3)	(4)	(5)	(6)	(7)	(8)
L1.V	0.36***		0.28***	0.27***		0.36**	0.34**	0.38**
	(0.10)		(0.10)	(0.09)		(0.15)	(0.16)	(0.16)
L2.V	0.18**		0.25***	0.27***		−0.38**	−0.40**	−0.39**
	(0.09)		(0.09)	(0.10)		(0.15)	(0.18)	(0.16)
L3.V	0.22***		0.17**	0.24***		0.09	0.13	−0.07
	(0.07)		(0.08)	(0.08)		(0.16)	(0.15)	(0.16)
L1.I		−0.03	−0.06**	−0.03	0.22		0.26	0.17
		(0.03)	(0.03)	(0.03)	(0.18)		(0.18)	(0.17)
L2.I		0.09***	0.07**	0.07**	0.25**		0.25**	0.23**
		(0.03)	(0.03)	(0.03)	(0.11)		(0.11)	(0.09)
L3.I		0.09***	0.07**	0.05*	0.02		−0.02	0.03
		(0.03)	(0.03)	(0.03)	(0.06)		(0.07)	(0.06)
q_1				−5.98***				13.37***
				(1.21)				(4.06)
q_3				−4.36***				3.88*
				(1.15)				(2.17)
Cons.	2.04***	7.60***	1.40	2.93***	6.76***	15.09***	6.16**	4.68*
	(0.53)	(1.62)	(0.91)	(1.01)	(1.91)	(4.05)	(2.63)	(2.46)
Obs.	201	146	154	154	147	163	147	147
Adj R-sq.	0.41	0.05	0.37	0.46	0.20	0.04	0.22	0.30
D-W stat.	2.10	2.40	2.02	2.14	2.11	2.46	2.12	2.10
Granger F			0.00	0.02			0.13	0.06

Notes:
Granger causality tests for monthly time series of initial returns and volume.
Non-financial IPOs in the LSE between June 1995 and May 2012 are used.
V is the monthly number of IPOs and I is the monthly average initial return of IPOs.
Li. signifies the ith lag of a monthly time series variable.
q_1 (q_3) is a dummy for the first (third) quarter, such that it is equal to 1 if the observation comes from a month in that quarter.
The dependent variable is V in models (1)–(4) and I in the rest.
Models (2) and (5) are Cochrane-Orcutt regressions, and the rest are ordinary least squares regressions.
D-W stat. is the Durbin-Watson statistic.
Granger F is the *p*-value of the Granger F test.
Robust standard errors are in parentheses.
*, **, and *** indicate significance at 10%, 5%, and 1% levels respectively.

shows that the first three lags of initial returns explain 20 percent of the time variation in this variable. In model (6), the first two lags of volume are significant at 5 percent. They remain significant at this level in models (7) and (8), but the Granger F tests suggest that the lags of volume are together insignificant at 5 percent.

These findings are broadly consistent with the US evidence provided by Lowry and Schwert. The UK evidence also suggests a lead–lag relationship between initial returns and volume, such that the lags of initial returns help predict volume, and not vice versa. Moreover, there is some evidence that the lead–lag relationship in the UK is positive as in the US. The second and third lags of initial returns have positive coefficients in models (2)–(4) (the first lag has a negative coefficient, but is significant only in model (3)).

3.2 The Relationship between Market Conditions and Volume

There is ample evidence on the positive relationship between market conditions and IPO activity. However, there are disagreements in the literature as to whether this relationship is due to rational or behavioral reasons. For instance, Pagano et al. (1998) study the decisions of Italian firms to go public and find that while firms become more likely to go public when the market-to-book ratios in their respective industries are high, their investments and profitability decline after their IPOs. They interpret this result as evidence for a behavioral explanation, such that firms time their IPOs to go public when the stocks in their industries are overvalued. On the other hand, Pástor and Veronesi (2005) offer a rational explanation based on a model of optimal IPO timing in which IPO waves emerge following improvements in market conditions. The basic idea is that when market conditions improve, many private firms that have been waiting to go public exercise their options around the same time, causing IPOs to cluster in time and form an IPO wave.

In this section, we investigate the UK evidence on the relationship between market conditions and volume. We use three variables that capture different aspects of market conditions. The first variable is the level of FTSE All-Share Index each month. The second is the standard deviation of daily returns on the FTSE All-Share Index each month. The third variable, which is a proxy for the real risk-free rate, is the difference between the official Bank of England rate and the expected inflation rate each month. Expected inflation rate estimates are obtained from the fitted values of an AR(12) process of the monthly log changes in Retail Price Index (RPI) as in Pástor and Veronesi (2005).[5] Since the theory links IPO activity to changes in market conditions, we modify these three variables accordingly. In particular, we calculate the monthly market return MR as the return on the FTSE All-Share Index, the change in market volatility ΔMV as the first difference of the standard deviation of daily returns, and the change in real risk-free rate ΔRF as the first difference of the real risk-free rate. Then, we regress IPO volume on these variables. The results are reported in the columns headed (1) to (3) in Table 4.3. Note that we include lags of IPO volume and dummies for the first and third quarters as in Table 4.2.

The results in models (1) to (3) match those obtained by Pástor and Veronesi. In particular, IPO volume is positively related to past market returns and negatively related to past changes in market volatility as predicted. This is because, increases in market returns and decreases in market volatility both imply a decrease in equity premium. Decreases in equity premium make the projects of firms more valuable inducing them to go public. Pástor and Veronesi's model predicts a negative relationship between the change in the real risk-free rate and volume, but their empirical results show a positive relationship. Our results in model (3) indicate that this relationship is weak and not clear in the UK.

The results of model (4) are consistent with Pagano et al. (1998). There is a strong positive relationship between the IPO volume and the lagged price-to-book value of the market. The model of Pástor and Veronesi also imply a positive relationship, but

Table 4.3 The relationship between market conditions and volume

	(1)	(2)	(3)	(4)	(5)
$L1.MR$	0.14**				0.11
	(0.07)				(0.07)
$L2.MR$	0.06				0.05
	(0.09)				(0.08)
$L3.MR$	0.23***				0.23***
	(0.08)				(0.08)
$L1.\Delta MV$		−2.48***			
		(0.69)			
$L2.\Delta MV$		−1.44			
		(0.88)			
$L3.\Delta MV$		−2.32***			
		(0.79)			
$L1.\Delta RF$			−0.14		
			(0.14)		
$L2.\Delta RF$			0.14		
			(0.14)		
$L3.\Delta RF$			0.22*		
			(0.13)		
$L1.P2B$				5.18***	4.91***
				(1.52)	(1.49)
$L1.V$	0.29***	0.29***	0.33***	0.25***	0.23***
	(0.09)	(0.09)	(0.09)	(0.09)	(0.09)
$L2.V$	0.22**	0.22**	0.21**	0.16*	0.16*
	(0.08)	(0.09)	(0.09)	(0.09)	(0.09)
$L3.V$	0.29***	0.32***	0.27***	0.21***	0.23***
	(0.07)	(0.07)	(0.07)	(0.07)	(0.07)
q_1	−4.86***	−5.45***	−5.18***	−4.29***	−4.69***
	(1.07)	(1.18)	(1.24)	(1.05)	(1.06)
q_3	−3.96***	−4.47***	−4.91***	−3.56***	−3.46***
	(0.96)	(0.94)	(1.22)	(0.97)	(0.95)
Cons.	3.62***	3.91***	4.18***	−3.86*	−3.59
	(0.68)	(0.68)	(0.76)	(2.24)	(2.18)
Obs.	201	201	201	201	201
Adj R-sq.	0.49	0.50	0.48	0.50	0.51

Notes:
OLS regression results. The dependent variable V is the monthly number of non-financial IPOs in the LSE between June 1995 and May 2012.
MR is the monthly return on the FTSE All-Share Index.
ΔMV is the first difference of the standard deviation of daily returns on the same index each month.
ΔRF is the first difference of the real risk-free rate. The real risk-free rate is the difference between the official Bank of England rate and the expected inflation rate each month.
Expected inflation rate estimates are obtained from the fitted values of an AR(12) process of the monthly log changes in RPI.
$P2B$ is the price-to-book value of Datastream's UK Total Market index (TOTMKUK) each month.
$Li.$ signifies the ith lag of a monthly time series variable.
q_1 (q_3) is a dummy for the first (third) quarter, such that it is equal to 1 if the observation comes from a month in that quarter.
Robust standard errors are in parentheses.
*, **, and *** indicate significance at 10%, 5%, and 1% levels respectively.

they argue that IPO volume should be more sensitive to changes in market conditions rather than levels of market conditions. They run a regression including past market returns and past level of the aggregate market-to-book ratio in the market, and indeed find that while past market returns are highly significant, past aggregate market-to-book ratio in the market is not. They interpret this result as evidence in favor of their rational explanation and against the behavioral market timing explanations. Our results in model (5) show that the past price-to-book value of the market remains highly significant even after including past market returns in the model. Therefore, the UK evidence does not rule out the behavioral explanation. However, this result has to be interpreted carefully, since high price-to-book values can simply imply the existence of valuable growth opportunities in the market rather than a misvaluation.

Overall, results of this section provide strong evidence that the activity in the UK IPO market is highly sensitive to the market conditions. Initial public offering volume increases following high market returns and low market volatility. Furthermore, IPO volume is closely linked to the market's price-to-book ratio.

4 HOT MARKETS IN THE UK

Hot and cold markets emerge naturally as a consequence of time variation in IPO volume. Hot markets are characterized by unusually high volume and initial returns, whereas cold markets are periods during which volume and initial returns are lower than usual. The literature offers various explanations on why hot markets emerge. Benveniste et al. (2002) present a model in which private firms in an industry enjoy an informational externality when firms in their industry go public, such that if the information revealed by the market is favorable, many more firms from the same industry go public. In this model, hot markets are periods in which IPOs from either the same industry or close industries cluster in time. Helwege and Liang (2004) do not find much evidence of industry concentration in hot markets that took place in the US.

An alternative explanation for hot markets is the market timing hypothesis. According to this hypothesis firms wait to go public during windows of opportunity when the cost of equity is temporarily low. Once such a window of opportunity arrives many firms seize it at the same time yielding a hot market. Alti (2006) tests this hypothesis and finds that hot market IPOs raise substantially more equity than their cold market counterparts. He also finds that hot market IPOs do not invest more than cold market ones ex post, suggesting that the reason hot market firms are raising more equity is not their superior growth opportunities.[6]

Note that the industry concentration and market timing stories can also be linked to each other. As mentioned earlier, Pagano et al. (1998) show that firms in an industry become more likely to go public when the market-to-book ratio of their industry rises. Like Alti (2006), they find that firms do not increase their investment levels after going public. In fact, they observe a decline in investment and profitability.

In the following subsections we first identify the hot markets in the UK. Then, we examine the level of industry concentration in UK hot markets and investigate whether UK firms raise more equity in hot markets.

86   *Handbook of research on IPOs*

4.1   Identifying Hot Markets between 1970 and 2012

We use the market-level quarterly data on new issues between 1970 and 2012. A limitation is that new issues include introductions and readmissions as well as IPOs. In other words, the quarterly time series of new issues and IPOs are not the same. However, an inspection of the firm-level data between 1995 and 2012, which is the period when we can calculate the quarterly number of IPOs, shows that the two time series have a very similar pattern. This is illustrated in panel A of Figure 4.3. Therefore, we assume that the quarterly series of new lists closely approximates the quarterly series of IPOs.

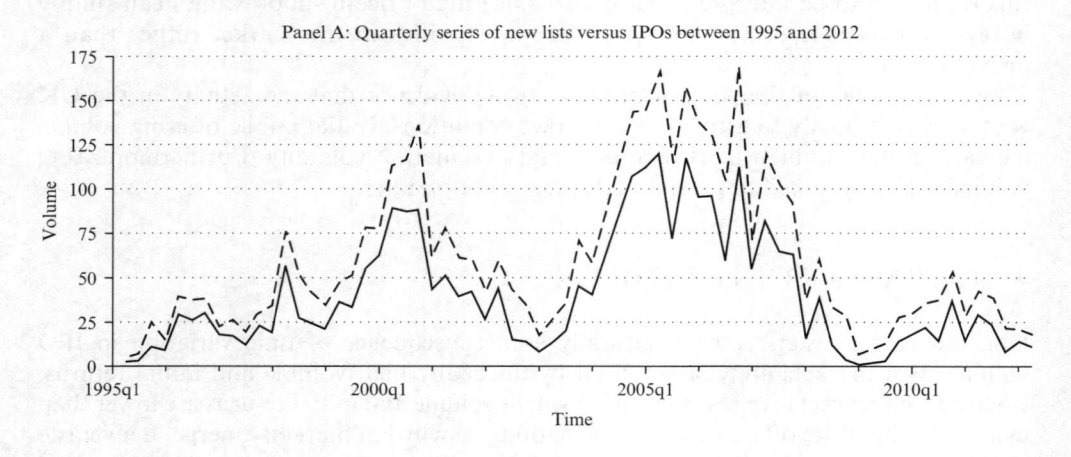

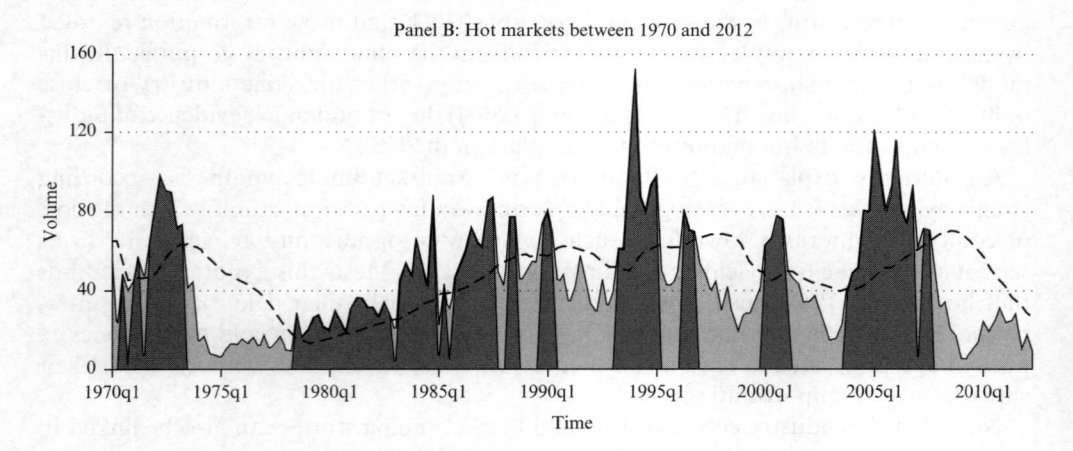

Notes:
In panel A the dashed line is the series of new lists in the LSE. The solid line is the series of IPOs in the LSE. The sample period is between June 1995 and May 2012. The sample includes new lists on AIM starting from June 1995 and those on the Main Market starting from January 1998.
In panel B, the area plot is the quarterly series of new lists in the LSE. Black and grey areas represent hot and cold markets respectively. The dashed line is the 20-quarter moving average volume.

Figure 4.3   Hot markets in the UK

Table 4.4 Descriptive statistics on quarterly series of new lists

	q_1	q_2	q_3	q_4	All	Count	K-Wp
Panel A: Volume							
Pre-AIM	18.5	33	27	36	27	101	0.06
Post-AIM	41	72	56	72	60	69	0.30
Panel B: Proceeds							
Pre-AIM	0.86	1.71	0.99	2.12	1.31	65	0.08
Post-AIM	1.96	4.95	2.95	3.38	3.02	69	0.06

Notes:
The sample is quarterly time series of new lists and their proceeds on the LSE between January 1970 and May 2012.
The series on proceeds start in 1972.
Proceeds are measured in £ billions of 2011.
Median values are reported for each quarter separately in columns q_1 to q_4 and for all quarters pooled in column All.
K-Wp is the Kruskal-Wallis p-value.
Pre-AIM is the period prior to the second quarter of 1995 and post-AIM is the remaining period when AIM has been in existence.

Descriptive statistics on quarterly series of new lists are provided in Table 4.4. The median number of new lists per quarter was 27 before the launch of AIM, which has more than doubled to 60 after its launch in 1995. There is evidence of seasonality in the series such that the median number of new lists is lower in the first and third quarters in both the pre- and post-AIM periods. The median value of proceeds raised by new lists also more than doubles after the launch of AIM, and it exhibits seasonality with lower figures in the first and third quarters in both the pre- and post-AIM periods.

We now move on to identifying hot markets in the UK using the quarterly series of new lists volume. The method of identifying hot markets varies across papers. Helwege and Liang (2004), Pástor and Veronesi (2005), and Alti (2006) use monthly IPO volume to detect hot markets, but each of these papers uses a different cut-off level to classify months as hot or cold. Yung et al. (2008) and Çolak and Günay (2011) identify hot and cold markets on a quarterly basis, whereas Bustamante (2012) identifies them on an annual basis. Furthermore, these methods differ in terms of the ways they smooth and deflate the time series of IPO volume. Banerjee et al. (2013b) compare these methods and propose a robust and intuitive method. We use their method in this chapter. This method is essentially akin to a moving-average trading rule, such that hot markets are periods during which short-run moving average of quarterly IPO volume exceeds its long-run counterpart by a sufficient margin. In particular, the method involves three parameters: s, l, and k, such that a quarter is classified as hot (cold) if the difference between its s-quarter short-run moving and l-quarter long-run moving average volume is higher (lower) than k standard deviations of volume in the past l quarters. We calibrate the method by setting $s = 1$, $l = 20$, and $k = 0$. In other words, a quarter is classified as hot (cold) if its volume exceeds (falls below) the average volume of past 20 quarters. Quarterly volume is adjusted for seasonality before applying the method.[7]

The hot markets identified using this method are presented in panel B of Figure 4.3. The first major hot market takes place in 1972, which is followed by a long cold market that lasts until 1979. The 1980s are characterized by a series of small hot markets. The market is cold for the first three years of the 1990s, but then a major hot market takes place between 1993 and 1994. After a short hot market in 1996, the next major hot market is in 2000, which coincides with the high-technology boom in the US. Finally, there is a long hot market between 2004 and 2006, which is followed by a long cold market that coincides with the credit crunch and financial crisis periods.[8]

4.2 Industry Concentration in Hot Markets

In this section we investigate whether hot markets in the UK are industry specific, such that in each hot market IPOs are concentrated in a narrow set of industries. To this end, we use the firm-level data, which includes the Industry Classification Benchmark (ICB) code of each IPO firm. Table 4.5 shows that between June 1995 and May 2012, 62.22 percent of 1718 non-financial IPOs took place in hot markets and the remaining 37.78 percent in cold markets. We identify 23 industries (four-digit ICB subsectors) with at least 20 IPOs.[9] In eight of these industries, more than 70 percent of the IPOs took place in hot markets. The figure exceeds 80 percent in the software, telecommunications equipment, mobile telecommunications, and electrical components and equipment industries.

At first sight, IPOs in some industries seem to be less clustered in hot markets than expected. For instance, one would expect IPOs in the Internet industry to be heavily clustered in hot markets, but 65.71 percent of the IPOs in this industry takes place in hot markets, which is barely larger than the sample average of 62.22 percent. However, the figure of 65.71 percent is deceiving as it is an aggregate figure for all hot markets. A closer look at the cross-section of hot markets tells a different story as we show next.

To further investigate industry concentration in hot markets, we run a logistic regression, such that the dependent variable *HM* is equal to 1 if the IPO took place in a hot market and 0 if it was in a cold market. The independent variables are a set of dummies for the 23 industries in Table 4.5. The odds ratio estimates of this model are reported in the second column of Table 4.6. The eight industries that were identified in Table 4.5 as having more than 70 percent of their IPOs in hot markets all have odds ratios that exceed 1 substantially. That is, the odds that a firm from one of these industries will go public in a hot market is much higher than the odds that it will go public in a cold market. While two industries have odds ratios less than 1, the difference between the odds ratio and 1 is not statistically significant for both industries. Therefore, the odds of going public in a cold market does not exceed those of going public in a hot market in any of the 23 industries. This is in contrast to Helwege and Liang (2004), who find that computer hardware and energy firms cluster in cold markets.

We further examine industry concentration by studying the 4 hot markets between June 1995 and May 2012 individually (see panel B in Figure 4.3): (1) 1996 Q2–Q4, (2) 2000 Q1–2001 Q1, (3) 2003 Q4–2006 Q4, (4) 2007 Q2–Q3. The results are reported in the third to the sixth columns of Table 4.6. HM_i is equal to 1 if an IPO took place in the ith hot market and 0 otherwise. We mentioned earlier that it is rather puzzling why IPOs in some industries, like the internet industry, are not as clustered in hot markets as expected. The results in Table 4.6 resolve this puzzle. The second column shows that while the odds that a firm went public in a hot market are 52 percent higher if that firm is in the Internet industry, the estimate is not statistically significant. This is because,

Table 4.5 Frequency of IPOs across industries and hot/cold markets

	Cold		Hot	
	Count	Percent	Count	Percent
OIL				
0533 Exploration and Production	39	42.86	52	57.14
0573 Oil Equipment and Services	9	40.91	13	59.09
MINING				
1773 Diamonds and Gemstones	7	30.43	16	69.57
1775 General Mining	30	35.29	55	64.71
1777 Gold Mining	15	35.71	27	64.29
ELECTRONIC AND ELECTRICAL EQUIPMENT				
2733 Electrical Components and Equipment	4	14.29	24	85.71
2737 Electronic Equipment	11	36.67	19	63.33
SUPPORT SERVICES				
2791 Business Support Services	38	41.30	54	58.70
2793 Business Training and Employment Agencies	14	38.89	22	61.11
HEALTH CARE				
4535 Medical Equipment	12	42.86	16	57.14
4573 Biotechnology	15	36.59	26	63.41
4577 Pharmaceuticals	15	29.41	36	70.59
MEDIA				
5553 Broadcasting and Entertainment	12	36.36	21	63.64
5555 Media Agencies	11	20.75	42	79.25
5557 Publishing	17	33.33	34	66.67
LEISURE				
5752 Gambling	5	20.83	19	79.17
5755 Recreational Services	22	51.16	21	48.84
TELECOMMUNICATIONS				
6535 Fixed Line Telecommunications	7	26.92	19	73.08
6575 Mobile Telecommunications	4	19.05	17	80.95
TECHNOLOGY				
9533 Computer Services	44	48.89	46	51.11
9535 Internet	12	34.29	23	65.71
9537 Software	19	18.10	86	81.90
9578 Telecommunications Equipment	3	12.00	22	88.00
Other industries	284	44.17	359	55.83
Total	649	37.78	1069	62.22

Notes:
The sample is 1718 non-financial IPOs in the LSE between June 1995 and May 2012.
Industry classification is based on four-digit ICB subsectors. Industries with at least 20 IPOs are reported.

there were no Internet firms in the first and last hot markets, and being an Internet firm decreased the odds of going public in the third market. In other words, Internet firms are not clustered in all hot markets, but in the second hot market only. Software firms are most heavily clustered in the second hot market as well. Firms in the remaining two industries of the technology sector, telecommunications equipment and computer

Table 4.6 Industry concentration in hot markets

	HM	HM_1	HM_2	HM_3	HM_4	HM_{3+4}
Exploration and Production	1.05	0.14*	0.23**	1.79**	1.04	1.84***
Oil Equipment and Services	1.14	0.62	0.48	1.32	1.79	1.73
Diamonds and Gemstones	1.81		0.96	2.97**		4.09***
General Mining	1.45		0.50	2.60***	0.43	2.65***
Gold Mining	1.42	0.32	0.25	2.55***	0.44	2.12**
Electrical Components and Equipment	4.75***	0.48	0.37	3.44***	2.99*	8.67***
Electronic Equipment	1.37	2.60*	0.35	1.27	0.62	1.10
Business Support Services	1.12	0.75	1.37	0.92	1.71	1.06
Business Training and Employment A.	1.24		2.88**	1.22		1.03
Medical Equipment	1.05		0.78	1.65	0.66	1.44
Biotechnology	1.37	0.67		2.00**	1.41	2.04**
Pharmaceuticals	1.90**	0.53	2.77***	1.23	1.12	1.28
Broadcasting and Entertainment	1.38		1.80	1.41	1.16	1.36
Media Agencies	3.02***	0.25	1.29	3.15***	0.70	2.81***
Publishing	1.58	1.41	6.51***	0.41**		0.31***
Gambling	3.01**		2.02	2.26*	1.63	2.41**
Recreational Services	0.76	1.71	1.64	0.51*	0.43	0.44**
Fixed Line Telecommunications	2.15*		2.40*	1.91	0.72	1.69
Mobile Telecommunications	3.36**		4.03***	2.10*		1.59
Computer Services	0.83	1.62	1.70	0.66*		0.50***
Internet	1.52		6.72***	0.66		0.50*
Software	3.58***		4.83***	1.49*	1.09	1.53**
Telecommunications Equipment	5.80***		2.52*	2.86**	1.56	3.72***
Cons.	1.26***	0.08***	0.10***	0.52***	0.06***	0.69***
Obs.	1718	1277	1677	1718	1462	1718
R-sq.	0.03	0.03	0.09	0.04	0.02	0.05
AUC	0.61	0.63	0.71	0.63	0.59	0.64

Notes:
Odds ratio estimates of logistic regression models.
The sample is 1718 non-financial IPOs in the LSE between June 1995 and May 2012. Four hot markets are identified during this period: (1) 1996 Q2–Q4, (2) 2000 Q1–2001 Q1, (3) 2003 Q4–2006 Q4, (4) 2007 Q2–Q3.
HM (HM_i) is a binary variable equal to 1 if the IPO took place in a (the ith) hot market.
Explanatory variables are industry dummies.
*, **, and *** indicate significance at 10%, 5%, and 1% levels respectively.
AUC is the area under the ROC curve.
Perfect predictor industries are dropped in each regression.

services, are also clustered to some extent in the second hot market. Furthermore, firms in the telecommunications sector, fixed line and mobile telecommunications industries, are heavily clustered in the second hot market too. Other industries that are particularly concentrated in this hot market and not in the others are pharmaceuticals, publishing, and business training and employment agencies. Therefore, the second hot market, which coincides with the high-technology boom period in the US, can be thought of as a result of the clustering of IPOs in technology and telecommunications sectors, coupled with clusterings in pharmaceuticals, publishing, and business training and employment agencies industries.

The third hot market, on the other hand, is dominated by firms in the mining and oil sectors. For instance, no diamonds and gemstones firms went public in the first or the last hot markets, and they were not more likely to go public in the second market, but their odds of going public in the third hot market were almost 200 percent higher. Biotechnology, media agencies, and electrical components and equipment are the other industries that are clustered in this hot market particularly. As a result, the third hot market can be viewed as a hot market of the mining and oil sectors that is supported by hot markets of the biotechnology, media agencies, and electrical components and equipment industries.

The first and fourth hot markets are shorter and have less IPOs than the second and third hot markets. These two smaller hot markets are not characterized particularly by any group of industries. However, the fourth hot market follows shortly after the third one with a gap of one quarter only. As a robustness check we combine the third hot market, the fourth hot market, and the one-quarter gap between them into a single hot market. The results reported in the last column of Table 4.6 suggest that the mining and oil sector still dominates the combined hot market. Biotechnology and media agencies industries remain heavily clustered as well. Not surprisingly, electrical components and equipment industry becomes even more heavily clustered, such that the odds of a firm going public in the combined hot market increases by 767 percent if the firm belongs to this industry.

We conduct further robustness checks. First, instead of running separate logistic regressions for each hot market, we run a multinomial logistic regression where the dependent variable HC is equal to 0 if the IPO took place in a cold market, or to i if it was in the ith hot market. We choose $HC = 0$ as the base case and estimate risk ratios relative to this case. The difference between separate logistic regressions and the multinomial regression is that in the former case the question is whether firms from a particular industry are more likely to go public in the ith hot market rather than any other time (that is, all other hot markets as well as cold markets); whereas in the latter case it is whether firms from a particular industry are more likely to go public in the ith hot market rather than in cold markets. The results of the multinomial regression are very similar to those in Table 4.6, so we do not report them for the sake of brevity. Furthermore, we run logistic regressions for each hot market using sectors, instead of industries, as explanatory variables. The conclusions do not change: technology and telecommunications sectors dominate the second hot market, oil and mining sectors dominate the third, and the electronic and electrical equipment sector is highly clustered in the third and fourth hot markets combined.

To summarize, the UK evidence of industry clustering in hot markets is much stronger than the US evidence provided by Helwege and Liang (2004). It seems that long hot markets with many IPOs are fueled by firms in close sectors and supported by clustering in a few other industries. Since 1995, the first major hot market that took place in the UK around 2000 is driven by technology and telecommunications sector and supported by pharmaceuticals, publishing, and business training and employment agencies industries. The second major hot market between 2004 and 2006 is driven by oil and mining sectors and supported by biotechnology, media agencies, and electrical components and equipment industries.

4.3 Proceeds Raised in Hot Markets

Market timing and investor sentiment hypotheses imply that IPOs cluster when the cost of equity is temporarily low. Moreover, IPO firms raise more equity during hot markets, since equity capital is relatively cheap during those periods. On the other hand, according to the capital demands hypothesis (see, for example, Lowry, 2003), if hot markets are periods during which firms have more growth opportunities, it is not surprising that they will raise more equity to invest in those opportunities. Therefore, all of these hypotheses predict that more equity will be issued during hot markets.

Table 4.7 provides descriptive statistics on median primary proceeds raised in hot, neutral, and cold quarters. In panel A, we see that the median primary proceeds raised in hot markets is about 25 percent higher (£10.08 million versus £8.12 million in 2011). Moreover, the median rises from £10.08 million to £1.06 million as we make our hot market definition stricter. While the figures in panel A provide some evidence that firms raise more equity in hot markets, they do not take firm size into account. It is quite a different matter when a firm with a market value of £20 million raises £10 million, versus another with a market value of £200 million raises the same amount. The figures in panel B control for this size effect. In particular we calculate primary proceeds raised as a percentage of post-IPO market value estimated at the offer price. The conclusion does not change. In hot markets, the median is about 3 percentage points higher (41.41 versus 38.67). Again, as the hot market definition becomes stricter the median rises from 41.41 to 42.35 percent and the gap between hot and cold markets widens to 5.7 percentage points.

More evidence on higher proceeds raised in hot markets is provided in Table 4.8. We

Table 4.7 Descriptive statistics on proceeds raised in hot, neutral, and cold markets

	H_0 Median	H_0 Count	$H_{0.5}$ Median	$H_{0.5}$ Count	H_1 Median	H_1 Count
Panel A: Proceeds in £ millions in 2011						
Cold	8.12	649	8.07	442	9.48	150
Neutral		0	8	452	8.54	967
Hot	10.08	1069	10.76	824	11.06	601
Panel B: Proceeds as a percentage of market value						
Cold	38.67	547	38.15	372	36.66	121
Neutral		0	38.87	395	39.20	862
Hot	41.41	977	42.12	757	42.35	541

Notes:
Median primary proceeds raised in cold, neutral, and hot markets.
The sample is 1718 nonfinancial IPOs in the LSE between June 1995 and May 2012.
In panel A, the primary proceeds are in millions of 2011 pounds.
In panel B, proceeds as a percentage of market value is equal to $100 \times (pro/(mv - pro))$, where pro is the primary proceeds raised by a firm, and mv is the firm's market value based on its offer price.
The cases where $mv = pro$ are excluded. H_i is a categorical variable equal to 1 (0) if the IPO took place in a quarter in which the volume of that quarter exceeds (falls below) the average volume of past 20 quarters by at least i standard deviations of those 20 quarters, and equal to 0.5 otherwise.

Table 4.8 Proceeds raised in hot markets

	Panel A: OLS regressions					Panel B: Median regressions		
	$\ln(pro_a)$		$\ln(pro_s)$		pro_a		pro_s	
H_0	0.31***		0.12**		1.94***		3.76**	
	(0.065)		(0.055)		(0.592)		(1.826)	
$H_{0.5}$	0.39***		0.24***		3.20***		5.28**	
	(0.076)		(0.062)		(0.557)		(2.234)	
H_1		0.44***		0.23**		3.54***		6.62**
		(0.106)		(0.088)		(0.774)		(3.154)
Elec.	0.07	0.09	−0.08	−0.08	2.42	1.88	3.29	2.87
	(0.155)	(0.156)	(0.119)	(0.118)	(1.603)	(1.290)	(4.699)	(5.059)
Health.	−0.32***	−0.32***	−0.26**	−0.27***	−0.98	−1.58*	−4.08	−4.92
	(0.118)	(0.117)	(0.104)	(0.105)	(1.165)	(0.936)	(3.478)	(3.785)
Leisure	0.15	0.14	0.02	0.01	−0.79	−0.80	4.02	4.20
	(0.193)	(0.191)	(0.154)	(0.153)	(1.500)	(1.208)	(4.586)	(4.943)
Media	−0.13	−0.13	0.02	0.01	−1.30	−1.35	−2.42	−2.67
	(0.124)	(0.125)	(0.099)	(0.100)	(1.107)	(0.892)	(3.363)	(3.630)
Mining	−0.20*	−0.19*	−0.15*	−0.16*	−1.67	−2.28***	−3.42	−4.35
	(0.113)	(0.112)	(0.086)	(0.086)	(1.070)	(0.862)	(3.199)	(3.449)
Oil	0.62***	0.61***	0.03	0.03	7.77***	8.67***	6.28*	5.41
	(0.131)	(0.130)	(0.094)	(0.094)	(1.194)	(0.961)	(3.581)	(3.841)
Support	−0.10	−0.11	0.02	0.02	−1.14	−1.02	2.69	0.77
	(0.121)	(0.121)	(0.109)	(0.108)	(1.130)	(0.910)	(3.406)	(3.669)

Table 4.8 (continued)

	Panel A: OLS regressions				Panel B: Median regressions			
	$\ln(pro_a)$		$\ln(pro_s)$		pro_a		pro_s	
Tech.	−0.16*	−0.18*	−0.17**	−0.17**	−1.13	−1.45**	−2.59	−4.16
	(0.092)	(0.092)	(0.073)	(0.074)	(0.871)	(0.719)	(2.657)	(2.870)
Telecom.	0.30	0.31	−0.34**	−0.34**	5.33***	4.81***	−8.49	−10.10*
	(0.230)	(0.230)	(0.169)	(0.167)	(1.769)	(1.458)	(5.655)	(6.010)
MM	2.95***	2.94***	0.39***	0.39***	105.76***	105.00***	5.48**	6.09**
	(0.080)	(0.080)	(0.071)	(0.071)	(0.702)	(0.576)	(2.306)	(2.476)
Con.	1.63***	1.59***	3.54***	3.54***	5.41***	4.34***	37.57***	36.14***
	(0.069)	(0.073)	(0.063)	(0.074)	(0.609)	(0.616)	(1.897)	(2.493)
Obs.	1718	1718	1524	1524	1718	1718	1524	1524
R-sq.	0.48	0.48	0.04	0.03	0.13	0.13	0.01	0.01

Notes:
OLS and median regression results.
The sample is 1718 non-financial IPOs in the LSE between June 1995 and May 2012.
pro_a is the primary proceeds raised by a firm in £ millions in 2011.
pro_s is equal to $100 \times (pro/(mv - pro))$, where pro is the primary proceeds raised by a firm, and mv is the firm's market value based on its offer price.
H_i is a categorical variable equal to 1 (0) if the IPO took place in a quarter in which the volume of that quarter exceeds (falls below) the average volume of past 20 quarters by at least i standard deviations of those 20 quarters, and equal to 0.5 otherwise.
The control variables are industry sector dummies (see Table 4.5).
MM is a dummy variable equal to 1 if the IPO firm is listed on the Main Market.
*, **, and *** indicate significance at 10%, 5%, and 1% levels respectively.

run a series of regressions that control for industry sectors and the market segment in which the IPO takes place (that is, Main Market versus AIM). In columns 2 to 7, we run OLS regressions. The dependent variable is the natural logarithm of proceeds in columns 2 to 4 and the natural logarithm of proceeds as a percentage of post-IPO market value estimated at the offer price in columns 5 to 7. The variables of interest are H_0, $H_{0.5}$, and H_1, which categorize IPOs as cold, neutral, or hot with an increasing level of strictness. As expected, the coefficients of these variables are positive significant. Moreover, the magnitudes of coefficients tend to increase as the hot market definition becomes stricter. As a robustness check we also run median regressions. We use the same dependent variables without taking the natural logarithms. The conclusions remain the same.

The evidence presented in this section suggests that UK IPOs raise more equity in hot markets. We estimate that median proceeds raised by firms that go public during the hottest periods can be more than 6 percentage points higher than those that conduct an IPO during the coldest periods. Overall, these results match the US evidence (see Alti (2006)).

5 CONCLUSION

In this chapter we show that the IPO market in the UK has a cyclical nature as in the US. The IPO volume varies substantially over time in the UK. For instance, while there were as many as 250 IPOs in 2005, the number of IPOs in 2009 was only five. The average monthly initial returns in the UK also exhibits substantial time variation reaching levels of 100 percent during the high-technology boom period of 2000, while averaging only 10 percent in 2001 following the burst of the dotcom bubble. Following Lowry and Schwert (2002), we investigate the relationship between IPO initial returns and volume in the UK. We find that periods of high initial returns lead to periods of high volume, which is the same pattern documented by Lowry and Schwert in the US.

After providing evidence for the cyclical nature of UK IPO market, we investigate the factors that drive the time variation in IPO activity in the UK. We find a strong link between market conditions and IPO volume. In particular, UK IPO volume is positively related to past market returns and negatively related to past changes in market volatility. These results agree with those in the US market obtained by Pástor and Veronesi (2005). However, unlike Pástor and Veronesi, we also find a strong relationship between IPO volume and past level of the market's price-to-book ratio. While this relationship is consistent with a rational explanation of IPO cycles, it also supports market timing explanations, such as the one offered by Pagano et al. (1998).

We also identify the hot IPO markets in the UK. Unlike Helwege and Liang (2004), who study the US hot markets, we find evidence of industry concentration in the UK hot markets. In particular, the hot market that took place during the high-technology boom period of 2000 mainly features IPOs from the technology and telecommunications sectors, while the hot market between 2004 and 2006 is characterized to a large extent by firms from the oil and mining sectors. Overall, our results lend support to models that predict industry clustering in hot markets such as Benveniste et al. (2002).

Finally, we compare the proceeds raised by UK firms in hot versus cold markets. We find that UK firms raise substantially higher amounts of proceeds during hot markets.

The result is robust to firm size, industry, and the market segment in which the firm's shares are listed. It is consistent with the US evidence provided by Alti (2006).

Overall, the IPO waves in the UK are driven by changes in market conditions. Furthermore, industry clustering contributes to the emergence of hot markets in the UK. The fact that IPO volume rises following improvements in market conditions supports the rational explanation of hot markets. However, it is not possible to rule out the market timing explanation, since IPO volume also rises when firm valuations are high in the market.

NOTES

1. Part of the decline in the number of listed firms on the Main Market since 1995 is due to transfers to AIM. Between 1995 and May 2012, 303 firms took this route, while only 130 firms took the opposite route.
2. A large proportion of the financial firms are investment trusts, venture capital trusts, and real estate holding and development firms.
3. Banerjee et al. (2011) offer an alternative theoretical explanation for this lead–lag relationship. In their model, time variation in initial returns and volume is due to changes in market conditions. Initial returns rise first as good firms lead IPO waves and signal quality with underpricing. Volume rises later when (and if) bad firms follow.
4. OLS regression of model (2) yields substantially autocorrelated residuals (the Durbin-Watson statistic is 0.97). Running Cochrane-Orcutt regressions, as in Ibbotson and Jaffe (1975), helps remedy this problem (the Durbin-Watson statistics becomes 2.40).
5. Pástor and Veronesi (2005) use the CPI. However, the CPI data goes back to 1996 in the UK, while our data starts in 1995. Therefore, we use the RPI data which goes back to 1947 instead.
6. On the other hand, Banerjee et al. (2013a) provide evidence that leaders in hot markets invest more *ex post* due to their superior growth opportunities. In their model, high-quality firms lead hot markets to signal quality. Similarly, Bustamante (2012) presents an IPO timing model, which shows that firms with better investment prospects accelerate their IPOs when the adverse selection problem is severe.
7. In particular, raw volume is regressed on dummies representing the quarters in a year. Then, the raw volume is divided by the volume predicted by the regression and re-meaned to have the same mean as the original series. This procedure is conducted separately for the pre- and post-AIM periods, since IPO volume experiences a permanent shift after the launch of AIM.
8. Vismara et al. (2012) detect a Europe-wide hot market between 2004 and 2006. They argue that AIM's success as an exchange-regulated market has contributed to the emergence of this hot market.
9. There are 92 non-financial subsectors in total.

REFERENCES

Alti, A. (2006), 'How persistent is the impact of market timing on capital structure?', *Journal of Finance*, **61** (4), 1681–710.
Banerjee, S., U. Güçbilmez and G. Pawlina (2013a), 'Leaders and followers in hot IPO markets', working paper, available at: http://ssrn.com/abstract=2020221 (accessed 19 April 2013).
Banerjee, S., U. Güçbilmez and G. Pawlina (2013b), 'Measuring IPO activity with implications for expected market returns', working paper, University of Edinburgh.
Benveniste, LuM., W.Y. Busaba and W.J. Wilhelm (2002), 'Information externalities and the role of underwriters in primary equity markets', *Journal of Financial Intermediation*, **11** (1), 61–86.
Brennan, M. and J.Franks (1997), 'Underpricing, ownership and control in initial public offerings of equity securities in the UK', *Journal of Financial Economics*, **45** (3), 391–413.
Bustamante, M.C. (2012), 'The dynamics of going public', *Review of Finance*, **16** (2), 577–618.
Chambers, D. and E. Dimson (2009), 'IPO underpricing over the very long run', *Journal of Finance*, **64** (3), 1407–43.
Çolak, G. and H. Günay (2011), 'Strategic waiting in the IPO markets', *Journal of Corporate Finance*, **17** (3), 555–83.

Hanley, K.W. (1993), 'The underpricing of initial public offerings and the partial adjustment phenomenon', *Journal of Financial Economics*, **34** (2), 231–50.

Helwege, J. and N. Liang (2004), 'Initial public offerings in hot and cold markets', *Journal of Financial and Quantitative Analysis*, **39** (3), 541–69.

Ibbotson, R.G. and J.F. Jaffe (1975), '"Hot issue" markets', *Journal of Finance*, **30** (4), 1027–42.

Levis, M. (1990), 'The winner's curse problem, interest costs and the underpricing of initial public offerings', *Economic Journal*, **100** (399), 76–89.

Loughran, T. and J.R. Ritter (2002), 'Why don't issuers get upset about leaving money on the table in IPOs?', *Review of Financial Studies*, **15** (2), 413–43.

Lowry, M. (2003), 'Why does IPO volume fluctuate so much?', *Journal of Financial Economics*, **67** (1), 3–40.

Lowry, M. and G.W. Schwert (2002), 'IPO market cycles: bubbles or sequential learning?', *Journal of Finance*, **57** (3), 1171–200.

Pagano, M., F. Panetta and L. Zingales (1998), 'Why do companies go public? An empirical analysis', *Journal of Finance*, **53** (1), 27–64.

Pástor, V. and P. Veronesi (2005), 'Rational IPO waves', *Journal of Finance*, **60** (4), 1713–57.

Rees, W.P. (1997), 'The arrival rate of initial public offers in the UK', *European Financial Management*, **3** (1), 45–62.

Vismara, S., S. Paleari and J.R. Ritter (2012), 'Europe's second markets for small companies', *European Financial Management*, **18** (3), 352–88.

Yung, C., G. Çolak and W. Wang (2008), 'Cycles in the IPO market', *Journal of Financial Economics*, **89** (1), 192–208.

PART II

PREPARATION FOR THE IPO

5 IPO offer price selection, institutional subscription, and the value of the firm: theory and evidence

Chitru S. Fernando, Vladimir A. Gatchev and Paul A. Spindt

1 INTRODUCTION

Once a firm that is going public has determined its market valuation and the amount of funds it plans to raise, finance theory has little to say about whether the firm's choice of an offer price level for its shares and the number of shares to offer affects shareholder wealth. Most studies assume that this selection is economically irrelevant. Therefore the attention that firms and markets pay to such 'mere accounting exercises' has frequently intrigued financial researchers.

Fernando et al. (2004) empirically analyze the informativeness of initial public offering (IPO) price levels and document systematic differences across similarly sized firms that pick different price levels when going public, showing that higher-priced IPOs use higher-reputation underwriters, have higher institutional ownership and manifest a lower probability of encountering financial distress.[1] Their empirical findings suggest that each firm selects its IPO offer price, which is one of the few variables that a firm directly controls at the IPO stage, to be consistent with its desired ownership structure, with firms that desire increased institutional participation and/or wish to make their shares less attractive to individual investors selecting higher IPO prices, and firms that wish to avoid institutional participation or explicitly desire increased individual investor participation selecting lower IPO prices. Brau and Fawcett (2006) provide chief financial officer (CFO) survey data that support the notion that firms are divided into two groups: firms that work with high-reputation underwriters who are selected in part for their institutional investor client base, and firms that work with low reputation underwriters who are selected in part for their retail investor client base. As in Fernando et al. (2004), Brau and Fawcett (2006) also show that their findings are not driven by differences in firm size. A similar clustering effect is observed by Fernando et al. (2005), who show that firms and underwriters associate by mutual choice, with high reputation underwriters matching with high quality firms and low reputation underwriters matching with low quality firms.

Despite the considerable empirical evidence that IPO offer price levels matter, especially from the standpoint of institutional investor subscription to IPOs, there is no theoretical rationale to explain why they matter. In this chapter we develop and empirically test a model that is aimed at filling this void in the literature, by establishing the relationship between IPO prices, ownership structure, and a firm's value.

There is a significant body of literature showing that ownership structure is an

102 *Handbook of research on IPOs*

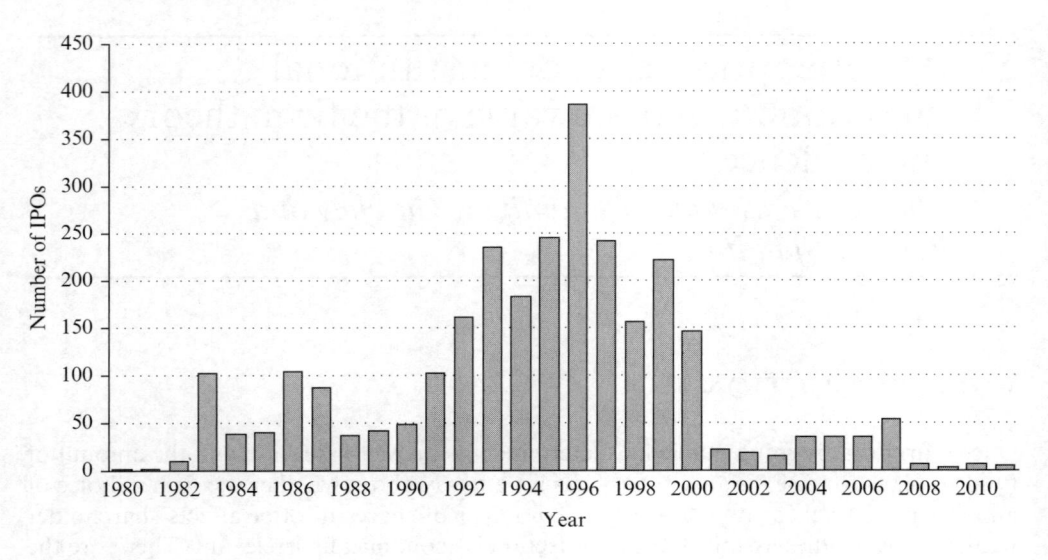

Notes:
The figure plots the number of sample IPOs by year, from 1980 to 2010.
The total number of IPOs is 2838 with a minimum of 1 in 1980 and a maximum of 387 in 1996.

Figure 5.1   Number of sample IPOs by year, from 1980 to 2010

important consideration driving the firm's IPO decisions.[2] Furthermore, in addition to Fernando et al. (2004), there is a considerable literature that provides some guidance on the question of whether firms prefer one price level to another and points to a link between share price levels and ownership. In particular, studies by Muscarella and Vetsuypens (1996), Fernando et al. (1999), and Schultz (2000) provide empirical support for the notion that lower share prices make stocks more attractive to retail investors. These findings are consistent with surveys of managers by Baker and Gallagher (1980) and Baker and Powell (1993), which report that maintaining a preferred price level is the primary motivation for stock splits. In the context of seasoned equity offerings (SEOs), D'Mello et al. (2003) find that firms that split receive higher proceeds on subsequent issues than non-splitting firms. In contrast, Falkenstein (1996), and Gompers and Metrick (2001) provide evidence that institutions avoid investing in low-priced stocks. While it has been the prevalent view that this institutional bias against low-priced stocks may be due to the illiquidity of these stocks (McInish and Wood, 1992; Brennan and Subrahmanyam, 1996; Gompers and Metrick, 2001) or because of a positive relation between price and size (Stoll and Whaley, 1983), the findings of Fernando et al. (2012a) for seasoned stocks suggest otherwise.

Figure 5.1 depicts the annual volume of IPOs in the 1980–2010 period, and Figure 5.2 depicts the range of offer price levels selected by these IPOs. Information generation by market intermediaries has been offered as a rationale for why firms might seek to set lower stock prices, but does not explain the wide cross-sectional variation in price levels that is observed in the market as illustrated in Figure 5.2. Merton (1987) predicts that broadening the base of investors who are familiar with a stock, which can be facilitated

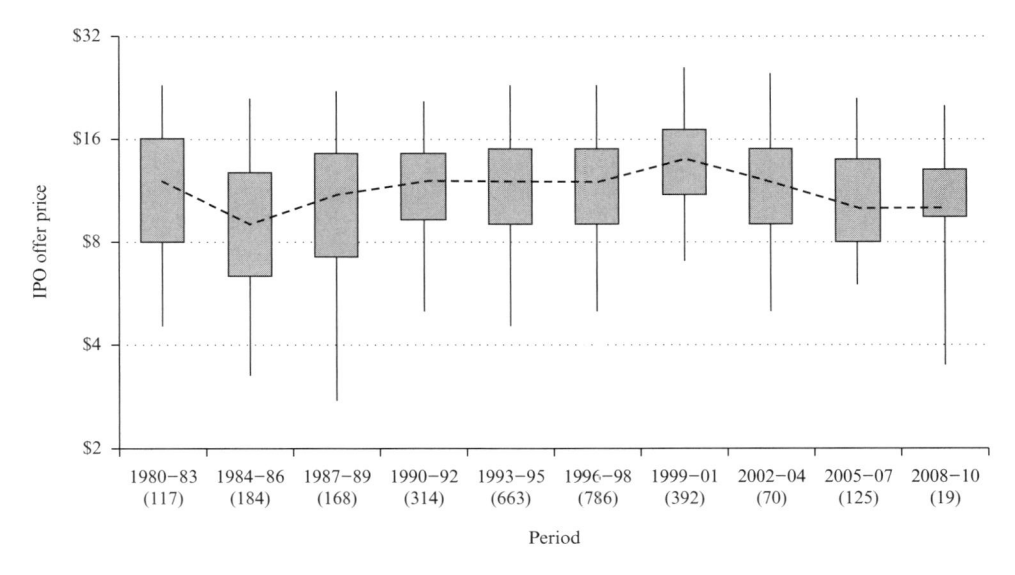

Notes:
The figure plots the distribution of IPO offer prices (in base-2 logarithmic scale) by three-year sub-periods.
The whiskers show the 2.5th to 97.5th percentiles.
The bars show the 25th to 75th percentiles.
The dashed line connects the median IPO offer prices.
For each period, the number of IPOs is shown in parenthesis.

Figure 5.2   Distribution of IPO offer prices by three-year sub-periods

by having a lower stock price and a higher number of shares, will lower its required rate of return. Building on this argument, Brennan and Hughes (1991) argue that non-linear brokerage commission schedules will induce firms to split their shares to generate higher brokerage revenues and thereby increase the incentive for analysts and brokers to generate information and promote their shares. Angel (1997) relies on the negative relation between share price and the relative tick size to develop a model in which lower prices and higher relative tick sizes provide higher incentives for analysts to promote the stock and help broaden the investor base of a firm. While Schultz (2000) does provide empirical evidence consistent with the notion that brokers promote stocks following stock splits, he also finds that this benefit is at least partly offset by the higher costs of trading incurred by the firm's shareholders.[3]

Furthermore, some investors, especially institutions, have their own means of information gathering about the firms they invest in and will not need to rely solely on the work of market intermediaries. Institutional investors dominate the US equity markets.[4] They have the ability to monitor the firms whose stocks they own and increase information availability about these firms, either by gathering their own independent information (for example, by employing buy-side analysts) or by positively influencing the information generation by sell-side analysts.[5] Thus, institutional ownership provides an alternative channel through which firms can disseminate information and create value by monitoring.[6] Consequently, as noted by Allen et al. (2000), we would expect firms (especially firms that perceive higher benefits from institutional ownership) to actively seek out institutional investors to hold their shares.

Extending the work of Brennan and Hughes (1991) and Angel (1997) to the IPO context to incorporate the information-gathering role of institutional investors offers the prospect of providing new insights into two well-documented findings in the literature: (1) the preference of institutional investors for higher-priced IPO stocks; and (2) the positive association between IPO offer price levels and the value of the firm.[7] Following the framework in Fernando et al. (2012a) for seasoned firms, we develop a model of IPO offer price determination by going-public firms that explicitly embodies the monitoring and informational benefits of institutional investment. Our model incorporates two types of investors: institutional and retail. Retail investors are unsophisticated and rely on outside sources, such as brokers and analysts, to provide them with information about stocks. In contrast, institutions monitor the firms whose stocks they own and help increase information availability about these firms by improving the effectiveness of analysts that cover the firm (Frankel et al., 2006; James and Karceski, 2006; Cornett et al., 2007; Ljungqvist et al., 2007; Ruiz-Mallorquí and Santana-Martín, 2011).

In our model, firms that go public select their IPO offer prices by trading off the benefits of institutional monitoring against the benefits of setting share prices that are more attractive to a broader shareholder base. As suggested by Parrino et al. (2003), there is considerable variation across firms in their perceived benefits from institutional ownership. Firms anticipating smaller benefits from institutional ownership set lower IPO prices to increase the relative spreads associated with trading their shares, and thereby induce more information generation by market intermediaries and a broader ownership structure.[8] Firms anticipating larger benefits from institutional ownership set higher IPO prices to decrease the all-in cost to investors of owning their shares. Firms that go public at higher IPO price levels have higher institutional ownership than firms with lower price levels, and higher priced firms will also have a higher value than lower priced firms.

In addition to providing new insights into the relations among and endogeneity associated with several key firm-specific variables such as institutional ownership, IPO offer price levels, underwriter reputation, stock market liquidity, and the value of the firm, our model also yields additional new empirical implications. First, while establishing a theoretical basis for the empirically observed positive relation between IPO prices and institutional ownership, we show that this relation exists independently of liquidity considerations, thus contradicting the widely held notion that higher liquidity is what drives institutions to hold higher-priced stocks. Second, our model implies that the share price level will be an indicator of a firm's value. Therefore, we would expect to find a greater propensity for institutions to invest in higher-priced IPOs and avoid penny-stock IPOs even in the absence of 'prudent-man' rules that constrain them to do so.[9]

We find strong empirical support for our theoretical predictions. IPO offer prices that firms choose when going public are positively and significantly related to institutional ownership and firm quality. It is especially important to note that this relation is robust to our control for stock market liquidity as measured by share turnover, which refutes the argument that the higher institutional ownership of high-priced stocks is driven by the higher liquidity of these stocks. The results are also robust to controls for firm size and exchange listing. We find that a one standard deviation increase in institutional ownership is associated with an increase in the IPO offer price of the firm by 10.4 percent.

Similarly, an increase in underwriter reputation from the median to the maximum reputational value in our sample leads to an increase in IPO offer prices by around 11 percent. Specifically, the value of IPO firms is positively related to the reputation of the lead IPO underwriter, with firms underwritten by the most reputable underwriter having a value that is approximately 9 percent higher than the value of the IPO firm that is underwritten by the underwriter with the median reputation rank in our sample. Further support for our theory is provided by the relation between firm value and institutional ownership and between firm value and the IPO offer price. We find that a one standard deviation increase in institutional ownership is associated with an approximately 2.3 percentage point increase in firm value. We also find that a one standard deviation increase in the (log) IPO offer price is associated with around a 12 percent increase in firm value.

Overall, our empirical findings provide strong support for our theory of IPO offer price determination. It is important to point out that, as demonstrated by our model, the empirical relations that we document are not causal but simply indicate that higher quality firms tend to have higher valuations as well as choose higher IPO offer prices, match with more reputed underwriters, and attract higher institutional ownership.

The rest of the chapter is organized as follows. We develop our model in section 2 and also discuss its empirical implications. Section 3 describes our sample and methodology. Section 4 presents the empirical results. Section 5 concludes.

2 THE MODEL AND EMPIRICAL IMPLICATIONS

In this section, we develop a simple model of IPO share price level selection by going-public firms that maximize firm value by taking into account the trade-offs associated with targeting institutional ownership versus a broader investor base.[10] We conclude the section by developing several empirical implications of our model.

2.1 The Economy

We consider a multi-stage economy with J risky assets (IPO firms), a riskless asset, and two types of risk-averse investors: institutional and retail. Within each investor type, there is a continuum of homogeneous investors. We assume that due to participation constraints all investors do not invest in all available IPO stocks, so that for each firm j, a proportion α_j of all investors are institutional investors and the remaining proportion $(1 - \alpha_j)$ are retail investors, where $\alpha_j \in (0,1)$. The α_j parameter is exogenous to our model and is motivated by existing literature that documents the effect of imperfect information and institutional constraints on investor participation. Merton (1987), for example, presents a model of asset prices in which each investor knows only about a subset of all available securities and therefore invests only in those securities.[11] In addition, existing literature presents significant evidence that prudent-man laws (see Del Guercio, 1996) and 'safety-net' considerations (see Badrinath et al., 1989) affect the decision of institutional investors to invest in some stocks but not invest in others. To incorporate the above-mentioned insights in our model, we allow the mix of institutional and retail investors to vary across firms. The equilibrium share ownership by each investor group will be determined endogenously as discussed below.

Risky asset payoffs are independently distributed, with each risky asset j having a random terminal payoff of $V\%_j$ that is normally distributed with mean μ_j and precision h_j, where h_j measures the firm's information quality and equals the inverse of the payoff variance. The riskless asset's return is normalized at zero. All investors in the economy have identical constant absolute risk aversion (CARA) preferences with CARA parameter'.[12] We examine the investment decision of a representative investor of each type, assuming for convenience that both investor types are endowed only with the riskless asset prior to trading in the risky asset.

Investment in the risky IPO assets is facilitated by market intermediaries, who we refer to collectively as 'analysts'.[13] In the case of IPOs, such analysts are typically employed by investment banks that underwrite and market the IPOs. As shown by Brennan and Hughes (1991) and Angel (1997), for a given firm size and in the presence of fixed per-share commissions, analysts will produce more information when the firm has more shares outstanding/a lower share price. Therefore, we assume that analysts jointly produce a signal of the final payoff of each firm with precision $S_j h_S$, where S_j is equal to firm j's number of shares outstanding. Conditional on the number of shares outstanding, S_j, the precision of final payoff for each firm j becomes $h_j + S_j h_S$. For analytical tractability, we also assume a trading cost structure where trading spreads are fixed at c per share.

In our model, institutions can both substitute for analysts by monitoring the firms they own and complement analysts by enhancing the quality of the information about firms that analysts generate. These benefits of having institutional shareholders will increase in proportion to their ownership in the firm. Therefore, for each firm j, institutional investment modifies the precision of firm payoffs by the multiplicative factor, $(1 + m_j \theta_I)$, where $m_j > 0$ is a parameter that captures the maximum extent to which institutions are able to positively affect a firm and θ_I is the fraction of the firm held by institutions, resulting in a final payoff precision of $(h_j + S_j h_S)(1 + m_j \theta_I)$.[14] This formulation directly captures potential institutional monitoring benefits as well as the idea advanced by Frankel et al. (2006) and Ljungqvist et al. (2007) that institutional investors induce analysts to generate more precise information about the firm. The firm's overall information quality will depend on both analyst coverage and institutional investment. The aggregate benefit of institutional investment, $(h_j + S_j h_S)(m_j \theta_I)$, will increase with institutional ownership θ_I, reflecting the fact that the influence of institutional investors on both firms and analysts will rise in proportion to their ownership in the firm. In determining their optimal ownership in the firm, institutional investors effectively trade off the benefits of increased monitoring and analyst information quality against the cost of decreased risk sharing. Therefore, we would expect IPO firms that are endowed with higher values of the institutional monitoring parameter, m_j, to target a higher institutional investor clientele.

2.2 Stages

The model consists of four stages. In the first stage IPO firms determine the number of shares outstanding to maximize the market value of the firm, which also determines the offer price per share. Setting lower share prices (and a higher number of shares outstanding) provide greater incentive for analysts to promote the firm's shares since the returns

IPO offer price selection 107

```
s = 1                    s = 2                        s = 3                        s = 4
├────────────────────────┼────────────────────────────┼────────────────────────────┤
```

- IPO firm *j* chooses number of shares outstanding S_j
- Payoff $V\%_j$ normally distributed with mean μ_j and precision h_j

- Analysts produce information about firm payoff. Added precision is jointly equal to $S_j h_S$
- Payoff precision becomes $h_j + S_j h_S$

- Ownership by investor type $i \in \{I, R\}$ is determined
- Investors pay a trading cost of c per share
- Firm market-clearing value Q_j is determined

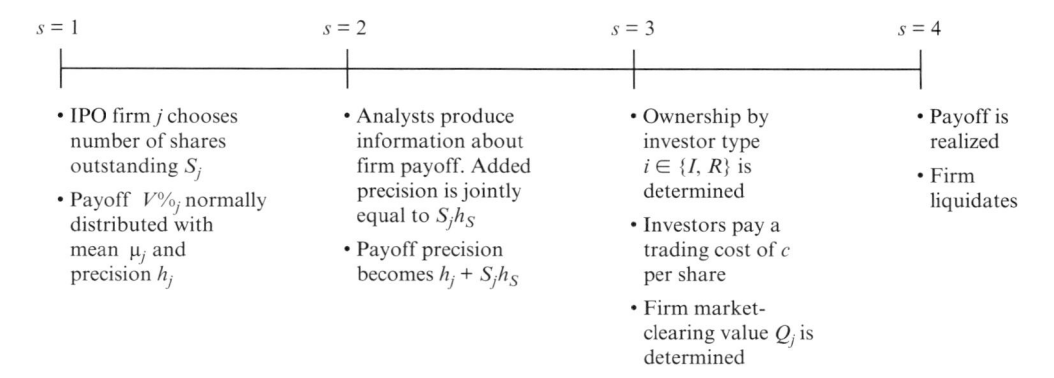

- Payoff is realized
- Firm liquidates

Figure 5.3   Four-stage model

to analysts increase with lower share prices under prevailing transactions cost structures. Therefore, a higher number of shares (and lower IPO share price) will increase the information generated by analysts about a firm but also the cost to shareholders of investing in the firm due to the higher trading spreads they will be required to pay. In the second stage, analysts produce information about each firm's terminal payoff. In the third stage, investors make their investment decisions regarding each IPO firm, which in turn determines the spreads earned by analysts and each firm's market-clearing valuation. In the final stage, firms' payoffs are realized and firms liquidate. The four stages are summarized in Figure 5.3. We solve the model recursively.

2.3 Optimal Investor Holdings and Equilibrium Valuations

The representative investor of type $i \in \{I, R\}$ has an initial endowment of the riskless asset denoted by $W_{0,i}$. The investor of type $i \in \{I, R\}$ solves:

$$\max_{\theta_{ij}} E\left[-e^{-\gamma W\%_i}\right], \tag{5.1}$$

where $W\%_i = W_{0,i} + \sum_{j=1}^{J} X_{ij} V\%_j - \sum_{j=1}^{J} X_{ij}(Q_j + cS_j)$. In the expression for investor wealth, X_{ij} measures how much each investor of type i invests in IPO firm j and is the choice variable with respect to which each investor maximizes wealth. Given our previous assumptions of atomistic investors and two investor types, the aggregate ownership of investors of type I in IPO firm j is $\theta_{Ij} = 2\alpha_j X_{Ij}$ and the aggregate ownership of investors of type R is $\theta_{Rj} = 2(1-\alpha_j) X_{Rj}$. The corresponding market clearing condition is that $\theta_{Ij} + \theta_{Rj} = 1$. In addition, Q_j is the market valuation of firm j at the trading stage and c is the per-share trading cost for investors.

Given the previous assumptions regarding the distribution of final firm payoffs, the portfolio optimization problem of each investor i can be stated as follows:

$$\max_{X_{ij}} \gamma E(W\%_i) - \frac{\gamma^2}{2} \text{Var}(W\%_i), \tag{5.2}$$

where

$$\operatorname{Var}(W\%_i) = \sum_{j=1}^{J} X_{ij}^2 \frac{1}{(h_j + S_j h_S)(1 + m_j 2\alpha_j X_{Ij})}. \quad (5.3)$$

The expression in (5.3) indicates that, all else equal, IPO firms with higher information quality (h_j), higher number of shares outstanding (S_j), and a higher benefit from institutional ownership (m_j) have a lower uncertainty of future values.

Solving for the optimal ownership weights and the equilibrium valuation of the IPO firm, subject to market clearing, we can state our results for the equilibrium ownership structure of the firm as follows:[15]

Proposition 1: The equilibrium ownership structure for each IPO firm j is given by

$$\theta_{Ij} = \alpha_j + \frac{\sqrt{1 + \alpha_j^2 m_j(2 + m_j)} - (1 + \alpha_j^2 m_j)}{(1 + \alpha_j) m_j} \quad (5.4)$$

$$\theta_{Rj} = 1 - \alpha_j + \frac{\sqrt{1 + \alpha_j^2 m_j(2 + m_j)} - (1 + \alpha_j^2 m_j)}{(1 + \alpha_j) m_j}. \quad (5.5)$$

For any $m_j > 0$, θ_{Ij} lies in the interval $(\alpha_j, 2\alpha_j/(1 + \alpha_j))$ and thus is always greater than 0 but less than 1 for any $\alpha_j \in (0,1)$. Furthermore, as can be seen from the foregoing, θ_{Ij} covers the whole interval between 0 and 1: when α_j approaches 0, θ_{Ij} also approaches 0 and when α_j approaches 1, θ_{Ij} also approaches 1. More importantly, for any $\alpha_j \in (0,1)$, as m_j increases, institutional ownership θ_{Ij} also increases while retail ownership θ_{Rj} decreases.

It is interesting to note that trading costs, which are the outcome of the number of shares/share price decision of the IPO firm, do not directly affect the manner in which ownership of any given firm is shared between institutional and retail investors. Therefore, in our model, there is no causal relation between trading costs and ownership structure. This result remains unchanged when we assume that institutional and retail investors have different trading cost structures, provided the differential is applied uniformly across all firms. Nonetheless, as we will show later, since IPO firms optimize their share price decision to maximize any potential benefit of institutional ownership, firms that have high (low) values of m_j will also have high (low) share prices in equilibrium, thereby leading to a positive association between institutional ownership and share prices. These results are in stark contrast to the existing empirical literature which assumes that the higher costs of trading low priced shares causes a lower institutional ownership of these shares relative to high priced shares.

We can state our result for the market valuation of each firm at the trading stage, conditional on the number of shares outstanding, as follows:

Lemma 1: The market valuation of each IPO firm j at the trading stage is given by

$$Q_j = \mu_j - cS_j - \frac{\gamma}{(h_j + S_j h_S)}\Gamma_1(m_j), \tag{5.6a}$$

where

$$\Gamma_1(m_j) = \frac{(1+m_j)\sqrt{1+\alpha_j^2 m_j(2+m_j)} - (1+\alpha_j m_j(2+m_j))}{2m_j(1-\alpha_j)^2} \tag{5.6b}$$

The expression for $\Gamma_1(m_j)$ reflects the effect of monitoring on the value of the firm. For $\alpha_j \in (0,1)$ and $m_j > 0$, $\Gamma_1(m_j)$ lies in the interval between 0 and $\frac{1}{2}$ and monotonically declines with m_j. As the institutional monitoring benefit (m_j) approaches 0, $\Gamma_1(m_j)$ approaches $\frac{1}{2}$ and the equilibrium price approaches a value with no monitoring benefits. As m_j increases, $\Gamma_1(m_j)$ decreases and the market value of the firm increases. It can be shown that $\lim_{m_j \to \infty} \Gamma_1(m_j) = 0$ so that in the limit uncertainty is resolved and risk does not affect the value of the firm.

Conditional on the IPO firm's choice of number of shares outstanding, firm value increases with the benefit of institutional ownership (m_j) and with the firm's information quality (h_j), while it decreases with investor risk aversion (γ). Given that institutional monitoring is positive, the proportion of institutional investors, α_j, has a positive effect on the value of the firm.

2.4 The Choice of Shares Outstanding

In the first stage, IPO firms choose the number of shares outstanding so as to maximize their value at the trading stage.[16] In doing so, firms have to balance offsetting effects. On the one hand, setting a low number of shares outstanding (leading to high share prices) reduces the cost of trading and increases the net returns to shareholders. On the other hand, a lower number of shares outstanding induces less information production by analysts, which results in higher uncertainty and lower valuations for the firm. Proposition 2 states the equilibrium result for the optimal number of shares that arises from these tradeoffs.

Proposition 2: The optimal number of shares outstanding, S^*_j, for each IPO firm j, is given by

$$S^*_j = \sqrt{\frac{\gamma \Gamma_1(m_j)}{ch_S}} - \frac{h_j}{h_S}. \tag{5.7}$$

As firm information quality (h_j) and institutional benefits (m_j) increase, the optimal number of shares outstanding decreases. We analyze the relation between equilibrium share prices and these variables in Proposition 3 below.

Solving the expression in (5.4) for m_j we obtain that

$$m_j = 2(\theta_{Ij} - \alpha_j)/(\theta_{Ij}(2\alpha_j - (1+\alpha_j)\theta_{Ij})). \tag{5.8}$$

Replacing for m_j in the expression for Proposition 2, we find that

$$S_j^* = \sqrt{\frac{\gamma \Gamma_2(\theta_{Ij})}{ch_S}} - \frac{h_j}{h_S}, \tag{5.9a}$$

where

$$\Gamma_2(\theta_{Ij}) = \frac{(1 - \theta_{Ij})(2\alpha_j - (1 + \alpha_j)\theta_{Ij})}{2(1 - \alpha_j)^2 \theta_{Ij}}. \tag{5.9b}$$

As we have shown above, equilibrium values of institutional ownership (θ_{Ij}) lie in the interval (α_j, $2\alpha_j/(1 + \alpha_j)$). For values of θ_{Ij} in this interval, $\Gamma_2(\theta_{Ij})$, and thus the optimal number of shares outstanding, monotonically decreases with institutional ownership. As we prove later in Proposition 4, this result gives rise to a positive association between share prices and institutional ownership. We should note, however, that this association is not causal.

The model also relates institutional ownership and IPO firm characteristics to equilibrium firm value. By substituting the optimal number of shares in (5.7) for the value of the firm expressed in Lemma 1, we obtain the expression for the equilibrium value of the firm, which we state in Proposition 3:

Proposition 3: The equilibrium value of the IPO firm is given by

$$Q_j^* = \mu_j + \frac{ch_j}{h_S} - 2\sqrt{\frac{\gamma c}{h_S} \Gamma_1(m_j)} \tag{5.10a}$$

or equivalently,

$$Q_j^* = \mu_j + \frac{ch_j}{h_S} - 2\sqrt{\frac{\gamma c}{h_S} \Gamma_2(\theta_{Ij})}. \tag{5.10b}$$

It is evident from (5.10b) that the maximized firm value is an increasing function of firm information quality (h_j) and of institutional ownership (θ_{Ij}). Furthermore, for $S_j^* > 0$, the value of the firm increases with the benefit of more shares outstanding (h_S). Note that (5.10b) does not imply that firms can increase their values by increasing institutional ownership. What it shows is that IPO firms with higher institutional monitoring benefits will have higher institutional ownership and higher values as the equilibrium outcome.

Our model also allows us to examine the relation between a firm's IPO share price and its expected cash flows, institutional monitoring benefits, and information quality. Proposition 4 provides the expression for a firm's equilibrium share price (expression (5.10b) divided by expression (5.9a)).

Proposition 4: The equilibrium IPO share price of the firm is given by

$$P_j^* = \frac{\mu_j - (ch_j/h_S)}{\sqrt{\dfrac{\gamma}{ch_S}\Gamma_2(\theta_{Ij}) - (h_j/h_S)}} - 2c. \tag{5.11}$$

The equilibrium IPO share price increases with the expected cash flows of the firm (μ_j), institutional ownership (θ_{Ij}, which proxies for institutional monitoring benefits), and the firm's information quality (h_j).[17] Putting together the comparative statics results for the value of the IPO firm and its IPO offer price, we can conclude that if the parameters in the model are not perfectly measured in practice (as we expect) there will be a positive association between the value of the IPO firm and its share price level. This is not because IPO share price levels directly affect firm value but because the factors that lead to a higher firm value also lead to a higher price per share.

2.5 Empirical Implications

Our theoretical framework gives rise to several empirical implications. Extending the prior literature, the model predicts that institutional ownership and IPO offer price per share will be positively correlated.

Empirically, we can also examine how the value of the IPO firm is affected by the firm's information quality and institutional ownership benefit. Expression (5.10b) of Proposition 3 predicts a positive relation between firm value and institutional ownership while expression (5.9a) following Proposition 2 predicts a positive relation between IPO offer price and institutional ownership. These two predictions combined suggest a positive association between firm value and IPO offer price. It should be noted that the latter relation is not causal. Rather, it stems from the fact that both IPO share price levels and firm value are positively affected by institutional monitoring benefits and the firm's information quality. Proposition 3 also predicts that the value of the firm would increase with the firm's information quality and with the accuracy of analyst forecasts.

Proposition 4 allows us to make empirical predictions about the cross-sectional differences in IPO price levels of firms. A firm's IPO offer price will increase with institutional ownership and the firm's information quality. This relation should hold even after controlling for measures of market liquidity. Examining expression (5.11), we do not find a clear relation between IPO offer price and the precision of analyst information. While it is true that the value of the firm monotonically increases with the precision of analyst information, the optimal number of shares outstanding first increases and then decreases as the precision of analyst information increases.

We test the above empirical predictions in Section 4 after describing our sample and variable definitions in the next section.

3 SAMPLE AND VARIABLES

Our main sample comes from Securities Data Corporation's (SDC's) New Issues database and covers 2838 initial public offerings between the years of 1980 and 2010. To ensure precise measurement of underwriter reputation for each IPO, we include only IPOs with a single lead underwriter. We only include firms with common stock (CRSP share codes 10 or 11) listed on NYSE/AMEX/Nasdaq (CRSP exchange codes 1, 2, or 3). We also require that firms have data available in the Center for Research in Security Prices (CRSP) daily and monthly files and the Compustat annual database.

The IPO offer price from the SDC New Issues database is our measure of the firm's preferred price range (see also Fernando et al., 2004). In addition, SDC provides data on total IPO proceeds, which we use as a measure of offer size. We measure firm size using the firm's market capitalization (first-day closing price times shares outstanding from CRSP) and total assets (Compustat item AT for the first fiscal year after the IPO date).

To measure the information quality of each firm (h_j), we use the standard deviation of daily returns for the first four months after the IPO. Firms with low standard deviation of daily returns have lower uncertainty and thus have more *ex ante* information available about their value.

While we do not have a direct measure of the precision of analyst information (h_S), we expect underwriter reputation to be highly correlated with such a precision. Highly reputable underwriters hire better analysts, who would then produce more precise information about the firm. In addition, high-reputation underwriters would be better able to assess the quality of the firm during the due diligence process and so would again generate more precise information about the firm.

The model developed in the previous section shows that institutional ownership increases monotonically with institutional benefits (m_j), which permits us to use institutional ownership as a direct measure of institutional benefits. We collect percentage institutional ownership data from the CDA Spectrum database of Thomson Financial, which consists of institutional 13F filings. Institutional ownership is measured at the end of the first quarter after the IPO date.

To measure the value of each IPO firm, we use the market value of assets to the book value of assets (value-to-assets) for the first fiscal year after the IPO. Asset market value is the sum of the book value of assets (Compustat item AT) and the market value of common stock (Compustat item PRCC_F times item CSHO) less the book value of common stock (equity (Compustat item SEQ, or item CEQ plus item PSTK, or item AT minus item LT) minus preferred stock (Compustat item PSTKL, or item PSTKRV, or item PSTK)) and deferred taxes when available (Compustat item TXDITC) net of post-retirement benefits when available (Compustat item PRBA). Because of its ease of calculation and because it is available for a large set of firms, this measure of firm value, which we and others refer to as Tobin's Q, is widely used in existing literature (see, for example, Kaplan and Zingales, 1997; Gompers et al., 2003; and the references therein). The value-to-assets measure is adjusted for the median value-to-assets of the firm's industry, where industries are defined as in Fama and French (1997).

The existing literature frequently uses share price level as a proxy for stock market liquidity. To control for liquidity differences in our sample while also studying the relation of IPO share price levels to other firm-specific variables, we employ the share turnover of the firm. We measure average daily share turnover using daily CRSP data for the first four months after the IPO. To address the overstatement of trading volume on the National Association of Securities Dealers Automated Quotations (NASDAQ) compared to trading volume on the New York Stock Exchange/American Stock Exchange (NYSE/AMEX) and to also control for other differences between the NYSE/AMEX and the NASDAQ, in our regressions we also use a dummy variable equal to one if an issue is traded on the NYSE/AMEX and equal to zero if it is traded on the NASDAQ.

Furthermore, existing research has shown that firm value, as measured by the industry-adjusted value-to-assets ratio, is positively related to the growth opportunities of the firm. We control for growth opportunities using the change in assets (Compustat item AT) from fiscal year t to year $t + 1$ relative to the IPO date and the research and development (R&D) expenses relative to total assets (Compustat item XRD divided by item AT) for fiscal year t. Research and development expenses are not available for a significant part of our sample. We make R&D expenses equal to zero when not available and at the same time we include a dummy variable indicating whether or not R&D expenses are missing. This allows us to estimate the coefficient for R&D expenses relative to assets only for firms with available R&D expenses and to estimate the other coefficients using all data for the remaining variables.

The reputation of the IPO's lead investment bank plays an important role during the IPO process. Among other financial services, investment banks provide certification and monitoring during the IPO and analyst coverage and market making after the IPO (see, for example, Fernando et al. (2005) and Fernando et al. 2012b). It is, therefore, important to incorporate the reputation of the lead underwriter and the effects that such reputation may have on the value of the firm and the choice of offer price. We use underwriter reputation as an overall measure of *ex post* firm quality, a measure of quality that reflects both the *ex ante* uncertainty about the IPO firm as well as the total benefit that the firm gains from external analyst coverage (in the language of our theoretical model, underwriter reputation is a measure of $h_j + S_f h_S$). Our measure of IPO underwriter reputation is based on Megginson and Weiss (1991). The measure is equal to the log of the lead underwriter's total underwritten IPO and SEO proceeds over the year of the IPO and the previous two years as a percent of the maximum log proceeds for any lead underwriter during the same period. Underwriter reputation ranges from 0 for underwriters with no offerings in the three years, to 100 for the underwriter with the highest IPO and SEO proceeds over the three-year window. To ensure that our tests are not driven by outliers, we winsorize all variables at the 1st and the 99th percentiles.

Table 5.1 reports the mean, median, and standard deviation for the variables discussed above. Both the average and median IPO offer prices in our sample are around $12 per share and have remained stable over the 30 years of our sample. The median firm in our sample is relatively small, with a market capitalization of approximately US$130 million and assets of approximately US$65 million. The total proceeds for the median IPO are around US$35 million or approximately 27 percent of the market capitalization of the firm. In the first quarter after the IPO, institutional investors own 17 percent of the median and 20 percent of the average IPO firm. Not surprisingly, the sample firms have relatively high asset growth rates, with the median firm growing at around 55 percent in the two years after the IPO. Most of the sample IPOs are listed on the NASDAQ with only around 18 percent listed on the NYSE or the AMEX.

Table 5.1   Descriptive statistics

Variable	Mean	Median	Standard deviation
IPO offer price	12.280	12.000	4.741
Log(IPO offer price)	2.426	2.485	0.422
Log(market capitalization in millions of dollars)	4.911	4.883	1.274
Log(total assets in millions of dollars)	4.260	4.179	1.349
Log(IPO proceeds in millions of dollars)	3.529	3.561	1.042
NYSE/AMEX dummy	0.177	0	0.381
Change in assets from year t to $t+1$, $(A_t - A_{t-1})/A_t$	0.515	0.557	0.306
R&D-to-assets (when available)	0.123	0.091	0.123
Percent institutional ownership	19.671	17.144	17.264
Log(1 + percent institutional ownership)	2.487	2.898	1.284
Percent standard deviation of daily returns	4.300	3.771	2.153
Log(percent standard deviation of daily returns)	1.342	1.330	0.501
Log(adjusted value-to-assets)	−0.334	−0.224	0.880
Log(0.01 + percent daily share turnover)	−2.081	−2.077	0.696
Megginson-Weiss lead underwriter reputation	87.882	89.799	8.862

Notes:
The table reports the mean, median and standard deviation for the variables used in subsequent analyses.
The sample of IPOs is obtained from the SDC New Issues database and covers 2838 single-lead IPOs between 1980 and 2010.
Additional data come from CRSP, Compustat, and CDA Spectrum.
The SDC New Issues database provides data on IPO offer prices and total IPO proceeds.
CRSP provides data on the market capitalization of the firm based on the first-day closing price, the standard deviation of daily returns estimated using returns during the first four months after the IPO, and average daily share turnover (shares traded divided by shares outstanding) for the first four months after the IPO.
Compustat provides data on the book value of firm assets and the R&D expenses relative to assets for the first fiscal year after the IPO.
The CDA Spectrum dataset provides data on institutional ownership in the first quarter after the IPO.
The value-to-assets of each firm is the market capitalization of equity plus the book value of total debt (from Compustat) divided by the book value of total assets.
We adjust the value-to-assets ratio by subtracting the annual industry median value-to-assets, where industries are defined as in Fama and French (1997).
The *Megginson-Weiss reputation* variable for each underwriter is based on Megginson and Weiss (1991) and is constructed as 100 times the log of the underwriter's total underwritten IPO and SEO proceeds divided by the maximum log proceeds for any underwriter during the same period.
For each underwriter, IPO and SEO proceeds are summed over the year of the IPO and the previous two years.
Underwriter reputation ranges from 0, for underwriters with no offerings in the past three years to 100 for the underwriter with the highest IPO and SEO proceeds over the past three years.
We further create an exchange dummy variable, based on CRSP data, equal to 1 if a stock is listed on the NYSE/AMEX and equal to 0 if it is listed on the NASDAQ. All variables are winsorized at the 1st and the 99th percentiles.

4   EMPIRICAL FINDINGS

In this section we present the results of our empirical tests of the hypotheses developed in section 2.5. In section 4.1 we examine the relation between firm value and several key variables, and in section 4.2 we examine the determination of IPO offer price levels.

In our tests we use panel data and estimate OLS regressions. Petersen (2009) presents evidence of a significant clustering of residuals across years in finance panel data sets. Failure to control for this year-level clustering leads to biased standard errors and therefore biased significance tests. In all our analysis, significance tests control for year-level clustering. In addition, in order to control for trends in the size of IPO proceeds and for trends in the overall size of firms over time, in subsequent analysis we include year fixed effects.

4.1 The Value of the Firm

Table 5.2 reports our findings on the links between firm value (as measured by the firm's value-to-assets) and other key variables of interest, such as the firm's information quality (measured by the standard deviation of daily returns), the reputation of the IPO's lead underwriter, institutional ownership, size, and IPO offer price levels.

Table 5.2 Regressions on value-to-assets of the firm

	Model (1)	Model (2)	Model (3)
Log(total assets in millions of dollars)	−0.044**	−0.078***	−0.129***
	(0.039)	(0.004)	(0.001)
Megginson-Weiss reputation of lead underwriter		0.009***	0.007**
		(0.001)	(0.011)
Log(1 + percent institutional ownership)	0.018*	0.006	
	(0.059)	(0.541)	
Log(IPO offer price)			0.284***
			(0.008)
NYSE/AMEX dummy	0.079*	0.075*	0.088**
	(0.063)	(0.079)	(0.028)
Change in assets from year t to $t+1$	0.404***	0.389***	0.357***
	(0.001)	(0.001)	(0.003)
R&D to assets	−0.049	−0.035	−0.016
	(0.219)	(0.366)	(0.709)
R&D to assets missing dummy	0.279	0.191	0.228
	(0.287)	(0.479)	(0.374)
Log(percent standard deviation of daily returns)	0.095	0.083	0.098
	(0.282)	(0.364)	(0.271)
R-squared	27.04%	27.60%	28.46%

Notes:
The table reports estimates from regression models, where the dependent variable is the industry-adjusted value-to-assets of the firm.
The value-to-assets ratio uses Compustat data in the first fiscal year after the IPO.
All explanatory variables are defined in Table 5.1.
The table also reports the R-squared of each model.
All models include year fixed effects. Significance levels are estimated based on standard errors adjusted for year-level clustering.
The sample in all models consists of 2718 IPOs between 1980 and 2010 with available data.
* Significance at the 0.10 level from a two-tailed t-test.
** Significance at the 0.05 level from a two-tailed t-test.
*** Significance at the 0.01 level from a two-tailed t-test.

Our findings provide significant support for our theory. Specifically, while firm value appears unrelated to the standard deviation of daily returns, value is positively related to the reputation of the lead IPO underwriter. In model (2) this relation is significant at the 0.01 level and the estimated coefficient shows that firms underwritten by the most reputable underwriter (the one with a reputation rank of 100) have a value that is approximately 9 percent higher than the value of the median IPO firm, which is underwritten by underwriters with a reputation rank of around 90. When the IPO offer price is included as an explanatory variable in the regressions, the relation between firm value and underwriter reputation remains statistically significant (at the 0.05 level) but the economic significance declines. According to our model, IPO offer price levels are related to the information quality of the firm and, therefore, it is not surprising that when share price is included as an explanatory variable the estimated effect of underwriter reputation on firm value declines.

Further support for our theory is provided by the relation between firm value and institutional ownership and between value and the share price of the firm. We find a positive and significant (at the 0.10 level) relation between firm value and institutional ownership in model (1).[18] Using the standard deviation of the institutional ownership variable from Table 5.1 and the estimated coefficient from model (1) of Table 5.2, we find that a one standard deviation (1.284) increase in institutional ownership is associated with an approximately 2.3 percentage point increase in firm value. Given the interrelatedness of institutional ownership and a firm's *ex post* quality (as measured by underwriter reputation), it is not surprising that including underwriter reputation in the model reduces the significance of the institutional ownership variable. Examining the IPO offer price coefficient in model (3), we find that firm value is significantly (at the 0.01 level) and positively related to the IPO offer price. More specifically, a one standard deviation (0.422) increase in the log offer price, is associated with around 12 percent increase in firm value. We would like to note that, as demonstrated by our model, this relation is not causal but simply indicates that higher quality firms tend to have higher valuations as well as choose higher IPO offer prices, match with more reputed underwriters, and attract higher institutional ownership.

When we examine the control variables we find that, consistent with existing literature, growth opportunities (as measured by asset growth) are positively related to the value of the firm, while size is negatively related to firm value (see, for example, Lang and Stulz, 1994).

4.2 IPO Offer Price Levels

Our last set of predictions concerns the determinants of differences in the IPO offer price levels of firms. These predictions are tested in Table 5.3. Our findings again provide significant support for our theory. Initial public offering offer prices are positively and significantly related to institutional ownership and firm quality. It is especially important to note that this relation is robust to our control for stock market liquidity as measured by share turnover. The results are also robust to controls for firm size and exchange listing.

In both model (2) and model (3) the relation between institutional ownership and IPO offer prices is significant at the 0.01 level. Examining the coefficient estimate of institutional ownership in model (3) of Table 5.3, we find that a one standard deviation (1.284)

Table 5.3 Regressions on IPO offer prices

	Model (1)	Model (2)	Model (2)
Log(total assets in millions of dollars)	0.176***	0.185***	0.155***
	(0.001)	(0.001)	(0.001)
NYSE/AMEX dummy	−0.042**	−0.029*	−0.032*
	(0.029)	(0.075)	(0.075)
Megginson-Weiss reputation of lead underwriter	0.011***		0.009***
	(0.001)		(0.001)
Log(percent institutional ownership)		0.081***	0.068***
		(0.001)	(0.001)
Log(0.01 + percent daily share turnover)	0.094***	0.070***	0.073***
	(0.001)	(0.001)	(0.001)
Log(percent standard deviation of daily returns)	−0.067*	−0.021	−0.045
	(0.059)	(0.466)	(0.180)
R-squared	54.62%	54.88%	57.40%

Notes:
The table reports estimates from regression models, where the dependent variable is the IPO offer price (natural logarithm).
All explanatory variables are defined in Table 5.1.
The table also reports the R-squared of each model.
All models include year fixed effects.
Significance levels are estimated based on standard errors adjusted for year-level clustering.
The sample in all models consists of 2838 IPOs between 1980 and 2010 with available data.
*   Significance at the 0.10 level from a two-tailed *t*-test.
**   Significance at the 0.05 level from a two-tailed *t*-test.
***   Significance at the 0.01 level from a two-tailed *t*-test.

increase in log institutional ownership is associated with an increase in the IPO offer price of the firm by 10.4 percent. At the median IPO firm this implies an increase in the offer price from around $12 per share to around $13.25 per share.

Initial public offering offer prices are negatively related to the standard deviation of daily returns in all three models. This relation is significant at the 0.10 level in model (1) but not significant at standard levels in model (2) and model (3), when we also control for institutional ownership. The economic effect of standard deviation of daily returns on IPO offer prices is also notable. For example, the estimated model (1) of Table 5.3 implies that a one standard deviation (0.501) increase in return volatility is associated with around a 3.4 percent decrease in the IPO offer price of the firm.

The relation between our other measure of *ex post* firm quality, underwriter reputation, and IPO offer prices is considerably stronger. In all specifications, the coefficient on underwriter reputation is significant at the 0.01 level. Interpreting the economic magnitude of the effect, we find that an increase in reputation from the median of 90 to the maximum of 100 leads to an increase in IPO offer prices by around 11 percent. For the median IPO firm, this means an increase in the offer price from $12 per share to $13.3 per share.

Overall, the findings in this section provide strong support for our theory. Both firm value and IPO offer prices are positively related to the firm's information quality and institutional ownership.

118 *Handbook of research on IPOs*

To control for the possibility that our results may be driven by some institutional investors being prevented from investing in low-priced stocks due to prudent-man or other constraints, we have replicated all our results while excluding all IPO firms with offer prices below $5 per share. The coefficient estimates and their significance are not affected in any noteworthy way by this change. The results are not reported for brevity.

5 CONCLUSIONS

We develop a model to explain the determination of IPO offer price levels and the observed relationships between IPO offer price, institutional ownership, underwriter reputation, and other IPO characteristics. Our model of IPO price determination explicitly incorporates the role of institutional investors in monitoring firms and improving information generation about these firms by market intermediaries. We show that firms and their underwriters select IPO offer price levels by trading off the relative costs and benefits of institutional ownership versus a more broad-based ownership structure. Firms that anticipate smaller net benefits from institutional ownership set lower share prices to make shares more appealing to retail investors and increase the trading revenue associated with trading their shares, thereby inducing more information generation by market intermediaries. In contrast, firms that anticipate larger net benefits from institutional ownership set higher IPO prices to decrease the cost to investors of owning their shares. In equilibrium, firms that go public at higher IPO offer prices have a higher institutional ownership and higher valuations than lower priced firms. In addition to establishing a theoretical basis for the empirically observed positive relation between IPO prices and institutional ownership, we show empirically that this relation exists independently of differences in size and market liquidity, which are widely believed to be the drivers for institutions to subscribe more to higher priced IPOs. Overall, while our empirical findings provide strong support for our theory of IPO offer price determination, it is important to point out that, as demonstrated by our model, the empirical relations that we document are not causal but simply indicate that higher quality IPO firms tend to have higher valuations as well as choose higher IPO offer prices, match with more reputed underwriters, and attract higher institutional ownership.

NOTES

1. Paralleling the findings of Fernando et al. (2004) for IPOs, the finance literature documents systematic relationships for both seasoned firms and IPOs between share price level and several important firm characteristics, such as ownership structure, probability of bankruptcy, performance, size, liquidity, trading volume. See, for example, Maloney and Mulherin (1992), Muscarella and Vetsuypens (1996), Falkenstein (1996), Angel (1997), Seguin and Smoller (1997), Schultz (2000), Gompers and Metrick (2001), Bradley et al. (2004), Dyl and Elliott (2006), and Fernando et al. (2012a).
2. See, for example, Booth and Chua (1996), Brennan and Franks (1997), Stoughton and Zechner (1998), and Mello and Parsons (1998).
3. Conroy et al. (1990), McInish and Wood (1992), and Stoll (2000) also provide evidence that stock splits are followed by an increase in trading costs and a reduction in market liquidity. Kadapakkam et al. (2005) document that lower-priced stocks have higher relative spreads even after decimalization, although the differences are lower in absolute terms. Moreover, the discussion and findings in Weld et al. (2009) and

Goldstein et al. (2009) suggest that despite the growth of discount brokerages, many brokers still charge fixed per-share commissions.
4. As noted by Gompers and Metrick (2001), institutional ownership of US stocks has grown dramatically over the past two decades. Brancato and Rabimov (2008) report that in 2005, institutional investors accounted for 61.2 percent of total US equity ownership and 67.9 percent of the ownership in the largest 1000 US firms.
5. See Frankel et al. (2006) and Ljungqvist et al. (2007) for further discussion of the influence of institutional investors on analyst performance, and Krigman et al. (1999), Wermers (2000), Cohen et al. (2002), Gibson et al. (2004), and Chen et al. (2011) for discussion of their superior information generating ability.
6. See, for example, Shleifer and Vishny (1986), McConnell and Servaes (1990), Smith (1996), Carleton et al. (1998), Gillan and Starks (2000), Allen et al. (2000), Hartzell and Starks (2003), Grinstein and Michaely (2005), and Boehmer and Kelley (2009) for a discussion of the benefits to a firm brought about by institutional ownership.
7. For the preference of institutions for higher priced stocks, see, for example, Falkenstein (1996), Gompers and Metrick (2001), and Fernando et al. (2004). For the relation between share price levels and firm value, see, for example, Seguin and Smoller (1997) and Fernando et al. (2004).
8. The benefits of institutional investment will vary widely across firms, depending on the extent and proprietary nature of firms' private information and the moral hazard problems associated with disclosing it (Brennan and Hughes, 1991), the cost of obtaining information through other channels (Diamond, 1985), the governance of the firm and the extent to which managerial behavior can be positively influenced by institutional investors (Denis and Serrano, 1996), and the costs incurred by firms due to institutional monitoring (Bushee, 1998).
9. See, for example, Badrinath et al. (1989) and Del Guercio (1996). Our argument here is similar to the 'ownership clientele' effect discussed by Allen et al. (2000), where higher quality firms attract relatively less-taxed institutional investors. As noted by Allen et al. (2000), such investors have a relative advantage in ensuring that the firms they invest in are well managed.
10. This model is derived from a similar model for seasoned stocks developed in Fernando et al. (2012b).
11. There is abundant evidence that investors invest only in a subset of all stocks. See, for example, Blume and Friend (1975), Kelly (1995), Barber and Odean (2000), Grinblatt and Keloharju (2001), and Goetzmann and Kumar (2008).
12. Our model can be extended to the case where institutional and retail investors have different risk preferences without qualitatively altering its main predictions. In the most plausible such extension – retail investors being more risk averse than institutional investors – the incentive for institutional investors to pay for analyst information will be further reduced since institutional investors' utility will not increase as much as the utility of retail investors from the reduction in risk ensuing from the information generated by analysts.
13. To avoid confusion and for brevity, we use the term 'analyst' to also include the 'broker' function, reflecting their dual (broker/analyst) role in the chapter and elsewhere – generating information and intermediating trades.
14. See Parrino et al. (2003).
15. All proofs are provided in the appendix to this chapter.
16. Because the mechanism by which IPO firms select an offer price is setting the number of shares outstanding, we pose the firm's optimization problem as one of selecting the number of shares rather than the IPO share price, noting that share price equals the firm's value divided by the number of shares outstanding.
17. These relations hold for positive firm value (Q_j^*) and positive number of shares outstanding (S_j^*).
18. For the general population of US firms, Gompers and Metrick (2001) find a positive relation between stock price performance and institutional ownership.

REFERENCES

Allen, F., A. Bernardo and I. Welch (2000), 'A theory of dividends based on tax clienteles', *Journal of Finance*, **55**, 2499–536.
Angel, J. (1997), 'Tick size, share price, and stock splits', *Journal of Finance*, **52**, 655–81.
Badrinath, S., G. Gay and J. Kale (1989), 'Patterns of institutional investment, prudence, and the managerial "safety-net" hypothesis', *Journal of Risk and Insurance*, **56**, 605–29.
Baker, K. and P. Gallagher (1980), 'Management's view of stock splits', *Financial Management*, **9**, 73–7.
Baker, K. and G. Powell (1993) 'Further evidence on managerial motives for stock splits', *Quarterly Journal of Business and Economics*, **32**, 20–31.

Barber, B. and T. Odean (2000), 'Trading is hazardous to your wealth: the common stock investment performance of individual investors', *Journal of Finance*, **55**, 773–806.
Blume, M.E. and I. Friend (1975), 'The asset structure of individual portfolios and some implications for utility functions', *Journal of Finance*, **30**, 585–603.
Boehmer, E. and E. Kelley (2009), 'Institutional investors and the informational efficiency of prices', *Review of Financial Studies*, **22**, 3563–94.
Booth, J. and L. Chua (1996), 'Ownership dispersion, costly information and IPO underpricing', *Journal of Financial Economics*, **41**, 291–310.
Bradley, D., J. Cooney, B. Jordan and A. Singh (2004), 'Negotiation and the IPO offer price: a comparison of integer vs. non-integer IPOs', *Journal of Financial and Quantitative Analysis*, **39**, 517–40.
Brancato, C. and S. Rabimov (2008), 'The 2008 institutional investment report', The Conference Board, New York.
Brau, J.C. and S.E. Fawcett (2006), 'Initial public offerings: an analysis of theory and practice', *Journal of Finance*, **61**, 399–436.
Brennan, M and J. Franks (1997), 'Underpricing, ownership and control in initial public offerings of equity securities in the UK', *Journal of Financial Economics*, **45**, 391–413.
Brennan, M. and P. Hughes (1991), 'Stock prices and the supply of information'. *Journal of Finance*, **46**, 1665–91.
Brennan, M. and A. Subrahmanyam (1996), 'Market microstructure and asset pricing: on the compensation for illiquidity in stock returns', *Journal of Financial Economics*, **41**, 441–64.
Bushee, B. (1998), 'The influence of institutional investors on myopic R&D investment behavior', *The Accounting Review*, **73**, 305–33.
Carleton, W., J. Nelson and M. Weisbach (1998), 'The influence of institutions on corporate governance through private negotiations: evidence from TIAA-CREF', *Journal of Finance*, **53**, 133–1362.
Chen, H., H. Nguyen and V. Singal (2011), 'The information content of stock splits', *Journal of Banking and Finance*, **35**, 2454–67.
Cohen, R., P. Gompers and T. Vuolteenaho (2002), 'Who underreacts to cash-flow news? Evidence from trading between individuals and institutions', *Journal of Financial Economics*, **66**, 409–62.
Conroy, R., R. Harris and B. Benet (1990), 'The effects of stock splits on bid-ask spreads', *Journal of Finance*, **45**, 1285–95.
Cornett, M., A. Marcus, A. Saunders and H. Tehranian (2007), 'The impact of institutional ownership on corporate operating performance', *Journal of Banking and Finance*, **31**, 1771–94.
D'Mello, R., O. Tawatnuntachai and D. Yaman (2003), 'Why do firms issue equity after splitting stocks?', *Financial Review*, **38**, 323–50.
Del Guercio, D. (1996), 'The distorting effect of the prudent-man laws on institutional equity investments', *Journal of Financial Economics*, **40**, 31–62.
Denis, D., J. Serrano (1996), 'Active investors and management turnover following unsuccessful control contests', *Journal of Financial Economics*, **40**, 239–66.
Diamond, D. (1985), 'Optimal release of information by firms', *Journal of Finance*, **40**, 1071–94.
Dyl, E. and W. Elliott (2006), 'The share price puzzle', *Journal of Business*, **79**, 2045–66.
Falkenstein, E. (1996), 'Preferences for stock characteristics as revealed by mutual fund portfolio holdings', *Journal of Finance*, **51**, 111–35.
Fama, E. and K. French (1997), 'Industry costs of equity', *Journal of Financial Economics*, **43**, 153–93.
Fernando, C.S., V.A. Gatchev and P.A. Spindt (2005), 'Wanna dance? How firms and underwriters choose each other', *Journal of Finance*, **60**, 2437–69.
Fernando, C.S., V.A. Gatchev and P.A. Spindt (2012a), 'Institutional ownership, analyst following, and share prices', *Journal of Banking & Finance*, **36**, 2175–89.
Fernando, C.S., S. Krishnamurthy and P.A. Spindt (1999), 'Is share price related to marketability? Evidence from open-end mutual fund share splits', *Financial Management*, **28**, 15–31.
Fernando, C.S., S. Krishnamurthy and P.A. Spindt (2004), 'Are share price levels informative? Evidence from the ownership, pricing, turnover and performance of IPO firms', *Journal of Financial Markets*, **7**, 377–403.
Fernando, C.S., A. May and W.L. Megginson (2012b), 'The value of investment banking relationships: evidence from the collapse of Lehman Brothers', *Journal of Finance*, **67**, 235–70.
Frankel, R., S. Kothari and J. Weber (2006), 'Determinants of the informativeness of analyst research', *Journal of Accounting and Economics*, **41**, 29–54.
Gibson, S., A. Safieddine and R. Sonti (2004), 'Smart investments by smart money: Evidence from seasoned equity offerings', *Journal of Financial Economics*, **72**, 581–604.
Gillan, S. and L. Starks (2000), 'Corporate governance proposals and shareholder activism: the role of institutional investors', *Journal of Financial Economics*, **57**, 275–305.
Goetzmann, W. and A. Kumar (2008), 'Equity portfolio diversification', *Review of Finance*, **12**, 433–63.

Goldstein, M., P. Irvine, E. Kandel and Z. Wiener (2009), 'Brokerage commissions and institutional trading patterns', *Review of Financial Studies*, **22**, 5175–212.
Gompers, P. and A. Metrick (2001), 'Institutional investors and equity prices', *Quarterly Journal of Economics*, **116**, 229–59.
Gompers, P., J. Ishii and A. Metrick (2003), 'Corporate governance and equity prices', *Quarterly Journal of Economics*, **118**, 107–55.
Grinblatt, M. and M. Keloharju (2001), 'How distance, language, and culture influence stockholdings and trades', *Journal of Finance*, **56**, 1053–73.
Grinstein, Y. and R. Michaely (2005), 'Institutional holdings and payout policy', *Journal of Finance*, **60**, 1389–426.
Hartzell, J. and L. Starks (2003), 'Institutional investors and executive compensation', *Journal of Finance*, **58**, 2351–74.
James, C. and J. Karceski (2006), 'Investor monitoring and differences in mutual fund performance', *Journal of Banking and Finance*, **30**, 2787–808.
Kadapakkam, P., S. Krishnamurthy and Y. Tse (2005), 'Stock splits, broker promotion, and decimalization', *Journal of Financial and Quantitative Analysis*, **40**, 873–95.
Kaplan, S. and L. Zingales (1997), 'Do investment-cash flow sensitivities provide useful measures of financing constraints?', *Quarterly Journal of Economics*, **112**, 169–215.
Kelly, M. (1995), 'All their eggs in one basket: portfolio diversification of US households', *Journal of Economic Behavior and Organization*, **27**, 87–96.
Krigman, L., W. Shaw and K. Womack (1999), 'The persistence of IPO mispricing and the predictive power of flipping', *Journal of Finance*, **54**, 1015–44.
Lang, L. and R. Stulz (1994), 'Tobin's Q, corporate diversification, and firm performance', *Journal of Political Economy*, **102**, 1248–80.
Ljungqvist, A., F. Marston, L. Starks, K. Wei and H. Yan (2007), 'Conflicts of interest in sell-side research and the moderating role of institutional investors', *Journal of Financial Economics*, **85**, 420–56.
Maloney, M. and J. Mulherin (1992), 'The effects of splitting on the ex: a microstructure reconciliation', *Financial Management*, **21**, 44–59.
McConnell, J. and H. Servaes (1990), 'Additional evidence on equity ownership and corporate value', *Journal of Financial Economics*, **27**, 595–612.
McInish, T. and R. Wood (1992), 'An analysis of intraday patterns in bid/ask spreads for NYSE stocks', *Journal of Finance* **47**, 753–64.
Megginson, W.L. and V.A. Weiss (1991), 'Venture capitalist certification in initial public offerings', *Journal of Finance*, **46**, 879–903.
Mello, A. and J. Parsons (1998), 'Going public and the ownership structure of the firm', *Journal of Financial Economics*, **49**, 79–109.
Merton, R. (1987), 'A simple model of capital market equilibrium with incomplete information', *Journal of Finance*, **42**, 483–510.
Muscarella, C. and M. Vetsuypens (1996), 'Stock splits: signaling or liquidity? The case of ADR "solo-splits"', *Journal of Financial Economics*, **42**, 3–26.
Parrino, R., R. Sias and L. Starks (2003), 'Voting with their feet: institutional ownership changes around forced CEO turnover', *Journal of Financial Economics*, **68**, 3–46.
Petersen, M. (2009), Estimating standard errors in finance panel data sets: comparing approaches', *Review of Financial Studies*, **22**, 435–80.
Ruiz-Mallorquí, M. and D. Santana-Martín (2011), 'Dominant institutional owners and firm value', *Journal of Banking and Finance*, **35**, 118–29.
Schultz, P. (2000), 'Stock splits, tick size, and sponsorship', *Journal of Finance*, **55**, 429–50.
Seguin, P. and M. Smoller (1997), 'Share price and mortality: an empirical evaluation of newly listed Nasdaq stocks', *Journal of Financial Economics*, **45**, 333–63.
Shleifer, A. and R. Vishny (1986), 'Large shareholders and corporate control', *Journal of Political Economy*, **94**, 461–88.
Smith, M. (1996), 'Shareholder activism by institutional investors: evidence from CALPERS', *Journal of Finance*, **51**, 227–52.
Stoll, H., (2000), 'Friction', *Journal of Finance*, **55**, 1479–514.
Stoll, H. and R. Whaley (1983), 'Transactions costs and the small firm effect', *Journal of Financial Economics*, **12**, 57–80.
Stoughton, N. and J. Zechner (1998), 'IPO mechanisms, monitoring and ownership structure', *Journal of Financial Economics*, **49**, 45–78.
Weld, W., R. Michaely, R. Thaler and S. Benartzi (2009), 'The nominal price puzzle', *Journal of Economic Perspectives*, **23**, 121–42.
Wermers, R. (2000), 'Mutual fund performance: an empirical decomposition into stock-picking talent, style, transactions costs, and expenses', *Journal of Finance*, **55**, 1655–703.

APPENDIX: MATHEMATICAL PROOFS

Proof of Proposition 1: The first order condition for institutional investors is:

$$\mu_j - Q_j - cS_j - \left[\frac{\gamma X_{Ij}(2 + m_j 2\alpha_j X_{Ij})}{2(1 + m_j 2\alpha_j X_{Ij})^2 (h_j + S_j h_S)}\right] = 0 \quad (5A.1)$$

and the first order condition for retail investors is:

$$\mu_j - Q_j - cS_j - \left[\frac{\gamma X_{Rj}}{(1 + m_j 2\alpha_j X_{Ij})(h_j + S_j h_S)}\right] = 0 \quad (5A.2)$$

The market clearing condition for any firm j is:

$$\theta_{Ij} + \theta_{Rj} = 1 \quad (5A.3)$$

Furthermore, by definition we have that:

$$\theta_{Ij} = 2\alpha_j X_{Ij} \quad (5A.4)$$

$$\theta_{Rj} = 2(1 - \alpha_j) X_{Rj} \quad (5A.5)$$

Substituting (5A.3), (5A.4), and (5A.5) into (5A.1) and (5A.2), and solving (5A.1) and (5A.2) for Q_j we get:

$$Q_j = \mu_j - cS_j - \left[\frac{\gamma \theta_{Ij}(2 + m_j \theta_{Ij})}{4\alpha_j(1 + m_j \theta_{Ij})^2 (h_j + S_j h_S)}\right] \quad (5A.6)$$

and

$$Q_j = \mu_j - cS_j - \left[\frac{\gamma(1 - \theta_{Ij})}{2(1 - \alpha_j)(1 + m_j \theta_{Ij})(h_j + S_j h_S)}\right] \quad (5A.7)$$

Equating (5A.6) and (5A.7) and then simplifying and solving the resulting expression yields the following two solutions for θ_{Ij}:

$$\theta_{Ij} = \left(\alpha_j + \frac{\sqrt{1 + \alpha_j^2 m_j(2 + m_j)} - (1 + \alpha_j^2 m_j)}{(1 + \alpha_j)m_j}, \alpha_j - \frac{\sqrt{1 + \alpha_j^2 m_j(2 + m_j)} + (1 + \alpha_j^2 m_j)}{(1 + \alpha_j)m_j}\right) \quad (5A.8)$$

The corresponding two solutions for θ_{Rj} become:

$$\theta_{Rj} = \left(1 - \alpha_j - \frac{\sqrt{1 + \alpha_j^2 m_j(2 + m_j)} - (1 + \alpha_j^2 m_j)}{(1 + \alpha_j)m_j}, 1 - \alpha_j + \frac{\sqrt{1 + \alpha_j^2 m_j(2 + m_j)} + (1 + \alpha_j^2 m_j)}{(1 + \alpha_j)m_j}\right) \quad (5A.9)$$

IPO offer price selection 123

However, only the first solution in each case satisfies the second order conditions for institutional and retail investors, which permits us to eliminate the second solution. QED.

Proof of Lemma 1: From (5A.7) we have that:

$$Q_j = \mu_j - cS_j - \left[\frac{\gamma(1-\theta_{Ij})}{2(1-\alpha_j)(1+m_j\theta_{Ij})(h_j + S_j h_S)}\right]$$

$$= \mu_j - cS_j - \left[\frac{\gamma}{(h_j + S_j h_S)} \frac{(1-\theta_{Ij})}{2(1-\alpha_j)(1+m_j\theta_{Ij})}\right] \quad (5A.10)$$

Substituting for θ_{Ij} and simplifying, we get:

$$Q_j = \mu_j - cS_j - \frac{\gamma}{(h_j + S_j h_S)}\Gamma_1(m_j), \quad (5A.11a)$$

where

$$\Gamma_1(m_j) = \frac{(1+m_j)\sqrt{1+\alpha_j^2 m_j(2+m_j)} - (1+\alpha_j m_j(2+m_j))}{2m_j(1-\alpha_j)^2}. \quad (5A.11b)$$

QED.

Proof of Proposition 2: The first order condition for Q_j (5A.11a) with respect to S_j is:

$$\frac{\gamma h_S}{(h_j + S_j h_S)^2}\Gamma_1(m_j) - c = 0 \quad (5A.12)$$

Solving for S_j yields two solutions,

$$S_j^* = -\left(\frac{\sqrt{\frac{\gamma\Gamma_1(m_j)}{ch_S}} + \frac{h_j}{h_S}}{\sqrt{\frac{\gamma\Gamma_1(m_j)}{ch_S}} - \frac{h_j}{h_S}}\right) \quad (5A.13)$$

The first solution does not satisfy the second order condition for maximizing the market value of the firm. QED.

6 The Canadian junior IPO market and the Capital Pool Company program
J. Ari Pandes and Michael J. Robinson

1 INTRODUCTION

Entrepreneurial firms are an important engine of growth in most developed economies, and fostering the development of smaller growth firms is an important economic objective. To develop their businesses, entrepreneurs need access to capital, and the debt market is often difficult to access since young firms lack the cash flows and collateral required by lenders. Thus, until a firm has grown to a certain size the entrepreneur must rely on equity capital, which is also difficult to attract due to the high costs of information asymmetry and the agency costs that exist between the entrepreneurs, management, and investors. A substantial body of academic research documents the important role that venture capital (VC) and private equity (PE) investors play in financing entrepreneurial firms.[1] Since these formal investors are specialized investors, they can alleviate the information gaps and costs that are prevalent in the private market. Specifically, VC and PE investors use their expertise to screen, advise, and monitor the entrepreneurial firms. However, only a small fraction of firms can attract VC and PE financing, and some firms might be averse to the strict oversight that accompanies such investment. Angel investors are another source of financing for entrepreneurial firms, but the amount of investment available from an angel investor tends to be lower than from a VC or PE investor in part because it is more difficult for an angel investor to alleviate the costs of information asymmetry and other agency issues.

To expand the pool of equity capital for entrepreneurial firms, many countries have created specialized stock markets that are devoted mainly to the financing of smaller growth companies. These junior, second-tier, stock exchanges apply less stringent listing rules and often do not require firms to demonstrate profitability. However, many of the companies listed on these exchanges are not early stage, and many are venture backed when they go public. Vismara et al. (2012) provide insight into Europe's second-tier markets, which focus on small company listings. Specifically, the authors examine the stock exchanges of the four largest European economics (Germany, France, Italy, and the UK) and note that these exchanges have launched 11 second-tier markets since 1995. Remarkably, only five currently exist. Moreover, the NASDAQ also set up a European market in the late 1990s, which ultimately failed to attract many listings. The recent high failure rate of junior equity markets in Europe suggests that they are prone to fail, for a number of reasons identified in earlier work by MacIntosh (1994) and Rasch (1994). Interestingly, however, Canada has a thriving public venture market that is one of the oldest and largest in the world. For over 100 years, the Toronto Stock Exchange's Venture Market (TSX-V) – the junior exchange of the senior Toronto Stock Exchange (TSX) – and its predecessor exchanges have facilitated the growth of early-stage companies by providing access to capital that is relatively liquid, while also offering institutional and retail investors a well-regulated market for making venture investments that have traditionally been exclusive to specialized VC or PE firms.

A particularly unique feature of the TSX-V is the Capital Pool Company (CPC) program, which is essentially a reverse merger listing vehicle for small-cap companies. The program marries experienced investors (with public markets experience) with private companies seeking capital by dividing the traditional IPO process in two: the creation of the CPC public vehicle shell and the qualifying transaction (QT), that is, the reverse merger or vending of the operating business into the CPC shell. From its inception as a regional development program in the province of Alberta in 1986, the CPC program has expanded across Canada and in recent years has increasingly attracted international listings. A notable example is the US firm ePals Corporation, an education technology and safe learning network firm with a savvy management team and strategic partnerships with leading US firms including Microsoft and IBM, which used the CPC program to go public in the summer of 2011. The CPC program is similar in concept to the US blind-pool programs that experienced a high degree of fraud in the 1980s. However, unlike in the US, the regulations and governance controls adopted in Canada mitigated much of the agency costs and fraud associated with this type of program. Indeed, the US has now adopted many of the features of the Canadian CPC program in what are now known as special purpose acquisition corporations (SPACs). A fundamental difference, however, between the US SPACs and the Canadian CPCs is that the latter is typically used by earlier stage companies in Canada on the TSX-V, whereas SPACs are used by later stage and larger companies listed on the senior US exchanges.

Since its inception in 1986 until 2010, 2090 CPCs[2] have been listed on the TSX-V with over 90 percent completing their QT, and 300 graduating to a more senior exchange – primarily the TSX. The growth of the Canadian CPC program is remarkable in light of the fact that the US blind pool market essentially disappeared following the adoption of strict regulations by the US Securities Exchange Commission (SEC), which passed the Securities Enforcement Remedies and Penny Stock Reform Act on 20 July, 1990.

This chapter describes the Canadian junior market (that is, the TSX-V) and how it has helped emerging private companies finance their growth opportunities through a going-public transaction. We present summary statistics for all TSX-V initial public offerings (IPOs) and show that the number of junior market IPOs in Canada is substantially larger than the number of IPOs in other comparable markets internationally, although the average IPO size is significantly smaller on the TSX-V compared to other international junior markets. We further show that large investment banks from the senior TSX exchange league tables are active participants in the junior market, which helps reduce the information and agency costs that are generally associated with early-stage companies. In addition, to highlight the unique characteristics of the CPC program, and also because CPC firms comprise the majority of all TSX-V IPOs, we examine this program in more detail. In particular, we show that CPC firms exhibit no more fraud than firms in other comparable markets, and that the majority of CPCs grow to become successful public firms. The objective of this chapter is not to provide a rigorous empirical analysis, but instead to provide a more descriptive summary of the Canadian junior IPO market and to highlight the size, scope, and longevity of the market.

2 THE CANADIAN JUNIOR MARKET

2.1 A Brief Background

The junior equity market in Canada has a rich history built on the success of regional stock exchanges that had specific expertise. The three main regional exchanges were the Alberta Stock Exchange (ASE), the Vancouver Stock Exchange (VSE), and the Winnipeg Stock Exchange (WSE), all of which began operations in the early twentieth century.[3] In 1999, the Canadian Venture Exchange (CDNX) was created by the merger of the Vancouver Stock Exchange and the Alberta Stock Exchange. The focus of the CDNX was junior companies, often resource and mining exploration companies, but also technology ventures. The Winnipeg Stock Exchange and the small-cap portion of the equities market of the Montreal Stock Exchange (MSE) were also later merged into the CDNX. In 2001, the Toronto Stock Exchange – specifically, the TSX Group – purchased the CDNX and renamed it as the TSX Venture Exchange (TSX-V). Thus, today the TSX is the senior Canadian equity market, while the TSX-V is a public venture capital marketplace for emerging companies.

An important difference between the TSX-V and the second markets in Europe, such as the Alternative Investment Market (AIM), Alternext by Euronext, the Freiverkehr in Germany, and the Mercato Alternativo dei Capitali (MAC) in Italy, are the different approaches to regulation.[4] The second markets in Europe are exchange regulated, meaning that specific requirements do not have to be met by companies seeking admission. More specifically, admission to the junior exchange requires that the company seeking admission appoints a Nominated Advisor (or Nomad) and a broker. The role of the Nomad is to assess whether the company is suitable for the market, and thus admission to an exchange ultimately rests on the analysis made by the Nomad. In contrast, Canadian stock exchanges, including the TSX-V, are regulated by the provincial securities regulator(s) (equivalent of the US Securities and Exchange Commission). Therefore, detailed requirements on market capitalization, public float, capital structure, and governance, must be met by companies seeking a listing. In addition to admission requirements, the TSX-V imposes stricter ongoing filing requirements compared to their European counterparts. This is perhaps why most of the IPOs on the exchange-regulated markets in Europe are offered exclusively to institutional investors, equivalent to private placements, as noted by Vismara et al. (2012). In contrast, retail investors regularly participate in junior IPOs and follow-on offerings in Canada.

2.2 Capital Pool Company Program

As discussed above, the majority of TSX-V IPOs are CPCs and so it is worthwhile examining this program in more detail. On the surface, the CPC program of the TSX-V[5] is similar to US blind-pool programs that were subject to a number of frauds during the 1980s. The program allows a newly created private company, which has no assets other than cash and no commercial operations, to conduct an initial public offering in order to raise start-up capital and list its securities for trading on the TSX-V. Once the initial public offering is completed, the CPC then has 24 months to identify and acquire a business or pool of assets using the funds raised from the distribution of its seed shares and from the IPO. The acquisition is called a 'qualifying transaction', and the exchange requires that following the QT, the resulting issuer must meet the TSX-V's applicable minimum listing requirements.

The CPC program had its genesis in a blind-pool program on the Alberta Stock Exchange (ASE) in 1986, at a time when falling energy prices had caused traditional financing to dry up for the junior energy firms, which formed an important part of the province's economic base. Between April and July of that year a small regional investment dealer took seven firms public as blind pools. Unfortunately, the principals of the second such firm, Audit Resources Inc., engaged in fraudulent trading practices that increased the firm's share price from $0.05 to $8.00 over a few months before regulators intervened and the fraud was discovered. Not only did investors lose money, but employees of the investment dealer got caught up in the fraudulent dealings and the investment dealer was permanently shut down later that year. By the time these problems with the program became apparent to the securities regulator, the Alberta Securities Commission (ASC), a further 14 blind pools had gone public. As will be shown below, almost 20 percent of these early Canadian blind pools were investigated for fraud during the first eight months of the program's existence and in half of the cases the firm's principals were found guilty of fraudulent behavior. In addition, only seven of the 21 (33.3 percent) blind pools turned into successful firms.

As a result of these early problems, the ASC placed a moratorium on new blind-pool stock offerings in October 1986 until the program could be reviewed. In November 1986, after a series of public hearings, the moratorium on blind pools was lifted, and a new set of regulations governing this form of financing were imposed. Importantly, the ASC and ASE borrowed VC control mechanisms to ensure the protection of outside investors' capital, and to provide the founders with a strong incentive to create value in the firm for all shareholders. The main governance mechanisms include: (1) escrow provisions for the firm's founders, which removes the incentive for short-term share price manipulation and early founder exit; (2) limits on the use of the firm's capital by the founders to prevent the misuse of corporate resources; (3) a veto provided to the outside shareholders over the use of proceeds to prevent investment in negative net present value (NPV) projects; and (4) a requirement to initiate a QT within a predefined time period to prevent shirking. Other regulations – some based on the VC diversification model – were designed to enhance secondary market liquidity. For example, each CPC is required to have a minimum of 200 arm's length shareholders, each of whom must purchase at least 1000 shares, and no one purchaser can buy more than 2 percent of the IPO shares. Finally, it was not a requirement of the regulations, but many underwriters provide secondary market support to a new CPC issue to enhance its trading liquidity for a short period following its IPO.

One key aspect of the long-term success of the CPC program has been the careful ongoing monitoring of the program's effectiveness and timely modifications to the regulations by the regulators and the stock exchange. For example, as the program was adopted by different jurisdictions across the country,[6] the maximum amount of post-IPO capital (that is, the sum of the seed and IPO capital) has been increased several times. From an initial value of $0.5 million, it was raised to $0.7 million on 1 March 2000, to $2.0 million on 15 January 2003, and to $5.0 million on 14 June 2010. As larger deals may take longer to complete, the CPC program increased the maximum time to complete a QT from 18 months to 24 months on 13 April 2005. Finally, to further increase the incentive of firm founders to complete a QT, the rule changes on 1 March 2000 required that all escrowed seed shares be cancelled if the firm was delisted before completing its QT.

3 DATA AND DESCRIPTIVE STATISTICS

Data on TSX-V IPOs are collected from the Financial Post (FP) Infomart database for the period 1 January 1993 to 31 December 2010. The FP database includes detailed offer characteristics, such as the offer price, the size of the offering, the book-runners in the offering, and the industry Standard Industrial Classification (SIC) code. In Table 6.1 we provide a yearly breakdown of the number of IPO offerings and IPO proceeds. We present the statistics for all IPOs, regular TSX-V IPOs, and for CPC IPOs. While there is variation in the number of offerings through time, with marked drops during the 1993

Table 6.1 Yearly number of IPOs and aggregate proceeds on the TSX Venture Exchange

	Total		Regular IPO		CPC IPO	
	N	Proceeds (MM$)	N	Proceeds (MM$)	N	Proceeds (MM$)
1993	110	152.09	54	141.14	56	10.95
1994	166	102.25	67	78.56	99	23.69
1995	152	128.24	61	105.85	91	22.38
1996	170	436.77	72	412.28	98	24.49
1997	264	219.77	119	183.18	145	36.60
1998	184	124.41	61	93.73	123	30.69
1999	142	111.71	43	83.78	99	27.93
2000	167	139.45	38	100.32	129	39.13
2001	124	83.08	19	47.26	105	35.82
2002	63	35.02	19	18.23	44	16.79
2003	52	72.64	23	55.31	29	17.33
2004	110	140.06	23	64.35	87	75.72
2005	123	150.07	38	93.26	85	56.81
2006	152	232.08	50	176.63	102	55.45
2007	239	436.15	58	350.51	181	85.64
2008	194	185.06	42	125.80	152	59.26
2009	74	77.64	22	58.41	52	19.23
2010	143	273.96	45	231.13	98	42.83
Total	2629	3100.46	854	2419.71	1775	680.75

Notes:
This table presents the yearly number of IPOs, which comprise regular IPOs and CPC IPOs, and the yearly aggregate proceeds from the IPOs on the TSX Venture Exchange (TSX-V) during the sample period, 1993–2010.
The data are collected from the Financial Post (FP) Infomart database.
N is the number of IPOs and Proceeds (MM$) is the aggregate IPO gross proceeds in millions of Canadian dollars.

Table 6.2 TSX Venture IPOs compared to European second market IPOs

	TSX-V	Reproduced from Vismara et al. (2012)			
		Paris B./Euronext	Deutsche Borse	Borsa Italiana	London
Panel A: Number of IPOs					
1995–97	586	121	22	1	175
1998–2000	493	324	328	37	274
2001–03	239	87	20	5	218
2004–06	385	102	49	15	786
2007–09	507	91	42	24	189
1995–2009	2210	725	461	82	1642
Panel B: Mean (median) IPO proceeds					
Commission-reg	1.16 (0.35)				
Seasoning		20.41 (11.14)	58.77 (32.79)	44.85 (27.84)	
New		29.08 (17.17)	99.44 (58.15)	169.66 (66.81)	
Exchange-reg		48.10 (2.32)	22.89 (15.47)	13.61 (13.15)	22.58 (10.67)

Notes:
This table compares the number of IPOs and the mean and median IPO proceeds on the TSX Venture Exchange (TSX-V) to the corresponding statistics reproduced from Vismara et al. (2012).
Panel A presents the number of IPOs for select time periods as in Vismara et al. (2012), and Panel B presents the mean (median) IPO proceeds for the different types of junior markets as defined in Vismara et al. (2012) for the period 1995–2009.
'Commission-reg' refers to a market that is regulated by the securities commission, which refers to the TSX-V in our sample.
'Seasoning' refers to the sequential segmentation model as defined in Vismara et al. (2012), for which small companies are expected to go public on a second-tier 'seasoning' market and, if the company is successful, move to the main market.
'New' refers to the sectorial exchange that only allowed admission to companies in the high-technology sector.
'Exchange-reg' refers to an exchange-regulated market as defined in Vismara et al. (2012), of which London's Alternative Investment Market is most commonly associated with.
In an exchange regulated market, the national listing authorities (equivalent to the US Securities and Exchange Commission) does not regulate the market.
The IPO proceeds from Vismara et al. (2012) are converted from euros to Canadian dollars at the average exchange rate in the respective year.

economic downturn and the post-Internet bubble downturn, 2002–04, the number of junior market IPOs has shown significant activity. Over the entire 1993–2010 sample period, there have been 2629 IPOs on the TSX-V, raising a total of $3.10 billion in proceeds. The sample comprises 854 regular IPOs and 1775 CPC IPOs, indicating the popularity of the CPC program in the Canadian junior market. The aggregate proceeds raised from regular IPOs during the sample period is $2.42 billion, while the aggregate proceeds raised from CPC IPOs is a substantially lower $680.75 million. This is consistent with the regulatory restrictions on the amount of proceeds raised in CPC IPOs, which as noted above has increased over time.

Table 6.2 compares the TSX-V with the second markets in Europe. To draw the comparison, we reproduce the statistics on the number of IPOs from Table 6.2 in Vismara et al. (2012) and the statistics on IPO proceeds from Table 6.3 in Vismara et al. (2012). To be consistent with Vismara et al. (2012), we have included – from their tables – statistics

Table 6.3 Industry distribution of the frequency and aggregate proceeds of TSX Venture Exchange IPOs

Industry	N	Proceeds (MM$)
Agriculture	1	0.45
Food products	3	3.23
Candy and soda	3	3.77
Beer and liquor	4	19.55
Tobacco products	–	–
Recreation	6	9.86
Entertainment	11	40.52
Printing and publishing	1	0.68
Consumer goods	3	4.01
Apparel	3	40.18
Healthcare	2	3.00
Medical equipment	11	28.00
Pharmaceutical products	28	134.33
Chemicals	3	5.79
Rubber and plastic products	3	3.59
Textiles	1	0.25
Construction materials	5	21.29
Construction	6	9.35
Steel works	2	5.38
Fabricated products	–	–
Machinery	11	18.12
Electrical equipment	1	35.00
Automobiles and trucks	2	2.02
Aircraft	1	0.90
Shipbuilding and railroad equipment	–	–
Defense	–	–
Precious metals	9	279.14
Non-metallic and industrial metal mining	413	797.82
Coal	–	–
Petroleum and natural gas	105	452.57
Utilities	4	12.43
Communication	10	35.04
Personal services	6	6.84
Business services	31	79.54
Computer hardware	7	11.33
Computer software	64	157.46
Electronic equipment	17	37.93
Measuring and control equipment	15	37.63
Business supplies	–	–
Shipping containers	–	–
Transportation	7	11.43
Wholesale	16	37.65
Retail	7	13.70
Restaurants, hotels and motels	–	–
Banking	3	3.50

Table 6.3 (continued)

Industry	N	Proceeds (MM$)
Insurance	3	8.44
Real estate	2	0.75
Trading	10	18.44
Other	14	28.82

Notes:
This table presents an industry distribution of TSX Venture Exchange (TSX-V) regular IPOs, that is, it does not include CPC IPOs.
Industry definitions are available on Professor Kenneth French's website.
N is the number of IPOs and Proceeds (MM$) is the aggregate IPO gross proceeds in millions of Canadian dollars.

on the different segmentation models that have existed in Europe over their sample period (1995–2009). In Table 6.2 we also restrict our sample period to 1995–2009, which is the same sample period used by Vismara et al. (2012), and we also convert their statistics on proceeds from euros to Canadian dollars. Panel A presents the number of IPOs and Panel B presents the mean (median) IPO proceeds.

The results in Table 6.2 are quite striking; Panel A shows that the number of IPOs on the TSX-V outnumber the number of IPOs in each of the four European countries examined by Vismara et al. (2012). Over the 1995–2009 period, TSX-V IPOs outnumber the Paris B/Euronext IPOs by 3.05×, the Deutsche Borse by 4.79×, the Borsa Italiana by 26.95×, and the London AIM by 1.35×. The results in Panel B are also telling; the mean proceeds for an IPO on the TSX-V is $1.16 million, and the median proceeds is $0.35 million. Of course, this includes both regular IPOs and CPC IPOs. While not reported in Table 6.2, we find the mean (median) proceeds for regular IPOs is $2.86 million ($1.13 million) and the mean (median) proceeds for CPC IPOs is $0.40 million ($0.30 million). Nevertheless, these values are significantly lower than the mean and median proceeds on each of the European second markets. In particular, the mean IPO proceeds on the Paris B/Euronext ranges from $20.41 million to $48.10 million depending on whether the market is seasoning, new, or exchange regulated. The median IPO proceeds ranges from $2.32 million to 11.14 million, depending on the market. For the Deutsche Borse, the mean IPO proceeds ranges from $22.89 million to $58.77 million and the median proceeds ranges from $15.47 million to $32.79 million, depending on the market. The Borsa Italiana also exhibits higher mean and median IPO proceeds compared to the TSX-V, with the mean proceeds ranging from $13.61 million to $44.85 million and the median proceeds ranging from $13.15 million to $27.84 million, depending on the market. Finally, the mean IPO proceeds on the London AIM market is $22.58 million and the median IPO proceeds is $10.67 million. Therefore, the Panel B results suggest that the TSX-V attracts companies that are much earlier in their development stage, which is consistent with a public venture market. In contrast, the European second markets appear to be tailored more for later stage companies, and as pointed out by Vismara et al. (2012), many of the companies listed on the European junior markets are venture-backed, which is not the case for TSX-V IPOs. Interestingly, many of the companies on the European second markets resemble the small-cap stocks on the senior TSX Exchange.

In Table 6.3 we provide an industry breakdown of the frequency and aggregate proceeds of TSX-V regular IPOs.[7] The industry of CPCs is only known at the time of the QT, and thus we do not know the industry of a CPC at the IPO.[8] Not surprisingly, given the mining and resource focus of the Canadian economy, 413 of the 854 IPOs (about 48.36 percent) are in the non-metallic and industrial metal mining industry. The second largest industry is the petroleum and natural gas sector, with 105 IPOs (about 12.30 percent). However, the junior market does not only attract mining and resource companies. In particular, the third, fourth and fifth most frequent IPOs are in the computer software, business services, and pharmaceutical products industries, respectively. We find a similar pattern in terms of proceeds, which are quite substantial in dollar terms. During our sample period (1993–2010), the non-metallic and industrial metal mining sector raised a non-trivial $797.82 million on the junior exchange. Interestingly, while the precious metals sector only had nine IPOs during the sample period, the proceeds are $279.14 million. Furthermore, the petroleum and natural gas sector raised $452.57 million, while the computer software sector raised $157.46 million.

One of the main challenges facing the success of a public venture market is attracting large and reputable underwriters to participate in junior equity issues, which is especially important since information and agency costs are so severe in this market. For example, several papers show that prestigious underwriters avoid the smaller and riskier new issues (for example, Beatty and Welch, 1996; Chemmanur and Fulghieri, 1994; Wolfe et al. 1994; Carter and Manaster, 1990) for several reasons. First, underwriters have reputational concerns, since they earn a return on built-up reputational capital. Second, the underwriting commission is typically a function of the issue size and larger underwriting firms are incentivized to participate in only the larger IPOs. Finally, as Rasch (1994) further notes, the low stock turnover of the smaller firms makes it unprofitable for brokerage firms to research these companies, since the costs associated with collecting and processing a firm's information is not recovered by brokerage commissions. Therefore, attracting high-quality underwriters is important to the success of a junior equity market.

In Table 6.4 we examine the underwriters participating in TSX-V IPOs. We assume that underwriters that are book-runners in the equity offerings of companies listed on the senior TSX exchange are larger and more reputable. Thus, we determine the underwriter rank from the league tables of underwriters participating in equity offerings on the senior TSX market. In Panel A we examine the number of IPOs underwritten by the 'Top 10' underwriters, the 'Top 20' underwriters, by underwriters appearing on the league tables ('On league'), and underwriters that do not appear on the league tables ('Off league'). In Panels B and C we examine the same categories but our variables of interest are the mean (median) IPO proceeds and mean (median) underwriter commission, respectively.

Focusing on Panel A, we find that 88, or 10.30 percent, of the regular IPOs are underwritten by investment banks that are among the ten largest on the senior TSX exchange, implying that there are some large underwriters from the TSX that are underwriting IPOs on the junior market. When we broaden the underwriter rank definition, we find that this number increases, where 287, or 33.61 percent, of the regular IPOs are underwritten by the largest 20 investment banks from the TSX league tables. We further find that 524, or 61.36 percent – well over half – of the regular IPOs are underwritten by an investment bank that at least appears on the league tables from the senior TSX market. Interestingly, when we turn to the CPC IPOs, which are perhaps the riskiest and certainly

Table 6.4   Underwriter characteristics of TSX Venture Exchange IPOs

	Regular IPOs	CPC IPOs
Panel A: Number (percent) of IPOs		
Top 10	88 (10.30)	182 (10.25)
Top 20	287 (33.61)	682 (38.42)
On league table	524 (61.36)	1241 (69.92)
Off league table	330 (38.64)	534 (30.08)
Total	854	1775
Panel B: Mean (median) proceeds ($MM)		
Top 10	5.59 (2.00)	0.52 (0.40)
Top 20	3.74 (1.28)	0.41 (0.30)
On league table	3.72 (1.26)	0.39 (0.30)
Off league table	1.43 (0.96)	0.37 (0.30)
Total	2.83 (1.07)	0.38 (0.30)
Panel C: Mean (median) commission (percent)		
Top 10	7.70 (8.00)	9.71 (10.00)
Top 20	8.55 (8.00)	9.81 (10.00)
On league table	8.59 (8.00)	9.83 (10.00)
Off league table	9.36 (10.00)	9.84 (10.00)
Total	8.88 (8.65)	9.84 (10.00)

Notes:
This table presents the number (percent) of IPOs in Panel A, the mean (median) IPO gross proceeds in Panel B, and the mean (median) underwriter commission in Panel C for regular IPOs and CPC IPOs for various underwriter rank classifications and for the full sample.
'Top 10' refers to the top ten underwriters from the TSX league tables of equity offerings.
'Top 20' refers to the top 20 underwriters from the TSX league tables of equity offerings.
'On league table' refers to an underwriter that appears on the TSX league tables of equity offerings.
'Off league table' refers to an underwriter that does not appear on the TSX league tables of equity offerings.
'Total' refers to the full sample.

the smallest IPOs, participation from the more reputable underwriters is just as high or even slightly greater than for the regular TSX-V IPOs. In particular, 182, or 10.25 percent of the CPC IPOs are taken public by an underwriter that ranks in the top ten from the TSX league tables; 682, or 38.42 percent of the CPC IPOs are taken public by an underwriter that ranks in the top 20 from the TSX league tables; and 1241, or 69.92 percent of the CPC IPOs are taken public by an underwriter that ranks on the TSX league tables. The strong participation by these large underwriters and the governance controls put in place by the regulators on blind pools are likely why the CPC program has exhibited such phenomenal growth over its 25-year history.

In Panel B we examine the mean and median proceeds for regular and CPC IPOs by underwriter type. Given the incentive structure for underwriting firms (that is, the dollar fee is a function of offer size), we would expect larger and more reputable underwriters to be associated with larger IPOs. Indeed, in Panel B we find that the mean and median proceeds are larger for underwriters that rank higher on the league tables for both regular IPOs and CPC IPOs. For regular IPOs, the mean and median proceeds for an IPO taken public by a 'Top 10' underwriter are $5.59 million and $2.00 million, respectively. For a 'Top 20' underwriter, the mean and median proceeds are $3.74 million and

$1.28 million, respectively. For an underwriter that appears on the TSX league tables, the mean proceeds is $3.72 million and the median proceeds is $1.26 million, while for an underwriter that does not appear on the TSX league tables, the mean (median) proceeds is substantially lower at $1.43 million ($0.96 million). Turning to the CPC IPOs, we find a very similar pattern. For a CPC IPO taken public by a 'Top 10' underwriter the mean and median proceeds are $0.52 million and $0.40 million, respectively; and for a CPC IPO taken public by a 'Top 20' underwriter the mean and median proceeds are $0.41 million and $0.30 million, respectively. More generally, for a CPC IPO taken public by an underwriter that appears on the TSX league tables, we find the mean proceeds to be $0.39 million and the median proceeds to be $0.30 million; and for a CPC IPO that is taken public by an underwriter that does not appear on the TSX league tables, the mean (median) proceeds is $0.37 million ($0.30 million), which is again consistent with the idea that larger and more reputable underwriters are associated with larger IPOs.

In Panel C we examine the commission (as a percentage of proceeds) charged by underwriters for TSX-V regular IPOs and CPC IPOs by underwriter type. For both the regular IPOs and the CPC IPOs, we find that the larger underwriters charge a lower commission than smaller underwriters. Focusing on the regular IPOs, we find that 'Top 10' underwriters charge an average commission of 7.70 percent and a median commission of 8.00 percent. For the 'Top 20' underwriters the mean commission of 8.55 percent is higher and the median commission of 8.00 percent is the same as for the 'Top 10' underwriters. Moreover, for an underwriter that appears on the TSX league tables, the mean and median commissions are 8.59 percent and 8.00 percent respectively, while for an underwriter that does not appear on the TSX league tables, the mean and median commissions are 9.36 percent and 10.00 percent, respectively. These findings suggest that more reputable underwriters tend to charger lower fees, which could be due to the fact that more reputable underwriters are associated with larger IPOs and hence there is an economies of scale effect. Alternatively, this could be due to the fact that more reputable underwriters take less risky firms public. We find the mean and median commissions to be higher for CPC IPOs compared to regular IPOs. Specifically, the 'Top 10' underwriters charge a mean commission of 9.71 percent and a median commission of 10.00 percent, respectively, and the 'Top 20' underwriters charge a mean commission of 9.81 percent and a median commission of 10.00 percent, respectively. For an underwriter that appears on the TSX league tables, the mean (median) commission is 9.83 percent (10.00 percent) and for an underwriter that is not on the TSX league tables, the mean commission is 9.84 percent and the median commission is 10.00 percent. The higher commission for CPC IPOs is consistent with an economies of scale effect, since CPC IPOs are generally smaller. The higher commission can also be due to the greater risk associated with CPC IPOs, since they are public shells with no operating history.

4 AN EXAMINATION OF THE CPC PROGRAM

As discussed above, the CPC program began in 1986, and since this program is so unique for a regulated stock market, and because it has been in existence for over 25 years, we have gathered detailed data for all blind pools prior to the program's inception, and for CPC firms that were listed on the ASE and its successor exchanges (the CDNX and TSX-V) since the program's inception. Therefore, the sample period in this section is from 18 April 1986 to 31 December 2010, which includes 21 blind pools before the CPC program's inception and 2,090 CPCs since the program's inception.

The CPC program actually developed as a regulatory response to a series of frauds in the then less-regulated blind-pool program between April and October of 1986, and so we first examine the effectiveness of the CPC regulations in reducing fraud in this market. Fraud can manifest itself in a number of different ways, including disseminating false financial or other information, otherwise manipulating the firm's stock price, or misusing corporate funds. The first two types of acts are criminal that are also subject to regulatory review, while the latter is likely more regulatory in nature. To determine which blind pools and CPC firms in our sample were the subject of a criminal investigation, we checked each firm against the Canadian Legal Information Institute (CanLII) database. This data source is maintained by the Federation of Law Societies of Canada and reflects any criminal investigations and/or convictions within Canada. Any regulatory investigations and/or sanctions were found in the provincial database for the jurisdiction in which the firm was registered and for the province in which it was listed. Finally, we also conducted a Factiva search of the overall Canadian blind-pool program. We restrict our analysis to the first five years following the listing of a firm as this is the critical period in the development of a blind-pool. The results on fraud are presented in Table 6.5.

Each row in Table 6.5 represents the percentage of total firms investigated and/or found guilty of fraudulent behavior within a given time period.[9] Specifically, First Commonwealth represents the period when the first seven blind pools were brought to market by the underwriter, First Commonwealth Securities, which was forced to cease operations soon after. Blind Pool Only includes all 21 blind pools that were listed in (Alberta) Canada before the development of the CPC program. ASE JCP Only represents the period of time when the CPC program was only available to Alberta investors. CDNX/TSXV CPC includes the period when the program was expanded to include other provinces in Canada. TSXV CPC is the period of time over which the program has been made available to investors in Canada's largest province, Ontario. Moreover, the first four of six columns in Table 6.5 capture whether criminal charges were brought against a firm or its founders or underwriters; whether a conviction was obtained on those charges; whether a firm or its founders or underwriters were the subject of any regulatory hearings; and whether those hearings resulted in any sanction. Finally, the last two columns provide a total percentage for both criminal or regulatory charges (adjusted for double counting), and a total percentage for criminal convictions or regulatory sanctions imposed.

One way of setting a benchmark level of fraud is to compare the Canadian blind pools with US blind pools during the same time period. Riemer (2007) notes that securities fraud in the US increased significantly in the 1980s, particularly in the penny stock market, where investors suffered billions of dollars in losses. Many of the penny stock firms went public using a blind-pool form of financing. Furthermore, in an early study of US blind pools, Stern and Bornstein (1986) show that out of 68 blind pools, only 23, or 33.8 percent, traded at a price above the initial subscription price, and the authors note that one blind-pool underwriter estimated that only 2 percent of these blind pools would

Table 6.5 Percentage of blind pools investigated for fraud and found to engage in fraudulent practices

	Calendar period	Criminal charges (%)	Criminal conviction (%)	Regulator hearing (%)	Regulator sanctions (%)	Criminal or regulator charges (%)	Conviction or sanctions (%)
First Commonwealth	04/18/1986–07/10/1986	14.29	14.29	14.29	0.00	28.57	14.29
Blind Pool Only	04/18/1986–12/30/1986	9.52	4.76	14.29	4.76	19.05	9.52
ASE JCP Only	12/31/1986–02/29/2000	0.38	0.09	2.72	1.78	2.82	1.88
CDNX/TSX-V CPC	03/01/2000–06/14/2002	0.00	0.00	0.85	0.00	0.85	0.00
TSX-V CPC	06/15/2002–12/31/2005	0.00	0.00	0.47	0.47	0.47	0.47

Notes:
This table reports the percentage of blind pools, or their principals or underwriters, which were the subject of a criminal investigation, criminal conviction, regulatory hearing or regulatory sanction, over a given period.
First Commonwealth and Blind Pool Only refer to periods when there were limited regulations on Canadian blind pools.
More specifically, First Commonwealth represents the period when the first seven blind pools were brought to market by the underwriter, First Commonwealth Securities, which was forced to cease operations soon after.
Blind Pool Only includes all 21 blind pools that were listed in (Alberta) Canada before the development of the CPC program.
ASE JCP Only represents the period of time when the CPC program was only available to Alberta investors. CDNX/TSX-V CPC includes the period when the program was expanded to include other provinces in Canada.
TSX-V CPC is the period of time over which the program has been made available to investors in Canada's largest province, Ontario. This later time period is restricted to the end of 2005 to allow there to be an examination of five years of trading subsequent to the IPO.

Source: Pandes and Robinson (2013).

ultimately become successful. By way of comparison, in Canada, Table 6.5 indicates that the rate of criminal or regulatory charges is 28.57 percent and the conviction or sanction rate is 14.29 percent over the less than three months of blind-pool offerings by First Commonwealth Securities, and the rate of criminal or regulatory charges is 19.05 percent, and the conviction or sanction rate is 9.52 percent for the first 21 blind pools before the development of the CPC program.

Table 6.5 further shows that the incidence of fraud in the blind pool market decreased significantly once the CPC regulations were enacted on 21 November 1986.[10] In particular, following the adoption of the CPC regulations, the annual rate of criminal or regulatory charges declined significantly to 0.21 percent, 0.37 percent and 0.13 percent for the next three time periods, respectively, and the conviction or sanction rates also dropped to 0.14 percent, 0.00 percent and 0.13 percent for the next three time periods, respectively. Thus, the CPC regulations significantly reduced the level of fraud in Canada's blind pool market. In fact, the CPC regulations lowered the level of fraud to the levels reported in other markets. Cumming and Johan (2013) report average annual fraud (ignoring delinquent filings) of 1.83 percent for NYSE firms, 4.41 percent for NASDAQ firms, 1.99 percent for US pink sheets, 0.33 percent for Canadian TSX firms, 0.10 percent for Canadian TSX Venture firms, 0.38 percent for UK LSE firms, and 0.10 percent for UK AIM firms.

As noted above, Stern and Bornstein (1986) estimated that only about 2 percent of US blind pools would turn into successful firms. Therefore, in Table 6.6 we provide further insight into the CPC Program by examining the percentage of successful CPCs during the sample period, 1986–2010. We measure success in two ways in Table 6.6: (1) success – the percentage of firms that completes a qualifying transaction and is either still listed on the exchange for the next five years, or if it is delisted due to an amalgamation, a takeover, or a graduation to a more senior exchange within five years following its QT; and (2) graduation – the percentage of CPCs that graduate to a more senior exchange at any time after its QT. The results in Table 6.6 show that prior to the adoption of the CPC regulations (on 21 November 1986) only 33.3 percent of the blind pools became successful public firms and less than 5 percent graduated to a senior exchange. Following the adoption of the CPC regulations, it can be seen that in most years the success rate is at least 70 percent, and the graduation rate is at least 15 percent. The Table 6.6 results thus indicate that the program has become viable from the perspective of both issuers and investors.

In Table 6.7 we present an industry breakdown of the frequency of CPCs at the time of the completion of the QT, when the reverse merger or amalgamation between the publicly traded CPC shell and the private operating company takes place, so that the industry is that of the operating company. Table 6.7 also presents the industry distribution of the aggregate proceeds at the CPC IPO. Since we do not have SIC codes for the firms, we categorize industries more broadly. The descriptive statistics show that while the program has attracted a large number of firms from the resource based industries, it has also been extensively used by firms from other industries. More specifically, while the energy industry and the mining industry both account for over 400 firms and over $140 million of IPO capital, there are over 300 industrial firms, 180 firms in high-technology industries, and over 100 manufacturing, services, and real estate firms. Overall, only 131 CPCs failed to complete a QT, which gives a QT completion rate (ignoring the 66 CPCs

Table 6.6 *Percentage of CPCs that are deemed to be successful and have graduated to a senior exchange*

Year	Success (percent)	Graduation (percent)
1986	33.33	4.76
1987	67.05	25.43
1988	61.94	13.55
1989	70.83	8.33
1990	100.00	25.00
1991	44.44	0.00
1992	64.71	23.53
1993	83.93	21.43
1994	77.78	27.27
1995	79.12	21.98
1996	71.43	19.39
1997	76.55	16.55
1998	70.94	20.51
1999	74.60	15.87
2000	74.58	13.56
2001	79.80	11.11
2002	70.00	15.00
2003	69.57	4.35

Notes:
CPCs are deemed to be successful if they remain listed for at least five years following the QT, or if they are delisted due to an amalgamation, a takeover, or a graduation to a more senior exchange within five years following the QT.
Graduation is defined as a CPC graduating to a more senior exchange at any time after its QT.
The year 1986 only includes blind pools listed prior to the adoption of the CPC program.
The years 1987 and onward include only blind pools under the CPC program.
The years 2004 to 2010 are not included in this table since we require five years after the QT to compute the success rate, and a firm has up to two years to complete the QT.

Source: Pandes and Robinson (2013).

that are still actively seeking a QT) of 93.5 percent. Thus, the CPC program has been used by firms drawn from a wide variety of industries.

5 SUMMARY AND CONCLUSIONS

The junior equity market in Canada, the Toronto Venture Stock Exchange, has evolved over the past 100 years to become one of the world's largest markets for development oriented, early stage firms to go public. While the average IPO size of TSX-V firms is small compared to IPOs in other international junior markets, the absolute number of firms going public on the TSX-V is substantially higher than the number of IPOs in these other junior markets. One key aspect of Canada's junior market has been the development of its Capital Pool Company (CPC) program, which is a highly regulated blind-pool program. Unlike the blind-pool experience in the US, where significant fraud

Table 6.7   Industry distribution of the frequency and aggregate proceeds of TSX Venture Exchange CPC IPOs

Industry	N	Proceeds (MM$)
Petroleum and natural gas	492	146.8
Manufacturing	114	52.6
Services	134	40.3
Real estate	103	34.1
Financial	35	11.1
Mining	438	140.3
Life sciences	76	36.8
Computer and other high technology	180	74.4
Industrial and other	321	96.6
Failed to complete a QT	131	34.1
Still a CPC (No industry yet chosen)	66	22.2
Total	2090	689.1

Notes:
This table presents an industry distribution of ASE, CDNX and TSX-V CPC IPOs where the industry is determined following the CPC firm's QT.
N is the number of firms.
Proceeds (MM$) is the aggregate IPO gross proceeds at the time of the CPC in millions of Canadian dollars.
The industry definitions are hand-collected.
The sample period is from 31 December 1986 to the end of 2010 (it ignores the 21 firms that went public as blind pools before the adoption of the CPC program).

was followed by the adoption of regulations that effectively shut down the market, the Canadian experience with blind pools illustrates how effective regulation through the enactment of VC-like governance mechanisms and the consequent presence of high-quality underwriters can balance the capital needs of early stage, entrepreneurial firms, while still serving to protect the interests of investors.

NOTES

1. See some excellent survey papers by Da Rin et al. (2013), Metrick and Yasuda (2011), and Gompers (2008).
2. In our analysis, we discriminate between the 21 blind-pool offerings that occurred before the CPC regulations were adopted in 1986, and the 2090 CPCs that occurred subsequent to the regulations being implemented. We further note that the 2090 CPCs in our sample are those that were listed on the Alberta Stock Exchange (ASE) and its successor exchanges, the Canadian Venture Exchange (CDNX) and the Toronto Venture Stock Exchange (TSX-V).
3. The Alberta Stock Exchange began operations in 1914, while the Vancouver Stock Exchange and the Winnipeg Stock Exchange opened in 1906.
4. The second markets in Europe have evolved over time and hence have had different names over time. We use the most recent exchange names. See table 6.1 in Vismara et al. (2012) for a detailed description of the evolution of the structure of European stock markets.
5. In the early years, the ASE program was called the Junior Capital Pool (JCP) program, but following the merger of the ASE and the VSE to form the CDNX, the program name was changed to the CPC program.
6. The program was expanded to British Columbia in 1999, to Manitoba and Saskatchewan in 2000, to Ontario and Quebec in 2002, and to Nova Scotia and New Brunswick in 2005.

7. Industry classifications are obtained from Professor Kenneth French's website: http://mba.tuck.dartmouth.edu/pages/faculty/ken.french/data_library.html (accessed 17 May 2013).
8. In section 4 we document the industry of a CPC at the time of the QT.
9. Owing to the need to examine a firm for five years after listing, our final time period ends on 31 December 2005.
10. Blind pools firms, which had begun their listing process prior to October, were allowed to go public in November and December and the first CPC firm was listed on 31 December 1986.

REFERENCES

Beatty, R.P. and I. Welch (1996), 'Issue expenses and legal liability in initial public offerings', *Journal of Law and Economics*, **39**, 545–602.

Carter, R.B. and S. Manaster (1990), 'Initial public offerings and underwriter reputation', *Journal of Finance*, **45**, 1045–64.

Chemmanur, T.J. and P. Fulghieri (1994), 'Investment bank reputation, information production, and financial intermediation', *Journal of Finance*, **49**, 57–79.

Cumming, D.J. and S.A. Johan (2013), 'Listing standards and fraud', *Managerial and Decision Economics*, forthcoming, available at: http://ssrn.com/abstract=2242449 (accessed 5 May 2013).

Da Rin, M., T. Hellmann and M. Puri (2013), 'A survey of venture capital research', in G. Constantinides, M. Harris and R. Stulz (eds), *Handbook of the Economics of Finance*, vol. 2 (part A), Amsterdam: North Holland, pp. 573–648.

Gompers, P. (2008), 'Venture Capital', in E. Eckbo (ed.), *Handbook of Corporate Finance*, vol. 1, Amsterdam: North Holland, pp. 481–509.

MacIntosh, J.G. (1994), 'Legal and institutional barriers to financing innovative enterprises in Canada', discussion paper, Government and Competitiveness Project, School of Policy Studies, Queen's University, Kingston, Ontario.

Metrick, A. and A. Yasuda (2011), 'Venture capital and other private equity: a survey', *European Financial Management*, **17**, 619–54.

Pandes, J. Ari, and M.J. Robinson (2013), 'Effective junior equity market regulation', unpublished working paper, SSRN website.

Rasch, S. (1994), 'Special stock market segments for small company shares in Europe – what went wrong?', Discussion Paper No. 94-13, Centre for European Economic Research (ZEW), Mannheim, Germany.

Riemer, D.S (2007), 'Special purpose acquisition companies: spac and span, or blank check redux?', *Washington University Law Review*, **85**, 931–67.

Stern, R.L. and P. Bornstein (1986), 'Ethereal equities', *Forbes*, **137** (6), March 24 40–42.

Vismara, S., S. Paleari and J.R. Ritter (2012), 'Europe's second markets for small companies', *European Financial Management*, **18**, 352–88.

Wolfe, G.A., E.S. Cooperman and S.P. Ferris (1994), 'An analysis of the underwriter selection process for initial public offerings', *Journal of Financial Research*, **17**, 77–90.

7. Investor protection and IPO survival in the Italian stock market
Mattia Cattaneo and Michele Meoli

1 INTRODUCTION

'How does better protection of outside investors (both shareholders and creditors) promote market development?' (La Porta et al., 2002, p.1147). This research question sanctioned the beginning of the law and finance literature and has captured the attention of many scholars in the past decade. Since the seminal work by La Porta et al. (1997), previous research has shown that an effective legal system supports the development of financial markets, and has then identified in laws and their enforcement one of the key mechanisms to protect outsider investors.

Despite the growing interest on the effects of regulation, researchers know relatively little about the impact of changes in investor protection on the evolution of financial markets. Prior scholars provided empirical evidence on the relationship between investor protection and stock market development either in a static perspective (for example, La Porta, 1997, 1998) or considering concise periods of time (for example, Armour et al., 2009). Nevertheless, considerable changes in laws relating to investor protection take a long time to become effective (Levine, 2011) and, thus, a long-run perspective is necessary to generate convincing evidence (Gehrig and Fohlin, 2006).

In this chapter we attempt to investigate whether changes in investor protection may affect the capital market development, in terms of initial pubic offering (IPO) survival, over a long period of time. The rational for looking at the IPO market is that it is seen as the bellwether for the development of the stock capital market (Fama and French, 2004) and laws have been identified as a main driver to ensure its growth (La Porta et al., 2002). In particular, we rely on the IPO survival because it is considered a good measure of capital market development over a long period of time (for example, Burhop et al., 2012). In fact, IPO survival indicates issuers' long-run financial strength (Krishnan et al., 2011), it measures post-IPO performance (Audretsch and Lehmann, 2005) and it may capture the extent to which investors support the long-run performance of listed firms with continuous availability of funds.

Relying on all the 879 IPOs listed in the Italian capital markets during the past 150 years, we therefore analyse the effect of the level of investor protection on the IPO survival. Such population offers the opportunity to examine the entire evolution of the Italian regulatory framework along the political and economic changes occurred over a long period of time. A competing-risks model is developed to analyse the determinants of survival for firms that were listed under a different level of investor protection, discriminating the cases of delisting for negative reasons from delisting due to mergers and acquisitions (M&As).

We find that the improvement in the level of investor protection that occurred in Italy increased the IPO survival over time. Specifically, the punctual evaluation of the level of investors' rights, measured by using the 'antidirector rights index' for shareholder protection and the 'creditor rights index' for creditor protection (La Porta et al., 1998), highlight that the level of shareholders and creditors protection contributes to explain the improvement of the IPO survival, and therefore the development of the Italian capital market.

Our perspective contributes to the former literature for several reasons. First, the Italian context represents an ideal framework to investigate the evolution of the phenomenon, because Italy has been characterized for a long time by a weak protection for both shareholders and creditors (La Porta et al., 1998), and evolved in a couple of decades (since the Draghi Reform[1] in 1998) into one of the developed countries in terms of investor protection. Second, Italy is a novel setting to analyse the impact of the level of investor protection on the capital markets, because while prior research investigated the historical dynamics of the stock capital markets of common-law countries (for example, Chambers and Dimson, 2009), our chapter examines the impact of investor protection on the capital markets of a civil-law country.

In the reminder of the chapter we first briefly review the literature on investor protection and IPO survival. Then, we accurately describe the evolution of the Italian regulatory framework to assess the different levels of investor protection in time. We present our methodology and the data and, lastly, we report the results and conclude.

2 INVESTOR PROTECTION AND IPO SURVIVAL

Outside investors financing firms face a concrete risk that the return of their investments will never materialize because of mechanisms affecting the expropriation of their wealth. Laws and their enforcement are identified in former literature among the key mechanisms to limit investors' expropriation (La Porta et al., 2000). When investors' rights are better protected by regulation, outsiders pay more for financial assets as equity and debts, because they believe that money investments and profits (interests or dividends) will come back. As a consequence, a higher level of investor protection improves the value of equity markets and supports the long-run performance of listed firms, because of the continuous availability of funds to fuel firms' growth (Shleifer and Wolfenzon, 2002). With particular reference to the IPO market, the law and finance theory (La Porta et al., 1997, 1998) predicts that a higher level of investor protection may limit the access to the capital markets to low quality firms, increasing their post-performance for the benefit of the stock market development. Because in the IPO market investors are assumed incapable to discern the quality of firm going public, a higher level of regulation should imply a lower risk of market for 'lemons' (Akerlof, 1970).

Only a few works explicitly study what the effects are of the regulation on the survival of newly listed firms. Simon (1989) investigates the impact of changes mandated by the Securities Act of 1933 on the five-year failure rates of newly listed firms on the New York Stock Exchange (NYSE) and other less-regulated US stock exchanges. Results give evidence that after that regulatory intervention, the failure rate of IPOs listed on the NYSE was quite low, similar to the previous period, while the failure rate of firms listed on the other US stock exchanges strongly dropped after the regulatory change. As far as the European evidence is concerned, Espenlaub et al. (2012) show that the survival rates of IPOs on the Alternative Investment Market (AIM), a London Stock Exchange market characterized by low regulatory requirements for firms going public, are largely comparable with those of heavily regulated US capital markets. Accordingly, using a comparative perspective, Burhop et al. (2012) find that the IPO failure rate was similar on the Berlin and the London capital markets at the beginning of the twentieth century, even if they were characterized by two different levels of regulation.

As a conclusion, results on the effect of regulation on IPO survival are poor and unconcluding. However, previous studies have a common limitation, since they refer to concise periods of time (maximum 15 years) and do not investigate the evolution of the investor protection in time. In practice, how investor protection evolves and its effects of the capital markets in terms of IPO survival is still an unexplored issue.

3 INVESTOR PROTECTION AND THE ITALIAN REGULATORY FRAMEWORK

In this chapter, we refer to two well-known indices first introduced by La Porta et al. (1998) to measure the level of investor protection in terms of shareholders' and creditors' rights. We introduce these indicators, show their composition, and then report their punctual changes along the history of the Italian capital market.

3.1 Investor Protection

When financing firms, two different classes of outside investors (shareholders and creditors) obtain rights and powers. Shareholders get the right to vote on key corporate matters, to select directors and to sue the directors and the firm. Creditors obtain the right to repossess collateral or to reorganize the firm that does not pay interest or that violates debt covenants. La Porta et al. (1998) formalize two indices to account for the protection of these different classes of investors: the antidirector rights index for shareholder protection and the creditor rights index for creditor protection.[2] Even if scholars provided alternative indicators to deal with investor protection (for example, La Porta et al., 2006; Djankov et al., 2007, 2008), recent eminent works still rely on these measures to investigate dynamics on the capital markets (for example, Bris and Cabolis, 2008; Dahya et al., 2008; Fogel et al., 2008; Spamann, 2010; Houston et al., 2010). Therefore, these two indices are still common and reliable measures to investigate the extent to which investors are protected in specific periods of time. Table 7.1 shows the composition of each index.

The antidirector rights index considers six mechanisms shareholders may rely on to protect themselves against expropriation. The creditor rights index is formed by four measures and contributes to designate the protection of creditors in a specific legal framework.

In the following paragraph we report the evolution of these two measures of investor protection since the foundation of the Reign of Italy, in 1861, noting their punctual change over time.

Table 7.1   Definition of independent variables

Variables	Definition
Antidirector rights index	Calculated by counting the following items, when verified: (1) the country allows shareholders to mail their proxy vote, (2) shareholders are not required to deposit their shares prior to the General Shareholders' Meeting, (3) cumulative voting or proportional representation of minorities on the board of directors is allowed, (4) an oppressed minorities mechanism is in place, (5) the minimum percentage of share capital that entitles a shareholder to call for an Extraordinary Shareholders' Meeting is less than or equal to 10 percent, or (6) when shareholders have pre-emptive rights that can only be waived by a shareholders meeting. The range for the index is from 0 to 6.
Creditor rights index	Calculated by counting the following items, when verified: (1) the country imposes restrictions, such as creditors' consent or minimum dividends, to file for reorganization; (2) secured creditors are able to gain possession of their security once the reorganization petition has been approved (no automatic stay); (3) the debtor does not retain the administration of its property pending the resolution of the reorganization; (4) secured creditors are ranked first in the distribution of the proceeds that result from the disposition of the assets of a bankrupt firm. The index ranges from 0 to 4

3.2   The Evolution of the Italian Regulatory Framework on Investor Protection

Several interventions reshaped the Italian stock markets regulation during its 150 years of history, transforming the Italian capital market from a completely self-regulated condition, with no form of investor protection, into an advanced system with efficient shareholders' and creditors' rights protection, comparable to that of most developed countries.

At the birth of the Reign of Italy, the Italian stock market was almost totally self-regulated; in other words it was characterized by a general lack of regulation and by a lot of frauds. The existing legal framework did not formalize any requirement in terms of information disclosure for listed firms. The first change in the Italian legal framework occurred in 1936, when the Law 375/36 (hereafter Bank Law) was approved, as a response to the crisis of 1929. Although no crucial changes in the investor protection occurred until 1942, scholars agree that Italian shareholders had pre-emptive rights that can only be waived by a shareholders' meeting before 1942 (La Porta et al., 1997; Enriques, 2003; Aganin and Volpin, 2005). We set the 'antidirector rights index' to 1 since 1936. Nevertheless, no changes affect creditors' protection.

In 1942, fundamental laws were introduced: the Royal Decree 262/42 (hereafter Civil Code) and the Royal Decree 267/42 (hereafter Bankruptcy Law). The stock market regulation improved dramatically, because requirements on shareholders' rights were introduced in limited liability companies. All shareholders acquired the right to vote at the annual shareholder meeting and approved the firms' annual report and directors. Specifically, in terms of 'antidirector rights index', the proportional representation on the board became an option available (Enriques, 2003). Therefore, such index is set equal to 2 after 1942.

Concerning creditor protection, the Royal Decree 267/42 (hereafter Article 182 *bis* proceeding) resembled in part the pre-packaged plan or reorganization under Chapter 11 of the US Bankruptcy Code by promoting the restructuring of firms (Manganelli, 2010). Secured creditors retained the priority rights without considering at what stage they enter the proceeding (*Codice di Procedura Civile*, Royal Decree 1443/40, Art. 528, enforced in 1942), whereas they were first ranked in the distribution of the proceeds. The courts could not impose the sale or distribution of the property until creditors secured by liens that were officially recorded (*Codice di Procedura Civile*, Royal Decree 1443/40, Art. 498, enforced in 1942) and the creditors' consent acted as a restriction for going into the reorganization. Concerning the possibility for debtors to retain the administration of their property, the Art. 167 of the Royal Decree 267/1942 allowed such right only when the debtor was admitted to the *Concordato Preventivo*, a minor Italian insolvency proceeding. As confirmed by La Porta et al. (1998) and in the update work of Djankov et al. (2007) the creditors' protection index is kept equal to 2 at least until 2003.

The real 'cornerstone' in shareholder protection was represented by the Legislative Decree 58/98 (hereafter Draghi Reform), explicitly focused on strengthening minority shareholders protection. This Law extended shareholders' decision rights, for example to cover defensive tactics during a takeover, and made an attempt to make it easier and less costly for shareholders to exercise voting rights. The threshold to call a shareholder meeting was reduced to 10 percent; an 'oppressed minority' mechanism was in place; only shareholders representing at least 5 percent of the shares might bring derivative suits; shareholders could cast their vote via mail and the loopholes in the takeover law were corrected (Aganin and Volpin, 2005; Enriques, 2009). The antidirector rights index is thus set to 5 after 1998.

The last important change in shareholder protection occurred in 2010, when Italy implemented the EU directive on shareholders rights (2007/36/EC, implemented in 2010 in Italy), whose primary objective was to encourage shareholders to actively participate in the company facilitating the exercise of voting rights. In particular, the shares were not more blocked before the meeting (record date 7 days before the meeting). Thus, the antidirector rights index is set to 6 after the entry into force of the EU 2007/36 directive in 2010.

Concluding, this brief overview identifies different increases in the level of investor protection during the entire history of the Italian capital markets, disentangling if the improvement in protection occurred in shareholders' or creditors' rights. Our aim, in this work, is that of examining how the changes in these indices have an impact, if any, on the survival of IPOs on the capital market. In particular, we wonder whether the increase in investor protection we detected analyzing the history of the Italian capital markets contributes to explain the increase in time of Italian IPO survival.

4 METHODOLOGY AND DATA

4.1 Methodology

In order to investigate the impact of investor protection on the development of the Italian capital markets development, our analysis is based on two main steps. First, we test whether there is an historical trend in the survival of newly listed firms. Second, we try to link the trend of IPO survival to the evolution of the investor protection standards, measured by the antidirector rights index and the creditor rights index.

The method traditionally employed in previous literature to assess the determinants of IPO survival is the survival analysis (Hensler et al., 1997; Jain and Kini, 2000, 2008; Espenlaub et al., 2012). In particular, we rely on the competing risk model,[3] an evolution of the Cox proportional hazard model, in order to discriminate different reasons for delisting. We aim to distinguish firms that were delisted following an M&A from the other reasons for delisting. In fact, M&As are not negative events for investors but, on the contrary, one of the reasons to go public is to take advantage of the market for facilitating valuation and divestment[4] (Högholm and Rydqvist, 1995). Nevertheless, a firm can be in compliance with an exchange's listing standards and voluntarily takes steps to delist its shares from the capital markets. Therefore, to check the robustness of our results, we also perform a sensitivity analysis using a competing risk model with three exits: delisting for negative reasons, delisting for voluntary choice, and delisting for M&As.

In competing risk models, as well as in other survival techniques, all observations that survive at the end of the analysis are treated as right censored. In our case, IPOs are considered as censored observations if they were not delisted on 31 December 2011.

4.2 Variables

Our analytical approach relies on a trend variable, and to two main independent variables to investigate the impact of the level of investor protection on IPO survival. First, by means of a historical trend, running from 0 (for IPOs in 1861) to 150 (for IPOs in 2011), we assess whether the change in IPO survival has simply followed a constant over time. Second, we measure the level of investor protection using the indicators provided by La Porta et al. (1998) concerning shareholders and creditors protection. In particular, the antidirector rights index is set to 0 before 1936, equals 1 for the period 1936–41, increases to 2 in 1942 (Enriques, 2003), jumps to 5 in 1998 (Aganin and Volpin, 2005; Enriques, 2009) and takes a value of 6 in 2010. The creditor rights index is set to 0 before 1942 and 2 after this year (La Porta et al., 1998; Djankov et al., 2007).

Nevertheless, the IPO survival is not determined only by the level of investor protection, but it is likely to be affected by several other determinants that we take into consideration through a large set of controls. Table 7.2 defines control variables, reporting data sources, and illustrating the rational for controlling for each determinant in our regression analysis. We report the correlation matrix in the appendix to this chapter.

Table 7.2 Definition of control variables

Variable	Definition	Data source	Rational for inclusion
Firm-level controls			
Age at IPO	Number of years between incorporation and IPO date	De Luca (2002)	IPOs suffer for a higher hazard rate when they go public a few years after the foundation, because of poorer experience and managerial competence (Jain and Kini, 1999)
Industry dummies	Set of binary variables that control for the issuer industry. Industries are defined by the first digit of the ICB code, zero is the reference case	De Luca (2002)	IPOs trade longer in some specific industries before delisting (Hensler et al., 1997)
Country-level controls			
GDP per capita	The real gross domestic product (GDP) scaled by the Italian population, at the time of each IPO	ISTAT	Measure of economic wealth. IPOs have more opportunities to raise capital in a well-developed economic system and may benefit for higher quality institutions and better shareholders rights (La Porta et al., 2006)
Mkt cap/GDP	The market capitalization of all listed firms, scaled by the Italian GDP, at the time of each IPO	De Luca (2002), Siciliano (2001)	Measure of size of the stock market relative to the size of the economy (Beck et al., 2000)
Listed firms/pop.	Number of publicly traded domestic companies scaled by population, at the time of each IPO	Mediobanca (2011), ISTAT	Measure of the weight of the equity market (Rajan and Zingales, 2003). The higher the ratio, the more mature is the capital market structure of a country with more services and facilities for listed firms

Table 7.2 (continued)

Variable	Definition	Data source	Rational for inclusion
Country-level controls			
Market return index	The total return of the Italian index including reinvested dividends, in the one year before each IPO	CONSOB (2011)	Measure of the market performances at the time of the IPO. In periods characterized by hot-issue returns, Espenlaub et al., (2012) argue that firms' survival time decreases
Public debt/GDP	Italian government debt, scaled by GDP, at the time of each IPO	Francese and Pace (2008)	Measure of the weight of fixed income securities in the market
Inflation	Change in the consumer price index, in the year prior to each IPO	ISTAT	Measure of the economic cycle. When the inflation rate exceeds some critical level, the only steady state may be the low activity one. Higher inflation rates lead to financial markets downturn (Huybens and Smith, 1999)
World War dummies	Binary variables equal to one if the IPO is performed during the two World Wars (1914–1918 or 1929–1945)	—	—
Internet bubble	Binary variable that equals one if the IPO is carried out in the period 1999–2000	—	—

Investor protection and IPO survival in the Italian stock market 149

4.3 Data and Sources

In this chapter we analyse the population of 879 Italian IPOs that went public over the full history of Italy since its foundation, in 1861, until the end of 2011, on the Milan Stock Exchange.[5]

Different datasets were used to obtain the information used in this study. The listing and delisting dates, the establishment and failure years, the industry identification, and the delisting reasons were collected referring to three sources: a publication by Mediobanca (2011)[6] for 1861–2010, the historical collection of De Luca (2002) for 1861–2000, which integrates the primary source of Mediobanca by punctually describing the industry and the history of each listed firm, and the EURIPO.[7] Additionally, three Italian institutions, Borsa Italiana, CONSOB and the Milan Chamber of Commerce, helped us in completing missing data, and in controlling the quality of our dataset.

Since our primary source of data contained the full population of listings in the Milan stock exchange, our first task consisted in identifying IPOs following the procedure of Chambers and Dimson (2009). We excluded introductions, new listings by firms with a dispersed and broad prior stockholder base, transfers of listings from other markets, the cross-listings of companies quoted on another exchange, and IPOs of closed-end-funds commonly known as investment trusts.

For each IPO firm we assessed the survival time after the listing, defined as the time elapsed from the IPO up to the suspension, liquidation or any other event leading to the delisting from a stock exchange, with the exception of transfers to another market.

Figure 7.1 reports the number of IPOs, the number of delisting and the number of

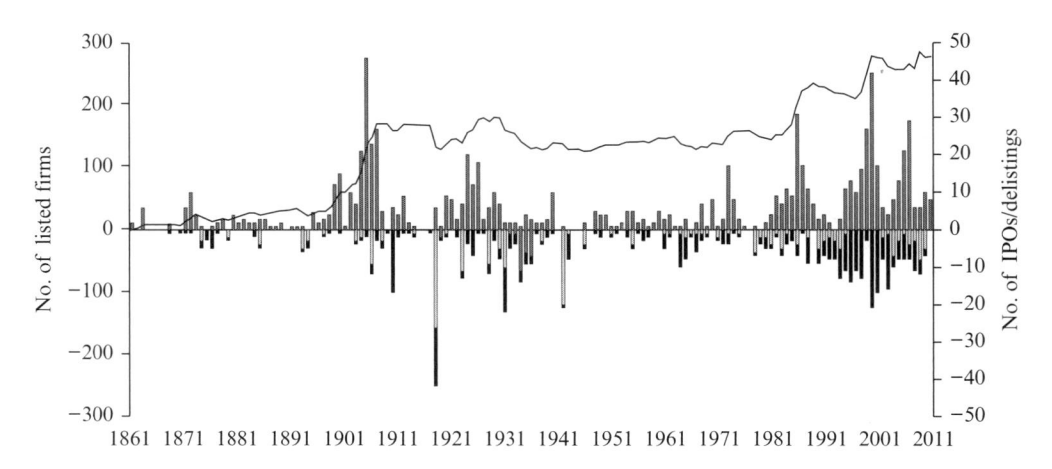

Notes:
X-axis represents years.
Vertical bars below the X-axis identify the number of delisted companies per year (M&As are in black, other delisting – failure, liquidation, bankruptcy and voluntary delisting – are in dark grey), while bars above the X-axis describe IPOs per year.
The curve above the X-axis represents the number of listed firms per year.

Figure 7.1   Number of IPOs and delistings in Italy during 1861–2011

listed companies from 1861 to 2011. The y-axis reports IPOs above zero, and the number of delisted firms below zero, distinguishing M&As from the other reasons for delisting. The figure shows how the IPO activity evolved over time according to a non-monotonic pattern, with a more developed capital market at the beginning and at the end of the century between 1927 and 1973.

5 EMPIRICAL EVIDENCE

Table 7.3 provides preliminary evidence on the investigated phenomenon considering the cumulative survival rates. It reports the survival rates of the population of Italian IPO firms, grouped by decades at the time of the listing respectively one, three, five and 10 years after the IPO. The survival rates are calculated using the non-parametric Kaplan-Meier method.[8] The values reported show that IPO survival largely varies in the different sub-periods, ranging from 39 percent to 87 percent for delisting within 10 years. Generally, the IPOs issued in the second part of the twentieth century, from 1951 to 2011, show a higher survival rate with respect to the IPOs issued from 1861 to 1950 (on average 78 percent versus 65 percent). The differences of the survival curves across these

Table 7.3 Cumulative survival rates

	Obs.	1 yr	3 yr	5 yr	10 yr
By decades					
1861–70	9	100	100	100	78
1871–80	31	97	74	48	39
1881–90	19	100	90	79	47
1891–00	43	100	100	91	79
1901–10	146	100	91	83	73
1911–20	32	100	100	94	59
1921–30	94	100	92	82	58
1931–40	31	100	100	81	77
1941–50	16	100	94	94	75
1951–60	27	100	96	93	70
1961–70	30	100	100	93	87
1971–80	36	100	100	100	83
1981–90	109	98	98	95	73
1991–2000	128	100	95	84	70
2001–11	128	100	97	93	85
Logrank	25.23				
	(0.032)				
Full sample	879	99	95	87	72

Notes:
The table reports the cumulative survival rates for the population of 879 IPOs listed during 1861–2011, classified by decades, calculated with the Kaplan-Meier method, for one year, three years, five years and 10 years after the IPO.
A log rank test is performed to assess the statistical significance of the differences among the survival curves (*p*-value in brackets).

different decades are statistically significant according to the log rank test (chi-square: 25.23, *p*-value: 0.032).

Table 7.4 reports the estimates for a competing risk model, regressing the survival time with respects to two possible exits: delisting for M&As, or delisting for negative reasons.

Model (1) includes the historical trend that is significantly associated with a lower incidence of delisting for negative reasons, and associated with a greater incidence of M&As. This result documents an improvement in the IPO survival over the full history of the Italian capital market. Among the control variables, the ratio between listed firms and population, the incidence of public debt over gross domestic product (GDP), and inflation, are all positively associated with a lower survival with respect to delisting for negative reasons.

In model (2) we add to the previous specification the indicator of minority shareholders' protection. We find that the antidirector rights index is strongly associated with a higher survival rate with respect to delisting for negative reasons. This result shows that the punctual improvements in terms of shareholders rights increased the average quality of the IPO firms. In practice, the increase in IPO survival is not only due to a continuous trend of evolution of the stock capital market, but rather for the changes in shareholder protection over time. An increase in investors' rights increases the propensity of shareholders to invest into newly public firms, because they feel they are facing a lower risk. Interestingly, the same indicator is negatively associated to a higher incidence of M&As. Contrary to delisting for negative reasons, when IPO companies will disappear due to being acquired, investors receive payment for their shares (Burhop et al., 2012). Delisting following M&As are indeed not negative events for investors, but the opportunity to perceive other strategic projects. For this reason, an increase in shareholders' rights is not necessarily associated with a decrease of M&A delistings over time. Among controls, market capitalization over GDP is negatively associated with the exit because of negative delisting.

Model (3) includes the creditor rights index for creditor protection that is associated with a lower incidence of delisting for negative reasons (at a 10 percent significance level) and a greater incidence of M&As, even if not significant. This result documents an increase in the IPO survival due to the changes occurred both in shareholders' rights and in the creditor protection on the Italian capital market. One may argue that, theoretically, the antidirector rights index and the creditor rights index do not necessarily operate in the same direction, since they measure the protection of different classes of investors. Nevertheless, as suggested by the literature (for example, La Porta et al., 1998), countries show that the shareholders and creditors protection is simultaneously higher or lower. Additionally, it is important to note that these two indices have a different level of significance, as the antidirector rights index impacts more on the IPO survival over time, in accordance to prior evidence (La Porta et al., 1998; Levine et al., 2000).

Finally, in order to check the robustness of our results we repeated the competing risk analysis splitting 'voluntary' cases of delistings from delistings for negative reasons, so that we obtain three exit cases: voluntary, M&As and other negative reasons. We classify a delisting as 'voluntary' if a firm is in compliance with an exchange's listing standards and voluntarily takes steps to delist its shares. Table 7.5 illustrates how results are confirmed for the two forms of exit considered, the M&A and the delisting for negative

Table 7.4 Competing risks model with two exits

	(1) Negative delistings	(1) M&As	(2) Negative delistings	(2) M&As	(3) Negative delistings	(3) M&As
Age at IPO	−0.115 (0.241)	0.087 (0.151)	−0.066 (0.222)	0.105 (0.138)	0.022 (0.212)	0.060 (0.157)
GDP per capita	0.137 (1.909)	−2.979 (2.373)	1.830 (1.970)	−1.034 (2.486)	0.587 (2.083)	−1.404 (1.527)
Mkt cap/GDP	−2.095** (0.953)	1.217 (0.879)	−1.727* (0.993)	1.122 (0.948)	−1.636 (1.002)	0.880 (0.822)
Listed firms/pop.	4.393 (3.497)	−1.505 (1.847)	2.677 (1.636)	−3.225 (1.981)	2.078 (1.617)	−0.626 (2.039)
Market return index	−0.004 (0.005)	−0.005** (0.003)	0.001 (0.002)	−0.002* (0.001)	0.003 (0.004)	−0.007** (0.003)
Public debt/GDP	0.013 (0.009)	−0.006 (0.007)	0.012 (0.008)	−0.008 (0.009)	0.014 (0.009)	−0.007 (0.007)
Inflation	0.015* (0.008)	−0.020** (0.010)	0.019** (0.009)	−0.016* (0.009)	0.020** (0.009)	−0.021** (0.010)
Time trend	−0.838*** (0.211)	0.930*** (0.359)	−0.611*** (0.228)	1.822*** (0.503)	−0.483** (0.242)	0.749 (0.473)
Antidirector rights			−0.236** (0.106)	−0.168** (0.075)		
Creditor rights					−0.327* (0.181)	0.118 (0.107)
Obs.	879	879	879	879	879	879

Notes:
Estimated coefficients for the competing risks models with two exits (delistings for negative reasons and delisting for M&As).
Model (1) controls for the historical trend; model (2) includes the indicator for shareholders' protection, the antidirector rights index; model (3) considers the creditor protection relying on the creditor rights index.
Robust standard errors are in parentheses.
Dummies for industries, World War I and World War II, and the Internet bubble are included in all models.
Stars identify significance level at less than 1% (***), 5% (**), and 10% (*).

Table 7.5 Competing risks model with three exits

	(1) Negative delisting	(1) M&As	(1) Voluntary delisting	(2) Negative delisting	(2) M&As	(2) Voluntary delisting	(3) Negative delisting	(3) M&As	(3) Voluntary delisting
Age at IPO	-0.033 (0.228)	0.087 (0.151)	-0.716 (1.249)	0.026 (0.204)	0.105 (0.138)	-0.358 (1.160)	0.075 (0.199)	0.060 (0.157)	-0.375 (1.168)
GDP per capita	-0.054 (2.058)	-2.979 (2.373)	-2.313 (6.347)	1.718 (2.090)	-1.034 (2.486)	-0.015 (4.075)	0.017 (1.961)	-1.404 (1.527)	-2.961 (8.527)
Mkt cap/GDP	-1.880** (0.873)	1.217 (0.879)	-1.485** (0.624)	-1.013 (0.937)	1.122 (0.948)	-3.767 (3.437)	-1.126 (0.991)	0.880 (0.822)	-1.109* (0.620)
Listed firms/pop.	2.792 (1.785)	-1.505 (1.847)	0.539 (3.982)	1.610 (1.863)	-3.225 (1.981)	-9.662 (7.126)	1.966 (1.823)	-0.626 (2.039)	0.126 (4.056)
Market return index	0.003 (0.003)	-0.005** (0.003)	-0.006 (0.007)	0.005 (0.006)	-0.002* (0.001)	-0.002 (0.010)	0.003 (0.003)	-0.007** (0.003)	-0.004 (0.009)
Public debt/GDP	0.007 (0.008)	-0.006 (0.007)	-0.852 (0.588)	0.016 (0.009)	-0.008 (0.009)	-0.100 (0.107)	0.010 (0.008)	-0.007 (0.007)	-0.074 (0.089)
Inflation	0.009 (0.011)	-0.020** (0.010)	0.014 (0.018)	0.011 (0.010)	-0.016* (0.009)	0.018 (0.018)	0.010 (0.010)	-0.021** (0.010)	0.016 (0.018)
Time trend	-0.807*** (0.227)	0.930*** (0.359)	0.278 (0.560)	-0.601** (0.247)	1.822*** (0.503)	0.159 (0.631)	-0.636*** (0.246)	0.749 (0.473)	0.246 (0.630)
Antidirector rights				-0.179** (0.087)	-0.168** (0.075)	-0.989 (0.964)			
Creditor rights							-0.239* (0.144)	0.118 (0.107)	-0.707 (0.868)
Obs.	879	879	879	879	879	879	879	879	879

Notes:
Estimated coefficients for the competing risks models with three exits (delistings for negative reasons, delisting for M&As and voluntary delisting).
Robust standard errors are in parentheses.
Dummies for industries, World War I and World War II, and the Internet bubble are included in all models.
Stars identify significance level at less than 1% (***), 5% (**), and 10% (*).

reasons, while with respect to the third exit, the voluntary delisting, regulation does not have a significant impact.

6 CONCLUSION

Former studies provide evidence of the different level of investor protection on the development of the capital market (La Porta et al., 1998, 2008). In particular, they compare the level of legal protection across different countries in order to investigate its effects on the capital market growth. Nevertheless, no studies have shown whether an improvement of the level of investor protection in the very long run contributes to the development of the internal capital market.

This work investigates the impact of the level of investor protection on the survival of all the IPOs carried out in the Italian capital market, from the birth of the Reign of Italy, in 1861, until 2011. We have the opportunity to investigate the evolution of this relationship using Italy as an ideal testing bed. Italy was characterized for a long time by a weak protection for outsider investors (La Porta et al., 1998), and evolved in a couple of decades into a developed country in terms of investor protection. Our results document a positive trend in terms of survival over the 150 years. This increase in the survival of IPOs is positively correlated to our measure for the level of shareholder rights in time, the 'antidirector rights index' and lesser with the creditor protection indicator, the 'creditor rights index' of La Porta et al. (1998). Our results show that the more the Italian system adopts investor protection measures, the higher is the survival of IPOs in the capital market. This can be due to the decrease in the number of low-quality firms accessing the market when a higher level of investor protection is implemented.

Regulatory authorities should recognize that the protection of shareholders' rights plays a significant role in fostering the growth of the IPO market, and ultimately the development of the entire capital market. Marginally, also creditor protection contributes to perceive such objective, even if a lower impact is documented. Although literature recognizes that excessive regulation is an obstacle to the development of capital markets (Modigliani and Perotti, 2000), we argue that focused regulatory interventions protecting the interest of minority shareholders may represent a strategic tool for governments to ensure their country's financial growth over time.

Future research could extend this study deepening the investigation of the long-run evolution of the Italian regulatory framework. In particular, the pattern of the cumulative survival rates in time (see Table 7.3) suggests a non-monotonic relationship between investor protection and IPO survival. While shareholders and creditors protection improved in time, the IPO survival rate does not seem to increase continuously through the decades. The suggested alternative way to investigate such dynamics is to focus on the impact of specific regulatory regimes over the history of the stock capital market. Future works will provide evidence whether the regulation may explain different patterns in the development of the stock capital market.

According to our approach, we recommend the implementation of an historical perspective to better evaluate the slow evolution of the regulatory framework in different legal systems. Since legal origins have such a pervasive influence on outcomes over the years (La Porta et al., 2008), a historical comparative approach across countries with different legal origins could be of interest to generalize our insights. In fact, the development of regulatory regimes requires sensitivity to the particular context and culture of the domain, and to the jurisdiction within which it is located (Murray and Scott, 2002).

NOTES

1. Also referred to as the Consolidated Law on Financial Intermediation, Legislative Decree. 58/98.
2. In the past two decades, over 100 works relied on these indicators to measure investor protection in different subject categories. For instance, the 'antidirector rights index' was used to investigate the effects of legal shareholder protection and firm evaluation (La Porta et al., 2002), dividend policy (La Porta et al., 2000), stock price informativeness (Morck et al., 2000), and financial crisis (Johnson et al., 2000). The 'creditor rights index' was considered to study the relationship between creditors protection and dividend policy (La Porta et al., 2000), culture (Stulz and Williamson, 2003), and deposit insurance on the risk premium (Bartholdy et al., 2003).
3. For details on methodology see Fine and Gray (1999).
4. In previous literature on IPO survival there is no shared consensus on this issue: companies delisted for M&As are considered either as non-survivors (Carpentier and Suret, 2011), as censored survivors (Jain and Kini, 2000) or are completely excluded from the analysis (Hensler et al., 1997). In our view, the correct method to consider M&A is that of looking at them as a 'competing' reason for delisting.
5. The Milan Stock Exchange (MSE) was founded by Eugène de Beauharnais, viceroy of the Napoleonic Kingdom of Italy, through decrees dated 16 January and 6 February 1808. In 1873, the MSE ranked higher, in trade volume, than Turin, Florence, Rome and Naples, but lower than Genoa. Nevertheless, during the industrialization process between 1895 and 1907 (Aganin and Volpin, 2005), a large number of firms went public on the MSE, making it the main stock exchange in Italy.
6. Mediobanca (2011), 'Shares listed and removed from list on Milan Stock Exchange from 1861 to 30 June 2011'.
7. The EURIPO database is managed by Universoft, a spin-off of the University of Bergamo (www.euripo.eu). It contains data on the companies that went public in Europe since 1985. See Vismara et al. (2012) for a description of this database.
8. The IPO survival rates are estimated non-parametrically using the Kaplan-Meier method:

$$s(t_j) = \left(\frac{n_j - d_j}{n_j}\right) s(t_{j-1})$$

where $S(t_j)$ is the probability of being listed at year t_j, $s(t_{j-1})$ is the probability of being listed at year t_{j-1}, n_j is the number of IPOs listed just before the year t_j (the risk set at t_j), d_j is the number of IPOs delisted during the year t_j.

REFERENCES

Aganin, A. and P. Volpin (2005), 'History of corporate ownership in Italy', in R. Morck (ed.), *The History of Corporate Governance around the World: Family Business Groups to Professional Managers*, University of Chicago Press, Chicago, IL and London, UK, pp. 325–61.

Akerlof, G.A. (1970), 'The market for "Lemons": quality uncertainty and the market mechanism', *Quarterly Journal of Economics*, **84** (3), 488–500.

Armour, J., S. Deakin, P. Sarkar, M. Siems and A. Singh (2009), 'Shareholder protection and stock market development: an empirical test of the legal origins hypothesis', *Journal of Empirical Legal Studies*, **6** (2), 343–80.

Audretsch, D.B. and E.E. Lehmann (2005), 'The effects of experience, ownership, and knowledge on IPO survival: empirical evidence from Germany', *Review of Accounting and Finance*, **4** (4), 13–33.

Bartholdy, J., G.W. Boyle and R.D. Stover (2003), 'Deposit insurance and the risk premium in bank deposit rates', *Journal of Banking & Finance*, **27** (4), 699–717.

Beck, T., A. Demirguc-Kunt and R. Levine (2000), 'A new database on financial development and structure', *World Bank Economic Review*, **14** (3), 597–605.

Bris, A. and C. Cabolis (2008), 'The value of investor protection: firm evidence from cross-border mergers', *Review of Financial Studies*, **21** (2), 605–48.

Burhop, C., D. Chambers and B.R. Cheffins (2012), 'Regulating IPOs: evidence from going public in London and Berlin, 1900–1913', University of Cambridge Faculty of Law Research Papers, No.2/2012. Cambridge: University of Cambridge.

Carpentier, C. and J. Suret (2011), 'The survival and success of penny stock IPOs: Canadian evidence', *Small Business Economics*, **36** (1), 101–21.

Chambers, D. and E. Dimson (2009), 'IPO underpricing over the very long-run', *Journal of Finance*, **64** (3), 1407–43.

Dahya, J., O. Dimitrov and J.J. McConnell (2008), 'Dominant shareholders, corporate boards and corporate value: a cross-country analysis', *Journal of Financial Economics*, **87** (1), 73–100.

De Luca G. (ed.) (2002), *Le società quotate alla Borsa valori di Milano dal 1861 al 2000* [*Listed Firms in the Milan Stock Exchange in the period 1861–2000*], Centro per la cultura d'impresa, Milan: Libri Scheiwiller.

Djankov, S., La Porta, R., López-de-Silanes, F. and A. Shleifer (2008), 'The law and economics of self-dealing', *Journal of Financial Economics*, **88** (3), 430–65.

Djankov, S., C. McLiesh and A. Shleifer (2007), 'Private credit in 129 countries', *Journal of Financial Economics*, **84** (2), 299–329.

Enriques, L. (2003), 'Off the books, but on the record: evidence from Italy on the relevance of judges to the quality of corporate law', in C.J. Milhaupt (ed.), *Global Markets: Domestic Institutions: Corporate Law and Governance in the New Era of Cross-Border Deals*, New York, Columbia University Press, pp. 257–94.

Enriques, L. (2009), 'Modernizing Italy's corporate governance institutions: mission accomplished?', European Corporate Governance Institute, Law Working Paper No. 123/2009.

Espenlaub, S., A. Khurshed and A. Mohamed (2012), 'PO survival in a reputational market', *Journal of Business Finance and Accounting*, **39** (3–4), 427–63.

Fama, E.F. and K.R. French (2004), 'New lists: Fundamentals and survival rates', *Journal of Financial Economics*, **73** (2), 229–69.

Fine, J.P. and R.J. Gray (1999), 'A proportional hazards model for the subdistribution of a competing risk', *Journal of the American Statistical Association*, **94** (446), 496–509.

Fogel, K., R. Morck and B. Yeung (2008), 'Big business stability and economic growth: is what's good for General Motors good for America?', *Journal of Financial Economics*, **89** (1), 83–108.

Francese, M. and A. Pace (2008), 'Il debito pubblico italiano dall'Unità a oggi. Una ricostruzione della serie storica' ['Italian public debt since the Unification. A reconstruction of the time series'], Banca d'Italia Occasional Paper No. 31.

Gehrig, T. and C. Fohlin (2006), 'Trading costs in early securities markets: the case of the Berlin stock exchange 1880–1910', *Review of Finance*, **10** (4), 587–612.

Hensler, D., R. Rutherford and T. Springer (1997), 'The survival of initial public offerings in the aftermarket', *Journal of Financial Research*, **20** (1), 93–110.

Högholm, K. and K. Rydqvist (1995), 'Going public in the 1980s: evidence from Sweden', *European Financial Management*, **1** (3), 287–315.

Houston, J.F., C. Lin, P. Lin and Y. Ma (2010), 'Creditor rights, information sharing, and bank risk taking', *Journal of Financial Economics*, **96** (3), 485–512.

Huybens, E. and B.D. Smith (1999), 'Inflation, financial markets and long-run real activity', *Journal of Monetary Economics*, **43** (2), 283–315.

Jain, B.A. and O. Kini (1999), 'The life cycle of initial public offering firms', *Journal of Business Finance & Accounting*, **26** (9–10), 1281–307.

Jain, B. and O. Kini (2000), 'Does the presence of venture capitalists improve the survival profile of IPO firms?', *Journal of Business Finance & Accounting*, **27** (9–10), 1139–76.

Jain, B. and O. Kini (2008), 'The impact of strategic investment choices on post-issue operating performance and survival of US IPO firms', *Journal of Business Finance & Accounting*, **35** (3–4), 459–90.

Johnson, S., P. Boone, A. Breach and E. Friedman (2000), 'Corporate governance in the Asian financial crisis', *Journal of Financial Economics*, **58** (1–2), 141–86.

Krishnan, C.N.V., V.I. Ivanov, R.W. Masulis and A.K. Singh (2011), 'Venture capital reputation, post-ipo performance, and corporate governance', *Journal of Financial and Quantitative Analysis*, **46** (5), 1295–333

La Porta, R., F. López-de-Silanes and A. Shleifer (2006), 'What works in securities laws?', *Journal of Finance*, **61** (1), 1–32.

La Porta, R., F. López-de-Silanes and A. Shleifer (2008), 'The economic consequences of legal origins, *Journal of Economic Literature*', **46** (2), 285–332.

La Porta, R., F. López-de-Silanes, A. Shleifer and R. Vishny (1997), 'Legal determinants of external finance', *Journal of Finance*, **52** (3), 1131–50.

La Porta, R., F. López-de-Silanes, A. Shleifer and R. Vishny (1998), 'Law and Finance', *Journal of Political Economy*, **106** (6), 1113–55.

La Porta, R., F. López-de-Silanes, A. Shleifer and R. Vishny (2000), 'Agency problems and dividend policies around the world', *Journal of Finance*, **55** (1), 1–33.

La Porta, R., F. López-de-Silanes, A. Shleifer and R. Vishny (2002), 'Investor protection and corporate valuation', *Journal of Finance*, **57** (3), 1147–70.

Levine, R. (2011), 'Regulating finance and regulators to promote growth', working paper, presented at the Federal Reserve Bank of Kansas City's Jackson Hole Symposium, Jackson Hole.

Levine, R., N. Loayza and T. Beck (2000), 'Financial intermediation and growth: causality and causes', *Journal of Monetary Economics*, **46** (1), 31–78.

Manganelli, P. (2010), 'Evolution of the Italian and US bankruptcy systems – a comparative analysis', *Journal of Technology and Law*, **5**, 237–62.

Mediobanca (2011), 'Shares listed and removed from list on Milan Stock Exchange from 1861 to 30 June 2011'.

Modigliani, F. and E. Perotti (2000), 'Security markets versus bank finance: legal enforcement and investors protection', *International Review of Finance*, **1** (2), 81–96.

Morck, R., B. Yeung and W. Yu. (2000), 'The information content of stock markets: why do emerging markets have synchronous stock price movements?', *Journal of Financial Economic*, **58** (1), 215–60.

Murray, A. and C. Scott (2002), 'Controlling the new media: hybrid responses to new forms of power', *The Modern Law Review*, **65** (4), 491–516.

Rajan, R.G. and L. Zingales (2003), 'The great reversals: the politics of financial development in the twentieth century', *Journal of Financial Economics*, **69** (1), 5–50.

Shleifer, A. and D. Wolfenzon (2002), 'Investor protection and equity markets', *Journal of Financial Economics*, **66** (1), 3–27.

Siciliano, G. (ed.) (2001), *Cento anni di borsa in Italia. Mercato, imprese e rendimenti azionari nel ventesimo secolo* [*One Hundred Years of the Stock Market in Italy. Financial Markets, Firms and Stock Returns in the Twentieth Century*], Bologna: Il Mulino.

Simon, C.J. (1989), 'The effect of the 1933 Securities Act on investor information and the performance of new issues', *American Economic Review*, **79** (3), 295–318.

Spamann, H. (2010), 'The "antidirector rights index" revisited', *Review of Financial Studies*, **23** (2), 467–86.

Stulz, R.M. and R. Williamson (2003), 'Culture, openness, and finance', *Journal of Financial Economics*, **70** (3), 313–49

Vismara, S., S. Paleari and J.R. Ritter (2012). 'Europe's second markets for small companies', *European Financial Management*, **18** (3), 352–88.

APPENDIX: CORRELATION MATRIX

Variables	1	2	3	4	5	6	7	9	10	11
1 Age at IPO	1.000									
2 GDP per capita	0.279*	1.000								
3 Mkt cap/GDP	0.227*	0.731*	1.000							
4 Listed firms/pop.	−0.137*	−0.135*	0.081	1.000						
5 Market return index	0.005	0.466*	0.781*	0.266*	1.000					
6 Public debt	0.209*	0.391*	0.521*	0.077	0.365*	1.000				
7 Inflation	0.098*	−0.038	−0.152*	−0.179*	−0.382*	−0.085	1.000			
9 Time trend	0.375*	0.880*	0.771*	−0.105*	0.406*	0.575*	0.069	1.000		
10 Antidirector rights	0.229*	0.780*	0.748*	−0.079	0.619*	0.529*	−0.081	0.830*	1.000	
11 Creditor rights	0.404*	0.812*	0.688*	−0.168*	0.337*	0.514*	0.078	0.921*	0.800*	1.000

Note: Correlation coefficients. Significant correlations at less than 1% are identified with *.

8 Underwriter reputation, bookbuilding and IPO duration
Hugh M.J. Colaco and Shantaram P. Hegde

1 INTRODUCTION

Consider the sample of firms that filed for an initial public offering (IPO) in the United States (US) in August 2000, at the end of the Internet bubble.[1] Of the 26 firms that filed to go public that month, 14 (or 54 percent) eventually withdrew. Contrast that with a withdrawal rate of only 24 percent for the 1986–2009 period.[2] While the greater riskiness of firms going public during the Internet bubble may partly account for the greater withdrawal rate, the above example also reflects the inability of underwriters (assigned with taking a firm public) to predict future market conditions. Since only 10 percent of firms that withdraw are successful in going public a second time (Dunbar and Foerster, 2008), the IPO timing decision is important.

Given the inability to forecast market conditions, Colaco and Hegde (2012) argue that a firm and its underwriter should prefer to spend less time in registration. Also, after filing their prospectus with the securities regulators that reveal some sensitive information about their business plans to the public, new firms face serious competitive threats that could erode growth prospects for their new products and services. Going public quicker also has post-IPO benefits. For one, analyst coverage would be available sooner. Also, NASDAQ OMX Group Inc. (the second largest US stock exchange operator) has implemented a rule from 23 April 2012 onwards reducing the waiting period for entry into the NASDAQ 100 index from a minimum period of one year to three months. Entry into the NASDAQ 100 index would undoubtedly increase the liquidity of the stock, especially for a firm that recently went public. So, the sooner a firm goes public, the quicker it would be eligible to be considered for inclusion into the NASDAQ 100 index, thus improving stock liquidity.

In this chapter, we first examine if high-reputation underwriters are able to extract good valuations for their client firms in terms of price and proceeds even though they take them public quickly as found in Colaco and Hegde (2012). This exercise sheds light on the value of information generated by underwriting services with respect to the price and quantity (number of shares) offered to public investors. Second, since the filing of amendments delays the firm in going public (Colaco and Hegde, 2012), we handcollect data on price and share amendments and examine their impact on the length of the IPO registration period (IPO duration, or IPOD), measured as the number of calendar days from the initial filing of the prospectus to the final offering of shares to the public. Price and share amendments may not necessarily convey the same information (Ang and Brau, 2003). Third, we examine whether IPOD is a signal of firm quality by examining post-IPO analyst recommendations. While the first point focuses on the role of the underwriter, the remaining two points focus on the firm. That is, price/share amendments and analyst recommendations are reasonably good indicators of firm quality. Thus, this chapter reflects the joint role that firms and underwriters play when a firm goes public.

2 IPOD AND UNDERWRITERS

2.1 Underwriter Reputation

Underwriters are assigned the primary responsibility of managing the bookbuilding process. We focus on three proxies for the value of underwriter services during the bookbuilding stage – amendments to the price and quantity of shares filed and the time it takes to complete the offering (IPOD). Further, our proxy for the quality of underwriting services is the reputation rankings of investment bankers. Given the significant reputational capital that they possess, high-reputation underwriters are expected to have 'better' relationships with institutional investors. As a result, they should be in a position to run an IPO more 'efficiently' as compared to low-reputation underwriters and discover the latent demand (that is, price and quantity preferences of investors) for the new issue more quickly. All else equal, this should translate into shorter IPODs (that is, shorter shelf life). High-reputation underwriters are also more likely to bundle IPOs to spread the costs of information production (Benveniste et al., 2002, 2003; Colaco et al., 2009). Bundling efficiency would imply a relatively short average IPO registration life since even a high-reputation underwriter would face resource constraints in terms of having multiple projects outstanding at any given time. Consider a well-established underwriter that takes 90 days, on average, to take a firm public and gets a new client every day. This implies that, on any given day, the underwriter has 90 clients. By contrast, another well-established underwriter that takes 60 days, on average, to take a firm public would, on any given day, be managing 60 clients, assuming a new client comes on board every day. The resources needed to support bookbuilding activities for the latter would most likely be significantly less than those for the former even allowing for economies of scale that the underwriter with 90 clients may be associated with. Further, the greater uncertainty associated with long project lives would impact the underwriter's reputational capital.

Since most IPOs in the US follow the bookbuilding method, underwriters bring their 'bookbuilding' expertise to an IPO. Many studies have examined the impact of underwriter reputation on underpricing as a way to reducing the information asymmetry between the firm and its prospective investors. While the relationship has been mostly negative (indicating underwriter certification), studies that use the 1990s as their sample period have found a positive relationship. This positive correlation has been partly attributed to the failure to treat underwriter reputation as endogenous (for example, see Habib and Ljungqvist, 2001; Fernando et al., 2005). Habib and Ljungqvist (2001) find that issuers choose prestigious underwriters because they (the underwriters) can use their reputational capital to reduce underpricing.

'One problem with using market share or a proxy like tombstone rankings to measure underwriter reputation or quality is that the specific tasks for which the underwriter is rewarded are undefined or, at best, ambiguous. What do higher quality underwriters promise and presumably deliver?' (Krigman et al., 2001, p. 247). As evidence of the impact of the reputational capital provided by the underwriter, Krigman et al. (2001) find that firms switch to higher-reputation underwriters at the SEO. Fernando et al. (2005) take the argument a step further and posit that the issuer–underwriter relationship is transactional rather than relationship based. The question posed in Krigman et al. (2001) is a valid one. Short IPOD is one such promise and delivery by high-reputation underwriters.

Why should high-reputation underwriters be associated with shorter IPODs? First, highly reputed underwriters have significant reputational capital. They have better relationships with institutional investors and, therefore, can manage an IPO more 'efficiently' (than less reputed underwriters). Second, because of their reputation, high-quality underwriters would also prefer not to be exposed to the market condition vagaries associated with longer registration periods. As mentioned in the introduction, a significant number of firms that filed to go public just before the Internet bubble ended eventually withdrew.

Benveniste et al. (2002, 2003) argue that underwriters bundle IPOs in order to spread the costs of information production among firms that go public in the absence of which no firm would want to take the lead in going public only to have other firms' free ride on that information. Colaco et al. (2009) find that bundling is greater for higher-quality underwriters. They argue that this association occurs because underwriters with high reputation have significant reputational capital at stake, so 'indirect' learning from contemporaneous IPOs is important given that 'direct' learning is unavailable at the time of the initial filing since bookbuilding has not yet begun.

2.2 Underwriter Efficiency

We examine the efficiency of highly reputed underwriters in terms of the time it takes to complete the offering and changes in the price and quantity of shares filed. Bouis (2009) and Colaco and Hegde (2012) find that high reputation underwriters are able to take firms public quicker. However, if highly reputed underwriters are not able to extract at least the same level of private information concerning uncertain investor demand during bookbuilding in a shorter period as their low-reputation counterparts, then taking a company public quicker may have limited advantages. Measuring underwriter efficiency during bookbuilding is not easy and information on the roadshow is typically not available unless there is access to proprietary data from an underwriter. As a result, we need to seek indirect measures. One such measure is the information provided by investors during bookbuilding. This is captured by the magnitude of the price update and, to some extent, the change in IPO proceeds between the initial filing and the offer. To capture underwriter efficiency, we construct a variable, daily value of information (DVI), which takes two formulations, as follows:

Formulation 1

$$DVI\,(Price) = \frac{Price\,update\, -\, Buy\,\&\,hold\,industry\,return\,from\,filing\,date\,to\,issue\,date}{IPOD} \times 100$$

where

$$\text{Price update} = \frac{\text{Offer price} - \text{Midpoint of initial price range}}{\text{Midpoint of initial price range}}$$

Formulation 2

$$DVI(\text{Proceeds}) = \frac{\text{Proceeds update} - \text{Buy \& hold industry return from filing date to issue date}}{IPOD} \times 100$$

where

$$\text{Proceeds update} = \frac{\text{Amount offered} - \text{Amount filed}}{\text{Amount filed}}$$

As noted earlier, DVI (Price) and DVI (Proceeds) capture the price, quantity and time dimensions of bookbuilding services. In formulation 1, the first term in the numerator, price update, captures the percentage price revision from initial filing to offer. Since this includes the impact of industry factors, we subtract the corresponding percent industry return from initial filing to offer to capture information specifically at the firm level. In essence, our objective is to isolate the incremental information generated by an issue over its registration period. We then divide this result by IPOD to obtain the value of information generated per day during registration. A positive DVI (Price) indicates that information generated during the roadshow has led to price improvements after controlling for contemporaneous industry returns, and vice versa. Since the ultimate objective of the firm is to raise a certain amount in proceeds, we perform the same analysis by using the change in proceeds rather than the change in price (formulation 2). It is worth noting that DVI (Proceeds) reflects changes in both price and quantity of shares offered (in addition to the waiting time – IPOD).[3]

3 DATA

The data used in this study is drawn from IPOs obtained from the Securities Data Corporation (SDC) New Issues database that were completed from 1986 to 2009. As with many previous studies of IPOs, unit offers, closed-end funds, American Depository Receipts (ADRs), spinoffs, reverse leveraged buyouts (LBOs), financial firms (Standard Industrial Classification (SIC) code 6xxx) and firms with an offer price less than $5 are excluded. We further exclude firms that do not have Center for Research in Security Prices (CRSP) shares codes 10 or 11 or do not have Compustat data. The SDC data has errors in the filing date which directly affects our measurement of IPOD. In his Table 1, Bouis (2009) reports a minimum registration period length of 20 days and a maximum of 1016 days after hand collecting the dates from Securities and Exchange Commission (SEC) filings. As a result, we check the SEC filings for the correct filing date and/or issue date for IPOs outside this range. IPO filings are available on the SEC website from May

Table 8.1   IPO duration (IPOD) by year

Year	N	Mean	SD	Min	P25	Median	P75	Max
1986	195	45.37	29.36	20	36	41	48	411
1987	141	47.45	32.16	20	35	41	50	268
1988	55	54.44	39.32	20	32	42	57	207
1989	51	59.63	60.25	28	37	43	54	446
1990	72	56.40	39.21	20	40.5	46	53.5	231
1991	173	61.28	45.26	20	42	47	58	307
1992	280	73.29	56.24	28	47	55	70	446
1993	362	75.32	70.52	20	47	55	64	446
1994	295	77.47	55.54	20	48	63	82	446
1995	365	70.05	59.14	22	47	56	69	446
1996	542	75.92	49.19	23	53	63	78	446
1997	363	92.36	59.40	23	61	71	98	446
1998	215	93.96	60.61	39	63	76	105	446
1999	380	94.66	65.24	25	65	75	93.5	446
2000	299	108.79	61.68	24	75	90	125	446
2001	52	157.48	108.02	24	82	121	191	446
2002	47	138.91	105.62	55	76	90	182	446
2003	45	126.64	116.74	29	69	80	114	446
2004	112	119.85	60.69	54	82.5	102.5	133.5	446
2005	113	141.15	85.54	20	83	104	174	446
2006	114	135.75	79.39	37	90	109	143	446
2007	108	138.28	83.83	38	88	104	163	446
2008	16	194.06	103.12	91	123.5	147.5	252.5	446
2009	35	237.66	170.65	30	87	113	446	446
Total	4430	87.46	69.39	20	50	66	94	446

Notes:
The sample includes completed IPOs from 1986 to 2009 after excluding unit offers, closed-end funds, ADRs, spinoffs, reverse LBOs, financial firms (SIC code 6xxx), firms with offer price less than $5 and firms that do not have CRSP share codes 10 or 11.
The table shows the summary statistics of IPOD (defined in the Appendix) based on the year in which the IPO was completed.

1996 onwards. We are unable to obtain the correct filing date and/or issue date for some firms that have an IPOD less than 20 days and go public before this period. To be consistent with the sample used in Bouis (2009), these firms are dropped from the sample. After accounting for the above and any other missing data, we are left with a final sample of 4430 completed IPOs. All dollar amounts are adjusted for inflation using the US GDP Implicit Price Deflator (year 2011 values = 100.00). Variables used in this study are defined in the Appendix to this chapter.

IPOD is measured as the number of calendar days between the filing date and the issue date. Table 8.1 shows the summary statistics of IPOD by year. IPOD is winsorized at its 99 percent value to minimize the effect of outliers. The average number of days taken to go public is 88 (median 66). The overall trend in IPOD has been rising particularly since the Internet bubble burst in 2000 and the passing of the Sarbanes–Oxley Act (SOX) in 2002. IPOD in the past 10 years has well exceeded 100 days, on average. Table 8.2 shows the industry wise breakdown of IPOD. We classify firms based on the 48 industry classifications obtained from Professor Ken French's website. The median firm in each industry mostly takes between 50 and 70 days to go public. The largest number of firms by far is in the business services industry (N = 1158) for which the median number of days taken to go public is 69.

We next highlight some other characteristics of the sample. We use the Loughran and Ritter (2004) updated measures of the Carter and Manaster (1990) underwriter reputation to rank each lead underwriter. Ranks range from 1 to 9, with higher ranks representing higher reputation lead underwriters. If there is more than one lead underwriter, we take the average underwriter rank. In Table 8.3, the median underwriter rank is 8 indicating that firms prefer to use high reputation underwriters. Gross spread as percentage price is the gross spread paid to the underwriters for each share sold as a percentage of the offer price. The median gross spread is 7 percent and the average is slightly higher. The (inflation-adjusted) average midpoint of the initial price range, measured as the sum of the low and the high of the range all divided by two, is 7.94 dollars while the average offer price is higher at 8.07 dollars. This indicates that IPO prices are adjusted upward, on average.

Amount filed is the initial number of shares filed times the midpoint of the initial price range in millions of dollars and is 47.63, on average. Amount offered is the number of shares offered times the offer price in millions of dollars and is 49.28, on average, indicating that the amount raised is higher than that expected initially. Total assets is the value of total assets in millions of dollars just prior to the IPO and is obtained from Compustat. Total assets is winsorized at its 1 percent and 99 percent values. Average total assets exceeds 80 million dollars. The median is much smaller at just over 14 million dollars. Age is the difference in years between the year when the firm completes the IPO and the founding year. The founding year is obtained from Professor Jay Ritter's website (http://bear.cba.ufl.edu/ritter/ipodata.htm) and described in Loughran and Ritter (2004). Age is winsorized at its 99 percent value to account for outliers.

The median firm age of the sample is seven years. Size of initial price range is the high minus the low of the initial price range all divided by the midpoint. This variable is a proxy for valuation uncertainty. The mean size of initial price range is 0.16.

In Table 8.4 panel A, we split our sample into high-reputation and low-reputation underwriters based on the median underwriter rank (8.0). A high- (low-) reputation underwriter is one with underwriter rank greater than or equal to (below) the median. DVI (Price), on average, is 0.08 percent for high-reputation underwriters and −0.02 percent for low-reputation underwriters. Both mean and median are significantly different for the two groups at less than the 1 percent level. Average DVI (Proceeds) is 0.24 percent for high-reputation underwriters and 0.03 percent for their low-reputation counterparts. Once again, the mean and median are significantly different for the two groups at the 5 percent and 1 percent levels respectively. The univariate results suggest that high-reputation underwriters are associated with higher price and proceeds per day than their low-reputation counterparts.

Note, however, that the univariate results for DVI could be driven by underwriter remuneration and firm specific factors and may not be indicative of the underwriter's ability to extract and synthesize information during bookbuilding (that is, underwriter

Table 8.2   IPOD by industry

Industry	N	Mean	SD	Min	P25	Median	P75	Max
aero	15	82.47	48.92	38	61	74	85	235
agric	13	74.23	46.11	29	46	55	103	197
autos	42	80.10	60.11	22	47	64.5	80	330
beer	12	70.17	25.03	45	54	64.5	79	137
bldmt	50	84.28	54.13	22	48	68	109	288
books	28	73.61	37.27	40	53	64	78.5	216
boxes	10	117.10	122.10	29	56	77.5	136	446
bussv	1158	90.15	67.96	20	55	69	98	446
chems	45	85.93	71.56	32	48	61	89	446
chips	336	83.15	69.63	21	48	63	86.5	446
clths	54	67.87	44.18	20	43	59.5	78	315
cnstr	45	79.69	44.33	35	47	67	97	240
coal	7	92.86	30.42	40	70	98	110	136
comps	232	85.81	74.60	20	49	63	91	446
drugs	315	102.03	82.76	22	53	76	117	446
elceq	41	84.00	67.97	22	48	64	92	411
fabpr	10	74.30	46.99	42	46	59	76	196
food	33	80.30	64.24	23	49	62	94	312
fun	68	87.84	58.62	30	53.5	68	100.5	330
gold	1	61.00	.	61	61	61	61	61
guns	3	64.33	12.01	52	52	65	76	76
hlth	169	95.92	70.11	20	49	70	120	427
hshld	59	87.49	84.40	28	49	60	77	446
labeq	76	72.20	49.37	29	46.5	56	78	324
mach	94	91.79	82.38	28	47	63.5	95	446
meals	112	78.98	42.96	30	52	63.5	90.5	328
medeq	228	88.46	73.89	31	50	64	90	446
mines	3	67.33	15.18	51	51	70	81	81
oil	86	103.99	83.28	27	56	74	113	433
other	32	92.78	80.79	20	51.5	71.5	103	439
paper	27	89.63	75.24	35	46	67	106	401
persv	75	98.83	74.98	21	55	74	112	446
rtail	273	75.70	57.77	20	44	62	84	446
rubbr	29	77.90	81.80	27	41	51	75	393
ships	9	57.89	19.95	20	56	61	62	90
smoke	5	64.60	12.42	50	57	66	67	83
soda	18	76.56	43.92	36	49	59.5	98	179
steel	42	71.62	43.55	34	46	59.5	71	233
telcm	211	92.12	74.10	20	54	69	96	446
toys	49	71.43	60.59	26	46	60	74	446
trans	106	93.97	96.41	30	48	62	86	446
txtls	23	82.87	72.33	36	54	62	78	389
util	25	84.76	56.21	28	46	73	87	261
whlsl	161	79.86	58.20	22	49	63	88	446
Total	4430	87.46	69.39	20	50	66	94	446

Notes:
The sample includes completed IPOs from 1986 to 2009 after excluding unit offers, closed end funds, ADRs, spinoffs, reverse LBOs, financial firms (SIC code 6xxx), firms with offer price less than $5 and firms that do not have CRSP share codes 10 or 11.
The table shows the industry-wise statistics of IPOD (defined in the Appendix).
The industry classifications are based on the 48 industry classifications from Ken French's website. Please refer to this website for full industry names: http://mba.tuck.dartmouth.edu/pages/faculty/ken.french/data_library.html.

Table 8.3 Summary statistics

Variable	N	Mean	SD	Min	P25	Median	P75	Max
IPOD	4430	87.46	69.39	20	50	66	94	446
Underwriter rank	4430	7.32	2.09	1	7	8	9	9
Gross spread as % price	4430	7.21	0.93	1	7	7	7	16
Midpoint of initial price range	4430	7.94	3.24	2.04	6.07	7.61	9.63	91.46
Offer price	4430	8.07	3.65	2.45	5.44	7.74	10.11	63.98
Amount filed	4430	47.63	93.47	0.54	12.04	22.38	49.68	2065.45
Amount offered	4430	49.28	110.21	0.88	11.07	23.27	48.93	3692.16
Total assets	4430	83.67	229.95	0.23	5.32	14.22	44.33	1616.2
Age	4430	14.06	18.57	0	4	7	15	95
Size of initial price range	4430	0.16	0.06	0	0.13	0.15	0.18	0.67

Notes:
The sample includes completed IPOs from 1986 to 2009 after excluding unit offers, closed-end funds, ADRs, spinoffs, reverse LBOs, financial firms (SIC code 6xxx), firms with offer price less than $5 and firms that do not have CRSP share codes 10 or 11. All variables are defined in the Appendix.

efficiency). To capture underwriter efficiency, we need to control for underwriter compensation, firm and other characteristics. So, we run two ordinary least squares (OLS) regressions with DVI (Price) and DVI (Proceeds) as the dependent variables. Our main explanatory variable of interest is Underwriter rank dummy, which equals one if a high reputation underwriter, and zero otherwise. We control for underwriter compensation (Gross spread as percentage price), firm size (Ln(Total assets)) and valuation uncertainty (Size of initial price range). We also include year dummies but exclude industry dummies since the dependent variable is industry adjusted.

Panel B reveals that there is a significant positive relationship between underwriter reputation and DVI (Price), after controlling for underwriter compensation by way of the gross spread, firm characteristics and time. This result shows that high-quality underwriters are indeed more efficient in managing the IPO process. That is, despite taking companies public quicker, high-reputation underwriters are able to extract significantly more value for their clients in terms of price. However, underwriter rank dummy is not significant in the DVI (Proceeds) regression indicating that underwriter reputation does not influence the proceeds generated per day during bookbuilding. We attribute this to the fact that DVI (Proceeds) implicitly assumes that all firms desire to increase proceeds at the offer from that stated initially. This may not always be the case. A cash-mindful firm that has very specific uses for the IPO proceeds may not wish to increase proceeds at the IPO even if demand during bookbuilding was very strong as a result of which price is raised. Such a firm would choose to offer fewer shares to receive the initial desired proceeds. Based on our measure, an underwriter associated with such a firm would be deemed to be relatively inefficient since proceeds did not change. Hence, DVI (Proceeds) should be viewed with caution. As regards the other regression results, there is some evidence that underwriter remuneration influences pricing. Our overall conclusion is that high-reputation underwriters generate better values for their clients (at least in terms of price) despite taking them public quicker.

Table 8.4 Daily value of information (DVI)

Panel A: DVI by underwriter reputation

Variables	High UW reputation			Low UW reputation			p-value of t-test	p-value of rank sum test
	N	Mean	Median	N	Mean	Median		
DVI (Price)	2847	0.08	0.04	1583	−0.02	0.00	<0.0001	<0.0001
DVI (Proceeds)	2847	0.24	0.04	1583	0.03	0.00	0.016	<0.0001

Panel B: Impact of underwriter reputation on DVI

Variables	(1) DVI (Price)	(2) DVI (Proceeds)
	OLS	OLS
Underwriter rank dummy	0.115***	−0.129
	(0.0354)	(0.207)
Gross spread as % price	0.0118*	−0.227
	(0.00658)	(0.184)
Ln(Total assets)	−0.0142	0.0572
	(0.00887)	(0.0614)
Size of initial price range	0.151	0.241
	(0.122)	(0.419)
Constant	−0.150*	1.258
	(0.0758)	(0.997)
Year dummies	YES	YES
Observations	4430	4430
Adjusted *R*-squared	0.085	0.002

Notes:
The sample includes completed IPOs from 1986 to 2009 after excluding unit offers, closed-end funds, ADRs, spinoffs, reverse LBOs, financial firms (SIC code 6xxx), firms with offer price less than $5 and firms that do not have CRSP share codes 10 or 11.
Ln refers to natural logarithm.
All variables are defined in the Appendix.
In panel B, standard errors (in parentheses) are adjusted for industry clustering.
*** $p < 0.01$, ** $p < 0.05$, * $p < 0.1$.

4 AMENDMENTS AND IPOD

While they play an important role, underwriters are not the sole determinants of the going public journey. Firms play an equal if not more important role in determining their fate. In this section, we take a closer look at amendments related to price and shares filed during registration since they reflect demand and thus may be associated with IPOD. This would be an indication that firms contribute to making the bookbuilding process more efficient.

Price amendments between the initial filing and offer may be upward, downward or both. Upward (downward) price amendments indicate strong (weak) demand while both reflect mixed demand. We expect upward price amendments to have short IPOD since

Table 8.5   Price and share amendments

Panel A: Price amendments					
Price amendment type	N	IPOD		Underwriter rank	
		Mean	SD	Mean	SD
Upward	392	85.62	60.61	8.22	1.37
Downward	282	124.29	87.94	7.15	2.09
Mixed	107	174.03	163.90	7.22	2.19
Total	781	111.70	95.97	7.70	1.85

Panel B: Share amendments					
Share amendment type	N	IPOD		Underwriter rank	
		Mean	SD	Mean	SD
Upward	318	108.12	98.93	7.24	2.23
Downward	178	133.37	110.32	7.24	2.12
Mixed	81	121.11	119.85	7.06	2.35
Total	577	117.73	106.06	7.21	2.21

Notes:
This subsample includes completed IPOs from 1993 to 2009 that amend price and/or shares after excluding unit offers, closed-end funds, ADRs, spinoffs, reverse LBOs, financial firms (SIC code 6xxx), firms with offer price less than $5 and firms that do not have CRSP share codes 10 or 11.
All variables are defined in the Appendix.

upward revisions in price reflect strong firm fundamentals and/or growth prospects. On the other hand, downward and mixed price amendments should have relatively long IPOD, reflecting weaker fundamentals or uncertain future prospects. We hand-collect price and share data for firms that amend price and/or shares from SEC filings for the period 1993 to 2009 to examine demand during the registration period more closely. The filings from 1993 to 1996 are obtained from Thomson Research, while those from 1996 onwards are from the SEC website.

In Table 8.5 panel A, we examine IPOD and underwriter rank for firms that amend the filed price upward, downward and mixed (that is, upward and downward or vice versa). Firms that file upward price amendments (indicating strong demand) take the least amount of time to go public (85 days, on average) and have the highest-reputation underwriters (8.22, on average). Firms that file downward price amendments (indicative of weak demand) take 124 days to go public, on average, and the mean underwriter reputation for this group is 7.15. Finally, firms that file mixed price amendments (indicating uncertainty) take the most amount of time to go public (174 days, on average) and have a mean underwriter reputation of 7.22, on average. In panel B, we examine the same for firms that amend the number of shares filed initially. Firms that amend shares upward go public quicker (108 days, on average) than firms in the other two categories. Underwriter rank does not vary very much among the three groups and is 7.21 for the three groups, on average. While share amendments reflect changes in demand for shares, they may also be filed for signalling reasons (Ang and Brau (2003)).

In Table 8.6 panel A, we examine the price trajectory for firms that amend price only (that is, no share amendments). Based on the mean, firms that amend price upward (downward) take 79 (114) days to go public while firms in the mixed group spend 147 days in registration. The results of the Tukey-Kramer pairwise comparisons test of difference in means show that the upward group is significantly different from each of the other two groups in terms of IPOD. Underwriter reputation is also significantly higher for the upward group as compared to the other groups. In panel A, primary shares (that is, newly created shares) and secondary shares (shares intended for sale in the IPO owned by existing shareholders) were allowed to be different in the offer as compared to the initial filing which may influence IPOD. So, in panel B, we do not allow primary and secondary shares to vary in the offer from that in the initial filing. The results are essentially the same. From panel C onwards, we allow for share amendments in addition to price amendments. Panel C examines IPOD and underwriter rank for share amendments in general while panel D focuses on upward share amendments. The results are mostly consistent to those found earlier. When downward share amendments are filed (panel E), only IPOD is significantly different for the downward and mixed groups. Finally, in panel F, we allow for mixed share amendments. Two of the three group comparisons are significant for IPOD but underwriter reputation is not significantly different between any groups. Our overall conclusion is that firms with an upward trajectory in price amendments (that is, intrinsically stronger firms) have lower IPOD and higher underwriter reputation as compared to firms with downward or mixed price amendments (intrinsically weaker firms). This shows that firm quality complements the role of underwriter reputation during bookbuilding and suggests that positive demand during registration enables the underwriter to finalize the demand schedule and take the firm public relatively quickly.

5 IPOD AND ANALYST RECOMMENDATIONS

If IPOD is a signal of firm quality, then short IPOD firms should be more likely to have Buy analyst recommendations than long IPOD firms following the IPO. This would be another indication that short IPOD firms are intrinsically stronger, thus contributing to making the bookbuilding process more efficient. To examine this issue, we obtain analyst estimates from Institutional Brokers' Estimate System (I/B/E/S) for 30 days, 60 days, 90 days and 120 days following the IPO. I/B/E/S recommendations are available only from 1993 and are not comprehensive. Recommendations are rated as follows: 1 = Strong Buy, 2 = Buy, 3 = Hold, 4 = Underperform, 5 = Sell. If there is more than one analyst recommendation for a given firm, the average recommendation is taken.

In Table 8.7 panel A, we find that 1114 of our sample firms had analyst coverage 30 days after the IPO. There are a total of 1846 recommendations for these 1114 firms, thus averaging 1.66 recommendations per firm. Firm coverage increases as time goes by as does the ratio of number of recommendations to number of firms. Note that affiliated analysts, analysts whose employers are members of the underwriting syndicate, are prohibited by the SEC from issuing recommendations for 25 days after the IPO (40 days after the IPO for managing underwriters from July 2002 onwards). Bradley et al. (2003)

Table 8.6 Price discovery trajectory

Panel A: Price amendments for firms that amend price only (N = 333)

Group 1	Group 2	IPOD Group 1 mean	IPOD Group 2 mean	IPOD Diff in means	IPOD TK-test	Underwriter rank Group 1 mean	Underwriter rank Group 2 mean	Underwriter rank Diff in means	Underwriter rank TK-test
Upward (N = 217)	Downward (N = 83)	79.3779	114.2651	34.8872	7.3970*	8.4777	7.512	0.9657	7.7902*
Upward (N = 217)	Mixed (N = 33)	79.3779	147.3333	67.9555	9.9523*	8.4777	7.5303	0.9474	5.2792*
Downward (N = 83)	Mixed (N = 33)	114.2651	147.3333	33.0683	4.3970*	7.512	7.5303	0.0183	0.0924

Panel B: Price amendments for firms that amend price only and both primary and secondary shares are the same in offer as initial filing (N = 294)

Group 1	Group 2	IPOD Group 1 mean	IPOD Group 2 mean	IPOD Diff in means	IPOD TK-test	Underwriter rank Group 1 mean	Underwriter rank Group 2 mean	Underwriter rank Diff in means	Underwriter rank TK-test
Upward (N = 195)	Downward (N = 70)	79.5282	120.0143	40.4861	7.6913*	8.4726	7.6786	0.7941	6.4251*
Upward (N = 195)	Mixed (N = 29)	79.5282	150.4828	70.9546	9.4368*	8.4726	7.7069	0.7658	4.3376*
Downward (N = 70)	Mixed (N = 29)	120.0143	150.4828	30.4685	3.6520*	7.6786	7.7069	0.0283	0.1446

Panel C: Price amendments for firms that amend both price and shares (N = 441)

Group 1	Group 2	IPOD Group 1 mean	IPOD Group 2 mean	IPOD Diff in means	IPOD TK-test	Underwriter rank Group 1 mean	Underwriter rank Group 2 mean	Underwriter rank Diff in means	Underwriter rank TK-test
Upward (N = 172)	Downward (N = 196)	92.1105	126.852	34.7416	5.4282*	7.8944	6.994	0.9003	6.0185*
Upward (N = 172)	Mixed (N = 73)	92.1105	161.9726	69.8621	8.1644*	7.8944	7.0616	0.8327	4.1636*
Downward (N = 196)	Mixed (N = 73)	126.852	161.9726	35.1206	4.1814*	6.994	7.0616	0.0676	0.3443

170

Panel D: Price amendments for firms that amend both price and shares and share amendments were upward only (N = 235)

Group 1	Group 2	IPOD Group 1 mean	IPOD Group 2 mean	IPOD Diff in means	IPOD TK-test	Underwriter rank Group 1 mean	Underwriter rank Group 2 mean	Underwriter rank Diff in means	Underwriter rank TK-test
Upward (N = 130)	Downward (N = 61)	85.1769	135.7705	50.5936	5.4470*	7.9192	6.4645	1.4547	6.6002*
Upward (N = 130)	Mixed (N = 44)	85.1769	145.2273	60.0503	5.7529*	7.9192	7.0341	0.8851	3.5734*
Downward (N = 61)	Mixed (N = 44)	135.7705	145.2273	9.4568	0.7989	6.4645	7.0341	0.5696	2.0278

Panel E: Price amendments for firms that amend both price and shares and share amendments were downward only (N = 139)

Group 1	Group 2	IPOD Group 1 mean	IPOD Group 2 mean	IPOD Diff in means	IPOD TK-test	Underwriter rank Group 1 mean	Underwriter rank Group 2 mean	Underwriter rank Diff in means	Underwriter rank TK-test
Upward (N = 22)	Downward (N = 100)	131.5455	126.39	5.1555	0.3308	7.8182	7.4283	0.3898	1.2529
Upward (N = 22)	Mixed (N = 17)	131.5455	193.3529	61.8075	2.8917	7.8182	7.3235	0.4947	1.1592
Downward (N = 100)	Mixed (N = 17)	126.39	193.3529	66.9629	3.8563*	7.4283	7.3235	0.1048	0.3023

Panel F: Price amendments for firms that amend both price and shares and share amendments were mixed (N = 67)

Group 1	Group 2	IPOD Group 1 mean	IPOD Group 2 mean	IPOD Diff in means	IPOD TK-test	Underwriter rank Group 1 mean	Underwriter rank Group 2 mean	Underwriter rank Diff in means	Underwriter rank TK-test
Upward (N = 20)	Downward (N = 35)	93.8	112.6286	18.8286	1.2874	7.8167	6.6762	1.1405	2.4851
Upward (N = 20)	Mixed (N = 12)	93.8	178.9167	85.1167	4.4675*	7.8167	6.7917	1.025	1.7145
Downward (N = 35)	Mixed (N = 12)	112.6286	178.9167	66.2881	3.7978*	6.6762	6.7917	0.1155	0.2108

Notes:
This subsample includes completed IPOs from 1993 to 2009 that amend price and/or shares after excluding unit offers, closed-end funds, ADRs, spinoffs, reverse LBOs, financial firms (SIC code 6xxx), firms with offer price less than $5 and firms that do not have CRSP share codes 10 or 11. All variables are defined in the Appendix.
TK-test is the Tukey-Kramer pairwise comparisons test of difference in means.

Table 8.7 IPOD and post-IPO analyst recommendations

Panel A: Analyst recommendations for all firms

	N	1	2	3	4	5	Total	Recommendations to firms ratio
30 days after IPO	1114	782	944	100	10	10	1846	1.66
60 days after IPO	2284	2131	2419	616	22	22	5210	2.28
90 days after IPO	2457	2587	2917	799	37	34	6374	2.59
120 days after IPO	2557	2983	3337	1024	46	49	7439	2.91

Panel B: Analyst recommendations based on Short and Long IPOD

	Short IPOD N	Mean	Median	Long IPOD N	Mean	Median	p-value of t-test	p-value of rank sum test
30 days after IPO	414	1.56	1.50	700	1.66	1.50	0.0023	0.0139
60 days after IPO	838	1.52	1.50	1446	1.73	1.67	<0.0001	<0.0001
90 days after IPO	928	1.53	1.50	1529	1.73	1.67	<0.0001	<0.0001
120 days after IPO	988	1.55	1.50	1569	1.73	1.67	<0.0001	<0.0001

Notes:
This subsample includes completed IPOs from 1993 to 2009 after excluding unit offers, closed end funds, ADRs, spinoffs, reverse LBOs, financial firms (SIC code 6xxx), firms with offer price less than $5 and firms that do not have CRSP share codes 10 or 11.
All variables are defined in the Appendix.
Panel A shows the number of analyst recommendations of each type.
The total number of recommendations is shown in the Total column.
N refers to the number of firms.
Panel B contains the summary statistics of analyst recommendations.

find that analyst coverage is initiated soon after the quiet period ends and most often with a favourable rating. Not surprisingly, then, a vast majority of recommendations are Buy or Strong Buy.

The key results are in panel B. Short (long) IPOD refers to IPOs whose IPOD is less than (greater than or equal to) the median IPOD. The mean recommendation is lower for short IPOD firms indicating that these firms are more likely to have Buy recommendations than long IPOD firms. For example, the mean analyst recommendation 60 days after the IPO is 1.52 for short IPOD firms and significantly higher (at less than the 1 percent level) for long IPOD firms (1.73). Similar results are observable for the 30 day, 90 day, and 120 day post-IPO period. In conclusion, short IPOD firms are more favoured by analysts.

6 CONCLUSION

We study the duration of the initial public offering (IPOD), defined as the amount of time firms spend in registration from the filing of the preliminary prospectus to the final public offering of shares. Based on a large sample of completed IPOs in the United States from 1986 to 2009, we find that high-reputation underwriters are more efficient than their low-reputation counterparts during the bookbuilding process and generate greater incremental value for their clients, while taking them public quicker. Further, using hand-collected data, we find that the trajectory in price amendments filed between the initial filing and offer influences IPOD. Finally, we find that short IPOD firms are more likely to have Buy analyst recommendations than long IPOD firms, which shows that short IPOD firms are intrinsically stronger.

NOTES

1. Lowry et al. (2010) define the Internet bubble as occurring between September 1998 and August 2000.
2. Numbers are based on our sample of completed and withdrawn/postponed IPOs from 1986 to 2009 after excluding unit offers, closed end funds, American Depository Receipts (ADRs), spinoffs, reverse leveraged buyouts (LBOs), and financial firms (SIC code 6xxx), and firms where the industry cannot be identified based on Fama and French (1997). In addition, the completed IPO sample excludes firms with an offer price below $5.
3. As stated in Lowry and Schwert (2004, p. 12), the initial price range is often not reported in the initial filing but in an amended filing later. Since the SEC filings before 1996 are not publicly available and because of our large sample size, we are unable to identify the initial pricing date for our sample of firms. To be consistent with industry return and IPOD which are each captured from the initial filing date to the issue date in the two formulations, we implicitly assume that Price update and Proceeds update each occur from the initial filing date to the issue date.

REFERENCES

Ang, J.S. and J.C. Brau (2003), 'Concealing and confounding adverse signals: insider wealth-maximizing behavior in the IPO process', *Journal of Financial Economics*, **67** (1), 149–72.
Benveniste, L.M., W.Y. Busaba and W.J. Wilhelm (2002), 'Information externalities and the role of underwriters in primary equity markets', *Journal of Financial Intermediation*, **11** (1), 61–86.
Benveniste, L.M., A. Ljungqvist, W.J. Wilhelm and X.Y. Yu (2003), 'Evidence of information spillovers in the production of investment banking services', *Journal of Finance*, **58** (2), 577–608.
Bouis, R. (2009), 'The short-term timing of initial public offerings', *Journal of Corporate Finance*, **15** (5), 587–601.
Bradley, D.J., B.D. Jordan and J.R. Ritter (2003), 'The quiet period goes out with a bang', *Journal of Finance*, **58** (1), 1–36.
Carter, R.B. and S. Manaster (1990), 'Initial public offerings and underwriter reputation', *Journal of Finance*, **45** (4), 1045–67.
Colaco, H.M.J., C. Ghosh, J.D. Knopf and J.L. Teall (2009), 'IPOs, clustering, indirect learning and filing independently', *Journal of Banking & Finance*, **33** (11), 2070–79.
Colaco, H.M.J. and S.P. Hegde (2012), 'Do firms that go public quickly perform better?', Aston Business School and University of Connecticut working paper.
Dunbar, C.G. and S.R. Foerster (2008), 'Second time lucky? Withdrawn IPOs that return to the market', *Journal of Financial Economics*, **87** (3), 610–35.
Fama, E.F. and K.R. French (1997), 'Industry costs of equity', *Journal of Financial Economics*, **43** (2), 153–93.
Fernando, C.S., V.A. Gatchev and P.A. Spindt (2005), 'Wanna dance? How firms and underwriters choose each other', *Journal of Finance*, **60** (5), 2437–69.
Habib, M.A. and A.P. Ljungqvist (2001), 'Underpricing and entrepreneurial wealth losses in IPOs: theory and evidence', *Review of Financial Studies*, **14** (2), 433–58.
Krigman, L., W.H. Shaw and K.L. Womack (2001), 'Why do firms switch underwriters?', *Journal of Financial Economics*, **60** (2–3), 245–84.
Loughran, T. and J.R. Ritter (2004), 'Why has IPO underpricing changed over time?', *Financial Management*, **33** (3), 5–37.

Lowry, M., M.S. Officer and G.W. Schwert (2010), 'The variability of IPO initial returns', *Journal of Finance*, **65** (2), 425–65.
Lowry, M. and G.W. Schwert (2004), 'Is the IPO pricing process efficient?', *Journal of Financial Economics*, **71** (1), 3–26.

APPENDIX: DEFINITION OF VARIABLES (BASED ON THE SEQUENCE IN WHICH THEY APPEAR IN THE TABLES OF THE CHAPTER)

All variables are obtained from Securities Data Corporation New Issue database (SDC) unless otherwise stated. All dollar values are adjusted for inflation using the GDP Implicit Price Deflator (year 2011 values = 100.00).

IPOD is the number of calendar days from the filing date to the issue date from SDC. IPOD is winsorized at its 99 percent value.

Underwriter rank is the ranking of the lead underwriter based on the Carter and Manaster (1990) ranking, updated on Professor Jay Ritter's website, and described in Loughran and Ritter (2004). If there is more than one lead underwriter, the average rank is taken.

Gross spread as % price is the gross spread paid to the underwriters for each share sold as a percent of the offer price.

Midpoint of initial price range is the sum of the low and the high of the initial price range all divided by two.

Offer price is the price at which the company goes public.

Amount filed is the initial number of shares filed times the midpoint of the initial price range in millions of dollars.

Amount offered is the number of shares offered times the offer price in millions of dollars.

Total assets is the value of total assets in millions of dollars just before the IPO and is winsorized at its 1 percent and 99 percent values.

Age is the difference in years between the year of the issue date and the founding year. The founding year is obtained from Professor Jay Ritter's website (http://bear.cba.ufl.edu/ritter/ipodata.htm) and described in Loughran and Ritter (2004). Age is winsorized at its 99 percent value.

Size of initial price range is the high minus the low of the initial price range all divided by the midpoint.

Daily value of information (Price) is price update minus equal-weighted buy and hold Ken French industry return between the initial filing and offer all divided by IPOD times 100. Price update is *Offer price* minus *Midpoint of initial price range* all divided by *Midpoint of initial price range*.

Daily value of information (Proceeds) is proceeds update minus equal-weighted buy and hold Ken French industry return between the initial filing and offer all divided by IPOD times 100. Proceeds update is *Amount offered* minus *Amount filed* all divided by *Amount filed*.

Underwriter rank dummy equals one if the lead underwriter rank equals or exceeds the median underwriter rank (high underwriter reputation), and zero otherwise (low underwriter reputation).

Upward refers to an increase in the price or share paths. As regards price, it reflects an increase in the price from midpoint of initial price range to offer via price amendment/s. For shares, it reflects an increase in the total number of shares (that is, primary and secondary) from the initial shares filed to the shares offered via share amendment/s. A price amendment is a change in the price range and occurs in an amended filing after the filing of the initial price range and before the filing of the offer price. A share amendment is a change in the total number of shares and occurs in an amended filing after the filing of initial shares and before the filing of shares offered.

Downward refers to a decrease in the price or share paths. As regards price, it reflects a decrease in the price from midpoint of initial price range to offer via price amendment/s. For shares, it reflects a decrease in the total number of shares (that is, primary and secondary) from the initial shares filed to the shares offered via share amendment/s.

Mixed refers to an increase and decrease or vice versa in the price or share paths. As regards price, it reflects an increase and decrease (or vice versa) in the price from midpoint of initial price range to offer via price amendment/s. For shares, it reflects an increase and decrease (or vice versa) in the total number of shares (that is, primary and secondary) from the initial shares filed to the shares offered via share amendment/s.

Analyst recommendation is classified as follows based on Institutional Brokers' Estimate System (I/B/E/S): 1 = Strong Buy, 2 = Buy, 3 = Hold, 4 = Underperform, 5 = Sell. If there is more than one analyst recommendation for a given firm, the average recommendation is taken.

Short (Long) IPOD refers to IPOs whose IPOD is less than (greater than or equal to) the median IPOD.

PART III

TRANSACTION STRUCTURE AND GOVERNANCE AT THE IPO

9 Corporate governance in newly listed companies
David B. Audretsch and Erik E. Lehmann

1 INTRODUCTION

Ever since the famous Berle and Means (1932) appraisal on the performance of large corporations, the term 'corporate governance' is used to describe questions of how to govern a firm or a company and is nowadays on everyone's lips and labels every organization. One of the most influential academic papers on corporate governance is the Jensen and Meckling (1976) approach. In this paper, the authors draw on the Berle and Means (1932) finding that corporations which are governed by managers instead of large shareholders, are underperforming. Jensen and Meckling (1976) put this finding in the context of the emerging literature on perfect contracts. Corporate governance is since then described as a contractual problem at the top of a firm to solve market imperfections. Oliver Hart (1995, p.678) mentioned that: 'Corporate governance issues arise in organizations whenever two conditions are present. First, there is an agency problem, or conflict of interest, involving members of the organization – these might be owners, managers, workers or consumers. Second, transaction costs are such that this agency problem cannot be dealt with through a contract.'

Within the past decades, a rich and fruitful literature, both theoretical and empirical, emerged, analyzing corporate governance problems in firms, in particular large and established listed companies (see Shleifer and Vishney, 1997; Lehmann and Weigand, 2000; Denis, 2001; Gugler, 2001; Becht et al., 2003). The starting point in this literature is that markets are incomplete, leading to externalities and unforeseen contingencies and thus gives managers leeway for opportunistic behavior. While the agency or perfect contract approach may help to internalize and weaken the costs of opportunistic behavior, unforeseen contingencies as a cause of governance problems could not be sufficiently solved by contracts. While externalities – opportunistic behavior of the management team at the cost of stakeholders – are seen as the predominant problem in corporate governance in large and established companies (Shleifer and Vishney, 1997), this may not necessarily hold for entrepreneurial and newly listed companies. These firms are mainly concerned with uncertainty, highly risky projects, lack of routines and networks and, most important, a lack of diversified projects to lower the risk of the firm (Audretsch and Lehmann, 2005; Audretsch et al., 2009). Instead of opportunistic behavior of the top management team, we argue that unforeseen contingencies could be named as the main source of corporate governance problems in entrepreneurial and newly listed firms, without neglecting the other problems.

Newly listed companies differ in relevant aspects from large and established companies in governing a firm. They are seldom managed by external managers without equity stakes in the firm but by owner-founders. Also, employees are more linked to the firm's assets and become increasingly critical of the success of the firm (see Audretsch et al., 2006a, 2006b). Without sufficient protection of employees' interests they tend to underinvest, to a firm's cost. Contracts are not sufficiently perfect as to guarantee employees' investment, and thus corporate governance concepts should also consider their interests besides those of the shareholders. This leads to the broader concept of stakeholder value and alters the aim of the top management team of the firm: to identify the relevant stakeholders and to pursue their interests, albeit their interests are still conflicting (Zingales, 1998).

An initial public offering (IPO) is therefore one of the most important events for a firm, often associated with a sharp change of its existing governance structure (Audretsch and Lehmann, 2005). An IPO is associated with an allocation of ownership rights, and thus shapes directly the property rights and the residual rights of control (Jensen and Meckling, 1976). Going public is the final stage of entrepreneurial firms in attracting equity. In the first stage, equity is often held by the entrepreneur or the entrepreneurial team. In the second stage, they may raise equity from some investors, such as venture capitalists or angel investors, with going public as the final stage. After being listed on the stock market, secondary or seasoned public offerings allow these firms to get access to additional equity to finance their growth in further stages (Gompers and Lerner, 2011).

During past decades, since the fall of the Iron Curtain, a new era has emerged, shifting the paradigm from the governed to the entrepreneurial firm (Audretsch and Thurik, 2001). Accompanied by technological changes, such as improvements in communications and computer technology and institutional changes, such as deregulation, these powerful forces changed the nature of the firm in two ways: they increased the importance of human capital relative to inanimate assets, and they have led to a break-up of the vertically integrated firms, in particular in the US (Rajan and Zingales, 2000, Audretsch and Thurik, 2001). The paradigm shift from the modern corporation to the entrepreneurial society is best described by Audretsch (2007) in terms of innovative activity being more important in generating economic growth than productive efficiency. This leads to a new type of entrepreneurial firms, the so called high-impact entrepreneurship as described by Acs (2011). The availability of financing, in particular private equity provided by venture capitalists, has made specialized human capital much more important and thus much more mobile (Gompers and Lerner, 2011).

With the increase in the importance of human capital, power has moved away from the top and is much more widely dispersed throughout the firm. The growing number of entrepreneurial firms where physical assets are less important than human capital and intangible assets, also shifts the perspective in corporate governance away from the owners of the physical assets – the shareholders – toward the owners of the human capital and intangible assets (Audretsch and Lehmann, 2006; Acs, 2011). Control over intangible and mobile assets becomes a greater source of power than control over physical assets since almost none of the control over rights can be allocated through contracts. Linking human capital and intangible assets as complementary assets to physical assets now generates the surplus and identifies the entrepreneur as one of the key persons in an entrepreneurial IPO firm.

Thus, corporate governance should refer to the design of institutions and mechanisms to make entrepreneurs and managers internalize the welfare of relevant stakeholders in the firm (Tirole, 2001). While traditional views of corporate governance mainly focus on the interests of shareholders as the only relevant stakeholders and thus principals, more recently a broader definition of corporate governance is gaining ground, integrating the interests of other stakeholders: those whose firm-specific investments lead to a hold-up problem and thus make them reluctant to make firm-specific investment (Rajan and Zingales, 2000; Lehmann, 2006). While the result of the agency problem is that investors will be reluctant to supply funds, the same holds for all stakeholders which make firm-specific investments that cannot be governed by a perfect contract (Hart, 1995; Rajan and Zingales, 1999). Since the outcome of such investments cannot be perfectly anticipated and fixed, entrepreneurs and managers could always act in their own interests to the cost of stakeholders. In addition to investors and financiers, we accordingly have to widen our scope of corporate governance to consider all stakeholders with firm-specific investments and, without loss of generality, could define corporate governance as the set of arrangements, either more market or hierarchically oriented, to ensure that investors – either suppliers of firm-specific financial or human capital – get a return on their investments.

In the following we will provide a short overview of corporate governance mechanisms in newly listed companies. Although such firms differ in large from the archetypical 'Berle-Means-Corporation' (Roe, 1994, p.93) in the corporate governance literature, our overview is also aligned to some extent to the framework provided by Shleifer and Vishny (1997). By this, we are able to highlight how newly listed companies differ from their counterparts, the large and established companies. Our approach differs from this traditional view in several ways. First, we distinguish between market mechanisms and hierarchical mechanisms. Secondly, we abstract from pure neoclassical theory in that market and their imperfections as the starting point in analyzing the existence of firms. Markets and hierarchies are two mechanisms to coordinate trade and exchange activities and the boundaries of the firm (the boundary between hierarchies and markets), and thus the governance structure is shaped by the cost and benefits of each of them.

The rest of the chapter is organized as follows. In the next section we provide a brief overview of governance in entrepreneurial and newly listed companies, starting with the separation of ownership and control and the resulting problems of moral hazard and adverse selection. The third section discusses mechanisms in corporate governance in entrepreneurial and newly listed companies.

2 GOVERNANCE PROBLEMS IN IPO FIRMS

2.1 The Separation of Ownership and Control

Starting with the entrepreneur as the owner-manager of the firm, Jensen and Meckling's (1976) work on the separation of ownership and control is the workhorse and starting point in nearly every study on corporate governance.[1] They first formalize the consequences if an owner-manager, who holds the entire assets of a firm, requires external financing for growth. They assume that the owner-manager receives benefits from consumption on the job as the manager of the firm. Selling equity shares – or residual cash-flow rights – to external investors leads to a separation of ownership and control, with the consequence that the costs of consumption on the job could be externalized to external investors and outside shareholders. This, however, lowers firm value and thus the market price of the shares. The possibility to externalize the costs of consumption of the job increases with the amount of shares offered to outside investors. The consequence is underinvestment of investors. Thus, capital markets should react at the time of the IPO according their beliefs and views about the costs of consumption of the job externalized by the top management team. Most prominent anecdotal evidence is provided by the Facebook IPO with a sharp decline in post-IPO performance on the stock market. The initial/long-run abnormal return phenomenon is extensively discussed in the theoretical and empirical literature, finding mixed evidence (see Ritter, 1991; Loughran and Ritter, 1995, 2002, 2004; Bonardo et al., 2010; Vismara et al., 2012).

The Jensen–Meckling approach has several implications which makes their paper (1976) one of the most cited in business and economics: both parties – investors and the owner-manager – can make investments, called agency costs, which lead to a better solution for both parties as long as the agency costs are lower than the gains from their investment. The standard approach is to view corporate governance as helping to overcome incentive problems between the manager and outside financiers (Vives, 2000, p. 4). This constitutes the basic problem as a principle agent problem between a principal – investor, financiers or, more generally, stakeholder – and the entrepreneur or manager as the agent, due to the presence of moral hazard and adverse selection. Literature focuses on several ways in which managers may not act in the firm's, or its owners', best interests (for surveys see Denis, 2001; Shleifer and Vishny, 1997; Gompers and Lerner, 2011). In the absence of perfect contracts between the relevant principal(s) and the entrepreneur or manager, the contract leaves the latter a lot of discretion since they have the power, the ability and the knowledge to run the firm. The consequence is managerial misbehavior, in that they may engage in all kinds of behavior that are detrimental to the firm.

Thus, the narrow view of corporate governance is how to ensure that managers follow the interests of shareholders. This view fits into the principal–agent paradigm that shareholders as the principal(s) have to solve two problems: the adverse selection problem of selecting good managers, and the moral hazard problem by checking that the managers put in appropriate effort and make their decisions in alignment with the interests of the principal(s) (Vives, 2000, p. 1).

2.2 Moral Hazard and Fraud in Entrepreneurial IPO Firms

While modern corporations are predominantly associated with problems of moral hazard behavior, entrepreneurial firms are characterized more by adverse selection problems. The artificial separation in the literature that moral hazard behavior is due to private information about (hidden) actions and adverse selection about hidden characteristics may serve as a workhorse for the analysis. Adverse selection and moral hazard are associated with different costs. While insufficient effort, extravagant investments or entrenchment strategies are not easy to discover in large firms, moral hazard behavior in entrepreneurial firms seldom attracts the attention of the public and thus still remains in the dark.

What we have in mind when we talk about corporate governance are more or less the scandals presented in the mass media, like excessive bonus payments, insider-trading and self-dealing. While excessive bonus payments are more prevalent in large and publicly held companies, and such misbehavior is frequently disseminated by the media press, owners of entrepreneurial firms are also accused of fraud and self-dealing activities (Audretsch and Lehmann, 2004). Owner-managers in entrepreneurial IPO firms as well as managers in large publicly traded corporations have incentives for moral hazard behavior if the expected utility exceeds the costs. They become criminals or engage in misbehavior not because their basic motivation differs from that of other persons, but because their benefits and cost differ (see Becker, 1968, p. 176). Moral hazard behavior constitutes the predominant problem in corporate governance, endogenously given by the opportunities, the incentives and the expected trade-off between the costs and benefits of managerial misbehaviour (see Bénabou and Tirole, 2007, p. 16f). Entrepreneurial and newly listed companies differ from large public companies with respect to the expected benefits from moral hazard behavior in several aspects:

- Insufficient effort – the problem in entrepreneurial firms is not that the entrepreneur or owner-manager wastes time for different tasks, but lack of investment in relationship-specific investments due to the double-sided moral hazard problem.
- Extravagant investments – entrepreneurial firms are organized around one idea; thus they are less diversified, and firm size as a signal of power and prestige may be relevant in later stages of the firms life cycle.
- Entrenchment strategies – entrepreneurial firms are invested in future or high-technology industries. Being taken over is one of the most favorable strategies for entrepreneurial firms and, thus, resisting takeovers to secure long-term positions by investment in anti-takeover mechanisms, such as in complex cross-ownership and holding structures, does not occur.
- Self-dealing – the importance of human capital and intangible assets relative to physical assets lowers the possibilities for self-dealing activities. Entrepreneurial firms are often far away from generating high cash flows or have to serve their financier, and thus self-dealing is limited.

Although the big scandals in the past years are linked to firms like ENRON, WorldCom or Parmalat, accounting scandals and fraud are more widespread in entrepreneurial firms. They may often use creative accounting techniques, even fraud, to increase their personnel wealth, particularly if quoted on the stock market. Beuselinck and Manigart (2007) study reporting quality in entrepreneurial and equity-backed firms. They find that reporting quality in such firms is the outcome of monitoring and governance by private equity investors and their ownership stakes in the firm. Their results show that financial reporting quality is a substitute for high ownership stakes. For a sample of all quoted firms in Germany from 1997 until 2006, Audretsch et al. (2009) found that about 20 percent are accused of having committed fraud within the first three years after IPO. Most interestingly, the chief executive officers (CEOs) of those firms are paid by stock options instead of owning large ownership shares, and the accused firms all came from industries with a low patenting intensity, such as media and life sciences.

2.3 Adverse Selection Problems in Entrepreneurial Firms

The problem of adverse selection is associated with private information about characteristics such as the ability of the entrepreneur or manager to run a firm. Those characteristics are more or less exogenously given, and literature suggests that adverse selection problems could be solved by self-enforcing contracts, incentive schemes, reputation, and signals such as guarantees. Adverse selection also occurs in large and public firms, in particular with respect to finding and selecting good managers. However, managers are selected as CEOs either because they climbed the job ladder within the firm, they showed abnormal performance on the market for managers or are selected by specialized head-hunters, or are through known social networks or personal contacts. Thus, private information about their quality in running and leading a company may be negligible relative to private information about the actions after the manager has been hired. Rather than adverse selection problems, the turnover of managers could be better explained by a mismatch between the principle and the hired manager (see Jovanovich, 1979).

The problem of adverse selection in entrepreneurial firms arises if mechanisms are designed in a way so that only bad qualities are selected.[2] Hellman (2007, p.83) points out that the entrepreneur's problem is how to assemble resources. If plenty of entrepreneurs compete for scarce resources like highly skilled employees or financial assets, the entrepreneur's challenge is to convince the resource providers to commit their resources to a new venture. Most of the entrepreneurs are unknown to their counterparts, employees, investors, financiers, or key supplier, and clients are involved in a 'chicken and egg problem' (Hellman, 2007, p.82), where the entrepreneurial firm needs to have credibility to get commitments from the providers of scare resources (key innovators, venture capitalists, alliance partners) but also needs to have commitment from partners in order to achieve credibility (see also Birley and Norburn, 1985). This opens the door for adverse selection problems, in particular if entrepreneurs are overconfident about their skills and their abilities, and overestimate future benefits and underestimate risk and costs. Then, financial resources are provided to the 'wrong' firms and key inventors leave their companies to get hired by entrepreneurial firms, lured by large ownership stakes and stock options.

3 MECHANISMS IN CORPORATE GOVERNANCE

Taking all these definitions and concepts together, interpreting the shareholder as one, but nonetheless a relevant, stakeholder, we can define corporate governance as a set of mechanisms and institutional designs to ensure that relevant investors (of either financial capital, human capital, or other assets) get a return on their investments. The main question is how to coordinate and motivate managers to behave accordingly. While free-market economists rely on the markets to motivate and coordinate people's (and firms') activities, others argue for a contractual and property rights approach and call for the emergence of institutions to coordinate and motivate people by internalizing the costs and benefits of their decisions. Zingales (1998, p.497) claims that the word 'governance' is synonymous with the exercise of authority, direction and control, and thus its use seems somewhat strange in the context of a free-market economy. Consequently, for free-market economists corporate governance problems could be solved by fostering market forces. If markets tend toward the perfect market model, then other mechanisms, such as governmental interventions, are obsolete or counterproductive by destroying incentives. Otherwise, the neoclassical approach assumes that in equilibrium, there are no profits, no entries and exits, and thus no opportunities and thus incentives for entrepreneurs (see Alvarez et al., 2011, for such a discussion; Buenstdorf, 2007). Also financial economists rely on the efficiency of market mechanisms, in particular in disseminating relevant information. If markets are sufficiently efficient in disseminating relevant information, then, there would be no room left for opportunistic behavior by the management team.

Following the microeconomic foundation of the firm, these mechanisms could and should thus be separated into 'market mechanisms' and 'authority' or institutional or hierarchical mechanisms. Similar transactions could take place either via exchanges on an anonymous market (Coase, 1937), or under the control of an authority. The set of mechanisms and institutional arrangements should also be spanned between these two extremes. Similar markets do not exist without a minimum of institutional mechanisms, such as computer-based trading; there exists no hierarchy without at least some market-based mechanisms. The most interesting question, not only in corporate governance of firms, is the optimal amount and mixture of market-based and institutional or hierarchical mechanisms. And this amount is endogenously given by the cost and benefits both of markets and hierarchies, because these costs vary and are shaped by technological developments, such as computer technology, learning by individuals and changes in social and political systems.

3.1 Market Mechanisms and the Role of Competition

It has long been argued that product and stock market competition act as a (perfect) mechanism in corporate governance (Scharfstein, 1988). Competition increases the probability of liquidation and thus managers work hard to avoid this (Schmidt, 1997). Badly performing firms will not survive and the market will be taken over by efficient firms and, at least, managers lose their jobs (Nalebuff and Stiglitz, 1983; Nickel, 1996). If managers waste resources in ways such that a firm's products are of lower quality compared to similar products of competing firms or are produced at higher costs, then product market competition or 'the economic grim reaper' (Baker and Kennedy, 2002) swamps those firms out of the market.

Entrepreneurial and newly listed companies are faced with the 'economic grim reaper': they are less diversified, too small to collude with others, victims of large incumbents in their strategic behavior in protecting market shares and reducing competition, and often too small to operate on a minimum efficient level (see Koppl and Minniti, 2011). Entrepreneurial and newly listed companies often survive a short time only and firm exit is not ostensibly caused by managerial misbehavior and an opportunistic misallocation of the scarce resources of the firm, but driven by bad luck, hazard, and a lack of managerial skills (see Jovanovic, 1982; Audretsch, 1995; Caves, 1998; Baker and Kennedy, 2002; Audretsch and Lehmann, 2005, 2008).

Providing access to equity capital for high-growth firms is only one aspect of stock markets as an economic institution (Vismara et al., 2012). The alterative is that stock markets also serve as an institution to reallocate productive resources from non-surviving firms to surviving firms. Schumpeter used the famous metaphor of 'creative destruction' describing that sustained equilibrium is not tolerated by innovative entrepreneurs, but also that entrepreneurial firms are the victims of market forces. Stock markets such as the National Association of Securities Dealers Automated Quotations (NASDAQ) in the US or the Neuer Market in Germany could then be interpreted as the main institution in a capitalist system to create and destroy existing structures (Audretsch and Lehmann, 2008). While large companies are often too-big-to-fail – such as General Motors – entrepreneurial and newly listed companies are often faced with the problem of being delisted or of leading a life as a penny stock at the stock market, unable to raise further capital for future investments. The process by which firms disappear from the stock market is not well understood. Baker and Kennedy (2002) provide a framework analyzing firm characteristics among surviving and non-surviving firms traded on the New York and American Stock Exchanges. They find that the 'economic grim reaper' (p. 324) kills at least underperforming firms. Fama and French (2001) use IPO data from the NASDAQ and find that new lists are delisted for poor performance at much higher rates than are all firms, and that only about one out of three new lists survived for 10 years. Audretsch and Lehmann (2005, 2008) show that delisting of entrepreneurial firms from the stock market are significantly shaped by the human capital of board members, lower innovation capacity and firm age. Survival on the stock market, and thus the ability to raise capital for further growth options, is positively shaped by the number of patents owned by the firm and the owner-manager, and by the share of board members having an academic degree.

If firms are not able to signal valuable gains in the future, investors sell their shares and stock market prices decline to zero. Capital markets, in particular when entrepreneurial and newly listed firms are far from serving the market with marketable products, serve as a substitute for the missing competition on the product market. If newly listed firms – due to bad luck, the wrong idea, mismanagement or insufficient management skills – are not able to spend their scarce resources optimally, the capital market serves as a complementary mechanism to the product market competition which speeds up the 'economic grim reaper'.

3.1.1 The market for corporate control in entrepreneurial firms[3]

The market for corporate control is of great importance in the corporate governance literature. If financial markets are sufficiently liquid that large equity stakes could be traded, the market for corporate control can be the superior mechanism in disciplining management (Manne, 1965). If managers waste firm resources, share prices decline on the stock market and it could be profitable for investors to buy the firm and replace the management. The fear of losing their jobs and their amenities would discipline managers to allocate scarce resources in the interest of the shareholders and owners of the firm.

While the market for corporate control may serve as a mechanism to discipline managers in large and publicly traded companies, this does not necessarily hold for newly listed companies. On the contrary, the market for corporate control offers the possibility to grow or survive in the market, either by the newly listed company being the target firm acquired by a larger incumbent or by acquiring other firms. Both can allow for access to resources that are critical for exploiting opportunities for further growth if takeovers are the only means by which this access can be accomplished. Thus, the market for corporate control not only serves as a mechanism to discipline poorly working managers, but also as a mechanism to lower transaction costs and costs of asymmetric information across target firms and acquirers.

There exists an emerging literature focusing on the interdependence between the IPO market and the market for corporate control (Bonardo et al., 2010). Initial public offerings can be part of a larger process of transferring control rights from the owner-manager of a privately held firm to another firm. They may also mitigate inefficiencies in the mergers and acquisition (M&A) markets for privately held targets (Ang and Kohers, 2001). These information asymmetries often seem to be prohibitively high especially in cases involving young firms with significant holdings in intangible assets the value of which has not yet been signaled (Shen and Reuer, 2005). Taking the firm public prior to its eventual sale, therefore, can significantly increase returns to its initial owners by reducing information asymmetries and, with that, reducing corresponding bid price discounts. Stock markets demand for standardized information disclosure, and stock prices as the aggregated information of several investors (Ellingsen and Rydqvist, 1997) reflect the market's evaluation of a firm's performance. Additionally, as Shen and Reuer (2005) argue, the presence of a resale market for a firm's shares reduces a potential investor's downside risk. Merger and acquisition transactions generally involve information asymmetries between targets and acquirers which are associated with adverse selection costs. Literature suggests several ways of coping with asymmetric information involved in corporate acquisitions, such as stock payments as opposed to cash (Eckbo et al., 1990) or an extended negotiation period allowing for a closer evaluation of the target (Coff, 1999).

Empirical research widely seems to support this important role the IPO plays in reducing information asymmetries connected with corporate mergers and acquisitions (Palepu, 1986; Lian and Wang, 2007). In addition to the signaling mechanism of discriminating high from low quality firms (Zingales, 1995) IPOs are a focal point for potential acquirers since entrepreneurial firms are often difficult to locate as potential targets (Palepu, 1986; Lian and Wang 2007). Brau et al. (2003) analyze firm owner's choice between an IPO and a takeover by a public acquirer. Their results show that the high-technology status of the private firm and the percentage of insider ownership, among others, positively influence the probability of a firm conducting an IPO. These findings are in line with the general assumption that young firms with large holdings of intangible assets, such as technologies or patents, need to signal their values as their acquisitions especially involve serious adverse selection risks.

There exists an emerging literature, both theoretical and empirical, pointing out that the market for corporate control serves as a matching mechanism between large and entrepreneurial firms (Hall, 1990; Bloningen and Taylor, 2000; Grimpe and Hussinger, 2008a; Norbäck and Persson, 2009; Lehmann et al. 2012). Entrepreneurial firms are assumed to be more likely to create breakthroughs but are not always able to bring the innovations to the market (Wright et al., 2004). In contrast, established and large firms have the financial resources but often provide only incremental innovations. Since start-up and entrepreneurial innovation is more radical than that of incumbents, Granstrand and Sjolander (1990) suggest a division of scientific labor between entrepreneurial firms and established firms that implicitly defines their roles as targets and acquirers. Accordingly, taking over the entrepreneurial firm may lead to a win-win situation for both parties (Gans and Stern, 2000). Thus, being taken over is not necessarily the nightmare of an entrepreneur and owner-manager but the most promising way to sell his or her shares (DeTienne and Cardon, 2012). Then, the market for corporate control does not act as a mechanism that disciplines bad managers but instead rewards entrepreneurial teams for their outstanding effort and quality. As Henkel et al. (2010) show, entrepreneurial firms may enter a contest with the winner being taken over by an incumbent firm. By choosing high-risk research and development (R&D) approaches they provide a signal to an incumbent firm – and thus are the winner of the beauty contest. Recent academic research focuses on this division of scientific labor and its impact on firm acquisitions (Colombo et al., 2010a, 2010b, Bonardo et al., 2011; Lehmann et al., 2012) and most of this literature points out that entrepreneurial firms are preferred acquisition targets because of their internally available technological capabilities, often measured by numbers of patents as a predictor for takeover probability (see also Powell, 1997; 2004).

Although acquisitions of entrepreneurial and newly listed companies are of great popularity in the academic literature, there exists only limited evidence on the performance of such acquisitions. Using event study methodology, Lehmann et al. (2012) find statistically significant abnormal returns for targets and bidders within a five-day window before the acquisition is made public. If the time window of the event study is enlarged, only shareholders of the target firms earn significant abnormal returns. Most other studies show dismal results in that a large number of acquired inventors leave the company after the acquisition and those that remain exhibit poor innovation outcome (see, for example Paruchuri et al., 2006; Kapoor and Lim, 2007).

Some studies tried to explain why these acquisitions often fail and have drawn attention to whether the acquired firm is kept as a separate entity or is integrated into the acquirer's organization (Kapoor and Lim, 2007; Puranam and Srikanth, 2007) or how post-deal decision autonomy is granted to the acquired key inventor. Colombo et al. (2010a) conclude that, while structural aspects of the post-merger deal reorganization are still important, one needs to go a step further to understand the dismissal empirical findings.

Lehmann et al. (2012) go a step further and contribute to this literature by analyzing how the likelihood of entrepreneurial firms being takeover targets is shaped by the specific role of the owner-manager of an entrepreneurial firm as the key inventor. This study differs thus from earlier work in that it explicitly distinguishes between the owner-manager as the owner of the intangible assets and the entrepreneurial firm as the legal entity. Like Grimpe and Hussinger (2008a) or Bonardo et al. (2010) they include the number of patents as a proxy for firm-specific knowledge and capabilities to create innovations, and thus give incentives to an incumbent firm to select an entrepreneurial firm as a takeover target. They distinguish whether the patents are owned by the owner-manager of the entrepreneurial firm or by the entrepreneurial firm as a legal entity and find compelling evidence that the likelihood of being a takeover target significantly decreases where the patents are owned by the owner-manager.

Bonardo et al. (2010) analyze a sample of European science-based entrepreneurial firms and conclude that the market for corporate control is active since most of the sampled firms are acquired after their IPOs, usually by companies operating within the same industries as their targets. This finding undermines the view that the market for corporate control does not primarily serve as a mechanism to discipline poorly performing management teams but to reallocate critical resources such as human capital and knowledge within industries.

The market for corporate control thus does not necessarily serve as a mechanism to discipline poorly working managers in newly listed companies but to reward entrepreneurs and entrepreneurial teams for past effort. If only successful entrepreneurial and newly listed companies are taken over, then the market for corporate control also mitigates adverse selection problems.

3.1.2 The market for managers in entrepreneurial firms

Following Fama (1980), the market for managers disciplines managers and prevents them from opportunistic behavior. If markets are sufficiently efficient, the shareholder value reflects the unobservable quality and effort of the managers. Competition in the market for managers is twofold: external and internal. While the external market values the manager's effort and quality by observing the shareholders' (or a firm's) value and the manager competes with other managers for remuneration and contracts, the internal market is based on competition within a given top management team of the respective firm. The competition on both markets will prevent managers from opportunistic behavior and thus induce them to invest the firm's resources and their effort in the best way to increase firm value. While the arguments put forth by Fama (1980) are intensively analyzed and discussed for large public companies, in particular in the context of takeover decisions,[4] empirical studies in the context of entrepreneurial and newly listed companies are scarce. One reason for this is that this kind of competition in entrepreneurial firms differs in several ways.

First, managers in entrepreneurial firms are often linked to their firms via family ties or they are the founders of their firms so that replacement against their will is often impossible. Secondly, entrepreneurial firms are often closely linked to the firm-specific human capital of the owner-manager, although he or she might lack general skills in management, marketing and finance.

Recent research in this under-studied field (DeTienne, 2010, p. 208) is more concerned with the strong link between managers and owners and firm performance in the short and long run and with entrepreneurial exit in general. Van Praag (2003) shows that firm survival and success are linked to the owners of the firm. She presumes that the person ('the man') makes the difference in firm performance, and not only firm-specific determinants or industry specific circumstances. The owner sets the conditions, the boundaries, the characteristics and creates the value of the firm. Her results show that business hazard varies with person-specific determinants such as age and past experience, but mostly with the motivation and enthusiasm with which a business venture is started. If such a business venture survives and grows, the problem of succession arises. Instead of replacing poorly performing managers, the major problem in privately held and entrepreneurial firms is the succession process and the selection of successor managers. Since replacement of managers in entrepreneurial firms is rather costly, more emphasis is put on the selection process of managers. Managers could either be selected from outside the firm and the family or internally recruited. Both strategies are associated with costs and benefits: while agency costs are assumed to be higher when selecting external managers, the internal recruiting strategy is limited by a smaller pool of relevant managers.

Another strand of the literature analyzes the exit strategies of founders and owner-managers in entrepreneurial firms (DeTienne and Cardon, 2012). While in large and publicly held corporations managerial replacement is often exogenously determined by the board of directors (Adams et al., 2010), entrepreneurial exit is an endogenous decision by the entrepreneur and owner-manager: they remove themselves (DeTienne, 2010, p. 208). Birley and Westhead (1993) propose that entrepreneurs exit through five different paths: sale to an independent party, management buyouts, sale to another business, an IPO or liquidation. Since entrepreneurial firms are strongly linked to the specific human capital of the founder and owner-manager, they may also step back from the active management of the firm and take a role on the board of directors. DeTienne and Cardon (2012) show that entrepreneurial exit paths are shaped by the specific human capital and prior experience of entrepreneurs. Their results confirm work on the lifecycle theory of the firm that different board members are needed on the board at different stages (Lynall et al., 2003). Board composition change and entrepreneurial exit reflect the firm's life cycle. If an entrepreneurial firm grows and acquires more resources, the initial human capital of the founder becomes diffused and has less impact on firm outcomes (DeTienne and Cardon, 2012).

While exits as described by Birley and Westhead (1993), DeTienne (2010) or DeTienne and Cardon (2012) are more or less voluntary exit decisions by the entrepreneur, there is one strand of literature analyzing the involuntary replacement of entrepreneurs: the venture capital literature. Although entrepreneurs have large ownership stakes in their firms, venture capitalists can force them to exit the firm involuntarily. In contrast to banks, venture capital firms, as the main financiers of entrepreneurial firms, possess the technical expertise and manpower which enables them to replace the original founder of the entrepreneurial firms with a new and more appropriate CEO (see Gorman and Sahlman, 1989; Hellmann and Puri, 2002; Ueda, 2004; Gompers and Lerner, 2011).

3.2 Authority and Institutional Mechanisms

3.2.1 Exit and voice

Institutional mechanisms are arrangements that point out that transaction costs of market mechanisms are prohibitively high so that the coordination of transactions occurs in alternative forms, like hierarchies. The existence of institutional mechanisms in corporate governance simply reveals that markets are imperfect and associated with high transaction costs. Institutional mechanisms could be summarized as mechanisms that help lowering the costs of monitoring and controlling firms, and come along in two basic forms, 'exit' and 'voice'.

Hirschman (1970) introduced the basic distinction between exit and voice in order to contrast the behavior of organization members who 'either vote with their feet when discontented with the evolution of their organizations or stay and try to improve things' (Tirole, 2006, p. 334). Exit, or passive control, aims at better measuring the manager's decisions and performance. While market mechanisms mainly focus on the market value of firms, passive control aims at measuring the manager's performance. The basic idea is that better information for the shareholders reduces the agency problem by reducing the incentive costs or the compensation for performance. If managers receive performance-based remuneration like direct ownership or stock options, their personnel wealth depends directly on the underlying value of the firm in the stock market. If shareholders, in particular large shareholders such as institutional shareholders, pension funds, or other block holders, receive additional informative signals, either from the markets, insiders of the firm or important shareholders and stakeholders, they may decide to disinvest when performance is poor or if expected future returns are lower than expected. This 'exit' option lowers the value of the shares and thus the recent and future earnings of the managers.

Passive control via exit plays an important role in the corporate governance debate in large and publicly quoted companies. In particular, institutional investors and pension funds are seen as key players in governing managers in such companies, but this has its costs. In particular, their degree of activism, their own value-maximizing strategies and investment managers potentially being short-term oriented and making biased decisions, casts doubts on their role in governing companies as the best of all shareholders (Vives, 2000; Gompers and Metrick, 2001).

3.2.2 Boards of directors in entrepreneurial and newly listed firms

The question of why firms are governed by boards of directors throughout the world is often answered by referring to legal requirements. However, also legal requirements are endogenous, and if boards of directors are associated with additional costs to a firm, firms without boards of directors should *ceteris paribus* have lower costs and thus outperform those with boards of directors. Even today, the media regularly chide boards for being insufficiently vigilant guardians of investors' money and of being too poorly performing in disciplining managers – as the accounting scandals in the dotcom era and the last financial crisis seem to prove. If boards were so bad, why hasn't the market caused them to improve, or even replaced the corporate form with less problematic forms of organization, Hermalin and Weisbach (2003) ask in their survey. They argue that boards are the second-best-efficient solution to the various agency problems confronting any organization with a potentially large divergence in interests among its members.

Thus, corporate governance problems do not only arise in firms with potentially divergent interests among managers and shareholders, but also in all other organizations. Their survey highlights the costs and benefits of boards of directors, board characteristics, and how characteristics, such as size and composition, shape board activities, such as CEO selection, CEO remuneration, and CEO replacement and turnover. They not only summarize existing theoretical and empirical evidence, but also provide an excellent framework for analyzing the board of directors within the corporate governance debate (see Adams et al., 2010). However, their survey mainly draws on large and publicly traded companies, and agency problems inherent in these. In particular, the board of directors in this discussion is mainly an economic institution to mitigate agency problems by selecting and monitoring managers. Thus, academic research focuses on the different goals of executives and shareholders, in that they face different risks and they differ in their incentives. Entrepreneurial firms are prone to such agency problems as well. Dominant shareholders, such as venture capitalists, are interested in protecting their investments and have a strong interest in monitoring entrepreneurial teams by controlling expenses and strategic decisions. Other stakeholders for example universities as technology providers, may wish to monitor entrepreneurial spin-offs in how their technology is commercialized (see Clarysse et al., 2007).

A major interest in academic research on the role of boards of directors in mitigating agency problems is in analyzing board composition (Zahra and Pierce, 1989). In Anglo-Saxon countries, board composition with respect to the numbers of insiders and outsiders is endogenous and is shaped by the CEO's bargaining power (Adams et al., 2010). Although empirical results are rather mixed, it is widely assumed that outsiders have a stronger incentive to monitor the top management team than insiders (see Deutsch and Ross, 2003). Thus, board composition is taken as an endogenous variable, analyzing the factors that shape the ratio of insiders on the board, such as past performance of the CEO which increases his or her bargaining power (Jain and Tabak, 2008).

Board composition is also considered as an exogenous variable, explaining top management selection, remuneration or dismissal. However, empirical evidence is rather mixed – since board composition and size are associated with costs and benefits (Huse, 1990, 2000), often expressed by an inverted U-shaped relationship between board characteristics and efficiency or performance (Daily and Dalton, 1993, Randøy and Goel, 2003).

Board compositions in entrepreneurial firms differ from those in large organizations but also from those in small and medium-sized firms, which are often dominated by family members on the board (Huse, 1990, 2000). In entrepreneurial firms, agency problems are assumed to be less pronounced and the role of the board of directors is not only reduced to the monitoring function but also entails the role of an active advisor (see Forbes and Milliken, 1999). Management and founding teams in entrepreneurial firms are less likely to concern themselves with issues of monitoring, but rather of mentoring. If entrepreneurial firms and their management teams are striving for growth, the use of external advisors on the board may be an opportunity to supplement the human capital of the management team with complementary experiences and skills. While it is also widely assumed that CEOs in small and medium-sized enterprises (SMEs) tend to adopt inappropriate governance structures, like lower numbers of outsiders, Dalton and Daily (1992) find the opposite for the fastest-growing entrepreneurial firms in their dataset. They interpret their findings in that CEOs of the most successful entrepreneurial firms recognize the need for professionalizing the firm by the use of outside experts, a strategy which affords outside resources and expertise without sacrificing effective control of the firm. Clarysse et al. (2007) show that large stakeholders such as venture capitalists or universities are more likely to develop boards with complementary skills. Audretsch et al. (2009) point to the strategic advantage of complementary skills of board members and show that those entrepreneurial firms outperform in abnormal returns and stock market survival (Audretsch and Lehmann, 2005). Brunninge et al. (2007) analyze the effects of board ownership and board composition on strategic change. They confirm that closely held firms exhibit less strategic change than do SMEs relying on more widespread ownership structures, and recommend that closely held firms could overcome this weakness by utilizing outside directors on the board or by extending the size of the top management team. The importance of the advisory role of boards of directors is also highlighted by Minichilli and Hansen (2007). They examine what effects a board of directors' involvement in the advice to management has in crisis. They point out that board member diversity becomes particularly important during crises as it provides the CEO with access to a more diverse pool of competencies and experiences.

An emerging literature investigates the dynamics of board composition in entrepreneurial firms and newly listed companies (Baker and Gompers, 2003). This research focuses on boards as a means by which entrepreneurial firms can manage external dependency and incorporate social exchange, on social networks and on resource dependence and other theories to improve our understanding of corporate governance in entrepreneurial firms (Uhlaner et al., 2007). In this context, board formation and evolution of board composition in academic spin-offs reached the attention of academics (Voharo et al., 2004; Björnali and Gulbrandson, 2010). Boards in academic spin-offs as entrepreneurial firms in transition are particularly interesting to study since these new ventures go through a number of stages of activity and need to develop resources and capabilities to enable their transition from a non-commercial environment to the market (Filatotchev et al., 2006; Björnali and Gulbrandson, 2010).

In contrast to large and publicly traded corporations, board composition in entrepreneurial firms attaches great importance to obtaining additional resources from outside the firm (Clarysse et al., 2007; Audretsch et al., 2009) instead of to monitoring the management team. As Björnali and Gulbrandson (2010, p. 93) point out, finding appropriate board members is a challenge for entrepreneurial firms in science-based industries with networks limited to peers within academia (Mosey and Wright, 2007; Hülsbeck and Lehmann, 2012). Audretsch and Stephan (1996) were among the first to point out that in science-based and high-technology industries board members access and absorb external knowledge and therefore need very different characteristics and qualifications.

Another distinction to large and publicly traded corporations lies in a firm's life cycle and its consequences on board composition. While most of the established firms have reached the 'maturity' levels within their life cycles (Lynall et al., 2003), entrepreneurial firms are, if at all, in the 'adolescence' phase of their life cycle. To move entrepreneurial firms forward to the next steps in the life cycle, new configurations of resources and capabilities must be obtained by attracting new external directors providing access to new resources (Björnali and Gulbrandson, 2010). Different board members are needed within shorter periods of time as compared to large and publicly traded firms in different stages (Vohora et al., 2004; Vanaelst et al., 2006). Board composition thus reflects changes in a firm's life cycle and the need for additional resources to exploit strategic advantage over rivals (Audretsch et al., 2009). Another step in the life cycle of entrepreneurial firms is the point, when shareholders of the firm, for example owners or venture capitalists, decide to sell the company to a competitor in order to secure financial gains out of the entrepreneurial firm. While mergers and acquisitions are often a synonym for an unfriendly takeover in the case of large and middle-sized companies, entrepreneurial firms, especially high-technology start-ups, choose this way to get remunerated for their effort. In this case, board composition could be a synonym for firm-value.

3.2.3 The presence of large shareholders

Small shareholders have little incentive to monitor management (Hart, 1995, p. 683). The cost of gathering information exceeds by far the benefits of an increased value of their shares. Beyond that, small or minority shareholders are far away from exerting power to control management, and they often lack the specific human capital to evaluate managers' actions and strategies. Concentrated ownership by large shareholders improves the control of managers by overcoming and mitigating the free-riding problem in corporate governance (Grossman and Hart, 1986; Hart, 1995) but also creates private benefits at the cost of minority shareholders, such as tunneling, adverse incentive effects (Rajan, 1992), the trade-off between liquidity and control (Bolton and Von Tadden, 1988), or risk-taking incentives biased toward too much risk.

While large shareholders and block-holders are well analyzed for large and publicly traded companies, their role and impact in entrepreneurial firms are little studied. Several large shareholders are identified and analyzed in the academic literature, for example banks and large creditors, and families or other firms, with mixed evidence (Lehmann and Weigand, 2000; Gugler, 2001; see also Audretsch and Lehmann, 2011).

Empirical studies analyzing the influence of large stakeholders mostly follow the same framework: a dummy variable indicates the type of shareholder, either a venture capital firm, commercial bank or the owner manager, among others, while the equity share is expressed either by the percentage of equity held by the respective type of shareholder or some measures of power within the group of all shareholders by using the Herfindahl Index. The endogenous variable measures the performance of the firm (where plenty of different performance measures are used).

3.2.4 Financial structure of entrepreneurial and newly listed firms

Hart (1995) highlights the corporate financial structure as an important source of discipline managers. Following the famous Modigliani–Miller theorem, entrepreneurial firms could either be financed via debt or equity. The conditions are best described by the Arrow–Debreu equilibrium model of frictionless markets which are perfectly competitive, without transaction costs, taxes and, most importantly, asymmetric information. In this Arrow–Debreu world, we have little or nothing to say about entrepreneurial financing choices. However, an implicit assumption of Modigliani and Miller (1958) is that markets are unhampered by taxes[5] and incentive problems. Abstracting from taxes, it is widely recognized that the decision to seek external financing and the type of financing are related to incentive problems caused by information asymmetries between the entrepreneur and the financier. Entrepreneurs have information about their character, capabilities and the quality of their project or firm that investors do not have. This leads to adverse selection effects and moral hazard behavior resulting in a pecking order of finance (Myers and Majluf, 1984). Equity and debt are associated with different costs for the firm which thus favors one kind of financing over the other. According to this pecking order theory, firms prefer to finance new projects with internal cash flows first and thus aim at signaling high project quality. They thereafter seek external debt and, finally, external equity capital. Financial resources or a firm's capital structure reflect adverse selection effects and thus serve as a signal for market participants. Equity financing and thus the dilution of ownership stakes is, given unused debt capacity, indicative a low-quality firm.

Banks and debt holders There are several aspects in that debt limits inefficient management (Hart, 1995, p. 685). Debt serves as a bonding or commitment device making it credible that the top management team will not expand its empire too much. In newly listed companies, debt may be put in place by the initial owner before the IPO or by active shareholders at a later stage. As providers of debt in entrepreneurial and newly listed companies, the role of banks is twofold: first, banks are seen as delegated monitors who exhibit specific human capital and expertise in monitoring and controlling managers, and second, banks act as large debt holders and are tough on managers after default (Dewatripont and Tirole, 1994). Although there is overwhelming evidence that banks as financial intermediaries play a major role in the reduction of information asymmetries and agency costs (Diamond, 1984), they may fail in providing debt when the degree of asymmetric information is too high. In this case, a profit-maximizing bank cannot capture the expected costs of debt by the interest rates of the loan (Stiglitz and Weiss, 1981). Entrepreneurial firms, operating in high-technology industries, are associated with high expected returns but are also associated with higher risk. According to the famous Stiglitz and Weiss approach (1981), they are faced with a higher moral hazard risk for the bank and with adverse selection effects. Banks cover their risks with interest rates. Unfortunately, the probability of bankruptcy increases not only with firm risk but also with increases in interest rates. This might lead to moral hazard behavior, such as gambling for resurrection and adverse selection effects of high-risk entrepreneurial firms. Thus, using asymmetric information, banks would chose an equilibrium interest rate which leads to credit rationing for firms which operate in industries, or choose projects which are associated with a higher risk as corresponding to the equilibrium interest rate. Thus, entrepreneurial firms are more or less restrained from receiving bank loans or debt.

Empirical evidence shows that entrepreneurial firms in science-based and high-technology industries suffer from insufficient funding (Kortum and Lerner, 2000). In particular the lack of collateral and reputation constrains the borrowing capacity of entrepreneurial firms (Lehmann et al., 2004). While ample literature has identified the importance of lending relationships for small and new firms as a mechanism compensating for their lack of credit history (Berger and Udell, 1990, 1998; Harhoff and Körting, 1998; Degryse and van Cayseele, 2000; Lehmann and Neuberger, 2001),[6] this does not hold for entrepreneurial firms largely based on intangible and non-physical assets, such as human capital, ideas, and intellectual properties (Rajan and Zingales, 2000; Fabel, 2004).

Typically, banks are almost always extensively represented on the supervisory boards of such companies. However, evidence on the effects of banks monitoring firms is mixed. On the one hand, banks can act as delegated monitors and use their experience and know-how to carefully monitor and control a firm. Additionally, according to the free-cash flow theory, debt increases the probability of default which managers work hard to avoid. On the other hand, banks follow their own interests at the firm's costs (Audretsch and Elston, 1997).

Debt This is another instrument to discipline managers and reduce agency costs since it implies the transfer of control over the firms' assets from the manager to the creditor (Hart, 2001). Debt makes it credible that managers will not expand their empires too much. According to the free-cash flow hypotheses (Jensen, 1986) debt increases the probability of default, and managers work hard to avoid it. Similar effects hold for leveraged buyouts (LBOs) where managers purchase firms which they finance with debt. There is ample evidence that debt disciplines managers in large and public corporations up to the point where debt overhang forces managers to invest in too risky projects and excessive risk-taking (see Hart, 2001). However, debt only plays a minor role as a governance mechanism in entrepreneurial firms. Debt as governance mechanism requires that managers return the free-cash flows to debt holders to avoid default. Since entrepreneurial firms are often far from having positive cash flows, debt holders and large creditors only play a minor role in them.

Venture capitalists Some authors cast doubt on the Stiglitz and Weiss (1981) approach and in particular the assumption of mean-preserving spreads of risk which results in credit rationing. De Meza and Webb (2000), among others, argue that banks may not be ill informed relative to the entrepreneurial team and, thus, equity finance could also serve as an indicator for high-quality projects. Lel and Udell (2002) suggest that the amount of debt held by an entrepreneur signals both his or her capability and personal guarantees, and venture capitalists may interpret debt as a quality signal solving the adverse selection problem and, thus, be less reluctant to invest in such entrepreneurial firms (Gompers and Lerner, 2001, 2011). Venture capitalists specialize in highly risky projects and play a crucial role in governing entrepreneurial firms. Profits are generated via a portfolio of firms where most of the ventures fail but some of the selected firms make spectacular profits, for example, Apple, Google, Intel or Microsoft, which initially received venture capital.

As mentioned above, entrepreneurial firms are characterized by the high risk of their projects and significant information asymmetries. This very nature of entrepreneurial firms prevents them from writing perfect contracts with investors or financiers in which obligations are specified in all relevant conceivable future contingencies (Hart and Moore, 1990), and thus the traditional principal–agency approach fails to govern entrepreneurial firms.

Like banks, venture capitalists are engaged in monitoring their firms. However, they differ from banks in controlling and monitoring firms in several important aspects. First, they take concentrated equity positions in the companies they finance, associated with seats on the boards, and thus actively monitor and control the management team. Secondly, they bring expertise and industry contacts and thus directly shapes firm performance (see Lehmann, 2004). Thirdly, funds are provided at several stages, and at each stage the firm is given just enough cash to reach the next stage. At each stage, the venture capitalist decides whether to stop funding without justification or to provide further funds for the next stage. Staging investments reduces agency costs and verifiability problems (Gompers, 1995; Bergemann and Hege, 1998). They also use the right to control future financing with pre-emptive rights to participate in new financing. Finally, they decide over the exit strategies: selling part or all of their shares in an IPO to other investors, such as pension funds or individual investors, or allowing the entrepreneurial firm to be purchased by a larger company (Cumming and MacIntosh, 2003).

The active role venture capitalists play in governing entrepreneurial firms is documented by the high rate of managerial displacement. Venture capitalists often have the right to demote or fire the top managers or CEOs if some key investment objective is not met, although the fired CEO is the initial founder of the start-up, with high ownership stakes in the firm. While active monitoring should lead to above average performance and positive externalities to other shareholders, it comes at a cost. Venture capitalists, in contrast to banks, contribute technological expertise which allows them to identify projects, but also to undertake the projects without the founder or initial entrepreneur (Ueda, 2004; Bottazi et al. 2008). This creates a double moral-hazard problem: entrepreneurs may underinvest in firm-specific investments after receiving the necessary financial resources in the first stages. Also the venture capitalist has an incentive to replace the entrepreneur. As Aghion and Bolton (1992) show, the double moral-hazard problem in financing entrepreneurship is particularly exacerbated in high-technology and science-based industries. As the relationship between the venture capitalist and the entrepreneurial firm develops over time, eventualities arise that could not easily have been foreseen or spelled out in an initial contract. Thus, neither the entrepreneur nor the venture capitalist undertakes first-best actions in order to enhance the expected outcome of the entrepreneurial firm or project (Kaplan and Strömberg, 2003, 2004).

The role as active monitors in governing entrepreneurial firms played by venture capitalists is not only associated with benefits, but also with costs. Thus, empirical evidence on the performance of venture backed firms is mixed and differs across countries and across different tax systems (Keuschnigg and Nielson, 2002, 2004). Black and Gilson (1998) point out the importance of an active stock market for the development of venture capital and thus the possibility to provide equity to entrepreneurial firms. Thus, performance of venture-backed entrepreneurial firms varies between countries with bank-based systems – for example, continental Europe – and those with more specialized markets. An active and specialized stock market thus may be a necessary condition for exit strategies but is by no means sufficient in explaining performance differences (Becker and Hellmann, 2003). In bank-based countries, such as Germany, public–private venture capitalists, with large private and public or state-owned banks as the major shareholders of venture capital firms, are the dominant form of venture capitalists. As Bascha and Waltz (2002) show, they often underperform as compared to private partnerships. Bottazzi and Da Rin (2002) analyze the role of venture capital in several European countries and find evidence suggesting that venture capital-backed entrepreneurial firms do not grow faster than those that are not backed by venture capital, while Lehmann (2004) confirms higher growth rates.

Universities and research institutes Since the end of the 1990s, spin-offs from universities and public research have received growing interest from policy-makers, altering the role of universities and research institutes from public institutes to private shareholders (see Mustar et al., 2006). Within this trend, a rich literature emerged highlighting the creation of academic spin-offs and start-ups (see Wright et al., 2004; Rothaermel et al., 2007). At the same time plenty of empirical studies analyzed the impact of universities spillovers on entrepreneurial firms' location and performance (Audretsch et al., 2004; Audretsch and Lehmann, 2005; Colombo et al., 2010a, 2010b). But only a few studies focus directly on the role of universities as major shareholders, finding, if at all, mixed empirical evidence.

Following the findings from corporate governance research, each type of shareholder is associated with specific costs and benefits. Unfortunately, these costs and benefits could hardly be separated in empirical studies and thus most studies fail to find compelling evidence either for a positive or a negative impact on firm performance. As a result, most studies conclude that 'shareholder X has no statistically significant impact on firm performance'.[7]

Costs and benefits should also be observed by universities or research institutes as large shareholders, in particular for university spin-offs and academic start-ups. The value-adding benefits of university or research institute affiliation are access to intangible sources of knowledge and human capital, and physical assets and resources such as laboratories. Universities and research institutes as large shareholders also provide access to emerging and future technologies, reduce the costs of developing new capabilities, to promote information sharing of tacit knowledge and offer important network connections. Strong academic support can also enhance the confidence and valuation of other stakeholders, like venture capitalists (Wright et al., 2007). Thus, science-based entrepreneurial firms with universities and research institutes as large shareholders should outperform entrepreneurial firms with other types of large shareholders.

Nevertheless, universities and research institutes as large shareholders may also have a downside. Foremost, academics as founders or members of the board of directors as representatives of the university may not have enough business and commercial experience to properly exploit innovations (Zahra et al., 2007). Representatives of universities or research institutes involved in governing and controlling university spin-off may not solely be motivated by pursuing a profit-maximizing strategy for the venture. Although there are well-known examples of the superior performance of universities as large shareholders, for example Harvard, Berkeley, or the Massachusetts Institute of Technology (MIT) in the US, there are only a few studies analyzing the performance of university-based entrepreneurial firms (see Bonardo et al., 2011).

Most of these studies implicitly assume that universities are the main large shareholders. Colombo et al. (2010a) examine the effects of a series of characteristics of local universities, such as scientific quality, on growth rates of academic start-ups and non-academic entrepreneurial firms and start-ups. They found compelling evidence that scientific quality, the 'type' of shareholder, matters for academic start-ups but not for the control group. One exception is Bonardo et al. (2011). They directly evaluate university-based entrepreneurial firms and compare them to several control groups. Based on a dataset of 499 high-technology and entrepreneurial firms from European countries, they found compelling evidence that affiliation with a university enhances valuation, in particular when academics are present in the top management team. For firms who publicize the fact that they are university based and have chosen to go public, the affiliation with a university is recognized as beneficial by investors. However, in the long run, university-based entrepreneurial firms underperform independent firms – revealing that the 'costs' of having a university or research institute as a large shareholder outweigh the benefits in the long run.

3.2.5 Legal regulations and tools

It is often argued from free-market economists and pure financial theorists that a market economy can achieve efficient corporate governance without government intervention. In such a free-market economy, the entrepreneur has an incentive to choose an efficient corporate governance structure that maximizes the aggregate returns to all stakeholders at the time of the IPO. Thus, an entrepreneur has an incentive to choose procedures for the selection of the best members of the board of directors, disclosure rules and other governance rules that maximize total surplus (Hart, 1995, p. 686). Bottazzi et al. (2009) develop a theoretical approach and empirical test of how the legal system affects the relationship between venture capitalists and entrepreneurs. They rely on the double moral-hazard framework and show how optimal contracts and investor actions depend on the quality of the legal system. Their empirical evidence, based on a sample of European venture capital deals, shows that with better legal protection, investors give more non-contractible support and demand more downside protection. They also find that the investor's legal system is more important than that of the company in determining investor behavior (see also Cumming et al., 2010).

However, it was not only the dotcom crisis in 2003 and, later, the financial crisis in 2007 that revealed the opposite, the need for statutory corporate governance rules. In the absence of perfect markets, and thus the existence of externalities and unforeseen contingencies, corporate governance problems arise that cannot be sufficiently solved without regulation. There is ample empirical evidence that 'law' matters in corporate governance all over the world (see LaPorta et al., 1998). In particular, countries differ in investor protection, insider trading legislation, financial regulation, as well as law enforcement (Cromme, 2005). Statutory corporate governance rules differ not only across countries but also within countries – in particular between listed and public companies on the one hand and private companies on the other. This leads to a 'one-size-fits-it-all' mentality of law-makers all over the world for listed and public companies (Arcot and Bruno, 2006). This lumps together entrepreneurial and newly listed companies with large and established corporations, although they differ in their causes and consequences of governance problems.

4 SUMMARY, CONCLUDING REMARKS AND SUGGESTIONS FOR FUTURE RESEARCH

In this survey we tried to summarize past and recent research on corporate governance and link them to entrepreneurial and newly listed companies. While corporate governance of large and public companies is an established field in business, management, finance, and economics, corporate governance mechanisms in newly listed companies are rather underestimated and lack theoretical and empirical evidence. Separating the corporate governance mechanisms in market-based mechanisms on the one hand, and institutional or hierarchical mechanisms on the other, may help as a workhorse for analyzing and studying corporate governance problems in companies. Since agency and transaction costs differ across firm characteristics, such as size, age, production technology and whether they are start-up firms, newly listed companies or large and established firms, the costs of corporate governance differ accordingly. Market mechanisms and institutional mechanisms in corporate governance are also associated with costs and benefits. Thus, there is no 'one-size-fits-it-all' mechanism in corporate governance which solves all the corporate governance problems. While some of the mechanisms attracted increasing interest by academic research in the past decade, such as the board of directors or the role of venture capitalists in governing entrepreneurial firms, other mechanisms, for example, the market for managers, the product market or large shareholders like universities, received less attention. In addition, some of the mechanisms are complementary, such as the market for corporate control and the market for managers, others, such as debt or investments in monitoring by directors, are substitutes. Academic research is far from providing sufficient solutions about the pros and cons of the different mechanisms in corporate governance, and how these mechanisms differ across newly listed companies and large and established firms.

With this survey we try to motivate and stimulate future research, both theoretically and empirically, to increase our understanding on the governance of entrepreneurial and newly listed firms and how and why governance mechanisms differ across different types of firms. While we assume that moral hazard is more prevalent in large and established firms and entrepreneurial firms suffer from adverse selection problems, future research could put this as a starting point – confirming the assumption or finding contrary evidence.

Further research is also required that examines the role of universities and research institutes as large shareholders of entrepreneurial firms, how their costs and benefits differ, and how they are represented within the board of entrepreneurial firms. In this context, the role of technology transfer offices could be examined as an intermediary between the university and research institution on the one hand, and the academic spin-off on the other. There remains also a paucity of evidence regarding the impact of universities and research institutions not only on the failure of entrepreneurial firms, but also on their performance. There is need for research that examines the rationales of the different large stakeholders and their interrelationship in governing entrepreneurial firms.

Finally, and perhaps the most important and promising, but also the most difficult, approach should be linking simultaneously the different mechanisms as described above into one theoretical and or empirical framework. Existing empirical and theoretical studies often analyze how one isolated mechanism – for example, the composition of the total management board – shapes firm performance. Mechanisms in corporate governance are endogenous and also interrelated either in a complementary or a substitutive way. Understanding these interrelated effects, together with empirical problems, such as the endogenous problem in datasets, offers this field of research a promising future for academics to provide helpful insights for both policy-makers and the most important person in an economy, the entrepreneur!

NOTES

1. See Audretsch and Lehmann (2011) for a discussion and collection of papers on this topic.
2. This follows directly from the well-known Akerlof analysis of the Lemon's market in used cars (Akerlof, 1970).
3. This section is mainly based on Audretsch and Lehmann (2007) and Lehmann et al. (2012).
4. Empirical studies highlight the turnover of managers in poorly performing firms and the replacement by insiders (Holmstrom and Kaplan, 2001) and outsiders (Denis and Denis, 1995; Weisbach, 1995; Parrino, 1997) in large corporations.
5. As mentioned by Hart (2001), if taxes are the main factors influencing the debt-equity ratio, we should see much higher debt-equity ratios than we actually do.
6. For an excellent reader see Degryse et al. (2009).
7. There exists compelling arguments why ownership structure could not shape firm performance. Demsetz (1983) argues that if ownership structure is chosen optimally, there could neither be a positive or negative effect from ownership structure on firm performance. However, this argument, or Demsetz Hypothesis, is based on (nearly) perfect market mechanisms which forces firms to choose the optimal governance structure or to fail.

REFERENCES

Acs, Z.J. (2011), 'High-impact entrepreneurship', in Z.J. Acs and D.B. Audretsch (eds), *Handbook of Entrepreneurship Research*, 2nd edn, New York: Springer Press. pp. 165–82.

Adams, R.B., B.E. Hermalin and M.S. Weisbach (2010), 'The role of boards of directors in corporate governance: a conceptual framework and survey', *Journal of Economic Literature* **48** (1), 58–107.

Aghion, P. and P. Bolton (1992), 'An incomplete contracts approach to financial contracting', *Review of Economic Studies*, **77**, 338–401.

Akerlof, G.A. (1970), 'The market for "lemons": quality uncertainty and the market mechanism', *The Quarterly Journal of Economics*, **84** (3), 488–500.

Alvarez, S.A., J.B. Barney and S.L. Young (2011), 'Debates in entrepreneurship: opportunity formation and implications for the field of entrepreneurship', in Z.J. Acs and D.B. Audretsch (eds), *Handbook of Entrepreneurship Research*, New York: Springer Press, pp. 23–46.

Ang, J. and N. Kohers (2001), 'The take-over market for privately held companies: the US experience', *Cambridge Journal of Economics*, **25** (6), 723–48.

Arcot, S.R. and G.V. Bruno, (2006), 'One size does not fit all, after all: evidence from corporate governance', paper presented at the 1st Annual Conference on Empirical Legal Studies, available at: http://ssrn.com/abstract=887947 or http://dx.doi.org/10.2139/ssrn.887947 (accessed December 2006).

Audretsch, D.B. (1995), *Innovation and Industry Evolution*, Cambridge, MA: MIT Press.

Audretsch, D.B. (2007), *The Entrepreneurial Society*, Oxford: Oxford University Press.

Audretsch, D.B. and J.A Elston (1997), 'Financing the German Mittelstand', *Small Business Economics*, **9** (2), 97–110.

Audretsch, D.B. and E.E. Lehmann (2004), 'Debt or equity: the role of venture capital in financing high-tech firms in Germany', *Schmalenbach Business Review*, **56**, 340–57.

Audretsch, D.B., and E.E. Lehmann (2005), 'The effects of experience, ownership, and knowledge on IPO survival: empirical evidence from Germany', *Review of Accounting and Finance*, **4** (4), 13–33.

Audretsch, D.B. and E.E. Lehmann (2006), 'Entrepreneurial access and absorption of knowledge spillovers: strategic board and managerial composition for competitive advantage', *Journal of Small Business Management*, **44** (2), 155–66.

Audretsch, D.B. and E.E. Lehmann (2007), Mergers and acquisitions in IPO markets: evidence from Germany, in G.N. Gregoriou and L. Renneboog (eds), *International Mergers and Acquisitions Activity Since 1990: Recent and Quantitative Analysis*, Amsterdam: Elsevier, pp. 169–79.

Audretsch, D.B. and E.E. Lehmann (2008), 'The Neuer Markt as an institution of creation and destruction', *International Entrepreneurship and Management Journal*, **4**, 419–29.

Audretsch, D.B. and E.E. Lehmann (eds) (2011), *Corporate Governance in Small and Medium-Sized Firms*, Cheltenham, UK and Northampton, MA, USA: Edward Elgar.

Audretsch, D.B. and P. Stephan (1996), 'Company-scientist locational links: the case of biotechnology', *American Economic Review*, **86** (3), 641–52.

Audretsch, D.B. and R.A. Thurik (2001), 'What's new about the new economy? sources of growth in the managed and entrepreneurial economies, *Industrial & Corporate Change*, **10**, 267–315.

Audretsch, D.B., M. Keilbach and E.E. Lehmann (2006a), *Entrepreneurship and Economic Growth*, Oxford University Press: Oxford.

Audretsch, D.B., M. Keilbach and E.E. Lehmann (2006b), 'The knowledge spillover theory of entrepreneurship and economic growth', *Economica e Politica Industriale*, 3, 25–45.

Audretsch, D.B., L. Klomp, E. Santarelli and A.R. Thurik (2004), 'Gibrat's Law: are the services different?', *Review of Industrial Organization*, **24**, 301–24.

Audretsch, D.B., E.E. Lehmann and L.A. Plummer (2009), 'Agency and governance in strategic entrepreneurship', *Entrepreneurship Theory and Practice*, **33** (1), 149–66.

Baker, G.P. and R.E. Kennedy (2002), 'Survivorship and the economic grim reaper', *Journal of Law, Economics, and Organization*, **18** (2), 324–61.

Baker, M. and P.A. Gompers (2003), 'The determinants of board structure at the initial public offering', *Journal of Law and Economics*, **66** (2), 569–98.

Bascha, A. and U. Walz (2002), 'Financing practices in the German venture capital industry: an empirical assessment', CFS Working Paper, 2002/08.

Becht, M., P. Bolton and A. Röell (2003), 'Corporate governance and control', in G.M. Constantinides, M. Harris and R.M. Stulz (eds), *Handbook of the Economics of Finance*, Amsterdam: North Holland, pp. 1–109.

Becker, G. (1968), 'Crime and punishment: an economic approach', *The Journal of Political Economy*, **76**, 169–217.

Becker, R. and T. Hellmann (2003), 'The genesis of venture capital: lessons from the German experience', in V. Kanniainen and C. Keuschnigg (eds), *Venture Capital, Entrepreneurship, and Public Policy*, Cambridge: MIT Press, pp. 33–67.

Bénabou, R. and J. Tirole (2007), 'Identity, dignity and taboos: beliefs as assets', CEPR Discussion Paper 6123, January.

Bergemann, D. and U. Hege (1998), 'Venture capital financing, moral hazard, and learning', *Journal of Banking & Finance*, **22** (6/8), 703–35.

Berger, A. and G. Udell (1990), 'Collateral, bank quality, and bank risk', *Journal of Monetary Economics*, **25**, 21–42.

Berger, A. and G.F. Udell (1998), 'The economics of small business finance: the roles of private equity and debt markets in the financial growth cycle', *Journal of Banking & Finance*, **22** (6/8), 613–73.

Berle, A.A. and G.C. Means (1932), *The Modern Corporation and Private Property*, New York: Macmillan.

Beuselinck, C. and S. Manigart (2007), 'Financial reporting quality in private equity backed companies: the impact of ownership concentration', *Small Business Economics*, **29**, 261–74.

Birley, S. and D. Norburn (1985), 'Small versus large companies: the entrepreneurial conundrum', *The Journal of Business Strategy*, **6** (1), 81–7.

Birley, S. and P. Westhead (1993), 'A comparison of new businesses established by "novice" and "habitual" founders in Great Britain', *International Small Business Journal*, **12** (1), 38–60.

Björnali, E. and M. Gulbrandsen (2010), 'Exploring board formation and evolution of board composition in academic spin-offs', *Journal of Technology Transfer*, **35** (1), 92–112.

Black, B.S. and R.J. Gilson (1988), 'Venture capital and the structure of capital markets: banks versus stock markets', *Journal of Financial Economics*, **47** (3), 243–77.

Bloningen, B.A. and C.T. Taylor (2000), 'R&D intensity and acquisitions in high technology industries: evidence from the US electronic and electrical equipment industries', *Journal of Industrial Economics*, **68** (1), 47–70.

Bolton, P. and E. von Thadden (1988), 'Blocks, liquidity, and corporate control', *Journal of Finance*, **53** (1), 1–25.

Bonardo, D., S. Paleari and S. Vismara (2010), 'The M&A dynamics of European science-based entrepreneurial firms', *The Journal of Technology Transfer*, **35** (1), 141–80.

Bonardo, D., S. Paleari and S. Vismara (2011), 'Valuing university-based firms: the effects of academic affiliation on IPO performance', *Entrepreneurship Theory & Practice*, **35** (4), 755–66.

Bottazzi, L. and M. Da Rin (2002), 'Venture capital in Europe and the financing of innovative companies', *Economic Policy*, **17**, 229–65.

Bottazzi, L., M. Da Rin and T. Hellmann (2008), 'Who are the active investors? Evidence from venture capital', *Journal of Financial Economics*, **89** (3), 488–512.

Bottazzi, L., M. Da Rin and T. Hellmann (2009), 'What is the role of legal systems in financial intermediation? Theory and evidence', *Journal of Financial Intermediation*, **18** (4), 559–98.

Brau, J.C., F. Bill and N. Kohers (2003), 'The choice of IPO versus takeover: empirical evidence', *Journal of Business*, **76**, 583–612.

Brunninge, O., M. Nordqvist and J. Wiklund (2007), 'Corporate governance and strategic change in SMEs: the effects of ownership, board composition and top management teams', *Small Business Economics*, **29** (3): 295–308.

Buenstorf, G. (2007), 'Creation and pursuit of entrepreneurial opportunities: an evolutionary perspective', *Small Business Economics*, **28**, 323–27.

Caves, R.E. (1998), 'Industrial organization and new findings on firm turnover', *Journal of Economic Literature*, **36** (4), 1947–82.

Clarysse, B., M. Knockaert and A. Lockett (2007), 'Outside board members in high tech start-ups', *Small Business Economics*, **29**, 243–59.

Coase, R.H. (1937), 'The nature of the firm', *Economica*, **4** (16), 386–405.

Coff, R.W. (1999), 'How buyers cope with uncertainty when acquiring firms in knowledge-intensive industries: caveat emptor', *Organization Science*, **10**, 144–61.

Colombo, M., D. D'Adda and E. Piva (2010b), 'The contribution of university research to the growth of academic start-ups: an empirical analysis', *The Journal of Technology Transfer*, **35** (1), 113–40.

Colombo, M., P. Mustar and M. Wright (2010a), 'Dynamics of science-based entrepreneurship', *The Journal of Technology Transfer*, **35** (1), 1–15.

Cromme, G. (2005), 'Corporate governance in Germany and the German corporate governance code', *Corporate Governance: An International Review*, **13**, 362–7.

Cumming, D.J. and J.G. MacIntosh (2003), 'A cross-country comparison of full and partial venture capital exits', *Journal of Banking & Finance*, **27** (3), 511–48.

Cumming, D.J., D. Schmidt and U. Walz (2010), 'Legality and venture governance around the world', *Journal of Business Venturing*, **25**, 54–72.

Daily, C.M. and D. Dalton (1993), 'Board of directors leadership and structure: control and performance implications', *Entrepreneurship: Theory and Practice*, **17** (3), 65–81.

Dalton, D. and C.M. Daily (1992), 'Financial performance of founder-managed versus professionally managed corporations', *Journal of Small Business Economics*, **30** (2), 25–34.

De Meza, D. and D. Webb (2000), 'Does credit rationing imply insufficient lending?', *Journal of Public Economics*, **78** (3), 215–34.

Degryse, H. and P. Van Cayseele (2000), 'Relationship lending within a bank-based system: evidence from European small business data', *Journal of Financial Intermediation*, **9** (1), 90–109.

Degryse, H., K. Moshe and S. Ongena (2009), *Microeconometrics of Banking: Methods, Applications and Results*, Oxford: Oxford University Press.
Demsetz, H. (1983), 'The structure of ownership and the theory of the firm', *Journal of Law and Economics*, **26**, 375–90.
Denis, D.J. and D.K. Denis (1995), 'Performance changes following top management dismissal', *Journal of Finance*, **50**, 1029–57.
Denis, D.K. (2001), 'Twenty-five years of corporate governance research . . . and counting', *Review of Financial Economics*, **10**, 191–212.
DeTienne D.R. (2010), 'Entrepreneurial exit as a critical component of the entrepreneurial process: theoretical development', *Journal of Business Venturing*, **25** (2), 203–15.
DeTienne, D.R. and M.S. Cardon (2012), 'Impact of founder experience on exit intensions', *Small Business Economics*, **38** (4), 351–74.
Deutsch, Y. and T.W. Ross (2003), 'You are known by the directors you keep: reputable directors as a signaling mechanism for young firms', *Management Science*, **49** (8): 1003–17.
Dewatripont, M. and J. Tirole (1994), 'A theory of debt and equity: diversity of securities and manager-shareholder congruence', *The Quarterly Journal of Economics*, **109** (4), 1027–54.
Diamond, D.W. (1984), 'Financial intermediation and delegated monitoring', *The Review of Economic Studies*, **51** (3), 393–414.
Eckbo, B., R. Espen M. Giammarino and R.L. Heinkel (1990), 'Asymmetric information and the medium of exchange in takeovers: theory and tests', *Review of Financial Studies*, **3**, 651–75.
Ellingsen, T. and K. Rydqvist (1997), 'The stock market as a screening device and the decision to go public', Working Paper Series in Economics and Finance 174, Stockholm School of Economics.
Fabel, O. (2004), 'Spinoffs of entrepreneurial firms: an o-ring approach', *Journal of Institutional and Theoretical Economics*, **160**, 416–38.
Fama, E.F. (1980), 'Agency problems and the theory of the firm', *Journal of Political Economy*, **88** (2), 288–307.
Fama, E.F. and K.R. French (2001), 'Disappearing dividends: changing firm characteristics or lower propensity to pay?', *Journal of Financial Economics*, **60** (1), 3–43.
Filatotchev, I., S. Toms and M. Wright (2006), 'The firm's strategic dynamics and corporate governance lifecycle', *International Journal of Managerial Finance*, **2** (4), 256–79.
Forbes, D. and F. Milliken (1999), 'Cognition and corporate governance: understanding boards of directors as strategic decision making groups', *Academy of Management Review*, **24**, 489–505.
Gans, J. and S. Stern (2000), 'Incumbency and R&D incentives: licensing the gale of creative destruction', *Journal of Economics and Management Strategy*, **9** (4), 485–511.
Gompers, P.A. (1995), 'Optimal investment, monitoring, and the staging of venture capital', *Journal of Finance*, **50** (5), 1461–89.
Gompers, P. and J. Lerner (2001), 'The really long-run performance of initial public offerings: the pre-Nasdaq evidence', *Journal of Finance*, **58** (4), 1355–92.
Gompers, P. and J. Lerner (2011), 'Equity financing', in Z.J. Acs and D.B. Audretsch (eds), *Handbook of Entrepreneurship Research*, New York: Springer Press, pp. 165–82, 2nd edn, pp. 183–214.
Gompers, P.A., and A. Metrick (2001), 'Institutional investors and equity prices', *Quarterly Journal of Economics*, **116** (1), 229–59.
Gorman, M. and W.A. Sahlman (1989), 'What do venture capitalists do?', *Journal of Business Venturing*, **4** (4), 231–48.
Granstrand, O. and S. Sjolander (1990), 'The acquisition of technology and small firms by large firms', *Journal of Economic Behavior and Organization*, **13**, 367–86.
Grimpe, C. and K. Hussinger (2008a), 'Pre-empting technology competition through firm acquisitions', *Economics Letters*, **100**, 189–91.
Grimpe, C. and K. Hussinger (2008b), 'Market and technology access through firm acquisitions: beyond one size fits all', ZEW Discussion Paper Series No. 08-037.
Grossman, S.J. and O.D. Hart (1986), 'The costs and benefits of ownership: a theory of vertical and lateral integration', *Journal of Political Economy*, **94**, 691–719.
Gugler, K. (2001), 'Corporate governance and performance', in K. Gugler (ed.), *Corporate Governance and Economic Performance*, Oxford: Oxford University Press, pp. 1–59.
Hall, B.H. (1990), 'The impact of corporate restructuring on industrial research and development', Brookings Papers on Economic Activity. Microeconomics 1990, pp. 85–135.
Harhoff, D. and T. Körting (1998), 'Lending relationships in Germany – empirical evidence from survey data', *Journal of Banking & Finance*, **22** (10/11), 1317–53.
Hart, O. (1995), 'Corporate governance: some theory and implications', *Economic Journal*, **195**, 678–89.
Hart, O. (2001), 'Financial contracting', *Journal of Economic Literature* **39**, 1079–100.
Hart, O. and J. Moore (1990), 'Property rights and the nature of the firm', *Journal of Political Economy*, **98**, 1119–58.

Hellmann, T. (2007), 'Entrepreneurs and the process of obtaining resources', *Journal of Economics & Management Strategy*, **16** (1), 81–110.
Hellmann, T. and M. Puri (2002), 'Venture capital and the professionalization of start-up firms: empirical evidence', *Journal of Finance*, **57**, 169–97.
Henkel, J., T. Rönde and M. Wagner (2010), 'And the winner is – acquired. Entrepreneurship as a contest with acquisition as the prize', CEPR Discussion Paper No. DP8147.
Hermalin, B.E. and M.S. Weisbach (2003), 'Boards of directors as an endogenously determined institution: a survey of the economic literature, *Economic Policy Review*, **9** (1), 7–26.
Hirschman, A.O. (1970), *Exit, Voice, and Loyalty*, Cambridge, MA: Harvard University Press.
Holmstrom, B. (1982), 'Moral hazard in teams', *Bell Journal of Economics*, **13** (2), 324–40.
Holmstom, B. and S. Kaplan (2001), 'Corporate governance and takeovers in the U.S.: making sense of the '80s and '90s', *Journal of Economic Perspectives*, Spring, 121–44.
Hülsbeck, M. and E.E. Lehmann (2012), 'Academic entrepreneurship and board formation in science-based firms', *Economics of Innovation and New Technology*, **21** (5–6), 547–65.
Huse, M. (1990), 'Board composition in small enterprises', *Entrepreneurship and Regional Development*, **2** (4), 363–73.
Huse, M. (2000), 'Boards of directors in SMEs: a review and research agenda', *Entrepreneurship and Regional Development*, **12** (4), 271–90.
Jain, B.A. and F. Tabak (2008), 'Factors influencing the choice between founder versus non-founder CEOs for IPO firms', *Journal of Business Venturing*, **23** (1), 21–45.
Jensen, M.C. (1986), 'Agency costs of free cash flow, corporate finance, and takeovers', *American Economic Review*, **76** (2), 323–9.
Jensen, M.C. and W.H. Meckling (1976), 'Theory of the firm: managerial behavior, agency costs and ownership structure', *Journal of Financial Economics*, **3** (4), 305–60.
Jovanovic, B. (1979), 'Job matching and the theory of turnover', *Journal of Political Economy*, **87** (5), 972–90.
Jovanovic, B. (1982), 'Selection and the evolution of industry', *Econometrica*, **50** (3), 649–70.
Kaplan, S.N. and P. Strömberg (2003), 'Financial contracting theory meets the real world: an empirical analysis of venture capital contracts', *Review of Economic Studies*, **70** (2), 281–315.
Kaplan, S.N. and P. Strömberg (2004), 'Characteristics, contracts, and actions: evidence from venture capitalist analyses', *Journal of Finance*, **59** (5), 2177–210.
Kapoor, R. and K. Lim (2007), 'The impact of acquisitions on the productivity of inventors at semiconductor firms: a synthesis of knowledge-based and incentive based perspectives', *Academy of Management Journal* **50** (5), 1133–55.
Keuschnigg, C. and S.B. Nielsen (2002), 'Tax policy, venture capital, and entrepreneurship', *Journal of Public Economics*, **87**, 175–203.
Keuschnigg, C. and S.B. Nielsen (2004), 'Start-ups, venture capitalists, and the capital gains tax', *Journal of Public Economics*, **88**, 1011–42
Koppl, R. and M. Minniti (2011), 'Market processes and entrepreneurial studies', in Z.J. Acs and D.B. Audretsch (eds), *Handbook of Entrepreneurship Research*, New York: Springer Press, pp. 165–182, 2nd edn, pp. 217–48.
Kortum, S. and J. Lerner (2000), 'Assessing the contribution of venture capital to innovation', *The RAND Journal of Economics*, **31** (4), 674–92.
La Porta R., F. Lopez-de-Silanes, A. Shleifer and R.W. Vishny (1998), 'Law and finance', *Journal of Political Economy*, **106** (6), 1113–55.
Lehmann, E.E. (2004), 'Does venture capital spur employment and growth?', *Small Business Economics*, **26**, 455–64.
Lehmann, E.E. (2006), 'Corporate governance in new enterprises or: why do some CEOs hold large equity stakes while others are paid through stock options?', *Zeitschrift für Betriebswirtschaftslehre Special Issue*, **5**, pp. 21–36.
Lehmann, E.E. and J. Weigand (2000), 'Does the governed corporation perform better? Governance structures and corporate performance in Germany', *European Finance Review*, **4** (2), 157–95.
Lehmann, E.E., T.V. Braun and S. Krispin (2012), 'Entrepreneurial human capital, complementary assets, and takeover probability', *Journal of Technology Transfer*, **37** (5), 589–608.
Lehmann, E., D. Neuberger and S. Räthke (2004), 'Lending to small and medium-sized firms: is there an east–west gap in Germany?', *Small Business Economics*, **23**, 23–39.
Lel, U. and G. Udell (2002), 'Financial constraints, startup firms and personal commitments', Kelley School of Business Working Paper, Indiana University.
Lian, Q. and Q. Wang (2007), 'The dual tracking puzzle: when IPO plans turn into mergers', EFA 2006 Zurich Meetings Paper.
Loughran, T. and J.R. Ritter (1995), 'The new issues puzzle', *Journal of Finance*, **50** (1), 23–51.

Loughran, T. and J.R. Ritter (2002), 'Why don't issuers get upset about leaving money on the table in IPOs?', *Review of Financial Studies*, **15**, 413–43
Loughran, T. and J.R. Ritter (2004), 'Why has IPO underpricing changed over time?', *Financial Management*, **33**, 5–37.
Lynall, M.D., B.R. Golden and A.J. Hillman (2003), 'Board composition from adolescence to maturity: a multitheoretic view', *Academy of Management Review*, **28** (3), 416–31.
Manne, H.G. (1965), 'Mergers and the market for corporate control', *Journal of Political Economy*, **73**, 110–20.
Minichilli, A. and C. Hansen (2007), 'The board advisory tasks in small firms and the event of crises', *Journal of Management and Governance*, **11** (1), 5–22.
Modigliani, F. and M.H. Miller (1958), 'The cost of capital, corporation finance and the theory of investment', *American Economic Review*, **48** (3), 261–97.
Mosey, S. and M. Wright (2007), 'From human capital to social capital: a longitudinal study of technology-based academic entrepreneurs', *Entrepreneurship Theory and Practice*, **31** (6), 909–35.
Mustar, P., M. Renault, M.G. Colombo, E. Piva, M. Fontes, A. Lockett, M. Wright, B. Clarysse and N. Moray (2006), 'Conceptualising the heterogeneity of research-based spin-offs: a multi-dimensional taxonomy', *Research Policy*, **35** (2), 289–308.
Myers, S.C. and N.S. Majluf (1984), 'Corporate financing and investment decisions when firms have information that investors do not have', *Journal of Financial Economics*, **13** (2), 187–221.
Nalebuff, B. and J. Stiglitz (1983), 'Information, competition, and markets', *American Economic Review*, **73**, 278–83.
Nickel, S. (1996), 'Competition and corporate governance', *Journal of Political Economy*, **104**, 724–46.
Norbäck, P.-J. and L. Persson (2009), 'The organization of the innovation industry: entrepreneurs, venture capitalists, and oligopolists', *Journal of the European Economic Association*, **7** (6), 1261–90.
Palepu, K.G. (1986), 'Predicting takeover targets', *Journal of Accounting & Economics*, **8**, 3–35.
Parrino, R. (1997), 'CEO turnover and outside succession. A cross-sectional analysis', *Journal of Financial Economics*, **46**, 165–97.
Paruchuri, S., A. Nerkar and D.C. Hambrick (2006), 'Acquisition integration and productivity losses in the technical core: disruption of inventors in acquired companies', *Organization Science*, **17** (5), 545–62.
Powell, R.G. (1997), 'Modeling takeover likelihood', *Journal of Business Finance & Accounting*, **24**, 1009–30.
Powell, R.G. (2004), 'Takeover prediction models and portfolio strategies: a multinomial approach', *Multinational Finance Journal*, **8**, 35–72.
Puranam, P. and K. Srikanth (2007), 'What they know vs. what they do: how acquirers leverage technology acquisitions', *Strategic Management Journal*, **28** (8), 805–25.
Rajan, R.G. (1992), 'Insiders and outsiders: the choice between informed and arm's-length debt', *The Journal of Finance*, **47** (4), 1367–400.
Rajan, R. and L. Zingales (1999), 'The politics of financial development', unpublished working paper, University of Chicago.
Rajan, R.G. and L. Zingales (2000), 'The governance of the new enterprise', in X. Vives (ed.), *Corporate Governance, Theoretical and Empirical Perspectives*, Cambridge: Cambridge University Press, pp. 201–27.
Rajan, R.G. and L. Zingales (2001), 'The firm as a dedicated hierarchie: a theory of the origin and growth of firms', *Quarterly Journal of Economics*, **116**, 805–51.
Randøy, T. and S. Goel (2003), 'Ownership structure, founder leadership, and performance in Norwegian SMEs: implications for financing entrepreneurial opportunities', *Journal of Business Venturing*, **18** (5), 619–37.
Ritter, J.R. (1991), 'The long-run performance of initial public offerings', *Journal of Finance*, **46**, 3–27.
Roe, M.J. (1994), *Strong Managers, Weak Owners: The Political Roots of American Corporate Finance*, Princeton, NJ: Princeton, University Press.
Rothaermel, F.T., S.D. Agung and L. Jiang (2007), 'University entrepreneurship: a taxonomy of the literature', *Industrial and Corporate Change*, **16** (4), 691–791.
Scharfstein, D. (1988), 'Product market competition and managerial slack', *RAND Journal of Economics*, **19**, 147–55.
Schmidt, K. (1997), 'Managerial incentives and product market competition', *Review of Economic Studies*, **64**, 191–214.
Shen, J.-C. and J. Reuer (2005), 'Adverse selection in acquisitions of small manufacturing firms: a comparison of private and public targets', *Small Business Economics*, **24**, 393–407.
Shleifer, A. and R.W. Vishny (1997), 'A survey of corporate governance', *Journal of Finance*, **52** (2), 737–83.
Stiglitz, J.E. and A. Weiss (1981), 'Credit rationing in markets with imperfect information', *American Economic Review*, **71** (3), 393–410.
Tirole, J. (2001), 'Corporate governance', *Econometrica*, **69**, 1–35.
Tirole, J. (2006), *The Theory of Corporate Finance*, New York: Princeton University Press.

Ueda, M. (2004), 'Banks versus venture capital: project evaluation, screening, and expropriation', *Journal of Finance*, **59** (2), 601–21.
Uhlaner, L., M. Wright and M. Huse (2007), 'Private firms and corporate governance: an integrated economic and management perspective', *Small Business Economics*, **29**, 225–41.
Van Praag, C.M. (2003), 'Business survival and success of young small business owners', *Small Business Economics*, **21** (1), 1–17.
Vanaelst, I, B. Clarysse, M. Wright and A. Lockett (2006), 'Entrepreneurial team development in academic spinouts: an examination of team heterogeneity', *Entrepreneurship Theory and Practice*, **30** (2), 249–71.
Vismara, S., S. Paleari and J.R. Ritter (2012), 'Europe's second markets for small companies', *European Financial Management*, **18** (3), 352–88
Vives, X. (2000), 'Corporate governance: does it matter?', in X. Vives (ed.), *Corporate Governance, Theoretical and Empirical Perspectives*, Cambridge: Cambridge University Press, pp. 1–21.
Vohora, A., M. Wright and A. Lockett (2004), 'Critical junctures in the development of university high-tech spinout companies', *Research Policy*, **33** (1), 147–75.
Weisbach, M.S. (1995), 'CEO turnover and the firm's investment decisions', *Journal of Financial Economics*, **37** (2), 159–88.
Wright, M., S. Birley and S. Mosey (2004), 'Entrepreneurship and university technology transfer', *The Journal of Technology Transfer*, **29** (3), 235–46.
Wright, M., K.M. Hmieleski, D.S. Siegel and M.D. Ensley (2007), 'The role of human capital in technological entrepreneurship, *Entrepreneurship Theory and Practice*, **31** (6), 791–806.
Zahra, S.A. and J.A. Pierce (1989), 'Boards of directors and corporate financial performance: a review and integrative mode', *Journal of Management*, **15** (2), 291–344.
Zahra, S.A., E.V. Velde and B. Larraneta (2007), 'Knowledge conversion capability and the performance of corporate and university spin-offs, *Industrial and Corporate Change*, **16**, 569–608.
Zingales, L. (1998), 'Corporate governance', in P. Newman (ed.), *The New Palgrave Dictionary of Economics and the Law*, vol. 1, London: Palgrave Macmillan, pp. 497–503.
Zingales, L. (1995), 'Insider ownership and the decision to go public', *Review of Economic Studies*, **62**, 425–49.

10 The allotment of IPO shares: placing strategies between retail versus institutional investors
Fabio Bertoni, Matteo Bonaventura and Giancarlo Giudici

1 INTRODUCTION

Underwriters hold a number of options in the placing of initial public offering (IPO) shares. They may choose how to partition the offering between retail investors and institutional investors. They may allot the shares through auctions (with or without price discrimination), lotteries, or discretionarily. They can set the price before or after the offering. They may increase the size of the placing (green-shoe option) or decrease it in case of undersubscription. They can also change the allocation scheme with respect to what is reported in the IPO prospectus (claw-back option).

In this chapter we review the literature related to IPO share allocation, with a particular focus on how allocation and pricing strategies interact. We also report some illustrative empirical evidence from the Italian IPO market. Italy offers an interesting environment to study how underwriters manage share allocations in response to information acquired in the IPO period. Italian IPOs are generally marketed through a hybrid offering, with book-building for institutional investors and an open offer for domestic retail investors. Generally, the IPO prospectus indicates the minimum number of shares to be allotted to retail investors, given the total number of offered shares. Claw-back clauses, disclosed in the prospectus, allow the underwriters to discretionarily shift a tranche of the offering between institutional and retail investors. Underwriters can increase (decrease) the portion of shares reserved to institutional investors if the demand from the public is weak (strong). By combining the claw-back option with the green-shoe option, the intermediaries can increase the number of shares allotted to one or both categories. Because, on average, IPOs leave some money on the table (Loughran and Ritter, 2002), by jointly setting the allocation and pricing of the offer, underwriters have the power to decide which category of investors will benefit more from this quick profit.

2 REVIEW OF THE LITERATURE

Ten years ago Ritter and Welch (2002, p. 1795) conjectured that 'research into share allocation issues is the most promising area of research in IPOs at the moment'. Yet no significant progress has been made in this field since then. A significant obstacle to the empirical work is that detailed data about IPO share allotment are generally not available. Existing studies rely on proprietary data obtained from private banks on a case-by-case basis, whose representativeness and generalizability are debatable. Moreover the practices and rules of the IPO process vary across countries, as illustrated in Table 10.1,

Table 10.1   Most common techniques of IPO share allotment and pricing around the world

Country	Description	References
Australia	Most of the IPOs are marketed at a fixed price published in the prospectus. The price and the amount of the offered shares cannot change. The shares are usually allocated among institutional and retail investors on a pro rata system based on the size of the bid	IPO prospectuses issued by local companies
Brazil	Book-building is the most common form of allocation process, and IPOs are hybrid, with a private placement for professional investors (domestic and international) and a public offering. The prospectus indicates a range of the total shares that must be assigned to retail investors	IPO prospectuses issued by local companies
China/ Hong Kong	In China government authorities imposes strict regulation on potential issuers' quality, IPO procedure, timing and pricing in order to stabilize the market. Shares may be allocated to domestic and foreign investors. In the Hong Kong exchange the share allotment mechanism is decided jointly by the IPO company and the lead manager (ballot is a form frequently used). Commonly a fraction of the offering is reserved to foreign investors	Fang et al. (2012)
France	Until the late 1990s the auction method has been the most popular. As the authorities permitted book-building in 1993, auctions have been gradually driven out. At the moment the most common technique is the hybrid offering, with two tranches for retail and professional investors	François Derrien (HEC Paris)
Germany	Book-building is the most common form of marketing IPOs. Shares are allocated in two different offerings, among institutional and retail investors	IPO prospectuses issued by local companies
India	Book-building is the dominant methodology and is carried out among three categories of investors: qualified institutional buyers (QIBs, who are allocated no more than 50% of the IPO shares), non-institutional investors (NIIs), and retail investors (RIIs, who are allocated no less than 35% of the IPO shares). The bids placed each day are published on the Internet and available to investors. The price is decided within a range. Allocation is decided on a pro rata basis in case of oversubscription, with no discretion. In case of undersubscription the firm can reallocate shares to any oversubscribed category	Arif Khurshed (University of Manchester)
Italy	Virtually all IPOs are 'hybrid'. A fraction of shares is allotted to institutional investors after book-building, and the remainder is allotted to retail investors (on a lottery basis in case of oversubscription). The price is generally decided after the offering. Only the smallest IPOs and placings on unregulated exchanges are allocated exclusively to institutional investors	Bertoni and Giudici (2012)
Japan	Until 1997 the allocation system was based on the allotment of half of the shares to institutional investors via discriminatory auction, and the remaining 50% to the public with a firm commitment contract. With the introduction of the book-building in the 2000s auctions have virtually disappeared. Retail investors are offered shares according to the policies of the investment bank	Kutsuna et al. (2009)

Table 10.1 (continued)

Country	Description	References
Singapore	The offering is divided into an 'Institutional Offering' and a 'Retail Offering' following the book-building process. The proportion of shares assigned to each category is established in the prospectus: however, the lead manager has full discretion in allocating the shares	IPO prospectuses issued by local companies
UK	Most of the IPOs are marketed through a placing which does not have a heavily publicized book-building run. Generally, retail investors are not invited to subscribe in a placing. Little is known about the effective allocation	Arif Khurshed (University of Manchester)
USA	Underwriters have full discretion in allotting IPO shares to institutional investors or retail investors. Contrary to European countries, up to 2012 the publication of research analysis on the IPO company was not allowed in the pre-deal marketing activity among institutional investors. Such restriction has been cancelled by the recent JOBS act. Book-building is dominant, although a few IPOs are auctioned	Jay R. Ritter (University of Florida)

although book-building and 'hybrid' offerings have become the most common techniques to market IPO shares.

Book-building has been adopted during the 1990s in the placement of IPO shares by almost all major financial markets (Ljungqvist et al., 2003). Under book-building, non-binding bids are collected by the issuing party among professional institutional investors. This process allows the underwriter to collect information to infer the demand function of IPO shares, allowing it to set the final offer price. The option to discriminate among different bidders in the placement of IPO shares is a key factor in this process. Such discretionary power may be used to reward investors revealing, during the pre-IPO period, their expectations about the value of the listing company (Benveniste and Spindt, 1989). Setting the price below the (perceived) fair market value results in oversubscription and positive initial returns for investors who get allotted the shares. Underwriters should then be more likely to assign shares of hot IPOs to investors whose bids reveal more information about the demand function. The most widely used empirical evidence to support these theories is the partial adjustment effect, first documented by Hanley (1993): underpricing seems to be highly correlated with the price revision, which implies that underwriters decide to offer underpriced shares when investors reveal a strong interest during the book-building phase.

Loughran and Ritter (2002, 2004) also posit that underwriters will attempt to underprice shares excessively and then allocate underpriced shares to institutional investors in return for commission business, as well as to dispense quick profits by allotting underpriced shares to favored customers and 'friends' (Liu and Ritter, 2007).

Another stream of the literature is devoted to analyzing the efficiency of book-building compared to alternative placing techniques, namely, auctions and fixed-price offerings. Auctions have been losing appeal around the world, although generally associated with lower underpricing. Sherman (2005) argues that institutional investors have relatively low incentives to gather information under auctions. Yet some theoretical models (Biais and Faugeron-Crouzet, 2002; Biais et al., 2002) show that properly structured auctions can give information-extraction incentives similar to those offered by book-building. Degeorge et al. (2010) also find that issuers extract valuable information from auction bids. While book-building is more costly than fixed-price IPOs, it can increase the amount of capital raised because it encourages institutional investors to release information about the demand for shares. Degeorge et al. (2007) and Gao and Ritter (2010) claim that book-building creates beneficial marketing effects, affecting the short-run elasticity of the demand curve.

The green-shoe option, which allows intermediaries to underwrite an additional portion of shares from pre-IPO shareholders or the issuing firm (typically 10 percent to 15 percent of the IPO size), is an additional discretionary option in the allocation strategy. Aggarwal (2003) shows that underwriters often short sell IPO shares to the participants. The short position is then covered either by exercising the green-shoe option in the case of positive initial returns, or by open-market repurchases in the case of weak initial returns, thus supporting the demand for shares and stabilizing the price.

A stream of the literature, that is particularly important for the objectives of this chapter, analyzes the discretionary options held by underwriters in IPO allocation and pricing. Most of the works focus on the underwriter's discretionary decision about the allocation of underpriced IPO shares among professional investors. In other words, given the total number of shares assigned to professional investors, they study why some bidders are allocated more shares than others. The model introduced by Benveniste and Wilhelm (1990) demonstrates that underwriters, given the opportunity to allocate shares between professional and retail investors, maximize the proceeds by using a combination of price and allocation discrimination.

Hanley and Wilhelm (1995), Sherman (2000), Cornelli and Goldreich (2001), Aggarwal et al. (2002), Ljungqvist and Wilhelm (2002), Boehmer et al. (2006) and Boreiko and Lombardo (2011) document empirical evidence that institutional investors are generally favored compared to retail investors in the allocation policy. Besides remunerating information disclosure, the preferential treatment for institutional investors can be justified as a way to reward participation in less attractive offerings, and compensate long-term investors. Rocholl (2009) analyzes the IPO allocation policy of a European investment bank and finds that institutional investors receive better allocations than retail investors because of their superior capability to detect underpriced issues. The author finds that professional investors are rewarded by favorable allocations in underpriced issues for their participation in offerings with weak demand. Jenkinson and Jones (2004) suggest that, in European IPOs, underwriters discriminate between long-term and short-term shareholders more than between informed and non-informed investors, as more informative bids (that is, limit bids) do not drive higher share allocations. Cornelli and Goldreich (2003) show that in the allocation process underwriters tend to penalize investors who immediately following previous listings sold IPO shares to take advantage of quick initial profits.

Bertoni and Giudici (2012) argue that the revision of the allotment scheme provides underwriters with an additional strategic option. When demand from uninformed retail investors is poor, issuers increase the number of shares allotted to institutions and revise downwards the offer price, increasing the odds that shares are underpriced. When demand from retail investors is large, instead, issuers decrease the allocation to institutional investors and revise optimistically the offer price, reducing the likelihood that shares are underpriced. Allocation and price revision are, in other words, endogenously determined by the underwriter. This mechanism, however, requires that demand from at least one category of investor is substantial. The endogeneity between allocation and price revision is instead absent when the offer size is reduced, due to poor demand from both categories of investors. In such a case, the degree of discriminatory power held by issuers is minimal, and the pricing decision does not depend on changes in allocation. We elaborate further on the interplay between allocation and pricing in the next section.

3 EMPIRICAL EVIDENCE FROM THE ITALIAN EXCHANGE

To exemplify the interrelation between allocation and pricing strategies in IPO placements we study a sample of Italian IPOs between 1997 and 2012. We include in the sample all IPOs filed in Italy in the period with the exclusion of real estate investment trusts (REITs) and listings on unregulated exchanges. The sample is composed of 206 IPOs, 193 of which (93.7 percent) are hybrid, involving both institutional and retail investors.

Table 10.2 reports descriptive statistics regarding the fraction of IPO shares initially reserved for retail and professional investors according to the prospectus allotment, which are compared to the effective allotment after the IPO.

The fraction of IPO shares reserved for institutions is much larger than the fraction reserved for retail investors. On average, only 25.66 percent of the prospectus allocation goes to retail investors. This percentage is decreasing over time and, since 2006, it has been below 20 percent. After the offering, there is a statistically significant increase in the number of shares assigned to retail investors, compared to the initial allocation declared in the prospectus (+3.33 percent).

Statistics reported in Table 10.2 include both hybrid and non-hybrid offers (one case in which the issue was reserved to retail investors and 12 cases in which only institutional investors were admitted to the offering). Therefore we report in the same table the sample mean excluding the latter IPOs and including only the 193 offerings in which both categories of investors are allotted shares (hybrid IPOs). The prospectus allotment to retail investors is 27.05 percent and increases to 30.64 percent in the final allocation. The increase is equal to +3.59 percent (significant at the 1 percent confidence level). In 39 hybrid IPOs, no variation between the *ex ante* allocation and the effective allocation is detected. The fraction of shares allotted to retail investors is larger than the prospectus allocation in 82 cases, and lower in 72.

Revisions in the initial allocation strategy can occur as soon as new information regarding the demand function is revealed by two categories of investors to the issuing firm and the underwriter in the pre-listing period. Changes may be related to exogenous factors (for example, insufficient demand or negative momentum) or endogenous factors controlled by the underwriter (for example, the willingness to favor one category of investors over the other). To investigate the causes of the adjustments in the allocation policy three different indicators can be introduced (Bertoni and Giudici, 2012).

The first is the oversubscription ratio, computed as the ratio between the number of

Table 10.2 Mean fraction of the IPO offer size reserved to retail and to institutional investors

Listing year	Number of IPOs	Prospectus allotment		Effective allotment		% shift toward retail investors (effective-prospectus)
		% allotted to retail investors (filed in prospectus)	% allotted to institutions (filed in prospectus)	% allotted to retail investors (effective)	% allotted to institutions (effective)	
1997	10	31.01	68.99	36.76	63.24	5.75*
1998	16	33.63	66.37	37.14	62.86	3.51**
1999	27	38.59	61.41	42.08	57.92	3.49***
2000	42	30.27	69.73	33.76	66.24	3.49**
2001	17	26.76	73.24	28.59	71.41	1.83
2002	6	21.67	78.33	28.14	71.86	6.47
2003	4	27.43	72.57	35.46	64.54	8.03**
2004	8	22.49	77.51	25.66	74.34	3.17
2005	15	20.04	79.96	26.60	73.40	6.56**
2006	21	17.70	82.30	17.60	82.40	−0.10
2007	29	15.85	84.15	16.84	83.16	0.99
2008	6	10.57	89.43	12.81	87.19	2.25*
2009	1	10.07	89.93	8.33	91.67	−1.74
2010	2	12.50	87.50	46.67	53.33	34.17
2011	1	10.00	90.00	8.71	91.29	−1.29
2012	1	10.00	90.00	10.61	89.39	0.61
Total	206	25.66	74.34	28.99	71.01	3.33***
Hybrid IPOs	193	27.05	72.95	30.64	69.36	3.59***

Notes:
The percentage is computed according to the *ex ante* declaration in the IPO prospectus ('prospectus allotment') and to the *ex post* effective allotment disclosed by the underwriting syndicate ('effective allotment').
The difference between the prospectus and the effective allotment for retail investors and the mean IPO initial return (defined as the percentage difference between the official price on the first day of trading and the IPO price) are also reported.
Sample: 206 IPOs listed on the Italian Exchange from 1997 to July 2012.
We report also mean values for 193 hybrid IPOs, obtained by excluding from the initial sample 12 IPOs in which retail investors are not allotted shares and 1 IPO in which only retail investors are allotted shares.
***, **, * significantly different from zero at the 99%, 95%, 90% confidence level, respectively.

shares requested by a single category of investors, and the number of shares intended for allocation. This variable is mostly exogenous, depending on the market momentum during the offering period, the underwriter can influence it to some extent through a marketing effort (for example, by offering bonus shares). Second, the demand satisfaction ratio, computed as the ratio between the shares allotted to, and those requested by, retail investors. The lower the demand satisfaction ratio, the larger is the rationing for retail investors. This ratio is under the control of the underwriter, which has the power to shift a fraction of the offering from one category of investors to the counterpart. Third, the IPO scaling ratio, representing the ratio between the prospectus offer size and the total number of shares sold by the underwriter. This ratio is lower than 1 when the underwriter exercises the overallotment option and short sells IPO shares, and it is larger than 1 when the underwriter decides to trim down the size of the offer. Note that offer size may be increased or reduced without affecting the proportion of shares allotted to the different categories of investors. Alternatively, the offer size may be adjusted for one category of investors only, leaving the number of shares assigned to the other unchanged.

Any revision in the IPO allocation policy, with respect to the prospectus allotment, may be described as a combination of the three factors above. First, if the shares booked by one category of investors are less than the size of the offering initially reserved to them, the final allocation will be adjusted to the low demand. In contrast, if the demand is larger than the offer size, the underwriter has the option to assign more shares. In this case, the underwriter has the opportunity to favor either institutional investors or retail investors in the revision of the allocation.

Table 10.3 reports the average values of the ratios defined above for the sample of 206 Italian IPOs, computed for retail investors and for institutions, respectively.

The demand for shares is larger than the offer size in most of the IPOs in the sample. On average, retail (institutional) investors bid 9.03 (5.93) times the number of shares they are allotted in the prospectus. Undersubscription is detected in only 28 cases by retail, and in only 16 cases by institutional investors. In six cases, none of the categories of investors fully subscribed their portions of the offering.

Considering the demand satisfaction ratio, strong rationing characterizes institutional investors that receive, on average, only 41.15 percent of the requested shares (conditional to the offer price) compared to 46.75 percent for retail investors (the difference is significant at the 5 percent confidence level). This confirms that the issuing firm and the intermediaries are used to set the final offer price such that they leave a strong discretionary power among the bidding investors, at the cost of leaving money on the table. Only in five cases have all institutional investors been allocated the number of shares they asked for. This occurs in 48 cases for small retail investors.

Considering the IPO scaling ratio, in 116 cases the offer size has been increased through the overallotment option. In 14 cases the offer size has been reduced due to insufficient demand for shares. In the remaining cases, the offer size remained constant.

Table 10.4 divides the sample in different groups, according to the oversubscription and IPO scaling ratios. We consider only the sample of 193 hybrid IPOs in which both retail and institutional investors are allotted shares. Average values for the demand satisfaction ratios, the price revision, the initial underpricing and the expected initial return for retail investors are also reported. The IPO price revision is defined as the percentage

Table 10.3 Statistics about oversubscription, demand satisfaction, and IPO scaling ratios

Category of investors	Sample size	Ratio	Mean (%)	Median (%)	Ratio < 1	Ratio = 1	Ratio > 1
Retail investors	194	Oversubscription	9.03*	3.81**	28 (14.4%)	–	166 (85.6%)
		Demand satisfaction	46.75**	31.23***	146 (75.3%)	(24.7%)	–
Institutional investors	205	Oversubscription	5.93*	3.08**	16 (7.8%)	–	189 (92.2%)
		Demand satisfaction	41.15**	34.25***	200 (97.6%)	5 (2.4%)	–
All investors	206	IPO scaling	97.33	94.32	116 (56.3%)	76 (36.9%)	14 (6.8%)

Notes:
The oversubscription ratio is the ratio between the number of shares requested by retail (professional) investors, during the offering and the number of shares initially assigned to the public (institutions), disclosed in the IPO prospectus.
The demand satisfaction ratio is the ratio between the total number of shares effectively allotted by the underwriters to the public (institutions) and the number of shares requested by retail (professional) investors, during the offering.
The IPO scaling ratio is the ratio between the total number of shares offered, net of the green-shoe option, according to the IPO prospectus (offer size), and the total number of shares effectively allotted by the underwriters.
Sample: 206 IPOs listed on the Italian Exchange from 1997 to July 2012 (194 with public offering, 205 with private placement).
***, **, * the difference between retail and institutional investors is significant at the 99%, 95%, 90% confidence level respectively (*t*-test for means, Wilcoxon signed-rank test for medians).

difference between the final offer price and the midpoint of the prospectus price range. We compute the IPO initial underpricing as the percent difference between the official market price at the end of the first day of trading, and the offer price. The expected return for retail investors is the initial IPO return weighted by the probability for retail investors to be assigned the requested shares, represented by their demand satisfaction ratio. This represents the 'real' expected return for small investors participating in the IPO, considering rationing effects.

Table 10.4 shows that for the six IPOs in which the offer size is reduced due to undersubscription from both the categories of investors, the price revision is negative and the mean initial return is significantly negative. When only retail investors undersubscribe the offering, their demand is fully satisfied, but on average the IPO price is negatively revised (this revealing negative information collected on the market) and shares are not significantly underpriced. When the offering is undersubscribed by institutional investors (but oversubscribed by retail investors) the revision of the IPO price is still negative, and the initial underpricing is again not significantly different from zero (in some cases significantly negative). In such cases the underwriter exercises the claw-back options allotting shares not requested by professional investors to the public. In four cases, the demand from retail investors has been so strong that the size of the IPO has been

Table 10.4 Categorization of hybrid IPOs by oversubscription and IPO scaling ratios

	Offer size compared to prospectus	Final allocation compared to prospectus	Number of IPOs	Demand satisfaction (retail) %	Demand satisfaction (institutions) %	Price revision %	Underpricing %	Initial expected return (retail) %
Undersubscription from both retail and institutional investors	Reduced		6	100.00	92.75	−17.15	−2.57*	−2.57*
Undersubscription from retail investors only	Reduced		4	100.00	71.32	−19.38	−1.49	−1.49
	Same		7	100.00	71.94	−22.30	4.77	4.77
	Increased		11	100.00	48.51	−11.41	2.31	2.31
Undersubscription from institutional investors only	Reduced		1	100.00	96.65	−11.05	−7.44	−7.44
	Same		4	100.00	85.64	−4.25	−3.37*	−3.37*
	Increased		4	78.08	75.84	−11.79	−0.34	−0.50
Oversubscription from both retail and institutional investors	Same	Same	39	24.37	25.32	+2.01	11.51***	0.93*
		More shares to retail investors	25	58.44	47.19	−3.77	3.49	−0.48
	Increased	More shares to both categories	37	37.64	31.76	−1.81	12.89***	2.08
		More shares to institutions only	35	18.54	25.36	+2.80	35.12***	2.32***
		More shares to retail only	1	9.92	29.25	+10.72	14.62	1.45
		More shares to retail, less shares to institutions	19	48.56	47.54	−6.13	2.31	0.12

Notes:
The demand satisfaction ratio is the ratio between the total number of shares effectively allotted by the underwriters to the public (institutions) and the number of shares requested by retail (professional) investors, during the offering.
Price revision is the percentage difference between the final offer price and the midpoint of the prospectus file range.
The underpricing is the percentage difference between the official price on the first day of trading and the IPO price.
The initial expected return is defined as the IPO initial return times the demand satisfaction ratio for retail investors.
Sample: 193 hybrid IPOs (that is IPOs in which both institutional and retail investors are allocated shares) on the Italian Exchange between 1997 and July 2012.
***, **, * significantly different from zero at the 99%, 95%, 90% confidence level, respectively.

increased albeit of the scarce demand by professional investors. One aspect that deserves to be highlighted is that, in all these cases, the importance of discretion in the allotment to institutions is so relevant that underwriters decide to leave a portion of their demand unsatisfied even when the demand is lower than expected in the prospectus.

In the remaining cases, the IPO is fully subscribed by both categories of investors. The underwriter has, in these circumstances, full discretionary power. In 39 cases the underwriter confirmed both the initial allocation and the offer size, in this case rewarding informed investors with underpriced shares. In 25 cases the underwriter confirmed the offer size but shifted shares to retail investors. This strategy is associated with negative information collected during book-building, as reflected by negative price (−3.77 percent). Remarkably, shares are not significantly underpriced in this case. Therefore, no reward is given to small investors, who get a negative average expected return, despite their important role in compensating poor demand from institutions.

Another strategy is to increase the offer size through the overallotment option.[1] In this scenario Table 10.4 shows that IPO shares are significantly underpriced (+35.12 percent on average) when additional shares are allotted exclusively to institutional investors (35 cases). A lower premium is recognized in the 37 cases in which both categories receive more shares compared to the prospectus allocation (+12.89 percent). When information collected during book-building is negative, more shares are assigned only to retail investors (19 cases) without underpricing.

The data strongly suggest that, consistent with the model by Benveniste and Spindt (1989), the underwriters' strategy is aimed at underpricing shares only when optimistic information is collected during the book-building phase. Such information is incorporated into the revision of the offer price. The reward for investors is a discount in IPO pricing, as is largely documented by the literature, but only for professional investors. Oversubscription from retail investors is not considered in pricing decision, but only to eventually compensate poor demand from institutions. This results in an adverse selection problem, and a rationing effect as described by Rock (1986).

Bertoni and Giudici (2012) run a set of regressions in order to find out the determinants of the demand satisfaction ratios, treating the price revision as an endogenous variable. They find that optimistic revision of the offer price and a shift in the allocation towards professional investors result in larger underpricing. When the demand for shares is poor and the offer is reduced, there is no significant correlation between IPO underpricing and allocation revision. However, when endogeneity between price and allocation revisions is considered, they are found to be negatively and significantly correlated. This result is significant only when the IPO is fully subscribed, suggesting that they represent alternative and competing options for the issuer because they both lead to a reduction in the discretionary power to allocate shares to institutional investors. In fact, an increase in the final IPO price determines a reduction in the demand for shares registered in the book, with the same effect of a supply increase. Feedback from small retail investors is determinant to which strategy will be pursued by the underwriter: in the case of poor demand from retail investors, the underwriter will most likely increase the allocation to institutions and reduce the offer price; when demand from retail investors is strong, however, it will most likely increase the offer price and reduce the allocation to informed investors, strengthening its discretionary power.

4 CONCLUDING REMARKS

The process of IPO share allocation is very complex. It depends on several factors and interacts with the pricing process. When both small retail investors and professional institutions are invited to join the offer (hybrid IPOs), information collected during book-building plays a crucial role in the decision about the final allocation and pricing, combined with the subscription from retail investors.

The literature highlights that positive information collected during book-building is rewarded with underpriced shares, and that institutional investors are generally favored in the allocation of hot IPOs. Considering the case of Italian IPOs, and analyzing the adjustments in the allocation policy alongside the revisions of the offer price, a number of interesting results emerge and shed new insights on IPO allocation strategies. First, underwriters preserve their discretion also when demand from institutions is poor. On average a part of the demand is never satisfied, also in case of undersubscription. Second, optimistic information collected during book-building is reflected in a preferential treatment for institutional investors. This favorable treatment can be implemented by underpricing the shares or by increasing the number of shares allotted. The data suggest that underwriters are more likely to increase the number of shares allotted to institutions when the overallotment option is exercised and when retail investors undersubscribe the offering. On the contrary, underwriters are more likely to increase the IPO price when the demand from retail investors is strong. This maximizes their bargaining power over professional investors. In fact, the underwriters may threaten to shift IPO shares to retail investors to convince informed investors to display optimistic bids in the book-building phase. If the demand from retail investors is poor, such a threat is less credible.

When pessimistic information is collected during the book-building phase, there is no need to issue underpriced shares and, if possible, a portion of the offering is shifted to retail investors. This helps the underwriter to exercise discriminatory power over professional investors, even when their demand is poor.

NOTE

1. Given the Italian institutional framework, the only way to increase the number of shares assigned to institutional investors when retail investors oversubscribe the IPO is the exercise of the overallotment option.

REFERENCES

Aggarwal, R. (2003), 'Allocation of initial public offerings and flipping activity', *Journal of Financial Economics*, **68**, 111–35.
Aggarwal, R., N. Prabhala and M. Puri (2002), 'Institutional allocation in initial public offerings: empirical evidence', *Journal of Finance*, **57**, 1421–42.
Benveniste, L.M. and P.A. Spindt (1989), 'How investment bankers determine the offer price and allocation of new issues', *Journal of Financial Economics*, **24**, 343–61.
Benveniste, L.M. and W.J. Wilhelm (1990), 'The comparative analysis of IPO proceeds under alternative regulatory environments', *Journal of Financial Economics*, **28**, 134–65.
Bertoni, F. and G. Giudici (2012), 'The strategic (re)allocation of IPO shares', SSRN Working Paper.

Biais, B. and A.M. Faugeron-Crouzet (2002), 'IPO auctions: English, Dutch, . . . French, and internet', *Journal of Financial Intermediation*, **11**, 9–36.

Biais, B., P. Bossaerts and J.C. Rochet (2002), 'An optimal IPO mechanism', *Review of Economic Studies*, **69**, 117–46.

Boehmer, B., E. Boehmer and R. Fishe (2006), 'Do institutions receive favorable allocations in IPOs with better long-run returns?', *Journal of Financial and Quantitative Analysis*, **41** (4), 809–28.

Boreiko, D. and S. Lombardo (2011), 'Italian IPOs: allocations and claw back clauses', *Journal of International Financial Markets, Institutions & Money*, **21**, 127–43.

Cornelli, F. and D. Goldreich (2001), 'Bookbuilding and strategic allocation', *Journal of Finance*, **56** (5), 2337–69.

Cornelli, F. and D. Goldreich (2003), 'Bookbuilding: how informative is the order book?', *Journal of Finance*, **58** (4), 1415–44.

Degeorge, F., F. Derrien and K.W. Womack (2007), 'Analyst hype in IPOs: explaining the popularity of book-building', *Review of Financial Studies*, **20** (4), 1021–58.

Degeorge, F., F. Derrien and K.W. Womack (2010), 'Auctioned IPOs: the US evidence', *Journal of Financial Economics*, **98**, 177–94.

Fang, J., H. Shi and H. Xu (2012), 'The determinants and consequences of IPOs in a regulated economy: evidence from China', *Journal of Multinational Financial Management*, **22**, 131–50.

Gao, X. and J.R. Ritter (2010), 'The marketing of seasoned equity offerings', *Journal of Financial Economics*, **97** (1), 33–52.

Hanley, K.W. (1993), 'The underpricing of initial public offerings and the partial adjustment phenomenon', *Journal of Financial Economics*, **34**, 231–50.

Hanley, K.W. and W.J. Wilhelm (1995), 'Evidence on the strategic allocation of IPOs', *Journal of Financial Economics*, **37**, 239–57.

Jenkinson, T. and H. Jones (2004), 'Bids and allocation in European IPO bookbuilding', *Journal of Finance*, **59** (5), 2309–38.

Kutsuna, K., J.K. Smith and R.L. Smith (2009), 'Public information, IPO price formation, and long-run returns: Japanese evidence', *Journal of Finance*, **64** (1), 505–46.

Liu, X. and J.R. Ritter (2007), 'Corporate executive bribery: an empirical analysis', working paper, available at: http://bear.warrington.ufl.edu/ritter/work_papers/BriberyDec42007.pdf (accessed 3 May 2013).

Ljungqvist, A.P.J. and W. Wilhelm (2002), 'IPO allocations: discriminatory or discretionary?', *Journal of Financial Economics*, **65**, 167–201.

Ljungqvist, A.P., T. Jenkinson and W.J. Wilhelm (2003), 'Global integration in primary equity markets: the role of U.S. banks and U.S. investors', *Review of Financial Studies*, **16** (1), 63–99.

Loughran, T. and J.R. Ritter (2002), 'Why don't issuers get upset about leaving money on the table in IPOs?', *Review of Financial Studies*, **15**, 413–43.

Loughran, T. and J.R. Ritter (2004), 'Why has IPO underpricing changed over time?', *Financial Management*, **33** (3), 5–37.

Ritter, J.R. and I. Welch (2002), 'A review of IPO activity, pricing, and allocation', *Journal of Finance*, **57** (4), 1795–828.

Rocholl, J. (2009), 'A friend in need is a friend indeed: allocation and demand in IPO bookbuilding', *Journal of Financial Intermediation*, **18**, 284–310.

Rock, K. (1986), 'Why new issues are underpriced', *Journal of Financial Economics*, **15**, 187–212.

Sherman, A.E. (2000), 'IPOs and long term relationships: an advantage of book building', *Review of Financial Studies*, **13**, 697–714.

Sherman, A.E. (2005), 'Global trends in IPO methods: Book building versus auctions with endogenous entry', *Journal of Financial Economics*, **78**, 615–49.

11 VC investment timing and IPO pricing
Jean-Sébastien Michel

1 INTRODUCTION

Traditional theories of initial public offering (IPO) underpricing assume market efficiency and treat the first-day closing price as the correct value of the IPO, which implies that IPOs are on average deeply underpriced at the offer. For example, Rock (1986) proposes a winner's curse interpretation whereby underpricing is necessary to induce uninformed investors to participate in the offering. Benveniste and Spindt (1989) link underpricing to truth-telling of investors in the book-building process. In both cases, firms with high information asymmetry require larger underpricing to either attract uninformed investors to participate in the offer or to encourage more information revelation.

Booth and Smith (1986) develop a certification hypothesis, whereby underwriters can reduce information asymmetry during the IPO process by certifying that the issue price is consistent with insider information about the firm's earnings prospects. A firm is willing to bond itself to a reputable underwriter because the reduced information asymmetry allows them to raise more money in the offer. Carter and Manaster (1990) and Carter et al. (1998) find empirical support for the certification hypothesis. In particular, Carter and Manaster (1990) shows that IPOs with more informed investor capital require higher returns. Since underwriter reputation reveals expected informed activity, they find that prestigious underwriters are associated with lower-risk offerings, have less incentive to acquire information, and are therefore associated with IPOs that have lower initial returns.

The model of Booth and Smith (1986) can apply not only to underwriters, but also to venture capitalists (VCs). Venture capitalists use various mechanisms to monitor the firms in which they invest, such as staging investment, requiring a presence on the board of directors, and structuring chief executive officer (CEO) compensation. These monitoring activities act to certify the firm when it goes public. Gompers (1995) finds that VCs concentrate their investments in early-stage companies where monitoring is most valuable. When the VC learns negative information about the firm, they cut it off from new financing. Firms that go public have therefore received more financing over more rounds than firms that do not go public. It is therefore not surprising that VC-backed IPOs have different initial pricing then non VC-backed IPOs.[1] Since VCs have inside information on the earnings prospects of the firms they are backing, and they participate in the IPO market repeatedly, they are in a position to credibly certify the firm to potential investors. Megginson and Weiss (1991) provide evidence of VC certification of IPOs by comparing a sample of VC-backed IPOs to a matched sample of IPOs between 1983 and 1987. The authors find that venture capital backing results in significantly lower initial returns and gross spreads.

While the early evidence supported the VC certification hypothesis, later studies cast some doubt on these findings. The grandstanding hypothesis of Gompers (1993) predicts that the relation between bringing companies public and fundraising ability should be stronger for young venture capital firms. Incremental IPOs attracts relatively more capital from investors for young VC firms than for old VC firms because the reputation of established VC firms is less affected by doing an IPO (Gompers (1996)). The incentive for young VCs is therefore to bring firms public early in order to prove themselves and increase the likelihood of raising new money. A cost of grandstanding is greater underpricing because of the greater information asymmetry inherent in the young firms being brought public (Muscarella and Vetsuypens, 1990). The evidence in Gompers (1996) suggests that companies backed by young VCs are younger and more underpriced at their IPO than those of old VCs, consistent with the grandstanding hypothesis. Lee and Wahal (2004) document that VC-backed IPOs experience larger first-day returns than comparable non-VC-backed IPOs after controlling for endogeneity in VC funding. The higher underpricing leads to larger future flows of capital into venture capital funds, especially after 1996, supporting the idea of grandstanding.

The evidence in Gompers (1996) and Lee and Wahal (2004) says that young VCs bring firms public that are younger than those brought to market by old VCs. However, what is of concern is not that young VCs bring young firms public. Given the number of specialized VC firms that have come into existence whose investments are bound to be in industries where young technology and pharmaceutical firms abound, it is not surprising that that young VCs bring young firms public. Rather, the concern is that young VCs bring firms public too early, regardless of whether they are young or old.

In this chapter, I examine the role of VC investment timing on short-run IPO pricing. More specifically, I look at the amount of time that passes between the date a firm files a prospectus to go public and the date it last received funding from one of its VCs, which I term the 'file delay', and its impact on the IPO's price adjustment and initial return. File delay provides a direct test of the grandstanding hypothesis because it is not based on a firm's age but rather on the amount of time between a firm's last round of financing and its decision to go public. It is also important for identification that the delay is calculated from the last financing round and not the first financing round, since companies at various stages of development and from various industries require different financing period lengths. However, once financing has ceased, the only decision remaining is when to take the firm public. Firms with very short file delay are therefore more likely to have been taken public too early relative to firms with longer file delays.

I find that lower file delay is associated with higher short-run IPO performance, consistent with the grandstanding hypothesis. In particular, the first-day return of the lowest quintile (bottom 20 percent) of file delay IPOs is 40 percent compared to 14 percent for the highest quintile (top 20 percent). Furthermore, lower file delay is associated with VCs that are younger and book-building periods which are longer. Overall, this evidence is consistent with the grandstanding hypothesis. This chapter contributes to the discussion about the role of venture capitalists in the IPO process in bringing companies they back to the market.

2 DATA AND SUMMARY STATISTICS

The sample is made up of 2964 venture capital-backed IPO firms from 1983 to 2011, which have a file date and round by round VC financing information available. IPOs must be covered by the Center for Research in Security Prices (CRSP) within the first 30 days of the offer. Additionally, unit offerings, closed-end funds, American depository receipts (ADRs), real estate investment trusts (REITs), shares of beneficial interest (SBIs) are eliminated.[2] Data on the IPOs of ordinary common shares are obtained from the Securities Data Company's (SDC) New Issues database. Data on venture capital-backed IPOs such as round-by-round financing, VC founding date and company founding date are obtained from the SDC's Venture Expert database. Share prices, share codes and shares outstanding after the offer are obtained from CRSP. All variables are described in detail in the appendix to this chapter.

Figure 11.1 shows the number of IPOs, as wells as the average file delay, price adjustment and initial return in calendar time. Many firms that end up going public haven't received any funds from their VC backers for years. From 1990 to 1995 and from 2002 to 2006, VC-backed firms that went public (1198 IPOs) had not received a penny from their VCs in over 2 (1.3) years in mean (median). In fact, 26 percent of VC-backed firms

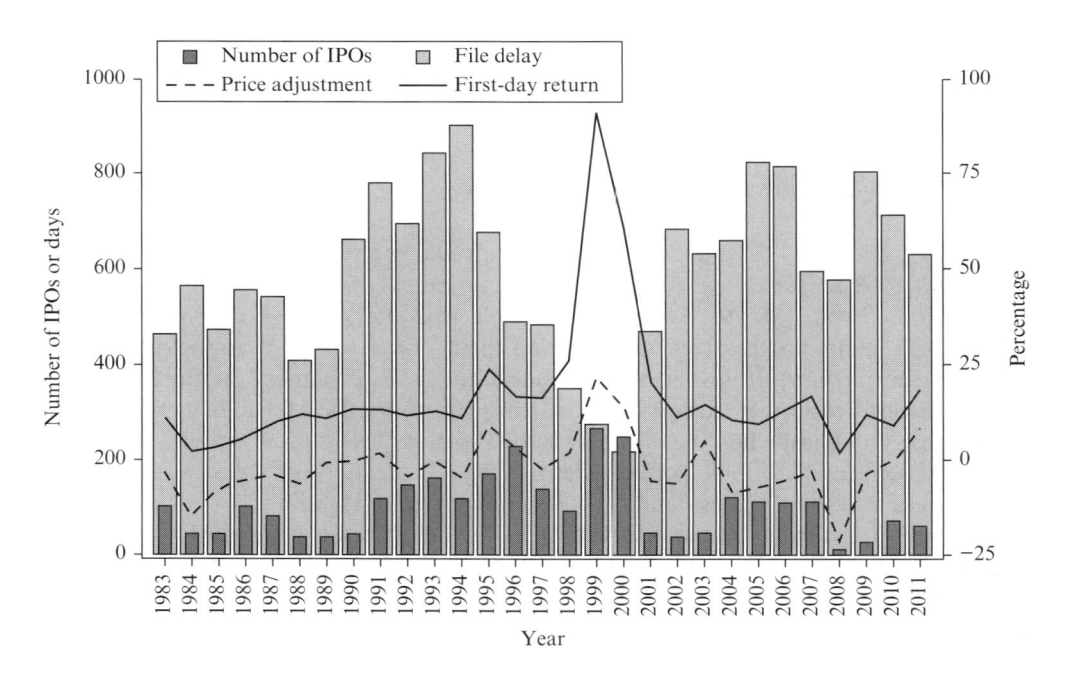

Notes:
This figure plots the yearly mean number of IPOs, file delay, price adjustment and first-day return.
All variables are described in detail in the appendix.
The sample includes VC-backed IPOs from 1983 to 2011.

Figure 11.1 Annual average number of IPOs, file delay, price adjustment and first-day return

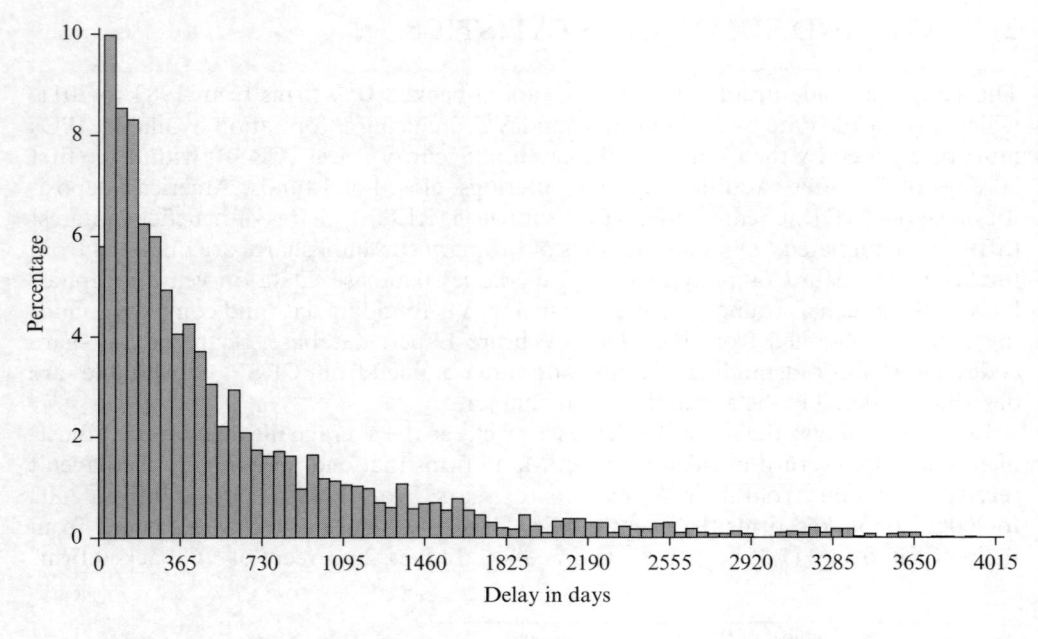

Notes:
This figure plots the frequency distribution of file delay.
All variables are described in detail in the appendix.
The sample includes VC-backed IPOs from 1983 to 2011.

Figure 11.2 File delay frequency distribution

going public between 1983 and 2011 had not received a penny from their VCs in the two years prior to their IPO. Just as surprising is how quickly firms are brought public in some periods. From 1983 to 1989 and from 1996 to 2001, VC-backed firms that went public (1479 IPOs) last received money from their VCs 1.1 (0.6) years before the file date in mean (median). It is difficult to reconcile the lack of financial support for some firms with certification. Focusing on short-run pricing, Figure 11.1 tells us that short-run returns are highest when the file delay is the shortest. This is most evident during the 1997–2001 technology bubble period when average file delay is at its lowest and short-run returns are at their highest, and is consistent with grandstanding.[3]

In Figure 11.2, I examine the distribution of file delay in the sample. Most firms (53 percent) decide to go public within a year of their last round of VC financing, but some decide to go public much later (16 percent go public more than three years after their last financing). Overall, after the first year, there is a gradual decline in the number of firms delaying their IPO.

Table 11.1 lists the summary statistics of the variables used in this chapter. The mean (median) file delay over the entire sample is 568.0 (326.5) days. Firms are slightly larger than those in the overall sample of IPOs with mean (median) assets of $252.7 ($54.2) million. Chemmanur and Krishnan (2011) finds assets of $154.9 ($21.7) million over the 1980 to 2003 period in the overall sample of IPOs. These firms are on average 9.8 years of age with 70 percent of them being technology firms. They are backed by 6.8 VC firms

Table 11.1   Summary statistics

	N	Mean	Std dev	Min	Median	Max
Panel A: market characteristics						
File delay (days)	2964	568.02	657.18	3	326.5	3880
Price adjustment (%)	2750	1.94	26.38	−67.74	0.00	220.00
First-day return (%)	2963	24.91	50.79	−53.03	9.21	626.67
Offer delay (days)	2964	98.21	198.35	1	68	6811
Panel B: firm characteristics						
TECH	2964	0.70	0.46	0	1	1
Assets (MM$)	2964	252.73	1156.70	0	54.20	28 406.50
Book-to-file	2748	0.28	0.33	−4.89	0.26	7.19
Firm age (years)	2799	9.79	12.73	0	6	102
Panel C: VC and deal characteristics						
VC age (years)	2948	18.08	9.00	0	17	124
Nbr firms	2964	6.83	5.54	1	5	41
Nbr rounds	2964	4.42	3.12	1	4	24
Total investment (MM$)	2812	101.76	361.79	0.00	27.45	7334.00
Stage level	2964	2.46	1.56	0	3	5

Notes:
This table reports the summary statistics of variables in this chapter.
All variables are described in detail in the appendix.
The sample includes VC-backed IPOs from 1983 to 2011.

on with an average VC age of 18.1 years. They receive 4.4 rounds of financing for a total investment of $101.8 million on average. Lastly, VC-backed firms tend to be about midway between the early and expansion stages of development when they receive their last round of VC financing.

3 RESULTS

3.1 Short-run Performance

In this subsection, I explore the relationship between the file delay and the stock's short-run performance. Specifically, the file delay is number of days between the last round of financing they receive and the date they file their prospectus. I capture short-run performance using two measures: price adjustment and first-day return. The price adjustment is the return between the mid-point of the file range and offer price, and the first-day return is the return between the offer price and the first-day closing price.

3.1.1 Bivariate results

I split the sample of VC-backed IPOs into quintiles based on the file delay, and examine both the price adjustment and the first-day return in Figure 11.3 and Table 11.2. Firms in the lowest file delay quintile (bottom 20 percent) file their prospectus on average 46 days after their last round of financing, and have a 6.6 percent

Figure 11.3 Average price adjustment and first-day return for file delay portfolios

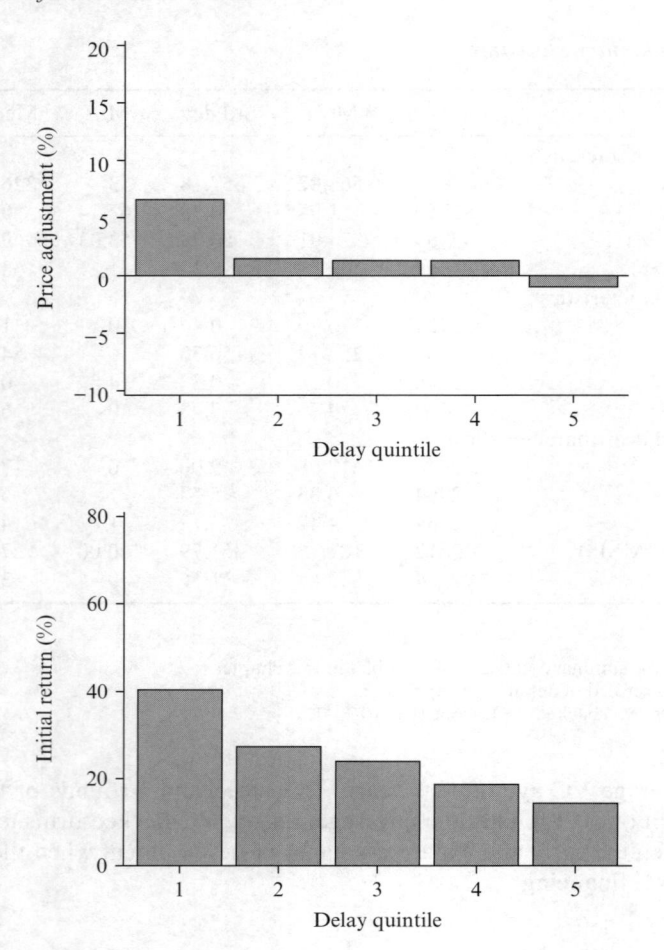

Notes:
This figure plots the price adjustment and first-day return for file delay quintile portfolios.
All variables are described in detail in the appendix.
The sample includes VC-backed IPOs from 1983 to 2011.

price adjustment and a 40.5 percent first-day return. However, firms in the highest file delay quintile (top 20 percent) file their prospectus on average 1654 days (4.5 years) after their last round of financing, and have a −1.0 percent price adjustment and a 14.4 percent initial return. These differences (7.6 percent and 26.2 percent, respectively) are economically significant and statistically significant at the 1 percent level. While these results are clearly supportive of the grandstanding, since firms that seem to be going public too early have much higher price adjustment and first-day returns than firms that go public later, conclusions are premature. I will control for other variables which may influence this relationship below (in particular, firm age which is 21.9 percent correlated with file delay).

Table 11.2 Short-run performance for file delay portfolios

	N	File delay (days)	Price adjustment (%)	First-day return (%)
Delay1 (low)	593	46.24	6.58	40.48
Delay2	594	161.41	1.40	27.21
Delay3	592	333.01	1.28	23.81
Delay4	593	647.64	1.30	18.73
Delay5 (high)	592	1653.92	−1.01	14.32
Delay5 − delay1		1607.68***	7.59***	26.16***
t-stat		(57.76)	(4.45)	(8.18)

Notes:
This table reports the means of price adjustment and first-day return for file delay quintile portfolios, as well as a high minus low delay hedge portfolio.
All variables are described in detail in the appendix.
The sample includes VC-backed IPOs from 1983 to 2011.
The numbers in parentheses are *t*-statistics based on simple *t*-tests for differences in means.
***, ** or * signify that the test statistic is significant at the 1, 5 or 10% level, respectively.

In Figure 11.4, I look at some VC characteristics which may be related to the file delay. Indeed, file delay is negatively related to the total number of rounds the IPO firm has received, with the bottom quintile receiving 5.6 rounds and the top quintile receiving 3.0 rounds (the difference is statistically significant at the 1 percent level). There are two ways to interpret this result. It is possible that firms that have received more rounds of financing are more ready to go public than firms that have received fewer rounds of financing, and so these firms delay filing their prospectus less. Another possibility is that VCs that have provided many rounds of financing are in a hurry to capitalize on their investment, and so they rush the firm into filing a prospectus. I also look at total investment provided to the IPO firm in order to see if will provide more insight, but it presents no remarkable pattern. Third, I look at the number of VCs that have backed the IPO. Firms in the lowest quintile of file delay have 4.2 more VCs than the highest quintile (this difference is statistically significant at the 1 percent level). It is possible that the greater number of rounds received by the IPO is driven by the firm having more VCs backers (the number of firms and the number of rounds are 67.1 percent correlated). Finally, I examine the IPO's development stage level at the time of the last round of financing, for all file delay quintiles.[4] The lowest file delay quintile IPOs are at a later stage of development than the highest quintile IPOs (3.2 versus 1.8, with the difference being significantly different from zero at the 1 percent level) when the firm receives its last round of financing prior to going public. This says that low file delay firms tend to be at the expansion stage whereas the high file delay firms tend to be between the seed stage and the early stage of development.

Overall, there is a strong relationship between the file delay and the number of rounds and VCs as well as the firm's stage of development. While I expect that filing too early should lead to greater uncertainty about the firm, I do not want to pick up the uncertainty which has already been documented for certain variables such as the number of rounds or firms.[5] I will control for these variables in the multivariate analysis below.

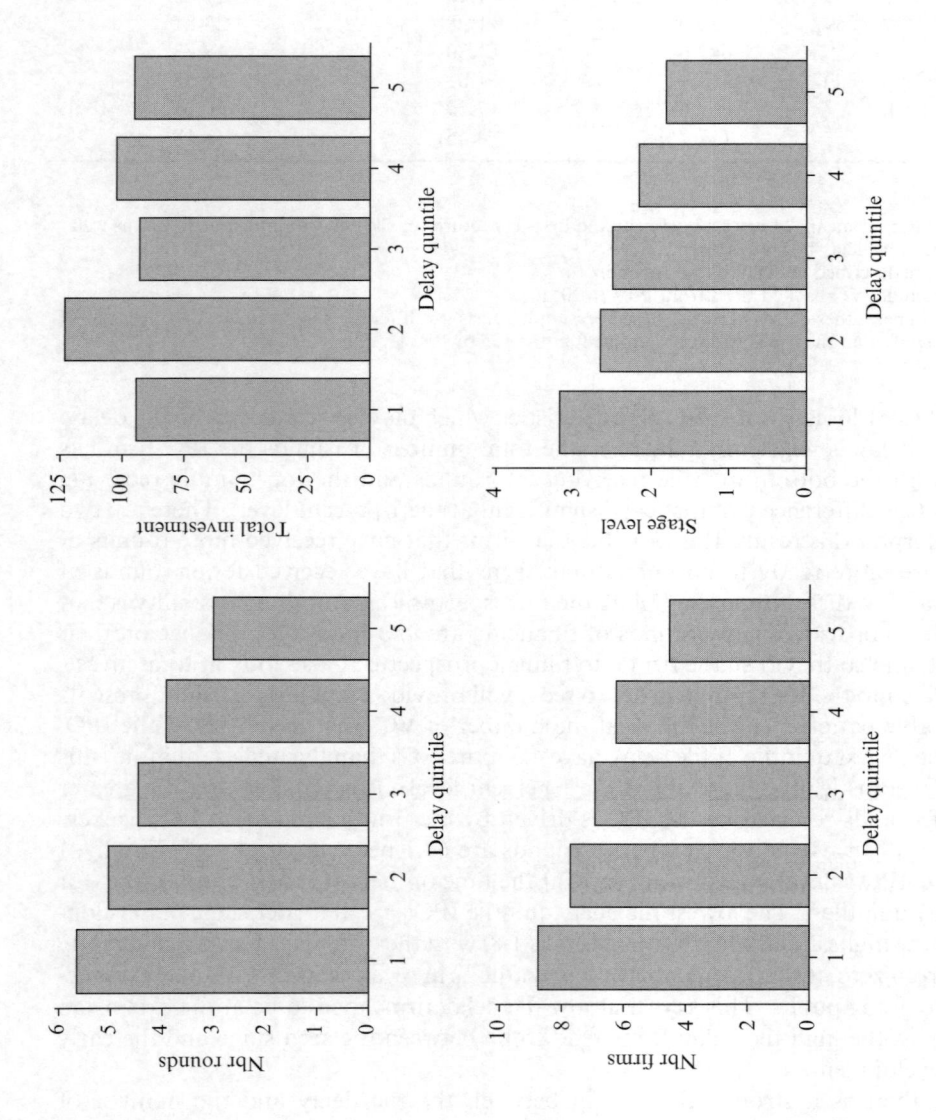

Notes:
This figure plots the mean number of rounds, total investment, number of firms, and stage level for file delay quintile portfolios.
All variables are described in detail in the appendix.
The sample includes VC-backed IPOs from 1983 to 2011.

Figure 11.4   VC characteristic averages for file delay portfolios

VC investment timing and IPO pricing 227

3.1.2 Trivariate results

To get a better idea of the subsample of IPOs where file delay is most important, on Figure 11.5 reports on the relationship between file delay and short-run performance for technology versus non-technology IPOs, large versus small IPOs, growth versus value IPOs, and young versus old IPOs. What is clear from these figures is that the impact of file delay is concentrated among young technology IPOs with high growth prospects. It will be important to control for these variables in the multivariate analysis since this is precisely what I do not want to capture: differences is short-run performance due to inherent firm differences. An unexpected result which comes out of these figures relates to assets. The file delay/short-run performance relationship is predominantly among large IPOs (that is, IPOs with more assets), a result which is somewhat contrary to those using technology, growth and age. This result is reassuring in the sense that it suggests that file delay is not solely positively related with uncertainty characteristics, to the extent that IPOs with more assets have lower uncertainty. Finally, it is interesting that in the subsample of technology, large, growth, or young IPOs, the impact of file delay on short-run performance is just as pronounced as in the overall sample. This result suggests that among non-technology, small, old, value firms, there is no apparent relationship between file delay and short-run performance.

3.1.3 Multivariate results

As mentioned above, controlling for the potentially confounding effects of important variables in the literature is important in order to properly test the grandstanding hypothesis. Table 11.3 reports multivariate ordinary least squares (OLS) regressions of short-run performance on file delay and various control variables. Price adjustment is examined in the first column, whereas first-day return is examined in columns 2 and 3 with and without price adjustment as an independent variable, respectively. The results are consistent with the bivariate analysis above. In the first column, file delay is negatively related to price adjustment and the coefficient is significant at the 1 percent level. A 1 percent decrease in file delay is associated with a 1.35 percentage point increase in price adjustment. Economically, a one standard deviation decrease in Ln(File delay) is associated with a 1.84 percentage point increase in price adjustment, controlling for other factors. Turning to first-day returns in the second column, I find that file delay is negatively related to first-day return and the coefficient is significant at the 1 percent level. A 1 percent decrease in file delay is associated with a 5.08 percentage point increase in first-day return. Economically, a one standard deviation decrease in Ln(File delay) is associated with a 6.93 percentage point increase in first-day return, controlling for other factors. In the third column, I add price adjustment as an independent variable in order to gauge the impact of file delay on first-day return, controlling for its indirect impact through price adjustment. The results are similar to those in the second column except that the magnitude of the coefficient on file delay is lower. A 1 percent decrease in file delay is associated with a 3.44 percentage point increase in first-day return. Economically, a 1 standard deviation decrease in Ln(File delay) is associated with a 4.69 percentage point increase in first-day return, controlling for price adjustment and other factors. These numbers are not trivial given the mean price adjustment in the sample

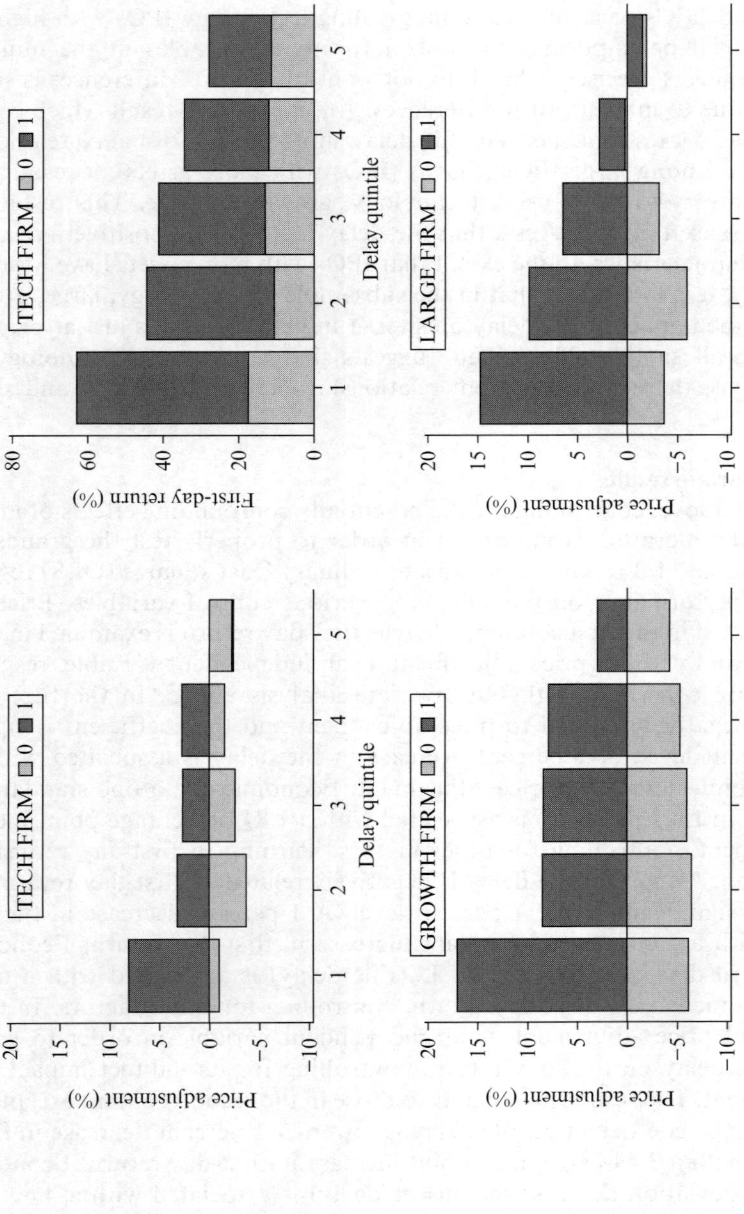
TECH FIRM
0
1
First-day return (%)
Delay quintile
TECH FIRM
Price adjustment (%)
Delay quintile
LARGE FIRM
Price adjustment (%)
Delay quintile
GROWTH FIRM
Price adjustment (%)
Delay quintile

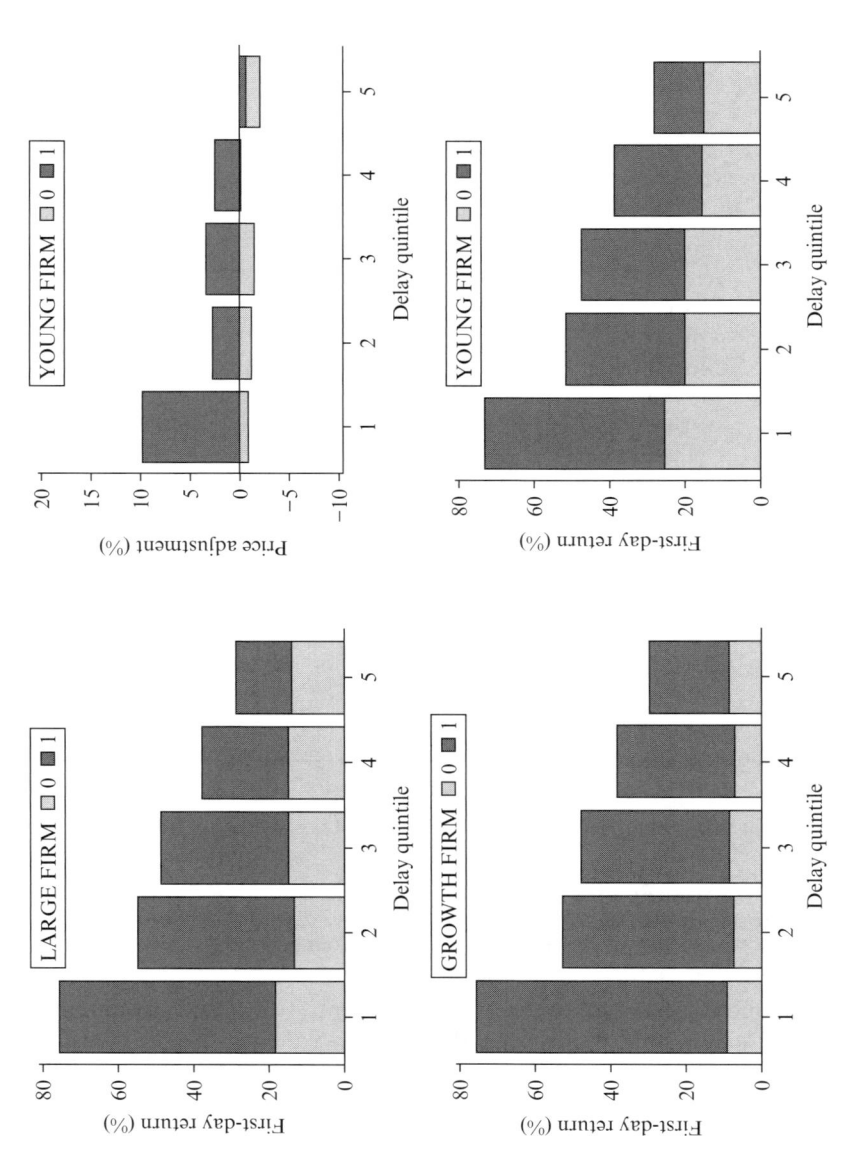

Notes:
This figure plots the mean price adjustment and first-day return for file delay quintile portfolios by technology (TECH FIRM), assets (LARGE FIRM), book-to-file (GROWTH FIRM), and firm age (YOUNG FIRM).
Except for technology, the dummy variables created represent being above or below the median.
All variables are described in detail in the appendix.
The sample includes VC-backed IPOs with a VC valuation available within three years of the file date, from 1983 to 2011.

Figure 11.5 Price adjustment and first-day return for file delay portfolios

Table 11.3 Short-run performance multivariate regressions

	Price adjustment Model 1	First-day return Model 1	First-day return Model 2
Ln(File delay)	−1.25***	−4.67***	−3.15***
	(−2.81)	(−5.37)	(−4.61)
TECH	4.47***	10.03***	4.60**
	(3.37)	(3.87)	(2.26)
Ln(Assets)	0.23**	0.97***	0.69***
	(2.30)	(4.96)	(4.49)
Book-to-file	6.63***	−1.61	−9.66***
	(3.81)	(−0.47)	(−3.61)
Ln(1+Firm age)	−2.55***	−4.34***	−1.25
	(−3.34)	(−2.90)	(−1.06)
Ln(Nbr firms)	0.41	6.05***	5.55***
	(0.44)	(3.38)	(3.96)
Nbr of rounds	−0.91***	−2.47***	−1.36***
	(−3.93)	(−5.43)	(−3.80)
Ln(Total investment)	0.49	2.02***	1.41**
	(1.29)	(2.67)	(2.39)
Stage level	1.47***	4.15***	2.37***
	(3.48)	(5.03)	(3.65)
Price adjustment			1.22***
			(39.39)
Intercept	7.11**	37.75***	29.11***
	(2.05)	(5.55)	(5.46)
Adj. R^2 (%)	4.10	8.69	43.85
N	2486	2486	2486

Notes:
This table reports the regressions of price adjustment and first-day return on Ln(File delay) and control variables.
All variables are described in detail in the appendix.
The sample includes VC-backed IPOs from 1983 to 2011.
The numbers in parentheses are simple *t*-statistics.
***, ** or * signify that the test statistic is significant at the 1, 5 or 10% level, respectively.

is 1.94 percent and the mean first-day return is 24.91 percent. The economic impact of file delay on price adjustment is 95 percent of the mean value (1.84/1.94), while the economic impact of file delay on first-day return is 28 percent of the mean value (6.93/24.91).

To summarize, the results in this subsection support the idea that the IPOs brought public too early by VCs have higher price adjustment and first-day returns than IPOs that are not brought public too early. While this is not a direct proof of the grandstanding hypothesis, it is a necessary condition. We examine the average age of the IPO's VCs in the next subsection to show that the firms that are brought public too early are indeed backed by young VCs who have an incentive to grandstand.

Table 11.4 VC Age multivariate regressions

	Model 1	Model 2	Model 3	Model 4
Ln(*File delay*)	−0.00	−0.01	0.03***	0.02**
	(−0.05)	(−1.25)	(4.43)	(2.43)
TECH		0.07***		0.04*
		(3.42)		(1.74)
Ln(*Assets*)		0.01***		0.01***
		(8.96)		(5.44)
Book-to-file		−0.05*		−0.03
		(−1.81)		(−1.00)
Ln(1+*Firm age*)		0.08***		0.07***
		(6.54)		(5.36)
Ln(*Nbr firms*)			0.01	0.03*
			(0.86)	(1.75)
Nbr of rounds			0.00	−0.00
			(0.85)	(−0.39)
Ln(*Total investment*)			0.08***	0.06***
			(14.44)	(10.01)
Stage level			0.01**	0.01**
			(2.27)	(2.12)
Intercept	2.84***	2.65***	2.35***	2.28***
	(74.90)	(55.40)	(45.21)	(39.38)
Adj. R^2 (%)	−0.03	5.12	9.20	10.21
N	2948	2572	2803	2478

Notes:
This table reports the regressions of Ln(1+*VC age*) on Ln(*File delay*) and control variables.
All variables are described in detail in the appendix.
The sample includes VC-backed IPOs from 1983 to 2011.
The numbers in parentheses are simple *t*-statistics.
***, ** or * signify that the test statistic is significant at the 1, 5 or 10% level, respectively.

VC age In Table 11.4, I examine the relationship between file delay and the average age of the VCs backing the IPO. To support the grandstanding hypothesis, there must be a positive relationship between file delay and VC age, such that young VC syndicates are bringing firms public too early. Model 1 tests the relationship between file delay and VC age without any control variables. The coefficient on Ln(File delay) is insignificantly different from zero. Model 2 adds to model 1 the IPO firm characteristics, which were found to be significantly related to file delay in Figure 11.5, as control variables. Again, I find that the relationship between file delay and VC age is insignificantly different from zero. The IPO firm characteristics are all significant on the other hand. Old, large, growth, and technology IPOs are all associated with older VC syndicates. In model 3, I add to model 1 the VC financing characteristics, which were found to be significantly related to file delay in Figure 11.4, as control variables. The results indicate that controlling for these VC financing characteristics elucidates the relationship between file delay and VC age. The coefficient on Ln(File delay) is significantly positive at the 1 percent level. The number of financing rounds, total VC investment in the IPO firm, and the IPO's growth stage

Table 11.5 Offer delay multivariate regressions

	Model 1	Model 2	Model 3
Ln(*File delay*)	−0.02**	−0.04***	−0.04***
	(−2.42)	(−3.17)	(−3.35)
TECH		0.07**	0.08**
		(2.12)	(2.34)
Ln(*Assets*)		0.01***	0.01***
		(3.34)	(3.49)
Book-to-file		−0.04	−0.03
		(−0.95)	(−0.70)
Ln(1+*Firm age*)		0.06***	0.06***
		(3.26)	(3.04)
Ln(*Nbr firms*)		−0.10***	−0.10***
		(−4.39)	(−4.37)
Nbr of rounds		−0.00	−0.00
		(−0.27)	(−0.52)
Ln(*Total investment*)		0.09***	0.09***
		(9.27)	(9.37)
Stage level		0.01	0.01
		(0.69)	(0.91)
Price adjustment			−0.00***
			(−3.24)
Intercept	4.39***	4.11***	4.12***
	(76.76)	(46.37)	(46.56)
Adj. R^2 (%)	0.00	6.14	6.50
N	2964	2486	2486

Notes:
This table reports the regressions of Ln(*Offer delay*) on Ln(*File delay*) and control variables.
All variables are described in detail in the appendix.
The sample includes VC-backed IPOs from 1983 to 2011.
The numbers in parentheses are simple *t*-statistics.
***, ** or * signify that the test statistic is significant at the 1, 5 or 10% level, respectively.

level are all significantly and positively related to VC age. Model 4 includes all control variables from models 2 and 3. The results are similar to those in Model 3, except that the magnitude of the coefficient on Ln(File delay) is slightly lower. Overall, the evidence shows that, controlling for differences in VC financing behavior, IPOs with shorter file delays are associated with younger VCs, consistent with the grandstanding hypothesis.

Offer delay An interesting question that comes out of the above analysis, especially given the first-day return differences are much larger than the price adjustment differences, is whether institutional investors in the primary market realize that some IPOs are being brought public too early. I examine this question in Table 11.5, by looking at the relationship between file delay and offer delay. The offer delay is the number of days between the file date and the offer date. If institutional investors are able to discern IPOs that go public too early, then it will take much convincing on the part of the firm, its

VC backers, and its underwriters in order to sell the entire allocation of shares. I therefore expect that IPOs that file their prospectus too early will have longer book-building periods (that is, offer delay) than IPOs that do not file too early. On the other hand, if institutional investors cannot distinguish between premature and non-premature IPOs, then I expect no relationship between file delay and offer delay, all other things being equal.

Model 1 tests the relationship between file delay and offer delay without any control variables. The coefficient on Ln(File delay) is significantly negative at the 5 percent level. This result says that IPOs with a short file delay have longer book-building periods, consistent with the idea that institutional investors can indeed discern these premature offers. Model 2 adds to model 1 the VC financing characteristics and IPO firm characteristics, which were found to be significantly related to file delay in Figures 11.4 and 11.5, as control variables. I find that the relationship between file delay and offer delay is even larger in magnitude than in model 1 and significant at the 1 percent level. The IPO firm characteristics are all significant except for the book-to-file ratio. The number of financing rounds is negatively and significantly related to the offer delay, while total VC investment is positively and significantly related to offer delay. Model 3 includes all control variables from model 2 along with the price adjustment, in order to test whether file delay has a direct impact above and beyond its indirect impact through price adjustment. The results are similar to those in model 2, except that the magnitude of the coefficient on Ln(File delay) is slightly higher. Overall, the evidence shows that, controlling for differences in VC financing behavior as well as firm characteristics, IPOs with shorter file delays are associated have longer book-building periods, suggesting that institutional investors are aware that they are being sold a premature IPO.

4 DISCUSSION

The results in this chapter suggest that younger VCs grandstand by bringing firms public too early, thus allowing them to raise future funds more easily. A byproduct of the grandstanding hypothesis is that firms brought to the market prematurely have more information asymmetry, and so require greater underpricing. Therefore the assumption underlying the grandstanding hypothesis is therefore that the first-day market closing price is efficient and the offer price is set low in order to induce investors to participate in the offering.

However, a literature has emerged that challenges the efficiency of the market in setting the aftermarket price (that is, it is possible that the first-day closing market price is set too high by market participants). Purnanandam and Swaminathan (2004) document that IPO prices are overvalued relative to intrinsic values. In a study of the role of underwriters in promoting IPO overvaluation, Chemmanur and Krishnan (2011) show a similar pattern of IPO market prices that are on average set too high initially and tend to converge to their intrinsic values in the long run. These studies list the divergence of opinion hypothesis of Miller (1977) as a potential explanation of the observed IPO price pattern. Miller (1977) predicts that in the presence of short-sales constraints, the price of a firm tends to reflect the valuations of the most optimistic investors, and thus tend to be upward biased. This is the case because pessimistic investors are forced out of the market when short sales are not available. Even when short sales are allowed after the offer, the view of pessimistic investors may not be reflected in the prices in the short run because there are limits to arbitrage in practice (Shleifer and Vishny, 1997). Ljungqvist et al. (2006) model IPO pricing assuming the existence of a fraction of sentiment-driven investors who are overoptimistic about the prospects of the IPO firms. Three recent studies examine the effect of investor sentiment on the overvaluation of IPOs. Using pre-offer bids from retail investors, Derrien (2005) finds evidence of overvaluation in French IPOs. Cornelli et al. (2006) use pre-IPO 'grey market' prices in a sample of European IPOs, and find evidence consistent with investors overvaluing IPOs in the short run. Michel (2012) finds that VC-backed IPOs with a higher return on recent VC investment have relatively poor long-run performance, and that this relationship is primarily driven by market conditions at the time of the VC investment, suggesting that IPO investors are too optimistic.

This overvaluation is potentially important in the context of the grandstanding hypothesis. If the first-day return is driven by overvaluation, then it is not a cost borne by the issuer (and the VC holding shares), in the sense that they are not pricing the offer below the intrinsic value. Indeed, young VCs may be benefiting from bringing firms public prematurely when stocks are overvalued. This alternate interpretation of the grandstanding hypothesis fits in nicely with the literature on market timing. In the market timing hypothesis, rational managers take advantage of the temporary mispricing caused by irrational investors, thereby affecting corporate policies. For example, Baker et al. (2007), assumes that arbitrage in securities markets is imperfect, and as a result, prices can be too high or too low. Rational managers perceive this mispricing and make decisions which maximize short-run value of the firm, but may also result in lower long-run values as prices correct to fundamentals. If young VCs push managers to go public when investors are overoptimistic, the firm would benefit from raising more capital, and VCs would benefit by being able to sell their shares at a higher price. This would also allow VCs to raise follow-on funds more easily. In this scenario, the relationship between firms going public prematurely and first-day returns would be driven by investor overoptimism and not by information asymmetry, although the two effects are not mutually exclusive. One can think of this alternative explanation as the 'market grandstanding' hypothesis, where grandstanding is linked to market timing instead of information asymmetry. Our results are also consistent with this alternate hypothesis.

5 CONCLUSIONS

In this chapter, I examine the role of VC investment timing on short-run IPO pricing. I find that lower file delay is associated with higher short-run IPO performance, consistent with the grandstanding hypothesis. Furthermore, lower file delay is associated with VCs that are younger and book-building periods which are longer. Overall, this evidence is consistent with the grandstanding hypothesis, but it is also consistent with a modified 'market' grandstanding hypothesis where grandstanding is associated with IPO overvaluation instead of information asymmetry. Research about the impact of venture capitalists on IPO pricing is important given venture capitalists have first contact with the firms they bring public, and so are arguably the most informed investors in the company.

NOTES

1. Among VC-backed IPOs, there is also variation in initial pricing. Focusing on venture-backed IPOs only, Li and Masulis (2007) find that initial returns decrease in the size of investment banks' pre-IPO equity holdings.
2. These issues are eliminated by retaining only issues with CRSP share codes equal to 10, 11 and 12.
3. In unreported tests, I find that the time-series correlation between file delay and initial return (price adjustment) is −54 percent (−34 percent).
4. Stage level equals 1 if the firm is at the 'seed' stage, 2 if the firm is at the 'early' stage, 3 if the firm is at the 'expansion' stage, 4 if the firm is at the 'late' stage, 5 if the firm is at the 'bridge loan' stage, and 0 otherwise.
5. In particular, it is possible that a greater number of rounds or firms are forms of risk sharing or risk management, which would suggest that the firms that are being backed are inherently riskier.

REFERENCES

Baker, M., R. Ruback and J. Wurgler (2007), 'Behavioral corporate finance', in E. Eckbo (ed.), *Handbook of Corporate Finance: Empirical Corporate Finance Vol. 1*, Amsterdam: Elsevier/North-Holland, ch. 4.

Benveniste, L. and P.A. Spindt (1989), 'How investment bankers determine the offer price and allocation of new issues', *Journal of Financial Economics*, **24**, 343–61.

Booth, J. and R. Smith (1986), 'Capital raising, underwriting, and the certification hypothesis', *Journal of Financial Economics*, **15**, 261–81.

Carter, R. and S. Manaster (1990), 'Initial public offerings and underwriter reputation', *Journal of Finance*, **45**, 1045–67.

Carter, R., F. Dark and A. Singh (1998), 'Underwriter reputation, initial returns, and the long-run performance of IPO stocks', *Journal of Finance*, **53**, 285–311.

Chemmanur, T. and K. Krishnan (2011), 'Heterogeneous beliefs, short sales constraints, and the economic role of the underwriter in IPOs', working paper, Boston College.

Cornelli, F., D. Goldreich and A. Ljungqvist (2006), 'Investor sentiment and pre-IPO markets', *Journal of Finance*, **61**, 1187–216.

Derrien, F. (2005), 'IPO pricing in "hot" market conditions: who leaves money on the table?', *Journal of Finance*, **60**, 487–521.

Gompers, P. (1993), 'The theory, structure, and performance of venture capital', unpublished PhD thesis, Harvard University, Cambridge, MA.

Gompers, P. (1995), 'Optimal investment, monitoring and the staging of venture capital', *Journal of Finance*, **50**, 1461–89.

Gompers, P. (1996), 'Grandstanding in the venture capital industry', *Journal of Financial Economics*, **42**, 133–56.

Lee, P.M. and S. Wahal (2004), 'Grandstanding, certification, and the underpricing of venture capital backed IPOs', *Journal of Financial Economics*, **73**, 375–407.

Li, X. and R. Masulis (2007), 'How do venture investments by different classes of financial institutions affect the equity underwriting process?', working paper, Vanderbilt University.

Ljungqvist, A., V. Nanda and R. Singh (2006), 'Hot markets, investors sentiment, and IPO pricing', *Journal of Business*, **79**, 1667–702.

Megginson, W.L. and K. Weiss (1991), 'Venture capitalist certification in initial public offerings', *Journal of Finance*, **46**, 879–903.

Michel, J. (2012), 'Return on recent VC investment and long-run IPO returns', *Entrepreneurship Theory and Practice*, forthcoming.

Miller, E. (1977), 'Risk, uncertainty, and divergence of opinion', *Journal of Finance*, **32**, 1151–68.

Muscarella, C. and M. Vetsuypens (1990), 'Firm age, uncertainty, and IPO underpricing: some new empirical evidence', SMU working paper.

Purnanandam, A. and B. Swaminathan (2004), 'Are IPOs really underpriced?', *Review of Financial Studies*, **17**, 811–48.

Rock, K. (1986), 'Why new issues are underpriced', *Journal of Financial Economics*, **15**, 187–212.

Shleifer, A. and R. Vishny (1997), 'The limits of arbitrage', *Journal of Finance*, **52**, 35–55.

APPENDIX: VARIABLE DEFINITIONS

Assets is the value of assets prior to the IPO in millions of dollars.
Book-to-file is the ratio of book value of equity and implied market value at the file date. The implied market value at the file date is given by shares outstanding after the IPO minus shares offered plus shares file, multiplied by the mid-point of the file range.
File delay is the number of days between the file date and the date of the last round of VC financing prior to the file date.
Firm age is the number of years between the firm founding date and the file date.
First-day return is the percentage difference between the mid-point of the file range and the offer price.
Nbr firms is the total number of VCs that have financed the firm.
Nbr of rounds is the total number of rounds of financing that the firm has received from VCs.
Offer delay is the number of days between the offer date and the file date.
Price adjustment is the percentage difference between the offer price and the first-day market closing price.
Stage level equals 1 if the firm received its last round of financing in its seed stage, 2 if it was received in its early stage, 3 if it was received in its expansion stage, 4 if it was received in its late stage, 5 if it was received in its bridge loan stage, and 0 otherwise.
TECH equals 1 if the firm is in a high-technology industry, and 0 otherwise.
Total investment is the total financing an IPO firm has received from all of its VCs.
VC age is the number of years between the VC founding date and the file date, averaged across all of the firm's VCs.

12 The underwriters of IPOs in Europe's second markets
Katrin Migliorati and Stefano Paleari

1 INTRODUCTION

Since 1995, most stock exchanges in Europe have launched second-tier markets with the aim to fulfil the needs of particular categories of firms. Among all the second markets, the London Alternative Investment Market (AIM) has attracted an impressive high number of new listings (Vismara et al., 2012). Even after the collapse of the Internet bubble, the AIM continued to attract new listings, while the US stock exchanges faced a permanent decline in IPO volume and other European second-tier markets closed. The attention on AIM has entitled increasing debate in the financial press on regulation and on the role of nominated advisors (that is, Nomads).

The AIM market is an exchange-regulated market (that is, unregulated) as defined by the European Financial Services Directive, meaning a market with minimal regulatory requirements for firms listed on these markets. The unique regulatory structure of the AIM relies on the shift of most of regulation from public authorities to private entities (that is, Nomads). Nomads represent the firm's key point of contact with the exchange and play a vital role in advising and guiding the company on both admission and ongoing services after the listing. They serve as gatekeepers and regulatory agents since a substantial part of regulation is outsourced to them (Espenlaub et al., 2012).

However, while a considerable body of the finance literature has focused on the role of underwriters as a valuable signal to reduce information asymmetries in markets characterized by uncertainty (Carter and Manaster, 1990; Carter et al., 1998), limited empirical research supports the Nomad system. In such context, information asymmetries between investors, firms and investment banks are emphasized due to minimal listing requirements and to Nomads who are chosen and paid by the firms themselves. Moreover, informational asymmetries may be also emphasized in a context that lacks a financial culture. For instance, Tokyo AIM was unsuccessfully launched in June 2009. The introduction of the Nomad system in Japan lock horns securities companies that may have been reluctant to take on responsibility that rests with them in case of scandals involving listed firms.

Understanding the type of Nomads is thus of particular importance as they are needed to certify and control the quality of new listings at all time, and as they play a crucial role in limiting informational problems and incentive conflicts (Espenlaub et al., 2012). In particular, no prior studies compare the role of investment banks taking companies public on the AIM unique market model relative to those on second regulated markets in continental Europe. Addressing this gap remains a major issue for academics, regulators and firms themselves, because the AIM regulatory model provides a unique setting in which to examine the potential effects of self-regulation on the role of Nomads.

We collect data on initial public offerings (IPOs) listed on the Europe second markets over the period 1995–2010. Our sample comprises 2373 IPOs listed on the AIM in UK or on second-tier regulated markets in France, Germany and Italy. These offerings are taken public by 198 different lead or co-lead investment banks. We identify several characteristics for investment banks referring to balance sheets and typology of banks. We investigate Nomad's characteristics relative to underwriter's characteristics on a second regulated market, and what the effects of the choice of Nomads are on IPO and bank performances.

Overall, our findings indicate significant differences between Nomads and underwriters that take companies public on second regulated markets. In univariate analyses, we find that Nomads are significantly younger, and smaller in terms of asset, equity values and number of subsidiaries. Further, Nomads are found to be significantly specialized in the IPO business, meaning that a substantial part of their revenues compared to those of the underwriters on second-tier regulated markets. We define the specialization in IPO business as the ratio between the value of the IPO business over the total amount of all deals made (equity, loan, bond and mergers and acquisitions – M&A). We further differentiate second-tier regulated markets at stock-exchange level to avoid country-specific biases. Indeed, across all markets, Nomads and investment banks are rarely US banks, and mostly domestic banks.

We validate our findings in a multivariate context. Previous literature has shown that issue and firm characteristics significantly affect the matching between underwriters and issuers (Fernando et al., 2005). For the same issuer and offering, a theory of Nomads acting to some extent as 'regulators' could predict a significant relation between Nomad characteristics and firm or bank performances. When considering firm performance, we find that Nomads characteristics are significantly (although not strongly) associated with underpricing. Specifically, being younger, smaller (in term of total assets) and specialized in the IPO business reduces the IPO underpricing. When considering bank performance, proxied by the average number of IPOs underwritten, we find that the propensity to take companies public increases significantly for smaller Nomads who are highly specialized in the IPO business. However, in Paris, Frankfurt and Milan, underwriters significantly increase their number of IPO mandates and are established banks. Overall, our findings suggest that the value of self-regulation demanded of Nomads significantly affects the characteristics of these players, in that they distinguish themselves from underwriters on second-tier regulated markets.

Our findings provide valuable new insights for new markets that aim to launch a model based on the Nomad system. The financial crisis in 2007/08 reignited the public debate on the Nomad system since capital markets agree on the need to support growing small and medium-size enterprises (SMEs) and the AIM market model serves as a model for small firms with high growth opportunities. For instance, in April 2012, the Financial Services Commission (FSC) in Korea announced its plan for creating the Korea New Exchange (KONEX) modelled on London's AIM and on Nomad's self-regulation structure. Also in Europe, New York Stock Exchange (NYSE) Euronext is being planned the creation of a new pan-European stock exchange ('Entrepreneurs' Exchange') dedicated to small companies, partly as a response to the Jobs Act ('jumpstart our business start-ups') in the US which eased the rules for small businesses raising equity capital for expansion.

In the reminder of the chapter we, first, briefly review related literature and institutional background on second markets and the AIM regulatory structure. Then, we turn to research design and data; we report empirical results and, lastly, conclude.

2 RELATED LITERATURE

Historically, firms going public in Europe on second markets had their pick during hot markets in comparison with cold ones (Vismara et al., 2012). Before the financial crisis in 2007/08, European second markets had indeed consistently failed following market downturns, with the exception of the UK AIM. As a result, the AIM unique regulatory model has been attracting increasing attention in both literature and public debate.

Several studies examine the effects of regulation on IPO activity, in particular following the drop in the US IPO volume relative to the higher number of firms listed on the AIM. Whether regulation is required to prevent market failure or boost the economy and capital market is still an open debate (for an excellent survey, see Leuz and Wysocki, 2008). Gao et al. (2012) document that the decline in US IPO activity is more related to the declining profitability of small companies rather than to the effects of regulation (the Sarbanes–Oxley Act of 2002 (SOX) and the 2003 Global Settlements). Inconsistent with the regulatory issues, Doidge et al. (2009) and Piotroski and Srinivasan (2008) find that listing choices by foreign firms choosing between US exchanges and the UK main market did not change due to SOX. In contrast, Piotroski and Srinivasan (2008) provide evidence that the decline in cross-listings on US exchanges relative to the UK AIM market may be due to SOX for small foreign firms. However, Doidge et al. (2009) suggest that small firms listed on the AIM would not have been eligible to list on a US exchange, either before or after SOX.

Second, a growing body of literature investigate the performance or the survival rate of AIM companies. Gregory et al. (2010) document a persistent long-run underperformance for UK companies over the period mid-1975 to 2004, using different methodologies in measuring abnormal returns. They found that this underperformance is concentrated in AIM stocks (and also in the now closed Unlisted Securities Market), particularly in smaller firms.

In analyzing the survival or performance of AIM newly listed stocks, limited research has considered the impact of Nomads. Espenlaub et al. (2012) examine determinants of IPO survival rates for new listings on the AIM and find that the reputation of Nomads (that is, proxied by Nomad's market share, credit score, profitability and age) extends expected survival time by about two years.

A related working paper accounts for Nomad characteristics. Gerakos et al. (2011) document that AIM stocks underperform significantly in comparison to companies listed on regulated exchanges in the US and the UK, and also relative to stocks traded on the lightly regulated 'Pink Sheets' in the US. In particular, the empirical analyses of Gerakos et al. (2011) compare across markets (that is, using stock market dummies) the potential association between firm performance or liquidity and types of Nomads (that is, Nomad as auditors or brokers, Nomad's numbers of listings, capital raising and number of subsequent delistings) finding only a minor association with the AIM listing illiquidity. However, none of these studies directly examine the characteristics of Nomads on the AIM in comparison to those of underwriters taking companies public on continental European second markets, which is the focus of our analysis.

3 THE INSTITUTIONAL FRAMEWORK

3.1 Second Markets

Stock exchanges in continental Europe are organized in segments, with a main market and different second markets. The regulatory regime of the second-tier markets is meant to fulfil the needs of particular classes of firms, mainly young and small companies. Second markets have less stringent requirements than main markets, with listing requirements more related to accounting thresholds to disclosure and governance.

A special category of markets is that of exchange-regulated (that is, unregulated) markets. While in regulated markets, national competent authorities define listing and trading rules, unregulated markets come under the authority of the exchange itself, except in the case of IPOs involving a public offer. The rules of the Transparency Directive do not apply to non-regulated Markets and European Union member states have generally not extended the applicability of the detailed rules of the Directive to those markets. Broadly speaking, unregulated markets require the minimal regulation for the firms listed on these markets of all the second markets. Since the launch of the exchange-regulated AIM in 1995 in London, the other stock markets in continental Europe opened similar 'unregulated markets'.

Overall, European second-tier regulated markets require a minimum market capitalization of €1 million, with the exception of France (€12–15 million on Second Marché), public float in a range of 10–25 per cent, firm age of around one year and IPO proceeds greater than €5 million. The AIM relaxes also these listing requirements (see Table 12.1).

3.2 Underwriters in Continental Europe

The existence of exchange-regulated markets covers the fundamental importance of the role of the investment bank. In second-tier regulated markets, companies hire an underwriter who mainly has to certify and advise the issuer, providing a package of services to the company (that is, supporting the company in preparing the listing and ensuring the company fulfils ongoing obligations).

In exchange-regulated markets, companies have instead to retain Nomads as their guide throughout the flotation process and as an advisor during their time as public companies. Nomads are required to vet, test suitability, and supervise the AIM firms at all times due to the 'light touch' regulation. They play a pivotal role serving as gatekeepers and regulators. A key implication is that the national listing authorities are not required to review and approve a firm's prospectus when its listing does not involve a public offer. In other words, on the AIM, neither the UK Listing Authority (UKLA) nor the London Stock Exchange (LSE) are required to approve the prospectus, and the exchange gives Nomads this responsibility.

Table 12.1 Main listing requirements on Alternative Investment Market (AIM) vs European second-tier regulated markets

| | AIM | Second-tier regulated markets ||||||
| | London | Paris || Frankfurt || Milan ||
		Second Marché	Nouveau Marché	Geregelter Markt	Neuer Markt	Mercato Ristretto Expandi	Nuovo Mercato Mtax
1 Public float	(Not closed) None	(18/02/2005) 10%	(18/02/2005) 20% (with at least 100 000 voting rights)	(11/2007) None (at least 10 000 shares)	(5/06/2003) 25% or 10% if IPO proceeds are greater than €5m (with at least 100000 shares)	(22/06/2009) 10%	(3/03/2008) 20% (with at least 100000 voting rights)
2 IPO proceeds (€ millions)			5		5	7.5	5
3 Minimum market cap (€ millions)	None	12/15				1	
4 Book value of equity (€ millions)	None		1.5	0.250	1.5		1.5
5 Shares newly issued	None	None	Half of the IPO shares	None	Half of the IPO shares		Half of the IPO shares
6 Firm age	None	2	None	3, exceptions possible	3	2	1

Notes:
This Table reports the major listing requirements for the AIM and the second-tier regulated markets in Paris (Second Marché, Nouveau Marché), Frankfurt (Geregelter Markt, Neuer Markt) or Milan (Mercato Ristretto/Expandi, Nuovo Mercato/Mtax). Closing dates of second markets are reported in parenthesis below the market name.

Pursuant to the AIM Rules for Companies, a Nomad is responsible to the exchange for assessing the appropriateness of an applicant for AIM, or an existing AIM company when appointed its Nomad, and for advising and guiding an AIM company on its responsibilities. The role of a Nomad is regulated by the 'AIM Rules for Nominated Advisers', which set out the eligibility, ongoing obligations and certain disciplinary matters. In particular, the Nomad should oversee and be actively involved in the preparation of the admission document and must satisfy him or herself that it complies with the AIM Rules for Companies. Furthermore, the exchange may take disciplinary action against the Nomad that may lead to the removal of nominated advisor status. In accordance with the procedures set out in the Disciplinary Procedures and Appeals Handbook the exchange may issue a warning notice, levy a fine, issue a censure, remove the Nomad from the register or publish the action the LSE has taken and the reasons for that action.

4 RESEARCH DESIGN

In the past two decades, the launch of second-tier markets in continental Europe has created a different route to raise funds at the IPO and in follow-on offerings (Vismara et al., 2012).

On 19 June 1995, a new market model was launched in London: the AIM, an exchange-regulated market characterized by minimal regulations. As mentioned in the previous section, the extremely light regulation on this type of market entails the outsourcing of part of the regulation to underwriters. In fact, the AIM distinguishes itself from other markets in that it requires AIM companies to retain a Nomad at all times (Espenlaub et al., 2012).

The existence of these unique players, who act to some extent as 'regulators', provides the ideal setting for investigating the role of Nomads in comparison to the role of underwriters on second-tier regulated markets. Nomads are responsible to the LSE for the appropriateness of the firm for AIM and for advising and guiding the AIM company. In particular, the admission on the exchange is cancelled if the AIM company ceases to have a Nomad and is not able to appoint a replacement Nomad. We refer to balance sheets and type of banks to investigate differences in the characteristics of Nomads compared to those of underwriters on second markets. We further differentiate second-tier regulated markets at stock-exchange level to avoid country-specific biases.

Initial public offerings have different resource bases and risk profile that are likely to impact the match with their investment banks that take companies public (Fernando et al., 2005). We also examine underwriter characteristics in a multivariate context. For the same issuer and offering, a theory of Nomads acting to some extent as 'regulators' would predict a significant relation between Nomad characteristics and IPO performance or investment bank performance relative to that between underwriter characteristics and IPO performance or investment bank performance on continental European second markets. Specifically, we examine the association between Nomad or underwriter characteristics with IPO underpricing and with the investment-bank IPO activity, accounting for other factors that can explain heterogeneity of underwriters.

5 DATA

We collect data on initial public offerings from the EURIPO database. We include issues marketed in the Europe's second markets from 1995 to 2010. Introductions (admissions with no initial offer), re-admissions, market transfers, and listings of companies already publicly listed on whatever stock exchange are excluded, as are IPOs of investment entities. We consider the population of 2472 companies that went public on the second markets in the UK, France, Germany and Italy. For the London Stock Exchange we use the AIM, for Paris Bourse we use Second Marché and Nouveau Marché, for Frankfurt Stock Exchange we use Geregelter Markt and Neuer Markt, and for Milan Stock Exchange we use Mercato Ristretto/Expandi and Nuovo Mercato/Mtax. After excluding 99 IPOs with missing data on proceeds and underwriter characteristics, we are left with a sample of 2373 IPOs. All proceeds exclude overallotment options, and we express all euro amounts in 2010 euros.

These offerings are taken public by 198 different lead or co-lead investment banks. Data on underwriters are collected from Bankscope, Fame and Thomson One Banker databases. For each bank we consider the statement of a mother bank integrating the statements of its controlled subsidiaries or branches with no unconsolidated companion, and additional consolidated statement (Bankscope database). In addition, the banks' websites are used to get the date of incorporation when absent on the above mentioned databases. We obtain investment bank Carter–Manaster rankings from Jay Ritter's website (http://bear.warrington.ufl.edu/ritter/ipodata.htm).

Figure 12.1 reports the average number of IPOs per year on the AIM and on second-tier regulated markets as a group in Paris, Frankfurt and Milan using the entire population of 2472 IPOs from 1995 to 2010. Among all of Europe's second markets, the AIM has succeeded in attracting the highest number of IPOs. During the sample period we

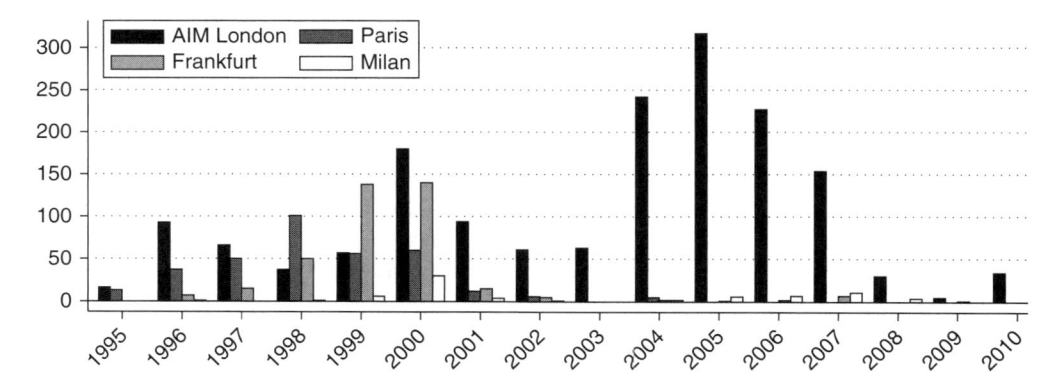

Notes:
The number of IPOs on the Alternative Investment Market (London) and second markets in Europe. This figure covers all the population of 2472 IPOs in the period 1995–2010, 1676 listed in AIM (London) and 796 listed on second-tier regulated markets in Paris (Second Marché, Nouveau Marché), Frankfurt (Geregelter Markt, Neuer Markt) and Milan (Mercato Ristretto/Expandi, Nuovo Mercato/Mtax). The sample comes from the Euripo database.

Figure 12.1   Number of IPOs on AIM and continental European second markets

Table 12.2 Descriptive statistics for the sample of IPOs

| | | Overall | AIM | Second-tier regulated markets ||||
				Paris	Frankfurt	Milan	Overall
Proceeds	Mean	35.2	24.9	21.4	81.0***	92.9***	56.4***
(€ millions)	25th percentile	4.7	3.1	6.8	24.2	18.7	10.6
	Median	11.9	7.9	11.9***	43.0***	40.7***	26.2***
	75th percentile	32.8	20.2	23.8	72.7	81.5	54.8
Mkt cap	Mean	107.8	58.9	90.3	283.2***	383.4***	211.1***
(€ millions)	25th percentile	15.6	10.1	28.8	67.9	66.2	40.6
	Median	39.4	26.7	50.3***	136.0***	135.0***	91.4***
	75th percentile	103.0	60.2	115.0	247.5	316.0	192.0
Secondary	Mean	4.7	3.2	9.6***	7.3***	5.6*	8.1***
	25th percentile	0.0	0.0	2.0	1.0	0.0	0.9
	Median	0.0	0.0	8.8***	5.1***	2.8***	6.0***
	75th percentile	6.0	0.0	14.2	10.5	7.2	11.8
Age	Mean	8.7	6.5	12.5***	11.8***	14.1***	12.3***
	25th percentile	1	0	4	3	4	4
	Median	4	2	9***	8***	11***	9***
	75th percentile	11	7	15	16	18	16
VC backed	Mean	0.53	0.62	0.38***	0.46***	0.31***	0.41***
No. of observations		2373	1598	330	372	73	775

Notes:
This table reports descriptive statistics for the sample of 2373 European IPOs during 1995–2010. 1598 IPOs are listed on the Alternative Investment Market (AIM) in London and 775 IPOs are listed on second-tier regulated markets in Paris (Second Marché, Nouveau Marché), Frankfurt (Geregelter Markt, Neuer Markt) or Milan (Mercato Ristretto/Expandi, Nuovo Mercato/Mtax).
The main sample covers the years between 1995 and 2010 and comes from the Euripo database.
The tests compare firms going public on AIM vs second-tier regulated markets.
The significance levels are based on *t*-statistics (mean), the Mann-Whitney *U*-test (rank), or a *Z*-test of equal proportions as required.
Statistical significance levels are at 1% (***), 5% (**), or 10% (*).

focus on, 1676 (67.8 per cent) out of 2472 IPOs took place on AIM. Second-tier regulated markets in Paris, Frankfurt and Milan account for the remaining 796 IPOs (32.7 per cent). In particular, 42.7 per cent IPOs took place in Paris, while 48.1 per cent in Frankfurt and 9.2 per cent in Milan. The IPO market tends to cluster in time with cycles of IPOs that are particularly evident on the AIM market. The first 'hot market' period reaches its peak in 2000 with 180 IPOs on the AIM, while the second, in 2005, reaches 317 IPOs, the highest number in the sample period. The average number of IPOs per year on the second-tier regulated markets fluctuates and reaches its peak during the technology bubble, respectively in Paris with 101 IPOs (in 1998), in Frankfurt with 140 IPOs (in 2000) and in Milan with 30 IPOs (in 2000).

Table 12.2 reports descriptive statistics on offering and firm characteristics for the IPO sample. A detailed description of all variables used in this study is reported in Table 12.3. Overall, companies going public on the AIM reveal statistically significant differences from firms going public on the second-tier regulated markets. However,

Table 12.3   Definitions of variables

Variable	Definition	Background	Data source
Underwriter characteristics			
Domestic	Dummy variable set equal to one when the country of the investment bank is equal to the country of the stock exchange where the IPO (brought to market by such underwriter) is listed	Proxy for the home-bias effect (Abrahamson et al., 2011)	Bankscope
US bank	Dummy variable set equal to one whether the underwriter is a US bank	Proxy for US-bank prestige (Torstila, 2001)	Bankscope
Carter–Manaster	Dummy variable set equal to one when the underwriter is associated at least once to Carter–Manaster rank	Proxy for US-bank prestige (Carter and Manaster, 1990)	Jay Ritter's website
Commercial bank	Dummy variable set equal to one when the underwriter is a commercial bank	Proxy for bank typology (Kim et al., 2008)	Bankscope
Co-leads (no.)	Average number of underwriter acting as co-leads for each issue	Proxy for bank syndicate	Prospectuses
No. subsidiaries (no.)	Number of recorded subsidiaries by each underwriter	Proxy for bank distribution power and size (Hayes, 1971)	Bankscope
Age (years)	Years between the listing date of a specific IPO and the incorporation date of the underwriter	Proxy for bank quality (Espenlaub et al., 2012)	Bankscope, website
Asset ($ billion 2010)	Average book value of total assets over the sample period adjusted for inflation	Proxy for bank size (De Haas and Van Lelyveld, 2010)	Bankscope
Equity ($ billion 2010)	Average book value of equity over the sample period adjusted for inflation	De Haas and Van Lelyveld (2010)	Bankscope
Equity/asset (%)	Ratio between book value of equity and total assets	Proxy for bank solvency (De Haas and Van Lelyveld, 2010)	Bankscope
IPO relevance (%)	Ratio between the value of the IPO business over the total amount of all deals made (equity, loan, bond and M&A)	Proxy for bank specialization in IPO business	Thomson One Banker
Controls			
Proceeds (€ million 2010)	Total proceeds not including the exercise of the overallotment option, adjusted for inflation (*source*: Eurostat)	Proxy for established firms (Carter et al., 1998)	Prospectuses and data from Euripo (www.euripo.eu)
Mkt Cap (€ million 2010)	Market capitalization at offer prices, adjusted for inflation (*source*: Eurostat)	Proxy for IPO demand or IPO firm quality (Krishnan et al., 2011)	Prospectuses and data from Euripo (www.euripo.eu)

Table 12.3 (continued)

Variable	Definition	Background	Data source
Controls			
Secondary (%)	Percentage of the total issue offered by current shareholders	Proxy for pre-offer demand (Carter et al., 1998)	Prospectuses and data from Euripo (www.euripo.eu)
Age (years)	Years since the incorporation to IPO	Proxy for IPO risk (Ritter, 1984)	Prospectuses, website
VC backed	Dummy variable set to one whether the firm is a venture backed issuer	Proxy for venture capital certification (Megginson and Weiss, 1991)	Prospectuses and data from Euripo (www.euripo.eu)

Notes:
For each IPO, we measure the average underwriter characteristic as the simple (unweighted) average across all its co-lead underwriters.
IPO relevance is yearly based.
All control variables were measured at the time of the IPO, as declared in the IPO prospectuses.
As second source for underwriter missing data, we use Thomson One Banker and Fame for UK banks.
In the regressions, No. subsidiaries, age (years +1), asset, proceeds are expressed as natural logarithms.
Jay Ritter's website is at http://bear.warrington.ufl.edu/ritter/ipodata.htm.

companies listed in Paris present, on average, similar values of market capitalization and of capital raised at IPO as companies listing on the AIM. While the average market capitalization is €58.9 million in London and €90.3 million in Paris, market capitalization reaches €283.2 million in Frankfurt and €383.4 million in Milan. In terms of IPO proceeds, AIM firms raise on average €24.9 million, almost the same amount as Paris firms (€21.4 million). Instead, Frankfurt and Milan firms raise significantly a larger amount of capital, more than €80 million. The average age of IPOs joining the AIM, measured as the number of years since incorporation to the listing, is around six years, while it is around 12 years on the second markets as a group and it ranges from 11 years (in Frankfurt) to 14 years (in Milan) on second markets. Secondary shares, measured as the percentage of the total issue offered by current shareholders, is on average 3.2 per cent on the AIM, while it ranges from 5.6 per cent (in Milan) to 9.6 per cent (in Paris) on second markets. Alternative Investment Market firms are statistically and significantly younger than companies listed on second markets and present lower values of secondary shares. Lastly, AIM firms are often venture-backed companies (62 per cent on average) in comparison to firms on other second markets (41 per cent on average).

6 EMPIRICAL RESULTS

6.1 Univariate Analysis of Underwriter Sample

In Table 12.4, we conduct a univariate examination of the characteristics of underwriters across stock markets. This analysis considers the possibility of heterogeneity in under-

Table 12.4 Statistics for Nomads versus underwriters in continental European second markets

	Overall	AIM	\multicolumn{4}{c}{Second-tier regulated markets}
	Mean	London	Paris	Frankfurt	Milan	Overall
Domestic (%)	90.10	94.12	86.67***	74.46***	97.26	81.81***
US bank (%)	3.24	2.00	4.85***	5.91***	9.59***	5.81***
Carter–Manaster	22.25	10.45	43.03***	47.31***	58.90***	46.58***
Commercial bank (%)	32.70	9.76	76.06***	84.68***	73.97***	80.00***
Co-lead	1.06	1.02	1.09***	1.09***	1.49***	1.13***
No. subsidiaries	341	127	1221***	833***	715***	893***
Age (years)	36	22	69***	68***	58***	67***
Asset ($ billions)	183	41	738***	504***	326***	536***
Equity ($ billions)	8.07	2.22	28.79***	19.64***	21.98***	22.04***
Equity/asset (%)	29.11	38.60	3.59***	6.80***	13.02***	6.79***
IPO relevance (%)	14.15	18.00	9.48***	5.05***	10.16***	7.07
Underwriter (no.)	198	127	43	40	30	90

Notes:
This table reports summary statistics of underwriters taking companies public on the Alternative Investment Market (AIM) in London and on second-tier regulated markets in Paris, Frankfurt and Milan.
The sample contains 198 underwriters who are lead or co-lead of at least one of the 2373 IPOs listed on second-tier regulated markets in Paris (Second Marché, Nouveau Marché), Frankfurt (Geregelter Markt, Neuer Markt) or Milan (Mercato Ristretto/Expandi, Nuovo Mercato/Mtax) during the period 1995–2010. Mean values of the underwriter characteristics are reported.
We follow Migliorati and Vismara [2012] for the data collection on underwriter characteristics.
The tests compare the characteristics of the underwriters taking public companies on the AIM versus continental European second markets (second markets include second-tier regulated markets in Paris, Frankfurt and Milan) overall and at national exchange-level.
Significant levels are based on *t*-statistics (mean), HSD-test (mean) or a *z*-test of equal proportions for the difference in means as required.
Tukey's HSD ('honestly significant difference' or 'HSD') is the approach specifically meant for comparing group means. It is based on the distribution of *q*, the studentized range, and the best for all-possible pairwise comparisons when sample sizes are unequal or confidence intervals are needed.
Statistical significance levels are at 1% (***), 5% (**), or 10% (*).

writer features across the AIM and Europe's second markets. We tests differences in characteristics of the underwriters taking companies public on the AIM versus second-tier regulated markets in Paris, Germany and Milan. We employ *t*-statistics (mean), Tuckey's test (mean) or a *z*-test of equal proportions for the difference in means as required.

This analysis considers the following variables as proxies for underwriter features. Domestic is a dummy variable set equal to one when the country of the investment bank is equal to the country of the stock exchange where the IPO (brought to market by such underwriter) is listed as a proxy for the home-bias effect (Abrahamson et al., 2011). US bank is a dummy variable set equal to one when the underwriter is a US bank (Torstila, 2001). Carter–Manaster is a dummy variable set equal to one when the underwriter is associated at least once to Carter–Manaster rank as a proxy for the US prestige of a bank (Torstila, 2001). Commercial bank is a dummy variable set equal to one when the underwriter is a commercial bank as a proxy for bank typology. The combination of traditional banking activities and underwriting activities may affect the degree of competitiveness in the investment banking industry (Kim et al., 2008). Moreover, commercial banks offering lending and underwriting services together may be less specialized but benefit from economy of scope and better diversify the risk than investment houses (Drucker and Puri, 2005). Co-lead is the average number of underwriters acting as co-leads for each issue. No. subsidiaries is the number of recorded subsidiaries by each underwriter as a proxy for its distribution power and size (Hayes, 1971). Age is measured as years between the listing date of a specific IPO and the incorporation date of the underwriter as proxy for underwriter quality (Espenlaub et al., 2012). Asset is the average book value of total assets over the sample period adjusted for inflation (expressed in $ billions 2010) as a proxy for bank size (De Haas and Van Lelyveld, 2010). Equity is the average book value of equity over the sample period adjusted for inflation (expressed in $ billions 2010). Equity/asset is the ratio between book value of equity and total assets, as a proxy for bank solvency (De Haas and Van Lelyveld, 2010). IPO relevance is the ratio between the value of the IPO business over the total amount of all deals made (equity, loan, bond and M&A) as a proxy for the degree of specialization of a bank in the IPO business.

Overall, underwriters taking companies public on the AIM (Nomads) reveal statistically significant differences from underwriters of IPOs on the second-tier regulated markets. Broadly speaking, across all stock markets we focus on, the home bias prevails and there are few US banks acting as co-leads. On average, the proportion of domestic underwriters is more than 85 per cent across all markets, while the proportion of US banks is less than 6 per cent, with a peak of 9.6 per cent in the Milan stock exchange. A related characteristic is the underwriter quality proxied by Carter–Manaster rank. Meoli et al. (2012) suggest that this classification of underwriters leads to overweight US banks. As such, we find that the proportion of IPOs underwritten by banks included in the Carter–Manaster ranking is lower for companies going public on the AIM. In terms of type and size of banks, Nomads are statistically significant smaller and younger than underwriters on second markets. On average, the number of subsidiaries and the age of Nomads are 127 and 22, respectively, in London, while they are around 90 and 67 for underwriters on the second markets as a group. In terms of bank size, Nomads have, on average, book values of total assets around $41 billion, while this value is on average $536 billion for underwriters on second markets and ranges from $326 (in Milan) to $738 billion (in Paris) on second markets. Lastly, Nomads are more focused on IPO business. The average value of IPO relevance is around 18 per cent for Nomads, while it is 7 per cent on the second markets as a group and it ranges from 5 per cent (in Frankfurt) to 10 per cent (in Milan) on second markets.

Overall, the findings reported in Table 12.4 are indicative of statistically significant differences between Nomads and underwriters on second-tier regulated markets in Paris, Frankfurt and Milan. Nomads are specialized financial boutiques, smaller, younger and mainly dedicated to the IPO business. On the other hand, underwriters of IPOs on second-tier regulated markets tend to be commercial banks with larger balance sheets and less specialization in the IPO activity.

6.2 Multivariate Analysis

In Table 12.5, we estimate regressions that examine the effects of Nomad's or underwriter's characteristics on IPO underpricing. The dependent variable is the underpricing defined as the percentage difference between the first-day closing price and the offer price. We include a number of controls variables, since comparing the characteristics across asset classes with different size and levels of risk may drive the heterogeneity among investment banks. A detailed description of all variables used in this study is reported in Table 12.3. Most of the control variables have the expected influence on underpricing. The results indicate that underpricing is rising in the proportion of the secondary shares and during 'hot periods' (that is, during the Internet bubble). It is decreasing with the issuer size (that is, total proceeds) and the firm risk (that is, issuer age).

As main explanatory variables we include our proxy for US bank and commercial bank, together with dummy variables built using decile of underwriter characteristics. Specifically, we include dummy variables set equal to one when the underwriter characteristic (that is, number of subsidiaries, age, assets and IPO relevance) is in the top decile of its distribution. Of primary interest is that Nomad's characteristics proxied asset and IPO relevance are significantly associated with underpricing, while none of the underwriter characteristics are significantly associated with IPO underpricing on second-tier regulated markets. Examining the coefficient estimate from specification (5) for the AIM case, we find that a one standard deviation decrease in the IPO relevance corresponds to around 3 per cent decrease in the IPO underpricing that has an average equals to 0.2.

In Table 12.6, we estimate poisson regressions with the average IPO activity of underwriters over the period 1995–2010. The dependent variable is the number of IPOs underwritten by each Nomad (on the AIM) or by each underwriter (on the second-tier regulated markets in Paris, Frankfurt or Milan). As independent variables, we include the following measures of underwriter characteristics: US bank and Commercial bank dummy variables and our proxies for bank – Age, Assets and IPO relevance. We include also a set of control variables for firm – and issuer – characteristics.

Looking at the independent variables, two results are worth noting. As to a firm, taking public younger issuers increases the number of IPO mandates for Nomads on AIM, while taking public smaller issuers (that is, total proceeds) increase the IPO activity for underwriters in Paris. These results confirm previous evidence (Table 12.2) that companies listed in Paris or on the AIM raise low amount of capital compared to companies in Frankfurt or Milan. As to an underwriter, we find that the propensity to take companies public increases significantly for smaller Nomads who are highly specialized in the IPO business. By contrast, in Paris, Frankfurt and Milan, underwriters increase significantly their number of IPO mandates being established banks. In the column labelled 'Values', incidence rate ratio are reported by exponentiating the poisson coefficients of the regressions. Looking at the economic relevance, our proxy for specialization in the IPO business is the most significant. For instance, the relative incidence rate of the Nomad IPO activity for a one-unit increase in his IPO relevance is 2.62, on the AIM.

While there is some evidence from the underpricing analysis that Nomads significantly differentiate themselves, Nomads experience higher number of IPO mandates having specific features that differ in comparison to those of underwriters on second-tier markets.

Table 12.5 Nomad versus underwriter characteristics and firm underpricing

Panel A: London

	(1)	(2)	(3)	(4)	(5)
Nomad characteristics					
US bank	0.19	0.11	0.20	0.18	0.12
Commercial bank	−0.01	−0.03	0.01	−0.01	−0.01
Top decile Ln (*No. of subsidiaries*)	0.01				0.06
Top decile Ln (1+*Age*)		0.11*			0.07
Top decile Ln (*Assets*)			−0.06*		−0.11*
Top decile IPO relevance				−0.06**	−0.06**
Control variables					
Ln(*Proceeds*)	−0.08***	−0.09***	−0.08***	−0.08***	−0.08***
Secondary	0.19***	0.18**	0.18**	0.18**	0.17*
Ln (1+*Age*)	−0.04***	−0.04***	−0.04***	−0.04***	−0.04***
VC backed	0.01	0.01	0.01	0.01	0.01
Internet bubble	0.3	0.31***	0.31***	0.3***	0.31***
Industry dummies	Yes	Yes	Yes	Yes	Yes
Constant	1.52***	1.54***	1.5***	1.52***	1.53***
No. of observations	1598	1598	1598	1598	1598
Adjusted R^2 (%)	9.5	9.7	9.6	9.6	9.9

Panel B: Second-tier regulated markets

	(1)	(2)	(3)	(4)	(5)
Underwriter characteristics					
US bank	0.13	0.14	0.13	0.13	0.13
Commercial bank	−0.04	−0.05	−0.03	−0.04	−0.06
Top decile Ln (*No. of subsidiaries*)	−0.03				0.02
Top decile Ln (1+*Age*)		−0.10			−0.10
Top decile Ln (*Assets*)			−0.04		−0.07
Top decile IPO relevance				−0.01	−0.08
Control variables					
Ln(*Proceeds*)	0.01	0.01	0.01	0.01	0.01
Secondary	0.29	0.28	0.29	0.30	0.31
Ln (1+*Age*)	−0.05	−0.05	−0.05	−0.05	−0.05
VC backed	−0.12**	−0.13**	−0.12**	−0.12**	−0.13**
Internet bubble	0.04	0.03	0.04	0.04	0.03
Industry dummies	Yes	Yes	Yes	Yes	Yes
Country dummies	Yes	Yes	Yes	Yes	Yes
Constant	0.13	0.11	0.13	0.15	0.12
No. of observations	775	775	775	775	775
Adjusted R^2 (%)	0.7	1.0	0.7	0.7	0.6

Notes:
This table reports the results from the regressions that investigate whether underwriter's characteristics affect the underpricing on the AIM (panel A) or on second-tier regulated markets (panel B).
The dependent variable is the underpricing defined as the percentage difference between first-day closing price and the offer price.
Underwriter characteristics (defined in Table 12.3) are set to one when the corresponding underwriter variable is in the top decile of its distribution.
Test for significance are based on robust standard errors. Industry (based on 1-digit Industry Classification Benchmark code) and country dummies are not reported.
Statistical significance levels are at 1% (***), 5% (**), or 10% (*).

Table 12.6 Number of IPOs annually underwritten and underwriter characteristics

	London		Paris		Frankfurt		Milan	
	Coeff	Values	Coeff	Values	Coeff	Values	Coeff	Values
Underwriter characteristics								
US bank	−0.87***	0.42	−0.79***	0.45	−0.90***	0.40	−1.11***	0.33
Commercial bank	−0.35***	0.70	0.28***	1.33	1.20***	3.31	0.22	1.25
Ln (1+*Age*)	0.01	1.00	0.04*	1.04	−0.08***	0.92	−0.04	0.96
Ln (*Assets*)	−0.11**	0.90	0.17***	1.19	−0.01	1.00	0.21**	1.23
IPO *relevance*	0.96**	2.62	0.84*	2.32	−5.23***	0.01	−2.64**	0.07
Control variables								
Ln(*Proceeds*)	0.01	1.01	−0.13***	0.88	0.01	1.00	0.10	1.11
Secondary	0.03	1.04	−0.68*	0.51	−0.50	0.61	−0.68	0.51
Ln (1+*Age*)	−0.07***	0.93	0.01	1.01	0.01	1.01	0.12	1.13
VC backed	−0.03	0.97	0.07	1.07	0.07	1.07	−0.08	0.92
Internet bubble	0.19***	1.21	−0.11	0.90	1.19***	3.30	0.87***	2.40
Constant	1.80***		2.32***		0.63		−2.12	
No. of observations	1598		330		372		73	
Pseudo R^2 (%)	5.5		7.7		3.8		3.5	
Mean value of dependent variable	7.13		4.99		10.43		3.86	

Notes:
This table reports the results of the regressions that investigate whether Nomad characteristics affect differently the propensity to take companies public compared to underwriter characteristics on continental European second markets.
The dependent variable is the average number of IPOs underwritten by each underwriter on a yearly basis, at stock-exchange level.
In the columns labelled 'Values', incidence rate ratio are reported by exponentiating the poisson coefficients of the regressions. These values measure the relative incidence rate of the dependent variable for a one-unit change in the explanatory variable.

7 CONCLUSION

This chapter compares the role of investment banks taking companies public on the AIM unique market model relative to those on second-tier regulated markets in continental Europe over the period 1995–2010. The AIM regulatory structure entails the outsourcing of substantial part of regulations on the nominated advisors (that is, Nomads) who are not just underwriters but act as 'regulators'. They are indeed demanded to advice and guide AIM companies at all time.

Relative to underwriters on the second-tier regulated markets in Paris (Second Marché and Nouveau Marché), in Frankfurt (Geregelter Markt and Neuer Markt), and in Milan (Mercato Ristretto/Expandi and Nuovo Mercato/Mtax), Nomads on the AIM are significantly younger and smaller – lower number of subsidiaries, total assets and equity. Nomads are more focused in the IPO business, with a significantly higher proportion of IPO-revenues in total revenues related to IPOs, equity, bond and M&A deals. Furthermore, we examine the association between underwriter characteristics and firm performance and investment bank performance to study underwriter characteristics in a multivariate context. We find that Nomads that are smaller and with higher expertise in IPOs (that is, higher IPO relevance) reduce underpricing. Furthermore, we find that the propensity to take companies public increases significantly for smaller Nomads who are highly specialized in the IPO business. By contrary, in Paris, Frankfurt and Milan, underwriters increase significantly their number of IPO mandates being established banks. For the same issuer and offering, we provide evidences that Nomads acting to some extent as 'regulators' predict a modest significant relation between their characteristics and IPO-underpricing, while a strong relation is found with their IPO activity, accounting for other factors that can explain heterogeneity of underwriters.

Our findings document that Nomads are smaller specialized financial boutiques mainly dedicated to the IPO business. On the other side, underwriters of IPOs on second-tier regulated markets tend to be commercial banks with larger balance sheet and less specialization in the IPO activity. Furthermore, underwriter size, type and IPO relevance act in an opposite direction on underwriter performance (that is, average number of IPOs underwritten on a yearly basis) in case of Nomads relative to underwriters on second-tier regulated markets.

Our results are of relevance for regulators of new markets modelled as the AIM regulatory structure. The recent failure of Tokyo AIM highlights the need of a system of Nomads acting as costly signals to certify and reduce uncertainty and information asymmetries between investors, issuers and underwriters. Stock markets with such minimum listing requirements and outsourced regulation need a Nomad system prone to take on the responsibility of a continuous monitoring of risky new listings. These results are of particular interest given the recent trend towards the launch of new markets for small companies (that is, the Korea New Exchange (KONEX) announced in April 2012, or the Entrepreneurs' Exchange announced in August 2012 by NYSE Euronext), following the 2007/08 financial crisis.

REFERENCES

Abrahamson, M., T. Jenkinson and J. Howard (2011), 'Why don't U.S. issuers demand European fees for IPOs?', *Journal of Finance*, **66** (6), 2055–82.
Carter, R.B. and S. Manaster (1990), 'Initial public offerings and underwriter reputation', *Journal of Finance*, **45** (4), 1045–67.
Carter, R.B., F.H. Dark and A.K. Singh (1998), 'Underwriter reputation, initial returns, and the long-run performance of IPO stocks', *Journal of Finance*, **53** (1), 285–311.
De Haas, R. and I. van Lelyveld (2010), 'Internal capital markets and lending by multinational bank subsidiaries', *Journal of Financial Intermediation*, **19** (1), 1–25.
Doidge, C., G.A. Karolyi and R.M. Stulz (2009), 'Has New York become less competitive than London in global markets? Evaluating foreign listing choices over time', *Journal of Financial Economics*, **91** (3), 253–77.
Drucker, S. and M. Puri (2005), 'On the benefits of concurrent lending and underwriting', *Journal of Finance*, **60** (6), 2763–99.
Espenlaub, S., A. Khurshed and A. Mohamed (2012), 'IPO survival in a reputational market', *Journal of Business Finance & Accounting*, **39** (3), 427–63.
Fernando, C.S., V.A. Gatchev and P.A. Spindt (2005), 'Wanna dance? How firms and underwriters choose each other', *Journal of Finance*, **60** (5), 2437–69.
Gao, X., J.R. Ritter and Z. Zhu (2012), 'Where have all the IPOs gone?', working paper, University of Florida.
Gerakos, J., M. Lang and M. Maffett (2011), 'Listing choices and self-regulation: the experience of the AIM', unpublished working paper, University of Chicago Booth School of Business.

Gregory, A., C. Guermat, F. Al-Shawawreh (2010), 'UK IPOs: long run returns, behavioural timing and pseudo timing', *Journal of Business Finance and Accounting*, **37** (5), 612–47.
Hayes, S.L. (1971), 'Investment banking: power structure in flux', *Harvard Business Review*, **49** (March/April), 136–52.
Kim, D., D. Palia and A. Saunders (2008), 'The impact of commercial banks on underwriting spreads: evidence from three past decades', *Journal of Finance and Quantitative Analysis*, **43** (4), 975–1000.
Krishnan, C.N.V., V.I. Ivanov and R.W. Masulis (2011), 'Venture capital reputation, post-IPO performance, and corporate governance', *Journal of Financial and Quantitative Analysis*, **46** (5), 1295–333.
Leuz, C. and P. Wysocki (2008), 'Economic consequences of financial reporting and disclosure regulation: a review and suggestions for future research', working paper, University of Chicago and MIT Sloan School of Management.
Megginson, W.L. and K.A. Weiss (1991), 'Venture capitalist certification in initial public offerings', *Journal of Finance*, **46** (3), 879–903.
Meoli, M., K. Migliorati, S. Paleari and S. Vismara (2012), 'The cost of going public: a European perspective', *International Journal of Economics and Management Engineering*, **2** (2), 1–10.
Piotroski, J. and S. Srinivasan (2008), 'Regulation and bonding: the Sarbanes–Oxley Act and the flow of international listings', *Journal of Accounting Research*, **46** (2), 383–425.
Ritter, J.R. (1984), 'The "hot issue" market of 1980', *Journal of Business*, **57** (2), 215–41.
Torstila, S. (2001), 'What determines IPO gross spreads in Europe?', *European Financial Management*, **7** (4), 523–41.
Vismara, S., S. Paleari and J.R. Ritter (2012), 'Europe's second markets for small companies', *European Financial Management*, **18** (3), 352–88.

PART IV

TRADING IN THE AFTERMARKET

13 Orphan versus non-orphan IPOs: the difference analyst coverage makes
Romain Boissin

1 INTRODUCTION

Numerous articles in academic journals or in the press have highlighted the importance of financial analysts' coverage of firms that are going public. Newly public firms rely on their underwriters throughout the IPO process, especially during the marketing phase. The underwriters' services include determining the offering price and the distribution of shares, but what is of particular importance for the issuer is receiving coverage through their financial analysts. During the initial public offering (IPO), investors are limited to information contained in the prospectus. As a result, the flow of information is restricted and sparse. Financial analysts can reduce these asymmetries. Indeed, coverage can transcend borders and financial markets and put the firm in the spotlight. Coverage is seen to add value by the firm because it can generate publicity, attract new consumers (Cliff and Denis, 2004), boost the share price (Chen and Ritter, 2000; Aggarwal et al., 2002), attract new investors, and reduce the cost of capital. However, coverage is not uniformly distributed and is mainly concentrated on large firms (as measured by their market capitalization). In the mid-2000s, 50 per cent of IPO firms were covered by a financial analyst and 35 per cent had no coverage.[1] Newly public firms often suffer from lack of analyst coverage even though it is widely accepted that, because coverage adds value, the allocation of resources to attract such coverage is a worthy investment.

This chapter addresses the resources at the disposal of IPO firms to attract financial analysts. We examine the long-run performance of orphan and non-orphan IPOs to explain what value has to be attributed to analyst coverage. We are interested in the added value of analyst coverage, making relevant distinctions between orphan IPO firms (those without analyst coverage within five years of their issuance) and non-orphan IPO firms (those with analyst coverage within five years of their issuance). This chapter addresses the question of the importance of analyst coverage for the long-run returns of IPO firms over the period from 1991 to 2010.

Over the years, academic research has noted the importance of analyst coverage. Krigman et al. (2001) suggested that the most important motivation for firms to switch underwriters between their IPO and a seasoned equity offering (SEO) is to obtain additional and influential analyst coverage. Loughran and Ritter (2004) and Cliff and Denis (2004) argued that the underpricing of newly public firms is positively related to analyst coverage. According to Loughran and Ritter (2004), the average underpricing of IPOs was 7 per cent in the 1980s, which doubled to 15 per cent from 1990 to 1998, before jumping to 65 per cent during the internet bubble. Part of this increase can be attributed to analyst coverage, which has grown more important over the years. Bradley et al. (2003) showed that the number of managing underwriters in a syndicate is a good indicator of the coverage enjoyed by newly listed firms at the time of their IPOs. Corwin and Schultz (2005) examined the syndicates of 1638 IPOs and found evidence that each additional co-manager results in 0.8 additional analyst recommendations within three months of the IPO. Bradley et al. (2008b), however, did not find incremental coverage to be related to improved long-run performance. Bradley et al. (2004) focused on the two-year post-issue performance (at the end of the IPO's quiet period) of IPOs that receive analyst coverage compared to those that do not. The authors found that orphans significantly underperformed compared to non-orphans during the period from 1996 to 1998.

Unlike Bradley et al. (2004), we analyse long-run performance from one to five years after the IPO. We measure the influence of analyst coverage on the long-run performance of IPO firms over a five-year horizon. We are then able to observe how long-run performance adjusts to analyst coverage. Our observation period is large and encompasses the period from 1991 to 2010. Our definition of an orphan IPO firm differs from that of Bradley et al. (2004) because the authors consider an IPO firm to be an orphan if 'there is an absence of a research report/analyst recommendation at the end of the quiet period by at least one underwriter in the managing syndicate'.

In US IPOs, during the one- to five-year horizon, we find a significant long-run abnormal performance by orphans (IPOs without analyst coverage) compared to non-orphans (IPOs with analyst coverage). For instance, by the fifth year after the IPO, buy-and-hold abnormal returns for orphans were a significant −52.95 per cent compared to −8.07 per cent for non-orphans, a difference that is statistically significant at the 1 per cent level. Further analysis reveals that this outperformance by non-orphans stems from high analyst coverage. Our results are robust after accounting for venture capital backing, underwriting syndicates, underpricing, institutional investor ownership, or operating performance variables.

The chapter is organized as follows. We first discuss the existing literature. In the third section, we describe the methodology, data and sample statistics. The fourth section presents the findings, and the last section concludes the chapter.

2 LITERATURE REVIEW

Khorana et al. (2009) examine the consequences of the loss of coverage for a firm over the period from 1983 to 2004. They find that firms that lose all analyst coverage are significantly more likely to get delisted. This study sheds light on the importance of analyst coverage for firms. To avoid such a situation, the firm may acquire the means to attract financial analysts during its IPO process. Previous studies have found that the underwriting syndicate and the presence of venture capitalists or institutional investors in the IPO, as well as underpricing, allow the firm to increase its probability of analyst coverage.

Krigman et al. (2001) reveal that changes in underwriters (between an IPO and an SEO) are made because the firm wants more reputable underwriters that will provide more coverage. The authors find that firms are more likely to make changes when analyst coverage is not to their liking. In addition, firms do not hesitate to allocate resources to improving their coverage. According to Ellis et al. (2005), almost 50 per cent of firms making an SEO change their lead underwriters. This change takes place not because of the reputation of the underwriter but for the coverage of analysts whose buy recommendation are often more favourable than those of their predecessors. Corwin and Schultz (2005) examine the underwriting syndicates of 1638 IPOs between 1997 and 2002 in the United States. They emphasize the importance of co-managers, stating that the addition of a co-manager to the syndicate increases analyst coverage within the three months after the IPO. Loughran and Ritter (2004) find that co-managers are included in syndicates exclusively to provide additional coverage.

The presence of venture capitalists in the IPO may encourage analysts to follow the firm. Several studies note a positive relationship between the presence of venture capitalists in the IPO and analyst coverage. Jain and Kini (2000) find that venture capitalists influence institutional investors, investment bankers and their analysts to ensure the success of the IPO process. This influence is the result of many interactions, especially with underwriters. Gompers and Lerner (1997) estimate that approximately 25 per cent of venture capitalists have an affiliation with underwriters. A venture capitalist involved in an IPO can advise its underwriter and vice versa.[2] These types of interactions also arise between venture capitalists and financial analysts. Therefore, venture capitalists can attract underwriters and thus facilitate analyst coverage. According to Chemmanur and Loutskina (2006), the presence of venture capitalists in an IPO leads 0.22 more analysts to follow the firm.

Rajan and Servaes (1997) and Aggarwal et al. (2002) argue that underpricing attracts an analyst following. Cliff and Denis (2004) find that underpricing is positively related to analyst coverage. The authors empirically examine the assumption that firms attract analyst coverage through underpricing. They study 1050 firms conducting an IPO and an SEO between 1993 and 2000 and find a strong correlation between underpricing and the frequency and quality of post-IPO analyst coverage. A total of 94 per cent of highly underpriced firms receive initial analyst coverage compared to 84 per cent of minimally underpriced firms. The authors conclude that underpricing compensates, in part, for expected analyst coverage. James and Karceski (2006) note that IPO firms that have not benefited from analyst coverage are significantly less underpriced (average of 27 per cent) compared with those covered by financial analysts (average of 72 per cent) over the period from 1999–2000. Das et al. (2006) show that IPOs with low (high) analyst coverage exhibit underpricing close to 13 per cent (47 per cent) over the period from 1986 to 2000. In contrast, Bradley et al. (2008a) do not establish any link between underpricing and analyst coverage following 683 IPOs from 1999 to 2000.

Ownership structure also affects analyst coverage. Bhushan (1989) and O'Brien and Bhushan (1990) find that the likelihood of analyst coverage is associated with the interests of institutional investors in the firm. The authors conclude that there is a positive relationship between institutional investor ownership and analyst coverage. Lang et al. (2004) and Boubaker and Labégorre (2008) indicate that analysts are reluctant to cover a firm managed by controlling family members. This is explained, in part, by the reliance of these firms on private communication channels rather than public disclosure, producing a poor informational environment.

3 METHODOLOGY, DATA AND SAMPLE STATISTICS

3.1 Methodology

The results of long-run performance studies are sensitive to methodological choices. We therefore present our results using two frequently used and recommended methodologies (Barber and Lyon, 1997; Brav and Gompers, 1997).

First, we use the calendar-time approach of Fama and French (1996). Their three-factor model assumes that the expected return on a portfolio in excess of the risk-free rate $[(ER_i) - R_f]$ is explained by the sensitivity of its return to three factors: (1) the excess return on a broad market portfolio $(R_M - R_f)$; (2) the difference between the return on a portfolio of small stocks and the return on a portfolio of big stocks (*SMB*, small minus big); and (3) the difference between the return on a portfolio of high-book-to-market stocks and the return on a portfolio of low-book-to-market stocks (*HML*, high minus low). Specifically, the expected excess return on portfolio i is,

$$E(R_i) - R_f = \alpha_i + \beta_i [E(R_M) - R_f] + s_i E(SMB) + h_i E(HML) + \varepsilon_i,$$

where $E(R_i)$ is the monthly return on the IPO portfolio, R_f is the one-month Treasury bill rate, $E(R_M)$ is the monthly return on an equally weighted market portfolio of the New York Stock Exchange (NYSE), the American Stock Exchange (AMEX) and the National Association of Securities Dealers Automated Quotations (NASDAQ) stocks, $E(SMB)$ is the difference between the returns on portfolios of small and big stocks (below or above the median), and $E(HML)$ is the difference between the returns on portfolios of high and low book-to-market stocks (above and below the 0.7 and 0.3 fractiles of book-to-market ratios).

Second, we use an event-time approach, as in the study of Brav and Gompers (1997). Fama and French (1992, 1993) have shown that the size and book-to-market portfolios are important determinants of the cross section of stock returns. We compare the performance of IPOs with that of size and book-to-market portfolios. Starting in January 1991, we use all NYSE, AMEX and NASDAQ stocks to create size quartile breakpoints with an equal number of firms in each size quartile. Size is measured by the number of shares outstanding multiplied by the stock price at the end of the preceding month. The monthly book-to-market data for each firm are extracted from the Datastream database. Within each size quartile, we create four book-to-market portfolios with an equal number of firms in each book-to-market quartile, resulting in 16 size and book-to-market portfolios. Equally weighted returns are calculated for each portfolio. To avoid comparing IPO firms with themselves, we eliminate IPO firms from the various portfolios for five years after their equity issues. Each issue is matched with its corresponding benchmark portfolio.

The long-run performance is calculated using the buy-and-hold abnormal return (BHAR) methodology. The difference between a return on a buy-and-hold investment in the sample firm and the return on a buy-and-hold investment in a portfolio with an appropriate expected return (*BHAR*) is

$$BHAR_{it} = \prod_{t=1}^{\tau} [1 + R_{it}] - \prod_{t=1}^{\tau} [1 + E(R_{it})]$$

where R_{it} is defined as the month t simple return of a sample firm and $E(R_{it})$ is the month t expected return of the sample firm (that is, the return of firm i's benchmark over the same period).

Long-run buy-and-hold abnormal returns are positively skewed and this positive skewness leads to negatively biased t-statistics. Lyon et al. (1999) recommend the use of a bootstrapped skewness-adjusted t-statistic to eliminate this skewness bias.

3.2 Data and Sample Statistics

The data come from different sources. We first identify firms that went public from 1991 to 2010 in the Thomson Financial Securities Data Company (SDC) Common Stock Initial Public Offerings database. Consistent with prior studies, we eliminate IPOs that are classified as American depository receipts (ADRs), real estate investment trusts (REITs) and closed-end funds, along with offerings that have a file range midpoint of less than €8 and financial services IPO firms (SIC code 6000–6999). Our sample contains 1265 IPOs. Analyst data are collected from the First Call database. Long-run performance is calculated using the Datastream monthly stock price database.

Table 13.1 presents descriptive statistics for our sample. Panel A shows the distribution of the IPO sample over the three sub-periods. Panel B provides the market capitalization of the IPOs in our sample at the end of the first month following the offering. Our sample offerings are substantially large in terms of market capitalization. We find that 63 per cent of our sample's IPOs raise $200 million or more and 25 per cent of the offerings have a capitalization ranging from $50 million to $200 million. Panel C documents that the industry composition of our sample is well-distributed, with the greatest concentration, 17 per cent, being in the business services industry.

Table 13.2 shows descriptive statistics for orphan and non-orphan IPOs. There are 253 IPOs classified as orphans and 1012 classified as non-orphans. The long-term debt of non-orphans is higher than that of orphan IPOs (significant at the 1 per cent level using w and t tests). The average orphan raises $309.61 million in its IPO, compared to $1067.46 million for the average non-orphan. This difference is statistically significant at the 1 per cent level. Like prior research, analyst coverage increases according to firm size. We find no significant differences in venture capital backing between orphan and non-orphan IPOs over the entire period. Orphans are associated with more underwriting syndicates, with a mean of 6.86 managing underwriters, compared to 6.48 for non-orphans (the difference is statistically significant using a w test). There is a weak relationship between analyst coverage and underpricing. For instance, orphans have initial returns of 13.85 per cent compared to 15.53 per cent for non-orphans. Non-orphans are more underpriced than orphans and the difference is statistically significant at the 10 per cent level using a w test. Non-orphans are associated with more institutional investor ownership than orphans. For instance, a mean of 73.89 per cent of the shares of IPOs with analyst coverage are held by institutional investors, compared to 31.74 per cent for orphan IPO firms. The difference is statistically significant at the 1 per cent level and is confirmed by both t and w tests.

Table 13.1   Description of the IPO sample

Panel A: Number of sample IPO firms by sub-period

1991/1998	301
1999/2000	122
2001/2010	842

Panel B: Sample IPO firms classified by market capitalization (price * shares) at the end of the first month following the offering

Market capitalization, in millions USD	Per cent of sample	Number of IPOs
Less than $50	11.78	149
$50–$99.9	9.09	115
$100–$199.99	15.89	201
$200–$399.99	21.50	272
$400–$999.99	23.16	293
Greater than $1000	18.58	235
All IPO firms	100.00	1265

Panel C: Industry distribution of sample IPO firms, by two-digit SIC code

	SIC code	Per cent of sample	Number of IPOs
Business services	(73)	17.00	215
Chemicals and allied products	(28)	11.78	149
Electronic equipment	(36)	10.83	137
Instruments	(38)	7.19	91
Oil and gas	(13)	4.74	60
Industrial equipment	(35)	3.87	49
Communications	(48)	2.92	37
Electric services	(49)	2.77	35
Management and related services	(87)	2.53	32
Water transportation	(44)	2.45	31
Miscellaneous retail	(59)	2.06	26
Other industries	(various)	31.86	403
All IPO firms		100.00	1265

4   RESULTS

Table 13.3 shows that IPO firms in the US have statistically significant long-run returns over the entire period. The mean returns of IPOs range from 4.22 per cent over the first year after their offerings to −16.40 per cent over the five-year horizon. Over the period from 1991 to 1998, similar to Ritter and Welch (2002), we find that IPOs have, on average, no abnormal returns regardless of the considered horizon. We also calculate long-run performance using the Fama–French three-factor model. The parameter of interest in this regression is the intercept, alpha. A negative intercept indicates that after controlling for market, size, and book-to-market factors in returns, a sample firm performed worse than expected. Intercepts (alpha) are positive regardless of the considered

Table 13.2   Descriptive statistics of orphan and non-orphan IPOs from 1991 to 2010

	Orphan	Non-orphan	t	w
IPO	253	1012		
AGE	17	23	1.2	0.2
LONG-TERM DEBT	129.63	431.17	2.6***	3.9***
SIZE	309.61	1067.46	2.7***	9.6***
VC AFFILIATION	5.95	38.51	−1.1	−1.1
UNDERWRITING SYNDICATE	6.86	6.48	−0.5	1.9**
UNDERPRICING	13.85	15.53	0.8	1.8*
INSTITUTIONAL INVESTORS	31.74	73.89	15.6***	11.8***

Notes:
This table provides characteristics of orphans and non-orphans. An orphan (non-orphan) is an IPO without analyst coverage (with analyst coverage).
IPO is the number of issuing firms.
AGE is the age in years of the issuing firm at the time of the offer.
LONG-TERM DEBT represents all interest-bearing financial obligations in millions, excluding amounts due within one year, at the offering date.
SIZE is the market capitalization in millions at the offering date.
VC AFFILIATION is the percentage of firms that are affiliated with venture capitalists.
UNDERWRITING SYNDICATE is the number of managing underwriters (lead plus co-managers).
UNDERPRICING is the percentage difference between the close on the first day of trading and the offer price.
INSTITUTIONAL INVESTORS is the percentage of shares held by institutional investors who hold 5% or more of the outstanding shares at the time of the offering.
Student's parametric *t*-tests and Wilcoxon (*w*) non-parametric tests are presented to estimate whether the difference between sample distributions is statistically significant.
*, ** and *** indicate significant differences at the 10%, 5% and 1% levels, respectively.

Table 13.3   Long-run performance of IPO firms

	1991–98		1999–2000		2001–10		1991–2010	
	Mean	*t*-stat	Mean	*t*-stat	Mean	*t*-stat	Mean	*t*-stat
BHAR (size & book-to-market adjusted)								
60-month returns	−12.94	−1.5	−56.13	−3.3***	−6.38	−1.4	−16.40	−3.5***
36-month returns	1.41	0.2	−36.09	−3***	−1.43	−0.5	−4.57	−1.5
12-month returns	5.85	1.5	−31.07	−3.3***	8.76	3.8***	4.22	2.2**
Fama–French Alpha	0.98	3***	1.47	1.7*	0.46	1.3	0.78	3.3***

Notes:
The long-run BHARs over the 12-, 36-, and 60-month returns are reported.
Fama–French is the alpha of running the Fama–French (1993) three-factor regression model.
Table presents 1265 IPOs made between 1991 and 2010.
A bootstrapped skewness-adjusted *t*-test is used to estimate whether the BHAR or the alpha are statistically significant.
*, ** and *** indicate significant differences at the 10%, 5% and 1% levels, respectively.

Table 13.4 Long-run performance of orphan and non-orphan IPO firms from 1991 to 2010

Type of abnormal return	N	Size and book-to-market adjusted						Fama–French	
		BHAR60 (%)	t-stat	BHAR36 (%)	t-stat	BHAR12 (%)	t-stat	Alpha (%)	t-stat
Full sample: 1991 to 2010									
Orphan	253	−52.95	−5.1***	−18.09	−2.1**	5.31	1.2	0.11	0.4
Non-orphan	1012	−8.07	−1.7*	−1.17	−0.4	3.95	2**	0.91	3.9***
Difference		44.87	4.6***	16.92	2.3**	−1.35	−0.3	0.75	2.9***
1991 to 1998									
Orphan	52	−67.16	−3***	−14.57	−0.5	−11.12	−1.3	0.26	0.7
Non-orphan	249	−1.62	−0.2	4.74	0.7	9.39	2.3**	1.07	3.2***
Difference		65.54	3.7***	19.32	0.9	20.51	2.3**	0.53	1.2
1999 to 2000									
Orphan	22	−141.25	−4.1***	−72.35	−2**	−54.80	−2.1**	−0.55	−0.4
Non-orphan	100	−37.41	−2.1**	−28.11	−2.1**	−25.85	−2.6***	1.96	2.3**
Difference		103.84	3.2***	44.24	2.1**	28.95	2.4***	2.50	2.9***
2001 to 2010									
Orphan	179	−17.19	−1.5	−10.97	−1.5	17.47	3.6***	−0.01	−0.1
Non-orphan	663	−3.72	−0.8	1.22	0.4	6.40	2.6***	0.55	1.5
Difference		13.47	1.3	12.19	1.5	−11.06	−1.9**	0.56	1.8*

Notes:
Table 13.4 presents the long-run performance of orphan and non-orphan IPO firms over the period from 1991 to 2010.
Long-run performance is computed as buy-and-hold abnormal returns over 12, 36 and 60 months.
A bootstrapped skewness-adjusted *t*-test is presented to estimate whether the BHAR or the difference between sample distributions are statistically significant.
*, ** and *** indicate significant differences at the 10%, 5% and 1% levels, respectively.

period. The Fama–French model shows that investing in IPO portfolios leads to a statistically significant (at 1 per cent level) 0.78 per cent return per month over the entire period.

We now distinguish IPO firms according to the level of analyst coverage. The findings are reported in Table 13.4. We find that market participants make a relevant distinction between orphan and non-orphan IPO firms over the entire period (1991–2010). For instance, the three-year return of non-orphans is −1.17 per cent, compared to −18.09 per cent for orphan IPOs, and the difference is statistically significant at the 5 per cent level. These findings are confirmed over the five-year returns. The Fama–French model shows that investing an equal amount in non-orphan IPO portfolios provides a 0.91 per cent return per month, which is statistically significant (at the 1 per cent level), compared to orphan IPO portfolios (monthly return of 0.11 per cent). The 1990s reveal that the differences between orphan and non-orphan IPOs appear in the first year following the offering. It is worth noting that the one-year returns show the analysts' ability to predict the long-run performance before the disclosure of financial statements. At the time of the IPO, investors are limited to the material information contained in the prospectus, and informational asymmetries are particularly high. In the first year after the offering, the non-orphans exhibit positive abnormal performance, while the orphans exhibit no abnormal performance. The Internet-bubble period (1999–2000) demonstrates similar findings. The 2000s reveal the opposite result, meaning that orphan IPOs exhibit higher returns than non-orphan IPOs in the first year after their issues. The difference is statistically significant at the 5 per cent level (not confirmed by the calendar-time approach). This could be attributable to recent scandals involving financial analysts; as a consequence, analyst coverage may have become worth less to investors.

Venture capital affiliation, underwriting syndication, institutional investor ownership and underpricing have been shown to influence the long-run performance of IPO firms. Therefore, if there is a relationship between analyst coverage and long-run performance, it may be a manifestation of these variables. We investigate these potential relationships by focusing on each of them individually.

The results of venture capital (VC) affiliation are presented in Table 13.5. We partition our sample into VC-backed IPOs and non-VC-backed IPOs. We find significant differences in the long-run performances of orphan and non-orphan VC-backed IPOs. Whatever the horizon and period considered, the long-run returns of non-orphan VC-backed IPOs outperform those of their orphan counterparts. The alpha of the Fama–French model presents similar findings but the difference in returns is not statistically significant. These results hold for non-VC-backed IPOs except in the 2000s, when investors paid no attention to analyst coverage.

From Table 13.6, we can see that non-orphan IPOs with large underwriting syndicates (IPOs in which the number of managing underwriters is above the median are classified as 'large'; otherwise, they are classified as 'small') outperform orphan IPOs. The one-year returns of non-orphan IPOs with large underwriting syndicates are −1.05 per cent compared to −32.05 per cent for orphan IPOs with large underwriting syndicates over the period from 1991 to 2010. The 31.60 per cent difference is significant at the 1 per cent level. These results hold for three- and five-year returns. An exception occurs during the past decade, when there is no difference between orphan and non-orphan IPOs with large underwriting syndicates. Panel B indicates that the difference between orphan and non-orphan IPOs with small underwriting syndicates is only statistically significant over a five-year horizon. However, we find that, over the period from 2001 to 2010, orphan IPOs with small underwriting syndicates exhibit better performances than their non-orphan counterparts during the first year after the issue. The difference of −25.52 per cent is statistically significant at the 5 per cent level (not confirmed by the calendar-time approach).

Table 13.7 shows that, over the entire period, highly underpriced non-orphan IPOs (IPOs with underpricing above the median level are classified as 'high'; otherwise, they are classified as 'low') outperform their orphan counterparts over the one- and five-year horizons (the differences are statistically significant at conventional levels). The alpha of the Fama–French model identifies significant differences between orphan and non-orphan highly underpriced IPOs, with an average return of −0.08 per cent per month for orphans compared to an average of 0.82 per cent per month for non-orphans. The difference of 0.86 per cent per month is statistically significant at the 1 per cent level. We find no differences between the long-run returns of orphan and non-orphan minimally

Table 13.5 Long-run performance by venture capital affiliation

Type of abnormal return	Size and book-to-market adjusted						Fama–French	
	BHAR60 (%)	t-stat	BHAR36 (%)	t-stat	BHAR12 (%)	t-stat	Alpha (%)	t-stat
Panel A: VC-backed IPOs								
Full sample: 1991 to 2010								
Orphan	−81.36	−3.1***	−30.96	−0.7	−26.70	−1.7*	0.27	0.5
Non-orphan	−15.45	−1.7*	−5.02	−0.7	4.13	0.9	1	2.7***
Difference	65.90	2.8***	25.94	0.9	30.83	2.3***	0.70	1.3
1991 to 2000								
Orphan	−87.15	−3***	−26.80	−0.5	−29.56	−1.4	1.05	1.3
Non-orphan	−20.82	−1.8*	−13.10	−1.3	−0.04	−0.1	1.75	3.8***
Difference	66.33	2.4***	13.70	0.4	29.52	2**	0.71	1.1
2001 to 2010								
Orphan	−23.39	−0.1	−51.73	−0.6	−12.43	−0.2	−0.41	−0.5
Non-orphan	2.32	0.2	12.34	1.3	13.09	2.3**	0.19	0.3
Difference	25.71	1.1	64.07	3.1***	25.52	1.2	0.60	0.7
Panel B: Non-VC-backed IPOs								
Full sample: 1991 to 2010								
Orphan	−87.05	−4.1***	−37.07	−2.2**	−17.42	−2.5***	−0.12	−0.3
Non-orphan	−0.01	−0.1	2.88	0.4	2.57	0.8	0.56	2.5***
Difference	87.04	4.4***	39.95	2.8***	19.99	2.9***	0.66	1.5
1991 to 2000								
Orphan	−90.57	−3.7***	−35.12	−2.3***	−20.39	−2.6***	−0.38	−0.8
Non-orphan	−4.38	−0.4	2.39	0.3	−1.26	−0.3	0.81	2.5***
Difference	86.19	4.4***	37.51	2.6***	19.12	2.5***	1.17	2.4***
2001 to 2010								
Orphan	−56.08	−0.4	−44.19	−0.5	−6.52	−0.4	0.10	0.1
Non-orphan	19.32	0.8	3.93	0.4	10.67	2.4***	0.28	0.9
Difference	75.40	1.1	48.12	1.2	17.20	1.1	0.18	0.2

Notes:
Table 13.5 presents the long-run performance of orphan and non-orphan IPO firms by venture capital affiliation over the period from 1991 to 2010.
Long-run performance is computed as buy-and-hold abnormal returns over 12, 36 and 60 months.
A bootstrapped skewness-adjusted *t*-test is presented to estimate whether the BHAR or the difference between sample distributions are statistically significant.
*, ** and *** indicate significant differences at the 10%, 5% and 1% levels, respectively.

underpriced IPOs over the entire period. Hence, analyst coverage has investment value only for highly underpriced IPOs.

Once we account for ownership structure, Table 13.8 shows that non-orphan IPOs with a high level of institutional investor ownership (IPOs with institutional investor ownership above the median level are classified as 'high'; otherwise, they are classified as 'low') outperform their orphan counterparts. The event-time approach indicates that the

Table 13.6 Long-run performance by an underwriting syndicate

Type of abnormal return								
	Size and book-to-market adjusted						Fama–French	
	BHAR60 (%)	t-stat	BHAR36 (%)	t-stat	BHAR12 (%)	t-stat	Alpha (%)	t-stat
Panel A: Large syndicate								
Full sample: 1991 to 2010								
Orphan	−115.61	−5.9***	−64.11	−2.6***	−32.65	−2.8***	0.22	0.5
Non-orphan	−16.20	−1.8*	−7.60	−1.5	−1.05	−0.3	0.97	2.5***
Difference	99.41	4.9***	56.52	3.9***	31.60	3.1***	0.50	1.2
1991 to 2000								
Orphan	−123.4	−5.6***	−69.57	−3.9***	−38.94	−2.4***	0.17	0.2
Non-orphan	−36.54	−2.1**	−20.16	−2.4***	−6.85	−1.2	1.65	2.5***
Difference	96.90	4.5***	49.41	3.6***	32.09	3.3***	1.1	1.5
2001 to 2010								
Orphan	−56.08	−0.3	−46.82	−0.5	−14.28	−0.8	0.20	0.3
Non-orphan	9.93	0.7	8.71	1.1	5.41	0.7	0.29	0.7
Difference	66.01	1	55.54	1.4	19.69	0.9	0.1	0.2
Panel B: Small syndicate								
Full sample: 1991 to 2010								
Orphan	−49.68	−2.1**	1.37	0.1	9.27	1.1	0.39	0.8
Non-orphan	3.15	0.4	8.28	1.5	2.61	1	1.00	4.3***
Difference	52.84	2.8***	6.90	0.4	−6.66	−0.7	0.55	1.2
1991 to 2000								
Orphan	−53.03	−1.9**	8.17	0.3	−8.45	−0.8	0.88	1.5
Non-orphan	5.06	0.5	13.21	1.4	6.39	1.5	1.28	3.8***
Difference	58.08	2.7***	5.03	0.2	14.84	1.4	0.34	0.7
2001 to 2010								
Orphan	−25.61	−0.1	−8.42	0.1	25.63	2.2**	−0.10	−0.1
Non-orphan	−3.14	−0.3	2.68	0.5	0.11	0.1	0.61	2**
Difference	22.47	1.2	11.11	0.6	−25.52	−1.9**	0.70	0.9

Notes:
Table 13.6 presents the long-run performance of orphan and non-orphan IPO firms by underwriting syndicate over the period from 1991 to 2010.
Firms with a number of managers above the median level are classified as large, otherwise small.
Long-run performance is computed as buy-and-hold abnormal returns over 12, 36 and 60 months.
A bootstrapped skewness-adjusted *t*-test is presented to estimate whether the BHAR or the difference between sample distributions are statistically significant.
*, ** and *** indicate significant differences at the 10%, 5% and 1% levels, respectively.

difference is statistically significant regardless of the considered horizon. However, in the 2000s, this difference is only statistically significant over a five-year horizon. Globally, these results hold for IPOs with a low level of institutional investor ownership.

In summary, these findings suggest that investors and market participants pay attention to analyst coverage when IPOs have large underwriting syndicates and are highly

Table 13.7 Long-run performance of orphan and non-orphan IPO firms by underpricing

Type of abnormal return	Size and book-to-market adjusted						Fama-French	
	BHAR60 (%)	t-stat	BHAR36 (%)	t-stat	BHAR12 (%)	t-stat	Alpha (%)	t-stat
Panel A: High underpriced								
Full sample: 1991 to 2010								
Orphan	−81.39	−3.6***	−28.40	−1.2	−13.56	−1.7*	−0.08	−0.2
Non-orphan	−5.42	−0.7	0.29	0.1	0.77	0.3	0.82	3.5***
Difference	75.97	4.3***	28.68	1.5	14.32	1.7*	0.86	2.4***
1991 to 2000								
Orphan	−79.58	−3.4***	−26.36	−0.8	−20.36	−1.9**	0.39	0.8
Non-orphan	−11.94	−1.2	−8.06	−1	−1.18	−0.3	1.13	3.5***
Difference	67.63	3.6***	18.29	0.9	19.18	2.1**	0.69	1.5
2001 to 2010								
Orphan	−105	−0.1	−35.98	−0.7	3.28	0.2	−0.54	−0.8
Non-orphan	12.15	1.2	10.15	2.1**	2.45	0.6	0.48	1.4
Difference	117.15	1.7*	46.14	1.1	−0.83	−0.1	0.99	1.7*
Panel B: Low underpriced								
Full sample: 1991 to 2010								
Orphan	−63.55	−2.3**	−44.98	−2.1**	−10.68	−0.8	−0.20	−0.3
Non-orphan	−10.18	−0.6	−3.70	−0.3	−4.17	−0.9	0.69	2.3**
Difference	53.36	1.6	41.28	1.6	6.51	0.5	0.95	1.5
1991 to 2000								
Orphan	−79.21	−2.7***	−31.79	−0.9	−24.91	−1.2	−0.23	−0.3
Non-orphan	−6.31	−0.3	13.76	0.8	4.96	0.5	0.81	1.7*
Difference	72.90	2**	45.55	1.5	29.87	1.6*	1.20	1.3
2001 to 2010								
Orphan	30.43	1.8*	−60.81	−1.9**	−0.64	−0.1	−0.37	−0.4
Non-orphan	−18.91	−0.8	−19.69	−2.3**	−9.41	−2.2**	0.45	1.2
Difference	−49.34	−1.3	41.12	1.7*	−8.77	−0.6	0.82	0.9

Notes:
Table 13.7 presents the long-run performance of orphan and non-orphan IPO firms by underpricing over the period from 1991 to 2010.
IPOs that are underpriced above the median level are classified as high, otherwise low.
Long-run performance is computed as buy-and-hold abnormal returns over 12, 36 and 60-months.
A bootstrapped skewness-adjusted *t*-test is presented to estimate whether the BHAR or the difference between sample distributions are statistically significant.
*, ** and *** indicate significant differences at the 10%, 5% and 1% levels, respectively.

underpriced. The differences between orphans and non-orphans persist in VC-backed and non-VC-backed IPOs and whatever the ownership structure of the IPOs (that is, those with a high versus low level of institutional investors). The 2000s reveals that the differences between orphan and non-orphan IPO firms are diminishing.

Next, we investigate the characteristics of analyst coverage by determining the number

Table 13.8 Long-run performance by institutional investor ownership

Type of abnormal return	Size and book-to-market adjusted						Fama–French	
	BHAR60 (%)	t-stat	BHAR36 (%)	t-stat	BHAR12 (%)	t-stat	Alpha (%)	t-stat
Panel A: High institutional investor ownership								
Full sample: 1991 to 2010								
Orphan	−53.70	−1	−26.66	−1.9*	−13.32	−1.7*	1.11	1.1
Non-orphan	19.42	2.3**	18.07	3***	12.43	3.1***	1.56	3***
Difference	73.12	2.8***	44.73	3.2***	25.75	3.1***	0.45	0.4
1991 to 2000								
Orphan	−46.09	−0.7	−33.08	−1.8*	−18.24	−1.7*	1.35	1.3
Non-orphan	17.04	1.8*	11.95	1.6	9.25	1.8*	1.75	5.9***
Difference	63.13	2.2**	45.03	3.3***	27.49	2.9***	0.25	0.2
2001 to 2010								
Orphan	−95.51	−1.3	−6.49	−0.1	2.15	0.1	0.48	0.2
Non-orphan	30.53	1.5	39.71	3.3***	23.67	3.2***	0.93	0.8
Difference	126.05	2**	46.20	1.2	21.54	1.5	0.87	0.3
Panel B: Low institutional investor ownership								
Full sample: 1991 to 2010								
Orphan	−83.76	−7.4***	−42.65	−2.7***	−15.41	−2.6***	−0.63	−0.9
Non-orphan	−24.78	−2.1**	−5.19	−0.4	−9.40	−1.6	−0.05	−0.1
Difference	58.97	4***	37.47	2.6***	6.01	0.8	0.65	1.6
1991 to 2000								
Orphan	−84.69	−6.8***	−42.85	−2.2**	−18.24	−2.7***	0.08	0.2
Non-orphan	−30.83	−2.2**	−6.59	−0.4	−14.73	−1.9*	0.26	0.5
Difference	53.87	3.5***	36.25	2.1**	3.50	0.4	0.36	0.8
2001 to 2010								
Orphan	−71.62	−0.9	−41.45	−1.1	2.01	0.1	−1.93	−1.4
Non-orphan	4.42	0.2	−0.65	−0.1	7.79	1	−0.74	−0.6
Difference	76.05	1.4	40.80	1.3	5.78	0.4	1.19	1.5

Notes:
Table 13.8 presents the long-run performance of orphan and non-orphan IPO firms by institutional investor ownership over the period from 1991 to 2010.
Firms with a percentage of shares held by institutional investors who hold 5% or more of the outstanding shares at the time of the offering that is above the median level are classified as high, otherwise low.
Long-run performance is computed as buy-and-hold abnormal returns over 12, 36 and 60 months.
A bootstrapped skewness-adjusted t-test is presented to estimate whether the BHAR or the difference between sample distributions are statistically significant.
*, ** and *** indicate significant differences at the 10%, 5% and 1% levels, respectively.

of financial analysts providing coverage. Numerous studies have documented a positive relationship between the coverage number and the subsequent short- and long-run performances (Bradley et al., 2003; Das et al., 2006). These findings are reported in Table 13.9. We find that IPOs with a high level of coverage (those with a coverage

Table 13.9 Long-run performance of non-orphan IPO firms based on analyst coverage

Type of abnormal return	Size and book-to-market adjusted							Fama–French	
	BHAR60 (%)	t-stat	BHAR36 (%)	t-stat	BHAR12 (%)	t-stat	Alpha (%)	t-stat
Full sample: 1991 to 2010								
High coverage	10.30	1.8*	9.80	2.5***	5.46	1.8*	1.13	4.6***
Low coverage	−29.88	−4.6***	−14.77	−3.2***	2.14	0.9	0.74	2.6***
Difference	40.18	5.3***	24.57	4.3***	3.31	0.8	−0.39	−1.7*
1991 to 2000								
High coverage	12.16	1.2	16.01	2**	8.08	1.6	1.56	4.8***
Low coverage	−41.27	−3.4***	−29.96	−3.1***	−11.45	−2.2**	1.01	2.5***
Difference	53.44	4.1***	45.97	4.5***	19.52	2.9	−0.54	−1.5
2001 to 2010								
High coverage	8.10	1.2	5.61	1.3	4.06	1.1	0.63	1.7*
Low coverage	−17.29	−3.3***	−4.27	−0.8	9.19	3.1***	0.49	1.2
Difference	25.40	3.2***	9.87	1.4	−5.12	−1.1	−0.14	−0.6

Notes:
Table 13.9 presents the long-run performance of non-orphan IPO firms based on analyst coverage over the period from 1991 to 2010. Those with an amount of analyst coverage above the median level are classified as high, otherwise low. Long-run performance is computed as buy-and-hold abnormal returns over 12, 36, and 60 months. A bootstrapped skewness-adjusted t-test is presented to estimate whether the BHAR or the difference between sample distributions are statistically significant. *, ** and *** indicate significant difference at the 10%, 5% and 1% levels, respectively.

Table 13.10   Definition of regression variables

Orphan	Dummy variable equals 1 if IPOs have analyst coverage and 0 otherwise
Syndicate	Dummy variable equals 1 if the number of managing underwriters is above the median level and 0 otherwise
Underpricing	Dummy variable equals 1 if an IPO's initial return is above the median level and 0 otherwise
VC backing	Dummy variable equals 1 if venture capitalists are affiliated with the IPO at the time of the offering and 0 otherwise
Institutional investors	Dummy variable equals 1 if the percentage of shares held by institutional investors who hold 5% or more of the outstanding shares at the time of the offering is above the median level and 0 otherwise
Coverage	Dummy variable equals 1 if the amount of coverage is above the median level and 0 otherwise
ROA	Natural logarithm of the change in return on assets. The change is measured 1, 3 and 5 years after the IPO date
Asset turnover	Natural logarithm of the change in asset turnover (sales divided by total assets). The change is measured 1, 3 and 5 years after the IPO date
Sales	Natural logarithm of the change in sales. The change is measured 1, 3 and 5 years after the IPO date
Capital expenditures	Natural logarithm of the change in capital expenditures. The change is measured 1, 3 and 5 years after the IPO date

number above the median level are classified as 'high'; otherwise, they are classified as 'low') perform better than IPOs with low coverage from three to five years after the IPO date. For instance, from 1991 to 2010, the five-year returns of IPOs with high coverage are 10.30 per cent compared with a −29.88 per cent for IPOs with low coverage. This difference is statistically significant at the 1 per cent level. This result holds for the 1990s and the 2000s.

To verify that the univariate results presented in Tables 13.4 through to 13.9 are robust in a multivariate setting, we report our regression model in Table 13.10. The dependent variable in the regression is the long-run performance of IPOs, as determined by the BHARs over one, three and five years. As Bradley et al. (2008b) note that a common oversight in examining analyst coverage is the endogenous problem between performance and analyst coverage. That is, the quality of an IPO is slowly revealed to the public through financial statements and other public sources after it has been issued. Therefore, other savvy investors could have predicted the long-run IPO performance. The analysts may just be jumping on the bandwagon when information is provided by other sources, such as financial statements. Our research model overcomes this obstacle.

Table 13.11 reports our regression results (corrected for heteroscedasticity and multicollinearity). We use a 2SLS regression model to account for the endogenous problem (that is, that the more valuable firms would likely attract more analysts). The coverage variable is endogenous, and we use instrument variables such as trading volume and intangibles that are known to influence analyst coverage but not long-run performance

Table 13.11 Cross-sectional regressions of long-run performance of IPOs from 1991–2010

	BHAR 60 803 observations	BHAR 36 1076 observations	BHAR 12 1265 observations
Intercept	−0.909**	−0.148	0.108
Orphan	1.274**	0.118	−0.089
Syndicate	−0.461***	−0.192***	−0.070
Underpricing	−0.013	0.070	0.042
VC backing	−0.067	−0.060	−0.036
Institutional investors	0.003	0.076	0.095
Coverage	0.161	0.222*	0.034
ROA	−0.014**	−0.004	0.004
Asset turnover	−0.002**	−0.003***	−0.009
Sales	0.002***	0.004***	−0.004
Capital expenditures	−0.001	−0.001***	0.001
Year fixed effects	Yes	Yes	Yes
Industry fixed effects	Yes	Yes	Yes

Notes:
The dependant variable is buy-and-hold abnormal return.
*, ** and *** indicate that the coefficient is significantly different from 0 at the 10%, 5% and 1% levels, respectively, using Student's *t*-test.
We use the 2SLS regression model.
The instrumented variable is coverage.
The instrument variables are trading volume and intangibles.

(Bhushan, 1989; O'Brien and Bhushan, 1990; Barth et al., 2001). The results of our model are statistically significant and it helps to explain the long-run performance of US IPOs.

We find non-orphan IPOs to be positively and significantly related to long-run performance over the five-year horizon, which is broadly consistent with the univariate analysis results given in Table 13.3. This finding reveals that market participants do not fully incorporate the perceived value of analyst coverage. Both the syndicate and operating performance variables explain a significant component of the long-run IPO performance regardless of the considered horizon. The other variables (such as underpricing, VC backing and institutional investors) fail to explain the long-run performance of US IPOs over the period from 1991 to 2010.

5 CONCLUSION

We examine the long-run performance of US IPOs carried out between 1991 and 2010 and find that the IPOs in our sample performed negatively relative to the comparison portfolio over this period, but this result varies substantially across sub-periods. We compare the long-run performance of firms that do not receive analyst coverage (orphans) to those that do (non-orphans). This abnormal long-run performance is considerably more severe for orphan IPOs than for non-orphan IPOs given a three- to five-year horizon. The evidence suggests that analyst coverage is indeed important to the issuing firm but the market does not fully incorporate the perceived value of this coverage. Once we control for other characteristics that have been shown to influence the long-run performance of IPOs, we find that investors and market participants pay attention to analyst coverage when IPOs have large underwriting syndicates and are highly underpriced. The difference between orphans and non-orphans persists in VC-backed and non-VC-backed IPOs, and whatever the ownership structures of the IPOs. Notably, however, the 2000s reveals that the difference between orphan and non-orphan IPO firms is diminishing. This trend may be attributable to scandals affecting analyst coverage, as both regulators and the financial press have identified analyst research that had been tainted by conflicts of interest.

Finally, multivariate regression analysis establishes that analyst coverage is significantly related to the long-run performance of IPOs, contrary to the study of Bradley et al. (2008b).

NOTES

1. 'Pour un nouvel essor de l'analyse financière indépendante sur le marché français', Autorité des Marchés Financiers (AMF), 2005.
2. Hoberg and Seyhun (2009) examine the collaboration between underwriters and venture capitalists in IPOs.

REFERENCES

Aggarwal, R., L. Krigman and K. Womack (2002), 'Strategic IPO underpricing, information momentum, and lockup expiration selling', *Journal of Financial Economics*, **66** (1), 106–37.
Barber, B. and J. Lyon (1997), 'Detecting long-run abnormal stock returns: the empirical power and specification of test statistics', *Journal of Financial Economics*, **43** (3), 341–72.
Barth, M., R. Kasznik and M. McNichols (2001), 'Analyst coverage and intangible assets' *Journal of Accounting Research*, **39**, 1–34.
Bhushan, R. (1989), 'Firm characteristics and analyst following', *Journal of Accounting and Economics*, **11** (2–3), 255–74.
Boubaker, S. and F. Labégorre (2008), 'Ownership structure, corporate governance and analyst following: a study of French listed firms', *Journal of Banking and Finance*, **32** (6), 961–76.
Bradley, D., K. Chan, J. Kim and A. Singh (2008b), 'Are there long-run implications of analysts' coverage for IPOs?', *Journal of Banking and Finance*, **32** (6), 1120–32.
Bradley, D., K. Chan, J. Kim and A. Singh (2004), 'Investment bankers, their analysts and orphaned IPOs', working paper, Clemson University.
Bradley, D., B. Jordan and J.R. Ritter (2003), 'The quiet period goes out with a bang', *Journal of Finance*, **58** (1), 1–36.
Bradley, D., B. Jordan and J.R. Ritter (2008a), 'Analyst behavior following IPOs: the "bubble period" evidence', *Review of Financial Studies*, **21** (1), 101–33.
Brav, A. and P. Gompers (1997), 'Myth or reality? The long-run performance of initial public offerings: evidence from venture and nonventure capital-backed companies', *Journal of Finance*, **52** (5), 1791–821.
Chemmanur, T. and E. Loutskina (2006), 'The role of venture capital backing in initial public offerings: certification, screening, or market power?', working paper, Boston College.
Chen, H. and J.R. Ritter (2000), 'The seven percent solution', *Journal of Finance*, **55** (3), 1105–31.
Cliff, M. and D. Denis (2004), 'Do initial public offering firms purchase analysts' coverage with underpricing?', *Journal of Finance*, **59** (6), 2871–901.
Corwin, S. and P. Schultz (2005), 'The role of IPO underwriting syndicates: pricing, information production, and underwriter competition', *Journal of Finance*, **60** (1), 443–86.
Das, S., R. Guo and H. Zhang (2006), 'Analysts' selective coverage and subsequent performance of newly public firms', *Journal of Finance*, **61** (3), 1159–85.

Ellis, K., R. Michaely and M. O'Hara (2005), 'Competition in investment banking: proactive, reactive, or retaliatory?', working paper, University of California.

Fama, E. and K. French (1992), 'The cross-section of expected stock returns', *Journal of Finance*, **47** (2), 427–65.

Fama, E. and K. French (1993), 'Common risk factors in the returns on stocks and bonds', *Journal of Financial Economics*, **33** (1), 3–56.

Fama, E. and K. French (1996), 'Multifactor explanations of asset pricing anomalies', *Journal of Finance*, **51** (1), 55–84.

Gompers, P. and J. Lerner (1997), 'Venture capital and the creation of public companies: do venture capitalists really bring more than money?', *Journal of Private Equity*, **1** (1), 15–30.

Hoberg, G. and H. Seyhun (2009), 'Do underwriters collaborate with venture capitalists in IPOs? Implications and evidence', working paper, University of Maryland.

Jain, B. and O. Kini (2000), 'Does the presence of venture capitalists improve the survival profile of IPO firms?', *Journal of Business Finance and Accounting*, **27** (9–10), 1139–76.

James, C. and J. Karceski (2006), 'Strength of analyst coverage following IPOs', *Journal of Financial Economics*, **82** (1), 1–34.

Khorana, A., S. Mola and P. Rau (2009), 'Is there life after loss of analyst coverage?', working paper, Purdue University.

Krigman, L., W. Shaw and K. Womack (2001), 'Why do firms switch underwriters?', *Journal of Financial Economics*, **60** (2–3), 245–84.

Lang, M., K. Lins and D. Miller (2004), 'Concentrated control, analyst following, and valuation: do analysts matter most when investors are protected least?', *Journal of Accounting Research*, **42** (3), 589–623.

Loughran, T. and J.R. Ritter (2004), 'Why has IPO underpricing changed over time?', *Financial Management*, **33** (3), 5–37.

Lyon, J., B. Barber and C. Tsai (1999), 'Improved methods for tests of long-run abnormal stock returns', *Journal of Finance*, **54** (1), 165–201.

O'Brien, P. and R. Bhushan (1990), 'Analyst following and institutional ownership', *Journal of Accounting Research*, **28**, 55–76.

Rajan, R. and H. Servaes (1997), 'Analyst following of initial public offerings', *Journal of Finance*, **52** (2), 507–29.

Ritter, J.R. and I. Welch (2002), 'A review of IPO activity, pricing and allocations', *Journal of Finance*, **57** (4), 1795–828.

14 Do directors trade after IPO lockup expiry?
Susanne Espenlaub, Marc Goergen, Arif Khurshed and Marko Remenar

1 INTRODUCTION

On 16 August 2012, Facebook's first lockup ended and more than 271 million shares became eligible for trading. The *Wall Street Journal* reported that, by 3.30 p.m. (New York time), more than 141 million shares had traded. This was three times the daily average over the last 30 days. By 4.00 p.m., Facebook's share price had fallen to $19.87, a drop of nearly 6.3 per cent compared with the closing price on the previous day.[1] The press speculated that the reason for the fall in Facebook's share price was that some of the directors and early investors were expected to sell their holdings. This speculation proved to be correct. Peter Thiel, one of the directors of Facebook, sold 20.1 million shares when the lockup expired.[2]

More generally, do directors of initial public offering (IPO) firms trade when lockups expire, and is their trading accompanied by a drop in the share price? In this chapter we answer this question by studying the trading behaviour of directors of 233 UK IPOs that came to the market during 1992–98. The reason why we study UK IPOs rather than US IPOs is that there is great variety in the characteristics of UK lockup agreements whereas in the US such agreements tend to have fairly similar characteristics. Given the greater diversity in terms of their lockup characteristics, UK lockup agreements are more likely to reflect the peculiarities of individual IPO firms and are therefore more likely to be perceived to be important by investors. Lockup agreements are important for at least three reasons. First, they ensure that the incentives of the firm's insiders and new shareholders are aligned for the duration of the lockup period, following the separation of ownership and control caused by the IPO. Second, they prevent directors from expropriating outside shareholders during a period of high uncertainty about the true value of the firm. Finally, they help the underwriter with their price support by temporarily limiting the supply of shares in the market.

Studies on US IPOs have found strong evidence of a significant price decline around the expiry day of lockups. Ofek and Richardson (2000), Field and Hanka (2001), Bradley et al. (2001), Brav and Gompers (2003) and Brau et al. (2004) report average abnormal returns of between −1 and −3 per cent around the lockup expiry of US IPOs. This finding is difficult to explain if the semi-strong version of the efficient market hypothesis holds. Conversely, Espenlaub et al. (2001) and Goergen et al. (2006) do not find significant abnormal returns around the lockup expiry of European (UK, France and Germany) IPOs.

To our knowledge, there is only one published study, by Espenlaub et al. (2001), on UK lockup agreements. The study highlights some major differences between UK and US lockup agreements. First, while US IPO lockup periods are mostly standardized at

180 days, UK IPO lockup periods have a substantial variation ranging from 158 days to 1095 days after the IPO. Second, expiry dates of UK lockups are frequently related to some company event, such as the announcement of the annual or interim results or the publication of the financial accounts, which while falling within a particular period has some uncertainty as to its exact date. This gives UK directors some discretion over the precise timing of the lockup expiry. Finally, there are also differences in terms of the legal restrictions faced by company insiders regarding share trading around announcements of price-sensitive information (see Fidrmuc et al., 2006).

A general expectation of the market would be that once the lockup agreements expire, insiders will sell at least some of their shares. Some studies from the US (Field and Hanka, 2001; Aggarwal et al., 2002; Brav and Gompers, 2003) look at insider trading around the lockup expiry. Field and Hanka (2001) find that trading increases temporarily to 80 per cent above average on the day following the expiry day and that trading increases permanently by 40 per cent after the expiry. They also document that lockup expiries in the US do not coincide with other events such as earnings announcements. This is different from the UK where Espenlaub et al. (2001) report that more than two-thirds of lockup agreements are tied in with the announcement of earnings or the publication of the annual results. In addition, UK regulation on insider trading (see Fidrmuc et al., 2006) imposes trading bans around earnings announcements and the publication of results. The existence of these trading bans and the resulting absence of trading around most expiries may then explain why Espenlaub et al. (2001), contrary to US studies, do not find significantly abnormal returns around the lockup expiry.

The aim of this chapter is to focus on the trading activities of directors around lockup expiries. Unlike the studies on the USA which focus on a much broader definition of insiders[3] and their trades at the time of lockup expiry, we only focus on directors' trading for two reasons. First, as Fidrmuc et al. (2006) argue, of all the insider trades, those by the directors usually have greater information content as compared to others. Second, in the UK only the directors are obliged to declare transactions carried out on their own accounts. We examine the share price performance around the lockup expiry and also the directors' trading activity by measuring the frequency of directors' transactions around the lockup expiry. We do not find evidence of a statistically significant drop in the share price of UK firms around the expiry of their lockup agreements. Further, contrary to what the above Facebook example suggests, we do not find evidence of large sales by directors at the time of the expiry. However, interestingly we find some cases of sales by directors predating the lockup expiry, sometimes as early as 50 weeks before the lockup expiry. This suggests that for some companies, the directors secure an early release from their original lockup. Our interviews with underwriters in the City of London show that it is indeed the case.

Finally, we look at the determinants of the likelihood of observing directors' sales on the day of the lockup expiry and soon thereafter. We find that the share price run-up before expiry, the size of the firm and the overall stock market run-up before the lockup expiry are the main predictors of directors' sales around the lockup expiry. We find limited evidence that characteristics of the IPO lockup agreements and IPO underpricing determine post-expiry director selling; this is in support of Brav and Gompers' (2003) signalling hypothesis according to which the level of underpricing and the length of lockups explain the likelihood of directors' sales at and after lockup expiry. Importantly, we only find evidence of such signalling when we examine actual expiry dates, allowing for the possibility of early release and selling prior to the expiry dates stipulated in the IPO prospectus.

The rest of the chapter is organized as follows. In the next section we analyse the institutional framework in relation to lockup agreements and directors' trades in the UK. In the third section we review the relevant literature and develop testable hypotheses. The fourth section describes the methodology and data used in this study. Section 5 presents and discusses our results. Finally, conclusions and suggestions for further research are presented in section 6.

2 BACKGROUND AND INSTITUTIONAL FRAMEWORK

2.1 Lockup Agreements in the UK

Contrary to the findings on the USA which suggest an increasing trend towards standardized lockup periods of 180 days, Espenlaub et al. (2001) report that for the UK there is great diversity not only with respect to the duration of the lockup period, but also with respect to the other lockup characteristics. First, UK IPOs frequently have separate lockup agreements for the different types of initial shareholders. Often, the directors are locked up for different periods of time than the other initial shareholders. Second, the lockup expiry date may be in the form of a specific calendar date (for example, 16 August 2012), as is the case in the USA, or it may be related to a specific corporate event, such as the earnings announcement or the publication of the annual report, whose exact date is as yet uncertain. Finally, lockups may also be staggered, that is, allow only for a gradual release of the locked shares across a series of consecutive expiry dates.[4]

To the opposite of the USA, which has no legal rules about lockup periods (Ofek and Richardson, 2000), in the UK certain types of companies are, or were in the past, subject to compulsory lockups. Until January 2000, lockup agreements were compulsory for UK mineral and scientific research-based companies, which did not satisfy the minimum age of three years required by the Official List of the London Stock Exchange (LSE). More specifically, the directors and other key employees of these companies were not allowed to sell shares either in the IPO or during the period of two years commencing with the first day of listing. Shareholders holding at least 10 per cent of the securities were not allowed to sell during the first six months following the IPO or until the publication of the semi-annual results, whichever was longer. Also, they could not sell more than 40 per cent of their holdings during the first two years following the IPO. Since January 2000, there has been no requirement for compulsory lockups in the UK.

2.2 Directors' Trading

In addition to the trading restrictions imposed by the lockup agreement, the directors of the company are also restricted by the 1977 Model Code of the London Stock Exchange and the 1985 Companies Act. According to the 1985 Companies Act, every company in the UK is required to keep a register of directors' interests, which has to be made available for inspection to the members of the firm and the general public. Directors must notify the company of any transactions carried out for their own account within five working days and the company must make an entry into the Company Register, which is available for public inspection, within three working days. Moreover, any listed company must notify the Stock Exchange of this information by the following day (see Fidrmuc et al., 2006, for more details on the UK regulation on insider trading).

The Model Code also specifies that a director must not deal in any securities of the listed company based on short-term considerations. Furthermore, a director must not deal during a 'close period' which covers the 60 days immediately before the announcement of the company's annual or semi-annual results.[5] Moreover, a director must not deal on any unpublished price-sensitive information at any time.[6]

3 LITERATURE REVIEW

Information on the lockup agreement can be found in the IPO prospectus. Hence, if the semi-strong version of the efficient market hypothesis is valid, this information should be reflected in the price as soon as it becomes publicly available. Thus, as argued by Ofek and Richardson (2000), Brav and Gompers (2003), Bradley et al. (2001), Brau et al. (2004) and Espenlaub et al. (2001), at the expiry of the lockup contract, on average the abnormal returns should be zero. Mohan and Chen's (2001) as well as Espenlaub et al.'s (2001) findings support this theoretical assertion. They do not find significant abnormal returns around the expiry.

In contrast, Ofek and Richardson (2000), Field and Hanka (2001), Bradley et al. (2001), Brav and Gompers (2003) and Brau et al. (2004) have all found evidence of a significant price decline around the expiry day. More specifically, Ofek and Richardson (2000), analysing a sample of 1053 US firms, find negative cumulative abnormal returns of 1.15 and 2.03 per cent on the day of the expiry and the period ranging from four days before the expiry, respectively, combined with substantial increases in the volume of shares traded on the expiry day and during the following 20 days. Price reversal does not occur after the lockup expiry, but trading volume subsides. They examine several plausible explanations, including bid-ask bounce, liquidity effects and biased expectations of supply shocks, but find little support for any of these. In an attempt to explain the magnitude of the share price drop, they also examine variables proxying for the incumbent shareholders' desire to diversify their holdings. They find that high-volatility stocks tend to have much larger price drops. Finally, they report that the decrease in the share price is consistent with a downward sloping demand curve for the shares.

Field and Hanka (2001) examine 1948 lockup agreements over 1988 to 1997. They report a statistically significant three-day abnormal return of −1.5 per cent and a permanent 40 per cent increase in trading volume. They find that the abnormal return and trading volume are roughly three times larger for venture capital (VC) backed firms than for firms without VC backing. They also conduct a robustness test and conclude that their results are driven solely by the lockup expiry and not by some other concurrent event (for example, earnings announcements).

Field and Hanka (2001) test the validity of several hypotheses that may explain the observed pattern in the returns. Consistent with the downward-sloping demand curve hypothesis, they find that the abnormal return is more negative when the trading volume is abnormally high. Furthermore, 17 per cent of firms in their sample have at least one insider sale in the two-week period centred on the expiry day. They find that the abnormal return is significantly more negative when insiders sell shares around the expiry of the lockup. However, since the return remains significantly negative in the absence of insider sales, they conclude that this phenomenon is not solely driven by unexpectedly large insider sales.

Bradley et al. (2001) examine the stock price behaviour around the lockup expiry for a sample of 2529 US firms during 1988–97. They report average abnormal returns of −0.74 per cent on the day of the expiry, with an average cumulative abnormal return of −1.61 per cent over the five-day period surrounding the expiry. Both figures are statistically significant. Moreover, they find that the negative abnormal returns are concentrated in firms with VC backing, with high-tech firms experiencing the most negative abnormal returns. In addition to industry and VC-backing, they examine the influence of firm size, post-IPO stock performance, underwriter reputation, volatility, percentage of shares locked up, length of the lockup and other variables. For the VC-backed sample, post-IPO stock performance, trading volume and volatility are the most significant explanatory variables. However, they find little or no significance of any of these potential explanatory variables for the case of IPOs without VC backing.

Studying 2794 US IPOs from 1988 to 1996, Brav and Gompers (2003) find a statistically significant buy-and-hold return of −1.7 per cent on day 1 (day 0 being the day of lockup expiry) combined with a significant increase in trading volume. They find that firms having potentially greater adverse selection problems lock their insiders in for a longer period. Also, the underpricing of the offering is substantially higher for firms that lock in more of their shares and lock them in for a longer period. Finally, they find that 15 per cent of the firms have insider sales prior to the expiration of the lockup. Brav and Gompers report that these sales occur in firms subject to less moral hazard, that is, larger firms, firms with high-quality underwriters and VC-backed firms. They conclude that lockups, as a commitment device, are less important for high-quality companies.

Brau et al. (2004) study a sample of 3049 IPOs from 1988–98 and find that cumulative abnormal returns are −1.9 per cent over the window covering the 10 days preceding the expiry as well as the expiry day. They offer two explanations for this observed anomaly. First, lockups may be used to mitigate informational asymmetries that exist between insiders and outsiders. Using firm size, underwriter reputation, growth opportunities and the inverse of the offer price as proxies for asymmetric information, they report evidence that greater informational asymmetry is related to larger negative abnormal returns. Second, they claim that at the lockup expiry there is a possibility of misalignment of insider and outsider incentives. This misalignment can decrease investors' demand for the shares and, subsequently, generate the negative abnormal returns. They find a significantly positive relationship between the percentage of management ownership after the IPO, their proxy for insider incentives, and the five-day cumulative abnormal returns.

So far, there exists only one published paper that examines UK lockup agreements. For a sample of 188 firms that went public on the London Stock Exchange during 1992–98, Espenlaub et al. (2001) find that non-managerial shareholders of high-technology firms, that is, firms that tend to have greater informational asymmetries, are more likely to be subject to lockup agreements. Moreover, they report that underwriter reputation acts as a signalling substitute for lockup agreements. Finally, they examine the stock performance around the lockup expiry day for a subsample of IPOs with clear-cut expiry dates. Consistent with the US findings, Espenlaub et al. report cumulative abnormal returns on the days around the expiry day ranging from −0.5 to −2.4 per cent. However, they also find that the abnormal returns around the expiry day are, in most cases, not statistically significant. One of the limitations of the Espenlaub et al. study is that it concentrates on lockup agreements with absolute expiry dates. In contrast, the study in this chapter also includes those agreements that expire on the day of a corporate event, such as the announcement or the publication of the annual results.

3.1 Testable Hypotheses

The efficient-market hypothesis predicts that on average abnormal share price movements around the expiry of the lockup agreements should be zero, and all information concerning lockup agreements should be incorporated in the opening share price on the first day of trading of the IPO.

Hypothesis 1: The abnormal returns at the time of the expiry of the lockup agreement should on average be equal to zero.

According to Field and Hanka (2001) and Brau et al. (2004), directors' sales can have a potentially strong impact on the share price, because they tend to convey bad news. Moreover, an increase in the supply of shares may drive their price down. Furthermore, agency costs of equity, caused by the lack of alignment of the interests of insiders with those of outsiders, are expected to decrease investor demand for the shares. Moreover, if current directors' sales are a predictor of future directors' sales, then even a slight increase in directors' sales could have a large impact on the stock price. If this effect drives the negative abnormal return that is observed around the expiry day, then the abnormal return should be confined to firms with director sales.

Hypothesis 2: The stock performance around the expiration of the lockup agreement is negatively affected by directors' sales around the expiry.

Brav and Gompers (2003) argue that insiders can essentially signal the quality of the firm using three variables: underpricing, the percentage of shares locked up, and the length of the lockup period. In a separating equilibrium, a high-quality issuer will underprice more, will agree to a longer lockup period, and/or agree to lock up a larger percentage of the shares. When the true value of the firm is revealed, insiders of high-quality firms will return to the market to recoup the cost from signalling firm quality. This leads to the following hypotheses:

Hypothesis 3a: The longer the lockup period, the greater is the likelihood of directors selling at and after the expiration of the lockup.

Hypothesis 3b: The larger the percentage of locked up shares, the greater is the likelihood of directors selling at and after the expiration of the lockup.

Hypothesis 3c: The higher the underpricing of the IPO, the greater is the likelihood of directors trading at and after the expiration of the lockup.

Alternatively, the directors, as the firm's initial shareholders, may just want to diversify their portfolios. According to Ofek and Richardson (2000), they are more likely to sell out after a large price run-up, or when the firm is highly risky and the benefits from portfolio diversification are therefore more substantial. Bolton and von Thadden (1998) model the optimal level of control and ownership concentration post-IPO and find that high-risk firms will end up being widely held given that the benefits from portfolio diversification accruing to the incumbent shareholders outweigh those of monitoring. This leads to the following two hypotheses:

Hypothesis 4: The larger the price run-up in the aftermarket of the IPO, the greater is the likelihood of directors trading at and after the expiration of the lockup.

Hypothesis 5: The higher the volatility of the share price prior to the expiration of the lockup, the greater is the likelihood of directors trading at and after the expiration of the lockup.

Finally, in order to control for other factors that may influence directors' trades at and after the expiry of the lockup agreement the models estimated in this study include a number of other potentially relevant variables. More specifically, the models control for prevailing stock-market conditions, the size of the firm, underwriter reputation, venture-capital backing, and industrial sector and issue year.

4 DATA SOURCES, VARIABLES AND METHODOLOGY

4.1 Sample Selection

The sample consists of IPOs conducted by UK companies on the London Stock Exchange during January 1992 to December 1998. In total there were 351 IPOs of non-financial and non-investment companies during this period, of which 112 were excluded for the following reasons: (1) the IPO prospectus did not make it clear which of the insiders were locked up, (2) there was no information on the individual shareholdings of insiders, (3) there was a lack of clarity on the number of shares locked up, (4) the date of the announcement/publication of interim/annual accounts was not traceable or (5) the firm was dead before the expiry of lockup. Six IPOs were excluded from the sample because the directors of these firms had no lockup agreements. The final sample consists of 233 IPOs.

Data on the lockup agreements, directors' shareholdings and other details about the IPOs are obtained from the offering prospectuses. The dates of earnings announcements were obtained from Factiva. The dates of the annual shareholders' meeting (AGM) and the dates when auditors signed the accounts were obtained from the annual reports. Data on directors' trades were obtained from the Directus database. Data on gross domestic product (GDP), the middle rate on the UK one-month

Treasury bill, the FT-All Share Index, and daily stock returns were obtained from DataStream.

4.2 Variables

4.2.1 Directors' trading

In order to examine directors' trading, we measure the frequency of directors' transactions (DTF). This measure is the one used by Park et al. (1995) in their study of insider trading activity surrounding annual earnings announcements. The directors' trading frequency in week t is:

$$DTF_t = 1/N_t \times \sum_{i=1}^{N_t} DTF_{i,t}$$

where $DTF_{i,t}$ is the number of directors' transactions in firm i in week t, and N_t is the number of firms in the sample in week t. The frequency of directors' purchases (DBF) and directors' sales (DSF) in week t is calculated as:

$$DBF_t = 1/N_t \times \sum_{t=1}^{N_t} DBF_{i,t}$$

$$DSF_t = 1/N_t \times \sum_{i=1}^{N_t} DSF_{i,t}$$

where $DBF_{i,t}$ is the number of directors' purchases in firm i in week t and $DSF_{i,t}$ is the number of directors' sales in firm i in week t.

All these weekly measures are computed for the period ranging from week -10 to week $+10$ with the week of the lockup expiry being week 0. The measures described above control for the change in the number of companies in the sample since they are based on N_t, that is, the number of companies in the sample in week t (as opposed to the total number of companies in the sample).

The second part of this study focuses on testing hypotheses three, four and five using binomial probit regressions with directors' sales as the dependent variable. In the probit regressions the dummy variable (*Sales*) is assigned a value of one if share sales by unlocked directors occurred during, at or up to two months after the lockup expiry, and zero otherwise.

4.2.2 Abnormal returns

The abnormal returns around the expiry of the lockup agreement are calculated using standard event-study methodology. The market-adjusted abnormal return for firm i on day t, $AR_{i,t}$, is calculated as:

$$AR_{i,t} = R_{i,t} - R_{m,t}$$

where $R_{i,t}$ is the daily return on the stock of firm i, and $R_{m,t}$ is the daily return on the market portfolio proxied by the FT-All Share Index. The cumulative abnormal return

Do directors trade after IPO lockup expiry? 283

from the start day t_s to the end day t_e for firm i within the event window t, $CAR_{i,t}$, is calculated as:

$$CAR_{i,t} = \sum_{t-t_1}^{t_1} AR_{i,t}$$

The lockup expiry day is considered to be day zero. Since the process of determining the exact lockup expiry dates is not always easy, due to several reasons, which will be described in the next section, four alternative event windows were used. The average cumulative abnormal return across all companies for the event period t, $ACAR_t$, is calculated as:

$$ACAR_t = 1/N_t \times \sum_{i-t}^{N_t} CAR_{i,t}$$

where N represents the number of firms in the sample.

4.2.3 Lockup expiry dates and the length of the lockup period

Table 14.1 shows the breakdown of lockup expiry dates in the sample according to their type. About one-third of the sample firms (34 per cent) had clear-cut expiry dates. The remaining firms had lockups tied to events such as announcement/publication of interim, preliminary or annual results and AGMs.

Given that two-thirds of our sample firms had expiry dates relative to a company announcement, we used several methods to determine the exact dates of the lockup expiry. As shown in Table 14.1, nearly 23 per cent of the expiry dates are related to the publication of annual accounts. Since the exact date of the publication of the accounts is not available, proxies had to be used. The date of the company's AGM was determined from the annual accounts. Three weeks were then subtracted from this date to obtain the approximate date of the publication of the accounts. If the AGM date was unavailable,

Table 14.1 Types of lockup expiry dates for directors

Type of the lockup expiry date	Percentage of the sample
Absolute expiry date	34.26
Relative expiry date, of which:	
• relative to the publication of annual accounts	23.11
• relative to the announcement of preliminary results	19.12
• relative to the announcement of interim results	10.36
• relative to the announcement of annual results	5.58
• relative to the combination of one absolute and one relative date (e.g. one year after the IPO or the announcement of annual results, whichever is earlier/later)	4.78
• relative to an AGM	2.79

Notes:
Expiry dates are based on the information stipulated in the IPO prospectuses of companies floated during 1992–98.
Absolute expiry dates refer to a fixed date after the IPO (such as 1 year after the IPO or 30 June 2000).

the date on which the auditors signed the accounts was used as a starting point. To arrive at the lockup expiry date in this case, three weeks would then be added to allow for the annual reports to be printed and distributed to the shareholders. While determining the proxies for the expiry dates, caution was taken to add extra days for holidays during the period of interest.

For the lockup expiry dates that were related to annual or interim announcements of preliminary results, the first step was to find a specific earnings-announcement date from the Factiva database. We found that in almost 77 per cent of the cases the date of the earnings announcement and the date when the auditors signed the accounts occur in the same week.[7] This regularity was then used to determine the earnings announcement dates for the dead companies. The date when the auditors signed the accounts was determined from the published accounts, an extra day would be added and this date would then be used as a proxy for the lockup expiry date. The same procedure was also adopted for the cases where the date of the earnings announcement obtained from Factiva was after the AGM.

Moreover, if the expiry date was related to the interim earnings announcement, and this date was not available from Factiva, six months were added to the date of the previous year's annual-earnings announcement to approximate the event date.

The length (or duration) of the lockup was calculated as the difference in days between the lockup expiry day and the date of the IPO. Table 14.2 describes the variables used in our regressions.

4.3 Descriptive Statistics

Descriptive statistics of the independent variables can be found in Panel A of Table 14.3. The average lockup duration is 491 days with half of the companies having a lockup duration of 441 days or longer. This is in marked contrast with the US where most firms have lockups of 180 days. Moreover, the high standard deviation of 189 days suggests that the lockup period in the UK varies substantially across firms.

The average stock performance before the lockup expiry, measured by the sum of stock returns from day −122 to day −1, is 3.49 per cent (market model adjusted return) with a standard deviation of 39.19 per cent. Average stock volatility in the sample is about 2 per cent. In line with the results obtained by previous studies (for example, Levis, 1995; Vismara et al., 2012), the average initial return of the IPOs in the sample is 10.36 per cent. On average, 45 per cent of the total shares outstanding post-IPO were held and subject to lockup agreements by insiders (directors and other shareholders with post-IPO shareholdings reported in the IPO prospectus).

Descriptive statistics on the two dummy variables included in the regressions are presented in Panel B of Table 14.3. The top ten underwriters, as classified by the Annual Broker Survey, underwrote 31 per cent of the sample. Furthermore, 52 per cent of all IPOs were venture-capital backed.

4.4 Methodology

To test Hypotheses 3 to 5 on the determinants of the probability of directors selling around the expiry of their lockup agreements, we use probit regressions with the binary

Table 14.2 Definitions of variables

Variable	Description
Sales1	Binary variable assigned a value of one if directors' sale occurred at or within eight weeks of the lockup expiry, and zero otherwise
Sales2	Binary variable assigned a value of one if directors' sale occurred before the lockup expiry, and zero otherwise
Sales3	Binary variable assigned a value of one if directors' sale occurred before or within eight weeks of the lockup expiry, and zero otherwise
Lockup duration	The number of days between the date of the IPO and the lockup expiry day
Insiders' shares locked up	The total number of ordinary shares held by insiders (directors and other shareholders listed in the IPO prospectus) and subject to a lockup agreement, as a fraction of the total number of shares outstanding after the IPO
Underpricing	The difference between the return on the stock on the first trading day and the return on the market over the ten day period prior to the IPO
Stock price run-up	Cumulative raw (discrete) stock returns from day -122 to day -1 relative to the expiry day (day 0)
Volatility	The standard deviation of raw discrete returns from day -122 days to day -1 relative to the expiry day (day 0)
Underwriter reputation	Dummy variable assigned a value of one if the underwriter of the issue was classified in the top ten in the year prior to the IPO and zero otherwise
VC backing	Dummy variable assigned a value of one if the firm was backed by a venture capitalist and zero otherwise
FTSE run-up	The change in the FT-All Share Index for the quarter preceding the lockup expiry date
Ln(Size)	Natural logarithm of the market capitalization of the firm based on the offer price
Expiry type	Dummy variable coded one if the expiry date is absolute and zero if it is relative or a combination of absolute and relative (see Table 14.1)

dependent variable *Sales* coded as one if director share sales reportedly took place around the expiry of directors' lockup agreements, and zero otherwise. Specifically, we use three versions of *Sales* relating to three different windows around the expiry date. The window for *Sales1* is the period from the week of the expiry (week 0) until eight weeks after the expiry (week 8). *Sales2* is coded one if directors' sales occurred before the lockup expiry and zero otherwise. Finally, *Sales3* is based on the combination of the previous two windows and is coded one if directors' sales occurred before or within eight weeks after the lockup expiry week, and zero otherwise.

Explanatory variables in the probit models are the duration of the lockup (hypothesis 3a), the fraction of directors' shares locked up (hypothesis 3b), IPO underpricing (hypothesis 3c), the stock-price and market (FTSE) run-up (hypothesis 4) and stock-price volatility (hypothesis 5) measured over the period from day -122 to day -1 relative

Table 14.3 Descriptive statistics for the 233 IPOs

Panel A

Variable	Mean	Standard deviation	Median	Minimum	Maximum
Lockup duration (days)	491.47	189.51	441.00	70.00	1203.00
Stock price run-up (%)					
Raw discrete returns	5.25	29.33	5.21	−76.31	144.10
Market-model abnormal returns	3.49	39.19	4.86	−146.32	171.56
Market-model abnormal returns (Scholes-Williams beta)	2.91	39.32	4.44	−146.20	171.66
Volatility (%)	1.90	1.44	1.49	0.16	7.89
Underpricing (%)	10.36	12.81	7.11	−16.42	70.18
Insiders' shares locked-up (%)	44.61	21.58	46.64	0.23	90.80
Size (£m)	7368.35	12476.12	4254.20	185.50	114689.44

Panel B

Dummy variable	= 1 (% of sample)	= 0 (% of sample)
Underwriter quality (1 if top ten)	31.38	68.62
VC backing (1 if VC backed)	52.30	47.70

to the expiry day (day 0). As stated above, we also control for firm size, underwriter reputation, VC backing, type of expiry date (dates set in absolute terms or relative to corporate events), and for year and industry effects.

5 RESULTS

5.1 Directors' Trading

The main body of this study focuses on the influence of directors' trades on the abnormal returns around the expiry and on the factors explaining directors' sales around the lockup expiry. We start by describing the directors' trading behaviour from week −10 to week +10 where week 0 is the week of lockup expiry. During this period, there was a total of 207 transactions by directors for our sample. Sixty of these transactions were purchases and 147 of these were sales. The directors' average weekly trading activity is reported separately for buy and sale transactions in Table 14.4 and is also depicted in Figure 14.1. Since the directors are free to buy further shares during the lockup period, their buying activity should not change significantly over the entire period of study. Conversely, their selling activity before the lockup expiry should be zero. Table 14.4 shows that the selling activity differs significantly from zero in most of the weeks around the lockup expiry. As expected, the selling activity is the highest in the week of expiry followed by week +1. However, an interesting result is that in some cases directors' selling starts much earlier than the actual lockup expiry stipulated in the IPO prospectus. Indeed, from week −6 there is selling activity. This shows that for some firms the

Table 14.4 Average transactions by the directors for the sample of 233 IPOs

Week	DBF (Buys)	DSF (Sells)
−10	0.0000	0.0000
−9	0.0040	0.0040
−8	0.0080	0.0000
−7	0.0000	0.0000
−6	0.0000	0.0319
−5	0.0558	0.0040
−4	0.0080	0.0040
−3	0.0080	0.0199
−2	0.0120	0.0159
−1	0.0040	0.0279
0	0.0279	0.1355
1	0.0159	0.1155
2	0.0040	0.0359
3	0.0159	0.0518
4	0.0159	0.0239
5	0.0199	0.0000
6	0.0040	0.0279
7	0.0159	0.0319
8	0.0080	0.0199
9	0.0120	0.0319
10	0.0000	0.0040

Notes:
Directors' buying activity (DBF) is measured as the number of buys in week t for the whole sample divided by the number of firms in the sample in week t.
Selling activity (DSF) is measured as the number of sells in week t for the whole sample divided by the number of firms in the sample in week t.
Week 0 is the week of the lockup expiry.

directors negotiate a release from their stipulated lockup. These results are confirmed by Figure 14.1, which shows the overall trading activity and the frequencies of sales and purchases by the directors.

We delve further into directors' pre-lockup selling activity by looking at the frequency of sales before the lockup expiry. The results in Table 14.5 are consistent with US evidence in that in over 86 per cent of IPO companies, there is no pre-expiry share selling by directors. Of the remaining 14 per cent of companies, over one-third (12 out of 32) have only a single sell transaction in the pre-expiry period. However, there is a tail of companies where directors make a substantial number of sales prior to expiry.

5.2 Stock Performance upon Lockup Expiry

Hypothesis 1 states that on average the abnormal returns around the expiry of the lockup agreement are equal to zero. To examine the stock performance around the expiry and to test hypothesis 1, we conduct an event study on our sample of 233 IPOs. The results are presented in panel A of Table 14.6. This table reports mean cumulative

288   *Handbook of research on IPOs*

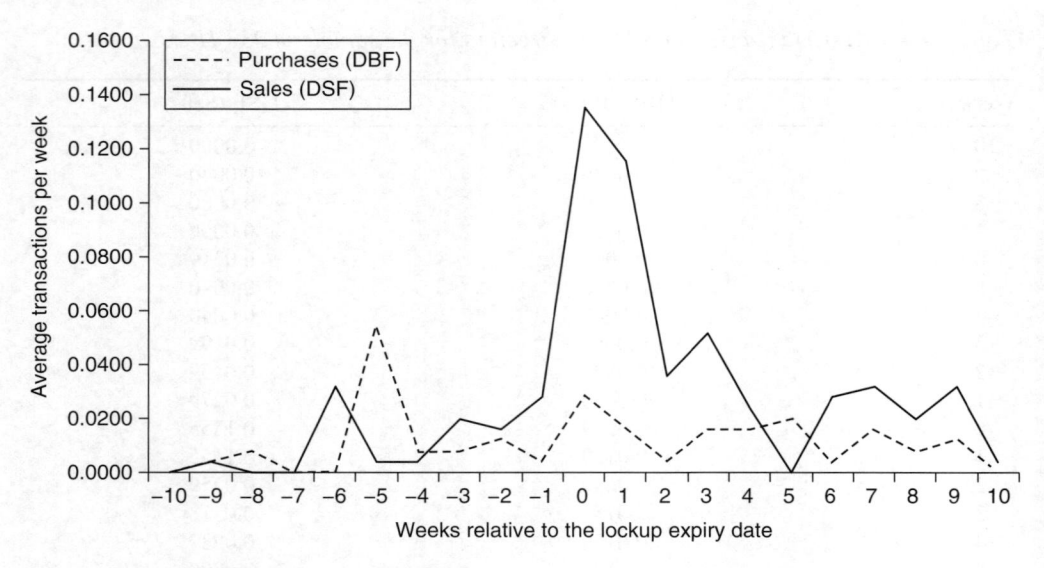

Figure 14.1   Directors' average weekly buy and sale transactions

Table 14.5   Share sales transactions by directors before the IPO lock-in expiry date

(1) No of selling transactions prior to lockup expiry	(2) Frequency of companies with given no. of pre-expiry sales	(3) Percentage of companies relative to total sample	(4) Cumulative percentage
0	201	86.27	86.27
1	12	5.15	91.42
2	7	3.00	94.42
3	4	1.72	96.14
4	1	0.43	96.57
5	1	0.43	97.00
6	2	0.86	97.85
7	2	0.86	98.71
8	1	0.43	99.14
9	1	0.43	99.57
13	1	0.43	100.00
Total	233	100.00	

Notes:
The sample comprises 233 UK IPOs issued during 1992–98.
The expiry dates refer to the lockup agreements of the directors in the IPO prospectuses.
For a given company, the lockup expiry is the earliest date on which a lockup agreement for a director of the company expires.
Column (2) shows the numbers of companies with a given number of share sales transactions by directors prior to the first expiry date stipulated for directors in the IPO prospectus.
201 out of the 233 companies have no pre-expiry share selling by the directors.
Column (1) only lists the number of sales transactions observed for a least one of the sample companies.

Do directors trade after IPO lockup expiry? 289

Table 14.6 *Univariate tests of abnormal returns around lockup expiry*

		Average cumulative market adjusted returns (*t*-statistics; test of zero mean)			
	Obs	Days (0, 1)	(0, 2)	(0, 3)	(0, 6)
Panel A					
Full sample	233	0.1604	−0.172	−0.235	−0.047
		(0.489)	(−0.478)	(−0.541)	(−0.091)
Panel B					
Subsample without directors' sales	192	−0.105	−0.402	−0.513	−0.333
		(0.316)	(1.030)	(−1.060)	(0.606)
Subsample with directors' sales	41	1.4032	0.9044	1.0668	1.2917
		(1.381)	(0.990)	(1.109)	(0.920)
p-values for equality of means test between the subsamples; one-tailed test <0		0.040**	0.084*	0.083*	0.116

Notes:
The sample comprises 233 UK IPOs conducted during 1992–98.
The analysis above presents the test of hypotheses 1 and 2. Event windows for CARs are expressed in days.
The sample is partitioned according to whether any directors' sales occurred within the first eight weeks after the lockup expiry or not.
* Significant at the 1% level.

abnormal returns (CARs) calculated over the two-, three-, four- and seven-day windows. The results show that there was no statistically significant decline in share prices around the lockup expiry. We also partitioned our sample according to the types of lockup (relative to earnings announcements, publications of annual accounts, and so on) but failed to find any significant changes in the share prices.[8] Therefore, we find support for hypothesis 1 in that the abnormal returns at the time of lockup expiry are not significantly different from zero.

In order to test hypothesis 2 and determine whether directors' sales influence the stock performance around the expiry of the lockup, we partition our sample into two sub groups, one subsample with directors' sales in the period of up to eight weeks after lockup expiry (weeks 0 to 8); and a second subsample without directors' sales in that period. The results are shown in Panel B of Table 14.6. Again the abnormal returns are not statistically significantly different from zero for either subsample. However, the difference in means test indicates that abnormal returns are significantly lower for the subsample without directors' sales. This is a puzzling finding and contrary to our expectations, and remains an issue for further research.[9]

5.3 Directors' Sales – Results

In order to test hypotheses 3(a), 3(b) and 3(c), 4 and 5, we estimate binomial probit models reported in Table 14.7. The dependent variables in the probit models focus on directors' selling after and/or before the lockup expiry. Model (1) uses a binary variable,

Table 14.7 Binomial probit results

Independent variables	Expected Sign	Model(1) Sales1	Model(2) Sales2	Model(3) Sales3
Constant		−4.78	−1.67	−3.17
		(−2.71)***	(−1.22)	(−2.77)***
Lockup duration	+	0.0003	0.001	0.0007
		(0.47)	(2.21)**	(1.33)
Insiders' shares locked up	+	−0.010	−0.001	−0.0009
		(−1.68)*	(−0.20)	(−0.20)
Underpricing	+	−0.406	0.808	1.12
		(−0.33)	(0.93)	(1.48)
Stock run-up before expiry	+	1.69	0.703	0.810
		(3.17)***	(1.65)*	(2.28)**
Volatility	+	−5.88	1.59	−5.07
		(−0.51)	(0.18)	(−0.65)
Ln(Size)		0.33	0.100	0.274
		(2.36)**	(0.70)	(2.49)**
FTSE run-up		0.058	−0.014	0.11
		(2.17)**	(−0.65)	(0.61)
Underwriter reputation		0.009	−0.17	−0.098
		(0.33)	(−0.07)	(−0.46)
VC backing		0.053	0.356	0.360
		(0.19)	(1.43)	(1.76)*
Expiry type		−0.714	−0.466	−0.279
		(−0.24)	(−1.68)*	(−1.26)
Year dummies		Yes	Yes	Yes
Industry dummies		Yes	Yes	Yes
No. of observations		233	233	233
Log likelihood		−95.29	−84.23	−122.67
Pseudo R^2		12.95	10.64	12.09

Notes:
In model (1), the dependent variable (*Sales1*) is a dummy variable taking a value of 1 if directors' sales occurred at or within eight weeks after the earliest lockup expiry date stipulated for directors, and zero otherwise.
For model (2), the dependent variable (*Sales2*) is a dummy variable taking a value of 1 if directors' sales occurred before the stipulated lockup expiry.
For model (3), the dependent variable (*Sales3*) is a dummy variable taking a value of 1 if directors' sales occurred anytime from before or within eight weeks after the stipulated lockup expiry.
The table reports the marginal effects and the figures in parentheses are *t*-statistics.
***, **, * significant at the 1%, 5% and 10% level, respectively.

Sales1, that equals unity for companies that reported directors' sales during the period ranging from the week with the earliest expiry date of directors' lockups to the eighth week thereafter. The results suggest that the likelihood of such selling increases with the run-up in the share price of the company and the run-up of the overall stock market: both variables have positive and significant coefficients (note, the table reports the marginal effects). This is consistent with hypothesis 4. There is also a size effect: the coefficient on the natural logarithm of firm size is positive and significant, indicating that directors are more likely to sell in larger companies. However, the only variable related to lockup agreement characteristics with a significant coefficient is the percentage of shares locked up for insiders (Variable (2)). Nevertheless, the coefficient has the wrong sign. Thus, we must reject hypothesis 3(b). Similarly, the statistical insignificance of the coefficients on the duration of the lockup agreement and on IPO underpricing leads us to reject hypotheses 3(a) and 3(c).

At first glance, these results suggest that, contrary to expectations, the features of the IPO lockup agreements and IPO underpricing do not play any role in determining the likelihood of post-expiry sales by directors. However, reflecting on the results reported in Tables 14.4 and 14.5 on the frequencies of directors' selling prior to the expiry dates stipulated in the IPO prospectuses, we realize that these stipulated expiry dates are clearly inappropriate cut-off points for companies with directors selling prior to that date, that is, companies that were likely granted an early release from the lockup by their underwriters. Therefore, we also estimate a probit model that aims to predict the probability of directors' selling prior to the stipulated expiry date: the dependent variable *Sales2* equals one for any company that reports sales transactions by its directors prior to the earliest expiry date stated in its IPO prospectus. While there still is a marginally significant effect of the share price run-up variable, there is now also a significant positive effect of the duration of the lockup agreement, in line with hypothesis 3(a). In addition, the coefficient on the dummy adjusting for the type of the expiry date, which is coded one if the expiry date is absolute and zero if it is relative (or a combination of absolute and relative), is now significant and negative. This suggests that companies with absolute lockup expiry dates are less likely to have directors sell shares before the expiry.

Finally, we re-estimate the probit model focusing on effective (rather than stipulated) expiry dates. Specifically, in model (3), we set the dependent variable *Sales3* as unity for any company that reports directors' sales prior to and up to week eight after the expiry of the earliest lockup agreement of directors. While the results are more similar to those from Model (1), in that there are positive share-price run-up and size effects, there is now also a significant and positive impact of VC backing. Also the t-statistics for the coefficients on lockup duration, underpricing and expiry type are now substantially larger, with the former two coefficients having the sign as predicted by hypotheses 3(a) and 3(c), respectively. However, the coefficients on these variables are still not statistically significant at conventional levels.

To summarize, there is some limited support for hypotheses 3(a) and 3(c) relating to the impact of lockup duration and IPO underpricing on post-expiry director selling. However, hypothesis 3(b) relating to the fraction of shares locked up by insiders must be rejected. In contrast, there is strong support for Hypothesis 4, the impact of the run-up in the price of the company stock. By contrast, there is no support for Hypothesis 5 on the role of the volatility of the stock. If the pre-IPO shareholders float the stock to diversify their portfolios (following the lockup expiry), then we expect insiders/directors to take account not only of stock performance but also of stock volatility. However, this latter proposition is not supported by the results of this study and we therefore reject hypothesis 5.

6 CONCLUSION

The directors, managers and other initial shareholders of most UK IPOs are subject to agreements which prevent them from selling their shares for a specified period. The terms of the lockup agreement, including the expiry date, are disclosed in the IPO prospectus. During the lockup period only a fraction of the shares outstanding can trade. On the expiry day, the directors and other locked-in shareholders are then suddenly allowed to sell. This can have a potentially large influence on the supply of shares in the market and the stock performance around the event.

We analyse a sample of 233 IPOs on the London Stock Exchange from 1992 to 1998. We find that there is directors' selling before the lockup expiry. This is in line with previous findings for the US (Brav and Gompers, 2003). Moreover, the increase in sales in the weeks immediately after the lockup expiry is substantial.

However, we find that the average cumulative abnormal return around the lockup expiry is not significantly different from zero irrespective of the type of expiry date and directors' selling activity around the expiry date. Nevertheless, in the UK, examining stock performance around the lockup expiry is not straightforward as two-thirds of lockup agreements are linked to corporate events, which while falling into specific periods, do not have clear dates. We find that, surprisingly, the subsample of companies with directors' sales has positive average cumulative abnormal returns at the lockup expiry whereas the subsample of companies without sales has negative abnormal returns. Moreover, the difference in abnormal returns between the two subsamples is significant. This aspect warrants further research.

We also attempt to explain the likelihood of directors' sales occurring during the period spanning from the week of the expiry of the lockup agreement to eight weeks later. Contrary to expectations, our results show the likelihood of directors' sales is unrelated to the features of the lockup agreement or to IPO underpricing. However, allowing for the effective expiry date to be different from that stipulated in the IPO prospectus, we do find some support for an effect of the lockup duration, the choice of expiry date, and IPO underpricing. Finally, returning to the example of Facebook, we found no evidence supporting the argument that, overall, sales by directors cause a drop in share price at the lockup expiry.

NOTES

1. See 'Facebook shares fall to new lows as lockup ends', *Wall Street Journal*, 16, August 2012.
2. See 'Early Facebook investor Peter Thiel unloads stake', *Wall Street Journal*, 20 August 2012.
3. In the US, the definition of insiders includes officers, directors, other key employees and shareholders holding more than 10 per cent of any equity class (Lakonishok and Lee, 2001).
4. For more details see Espenlaub et al. (2001), tables 14.2–14.4.
5. Companies that publish quarterly results are subject to a close period of 30 days before the publication of the quarterly results.
6. The Model Code also takes into consideration dealings in exceptional circumstances and dealings by connected persons, investment managers and relevant employees. In 1994, the Criminal Justice Act of 1993, which prohibits insider trading, was appended to The Model Code. The Model Code is included in chapter 9 ('Continuing obligations') of the Listing Rules.
7. The method is described in detail in Table 14.A1.
8. These results are not reported in the table but available from the authors.

9. The results for the abnormal returns at the expiry for the full sample and the two subsamples are robust to changes in the research design, specifically to controls for risk and thin trading. Results based on the market model and using Scholes-Williams adjusted betas are qualitatively identical; they are not reported but are available from the authors.

REFERENCES

Aggarwal. R.K., L. Krigman and K.L. Womack (2002), 'Strategic IPO underpricing, information momentum, and lockup expiration selling', *Journal of Financial Economics*, **66**, 105–37.
Bolton, P. and E.-L. von Thadden (1998), 'Liquidity and control: a dynamic theory of corporate ownership structure', *Journal of Institutional and Theoretical Economics*, **154**, 177–211.
Bradley, D.J., B.D. Jordan, I.C. Roten and H.C. Yi (2001), 'Venture capital and IPO lockup expiration: an empirical analysis', *Journal of Financial Research*, **24**, 465–92.
Brau, J.C., D.A. Carter, S.E. Christophe and K.G. Key (2004), 'Market reaction to the expiration of IPO lockup provisions', *Managerial Finance*, **30**, 87–103.
Brav, A. and P.A. Gompers (2003), 'The role of lockups in initial public offerings', *Review of Financial Studies*, **16**, 1–29.
Espenlaub, S., M. Goergen and A. Khurshed (2001), 'IPO lock-in agreements in the UK', *Journal of Business Finance and Accounting*, **28**, 1235–78.
Fidrmuc, J.P., M. Goergen and L. Renneboog (2006), 'Insider trading, news releases, and ownership concentration', *Journal of Finance*, **61**, 2931–73.
Field, L.C. and G. Hanka (2001), 'The expiration of IPO share lockups', *Journal of Finance*, **56**, 471–500.
Goergen, M., L. Renneboog and A. Khurshed (2006), 'Explaining the diversity in shareholder lockup agreements', *Journal of Financial Intermediation*, **15**, 254–80.
Lakonishok, J. and I. Lee (2001), 'Are insiders' trades informative?', *Review of Financial Studies*, **14**, 79–112.
Levis, M. (1995), 'Seasoned equity offerings and the short- and long-run performance of initial public offerings in the UK', *European Financial Management*, **1**, 125–46.
Mohan, N.J. and C.R. Chen (2001), 'Information content of lock-up provisions in initial public offerings', *International Review of Economics and Finance*, **10**, 41–59.
Ofek, E. and M. Richardson (2000), 'The IPO lockup period: implications for market efficiency and downward sloping demand curves', working paper, Stern School of Business, New York University.
Park, S., H.J. Jang and M.P. Loeb (1995), 'Insider trading activity surrounding annual earnings announcements', *Journal of Business Finance and Accounting*, **22**, 587–614.
The London Stock Exchange Listing Rules (Purple Book).
Vismara, S., S. Paleari and J.R. Ritter (2012), 'Europe's second markets for small companies', *European Financial Management*, **18**, 352–88.

APPENDIX

For all the companies in the sample, which could be found on Factiva, regardless of the type of their lockup expiry date, earnings announcement dates, in some cases for a few subsequent years, were collected. Furthermore, the dates when the auditors signed accounts as true and fair were collected from the published annual accounts for the same companies. Finally, those two dates were compared. The results are presented in Table 14.A1.

It is clear from the table in more than 65 per cent of all the cases that were examined the date of earnings announcement and the date when the auditors signed the accounts as true and fair differ slightly. Nevertheless, in almost 77 per cent of the cases those two events occurred in the same week.

Table 14.A1 Comparison of earnings announcements (EAs) dates and dates when auditors signed the accounts

The date of EA and the date auditors signed the accounts	Number of cases	Percentage	Cumulative Percentage
Same day	19	36.54	36.54
Within a day	15	28.85	65.38
Within a week	6	11.54	76.92
Week–month	8	15.38	92.31
More than a month	4	7.69	100.00
Total	52	100.00	

15 Venture capital and IPO waves in Europe: an analysis of firm and performance characteristics
Wolfgang Bessler and Martin Seim

1 INTRODUCTION[1]

Venture capital (VC) is one of the most important financing sources for entrepreneurial start-up firms. A large body of theoretical and empirical literature documents venture capitalists' ability to carefully screen new ventures, monitor management and provide strategic and operating advice to their portfolio firms (Gompers and Lerner, 1999; Metrick and Yasuda, 2011). In addition, venture capitalists mitigate information asymmetries between the entrepreneur and the VC firm as well as between the VC firm and its investors (Sahlman, 1990). Venture capital-financed firms also grow more rapidly and have higher survival probabilities compared to non-VC-financed firms, demonstrating the importance of venture capital for economic growth (Jain and Kini, 2000; Bessler et al., 2012d; Puri and Zarutskie, 2012). This is supported by the observation that an increase in employment and new job creation is strongly related to the growth rate of start-up firms but not to small firms per se (Haltiwanger et al., 2010). To raise sufficient venture capital in an economy, however, VC firms must have profitable exit opportunities. Historically, the preferred exit channel for VC firms was to take their portfolio firms public. In this case, venture capitalists sold their shares in the stock market either at the time of the initial public offering (IPO) or in the secondary market later on (Brav and Gompers, 2003). The profitability and success of this exit strategy strongly depends on the intrinsic value of the portfolio firm but also on investor sentiment and the development of capital markets. Moreover, a vibrant venture capital industry is a prerequisite for successful VC exit strategies (Black and Gilson, 1998).

The focus of this study is on European firms that went public between 1996 and 2010 and were backed by a reputable venture capitalist. In contrast to existing studies that either cover a shorter sample period or focus on specific countries or different IPO subgroups, our study provides an empirical analysis of the going public activity of venture-backed firms for 14 European countries. We analyze firm characteristics as well as underpricing and long-run performance differences between two IPO waves and stock market cycles. The first IPO wave covers the 'new economy' period from 1996 to 2003, while the second wave spans the period between 2003 and 2010.

While we focus on the last two VC and IPO waves in Europe, it is still important for our research question to compare the IPO activity in Europe to that in other regions such as the US and Asia (China, Hong Kong and Singapore) to provide a perspective on future IPO activity. Therefore, we present in Figure 15.1 the IPO activity in Europe, the US, and Asia for the period from 1980 to 2010. The graphs reveal that during the last three decades two major IPO waves occurred in the US (1980–87 and 1991–2000) with low IPO activity and no pronounced wave thereafter. Two IPO waves occurred in

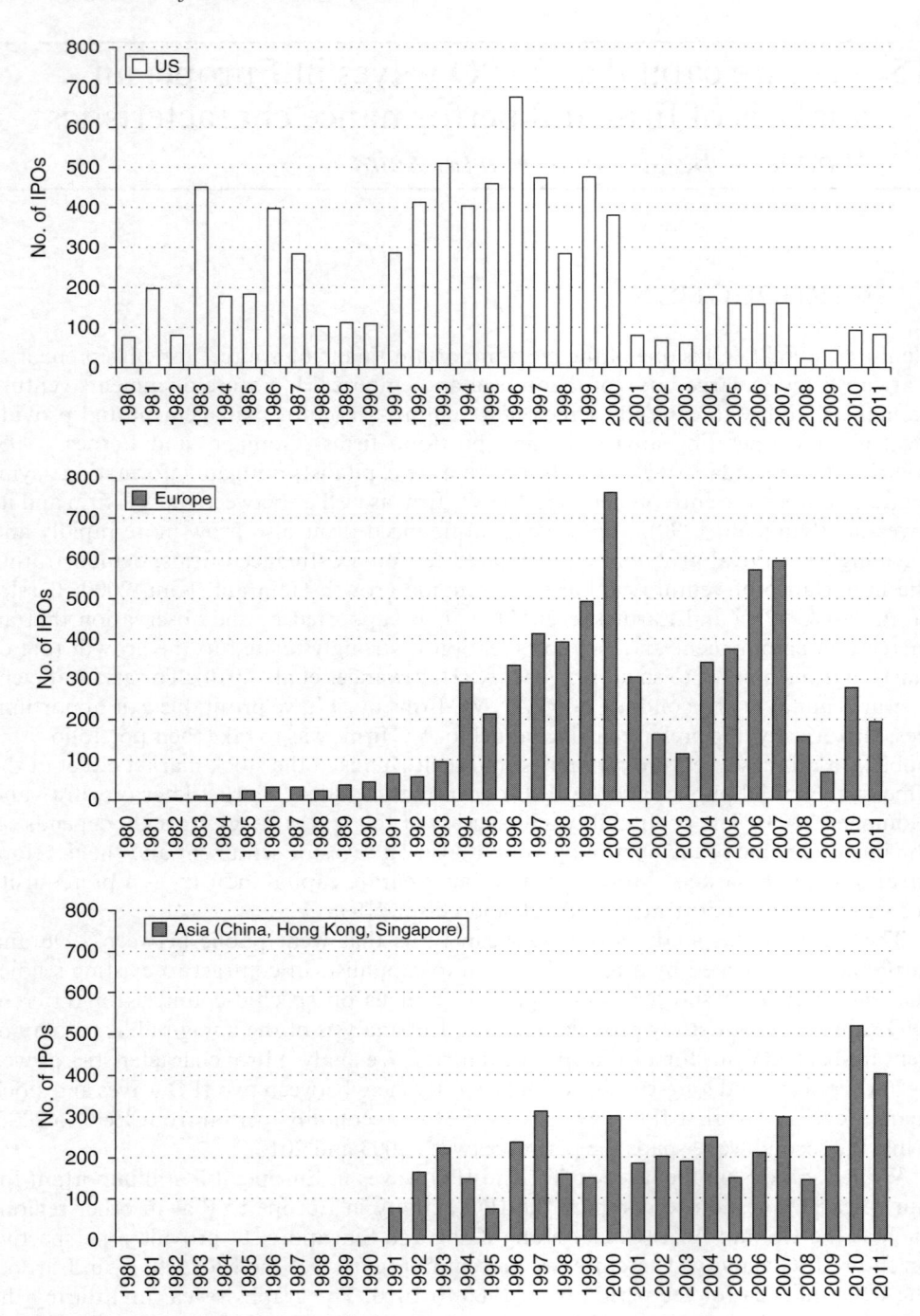

Figure 15.1 IPO waves in the US, Europe, and Asia (China, Hong Kong, Singapore)

Europe (1994–2001 and 2004–08) with low IPO activity since then. Finally, there was also a higher IPO activity in Asia since 1992 which started to gain a stronger momentum in recent years.

Figure 15.1 underscores the recent evidence on the dramatically declining IPO activity in the US during the past decade (Gao et al., 2011) and the still strong IPO activity in Europe during the same period (Vismara, et al., 2012). This dramatic decline in the US during the last decade has been viewed as an 'IPO crisis', because it appears that going public has lost its appeal and importance as an exit route during the last decade. A number of factors may have contributed to this 'IPO crisis': significant changes in regulation following the Enron debacle, a reduction of both analyst coverage and number of analysts due to severe conflicts of interest in the investment banking industry as well as a rapidly increasing market share of high-frequency trading that is concentrated in larger and liquid stocks (Weild and Kim, 2009, 2010). While regulatory changes may have prevented small capitalization firms from going public and may have contributed to the decline in the number of IPO in the US, Gao et al. (2011, p. 5) suggest that 'firms are being acquired rather than going public because in many industries a small firm is worth more as part of a larger organization than as an independent firm, whether it is public or private'. Gao et al. (2011) even predict that the IPO volume in the US will not return to the levels of the 1980s and 1990s. However, these results run counter to the IPO activities in Europe, because Europe still experienced an IPO wave during the past decade, including a substantial number of venture-backed IPOs. In fact, we document a slightly increasing number of venture-backed IPOs in the post-'new economy' period.

Our empirical findings for IPOs in Europe are as follows: comparing first (1996–2003) and second wave (2003–08), we find that first wave IPOs are more heavily underpriced and exhibit a superior stock price performance during the first year after going public. First-cycle IPOs are more risky, have higher market-to-book ratios, and higher pre-IPO market values, thereby reflecting investors' (over-)optimism in the first period. In contrast, second-cycle IPOs (2003–10) are older when going public, are taken public after significant overall stock market increases, and, most importantly, outperform first-cycle IPOs in terms of operating performance up to three years after going public. These findings suggest that during the first period venture capitalists were financially more successful in taking their portfolio firms public. During the second IPO wave, venture capitalists only sold the more profitable portfolio firms in the public equity markets. This result can be mainly inferred from the significantly superior operating performance of second-cycle IPOs. In addition, second-cycle IPO are also larger in terms of total assets and exhibit larger research and development (R&D) spending which might indicate a higher long-run success. Although the second IPO wave was characterized by better economic conditions, valuation multiples seemed more appropriate and realistic compared to first-cycle IPOs. Interestingly, our results for Europe differ from recent evidence for the US especially with regard to firm profitability and IPO activity.

The remainder of the chapter is organized as follows. In section 2 we briefly review the literature on venture capital (2.1.), initial public offerings (2.2), and the interaction between venture capital and IPOs (2.3). Section 3 describes our dataset. We present the methodology and the results on underpricing and long-run performance in section 4. Section 5 contains a detailed analysis of the determinants of short- and long-run returns and explores the differences of firm characteristics of venture-backed IPOs between both periods, while section 6 provides additional robustness tests. In Section 7 we offer our perspective on future IPO activity and its consequences. Section 8 concludes.

2 LITERATURE REVIEW

2.1 Importance of Venture Capital

Theoretical and empirical research on venture capital highlights its importance for start-up firms and economic growth. The ability of venture capital firms to select promising ventures, to provide strategic advice to entrepreneurs, and to monitor these firms efficiently should all contribute to the success of VCs' portfolio firms (Barry et al., 1990; Sahlman, 1990; Gompers and Lerner, 1999; Metrick and Yasuda, 2011). Consequently, venture capitalists' involvement usually results in higher growth rates and increases the survival probability of venture-backed compared to non-venture-backed firms (Jain and Kini, 2000; Bessler et al., 2012d; Puri and Zarutskie, 2012). In addition, venture capitalists support innovation, patenting activity and patent quality, and contribute significantly to the creation of new firms and employment (Kortum and Lerner, 2000; Lerner et al., 2011; Bernstein, 2012).

Traditionally, there have been substantial differences between the US and the European venture capital industries. In the US, high-quality capital markets supported the success and growth of the venture capital industry and offered thriving exit opportunities (Black and Gilson, 1998). In contrast, the exit opportunities were less developed in Europe for decades. However, the opening of new stock market segments for entrepreneurial and technology start-ups in many European countries (for example, Germany, France, and Italy) between 1996 and 2000 resulted in attractive exit opportunities for venture capitalists and other early-stage investors. This growth of European venture capital markets narrowed the gap between the US and Europe (Bessler et al. 2010; Da Rin et al., 2006). Nevertheless, it seems that US venture capitalists still outperform their European counterparts, which is often attributed to differences in the contracting behavior and access to expert knowledge of US venture capitalists as opposed to VCs in Europe (Hege et al., 2009).

Especially in the US, going public as the preferred exit route for venture capitalists may have been negatively affected by the regulatory changes that have occurred as a consequence of the 'new economy' bubble and other market irregularities such as the Enron scandal and conflicts of interest in the investment banking industry. Since then trade sales have become the preferred exit route for venture capital firms. In the US, the share of IPOs relative to trade sales and secondaries as an exit route dramatically declined from roughly 40 percent to below 20 percent subsequent to economy period (NVCA, 2010; Schwienbacher, 2010; Sousa, 2010; Gao et al., 2011). Moreover, Lerner (2011) and Kaplan and Lerner (2010) note that the evolution of venture capital and private equity over the next years is uncertain, which might negatively affect the size of the VC industry. In Europe, investments rapidly increased over time, whereas exits remained roughly at the same level before and after the 'new economy', reflecting 'a recipe for low realized returns and unhappy investors', at least over the last decade (Lerner, 2011, p. 11). Nevertheless, a substantial number of venture capitalists in the 'new economy' Europe still exit their portfolio firms by taking them public. Overall, the positive role of venture capitalists should be reflected in moderate initial returns as well as in a superior long-run operating and financial performance of IPOs.

2.2 Initial Public Offerings

There is an immense body of theoretical and empirical literature on initial public offerings which focuses on motives and ownership structures, underpricing and long-run financial and operating performance, hot and cold issue markets, lock-up periods, agency problems in underwriter and analyst behavior, and, of course, the benefits of venture capitalists' involvement (for a review see Ritter, 2002). Since the most important current topics on IPOs are addressed in other chapters of this book, in this section we focus only on those issues that are closely related to our own research questions. These are venture capital cycles and IPO waves as well as empirical evidence on IPOs in European countries.

During the past decade there has been growing evidence that financing and investment activities of firms occur in waves. Whether this suggests herd behavior or market timing abilities of management remains an open question. Our research contributes to the existing literature on corporate financing waves by analyzing venture capital cycles and IPO waves in Europe and by relating our findings to those for the US and Asia (see Figure 15.1). While some research on investment and financing waves focuses on merger and acquisition (M&A) activities (Andrade et al., 2001; Rhodes-Kropf et al., 2005; Alexandridis et al., 2012; Bessler and Zimmermann, 2012a) or seasoned equity offerings (Choe et al., 1993), others report that share repurchases also occur in waves (Dittmar and Dittmar, 2008). Whether IPOs also occur in waves is examined by Ritter (1984) and Lowry (2003) for the US. An integrating perspective of these different corporate financing waves is provided by Rau and Stouraitis (2011). Hence, analyzing whether IPOs in Europe occur in waves and whether there are significant differences in firm characteristics and performance of IPOs between these waves is an important but unexplored issue.

Although IPOs in Europe have been analyzed in a number of studies, most research focuses on a single country instead of Europe as an integrated financial market. Given that financial markets and economic activities as well as the legal environment were only partially integrated in Europe before the introduction of a common currency in 2000, it is not surprising that country studies dominate in the literature up to recently. For Germany, for example, Tykvová (2003), Bessler and Kurth (2007), Bessler and Bittelmeyer (2008), Bessler and Stanzel (2009) as well as Bessler et al. (2012a) investigate IPOs with respect to various issues such as venture capital, lock-up periods, innovation and patents, analyst behavior as well as share repurchases. For France, Goergen et al. (2009) analyze the determinants for underpricing of IPOs and Meoli et al. (2010) and Bonardo et al. (2011) study the valuation and performance of IPOs for Italy, whereas Levis (2011) and Appadu et al. (2012) 'among others' examine private equity and the financial policy and performance of IPOs in the UK. An earlier study on European IPOs by Gajewski and Gresse (2006) ends in 2004 and does not distinguish between IPO waves. In particular, the extreme valuations during the new economy bubble are not examined separately. Vismara et al. (2012) analyze IPOs in Europe from 1995 to 2009, but their emphasis is on junior market segments. In recent studies, Bessler and Seim

(2012) and Bessler et al. (2012d) analyze the underpricing and the long-run performance of venture-backed IPOs relative to non-ventured-backed IPOs in Europe as well as the survival probability relative to private equity-backed IPOs. The influence of going public on corporate growth strategies, that is, external or internal growth, is analyzed in Bessler and Zimmermann (2012b). Overall, it seems of interest to gain more insights and empirical evidence of the importance of venture capital cycles and IPO waves as well as a better understanding of the interaction between VC exit strategies and IPO activities in Europe.

2.3 Venture Capital and Initial Public Offerings

Given venture capitalists' unique experience in advising and monitoring start-up firms, VC-backing should provide a positive signal to outside investors and VC investments should certify the value of their portfolio firms. Certification may also be conducted by the underwriter in the primary as well as the secondary market (Carter et al., 1998; Bradley et al., 2008; Bessler and Stanzel, 2009; Dong et al., 2011) and even by the IPO's larger customers (Johnson et al., 2010). This positive certification role of venture capitalists should be reflected in a lower underpricing of venture-backed compared to non-venture-backed IPOs (Megginson and Weiss, 1991; Brav and Gompers, 1997). Moreover, there is evidence that venture capitalists significantly contribute to the development of entrepreneurial firms over their life cycle by offering strategic and operational advice even beyond the IPO, which should also lead to superior long-run returns and performance of venture-backed IPOs (Lerner, 1994; Gompers and Lerner, 1998; Doukas and Gonenc, 2005). These empirical results suggest superior skills of venture capitalists and also reflect their ability of monitoring and supporting companies. However, this role may be limited to experienced venture capitalists (Barry et al., 1990), and the superior performance of venture-backed IPOs may hold only for the period up to the end of the lock-up period (Brav and Gompers, 2003). Given that European venture capital firms are often perceived as being relatively inexperienced and differences in VC reputation are hardly noticeable, at least during the earlier years of our sample period, the certification role of venture capital in some European countries such as Germany appears to some extent questionable (Bessler and Kurth, 2007), although there is some recent evidence of the superior performance of venture-backed IPOs in Europe (Bessler and Seim, 2012).

In contrast, Francis and Hasan (2001) and Lee and Wahal (2004) document larger initial returns for venture-backed IPOs while Abukari and Jog (2011) do not find differences in the long-run performance of VC- and non-VC-backed IPOs. In support of these findings, Gompers (1996) argues that some VCs take their portfolio firms public when market conditions are favorable, following a relatively short investment period. This approach allows them to accelerate fund raising for new investments and to generate considerable returns for their investors. According to this 'grandstanding' hypothesis, younger venture capitalists bear the cost of high underpricing in order to build up reputation relative to more experienced VC firms. Therefore, given that European venture capitalists appear to be less sophisticated compared to their US counterparts (Hege et al., 2009), grandstanding might be more pronounced in the European venture capital industry (Tykvová, 2003). Moreover, the findings of Hsu (2010) corroborate the grandstanding hypothesis in that venture capitalists generally shorten incubation periods, that is, the time interval for which venture capitalists stay invested prior to an IPO. Hence, stronger incentives to grandstand should lead to inferior long-run performance and decreasing survival rates of these IPOs as documented by Hamza and Kooli (2011).

Based on this literature it seems fair to conclude that the research on venture capital, initial public offerings and the interaction between venture capital and initial public offerings in Europe has increased during the last decade. However, most studies focus on specific countries or aspects and hence there is little European-wide empirical evidence on the importance of venture capital and its impact on market valuation (underpricing) and long-run-performance of venture-backed IPOs. We therefore analyze the performance of venture capital-backed IPOs for a group of European countries over an extended time period and compare our findings to those for the US.

3 DATA AND SAMPLE OVERVIEW

This study is based on an initial sample of more than 400 venture-backed European firms that went public on European stock exchanges between January 1996 and June 2010. This period includes two complete stock market cycles and IPO waves and ends with the financial crisis. The IPO data is from Thomson One and is matched with information from the VentureXpert database. Only firms that were backed by a reputable venture capitalist are included. Thus, the venture capital firms are either a member of the European Venture Capital Association (EVCA) or of the major national venture capital organizations in Europe. We excluded those IPOs with inconsistent information in Thomson One and VentureXpert. Stock returns and balance sheet data are collected from Thomson Datastream and are all converted into euros. Additional information on a country's venture capital investment relative to gross domestic product (GDP) is provided by EVCA. We follow the usual approach in the academic finance literature and exclude all firms from the banking and insurance sector (for example, 4-digit SIC code 6000), because they are differently regulated. We also exclude penny stocks (that are, all IPOs with an offer price of less than €1). This leaves us with a final sample of 382 venture-backed IPOs. For these IPOs we are able to calculate the underpricing which, from the investors' perspective, is the initial or first day return. Calculating long-run returns (buy-and-hold return – BHR) and long-run performance (buy-and-hold abnormal return – BHAR) requires stock return data for at least 750 trading days, that is, three years after the IPO. This requirement reduces the sample size to 363 venture-backed IPOs. For the European market and country indices we use the Datastream European market and country indices prior to 2001 and the Morgan Stanley Capital International (MSCI) Europe market and country indices after 1 January 2001. This approach had to be used because the MSCI Europe market and country indices are, on a monthly basis, only available prior to 2001. The annual distribution of the number of IPOs together with a broad European stock market index is presented in Figure 15.2. The number of IPOs closely follows the stock market performance. It appears that venture capitalists took their portfolio firms public especially during the 'new economy' period, at the end of the 1990s, and in the period from 2005 to 2007. These were environments of generally positive market sentiment that offered successful listings and exit opportunities.

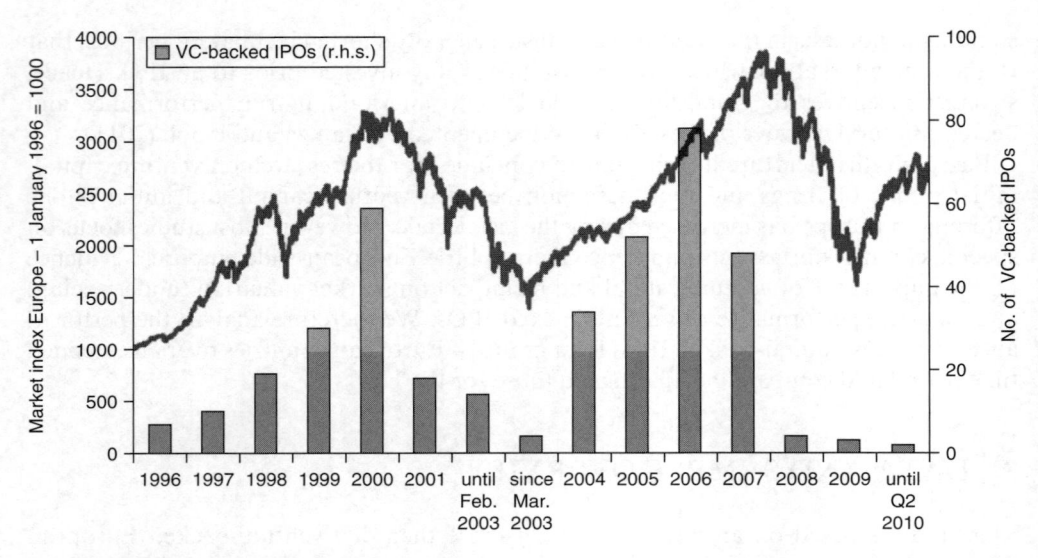

Figure 15.2   Number of VC-backed IPOs over time and European stock market index

To analyze the differences between the two stock market cycles and IPO waves, we partition our sample into two groups. As a breakpoint we use March 2003, which was the month of the lowest stock market level in Europe during that period. All venture-backed firms that went public prior to March 2003 belong to the first IPO wave, while portfolio firms that went public later than February 2003 are part of the second cycle. Therefore, the first IPO wave spans the time period from 1996 to early 2003, including the 'new economy' period. In this time period, we first observe an increase in the annual number of firms going public of up to nearly 60 IPOs in the year 2000. This number decreases to less than 20 venture-backed IPOs in 2001 and even falls below 10 IPOs in 2003. The second IPO wave shows similar dynamics with the number of IPOs strongly increasing since 2004. In 2006, nearly 80 European firms that were backed by a reputable venture capitalist went public on European exchanges. Interestingly, the following decrease in IPO activity is, in relative terms, even more dramatic than during the 'new economy' period. During the financial crisis in 2008 and 2009, only a small number of firms went public, probably due to investor pessimism and low confidence in financial markets, but also due to the low stock market valuations. On a relative basis, the figure for 2008 is only about 10 percent of the number of IPOs in 2006. Therefore, at a first glance, we observe two pronounced IPO waves and stock market cycles. The interesting research question and the main focus of our empirical analysis is whether these periods are similar or whether there are significant differences between both periods with respect to underpricing, short- and long-run performance, and firm characteristics.

The empirical analysis is divided into two parts. First, we perform some univariate tests on underpricing and long-run performance. Second, we conduct multivariate analyses to provide evidence on the impact of firm characteristics on performance, and to test whether there are significant differences in firm characteristics across both IPO waves.

4 UNDERPRICING AND LONG-RUN PERFORMANCE

4.1 Methodology

Underpricing is defined as the return an investor realizes by getting shares allocated in the primary market and selling them in the secondary market at the end of the first day of trading. Hence, underpricing (UP) for firm i is the percentage change from the offer price $P_{i,OP}$ to the closing price $P_{i,CP}$ on the first trading day (Loughran and Ritter, 2004; Ritter, 1984):

$$UP_i = \frac{P_{i,CP} - P_{i,OP}}{P_{i,OP}} \qquad (15.1)$$

For the regression analyses we also calculated three day and five day initial returns. The long-run performance of IPO firms is analyzed by calculating buy-and-hold abnormal returns on a daily basis:

$$BHAR = \frac{1}{n}\sum_{i=1}^{n}\left[\left(\prod_{t=1}^{T}(1+R_{i,t})\right) - \left(\prod_{t=1}^{T}(1+R_{M,t})\right)\right] \qquad (15.2)$$

Abnormal returns are calculated from the second trading day until 750 trading days (about three years) after the IPO. The BHAR performance compares the average performance of a buy-and-hold investment in a portfolio consisting of all IPOs to the buy-and-hold investment in an appropriate benchmark portfolio. As our analysis consists of IPOs that are listed on different European exchanges, country-specific risk and return characteristics are controlled for by using country-specific benchmarks. Therefore, we use the local MSCI indices to calculate the BHAR. As MSCI indices are available only on a monthly basis prior to January 2001, we use information from Datastream to calculate the daily returns of country indices for the period from 1996 to 2000. As a robustness check we replicated our calculations using the MSCI Europe as the benchmark index. The results remain qualitatively the same. Because some IPOs delist or are acquired within three years after going public, the required return data is not available for 750 trading days. In these cases the returns of IPOs are set equal to the respective market index after the delisting date. Consequently, the weight of each of the remaining IPOs does not change and the sample size remains the same for the whole period of 750 trading days. As another robustness check we also repeated our calculations by dropping dead stocks from the portfolio and calculating BHAR with the remaining IPOs. Again, the results do not change qualitatively. Because some IPO firms, especially those that went public on the 'new markets' in Europe, are characterized by some extreme returns, it is important to Winsorize the raw returns as well as the abnormal returns at the upper and lower 1 percent (and alternatively at the 2 percent) percentiles of the return distribution.

To test for statistical significance, we employ a bootstrapped version of the skewness adjusted t-test in order to correct for the positive skewness in UP and in $BHAR$. Following Lyon et al. (1999), we draw 1000 samples of size $m = n/4$ to calculate the critical values of the transformed t-statistic:

304   *Handbook of research on IPOs*

$$t_{sa} = \sqrt{m}\left(S + \frac{1}{3}\hat{\gamma}S^2 + \frac{1}{6m}\hat{\gamma}\right), \tag{15.3}$$

with

$$S = \frac{\overline{AR_\tau}}{\sigma(AR_\tau)} \quad \text{and} \quad \hat{\gamma} = \frac{\sum_{i=1}^{m}(AR_{i,\tau} - \overline{AR_\tau})^3}{m\sigma(AR_\tau)^3}. \tag{15.4}$$

In all tables we report the test statistics of the skewness adjusted *t*-test (indicated by t_{sa}) and the respective significance levels. This is complemented by the signed-rank test (z_{sign}) proposed by Wilcoxon (1945) which tests whether the median of the respective return distribution differs significantly from zero. In addition, a conventional two-sample *t*-test (t_{diff}) and the rank-sum test (z_{rank}) are used to test for differences between the two IPO waves.

4.2 Analysis of Underpricing and Long-run Performance

The size of the average annual underpricing is presented in Figure 15.3. Similar to the co-movement of the number of IPOs and the stock market index in Figure 15.2, the size of the underpricing also strongly fluctuates over time. Interestingly, the dynamics and positive correlation between the number of IPOs and the magnitude of the underpricing are much stronger during the first period. During the second period, underpricing substantially decreases and is much smaller compared to the results reported in other empirical studies covering many different countries during earlier periods (Ritter, 2003; Loughran and Ritter, 2004).

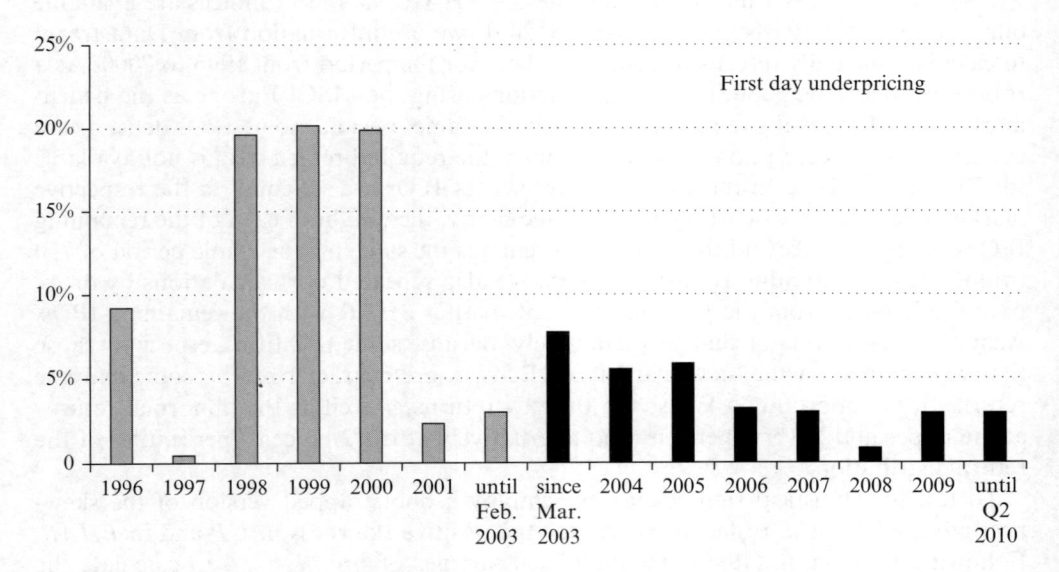

Figure 15.3   Underpricing of VC-backed IPOs according to year of IPO

Table 15.1 Descriptive statistics: underpricing

	Mean	Median	Std dev.	t_{sa}	z_{sign}	t_{diff}	z_{rank}
Panel A: One-day underpricing							
Full sample (n = 382)	8.47%	0.79%	23.95%	12.67***	8.19***	–	–
First cycle (n = 157)	14.64%	1.33%	34.89%	9.58***	5.82***	−3.68***	−2.05**
Second cycle (n = 225)	4.15%	0.53%	9.09%	7.63***	5.91***		
Panel B: Three-day underpricing							
Full sample (n = 382)	8.91%	1.26%	24.95%	10.86***	6.75***	–	–
First cycle (n = 157)	15.49%	4.91%	35.36%	7.87***	4.97***	−3.81***	−2.01**
Second cycle (n = 225)	4.32%	0.56%	11.69%	5.75***	4.77***		
Panel C: Five-day underpricing							
Full sample (n = 382)	9.26%	1.94%	26.51%	10.50***	6.31***	–	–
First cycle (n = 157)	15.99%	4.65%	37.35%	7.73***	4.68***	−3.67***	−1.94*
Second cycle (n = 225)	4.57%	1.19%	13.05%	5.68***	4.39***		

Note: * $p < 0.1$, ** $p < 0.05$, *** $p < 0.01$.

During the 'new economy' period, the highest level of underpricing or average initial returns was about 20 percent. During the second period, in contrast, underpricing ranged between 3 percent and 7 percent. Additionally, Table 15.1 provides test statistics of average initial returns measured over 1, 3, and 5 trading days. The first row of each of the three panels indicates that mean and median initial returns are significantly different from zero. For example, average 1, 3, and 5 day initial returns amount to 8.47 percent, 8.91 percent, and 9.26 percent, respectively. The median is always below the mean indicating that the return distribution is positively skewed and includes some extreme initial returns. Because underpricing is an important source of returns to pre-IPO investors and investors that got shares allocated at the time of the IPO, we analyze underpricing and long-run performance separately in the univariate as well as in the multivariate setting. This makes our research comparable to related studies that either investigate underpricing or long-run returns and performance.

In Figure 15.4 we present the BHR (solid line) and the BHAR (dashed line) excluding first day returns. In principle, both BHR and BHAR are similar in that the performance measures strongly increase up to the end of the first year (250 trading days). After one year most of the investors are allowed to exit from their investment due to the expiration of the lockup period. In some cases venture capital firms are even obliged to exit from their investment. Subsequently, the returns steadily decline up to the end of the 750-days holding period (that is, three years).

Table 15.2 shows the test statistics for BHR (panel A) and BHAR (panel B) for different holding periods. Again, the first row of each holding period includes the results for the full sample. As expected, for holding periods of 125 and 250 trading days, both performance measures indicate a significant outperformance, while for longer holding periods of 500 and 750 trading days the mean BHR and BHAR are not significantly different from zero. Interestingly, the test statistics of the signed-rank median test reveal that for the two- and three-year holding periods the median performance is significantly

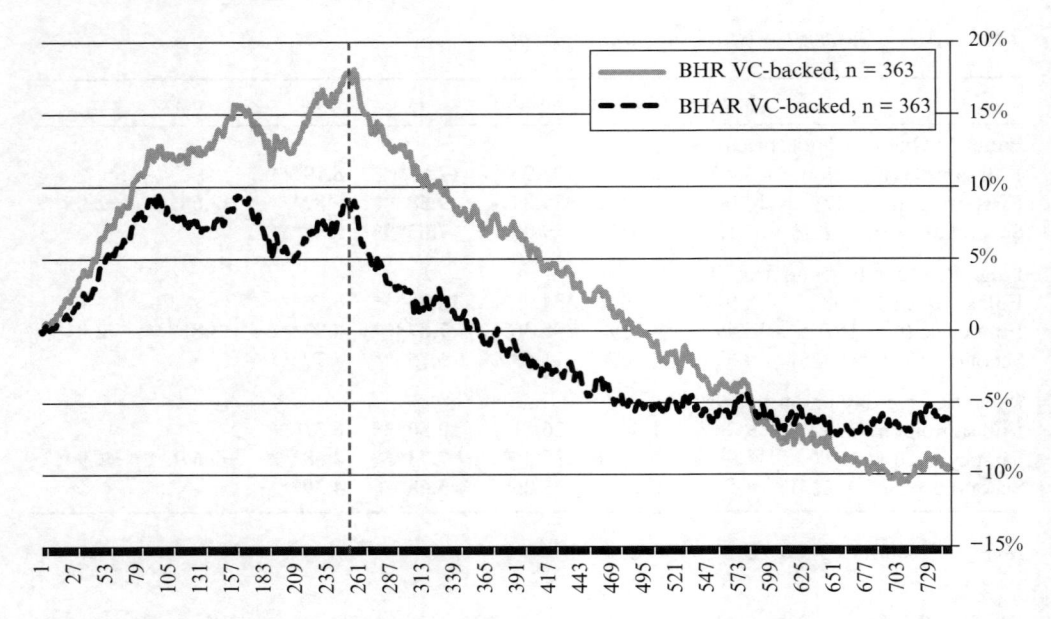

Figure 15.4 Long-run performance and abnormal performance of VC-backed IPOs

negative. But the most puzzling result is that for 250 trading days the mean BHAR of 8.71 percent is significantly positive, while the median BHAR of −9.18 percent is significantly negative. In spite of the Winsorization procedure, which should reduce the influence of outliers, the performance distributions are obviously extremely skewed. Because of this observation, we also Winsorized all returns at the upper and lower 2 percent percentiles. Although this reduced the magnitude of the peaks in the return series, the general patterns and conclusions remain the same. Overall, our results for the entire sample period from 1996 to mid-2010 reveal that venture-backed IPOs experience relatively high levels of underpricing and generate, at least for some time period after the IPO, positive returns.

4.3 Analysis of Different IPO Waves and Stock Market Cycles

Having investigated the full time period, we now focus on analyzing whether there are significant differences in the short- and long-run financial performance between the two IPO waves and stock market cycles. For this we partition our sample into the two stock market cycles. We find significant differences in underpricing as well as in long-run returns. Figure 15.2 and Table 15.1 clearly reveal the differences in underpricing between both IPO waves. Average and median levels of underpricing are significantly larger for first period IPOs for each of the three initial return intervals. For example, the underpricing for the first period is, on average, 14.65 percent, whereas it is only 4.15 percent for the second period. However, it seems that most of the differences in IPO underpricing are attributable to the hot market phase of the 'new economy' period (1998–2000). An analysis of the long-run performance also suggests substantial differences between both

Table 15.2   Descriptive statistics: long-run performance

	Mean	Median	Std dev.	t_{sa}	z_{sign}	t_{diff}	z_{rank}
Panel A: Buy-and-hold returns (BHR)							
125 trading days							
Full sample (n = 363)	12.70%	−1.78%	68.31%	**4.10***	0.93	–	–
First cycle (n = 157)	17.72%	−8.75%	94.40%	**2.63***	−0.67	−1.11	**2.70***
Second cycle (n = 206)	8.87%	1.50%	37.75%	**3.52***	**2.54**		
250 trading days							
Full sample (n = 363)	17.28%	−4.61%	99.83%	**3.85***	0.31	–	–
First cycle (n = 157)	20.28%	−17.86%	131.43%	**2.20**	−1.43	−0.46	**3.25***
Second cycle (n = 206)	15.00%	3.37%	66.64%	**3.89***	**2.22**		
500 trading days							
Full sample (n = 363)	−0.38%	−33.89%	112.08%	−0.03	**−4.08***	–	–
First cycle (n = 157)	−3.57%	−51.18%	144.27%	−0.23	**−4.12***	0.44	**4.12***
Second cycle (n = 206)	2.06%	−20.12%	79.55%	−0.40	−1.50		
750 trading days							
Full sample (n = 363)	−9.64%	−47.26%	112.62%	−1.40	**−5.60***	–	–
First cycle (n = 157)	−8.70%	−65.53%	137.54%	−0.66	**−3.41***	−0.13	**3.38***
Second cycle (n = 206)	−10.36%	−37.94%	89.43%	−1.49	**−4.40***		
Panel B: Buy-and-hold abnormal returns (BHAR)							
125 trading days							
Full sample (n = 363)	7.70%	−4.32%	63.59%	**2.51**	−1.33	–	–
First cycle (n = 157)	16.81%	−8.72%	86.96%	**2.74***	−0.59	**−2.18***	0.92
Second cycle (n = 206)	0.76%	−2.34%	35.68%	0.30	−0.90		
250 trading days							
Full sample (n = 363)	8.71%	−9.18%	91.47%	**1.95***	**−2.18**	–	–
First cycle (n = 157)	18.11%	−12.94%	118.73%	**2.15**	−1.51	−1.59	1.21
Second cycle (n = 206)	1.55%	−4.83%	62.69%	0.36	−1.28		
500 trading days							
Full sample (n = 363)	−7.62%	−17.00%	68.73%	−0.76	**−5.57***	–	–
First cycle (n = 157)	−1.65%	−41.05%	134.45%	−0.09	**−4.10***	−0.51	**2.71***
Second cycle (n = 206)	−5.03%	−25.03%	102.34%	−1.43	**−3.55***		
750 trading days							
Full sample (n = 363)	−6.33%	−28.56%	100.69%	−1.00	**−5.71***	–	–
First cycle (n = 157)	−1.88%	−35.02%	121.58%	−0.13	**−3.37***	−0.70	1.41
Second cycle (n = 206)	−9.72%	−21.25%	81.42%	−1.24	**−4.47***		

Note: * p < 0.1, ** p < 0.05, *** p < 0.01.

periods. This is illustrated in Figure 15.5 and Figure 15.6, where the BHR, are presented excluding and including underpricing, respectively.

The BHR at the end of the first year for the first IPO wave (solid line in Figure 15.5) is similar to the BHR of the second wave (dashed line). However, there are significant differences during the first year after the IPO. While the second period BHR monotonically increases to 15.00 percent during the 250 trading days, the first period BHR (20.28 percent after one year) exhibits some volatility and ups and downs over the first year period as well as for the other periods, which can be inferred from the statistics in

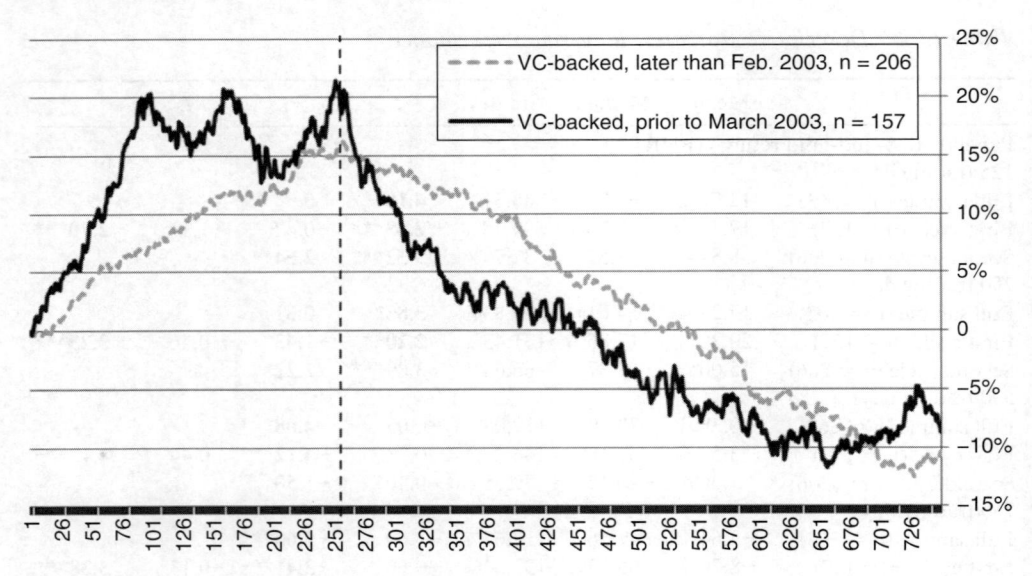

Figure 15.5   Long-run performance of VC-backed IPOs: excluding underpricing

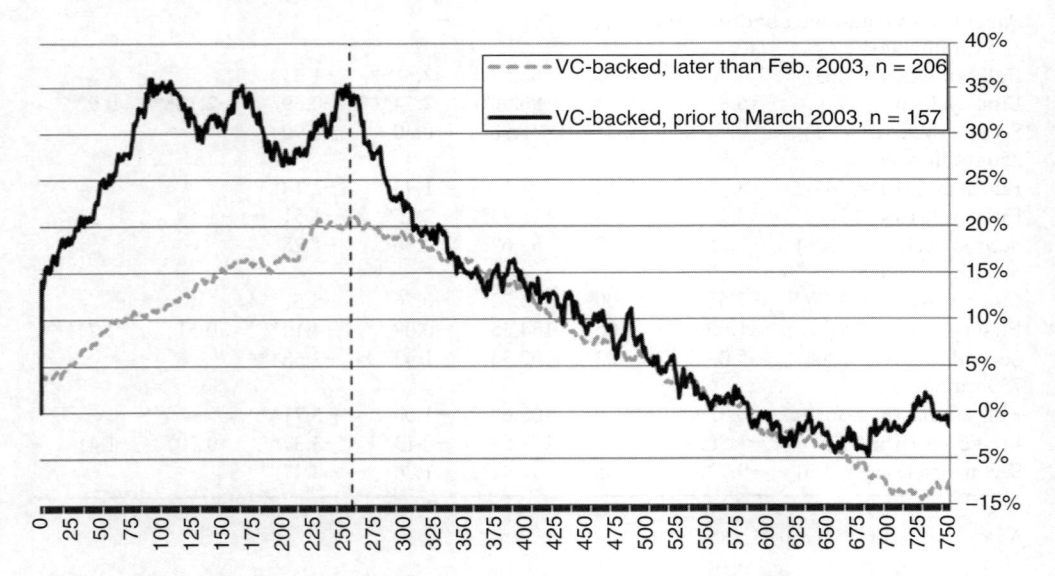

Figure 15.6   Long-run performance of VC-backed IPOs: including underpricing

Table 15.2. Therefore, the pronounced volatility in stock returns of first period IPOs probably accounts for the insignificant differences in the mean between both periods despite return differences of up to 9 percent for the 125 trading day interval. Moreover, the test statistics for the rank-sum test indicate that the median second period BHR is significantly larger compared to the first period IPOs for all holding periods (panel A of Table 15.2). Figure 15.6 shows the BHR including underpricing across both periods.

Most notably, there are no differences between first and second period IPOs beyond one year or 250 trading days. In contrast, the extraordinary performance differences during the first year of trading are obviously due to the magnitude of underpricing, which is significantly higher during the first period. In order to better understand the reasons for the performance distribution through time, we also analyze the reasons for the pronounced peaks of first cycle IPOs during the first year post IPO after 80, 125 and 250 trading days (the results are not reported here but are available on request). Our analysis reveals that the peaks are country specific in that the performance of VC-backed IPOs in the three largest capital markets in our sample, that is, the UK, France, and Germany, reach their peak level at these three holding period dates. Hence, we observe the weighted average of these three performance peaks.

From this analysis we can conclude that the major differences between the two periods are due to the fact that investors were either more optimistic during the first period or more pessimistic during the second period. This is especially true for the first year subsequent to the IPO, where first period IPOs have high initial returns and start trading at extreme premiums in the secondary market relative to their offering prices in the primary market. One possible explanation is that more private investors were actively involved during the first period and more institutional investors during the second period. Therefore, institutional investors and 'potentially' investment banks were less optimistic in the second period than during the first period, causing initial and first-year returns to be lower during the second IPO wave. However, in the long-run the returns appear to be quite similar. The reasons for these substantial differences in initial returns and long-run performance between both IPO waves are analyzed next.

5 FIRM CHARACTERISTICS

So far, our analysis revealed some notable differences in underpricing and long-run performance between both IPO waves in Europe. Consequently, these results suggest different market-wide factors and changing firm characteristics of venture-backed IPOs over time that might explain the differences in underpricing and long-run performance. We now analyze these effects in more detail in order to obtain further insights into the factors that influence both underpricing and long-run performance. First, the methodological framework is explained in section 5.1. Then, our results on IPO underpricing and long-run performance are related to the hypotheses discussed in the literature section. After analyzing the entire sample period, each sub-sample period is examined separately (section 5.2). Finally, the multivariate analyses (section 5.3) aim at detecting differences between the two IPO periods and the apparent changes in the exit behavior of venture capital firms. In particular, we investigate the pre and post IPO characteristics and the operating performance of our sample firms. Moreover, the outcome of section 5.2 and 5.3 allows us to analyze the interaction between financial and operating performance.

5.1 Cross-sectional Regressions and Logit Models

To explain the magnitude of the underpricing and long-run performance of IPO firms we employ ordinary least squares (OLS) cross-sectional regressions (15.5) and then compare our findings to previous studies. The respective performance measure of each firm (Y_i) is regressed on a constant, some binary dummies (D), and a set of explanatory variables in the matrix X.

$$Y_i = \beta_0 + \sum_{d=1}^{l} \beta_d D_{d,i} + \sum_{j=l+1}^{k} \beta_j X_{j,i}, \qquad (15.5)$$

We also employ logit regression models (15.6) to investigate the pre and post IPO firm characteristics that are important in differentiating venture-backed IPOs between both periods (Greene, 2011, p. 721ff.):

$$Prob(Y_i = 1) = \frac{e^{\beta_0 + \sum_{d=1}^{l} \beta_d D_{d,i} + \sum_{j=l+1}^{k} \beta_j X_{j,i}}}{1 + e^{\beta_0 + \sum_{d=1}^{l} \beta_d D_{d,i} + \sum_{j=l+1}^{k} \beta_j X_{j,i}}} \qquad (15.6)$$

In equation (15.6), Y_i is a binary variable that is set to 1 for venture-backed IPOs of the first period and is set to zero for the second period IPOs. As opposed to a probit specification, the logistic distribution has considerably heavier tails than the normal distribution and is therefore better suited to deal with the wide variation in some variables as is the case in our sample. In contrast to a univariate comparison of firm characteristics for distinguishing between the two time periods of venture-backed IPOs, this multivariate framework directly accounts for the correlation structure of the variables under investigation. As we compare the characteristics of IPOs over time we must not interpret the logit model in the sense of a binary choice model. Rather, our focus is on the multivariate comparisons across the two waves. To control for potential heteroskedasticity, we estimate both OLS and logit regressions with White (1984) standard errors. We also control for the presence of industry effects in both OLS and logit regressions and include dummy variables for IPOs from the technology sector according to the definition of Loughran and Ritter (2004), the manufacturing industry, and IPOs from the trade and services sectors. The variables that enter the different regression models are explained in Table 15.A1 in the Appendix to this chapter. We do not report the results for the industry dummies here as they are insignificant in virtually all cross-sectional and logit regressions. The only exception is that significantly more technology stocks went public during the first IPO wave compared to the second wave. However, this outcome was expected, given the objectives of these newly created stock market segments.

5.2 Determining Factors of Underpricing and Long-run Performance

5.2.1 Underpricing

We estimate cross-sectional regressions on IPO underpricing for one-, three-, and five-day initial returns. In Table 15.3 the results for the full sample (panel A) and for the two IPO sub-periods (panel B and panel C) are reported. The results in panel A reveal that IPO underpricing is significantly higher for companies that went public during the first hot market phase, covering the time period from 1998 to 2000. The dummy variable capturing the effects of the second hot market phase does not indicate higher initial returns for venture-backed IPOs during the period from 2005 to 2007. This is not surprising given the results from the descriptive analysis in Figure 15.2. Moreover, venture-backed

Table 15.3 Regression results: underpricing

	Dependent variable: underpricing (UP)									
	Panel A: full sample			Panel B: first cycle			Panel C: second cycle		
	1-day UP	3-day UP	5-day UP	1-day UP	3-day UP	5-day UP	1-day UP	3-day UP	5-day UP
Hot-dummy: 1998–2000	**0.1239*****	**0.1288*****	**0.1372*****	**0.1442*****	**0.1458*****	**0.1522*****			
Hot-dummy: 2005–07	−0.0094	−0.0113	−0.0079				−0.0145	−0.0196	−0.0151
VC invest. rel. GDP	**0.0562*****	**0.0846*****	**0.0856*****	0.0427	0.0831	0.0967	**0.0602*****	**0.0842*****	**0.0851*****
Main market dummy	−0.0222	−0.0329	−0.0294	−0.0558	−0.1058	−0.1015	0.0025	0.0241	0.0257
Market run-up	0.2227	0.2472	0.2706	0.2697	0.3383	0.3463	0.0529	−0.0384	0.0547
Return vola (ex-ante risk)	1.2839	**2.1364***	**2.3644***	1.1068	1.7682	2.0615	**1.5078****	**2.4309****	2.6505
Age	−0.0011	−0.0029	0.0040	−0.0001	−0.0104	0.0004	0.0007	0.0016	0.0046
Market-to-book	−0.0094	−0.0099	−0.0154	−0.0009	0.0024	−0.0104	−0.0084	−0.0118	−0.0167
Market value	0.0085	0.0123	0.0011	0.0306	0.0377	0.0170	−0.0033	−0.0034	−0.0088
Const	−0.0272	−0.0976	−0.0558	−0.1028	−0.2069	−0.1225	0.0141	−0.0296	−0.0092
Adj. R²	8.90%	12.85%	10.83%	−0.05%	6.30%	3.36%	9.07%	12.70%	10.47%
F-test	3.3112	3.2926	3.1341	2.2491	1.9425	1.841	3.3725	3.3272	2.8597
N	350	350	350	137	137	137	213	213	213

Note: * $p < 0.1$, ** $p < 0.05$, *** $p < 0.01$.

IPOs which experience substantial volatility in the secondary market returns during the first two months exhibit higher initial returns. This is especially true for the three- and five-day return windows. This finding is in line with the predictions of Beatty and Ritter (1986) and empirical results of Jog and Wang (2002) for Canada, who argue that high-risk stocks should exhibit higher underpricing. Finally, the lagged ratio of venture capital investment relative to GDP of the country in which the firm went public is positive and highly significant for all three underpricing measures. This observation is referred to as 'grandstanding' in the venture capital literature.

The 'grandstanding' hypothesis is based on the observation that when venture capital investment is at relatively high levels, VC firms might be encouraged to bring their portfolio firms earlier to the public equity market in order to liquidate their engagements and to return funds to their investors earlier, while bearing the cost of higher underpricing (Gompers, 1996; Lee and Wahal, 2004). The results for the 'new economy' period, with the opening of new stock market segments for young growth firms in Europe, are supported by findings for the grandstanding hypothesis in Asia. Hibara and Mathew (2004), for example, provide evidence for Japan in that subsequent to the opening of the new stock market segment, IPOs backed by less experienced VCs were younger when going public and were more underpriced. Indeed, one might argue that a venture capitalist would not take its portfolio firm public after this very short investment horizon of one year only.

Therefore, we ran the regressions with two-, three-, and four-year average investment to GDP ratios and the results became even stronger. However, we do not have time series information on investment to GDP prior to 1996. Hence, including longer lags would lead to a substantial reduction in the number of observations.

Turning to panel B and panel C, we find that only the hot market dummy for IPOs for the period from 1998 to 2000 has explanatory power for IPO underpricing (panel B). This provides further evidence for larger amounts of money left on the table according to Loughran and Ritter (2002). Interestingly, if the venture capital industry was less developed at the beginning of our sample period compared to the more recent IPO wave, grandstanding should be observable especially during the first IPO wave, because at that time venture capitalists should be more concerned about their reputation. In contrast, lagged venture capital investment exerts a positive and significant influence on underpricing, especially for second-period IPOs (panel C). Similarly, risk significantly increases underpricing of venture-backed IPOs in the second wave only.

Overall, we document that the differences in underpricing for second-period IPOs are related to common theories discussed in the venture capital and IPOs literature, while first-cycle underpricing is driven by the hot market phase from 1998 to 2000. At least to some extent, Loughran and Ritter's (2002) 'money left on the table' argument may explain underpricing of first cycle IPOs, because these firms do not seem to be aggressively bargaining about the offer price during the hot market phase. Consequently, we observe higher levels of underpricing. The strategies of the underwriter may explain this phenomenon as well. For the US, Goldstein et al. (2011) estimate that about US$82 billion were left on the table during the period between 1999 and 2005. Given the differences in IPO underpricing and initial returns, we proceed in the following section with an analysis of the long-run performance to provide further insights into the question whether IPOs had different performance characteristics in these two cycles.

5.2.2 Long-run performance

The results for the long-run return analysis where the dependent variables are the buy-and-hold returns for four different holding periods are provided in Table 15.4. Again, we show the full sample results (panel A) and the coefficient estimates for each sub-sample separately (panel B and panel C). We ran regressions with both, raw returns (BHR) and abnormal returns (BHAR). However, we only present the results for the raw returns as the dependent variable because we are interested in explaining the absolute performance differences between the two IPO cycles and less in comparing in the relative performance. The results for abnormal returns (BHAR) are qualitatively the same and are available upon request. Similar to the analysis of IPO underpricing and initial returns, we control for industry effects and find no impact on long-run performance.

For the full sample (panel A), we document significantly higher returns for the period of up to 250 trading days or about one year, but strongly decreasing returns for the overall three-year holding period of hot market IPOs. Disentangling this effect, especially the first hot-market phase led to a very strong performance up to one year post IPO, while IPOs of the second hot-market phase show a significantly negative performance over the two- and three-year holding periods (panel B and panel C). This may be attributable to the financial crisis that hit the market in late 2007. Similar to the results for the underpricing analysis, larger lagged venture capital investments relative to GDP decrease stock returns especially for longer investment horizons of one to three years in both cycles (panel A, panel B, and panel C). This finding again supports the grandstanding hypothesis in that portfolio firms were taken public by venture capitalists for reputational concerns rather than for certification reasons. This is reflected in the inferior long-run returns and supports our conclusions from the underpricing analyses. Moreover, younger venture-backed IPOs exhibit an inferior long-run performance. This is also observed for second period IPOs (panel C). Overall, these findings are in line with Ritter (1991) who attributes this relationship to a general over-optimism of investors in younger IPO firms.

The analysis of the market run-up prior to the IPO offers additional interesting insights. According to Ritter (1991) hot market IPOs, that is, firms going public after strong market increases and potentially higher initial returns, underperform in the long run. While for the full sample the pre IPO market return does not contribute to the explanation of the long-run performance (panel A), it becomes significant in both sub-periods. For the first period IPOs market returns and long-run performance are positively correlated (panel B). However, the pre IPO market performance exerts a negative influence on long-run returns for second period IPOs (panel C). Given the fact that for both periods the respective hot-market phase of a stronger performance was followed by market downturns, this finding is surprising. We would have expected a similar relation between long-run performance of IPOs and market returns in both cycles. Moreover, while IPO return volatility has a significantly negative impact on long-run returns over two and three years for first period IPOs (panel B), the higher volatility positively influences the performance of second period IPOs, at least for the first year after going public.

Table 15.4 *Regression results: long-run performance*

Dependent variable: long-run performance (BHR)

	Panel A: full sample				Panel B: first cycle				Panel C: second cycle			
	125 days	250 days	500 days	750 days	125 days	250 days	500 days	750 days	125 days	250 days	500 days	750 days
Hot-Dummy: 1998–2000	**0.3419*****	**0.5461*****	0.2504	−0.2687	**0.4919*****	**0.5482*****	0.3770	−0.1675				
Hot-Dummy: 2005–07	**0.1675*****	**0.1521***	−0.1419	**−0.6218*****					−0.0011	0.0748	**−0.2812****	**−0.7315*****
VC Invest. rel. GDP	−0.0111	−0.1829	**−0.3726*****	**−0.2520****	−0.2457	**−0.5329***	**−0.6431***	−0.4212	0.0114	−0.0933	**−0.2890*****	**−0.2174****
Main market dummy	0.0292	0.1433	0.0888	0.0354	−0.0421	0.0317	0.0657	−0.0200	**0.1371***	0.2106	0.0615	0.0552
Market run-up	−0.2562	1.2192	0.9387	1.2952	−0.0265	**3.2315****	2.6376	**2.1460***	**−1.4739*****	**−3.1019*****	**−2.8069****	−0.8258
Return vola (ex-ante risk)	3.7754	−2.0781	**−14.8362*****	**−12.9025*****	2.4749	−4.4100	**−17.0169*****	**−13.5848*****	**9.2137****	**9.3237****	0.4796	−3.4189
Age	0.0392	**0.1632*****	**0.1862*****	**0.1459*****	−0.0438	0.1315	0.1563	0.1214	**0.0697****	**0.1328****	**0.1424****	**0.1122***
Market-to-book	−0.0317	−0.0501	−0.0231	−0.0813	−0.1228	−0.1853	−0.2683	**−0.2324****	0.0163	0.0082	0.0805	0.0162
Market value	−0.0050	−0.0981	−0.0322	0.0110	0.0546	−0.1366	−0.1007	−0.0559	−0.0396	−0.0440	0.0618	0.0925
Const	**0.7660*****	**1.1788*****	**1.3286*****	**1.4950*****	0.5485	**1.5239***	**1.6992*****	**1.6872*****	**0.9437*****	**1.0283*****	**0.9765*****	**1.1995*****
Adj. R^2	1.79%	2.93%	7.60%	11.08%	0.87%	4.75%	10.51%	10.85%	10.06%	9.37%	11.19%	13.71%
F-test	1.8326	1.8087	4.6642	8.357	2.7242	2.2293	2.1515	4.9417	2.1404	2.4657	4.0869	6.1055
N	335	333	328	311	137	136	135	129	198	197	193	182

Note: * $p < 0.1$, ** $p < 0.05$, *** $p < 0.01$.

5.3 Differences in IPO Firm Characteristics Pre- and Post-going Public

While the overall results are generally in line with the findings in previous studies of IPOs and venture capital, our analysis of long-run returns reveals differences between first and second period venture-backed IPOs with respect to risk and market returns. Therefore, we investigate in more detail the significant factors explaining the differences between IPO firms. The emphasis in our analysis is on valuations and firm characteristics at the time of the IPO and on measures of operating performance in the post IPO period. First, we investigate to which extent first and second period IPOs are different with regard to firm characteristics and stock market conditions surrounding the time of the IPO (section 5.3.1). Second, we provide evidence on the post-IPO operating performance for both IPO waves (section 5.3.2). Here, we identify the relationship between pre-IPO firm characteristics and long-run operating performance for both IPO waves.

5.3.1 Differences in IPO characteristics pre IPO

In Table 15.5 we provide an overview of the explanatory variables for the full sample. We then partition the sample according to whether the respective firm went public during the first or the second IPO cycle. Moreover, Table 15.6 reveals that there are considerable differences between both IPO cycles on the basis of univariate comparisons. It needs to be mentioned, however, that our proxy for *ex ante* risk is '*Return Volatility*' which is measured subsequent to the IPO and is strictly speaking no pre-IPO variable. Pre-IPO firm and market characteristics in a multivariate setting are provided in Table 15.7. As first-period IPOs enter the logit model with a value of 1, a positive sign on the logit coefficient estimates indicates a higher value of this variable for first-period IPO firms compared to second-period IPOs.

Venture-backed firms taken public during the first IPO wave compared to the second IPO wave reveal a much higher return volatility in the first two months of trading. They are also larger in terms of pre-IPO market capitalization. This measure is not influenced by underpricing, which is much larger in the first period (see Table 15.1) and therefore not biased towards first-cycle IPOs. Interestingly, stock market returns prior to the IPO are on average higher during the second stock market cycle, indicating that the 'new economy' period peak was less pronounced in comparison to the increasing stock market levels prior to the financial crisis. This result also becomes evident in Figure 15.2. This means that VC-backed IPOs of the second cycle are taken public subsequent to strong overall stock market increases. In addition, the ratio of venture capital investment relative to GDP is also higher during the second IPO wave. This finding can be attributed to the overall growth of the venture capital industry and VC investments (Lerner, 2011) and might highlight the pressures of venture capitalists to exit from their portfolio firms at a certain point in time.

More recently, this issue has gained in importance. Despite the common belief that going public is the most frequently used and most successful exit venue for venture capitalists, IPOs as an exit route have been partially replaced by trade sales and secondary offerings during the past decade in Europe. These changes in exit behavior are even more dramatic for the US (Schwienbacher, 2010; Sousa, 2010; Gao et al., 2011; Bessler et al., 2012c). One reason might be that many firms are not ready to go public because they are either too small or their ideas and innovation are not fully converted into products yet.

Table 15.5 Descriptive statistics: firm characteristics pre-IPO

	Full sample (max number of obs. = 382)			First cycle (max number of obs. = 157)			Second cycle (max number of obs. = 225)		
	Mean	Median	Std dev.	Mean	Median	Std dev.	Mean	Median	Std dev.
VC invest. rel. GDP	0.45%	0.23%	0.44%	0.31%	0.19%	0.28%	0.54%	0.36%	0.50%
Age	2.54	2.30	1.04	2.30	2.20	0.96	2.71	2.48	1.06
Market-to-book	1.17	1.17	0.79	1.36	1.33	0.67	1.03	1.05	0.84
Market value	4.99	4.92	1.24	5.15	5.05	1.13	4.87	4.85	1.30
Market run-up	3.24%	4.16%	6.96%	1.91%	2.42%	8.44%	4.16%	4.73%	5.53%
Return vola (ex-ante risk)	2.75%	2.21%	1.97%	3.78%	3.27%	2.35%	2.03%	1.80%	1.22%
Main market dummy	56.02%			50.96%			59.56%		
First cycle dummy	41.10%			n.a.			n.a.		
Hot-Dummy: 1998–2000	28.27%			68.79%			n.a.		
Hot-Dummy: 2005–07	46.60%			n.a.			79.11%		

316

Table 15.6 Test statistics: firm characteristics pre-IPO

| | Comparison between first- and second-cycle IPOs ||||
| | Difference in || Test statistic ||
	Mean	Median	t-test	z-score
VC invest. rel. GDP	0.24%	0.18%	(5.785)***	(4.113)***
Age	0.42	0.29	(4.015)***	(3.997)***
Market-to-book	−0.33	−0.28	(−4.228)***	(−5.384)***
Market value	−0.28	−0.20	(−2.223)**	(−2.211)**
Market run-up	2.25%	2.31%	(2.933)***	(3.403)***
Return vola (ex-ante risk)	−1.75%	−1.47%	(−8.580)***	(−8.430)***

Note: * p < 0.1, ** p < 0.05, *** p < 0.01.

Table 15.7 Logit regression: comparison of characteristics pre-IPO

	Dependent variable: 1 for first-cycle IPOs; 0 for second-cycle IPOs
VC invest. rel. GDP	−1.2401***
Main market dummy	−0.5417
Market run-up	−9.3820***
Return vola (ex-ante risk)	73.5337***
Age	−0.4062***
Market-to-book	0.4462*
Market value	0.4355***
Const	−3.6772***
Pseudo R^2	35.34%
Chi^2	76.8373
N	350

Note: * p < 0.1, ** p < 0.05, *** p < 0.01.

In addition, going public may not always turn out to be the highest valued exit alternative if innovation and business models are not sufficient for a successful self-sustainable business entity. Moreover, in a rapidly changing technological and innovative environment, small firms may not be able to convert their ideas into products and scale their production and distribution capabilities quickly enough to be successful in a dynamic, highly competitive business environment. Consequently, firms may not be able to generate the high growth rates that are required by the stock market and therefore cannot offer investors the prospect of superior returns. In these cases, a trade sale might be the less risky and more valuable exit opportunity for early stage investors.

In addition, second-period IPOs are significantly older when going public compared to first-period IPOs. And valuations in terms of the market-to-book ratio (calculated using the market value measured pre IPO and therefore not influenced by underpricing) are significantly higher for first period IPOs. Hence, if the market-to-book ratio is a good

Table 15.8 Logit regression: comparison of characteristics post-IPO

	Dependent variable: 1 for first-cycle IPOs; 0 for second-cycle IPOs			
	End of IPO year	$t+1$	$t+2$	$t+3$
Sales-to-assets	0.1626	0.2125	0.2387**	0.1421
Cash flow-to-assets	−3.6596***	−2.9688***	−1.2367*	−1.6265*
R&D-to-assets	−4.3964**	−4.3328***	−1.4997	−1.8343
CAPEX-to-assets	7.5006***	5.2754***	4.8809**	5.5209
Total assets	0.0078	0.0530	−0.1035	−0.0969
Market-to-book	0.0579**	0.1295***	0.0393*	0.0149
Const	−2.6699**	−3.4002***	−1.0203	−0.3253
Pseudo R^2	13.27%	14.12%	7.58%	4.37%
Chi^2	50.6563	50.6706	28.3365	12.4567
N	342	344	339	277

Note: * $p < 0.1$, ** $p < 0.05$, *** $p < 0.01$.

indicator for an IPO's growth prospects, we would expect a superior financial performance in terms of increasing stock prices but also a higher profitability of these IPOs. This issue is investigated next.

5.3.2 Differences in IPO operating performance after going public

The following analysis provides a multivariate comparison of operating performance measures and firm characteristics subsequent to the IPO. The results are presented in Table 15.8. According to the setup in section 5.3.1, the first period IPOs again enter the logit model with a value of 1, while second period IPOs are assigned a value of zero. In the logit regressions the variables enter the regression at the end of the IPO year and at the end of every of the following three years after going public. The sample size varies because for some firms we do not have IPO year balance sheet data. Other firms drop out of the sample due to delisting, which is most pronounced at the end of the third year after the IPO where the sample size decreases by almost 20 percent. In contrast to our findings in section 5.3.1, the results reveal that first-period IPOs do not outperform second-period IPOs. In general, the operating performance of the first-period IPOs is inferior compared to firms that went public during the second period.

The results reveal that up to two years after the IPO, first-period IPOs exhibit a significantly higher market-to-book ratio, suggesting greater growth opportunities and investor optimism. This is in line with the pre-IPO analysis in section 5.3.1 and supports our findings for underpricing and initial returns. In contrast, the market-to-book ratio does not help to differentiate between first and second period IPOs over longer time horizons. Moreover, while second period IPOs invest more in R&D activities, at least up to one year post IPO, first period IPOs have larger capital expenditures. However, the significantly higher capital expenditures of first period IPOs up to two years post IPO do not seem to contribute to overall firm performance. The most striking result is that operating cash flow to total assets is significantly negative over the four time intervals, indicating the superior operating performance of second-cycle IPOs. In results not reported here, univariate tests reveal that the return on assets (ROA) is also significantly higher for second-cycle IPOs for some time periods. However, due to multicollinearity issues we dropped ROA from our logit regressions. As a robustness check, we included in the logit regressions either (1) dummy variables for the countries with the highest IPO activity, that is, the UK, Germany, and France, or (2) excluded countries with a low IPO activity, during our sample period to make sure that the results are not driven by country effects. The results remain qualitatively the same.

This result is also consistent with our performance analyses in section 4.3, because second-cycle IPOs exhibit less volatile returns and these returns are even slightly higher than for first-cycle IPOs for longer horizons if underpricing is excluded. Moreover, cash flow is the only variable that significantly distinguishes first and second cycle IPOs at the end of the third year after going public. This means that second period IPOs are more profitable for at least three years after going public, which is consistent with the notion that venture capitalists were only able to take the most successful portfolio firms public during the second IPO wave. Another interpretation of our results is that companies were taken public much earlier in their company life cycle during the first period. *Ex post* this might have been too early, given their growth prospects and chances to succeed. However, the high stock market level and the investors' euphoria during the 'new economy' period may have convinced many managers, venture capitalists, and investment bankers to time the market and take these companies public in an extremely favorable and over-optimistic stock market environment. These findings support our hypothesis of differences in firm characteristics during the first and second IPO period.

Our results also support the findings of Jain and Kini (1994) who reason that post IPO operating performance generally declines and hence stands in contrast to high valuation multiples and market-to-book ratios at the time of the IPO. One reason is investors' ambitious expectations regarding future earnings growth opportunities. In our context, IPOs with presumably the highest growth opportunities as measured by the pre IPO market-to-book ratio, that is, first period IPOs, show significantly lower profitability in terms of operating cash flow to assets and return on assets. This suggests that especially investors of first-period IPOs might have been overly optimistic about future growth opportunities and valued these IPOs at substantial premiums. This IPO-euphoria during the late 1990s even amplified this over-optimism and venture capital firms took advantage of this window of opportunity by taking their portfolio firms public and by profiting from this high-valuation environment. However, expected growth opportunities did not materialize in the long run but still resulted in overly optimistic stock valuations up to one year after the IPO which, however, reverted in the following years. In contrast, during the second-cycle venture capitalists were only able to sell the most mature and promising portfolio firms to the equity market. This was an environment of positive investor sentiment and a good economic perspective. Consequently, these IPOs turned out to be more profitable with more realistic valuation multiples compared to first period IPOs.

Moreover, we perform additional analyses for both periods and compare our results to the recent findings for the US. Gao et al. (2011) report a substantial decline in the number of IPOs subsequent to the 'new economy' period, which is mainly due to small firms that abstain from going public. While the number of IPOs in general also decreased in Europe in recent years, although to a much lesser extent (see Figure 15.1), we document a pronounced wave of VC-backed IPOs post the 'new economy' period as is evidenced in Figure 15.2. As in Gao et al. (2011), we split the IPO sample into groups of large and small IPOs and choose €50 million of sales during the IPO year as the breakpoint. While a higher fraction of large IPOs occurred during the second IPO wave, we find that the overall number of IPOs in Europe is even increasing during the second wave. This observation clearly contradicts the findings and conclusions of Gao et al. (2011) for the US and reveals that the IPO activity and IPO waves in Europe are quite different from those in the US during the past decade.

Furthermore, there is evidence of a decline in the profitability of especially smaller IPOs in the US during the last decade. Given the arguments provided above with respect to the changing competitive environment, it seems possible that the business ideas of smaller firms can only be successfully converted and exploited in the long run when these firms become part of a larger organization and therefore trade sales and not going public has become the preferred exit route of early stage investors. In contrast, while the relative share of IPO exits of both US and European venture capitalists is decreasing (NVCA, 2010; Schwienbacher, 2010; Sousa, 2010; Bessler et al., 2012c), we find an increasing profitability of those VC-backed firms that eventually go public over time. Because Gao et al. (2011) do not explicitly differentiate between VC and non VC-backed IPOs, we cannot perform a more detailed comparison of their and our results.

6 ROBUSTNESS TESTS

In the results presented so far, we define a venture-backed IPO via the VentureXpert database if there was a capital investment by a venture capital or private equity firm prior to the IPO. Thus, we do not differentiate between different types of venture capital. Metrick and Yasuda (2011) notice that both VC and PE firms are similar as they are financial intermediaries, act in an environment of a high degree of information asymmetry, and often condition their investments on contractual provisions. VC and PE firms, however, differ with regard to the instruments used to improve the performance of their portfolio firms. Supporting evidence was recently provided by Levis (2011) documenting that PE-backed IPOs in the UK perform better than VC-backed IPOs. This finding underlines the notion that PE firms invest in more mature firms with an already established business model, restructure these firms, and provide sophisticated advice which eventually results in an improved performance. Moreover, given that providers of risk capital in the second IPO wave were only able to bring the most mature and profitable portfolio firms to the public market, our results might be driven by later (PE) stage investments rather than early (VC) stage investments.

However, the distinction between VC and PE firms seems not that straightforward as argued by Levis (2011). In contrast to the US, there is a substantial overlap of both groups in the UK which might be the case for continental Europe as well. To control for the impact of potential differences between VC and PE investments, we search the VentureXpert database for the stage of the last investment round pre IPO. This procedure identifies 144 out of the 382 IPOs as PE investment rounds. We dropped all PE investment rounds and re-ran the cross-sectional and logit regressions, and our results remain largely the same. However, there is one notable exception. Age is no longer significant in the regressions that explain long-run returns. Moreover, while second-cycle IPOs are still older than first-cycle IPOs when going public, this difference turns insignificant in the logit model specification. In results not reported here, we perform a chi-square test of independence of age and investment stage and reject the null hypothesis of independence at the 1 percent significance level, that is, PE firms fund more mature firms, which is not surprising. Bessler et al. (2012d) also investigate the influence of VC and PE on the survival profile of IPOs in Europe. Their hazard analyses reveal that VC/PE-backed companies exhibit a significantly higher likelihood of survival of more than 6 percent, and the survival duration is extended by roughly 20 percent. Moreover, when differentiating between VC and PE, the positive impact of overall VC/PE-backing on survival rates is mainly driven by VC investments, while the survival rates of PE-sponsored IPOs do not significantly differ from non-sponsored firms. Again, this highlights that the positive effects of risk capital are due to VC investments rather than PE.

Overall, after restricting our IPOs to being backed with early stage risk capital only, our main finding of significant differences between first- and second-cycle IPOs with regard to pre- and post-IPO firm characteristics, underpricing, and long-run returns remain stable. While first-cycle IPOs still exhibit higher valuations when going public, second-cycle IPOs eventually are the more profitable firms in the long run. They were also valued much more conservatively at the time of the IPO.

7 A PERSPECTIVE ON FUTURE VC ACTIVITY AND IPO WAVES

The empirical findings in our study and in other recent studies for Europe (Schwienbacher, 2010; Sousa, 2010; Bessler and Seim, 2012; Vismara et al., 2012) and for the US (Gao et al., 2011) raise a number of interesting questions with respect to future VC and IPO activities. First, will going public again become an attractive exit route for VCs in the US, given the observation that the last IPO wave occurred at the end of the 1990s, and venture capitalists seem to have shifted to trade sales as the preferred exit route during the last decade? Secondly, given the fact that the last venture capital and IPO waves in Europe were observed during the 1996–2002 and 2003–08 periods, will there be another IPO wave when European economies recover from the current financial crisis, or will there be a dramatic shift to trade sales, given that trade sales have already gained a significant share as a VC exit channel (Bessler et al., 2012c)?

The decline in IPO activity in the US has been attributed to regulatory changes but also to changes in the financial 'ecosystem' (Weild and Kim, 2009, 2010). The question is whether a similar down-turn will occur in Europe as a consequence of the current regulative initiatives for banks and securities markets and restrictions on providers of risk capital such as venture capital funds. It also seems possible, however, that even without additional regulations in the US and Europe, IPOs may have lost their appeal and are no longer an attractive exit route for venture capitalists. This is based on the observation that most of the portfolio firms may not generate new business ideas that are sufficient for creating a self-sustainable company. If the firm's value due to its new ideas, innovation, patents or new products is higher when being integrated into a larger company, trade sales become the preferred exit channel for early stage investors such as venture capitalists. Given these facts, there is currently little hope that the number of IPOs will start to increase in the near future and return to previous levels. Consequently, we may not observe another IPO wave in the US soon (Gao et al., 2011). Similar reasoning applies to Europe (Lerner, 2011), which has been the focus of this study. Interestingly, we observed an increasing IPO volume in emerging markets during the last decade, offsetting the declining IPO activity in developed markets.

In the future, Asian and perhaps Latin American countries may emerge as the continents with the highest growth potential and the necessary funding to support new business ideas and innovation, which may eventually result in firms going public. It is therefore not surprising that a study by PwC (2011) predicted that the largest number of IPOs during the next decade will occur in China, India, Brazil, and Hong Kong, with the US lagging behind. European venture capital firms are already raising funds in Asia for investments in the US and in Europe, given the currently extremely negative sentiment and the lower inflows from new funds and from funds generated from exits. Future research needs to evaluate whether these changes in the venture capital industry and in financial markets as well as changes in the characteristics of venture-backed IPOs and in the exit behavior of venture capitalists will continue when stock market valuations increase and economic activity recovers in the US and in Europe.

8 CONCLUSION

In this study we analyze the performance and firm characteristics of venture-backed IPOs in Europe for the period from 1996 to 2010. Covering two complete stock market cycles and IPO waves for 14 European countries, we explore whether there are significant differences between these two periods. The first IPO wave (1996–2003) includes the 'new economy' period, while the second wave (2003–10) is characterized by overall excellent market and firm fundamentals. In the empirical part we first analyze initial returns and the long-run performance to gain insights into possible differences in performance characteristics between IPO firms in the first and in the second cycle. Next, we compare firm-specific characteristics between both periods as well as market-wide characteristics prior to and subsequent to the IPO in a multivariate framework. Our study offers new and interesting insights into the development of European VC and IPO markets during the past two decades. In addition, and most importantly, we compare the results of IPO waves for European countries to findings reported in recent studies for the US. These studies find that the last IPO wave in the US occurred at the end of the 1990s, with a declining IPO activity since then. Looking forward, there seems hardly any reason to believe that another going-public wave will emerge in the US in the near future (Gao et al., 2011).

Our results for Europe reveal that first-period IPOs have a significantly higher underpricing and a superior long-run performance at least for the first year after going public. These results are due to optimistic investor expectations and high valuations of first period IPOs. For holding periods longer than one year, however, no significant differences between both periods are observed. Nevertheless, first-period IPOs are more risky, have higher market-to-book ratios, and higher market values of equity, reflecting investors' optimistic growth expectations. In contrast, second-period IPOs are older when going public and are usually offered subsequent to overall stock market increases. Most interestingly, second-period IPOs are larger in terms of total assets, engage more in R&D spending, and are more profitable for the first three years after going public. Overall, IPOs in the second period reveal different characteristics than companies that went public during the first IPO wave. These empirical results provide evidence for significant changes in firm and performance characteristics over time.

From the venture capitalists' perspective, given the higher underpricing and the superior first-year returns during the 'new economy' period, *ex post* taking these portfolio firms public was an optimal and profitable exit strategy. During the second IPO wave, it appears that venture capitalists only had the opportunity to sell the most mature and profitable portfolio firms in the public equity market. Consequently, they began to rely more on alternative exit channels such as trade sales and secondary purchases. This is a trend that has been observed in the US for the past decade, revealing the fundamental differences between the European und US markets during that period. Whether this constitutes a fundamental change in exit strategies of venture capital firms as well as in the capital market environment in Europe needs to be explored in future studies.

NOTE

1. We are grateful to the European Venture Capital Association, SIX Swiss Exchange, London Stock Exchange, NYSE/Euronext, NASDAQ/OMX and Deutsche Börse for providing the data and discussions. We thank the participants at the 2011 Interdisciplinary European Conference on Entrepreneurship Research (IECER), Munich, where we received the IECER 'Best Paper Award', for their helpful comments. We are thankful to Jay Ritter for providing the IPO data on his homepage.

REFERENCES

Abukari, K. and V. Jog (2011), 'Long term performance and predictability of initial public offerings (IPOs)', working paper, Carleton University.
Alexandridis, G., C. Mavrovitis and N. Travlos (2012), 'How have M&As changed? Evidence from the sixth merger wave', *European Journal of Finance*, **18** (8), 663–88.
Andrade, G., M. Mitchell and E. Stafford (2001), 'New evidence and perspectives on mergers', *Journal of Economic Perspectives*, **15** (2), 103–20.
Appadu, N., A. Faelten and M. Levis (2012), 'The first 1000 days in the life of an IPO', working paper, Cass Business School.
Barry, C., C. Muscarella, J. Peavy and M. Verstuypens (1990), 'The role of venture capital in the creation of public companies: evidence from the going public process', *Journal of Financial Economics*, **27** (2), 447–71.
Beatty, R. and J. Ritter (1986) 'Investment banking, reputation, and the underpricing of initial public offerings', *Journal of Financial Economics*, **15** (1–2), 213–32.
Bernstein, S. (2012), 'Does going public affect innovation?', working paper, Harvard Business School.
Bessler, W. and C. Bittelmeyer (2008), 'Patents and the performance of technology firms: an empirical analysis of initial public offerings in Germany', *Financial Markets & Portfolio Management*, **22** (4), 323–56.
Bessler, W. and A. Kurth (2007), 'Agency problems and the performance of venture-backed IPOs in Germany: exit strategies, lock-up periods, and bank ownership', *European Journal of Finance*, **13** (1), 29–63.
Bessler, W. and M. Seim (2012), 'The performance of venture-backed IPOs in Europe', *Venture Capital: An International Journal of Entrepreneurial Finance*, **14** (4), 215–39.
Bessler, W. and M. Stanzel (2009), 'Conflicts of interest and research quality of affiliated analysts in the German universal banking system: evidence from IPO underwriting', *European Financial Management*, **15** (4), 757–86.
Bessler, W. and J. Zimmermann (2012a), 'Acquisition activities of initial public offerings in Europe: an analysis of exit and growth strategies', working paper, University of Giessen.

Bessler, W. and J. Zimmermann (2012b), 'Growth strategies of entrepreneurial firms after going public: a European perspective', working paper, University of Giessen.
Bessler, W., W. Drobetz and M. Seim (2012a), 'Share repurchases of initial public offerings: motives, valuation effects, and the impact of market regulation', *European Journal of Finance*, July, doi: 10.1080/1351847x.2012.698991 (accessed 26 May 2013).
Bessler, W., W. Drobetz and M. Seim (2012b), 'Equity issues and stock repurchases of initial public offerings', working paper, University of Giessen.
Bessler, W., J. Holler and M. Seim (2010), 'Venture capital and private equity in Germany', in D. Cumming (ed.), *Private Equity: Funds Types, Risk and Returns, and Regulation*, Hoboken, NJ: Wiley, pp. 511–53.
Bessler, W., J. Holler, M. Seim and J. Zimmermann (2012c), 'From ideas to product: financing innovation and getting access to innovation', in D. Cumming (ed.), *The Oxford Handbook of Venture Capital*, Oxford: Oxford University Press, pp. 627–67.
Bessler, W., M. Seim and J. Zimmermann (2012d), 'The survival of initial public offerings in Europe: the impact of venture capital and private equity', working paper, University of Giessen.
Black, B. and R. Gilson, (1998), 'Venture capital and the structure of capital markets: banks versus stock markets', *Journal of Financial Economics*, **47** (3), 243–77.
Bonardo, D., S. Paleari and S. Vismara (2011), 'Valuing university-based firms: the effects of academic affiliation on IPO performance', *Entrepreneurship Theory and Practice*, **35** (4), 755–76.
Bradley, D., B. Jordan and J.R. Ritter (2008), 'Analyst behavior following IPOs: the "bubble period" evidence', *Review of Financial Studies*, **21** (1), 101–33.
Brav, A. and P. Gompers (1997), 'Myth or reality? The long-run underperformance of initial public offerings: evidence from venture and non-venture capital-backed companies', *Journal of Finance*, **52** (5), 1791–821.
Brav, A. and P. Gompers (2003), 'The role of lock-ups in initial public offerings', *Review of Financial Studies*, **16** (1), 1–29.
Carter, R., F. Dark and A. Singh (1998), 'Underwriter reputation, initial returns, and the long-run performance of IPO stocks', *Journal of Finance*, **53** (1), 285–311.
Choe, H., R. Masulis and V. Nanda (1993), 'Common stock offerings across the business cycle: theory and evidence', *Journal of Empirical Finance*, **1** (1), 3–31.
Da Rin, M., G. Nicodano and A. Sembenelli (2006), 'Public policy and the creation of active venture capital markets', *Journal of Public Economics*, **90** (8–9), 1699–723.
Dittmar, A. and R. Dittmar (2008), 'The timing of financing decisions: an examination of the correlation in financing waves', *Journal of Financial Economics*, **90** (1), 59–83.
Dong, M., J.-S. Michel and J.A. Pandes (2011), 'Underwriter quality and long run IPO performance', *Financial Management*, **40** (1), 219–51.
Doukas, J. and H. Gonenc (2005), 'Long-term performance of new equity issuers, venture capital and reputation of investment bankers', *Economic Notes*, **34** (1), 1–34.
Francis, B. and I. Hasan (2001), 'The underpricing of venture and non-venture capital IPOs: an empirical investigation', *Journal of Financial Services Research*, **19** (2–3), 99–113.
Gajewski, J.-F. and C. Gresse (2006), 'A survey of the European IPO market', working paper, European Capital Markets Institute.
Gao, X., J.R. Ritter and Z. Zhu (2011), 'Where have all the IPOs gone?', working paper, University of Florida.
Goergen, M., A. Khurshed and L. Renneboog (2009), 'Why are the French so different from the Germans? Underpricing of IPOs on the Euro new markets', *International Review of Law and Economics*, **29** (3), 260–71.
Goldstein, M., P. Irvine and A. Puckett (2011), 'Purchasing IPOs with commissions', *Journal of Financial and Quantitative Analysis*, **46** (3), 1193–225.
Gompers, P. (1996), 'Grandstanding in the venture capital industry', *Journal of Financial Economics*, **42** (1), 133–56.
Gompers, P. and J. Lerner (1998), 'Venture capital distributions: short-run and long-run reactions', *Journal of Finance*, **53** (6), 2161–83.
Gompers, P. and J. Lerner (eds) (1999), *The Venture Capital Cycle*, Cambridge, MA: MIT Press.
Greene, W. (ed.) (2011), *Econometric Analysis*, 7th edn, Boston, MA: Pearson.
Haltiwanger, J., R. Jarmin and J. Miranda (2010), 'Who creates jobs? Small vs. large vs. young', working paper, University of Maryland.
Hamza, O. and M. Kooli (2011), 'Does venture capitalists reputation improve the survival profile of IPO firms?', working paper, University of Montreal.
Hege, U., F. Palomino and A. Schwienbacher (2009), 'Venture capital performance: the disparity between Europe and the United States', *Finance*, **30** (1), 7–50.
Hibara, N. and P. Mathew (2004), 'Grandstanding and venture capital firms in newly established IPO markets', *Journal of Entrepreneurial Finance*, **39** (3), 77–85.
Hsu, S. (2010), 'Industry technological changes, venture capital incubation, and post-IPO firm innovation and performance', working paper, University of Wisconsin Milwaukee.

Jain, B. and O. Kini (1994) 'The post-issue operating performance of IPO firms', *Journal of Finance*, **49** (5), 1669–726.
Jain, B. and O. Kini (2000), 'Does the presence of venture capitalists improve the survival profile of IPO firms', *Journal of Business Finance & Accounting*, **27** (9–10), 1139–76.
Jog, V. and L. Wang (2002) 'Aftermarket volatility and underpricing of Canadian initial public offerings', *Canadian Journal of Administrative Sciences*, **19** (3), 231–48.
Johnson, W., J.-K. Kang and S. Yi (2010), 'The certification role of large customers in the new issues market', *Financial Management*, **39** (4), 1425–74.
Kaplan, S. and J. Lerner (2010), 'It ain't broke: the past, present, and future of venture capital', *Journal of Applied Corporate Finance*, **22** (2), 36–47.
Kortum, S. and J. Lerner (2000), 'Assessing the contribution of venture capital to innovation', *RAND Journal of Economics*, **31** (4), 674–92.
Lee, P. and S. Wahal (2004), 'Grandstanding, certification and the underpricing of venture capital backed IPOs', *Journal of Financial Economics*, **73** (2), 375–407.
Lerner, J. (1994), 'Venture capitalists and the decision to go public', *Journal of Financial Economics*, **35** (3), 293–316.
Lerner, J. (2011), 'The future of private equity', *European Financial Management*, **17** (3), 423–35.
Lerner, J., M. Sorensen and P. Strömberg (2011), 'Private equity and long-run investment: the case of innovation', *Journal of Finance*, **66** (2), 445–77.
Levis, M. (2011), 'The performance of private equity backed IPOs', *Financial Management*, **40** (1), 253–77.
Loughran, T and J.R. Ritter (2002), 'Why don't issuers get upset about leaving money on the table in IPOs?', *Review of Financial Studies*, **15** (2), 413–43.
Loughran, T. and J. Ritter (2004) 'Why has IPO underpricing changed over time?', *Financial Management*, **33** (3), 5–37.
Lowry, M. (2003), 'Why does IPO volume fluctuate so much?', *Journal of Financial Economics*, **67** (1), 3–40.
Lyon, J., B. Barber and C.-L. Tsai (1999), 'Improved methods for tests of long-run abnormal stock returns', *Journal of Finance*, **54** (1), 165–201.
Megginson, W.L. and K. Weiss (1991), 'Venture capitalist certification in initial public offerings', *Journal of Finance*, **46** (3), 879–903.
Meoli, M., S. Paleari and S. Vismara (2010), 'The valuation of IPOs in the European legal framework', working paper, University of Bergamo.
Metrick, A. and A. Yasuda (2011), 'Venture capital and other private equity: a survey', *European Financial Management*, **17** (4), 619–54.
National Venture Capital Association (NVCA) (2010), *National Venture Capital Association – Yearbook 2010*.
PricewaterhouseCoopers (PwC) (2011), 'Capital markets in 2025 – the future of equity capital markets', available at http://www.pwc.com/capitalmarkets2025 (accessed 23 Jan. 2012).
Puri, M. and R. Zarutskie (2012), 'On the lifecycle dynamics of venture-capital- and non-venture-capital-financed firms', *Journal of Finance*, **67** (6), 2247–93.
Rau, P. and A. Stouraitis (2011), 'Patterns in the timing of corporate event waves', *Journal of Financial and Quantitative Analysis*, **46** (1), 209–46.
Rhodes-Kropf, M., D. Robinson, and S. Viswanathan (2005), 'Valuation waves and merger activity: the empirical evidence', *Journal of Financial Economics*, **77** (3), 561–603.
Ritter, J. (1991), 'The long-run performance of initial public offerings', *Journal of Finance*, **46** (1), 3–27.
Ritter, J.R. (1984), 'The "hot issue" market of 1980', *Journal of Business*, **57** (2), 215–40.
Ritter, J.R. (2003), 'Differences between European and American IPO markets', *European Financial Management*, **9** (4), 421–34.
Sahlman, W. (1990), 'The structure and governance of venture capital organizations', *Journal of Financial Economics*, **27** (2), 473–521.
Schwienbacher, A. (2010), 'Venture capital exits', in D. Cumming (ed.), *Venture Capital – Investment Strategies, Structures, and Policies*, Hoboken, NJ: Wiley, pp. 389–405.
Sousa, M. (2010), 'Why do private equity firms sell to each other?', working paper, Oxford University.
Tykvová, T. (2003), 'Is the behavior of German venture capitalists different? Evidence from the Neuer Markt', working paper, Centre for European Economic Research.
Vismara, S., S. Paleari, and J.R. Ritter (2012), 'Europe's second markets for small companies', *European Financial Management*, **18** (3), 352–88.
Weild, D. and E. Kim (2009), 'A wake-up call for America', Grant Thornton Capital Market Series.
Weild, D. and E. Kim (2010), 'Market structure is causing the IPO crisis – and more', Grant Thornton Capital Market Series.
White, H. (ed.) (1984), *Asymptotic Theory for Econometricians*, San Diego, CA: Academic Press.
Wilcoxon, F. (1945), 'Individual comparisons by ranking methods', *Biometrics Bulletin*, **1** (1), 80–83.

APPENDIX

Table 15.A1

	Variable	Description
Variables that enter underpricing, long-run performance regressions, and the comparison of IPOs pre IPO	First cycle-dummy	1 for all venture-backed IPOs that took place prior to March 2003, zero otherwise
	Hot-dummy: 1998–2000/ Hot-dummy: 2005–07	The sample period is characterized by distinct hot and cold issue market periods as is evidenced in Figure 15.3. In order to account for the increasing and declining stock market periods the Hot-9800 (Hot-0507) dummy is set to 1 if the IPO took place between 1998 and 2000 (2005 and 2007), and zero otherwise
	VC invest. rel. GDP	This variable represents the one year lagged relation between venture capital investment and GDP in the respective country where the IPO took place
	Main market dummy	Dummy variable that takes the value 1 for all venture-backed IPOs on main markets, zero otherwise
	Market run-up	The performance of the respective country market index in the 60 trading days (three months) preceding the IPO
	Return vola	The standard deviation of the daily returns in the first two months of trading in the secondary market, beginning after ten trading days
	Market-to-book	Market-to-book ratio based on the offer price of the IPO, Winsorized at the 1% level and logarithmized
	Market value	Market value of equity based on the offer price of the IPO, Winsorized at the 1% level and logarithmized
	Age	Natural logarithm of age+1 of the IPO, where age is the number of years between foundation and IPO date
	Tech-dummy	Dummy variable that takes the value 1 for technology IPOs. The classification is based on the 3-digit SIC code according to Loughran and Ritter (2004)
	Manufac-dummy	Dummy variable that takes the value 1 for IPOs of the manufacturing industry. The classification is based on the 3-digit SIC code
	Trade & service-dummy	Dummy variable that takes the value 1 for IPOs of the trade or service industry. The classification is based on the 3-digit SIC code
Post-IPO comparison of operating performance	Sales-to-assets	Ratio of sales to total assets, Winsorized at the 1% level
	Cash flow-to-assets	Ratio of net cash flow from operations to total assets, Winsorized at the 1% level
	R&D-to-assets	Ratio of R&D expenditures to total assets. Missing values are set to zero, Winsorized at the 1% level
	CAPEX-to-assets	Ratio of capital expenditures to total assets, Winsorized at the 1% level
	Total assets	The natural logarithm of total assets in thousands of EUR, Winsorized at the 1% level
	Market-to-book	Market-to-book ratio, Winsorized at the 1% level

16 IPO pricing and ownership structure: the business-group effect
Aharon Cohen Mohliver, Gitit Gur-Gershgorn and Shinjinee Chattopadhyay

1 INTRODUCTION

When firms first go public, they tend to experience a surge in share price. Academics have been documenting this phenomenon, and trying to explain it, since the 1970s (Ibbotson, 1975; Reilly, 1973; Ritter, 1998; Ritter and Welch, 2002; Stoll and Curley, 1970). Citing studies produced as early as 1957, Stoll and Curley (1970) make these observations on this 'remarkable price appreciation':

> *In the short run*, the stocks in the sample showed a remarkable price appreciation. Between the initial offering date and the first market date, the average 6-month rate of return for all companies in the sample, over and above the 6-month rate of return on the Standard and Poor's Index, was 42.4 percent.
> On the average, an investor would have done almost 50 percent better per 6-month period by buying new small issues at the *offering price* [italics in original] than by investing in a portfolio of larger stocks. (Stoll and Curley, 1970, p. 7)

This phenomenon, commonly referred to in the IPO literature as 'first-day return' or 'underpricing', is both persistent and global. It has been a constant from the very first studies conducted in the 1950s through the dotcom bubble. In a cross-country comparison, each and every country studied showed average initial public offering (IPO) prices increasing[1] from the offer stage to market close on the first day's trading. In fact, first-day return is so prevalent that Ritter and Welch, in their review paper (2002), assert that 'We know of no exceptions to the rule that the IPOs of operating companies are underpriced, on average, in all countries' (p. 1802).

The counterparty in an IPO is the issuing firm. When prices rise on the first day of trading, this translates into a transfer of (potential) capital from the issuing firm to investors in the IPO. The literature commonly refers to this as 'money left on the table'. The rationale behind 'leaving money on the table' varies according to the theoretical lens used. Signaling theories suggest that good firms signal their quality by willingly leaving money on the table for investors (Welch, 1989). One strand of the literature suggests that firms undertake a 'book-building' exercise to gauge investor interest before they issue an offer price, and underpricing is merely compensation to investors for revealing private information on their preferences (Benveniste and Spindt, 1989; Benveniste and Wilhelm, 1990). Another relates to preferential share allocation: underwriters allocate shares to favored business partners as a quid pro quo to strengthen the relationship and in expectation of repeated interaction (Cornelli and Goldreich, 2001; Ljungqvist and Wilhelm Jr, 2002).

In this chapter, we argue that the ownership structure of an economy, particularly dominant business groups, is a key source of heterogeneity of IPO underpricing between economies and can help shed light on some of the debates within the IPO pricing literature. We incorporate the concept of dominant groups' market power by allowing for heterogeneity in the corporate ownership structure of the economy where the IPO is issued. Based on empirical facts, we suggest that the ownership structure of an economy should be incorporated into existing theories on IPO underpricing.

We make two main observations. First, we show that over and above predictors such as market size, legal origin and corruption, the extent of underpricing and the resulting amount of money left on the table is smaller when the economy comprises fewer family-owned business groups. If the number of family-owned groups increases by one, underpricing decreases by .61 percentage points. Secondly, we show that as the average number of pyramidal layers within business groups increases, the average underpricing decreases. If the average number of pyramidal layers increases by one, average IPO underpricing decreases by 28.3 percentage points.

Both the number of family-owned groups and the number of pyramidal layers are proxies of the distribution of power, competition and control within an economy. Past literature suggests that as a family-owned group gains additional layers, it separates ownership from control by diluting ownership with non-family shareholders. This is explained as an indication both of optimizing ownership structure for rent extraction (Almeida and Wolfenzon, 2006a) and of the increased ability to 'tunnel' funds from one group firm to another (Bae et al., 2002; Bertrand et al., 2002; Jiang et al., 2010; Johnson et al., 2000).

We find that when economic power becomes concentrated in the hands of fewer agents, the average level of IPO underpricing decreases, leaving less money on the table for participating institutional investors. We conjecture that this indicates the greater influence of the business group on institutional investors who depend on the group for business unrelated to the IPO (such as pension-fund management, insurance and loans). Similar types of agency behavior have been documented among US mutual funds voting at shareholders' meetings for companies whose 401(k) portfolios they manage (Davis and Kim, 2007).

We also view our findings as supporting existing theories on asymmetric information. Past literature suggests that one reason for underpricing is that high-quality firms 'signal' their quality by leaving money on the table. As the number of groups in an economy increases, intensifying competition makes it more important to send such signals, and underpricing increases. In a more general sense, the more pyramidal business groups there are in an economy, the more costly it is to assert each group's true quality – and since there is a clear 'group' component to a single firm's performance (Bertrand et al., 2002; Chang and Hong, 2000), this should be reflected in the pricing of the IPO. The second theory that may speak to such evidence is that on book-building: as the number of groups increases, competition for investors also increases, and therefore investors are compensated more for revealing private information.

We next examine how IPO underpricing varies with the average number of pyramidal layers in the economy, which we consider as a proxy for the degree of separation between ownership and control (Claessens et al., 2000; Morck et al., 2005). We control for the market size of the economy and anti-director measure, following past literature.

Corruption is also likely to affect underpricing, and is therefore included as a control. We also control for legal origin, since it has been found to be strongly correlated with the strength of small investors and the institutions protecting them.

Theories on agency conflict and asymmetric information predict lower underpricing when there is a greater separation between ownership and control. Previously, authors have theorized that when groups have more pyramidal layers, firms are more likely to divert cash in order to benefit the owners of the groups (Almeida and Wolfenzon, 2006b). We find support for this theory. When there are more pyramidal layers, more funds are diverted into the firm and less money is left on the table.

The chapter is organized as follows. We begin with a review of the literature on business groups, their financing constraints and how they function. We then move on to discuss the IPO underpricing phenomenon, why it happens and the various agency conflicts that are associated with it. Finally, we present the data and results, a discussion and our conclusion.

2 BUSINESS GROUPS AROUND THE WORLD, INTERNAL DEALINGS AND FINANCING CONSTRAINTS

With few exceptions,[2] corporate ownership around the world follows one of two archetypal structures: the Anglo-Saxon diverse-ownership structure, which is common in the English-speaking world (predominantly in the US and the UK), and the business-group structure that prevails in other economies around the world. In business-group economies, large portions of public and private corporations are held by a small number of individuals or families. This ownership structure was first observed by Leff (1978) with regard to the ownership structure in South America, but was not explored extensively by academics until the publication of two seminal papers by La Porta et al. in the late 1990s that observed both the prevalence of this structure and its dependence on the distantly determined legal origins of the country (La Porta et al., 1998, 1999). Subsequently, researchers began to map individual economies, and established that business groups are dominant and common in both developing and most developed economies (Barca and Becht, 2001; Claessens et al., 2000; Faccio and Lang, 2002; La Porta et al., 1999; Sacristan-Navarro and Gomez-Anson, 2007).

Several explanations have been put forward to account for this discrepancy in ownership structure. The foremost theory focuses on inefficient institutions being substituted early in the countries' development, followed by a political and economic entrenchment that precludes a shift toward diversified ownership structure. Emerging economies are often characterized by poorly developed institutions or financial intermediaries alongside well-functioning product and labor markets. This lack of developed institutions increases the cost of establishing contractual relationships and acquiring capital (Khanna and Yafeh, 2007). Large business groups can mitigate some of these problems by allocating capital more efficiently within the group rather than entrusting it to underdeveloped external institutions (Chang and Hong, 2000; Khanna and Yafeh, 2007; Khanna and Rivkin, 2001).

Business groups compete with each other in various markets: goods, labor, access to government benefits and contracts and in financing their activities. In some of these markets, they often control mechanisms through which they can obtain preferential access. When financing their activities, for example, groups often influence banks, insurance companies and asset-managing firms. Khanna and Palepu (2000) find that in India, firms affiliated with business groups have better access to international sources of capital than non-affiliated firms. Weaker regulation also helps groups gain preferential access to capital (La Porta et al., 1998).

The literature finds much evidence of internal business within groups. Shin and Park (1999), for example, find that investments made by firms within a business group are less sensitive to their own cash flow (compared to non-group affiliated firms) but are highly sensitive to the cash flow of other firms in the group. They interpret this finding as pointing to an internal capital market within the groups, in which funds flow between firms that are unrelated except for their membership of the group. In a similar vein, Chang and Hong (2000) show that various forms of internal business exist within Korean groups, including debt guarantees, internal trade and equity investments. Gopalan et al. (2007) find that intra-group loans are common among Indian business groups, with lending usually flowing from stronger firms to weaker ones in the same group. Such loans come with zero-interest terms, and are most common when firms are hit by negative earnings shocks. The authors also find that such loans reduce the probability of future bankruptcy of firms. These and other related papers suggest that firms in business groups are not unrelated, but rather assist each other in ways that are not observed in diversified-ownership economies.

It is important to note that while intragroup capital markets create better financing possibilities for affiliated firms, they can reduce the efficiency of capital allocation in the wider economy – even when they are efficient in allocating funds within the group (Almeida and Wolfenzon, 2006a). Critically, Almeida and Wolfenzon show that a group's choice of a pyramidal structure (as opposed to dual-class shares, which offer the same equity control) can be explained theoretically as an attempt to maximize the ultimate owner's potential extraction of cash-flow gains (Almeida and Wolfenzon, 2006b). Divergence of cash-flow rights from control rights has also been tied to agency problems at the firm level for firms controlled by a group, where the controlling shareholder's interests diverge from those of minority shareholders as the cash-flow rights of the major shareholder diminish (Morck et al., 2005).

Intragroup dealings such as capital allocation, debt guarantee and internal trade can work to the benefit of the group – or to the benefit of the group owner, by diverting funds from firms in which they have only modest cash-flow rights to others in which their cash-flow rights are larger. This phenomenon is known as 'tunneling' – a term first used by Friedmen et al. (2003).

There is mounting evidence that business groups around the world make use of tunneling. Bae et al. (2002) show that while minority holders of Korean business groups tend to lose out during a merger or acquisition, the controlling shareholders of the group benefit through value added to other firms within the group. Bertrand et al. (2002) find that in a sample of Indian business groups, more than 25 percent of the marginal rupee value of profits in low-cash-flow firms are ferreted away through tunneling. Bertrand et al. (2008) study Thai business groups and find that the sons of business founders exert great control over their businesses, especially after the founder dies. They also find that such control is associated with lower firm-level performance. They hypothesize that there is an inter-generational dilution of control and ownership, leading to a 'race to the bottom' in tunneling resources out of group firms.

The key question about tunneling is why it exists in the first place. Why do minority shareholders continue to buy into firms offering low cash-flow rights, despite the evidence that tunneling takes place? Bertrand et al. (2002) propose a few explanations. They suggest that these firms may provide other benefits that offset investors' losses from tunneling, such as political contacts that are especially valuable in emerging economies. A second explanation is that shareholders are not *ex ante* informed which firms offer high or low cash flow. The third is that efficient markets ultimately absorb the effects of tunneling through the growth of firms following acquisitions. These explanations all apply not only to tunneling funds from lower cash-flow firms to those higher up in the pyramid, but also to tunneling funds from institutional investors, both inside and outside the group, to firms that are publicly traded.

Morck et al. (1998) argue that when business groups form a significant percentage of operational firms within an economy, the poor corporate governance and agency conflicts within firms impede overall economic growth. In a different paper, Morck and Yeung (2003) suggest that family businesses and groups invest more in political lobbying than in innovation or creative destruction, which also contributes to economic stagnation.

It is becoming increasingly clear that business groups use their unique structures of ownership and control to facilitate better access to funds for their member firms and to increase the wealth of the individuals who control them. This complex relationship between firms within a group, and between the group and its environment, can manifest itself in the actions taken by investors considering trades offered by business-group firms.

We postulate that groups' use of intragroup capital markets, bank loans and trade to finance their activities, combined with agency conflicts affecting asset managers' investment decisions, leads to heterogeneous compensation for IPO investors. Agency-driven behavior in fund management is a well-documented phenomenon. Davis and Kim (2007) showed that even in highly regulated and transparent markets such as the US, there is a positive association between business ties and the propensity of mutual funds to vote with management. This behavior is prominent until votes are mandatorily published, at which point it disappears. Analysts issue a disproportionally high number of 'buy' recommendations for IPOs underwritten by their firm (Michaely and Womack, 1999), and are slower to downgrade their recommendations than unaffiliated analysts (O'Brien et al., 2005). Affiliated analysts issue more optimistic growth forecasts (Dechow et al., 2000). Interestingly, Bradshaw et al. (2006) demonstrate that over-optimism is positively related to net corporate financing activities.

In business-group economies, IPOs for individual firms affiliated with groups are rarely independent of other firms in the group. Agent-based behavior that benefits the group can therefore show up as increased participation in IPOs from firms in the same group, as compared with non-group related IPOs. This enables the group to infuse the firm with investor capital while also maintaining control over future proxy voting. The group's asset managers maintain a consistent strategy of heightened participation, which results in higher pricing for all the group's IPOs.

3 UNDERPRICING: THEORIES AND EXISTING EVIDENCE

Stoll and Curley (1970), Logue et al. (2002), Reilly (1973) and Ibbotson (1975) were among the first to show evidence on IPO underpricing. On average, IPOs are more likely to be underpriced than not. Ritter and Welch (2002) find that, in the US market, the average first-day return or underpricing is 18.8 percent. The comparable daily market return is an average of 0.05 percent, so market misevaluation is unlikely to explain this large number. Several explanations for underpricing have been put forth in past literature.

A number of papers theorize or document evidence based on asymmetric information. They argue that when the issuer is better informed about the quality of the firm than investors, underpricing functions as a mechanism for signaling this quality to the market. The implication is that only high-quality firms would agree to leave money on the table. Later, the issuer can recover the cost via additional issues (Welch, 1989), market response to future dividend announcements (Allen and Faulhaber, 1989) or analyst coverage (Chemmanur, 1993).

According to Amihud et al. (2001), another reason for underpricing IPOs is to use the resulting oversubscription as a signal of investor interest. The authors find that IPOs tend to be either heavily oversubscribed or undersubscribed, depending on how investors judge the sentiment of other investors. Overpricing means that some investors are priced out, which signals lack of interest to other investors. Underpricing makes undersubscription less likely, and is a preferred strategy for a 'noisy' environment where investors' decisions are not mutually independent and information on subscription is available.

However, there is also some evidence against signaling theories. Jegadeesh et al. (1993) find that neither underpricing nor post-first-day returns tend to lead to future issuing activity. Michaely and Shaw (1994) find no evidence of higher dividends following greater underpricing; nor do they find that firms with greater underpricing are more likely to return to the market for a second offering. Although popular, signaling theories appear to fall short in some instances.

An important theme in the literature on IPO underpricing relates to conflict of interest, and particularly the role of 'book-building'. Benveniste and Spindt (1989), Benveniste and Wilhelm (1990) and Spatt and Srivastava (1991) argue that the practice of 'book-building' allows underwriters to obtain information from informed investors. First, they set a preliminary price range for the offer, before going on a 'roadshow' with issuers to market the company to potential investors. The underwriters record indications of interest and use them to gauge demand for the share, revising the offer price upwards if demand is strong. However, since investors know that expressing interest results in a higher offer price, they must be offered incentives in return for revealing how much they are willing to pay; IPO share allocations and underpricing are among such incentives. Hanley (1993) was the first to document the mechanism of book-building empirically, by showing that the degree of underpricing is positively related to the percentage revision in offer price from the original offer price. Ritter and Welch (2002) show that in the period from 1980 to 2001 the average underpricing was 53 percent in those cases when the offer price exceeded the upper limit of the price range originally filed. This is significantly above the 12 percent for

IPOs priced within their filing range, or the 3 percent for IPOs that adjust their offer price downward.

On a related theme, news publications including the *Wall Street Journal* (Pulliam and Smith (2000)) have speculated that underwriters deliberately leave money on the table and also allocate shares preferentially to investors of their choice. Since underpricing creates an excess demand for shares, issuers and underwriters can pick and choose who to allocate shares to. In the academic literature, Sherman and Titman (2002) have argued that share allocation is one of the methods by which investors are compensated for revealing costly information during the 'book-building' process. Loughran and Ritter (1994) suggest that underwriters do not always distribute shares equitably, but allocate them preferentially to their favored buy-side clients when they are in a position to do so. But if firms know this, why are they still content to leave money on the table? The authors use prospect theory (Kahnman and Tversky, 1979) to argue that firms will be more tolerant of underpricing if they know that their post-market valuation will be higher than expected. The larger a post-market revision they anticipate, the less likely they are to negotiate with underwriters on the offer price. Ritter and Welch (2002) report that $66 billion was left on the table during the Internet bubble, and that IPO allocation shares accounted for as much as 10 percent of shares traded during this period.

While there is no clear evidence on how shares are allocated among the various parties, there is some evidence on how institutional investors, who are better informed clients, benefit from share allocation. Hanley and Wilhelm (1995) showed that they benefit significantly from the short-run benefits of IPO underpricing – but at the cost of participating in less attractive offerings. Aggarwal et al. (2002) look at US offerings between 1997 and 1998 and report similar findings, while Cornelli and Goldreich (2001) look at UK offerings and also reach the same conclusion.

Since institutional investors are also potential block-holders with voting rights, share allocation during IPOs gives them the power to influence the long-term performance of the firm. For example, Brennan and Franks (1997) look at a sample of 69 British firms and find that when shares are distributed more widely among minority holders, the founder is less likely to be ousted from the firm. Stoughton and Zechner (1998) suggest that the promised benefit of underpricing not only attracts large institutional investors, but also incentivizes them to take control of management and monitor the firm's activities more closely. Mello and Parsons (1998) develop a model to show that rather than allocating all shares to institutional investors, it is optimal for a firm to issue dispersed holdings to small and passive investors, before marketing the controlling blocks to larger and more active shareholders.

We propose a similar argument. Preferential business partners acting as institutional investors compensate the group through higher IPO pricing, in the hope of receiving future business from companies affiliated with the group. When these investors are under the group's control, the business-group literature suggests this may cause conflicts of interest that will be reflected in a similar price pattern. The stronger the control exerted by business groups over the economy, the less is the money left on the table through IPOs.

4 DATA

We use data on average underpricing spanning 35 countries gathered by Loughran et al. (1994) from various papers independently documenting underpricing around the world. We only use countries for which we could find ownership data, namely Argentina, Australia, Austria, Belgium, Brazil, Canada, Chile, Denmark, Finland, France, Germany, Greece, Hong Kong, India, Indonesia, Ireland, Israel, Italy, Japan, Malaysia, Mexico, the Netherlands, Norway, the Philippines, Portugal, South Africa, Spain, Sri Lanka, Sweden, Switzerland, Taiwan, Thailand, Turkey, the UK and the US. We could not find either detailed ownership mapping, anti-director rights or corruption measures for Bulgaria, China, Cyprus, Egypt, South Korea, Singapore, Poland, Jordan, Nigeria, Russia, or Saudi Arabia, and therefore excluded those countries from the analysis. Our data covers samples that range between 20 IPOs (Argentina) and 12 246 IPOs (US). The mean underpricing for the countries in the sample is 23.86 percent, with a minimum of 4.4 percent and a maximum of 88.5 percent. We match this data to corporate ownership characteristics in these economies based largely on mapping done by Masulis et al. (2011). In their study, the authors used data on 28 635 firms in 45 countries to construct a comprehensive map of ownership structures. They found that of the 28 635 firms, 3007 were controlled by business groups (using a holdings threshold of at least 20 percent of voting rights, or 10 percent if the owners held additional control mechanisms such as chief executive officer or chairman positions). They report two variables that are central to our analysis: average pyramid layer depth, defined as the average number of pyramid layers across all firms in the economy, and the number of family groups, defined as the number of family-controlled business groups in the economy. The average number of pyramidal business groups in the sample is 16.5, ranging from one group (Austria) to 61 groups (South Korea). The average pyramid layer depth is 0.23, with a minimum layer depth of 0.029 (Switzerland) and a maximum of 0.89 (Israel). Together, these two variables allow us to proxy the extent to which groups have the incentive and power to influence the allocation and pricing of their IPOs. We can also proxy the information cost relating to each group (which we postulate increases as the number of business groups increase). On average, the more layers a pyramidal group has, the greater the separation between ownership and control, and the more prevalent conflicts of interest are (Almeida and Wolfenzon, 2006; Claessens et al., 2000; Morck et al., 2005). The more business groups there are in an economy, the less power each individual group has vis-à-vis institutional investors and underwriters, both directly (through the control of financial intermediaries) and indirectly (through the ability to restrict or enhance future business with external intermediaries).

The functioning of capital markets is highly influenced by the quality of institutions that regulate trades, the strength and origin of legal institutions and the level of corruption in the economy.

To reflect legal and economic risk, we use IHS Global Insight data. Legal risk is defined as 'an assessment of whether the necessary business laws are in place, and whether there are any outstanding gaps', while economic risk is defined as the 'assessment of the economic stance of the government and economy – whether market forces can operate properly and how actively the current government encourages this'. Global Insight employs both foreign and local experts to assess country-specific risk. Since it is frequently used by businesses themselves, it poses an endogeneity concern if analyzed independently; we therefore retain this data as control variables.

For legal origin, we use the classification introduced by La Porta et al. (1998) to account for unobserved similarities in the legal framework surrounding IPOs, and the anti-director rights index to account for the expected marginal power of investors who buy into the IPO.[3]

Finally, to model corruption, we use data from the Transparency International Group[4] covering all 35 countries in our analysis. This data is much like the International Country Risk Guides and Business International data, both of which are used widely in the literature (Morey et al., 2009; Sachs and Warner, 1997; Simon et al., 1998). The corruption data used is based on the perception of informed insiders, or on surveys of the perception of corruption in the general population, and takes the form of a 'corruption score' ranging from 2.3 (high corruption) in the Philippines to 9.3 (low corruption) in Sweden.

We estimate an ordinary least squares (OLS) regression, predicting IPO underpricing by the structure of corporate ownership (average depth of pyramid layers and number of pyramidal business groups), market size, legal origin and anti-director rights. We introduce corruption, economic risk and legal risk in different models to avoid multicollinearity. The results are reported in Tables 16.1 and 16.2

Anti-director rights have no significant effect on the pricing of the IPO, while the legal origin of the country is significant for the countries with French legal origin (Argentina, Belgium, Brazil, Chile, France, Greece, Indonesia, Italy, Mexico, the Netherlands, Philippines, Portugal, Spain and Turkey).

Corruption is positively related to underpricing, suggesting that when economies are perceived as more corrupt, the average price discount sought by investors is higher. Economic and legal risks also increase the average underpricing. (See Figures 16.1, 16.2 and 16.3). We can attribute the difference in magnitude to the different methodologies and scales used by the institutions collecting the data. The range of the economic and legal risk scales is 1–5, with a standard deviation of 0.74 and 0.64 respectively. This implies that two standard deviations out, IPOs are discounted by 20 percent in economies where the economic risk is high – a significant discount in a sample where underpricing is centered at 23 percent with a standard deviation of 18 percent.

The number of business groups is positively related to the amount of money that is left on the table for investors, increasing by an average of 0.6 percentage points for each additional business group. The variance on the number of pyramidal family groups (Figure 16.4) is large, ranging from 1 to 61 with a mean of 16.5. This implies that two standard deviations out in the number of pyramidal business groups increases the average underpricing by 15 percent.

The average pyramid layer is marginally significant, but interestingly loses significance when we introduce the variable capturing the countries' level of legal risk (Figure 16.5). Since much of the gains to tunneling are contingent on weak enforcement of contracts and weak legal protection, the loss of significance when legal risk is modeled suggests that tunneling may be a factor in IPOs being less underpriced in these economies. The average pyramid layer is 0.229 and the variable ranges from 0.029 to 0.89 in our sample with a variance of 0.175. This implies that two standard deviations out on the group pyramid layer, the average underpricing drops by 9.9 percent.

Table 16.1 Descriptive statistics and correlation table for continuous variables

	Mean	SD	First-day return	Average pyramid layer	No. of pyramidal family groups	Market value	Corruption	Economic stability	Legal stability
First day return	0.22	0.17	1.0000						
Average pyramid layer	0.23	0.18	−0.0502	1.0000					
No. of pyramidal groups	15.9	11.3	0.5467	−0.0185	1.0000				
Market value (US $millions)	1136	2706	−0.0223	−0.2790	0.4163	1.0000			
Corruption	1.39	2.24	0.3345	0.3555	0.1937	−0.1421	1.0000		
Economic stability	2.08	0.75	0.5360	0.3897	0.4329	−0.1395	0.7317	1.0000	
Legal stability	1.61	0.65	0.4020	0.2291	0.1473	−0.1907	0.8856	0.7272	1.0000

Table 16.2 Results for an OLS regression of first-day return

Variables	(1) First-day return	(2) First-day return	(3) First-day return	(4) First-day return
Average pyramid layer		−0.283*	−0.305*	−0.189
		(0.157)	(0.164)	(0.149)
No. of pyramidal family groups		0.00614**	0.00606*	0.00574*
		(0.00296)	(0.00310)	(0.00292)
Mktw	−1.03e−08	−2.30e−08*	−2.04e−08	−1.86e−08
	(1.24e−08)	(1.18e−08)	(1.24e−08)	(1.19e−08)
Llsvantidirector	0.00295	0.000467	−0.00525	0.00405
	(0.0288)	(0.0232)	(0.0237)	(0.0228)
Legal origin = French	−0.143*	−0.181**	−0.114	−0.159**
	(0.0836)	(0.0719)	(0.0694)	(0.0678)
Legal origin = German	−0.0345	−0.0447	−0.0464	−0.0238
	(0.106)	(0.0916)	(0.0938)	(0.0906)
Legal origin = Scandinavian	−0.168	−0.0327	−0.0480	−0.0344
	(0.109)	(0.0950)	(0.0963)	(0.0924)
Corruption		0.0414**		
		(0.0153)		
Eco risk			0.106**	
			(0.0441)	
Leg risk				0.138***
				(0.0463)
Constant	0.313**	0.570***	0.0796	0.0395
	(0.125)	(0.171)	(0.139)	(0.135)
Observations	35	35	35	35
R-squared	0.150	0.518	0.496	0.539
Adj. R-square	0.0034	0.369	0.340	0.397

Notes:
Standard errors in parentheses.
*** $p < 0.01$, ** $p < 0.05$, * $p < 0.1$.

This chapter examines the way ownership structure of firms affect average IPO underpricing, potential agency conflicts and information effects within an economy. In many countries, markets are dominated by family-owned business groups rather than smaller independent firms, and both agency conflicts and information friction manifest differently within these economies.

In previous literature, IPO underpricing has been posited as a reward for investors for sharing private information, a signal to investors of the firm's quality or a way to increase demand among investors. These explanations are supported by our findings in the previously unexplored context of ownership heterogeneity. We find that greater underpricing is associated with lower numbers of pyramidal layers within business groups in the economy. We postulate that lower underpricing may indicate more tunneling: business groups with more pyramidal layers are more likely to divert funds within the group, as has been shown in previous research. In the context of IPO pricing, this would imply leaving less money on the table for participating investors when firms

338 *Handbook of research on IPOs*

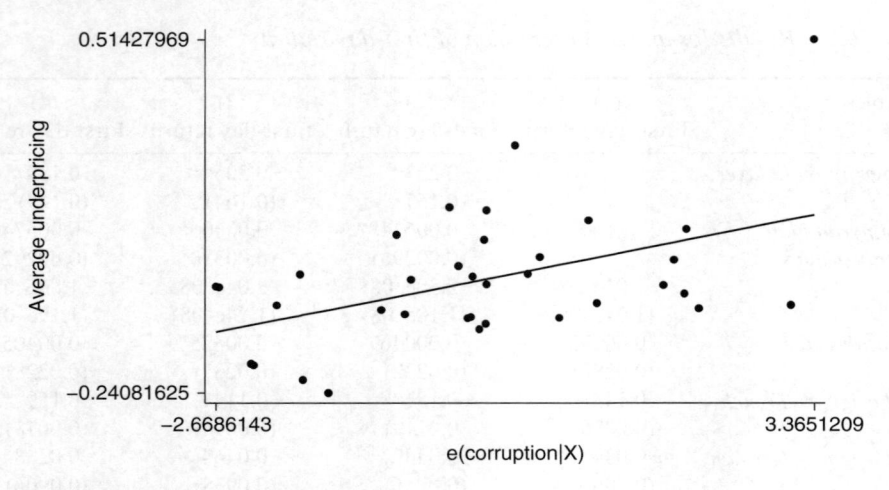

Note: Coef. = .04135868; se = .01532156; t = 2.7.

Figure 16.1 Marginal effect of corruption on underpricing (model 2)

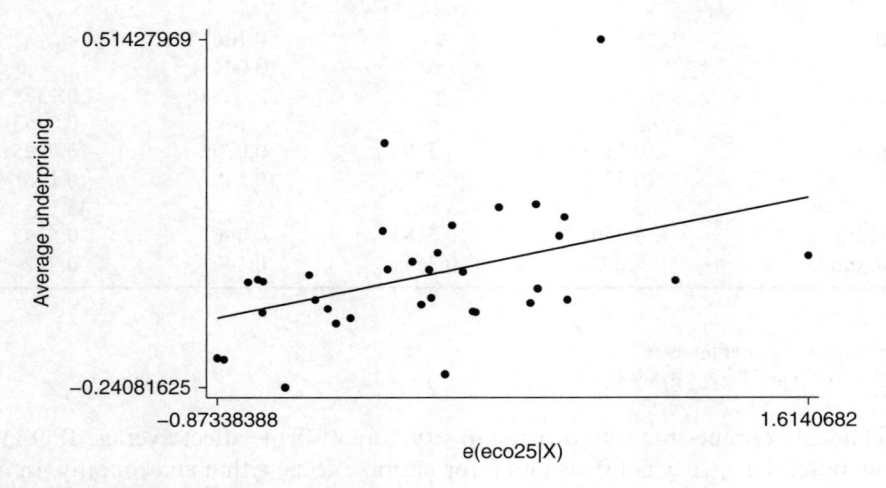

Note: Coef. = .10642804; se = .04409404; t = 2.41.

Figure 16.2 Marginal effect of Economic Risk on underpricing (model 3)

go public. A second possible explanation for this finding is that factors endogenous to the group-ownership model change the information gathering characteristics investors provide during the IPO. A third possible explanation is that inherent advantages of group ownership are reflected in the risk characteristics of the IPO, providing more stable but lower underpricing across group firms, we mention a few such advantages in this chapter.

There is the evidence of co-insurance within firms belonging to the same group, or between layers of the same group. Since there is evidence that intragroup loans at low

IPO pricing and ownership structure 339

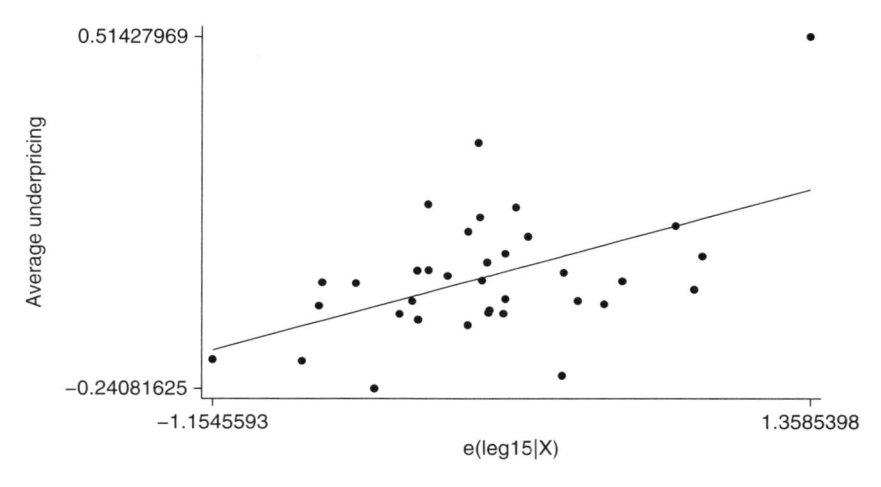

Note: Coef. = .13758388; se = .04625517; t = 2.97.

Figure 16.3 Marginal effect of legal risk on underpricing (model 4)

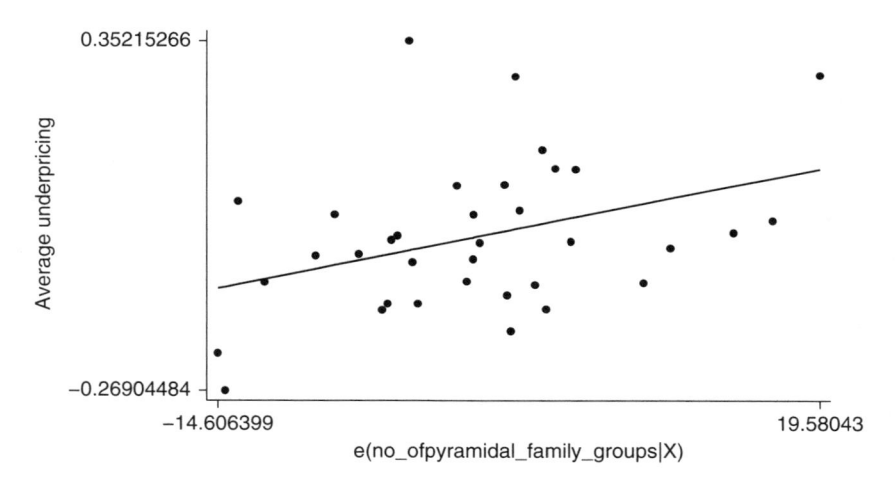

Note: Coef. = .00614042; se = .00296399; t = 2.07.

Figure 16.4 Marginal effect of number of pyramidal family groups on underpricing

interest rates are prevalent among business groups, there may be less reason to leave money for investors.

A second argument we present is based on reputation. Large pyramidal business groups with more layers separating ownership from control are often well known, with established reputations within the economy. This would also lead them to leave less money on the table, because they have less need to signal their quality to the market than independent firms. The same holds for building demand during an IPO: membership of a business group with a large number of pyramidal layers may signal high quality in itself,

Figure 16.5   Marginal effect of average pyramid layer on underpricing (model 2)

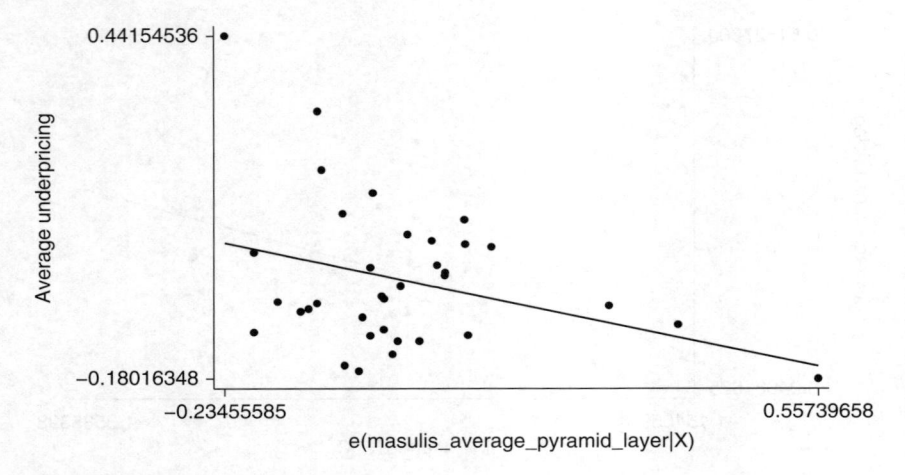

Notes: Coef. = −.28327002; se = .1567171; t = −1.81.

therefore generating greater demand for shares and reducing the need to compensate investors and to underprice the IPO.

It is important to understand that there are potential welfare consequences of funds being diverted. Lower IPO underpricing can reduce the returns to being a non-family shareholder, thereby affecting economic growth and development. It can also reduce transparency in terms of the firm's financial health or accounting practices, which can lead to potentially harmful consequences.

Higher underpricing is also associated with a larger number of business groups within an economy. We postulate that competition drives this finding; the larger the number of groups, the greater the competition for investor funds and share purchases during an IPO. Therefore, the need to signal quality increases as competition increases.

Our third finding is that underpricing increases as endemic corruption increases, which suggest interesting future avenues of inquiry. Do more corrupt countries have a higher concentration of groups with more pyramidal layers? Is corruption a proxy for the prevalence of tunneling, and lower returns for shareholders? Or, more generally, do investors demand a higher premium at IPO because the future benefits or costs of economic corruption are not yet revealed?

Initial public offering pricing is a vast literature, encompassing multiple time periods, industries, countries and firms, but the theme of heterogeneity in ownership structure remains relatively underexplored. We believe that it holds the key to resolving many of the unanswered questions and competing theories in the field.

5   CONCLUSION

This chapter demonstrates links between firm ownership structure and the average IPO underpricing in an economy. We aim to exhibit new avenues of exploring the effects of market competition, information asymmetry, power and conflicts of interest on IPO pricing. Using a cross-country analysis based on two independent datasets, we show that the amount of money "left on the table" for investors decreases with the degree of concentration of ownership within the economy. We also show that the greater the degree of separation between power and equity ownership, the smaller the average IPO underpricing. We view these findings as providing support for IPO pricing theories based on share allocation, social control and power.

NOTES

1. These papers all exclude IPOs of funds and non-operating companies.
2. Several economies are structured in a hybrid fashion, where ownership is concentrated not in the hands of individuals, but rather in holding corporations and banks that are themselves held by the affiliated firms. Japan's *keiretsu* and the German *konzerns* are prominent examples.
3. We included either the La Porta et. al. (1999) index or the index published by Spamann (2008). Neither was significant in our model.
4. Corruption Index 2011. Transparency International. Retrieved 24 Sept. 2012 (UTC).

REFERENCES

Aggarwal, Reena, Nagapuranand Prabhala and Manju Puri (2002), 'Institutional allocation in initial public offerings: empirical evidence', NBER Working Paper No. 9070.
Allen, Franklin and Gerald R. Faulhaber (1989), 'Signaling by underpricing in the IPO market', *Journal of Financial Economics*, **23**, 303–24.
Almeida, Heitor and Daniel Wolfenzon (2006a), 'Should business groups be dismantled? The equilibrium costs of efficient internal capital markets', *Journal of Financial Economics*, **79**, 99–144.
Almeida, Heitor and Daniel Wolfenzon (2006b), 'A theory of pyramidal ownership and family business groups', *Journal of Finance*, **61**, 2637–80.
Amihud, Yakov, Shmuel Hauser and Amir Kirsh (2001), 'Allocations, adverse selection and cascades in IPOs: evidence from Israel', working paper, New York University.
Bae, Kee-Hong, Jun-Koo Kang and Jin-Mo Kim (2002), 'Tunneling or value added? Evidence from mergers by Korean business groups', *Journal of Finance*, **57**, 2695–740.
Barca, F. and M. Becht (2001), *The Control of Corporate Europe*, Oxford: Oxford University Press.
Benveniste, Lawrence M. and Paul A. Spindt (1989), 'How investment bankers determine the offer price and allocation of new issues', *Journal of Financial Economics*, **24**, 343–61.
Benveniste, Lawrence M. and William J. Wilhelm (1990), 'A comparative analysis of ipo proceeds under alternative regulatory environments', *Journal of Financial Economics*, **28**, 173–207.
Bertrand, Marianne, Simon Johnson, Krislert Samphantharak and Antoinette Schoar (2008), 'Mixing family with business: a study of Thai business groups and the families behind them', *Journal of Financial Economics*, **88**, 466–98.
Bertrand, Marianne, Paras Mehta and Sendhil Mullainathan (2002), 'Ferreting out tunneling: an application to Indian business groups', *Quarterly Journal of Economics*, **117**, 121–48.
Bradshaw, Mark T., Scott A. Richardson and Richard G. Sloan (2006), 'The relation between corporate financing activities, analysts' forecasts and stock returns', *Journal of Accounting and Economics*, **42**, 53–85.
Brennan, M.J and J. Franks (1997), Underpricing, ownership and control in initial public offerings of equity securities in the UK', *Journal of Financial Economics*, **45**, 391–413.
Chang, Sea Jin and Jaebum Hong (2000), 'Economic performance of group-affiliated companies in Korea: Intragroup resource sharing and internal business transactions', *Academy of Management Journal*, **43**, 429–48.
Chemmanur, Thomas J. (1993), 'The pricing of initial public offers: a dynamic model with information production', *Journal of Finance*, **48**, 285–304.
Claessens, Stijn, Simeon Djankov and Larry H.P. Lang (2000), 'The separation of ownership and control in East Asian corporations', *Journal of Financial Economics*, **58**, 81–112.

Cornelli, Francesca and David Goldreich (2001), 'Bookbuilding and strategic allocation', *Journal of Finance*, **56**, 2337–69.
Davis, Gerald F. and E. Han Kim (2007), 'Business ties and proxy voting by mutual funds', *Journal of Financial Economics*, **85**, 552–70.
Dechow, Patricia M., Amy P. Hutton and Richard G. Sloan (2000), 'The relation between analysts' forecasts of long-term earnings growth and stock price performance following equity offerings', *Contemporary Accounting Research*, **17**, 1–32.
Faccio, Mara and Larry H.P. Lang (2002), 'The ultimate ownership of Western European corporations', *Journal of Financial Economics*, **65**, 365–95.
Friedman, Eric, Simon Johnson and Todd Mitton (2003), 'Propping and tunneling', *Journal of Comparative Economics*, **31** (4), 732–50.
Gopalan, Radhakrishnan, Vikram Nanda and Amit Seru (2007), 'Affiliated firms and financial support: evidence from Indian business groups', *Journal of Financial Economics*, **86**, 759–95.
Hanley, Katherine Weiss (1993), 'The underpricing of initial public offerings and the partial adjustment phenomenon', *Journal of Financial Economics*, **34**, 231–50.
Hanley, Katherine Weiss and William J. Wilhelm Jr (1995), 'Evidence on the strategic allocation of initial public offerings', *Journal of Financial Economics*, **37**, 239–57.
Ibbotson, Roger G. (1975), 'Price performance of common stock new issues', *Journal of Financial Economics*, **2**, 235–72.
Jegadeesh, Narasimhan, Mark Weinstein and Ivo Welch (1993), 'An empirical investigation of IPO returns and subsequent equity offerings', *Journal of Financial Economics*, **34**, 251–77.
Jiang, Guohua, Charles M.C. Lee and Heng Yue (2010), 'Tunneling through intercorporate loans: the China experience', *Journal of Financial Economics*, **98**, 1–20.
Johnson, Simon, Rafael La Porta, Florencio Lopez-de-Silanes and Andrey Shleifer (2000), 'Tunneling', *American Economic Review*, **90**, 22–7.
Kahneman, D. and A. Tversky (1979), 'Prospect theory: an analysis of decision under risk', *Econometrica*, **47**, 263–91.
Khanna, Tarun and Krishna Palepu (2000), Is group affliation profitable in emerging markets? An analysis of diversified Indian business groups, *Journal of Finance*, **55**, 867–91.
Khanna, Tarun and Jan W. Rivkin (2001), 'Estimating the performance effects of business groups in emerging markets', *Strategic Management Journal*, **22**, 45–74.
Khanna, Tarun and Yishay Yafeh (2007), 'Business groups in emerging markets: paragons or parasites?', *Journal of Economic Literature*, **45**, 331–72.
La Porta, Rafael, Florencio Lopez-De-Silanes and Andrei Shleifer (1999), 'Corporate ownership around the world', *Journal of Finance*, **54**, 471–517.
La Porta, Rafael, Florencio Lopez-de-Silanes, Andrei Shleifer and Robert W. Vishny (1998), 'Law and finance', *Journal of Political Economy*, **106**, 1113–55.
Leff, Nathaniel H. (1978), 'Industrial organization and entrepreneurship in the developing countries: the economic groups', *Economic Development and Cultural Change*, **26**, 661–75.
Ljungqvist, Alexander P. and William J. Wilhelm Jr (2002), 'IPO allocations: discriminatory or discretionary?', *Journal of Financial Economics*, **65**, 167–201.
Logue, Dennis E, Richard Rogalski, James Seward and Lynn Forster-Johnson (2002), 'What's special about the role of underwriter reputation and market activities in IPOs?', *Journal of Business*, **75**, 213–43.
Loughran, Tim, Jay R. Ritter and Kristian Rydqvist (1994), 'Initial public offerings: international insights', *Pacific-Basin Finance Journal*, **2**, 165–99.
Masulis, Ronald W., Peter K. Pham and Jason Zein (2011), 'Family business groups around the world: financing advantages, control motivations and organizational choices', *Review of Financial Studies*, **24**, 3556–600.
Mello, A.S. and J.E. Parsons (1998), 'Going public and the ownership structure of the firm', *Journal of Financial Economics*, **49**, 79–109.
Michaely, Roni and Wayne F. Shaw (1994), 'The pricing of initial public offerings: tests of adverse selection and signaling theories', *Review of Financial Studies*, **7**, 279–319.
Michaely, Roni and Kent L. Womack (1999), 'Conflict of interest and the credibility of underwriter analyst recommendations', *Review of Financial Studies*, **12**, 653–86.
Morck, Randall and Bernard Yeung (2003), 'Agency problems in large family business groups', *Entrepreneurship Theory and Practice*, **27**, 367–82.
Morck, Randall, David Stangeland and Bernard Yeung (1998), 'Inherited wealth, corporate control, and economic growth: the Canadian disease', in Randall Morck (ed.), National Bureau of Economic Research Conference, NBER Working Paper No. W6814.
Morck, Randall, Daniel Wolfenzon and Bernard Yeung (2005), 'Corporate governance, economic entrenchment, and growth', *Journal of Economic Literature*, **43**, 655–720.
Morey, Matthew, Aron Gottesman, Edward Baker and Ben Godridge (2009), 'Does better corporate govern-

ance result in higher valuations in emerging markets? Another examination using a new data set', *Journal of Banking & Finance*, **33**, 254–62.
O'Brien, Patricia C., Maureen F. McNichols and L.I.N. Hsiou-Wei (2005), 'Analyst impartiality and investment banking relationships', *Journal of Accounting Research*, **43**, 623–50.
Pulliam, Susan and Randall Smith (2000), 'Linux deal is focus of IPO-commission probe', *Wall Street Journal*, 12 December, C1.
Reilly, Frank K. (1973), 'Further evidence on short-run results for new issue investors', *Journal of Financial and Quantitative Analysis*, **8**, 83–90.
Ritter, Jay R. (1998), *Initial Public Offerings*, Boston, MA: WGL/RIA.
Ritter, Jay R. and Ivo Welch (2002), 'A review of IPO activity, pricing, and allocations', *Journal of Finance*, **57**, 1795–828.
Sachs, Jeffrey D. and Andrew M. Warner (1997), 'Fundamental sources of long-run growth', *American Economic Review*, **20**, 247–65.
Sacristan-Navarro, Maria and Silvia Gomez-Anson (2007), 'Family ownership and pyramids in the Spanish market', *Family Business Review*, **20**, 247–65.
Sherman, Ann and Sheridan Titman (2002), 'Building the IPO order book: underpricing and particpation limits with costly information', *Journal of Financial Eonomics*, **65**, 3–29.
Shin, Hyun-Han and Young S. Park (1999), 'Financing constraints and internal capital markets: evidence from Korean chaebols', *Journal of Corporate Finance*, **5**, 169–91.
Simon, Johnson, Daniel Kaufmann and Pablo Zoido-Lobatón (1998), 'Regulatory discretion and the unofficial economy', *American Economic Review*, **88**, 387–92.
Spamann, Holger (2008), 'Law and finance revisited', American Law & Economics Association Annual Meeting, John M. Olin Center For Law, Economics and Business.
Spatt, Chester S. and Sanjay Srivastava (1991), 'Preplay communication, participation restrictions and efficiency in initial public offerings', *Review of Financial Studies*, **4**, 709–26.
Stoll, Hans R. and Anthony J. Curley (1970), 'Small business and the new issues market for equities', *Journal of Financial and Quantitative Analysis*, **5**, 309–22.
Stoughton, N.M. and Josef Zechner (1998), 'IPO-mechanisms, monitoring and ownership structure', *Journal of Financial Economics*, **49**, 45–77.
Welch, Ivo (1989), 'Seasoned offerings, imitation costs, and the underpricing of initial public offerings', *Journal of Finance*, **44**, 421–49.

PART V

THE AFTERMARKET PERFORMANCE OF IPOS

17 Acquisitions, SEOs, divestitures and IPO performance
Naaguesh Appadu, Anna Faelten and Mario Levis

1 INTRODUCTION

Since the early 1990s, when Ritter (1991) first documented the aftermarket underperformance of initial public offerings (IPOs), a considerable amount of empirical research across many countries[1] has corroborated his findings and highlighted some significant differences in performance across different types of IPOs.[2] Post-event market underperformance, however, is not a unique feature of IPOs. A number of studies, for example, report that firms with seasoned equity offerings (SEOs) underperform in comparison to similar non-issuing firms in the three-year period following the issue (Loughran and Ritter, 1995; Spiess and Affleck-Graves, 1995; Iqbal et al., 2006). Furthermore, despite the positive initial returns for firms announcing acquisitions, there is considerable evidence suggesting negative post-event performance at least for stock-financed acquisitions (Loughran and Vijh, 1997; Rau and Vermaelen, 1998; Wiggenhorn et al., 2007).

Raising additional equity capital and acquisitions are quite common among recently listed firms. Survey evidence of US and European chief financial officers (CFOs) on the motivation of IPOs (Brau and Fawcett, 2006; Bancel and Mittoo, 2009) and the actual record of corporate activity of recent IPOs (Hovakimian and Hutton, 2010b) suggest that such activities are an integral part of future strategy for growth. Divestitures are also widely used by firms in general as part of an overall strategic plan and are often related to recent acquisitions. In contrast to SEOs and acquisitions, however, they tend to be value enhancing (Dranikoff et al., 2002; Hollowell, 2009; Lee and Madhavan, 2010). Given the similarities in the post-event performance patterns of IPOs and acquisitions, Brau et al. (2012) argue that acquisitions by recently listed firms may account for the aftermarket underperformance of IPOs. A similar type of argument could apply to SEOs as well.

In spite of the considerable evidence on the extent of individual corporate activity, in terms of acquisitions, seasoned equity offerings and divestitures by recently listed firms, there is still relatively limited empirical evidence on the implications of the range of such activities on subsequent performance.[3] The purpose of this chapter is to investigate the pattern of these three types of follow-on corporate activities during the three-year period after flotation and their implications on the long-run aftermarket performance of recent IPOs.

In this chapter, we test and find support for strong linkages in the type, timing and pattern underpinning the different kinds of post-IPO corporate event; furthermore, we also show that such characteristics of corporate events have a defining effect on the aftermarket performance of IPO companies. Recent IPO firms involved in a series of acquisitions and/or seasoned equity offerings perform relatively better in comparison to others who remain either totally inactive or just have a single, probably opportunistic, event without a coherent plan for future growth. This could also be the result of an inherent sample bias as firms that realize their set objectives of a recent completed corporate transaction are unlikely to return for more at least in the immediate future. In this sense, the superior performance of the firms displaying a pattern of continued corporate activity is to be expected. By showing that the aftermarket performance of IPO companies relates both to the pattern and underlying motivation of their follow-on transactions, we highlight an additional important dimension of the long-standing debate on IPO firms' aftermarket performance. More specifically, we argue that a public listing on its own is not necessarily the determining factor of aftermarket performance; instead, the newly listed firms' competitive position and management's ability to utilize their public status to pursue growth opportunities have a defining impact on future performance.

We start our analysis by providing a detailed account of the types of corporate event undertaken by IPO firms within the first three years of their listing. We find that a total of 82 percent of the IPO companies in our sample were involved in at least one of the three types of corporate event, while half of them had at least one acquisition or SEO. Overall, acquisitions, either in cash, stock, or both, were by far the most popular type of corporate event, accounting for 54 percent of all of the events in the sample.

In the rest of the chapter, we examine the underlying characteristics of each of the three types of corporate event. We find that the IPO firms mostly involved in acquisitions are larger and more profitable, with a strong market debut and good recent stock performance at least for stock-financed transactions. Seasoned equity offerings also come early after the IPO at times of positive market sentiment following a recent run of good stock performance, but on average are the less profitable IPO firms that raise additional equity capital. Divestitures, on the other hand, come later and involve considerably larger firms often listed on the Main market have low cash balances. We also find that the underlying motivation for the same type of transaction may change over time. An acquisition, SEO, or a divestiture, for example, are sometimes driven by pure demand for capital, while at other times they occur predominantly due to market timing considerations.

Second, we investigate the aftermarket performance of IPO companies on the basis of the type and pattern of their follow-on corporate activities, in terms of acquisitions, SEOs, and divestitures. We find strong evidence that IPO firms that engage in a number of SEOs and acquisitions during the three-year post-IPO period perform significantly better than their inactive counterparts. Although a casual comparison of our results with the evidence of previous studies may indicate noticeable inconsistencies, these are due to differences in the sample characteristics and the methodological approach between this and other studies. More specifically, instead of examining a specific type of corporate event in isolation, we take a rounded view of a firm's follow-on corporate event activities and their implications for performance. Our rationale for this integrated approach reflects our underlying view that a series of follow-on corporate activities is a better indicator of a firm's planned strategy for growth.

To the best of our knowledge, this is the first study that explicitly recognizes and traces the activity and patterns of three of the most common types of event during a three-year period in the aftermarket. By examining the underlying company characteristics, patterns and motivation behind each of the three types of event over different time periods after the IPO, we show that the drivers behind them differ not only across the three events but for each specific event over different time periods. More generally, we also contribute to the literature by showing that the average aftermarket underperformance of IPO companies conceals a wide range of diverse performances that relate to the timing and type of their follow-on decisions during the first three years after flotation.

The rest of the chapter is organized as follows. Section 2 provides a review of the related literature. Section 3 describes the data and methodology, and section 4 provides a detailed mapping of the type and sequence of the three corporate events during the three-year period following the IPO. Section 5 examines the underlying characteristics of acquisitions, SEOs and divestitures, and section 6 reports on IPO companies' aftermarket performance according to different types of corporate activity. Finally, in section 7 we summarize the results and highlight the key conclusions and potential implications of our study.

2 RELATED LITERATURE

The popularity of follow-on corporate activity by newly listed firms is consistent with the view that an IPO is the first step towards a long-term plan for growth. An IPO, for example, offers the opportunity to raise the cash or use the publicly traded stock for future acquisitions (Mikkelson et al., 1997; Brau et al., 2003) and reduce information asymmetry (Eckbo et al., 1990). The survey of chief financial officers by Brau and Fawcett (2006) provides considerable support for the latter position. Capital infusion and alleviation of information uncertainty, however, are not the only links between an IPO and a merger. A public listing may also facilitate a subsequent stock merger by reducing valuation uncertainty and leading to more efficient acquisition strategies (Hsieh et al., 2011).

Recent empirical evidence by Hovakimian and Hutton (2010a) and Celikyurt et al. (2010) provides even further support for the importance of acquisitions for newly listed firms. They show that the future growth of IPO firms is mainly through acquisitions rather than capital expenditure or R&D; IPO firms are also more prolific acquirers in comparison to their more mature counterparts within their industry (Maksimovic et al., 2010).

Acquisitions may also stimulate demand for additional capital, leading to further capital-raising rounds. Welch (1989), for example, finds significantly higher levels of secondary issue offerings among recently floated firms than one would expect among a random sample of firms. The surge in post-IPO acquisitions, however, may also lead to divestitures as certain parts of the acquired assets, which do not fit into the newly developed entity, may be disposed of to improve profitability. Divestitures, of course, could also be related to market feedback and the enhanced liquidity enjoyed by the public listing.

The poor aftermarket performance of acquisitions and seasoned equity offerings is often attributed to the market misevaluation hypothesis (Shleifer and Vishny, 2003; Baker et al., 2003), which leads to opportunistic behavior and the tendency of managers to exploit their informational advantage by timing their financing and investment decisions to take advantage of overvalued stock prices.[4] A number of studies provide evidence that is broadly consistent with the market timing of IPOs and SEOs (Levis, 1995; Loughran and Ritter, 1995; Jiang, 2008; Kim and Weisbach, 2008), acquisitions

(Loughran and Vijh, 1997; Rhodes-Kropf et al., 2005) and even divestitures (Brauer and Stussi, 2010).

Financing and investment decisions may also be motivated by feedback received from the market that helps in the pursuit of expected growth opportunities. Jegadeesh et al. (1993), for example, show that IPOs followed by high returns are associated with a higher probability of follow-on SEOs within three years of the IPO. More recently, Hovakimian and Hutton (2010b) also report that firms with high post-equity-issue returns are more likely to return to the market for additional rounds of equity financing. They argue that these results are consistent with the market feedback hypothesis in that high post-issue returns encourage managers to return to the market for additional funding. It is important to note, however, that such a pattern of follow-on equity issues may also be the direct outcome of strategic (demand for capital) rather than opportunistic (overvaluation) transactions.

Lowry and Schwert (2002) highlight an additional dimension of the market feedback hypothesis by reporting that IPO volume and average initial returns are highly autocorrelated, that is, companies tend to go public following periods of high initial returns. Both the cycles of initial returns and the lead-lag relationship between initial returns and IPO volume are predominantly driven by information learned during the registration period. More positive information results in higher initial returns and more companies filing IPOs soon thereafter. Recent increases in the price of acquiring firms as a result of either positive market feedback or overvaluation is likely to affect stock but not cash-based acquisitions (King et al., 2008).

Finally, it is also interesting to note that all three types of corporate event (IPOs, acquisitions and SEOs) are not only moving in cycles of their own but, given that the underlying drivers of individual corporate events are broadly similar, there is a significant overlap among them. Lowry (2003), for example, finds that IPO volume fluctuates substantially over time and relates to firms' demands for capital and investor sentiment; Howe and Zhang (2010) show a similar pattern for SEOs. Furthermore, Colak and Tekatli (2010) find that a common factor related to the business cycle can explain a significant proportion of individual corporate events. Moreover, Rau and Stouraitis (2011) find that such corporate event waves are closely linked and even follow certain patterns. For example, SEOs precede IPOs, which are followed by stock-financed merger waves, followed in turn by stock repurchase activity. The speed and sequence of corporate event waves may have important implications for the timing of financing and investment decisions. More specifically, a recently floated firm that timed its listing at a 'window of opportunity' for IPOs is likely to be involved soon afterwards in some type of acquisition if the IPO and merger and acquisition (M&A) waves overlap. In such cases, acquisitions by IPO firms are likely to take place within a short time period after flotation.

It is important to note two recent papers that focus explicitly on the long-run performance for firms with follow-on corporate events. Brau et al. (2012) find that IPO companies that acquire within a year of going public significantly underperform in the three years following flotation; on the other hand, non-acquiring IPO firms or those that wait for more than a year after the IPO to become acquirers do not significantly underperform over the same time period. Their paper, however, differs from ours not only on its focus on acquisitions only, but more importantly on its implicit assumption that acquisitions are the only type of follow-on corporate transactions made by recently listed firms. Furthermore, they do not distinguish between cash and stock acquisitions, a feature that is usually associated with differences in performance (Loughran and Vijh, 1997; Carrow et al., 2004). In contrast Bessler and Zimmermann (2011), using a pan-European IPO sample,[5] show positive aftermarket long-run performance for acquiring IPO firms. Their study, however, also ignores any other type of corporate activities that the recent IPOs may have been involved after the listing. Billett et al. (2011) also provide a wider perspective on subsequent corporate activities by examining the implications of a variety of follow-on security issuances on long-run performance. Their results suggest that negative post-issuance returns are related to the number of different types of security issued; in the case of IPOs, they find that firms that go through a series of post-IPO financing rounds, in the form of bank loans, follow-on SEOs, public debt issues, or private placements of equity significantly underperform. Their evidence implies that undertaking such activities without a strong strategic objective leads to disappointing performance.

3 DATA AND METHODOLOGY

This study is based on a sample of 1504 non-financial IPOs listed on the two London markets, the Official List (often referred to as the Main market) (276 IPOs) and the Alternative Investment Market (AIM) (1228 IPOs) during the period from January 1995 to March 2008. The basic sample of IPOs originates from London Stock Exchange statistics and covers industry classification, market capitalization, amount raised, and issue price. The data on the follow-on acquisitions (cash and stock), SEOs, and divestitures within the three years after flotation are from Bloomberg and cover the period January 1995 to December 2010. We analyze the entire universe of all completed acquisition and SEO transactions with a stated deal value amount.[6] The financial accounts, stock price returns and macroeconomic data is from Datastream.

Long-term aftermarket performance estimates are based on buy-and-hold abnormal returns (BHARs) for each IPO.[7] These are computed as:

$$BHAR = \frac{1}{N}\sum_{i=1}^{N}\left[\left(\prod_{t=1}^{T}(1 + r_{it})\right) - \left(\prod_{t=1}^{T}(1 + r_{bt})\right)\right] \quad (17.1)$$

where: r_{it} and r_{bt} are the raw returns on IPO i and the selected benchmark b at event month t.

We estimate BHARs using the FTSE All-Share Index for all IPOs listed on the Main market and the Small Cap index for IPOs listed on AIM. Given the concentration of certain industries in our IPO sample we also estimate industry-adjusted BHARs based on the 10 broad FTSE sector indices. The null hypothesis that the mean BHARs are equal to zero is tested using the skewness-adjusted t-statistic with bootstrapped p-values as suggested by Lyon et al. (1999) and adapted by Jelic et al. (2005).

We also assess aftermarket performance using the Fama and French (1993) three-factor model with equal- and value-weighted returns as follows:

352 *Handbook of research on IPOs*

$$R_{pt} - R_{ft} = a_i + b_i(R_{mt} - R_{ft}) + s\,SMB_t + h\,HML_t + e_t \qquad (17.2)$$

The three factors are ($R_{mt} - R_{ft}$) the excess return on the value-weighted market portfolio, (*SMB*) the return on a portfolio formed by subtracting the return on a large from the return on a small firm portfolio. High minus low (*HML*) is the return on UK-listed high book-to-market return minus the return of the low book-to-market portfolio and R_f is the 90-day UK Treasury bill rate. The *SMB* and *HML* portfolios were constructed using a two-by-three grouping rebalanced every six months throughout the sample period.

4 DESCRIPTIVE STATISTICS OF IPOS AND FOLLOW-ON CORPORATE EVENTS

4.1 Annual Distribution of IPOs and Corporate Events

Table 17.1 provides details of the annual distribution of the sample of 1504 IPOs during the period January 1995 to March 2008 and their follow-on corporate activities in

Table 17.1 Annual distribution of IPOs, acquisitions, SEOs, and divestitures

Year	IPOs No.	IPOs Amount raised (£m)	Acquisitions No.	Acquisitions Value (£m)	SEOs No.	SEOs Value (£m)	Divestitures No.	Divestitures Value (£m)*	All events No.	All events Value (£m)
1995	11	53							–	–
1996	82	419	1	127	9	244	0		10	371
1997	53	273	2	1	12	92	1		15	93
1998	71	7119	47	485	25	220	5		77	705
1999	77	10951	98	668	32	270	21		151	939
2000	201	9276	189	3090	59	2072	20		268	5162
2001	78	4891	170	1503	35	957	53		258	2460
2002	54	3984	118	852	48	935	41		207	1787
2003	50	2586	61	3536	31	1437	33		125	4973
2004	214	4375	81	1073	25	805	20		126	1878
2005	261	8471	168	3126	68	1932	39		275	5058
2006	200	13534	234	7604	167	3409	43		444	11013
2007	144	11096	273	5043	225	4235	69		567	9278
2008	8	170	108	2556	108	1898	57		273	4454
2009			22	6696	47	1066	23		92	7762
2010			14	1787	22	524	9		45	2312
2011			1		2	23	2		5	23
All	1504	77197	1587	38146	915	20120	436		2938	58266

Notes:
The total sample of 1504 IPOs during the period 1995–2008 raised a total of £77.2 billion and involved 1587 acquisitions worth £38.1 billion, 915 SEOs raising £20.1 billion, and 436 divestitures. In total, the sample of IPO firms was involved in 2938 corporate events in the three-year period after flotation, worth £58.3 billion, excluding the value of divestitures.
* Data for the value of divestitures is not available.

terms of acquisitions, SEOs, and divestitures. It shows significant variations in both the volume of IPOs and follow-on events during the sample period. The first wave of IPOs ended in the middle of 2000 with the burst of the technology bubble; the market started growing again in 2004 with 218 issues that year and continued for three years until mid-2007, with the peak year being 2005 with 270 issues.[8] In sharp contrast to the strong and almost immediate involvement of a large number of recently listed IPO firms in a frantic spree of acquisitions during 1999–2001, the 2004–06 cohort was relatively modest and it took almost two years for follow-on acquisitions to peak again. This new wave of IPOs was also different from 1999–2000 as it was followed by strong SEO activity (333 issues) in the subsequent two years. On the other hand, the volume of divestitures appears relatively stable during the entire sample period.[9] The differences in the patterns of the follow-on events between the two waves reflect, to a certain extent, the type and characteristics of the two IPO groups and the corresponding market sentiment at the time. The 1999–2000 wave of IPOs, for example, was dominated by small technology firms listing on AIM, raising modest amounts of capital at relatively high valuations; in contrast, the 2004–06 cycle was considerably more diverse in terms of industry distribution and market size. Both cycles of IPO, acquisition and SEO activity coincided, however, with corresponding strong market performances.

The 1504 IPO firms in our sample were involved in 2938 corporate events during the three-year period after flotation, resulting in an average of 1.9 events per IPO firm. Consistent with the literature on the importance of acquisitions as one of the key objectives for an IPO, more than 50 percent of the follow-on corporate events (1587) were acquisitions. In contrast, however, with the CFOs' view that IPOs provide 'currency' for acquisitions, unreported results show that pure cash transactions accounted for 41 percent of all acquisitions while pure stock acquisitions accounted for only 14 percent; the 'currency' argument, however, receives considerable support from the 708 acquisitions (45 percent of the total) that were completed by a combination of cash and stock.

Table 17.2 provides summary statistics of the number of corporate events for each of the three years following an IPO. It is immediately apparent that each of the three types of corporate event follows a distinct timing pattern. In sharp contrast to divestitures, for example – almost half of which occur during the third year after flotation – 45 percent of the total number of acquisitions completed within the first 12 months and then gradually decline during the second (32 percent) and third years (23 percent). This pattern of activity is consistent with the notion that firms are indeed using public listing as part of a strategic move for growth through acquisitions. On the other hand, the broadly even distribution of SEOs across the three years suggests that firms raise additional equity at regular intervals in order to fund ongoing operations and possibly cash acquisitions.

4.2 Volume, Pattern and Timing of Follow-on Corporate Events

Table 17.3 provides details on the pattern and timing of corporate events by IPO firms during the three-year period following flotation. First, it is worth noting that out of a total of 1504 IPOs, only 1277 were still listed at the beginning of the third year; a sizeable proportion (15 percent) of the original sample were delisted either voluntarily, that is, as a result of transfer to the Main market, a merger, going private again or bankruptcy. More specifically, Table 17.3 shows the number and proportion of IPO firms that were

Table 17.2 Annual number of events announced in the three years after flotation

	Year 1	Year 2	Year 3	TOTAL
Acquisitions				
Number	715	503	369	1587
% of total by year	(45)	(32)	(23)	(100)
% of total by type	(67)	(49)	(43)	(54)
SEOs				
Number	274	346	295	915
% of total by year	(30)	(38)	(32)	(100)
% of total by type	(26)	(34)	(34)	(31)
Divestitures				
Number	71	168	197	436
% of total by year	(16)	(39)	(45)	(100)
% of total by type	(7)	(17)	(23)	(15)
All				
Number	1060	1017	861	2938
% of total by year	(36)	(35)	(29)	(100)
% of total by type	(100)	(100)	(100)	(100)

Notes:
The total sample of 1504 IPO firms during the period 1995–2008 was involved in 2938 corporate events during the first three years after flotation.
Acquisitions account for 54% of the total number of events (2938) during 1995–2011, while SEOs and divestitures account for 31% and 15% respectively.
The majority of acquisitions (45%) occur within the first year of listing, while a larger number of divestitures (45%) take place in the third year after going public.
SEOs are distributed evenly across the three years.

involved in each of the three types of corporate event during the first six months and at one, two, and three years after flotation. The percentage estimates are based on the number of live IPO firms at the end of each of the four periods. For example, 625 IPO firms, or 49 percent of those still alive at the end of the three-year period, were not involved in any acquisitions. On the other hand, 652 (51 percent of the surviving IPO firms) made at least one acquisition within the three-year period, while 124 (10 percent of the surviving) made at least four.

Acquisitions clearly emerge as the most popular type of activity, particularly within 12 months of flotation; a total of 28 percent and 41 percent of the IPO companies in the sample had at least one such event within first 12 and 24 months, respectively, and by the end of the third year, more than half (51 percent) had concluded one such transaction. However, although the pattern of post-IPO acquisition activity in the UK is broadly comparable to the US, the average number of takeovers per IPO is still lower. Celikyurt et al. (2010), for example, report that 54.7 percent of IPO firms in the US conduct at least one acquisition within the first year and 71.5 percent within three years. Moreover, while they find that the average number of acquisitions during the first IPO year is 0.65, increasing to 3.35 by the end of the third year, the equivalent average level of acquisition activity in the UK is 0.48 for the first year, increasing to 1.04 by the third year. Their sample, however, includes only 1295 IPOs with total proceeds equal to or greater than

Table 17.3 Summary statistics of corporate events following an IPO

	Months 0–6 No.	Months 0–6 %	Years 0–1 No.	Years 0–1 %	Years 0–2 No.	Years 0–2 %	Years 0–3 No.	Years 0–3 %
Total no. of IPOs	1504							
End of period: IPOs	1495	99%	1475	98%	1388	92%	1277	85%
Delisted IPO firms	9	1%	29	2%	116	8%	227	15%
IPO firms conducting no:								
Acquisitions	1253	84%	1069	73%	824	59%	625	49%
SEOs	1378	92%	1225	83%	887	64%	632	50%
Divestitures	1465	98%	1450	98%	1225	88%	977	77%
Events at all	1162	78%	889	60%	484	35%	213	17%
IPO firms making at least one:								
Acquisition	242	16%	406	28%	564	41%	652	51%
SEO	117	8%	250	17%	501	36%	645	50%
Divestiture	30	2%	58	4%	163	12%	280	22%
IPO firms making at least two:								
Acquisitions	69	5%	155	11%	267	19%	344	27%
SEOs	5	0%	23	2%	106	8%	215	17%
Divestitures	2	0%	10	1%	42	3%	80	6%
IPO firms making at least three:								
Acquisitions	24	2%	73	5%	143	10%	204	16%
SEOs	0	0%	1	0%	11	1%	48	4%
Divestitures	0	0%	3	0%	15	1%	38	3%
IPO firms making at least four:								
Acquisitions	9	1%	34	2%	85	6%	124	10%
SEOs	0	0%	0	0%	2	0%	7	1%
Divestitures	0	0%	0	0%	8	1%	19	1%

Notes: The sample of 1504 IPOs during the period 1995–2008 were involved in different types of corporate events in the three years following flotation. An event can be an acquisition, an SEO or a divestiture during the first six, 12, 24, or 36 months. From a total of 227 IPO companies, 15% of the initial sample were delisted by the end of the three-year period after flotation, and about 50% of the initial sample of IPO companies by the end of the three-year period were not involved in any acquisitions or SEOs; a large proportion of the IPO companies (77%) were not involved in any divestitures. Overall, during the three-year period in the aftermarket, only 17% were not involved in any type of corporate event, while small minorities of 10%, 1%, and 2% were involved in more than four acquisitions, SEOs, or divestitures respectively.

$100 million. Hovakimian and Hutton (2010a), on the other hand, using a larger sample of 5771 IPOs that includes smaller companies and over a longer time period, find that only 19 percent and 36 percent of the IPO firms in their sample completed at least one acquisition by the first and third years of their IPO, respectively. This is a level of activity considerably lower than the equivalent 28 percent and 51 percent rates of activity which we report in Table 17.3 for the UK. They also find that the average number of acquisitions per IPO is just 0.74, considerably lower than in the UK.

Seasoned equity offerings start relatively slowly, with only 17 percent having an additional equity issue in the first 12 months, but their frequency grows rapidly during the second and third years. In fact, by the end of the third year, 50 percent of the surviving

IPO firms had raised additional equity through at least one SEO, a proportion almost identical to those involved in a least one acquisition; a further 17 percent and 4 percent of the surviving IPOs had two or three SEOs respectively by the third year of listing. Overall, however, the average number of SEOs from our original sample of IPOs is only 0.6 in comparison to 1.04 acquisitions per IPO. The pattern of SEO activity in our sample is consistent with Hovakimian and Hutton (2010b), who use a broader sample of equity issues not related to IPOs only, finding that 50 percent of the issues are by firms that issue once, 26 percent by those issuing twice and 13 percent three times. The slow start and subsequent gradual increase in the number of SEOs could be related to the emerging need for funds for further acquisitions and capital expenditure but could also be related to recent price movements. Table 17.3 also shows that a remarkable 77 percent of the surviving sample IPO companies did not complete a single divestiture during the three-year period. Only 4 percent made a divestiture within the first year of listing but, although their popularity increased gradually over time, only 23 percent of the IPO firms still alive at the beginning of the third year were involved in at least one such event by the end of the three-year period. Finally, it is worth noting that the overall volume of acquisitions and SEOs in our sample of IPOs is very similar to the equivalent level of activity across Europe (Vismara et al. 2012).

Table 17.4, in the broad shape of a decision tree, offers a different perspective on post-IPO corporate activity by tracing the pattern of the first three post-IPO corporate events. For each step, there are five options: acquisition, divestiture, SEO, no event, or delisting. The first event for 500 (33 percent) of the total of 1504 IPO firms in the initial sample was an acquisition, 29 percent an SEO, and 9 percent a divestiture. At the same time, 87 firms (5 percent) were delisted before they had undertaken any corporate activity, while almost a quarter (353 firms or 24 percent) of the whole sample was not involved in any corporate activity during the first three years of public life.

Table 17.4 also shows that 46 percent of firms (230) with an acquisition as their first event followed it up with a second acquisition, while 52 percent (122) even made a third acquisition during the three-year period following flotation. At the same time, 19 percent of the IPO firms starting with an acquisition as their first corporate event followed it up with an SEO and then either switched to yet another acquisition (36 percent), opted for a divestiture (4 percent), or proceeded with another SEO (16 percent). We also observe a broadly similar interchanging pattern for IPO firms starting with an SEO or a divestiture as their first event. For example, 435 IPO firms (29 percent of the total), raised additional equity as their first corporate event; 25 percent of these followed it up with a second fundraising round and 19 percent even had a third one. At the same time, a sizeable proportion (23 percent) probably used at least some of the proceeds of their first SEO for an acquisition as their second event.

Overall, the evidence suggests that the type of the first corporate event sets the pattern for the follow-on activities. For example, more than half of the IPO firms starting with an acquisition are involved in more acquisitions as their second and third events. Moreover, 54 percent of IPO firms starting with a divestiture are also more likely to be involved in two more such transactions later on. A broadly similar, but with a less pronounced pattern, is also observed for SEOs. Such repetitive patterns of the same type of event may be related to positive market feedback and subsequent positive performance, as reported for SEOs by Hovakimian and Hutton (2010b), or may be part of a predefined strategic

Acquisitions, SEOs, divestitures and IPO performance 357

Table 17.4 Patterns of post-IPO corporate event activity

	Event 1	Event 2	Event 3
1504 IPOs		Acquisition (230; 46%)	Acquisition (122; 52%) SEO (28; 12%) Divestiture (21; 10%) No event (55; 24%) Delist (4; 2%)
	Acquisition (500; 33%)	SEO (95; 19%)	Acquisition (35; 36%) SEO (15; 16%) Divestiture (4; 4%) No event (37; 40%) Delist (4; 4%)
		Divestiture (27; 16%)	Acquisition (8; 20%) SEO (3; 13%) Divestiture (5; 16%) No event (8; 32%) Delist (3; 13%)
		No event (121; 24%) Delist (27; 5%)	
		Acquisition (106; 24%)	Acquisition (36; 34%) SEO (24; 23%) Divestiture (5; 5%) No event (34; 32%) Delist (7; 6%)
	SEO (435; 29%)	SEO (111; 25%)	Acquisition (18; 16%) SEO (21; 19%) Divestiture (6; 5%) No event (62; 56%) Delist (4; 4%)
		Divestiture (34; 8%)	Acquisition (4; 11%) SEO (5; 15%) Divestiture (9; 26%) No event (12; 37%) Delist (4; 11%)
		No event (160; 37%) Delist (28; 6%)	
		Acquisition (16; 12%)	Acquisition (6; 38%) SEO (3; 18%) Divestiture (1; 6%) No event (6; 38%) Delist (0; 0%)
	Divestiture (129; 9%)	SEO (29; 22%)	Acquisition (0; 0%) SEO (4; 14%) Divestiture (7; 24%) No event (17; 59%) Delist (1; 3%)
		Divestiture (25; 20%)	Acquisition (0; 0%) SEO (0; 0%) Divestiture (13; 54%) No event (11; 42%) Delist (1; 4%)
		No event (45; 36%) Delist (14; 10%)	
	No event (353; 24%) Delist (87; 5%)		

Notes:
This table illustrates the pattern of corporate events for the 1504 newly listed firms.
After listing, there are five possible options: acquisition, SEO, divestiture, no event, or delisting. Delisting incorporates bankruptcy, delisting, and takeover. Each option is available three consecutive times, event 1, event 2, and event 3. The table therefore becomes a decision tree illustration in that each event step (1–3) shows the number of firms following a given path of the five options available.
The numbers in brackets correspond to the number of firms following the given path together with the corresponding probability for the sample.

plan for growth. We explore the potential implications of such patterns of serial behavior on long-term performance in section 5. Finally, it is worth noting that a total of 28 firms – 7.2 percent of the surviving firms – were delisted after completing three events.

5   THE LIKELIHOOD OF AN ACQUISITION, SEO OR DIVESTITURE

In this section we investigate the firm and market characteristics related to each of the three types of corporate event. Table 17.5 presents summary statistics on the size and key operating characteristics for our sample of IPOs, in both the Main and AIM markets, by the type of their first corporate event, and for the group of IPO firms without any corporate activity during the three years after flotation. More specifically, it reports the median values for underpricing, market value, and equity proceeds as well as a number of key performance indicators. In general, we find no fundamental differences in the characteristics of the IPO firms involved in different types of corporate event; this applies to firms in both the Main and AIM markets, in spite of the obvious differences in the absolute values of their size-related characteristics. There are, however, some subtle differences between corporate-event active and inactive IPO firms. The latter group, for example, consists of relatively larger firms in terms of assets and sales, which are more profitable, at least in the Main market, both in absolute and relative terms, and operating in more mature industries as indicated by their assets' tangibility. On the other hand, recently listed firms involved in acquisitions and SEOs are relatively smaller in terms of sales and somewhat less profitable.

We use logit panel regressions to assess separately the likelihood of an acquisition – financed by cash, stock or mixed – SEO, or divestiture as a function of company-specific characteristics and market conditions. In the logit regression (17.3), the dependent variable is set to one when there is an event during each of the six-month intervals within the three years after going public or 0 otherwise. Thus, the same IPO firm may be included in any of the six logit regressions if it was involved in different types of event during that period.

$$A_{it} = a_i + \beta_1 Timing + \beta_2 IPOProceeds + \beta_3 EquityProceeds(-6M) + \\ \beta_4 Profitability(-1Y) + \beta_5 Leverage(-1Y) + \beta_6 Tangibility(-1Y) + \\ \beta_7 Return(-3M) + \beta_8 MarketSentiment(-3M) + \beta_9 GDPGrowth(-6M) + \\ \beta_{10} FDR + \beta_{11} PreviousEvent(-1) + \beta_{12} Market + \beta_{13} Sales(-1Y) + \varepsilon_{it} \quad (17.3)$$

The independent variables relate to the three hypotheses while company characteristics are used as control variables. According to the financing hypothesis, the probability of acquisition increases with the availability of IPO proceeds (money raised at flotation scaled to total assets), the proceeds of previous equity issues (equity raised scaled to total assets), profitability (earnings before interest, tax, depreciation and amortization, EBITDA, scaled to total assets), leverage (total debt scaled to total assets) and asset tangibility (property plant and equipment scaled to total assets). On the other hand, the probability of acquisition declines with the time period lapsed since the IPO (the number of six-month intervals since the IPO).

Table 17.5 Operational characteristics for the IPO firms at the time of listing

	Acquisitions Cash		Stock		Hybrid		SEOs		Divestitures		No Event	
	Main	AIM	Main	AIM	Main	AIM	Main	AIM	Main	AIM	Main	AIM
Underpricing												
Median	8%	10%	10%	9%	8%	10%	8%	8%	8.3%	7.7%	9%	7.3%
No. obs.	80	256	18	129	59	274	89	489	55	184	54	355
MV at offer (£m)												
Median	430	20	535	13	204	16	490	19	674	22	157	17
No. obs.	98	268	22	149	68	291	114	531	82	198	67	373
IPO proceeds (£m)												
Median	94	5	67	3	64	4	115	4	188	6	54	5
No. obs.	98	268	21	149	67	290	112	530	81	198	67	373
Total Assets (£m)												
Median	104	10	48	5	63	7	147	7	266	9	59	6
No. obs.	88	266	21	146	65	286	107	521	68	190	64	357
Sales (£m)												
Median	104	10	48	5	63	7	147	7	266	9	59	6
No. obs.	88	266	21	146	65	286	107	521	68	190	64	357
EBITDA (£m)												
Median	12	0.6	2	−0.1	5	0.1	19	−0.3	27	−0.2	4	0.04
No. obs.	88	231	19	128	62	249	104	464	165	169	63	309
IPO proceeds/TA												
Median	63%	56%	104%	67%	86%	54%	63%	71%	49%	57%	82%	77%
No. obs.	85	263	15	139	63	274	102	495	66	181	60	340

Table 17.5 (continued)

	Acquisitions Cash		Stock		Hybrid		SEOs		Divestitures		No Event	
	Main	AIM	Main	AIM	Main	AIM	Main	AIM	Main	AIM	Main	AIM
Sales/TA												
Median	94%	68%	70%	18%	47%	60%	71%	18%	67%	18%	68%	38%
No. obs.	82	219	19	119	59	232	99	448	66	164	54	284
Leverage (TD/TA)												
Median	15%	7%	14%	18%	5%	6%	14%	3%	15%	3%	13%	3%
No. obs.	87	232	20	123	63	249	106	456	65	166	62	296
Cash/TA												
Median	15%	19%	55%	28%	26%	22%	18%	33%	12%	22%	18%	28%
No. obs.	84	219	18	119	61	238	103	437	63	163	61	271
Tangibility/TA												
Median	18%	8%	7%	7%	8%	6%	19%	7%	18%	7.5%	26%	8%
No. obs.	85	217	19	112	54	234	104	421	64	159	61	269
EBITDA to sales												
Median	16%	7%	8.2%	−8.3%	13%	4%	17%	−18%	16%	−0.8%	11%	4.4%
No. obs.	88	209	19	128	62	235	100	346	63	132	62	265
EBITDA/TA												
Median	15%	7%	−1.3%	−9%	12%	1.4%	−8%	−7%	11%	−4%	13%	1%
No. obs.	88	231	22	149	62	249	104	463	65	169	63	308

Notes:
The table reports key operational characteristics for the sample of 1504 IPOs in the Main and AIM markets during the period 1995–2007, according to the type of their first corporate event since flotation.
The source of data for all balance items are the IPO prospectuses which are based on the last published accounts before going public.
The number of observations varies across items depending on data availability.

The market timing hypothesis posits that the likelihood of stock acquisitions increases with recent stock price performance, market sentiment (the average discount of investment trusts over a three-month period before the event) and general economic conditions (gross domestic product, GDP, and growth over the previous six months). First day returns (underpricing) could also be an important determinant of acquisition activity, either as an indicator of market feedback or as another proxy for market misevaluation. We also include a dummy variable to control for the occurrence of a previous similar event as a proxy of reduced adverse selection costs and an indication of an established strategic plan for future growth; our set of control variables also includes the listing market (Main or AIM) and a log of sales as a proxy for size.

Table 17.6 reports the logit regressions for each of the three main corporate events and separate results for acquisitions according to the method of payment, that is, cash, stock, and hybrid. It is worth noting that the market timing and feedback hypotheses are to a certain extent relevant for all three types of event while the financing hypothesis relates to acquisitions and SEOs only. More specifically, we find a negative and significant coefficient for timing across all types of acquisition and SEO, suggesting that an early engagement in such transactions is indicative of a pre-planned strategy for future growth. Divestitures, on the other hand, take place later in public life, suggesting that such events are in response to firm performance and market conditions rather than part of a predefined plan. In contrast to Hovakimian and Hutton (2010a) and Celikyurt et al. (2010), who report a positive and significant coefficient for cash acquisitions, we find positive but not significant coefficients, suggesting that IPO proceeds are not the dominant source of funds for acquisitions. Instead, our evidence demonstrates strong support for the financing hypothesis in terms of the positive and significant coefficient of the additional equity proceeds for cash and hybrid acquisitions; thus, recent IPO firms use their public status to raise additional equity capital (SEOs) to fund cash and mixed acquisitions. Stock acquisitions of course also use their public listing to generate currency for acquisitions, as suggested by Brau and Fawcett (2006)'s CFOs' survey. The positive and significant profitability coefficient for cash acquisitions suggests that internally generated funds are another important source of finance for cash and hybrid acquisitions. On the other hand, the corresponding negative coefficient for SEOs and divestitures indicates that such corporate events are more likely to be motivated by the need for some type of corporate restructuring to address their poor profitability at that point in time. Klein and Rosenfeld (2010), for example, find that poor performance and underinvestment in subsidiaries are the key motivations for spin-offs and the subsequent improvement in the parents' performance.

There is also considerable evidence in support of both the market timing and market feedback hypotheses across all three types of corporate event. In contrast to Hovakimian and Hutton (2010a), we find that only stock acquisitions are affected by market timing exactly as predicted by the market timing hypothesis. The probability of stock acquisitions and SEOs, for example, is significantly higher for issuers with strong recent price performance and in the case of stock and hybrid acquisitions for IPO companies with a particularly successful market debut in terms of first day performance. Celikyurt et al. (2010) also report that firms with higher first-day returns conduct more stock-financed acquisitions in the years following an IPO. Further support for the importance of market

Table 17.6 The likelihood of an acquisition, SEO, or divestiture

	All acquisitions	Cash acquisitions	Stock acquisitions	Hybrid acquisitions	SEOs	Divestitures
Timing	−0.091	−0.071	−0.136	−2.229	−0.094	0.273
	(−8.96)***	(−6.21)***	(−2.40)**	(−6.18)***	(−3.80)***	(5.74)***
IPO proceeds	−0.024	0.002	0.012	−0.166	−0.071-	−0.016
	(−1.68)*	(0.16)	(0.162)	(−2.41)**	(−1.68)*	(−0.22)
Equity proceeds	0.332	0.186	0.348	0.672		−0.216
	(5.34)***	(3.48)***	(1.89)*	(5.41)***		(−0.89)
Profitability	0.183	0.258	−0.298	0.402	−0.383	−0.664
	(3.23)***	(3.44)***	(−1.29)	(1.97)**	(−3.12)***	(−3.58)***
Sales	0.031	0.047	−0.063	0.038	−0.026	0.116
	(3.71)***	(4.71)***	(−1.46)	(1.42)	(−1.18)	(2.60)***
Leverage	0.038	0.045	0.029	0.208	−0.190	0.465
	(0.67)	(0.72)	(0.11)	(1.22)	(−1.18)	(2.31)**
Tangibility	−0.335	−0.210	−0.604	−1.615	0.370	0.057
	(−4.46)***	(−2.51)**	(−1.53)	(−5.01)***	(1.99)**	(0.17)
−3M return	0.0836	0.081	0.348	−0.011	0.356	0.119
	(2.04)**	(1.84)*	(2.17)**	(−0.08)	(4.21)***	(0.71)
Underpricing	0.086	0.039	0.233	0.119	−0.040	0.227
	(3.03)**	(1.33)	(2.34)**	(1.58)	(−0.01)	(2.39)**
Previous event	0.531	0.362	0.575	1.232	0.314	0.041
	(11.82)***	(7.75)***	(2.69)***	(10.59)***	(2.64)***	(0.19)
Market sentiment	1.669	1.331	−1.480	7.176	7.22	4.04
	(3.28)***	(2.34)**	(−0.53)	(4.13)***	(5.09)***	(1.79)*
GDP growth	6.253	2.659	9.506	9.20	−21.92	1.88
	(2.55)***	(0.94)	(0.72)	(3.12)***	(−3.58)***	(0.19)
Market listing	0.034	0.063	0.034	−0.013	0.181	0.66
	(0.77)	(1.30)	(0.13)	(−0.85)	(1.59)	(3.51)***
Intercept	−0.818	−1.414	−3.909	−2.070	−0.959	−6.69
	(−5.62)***	(−7.80)***	(−5.81)***	(−5.15)***	(−2.31)**	(−5.85)***
R−squared	0.099	0.092	0.034	0.126	0.025	0.072
Observations	7059	7059	7059	7059	7059	7059

Notes:
The table reports estimates from logit panel regressions where the dependent variable is a dummy variable which takes the value of '1' if there is an event during the six month period and '0' otherwise.
Timing is the number of six-month time intervals since the IPO.
IPO proceeds is the money raised scaled to total assets.
Equity proceeds is the primary equity capital (SEO) raised in the six-month period scaled to total assets.
Profitability is EBITDA scaled to total assets of the latest available in the calendar year six months prior (LACY-6M).
Sales is the logarithm of revenues (LACY-6M).
Leverage is the total debt scaled to total assets (LACY-6M).
Tangibility is property plant and equipment scaled to total assets (LACY-6M).
Return is the three-month share price return prior to the six-month period.
Underpricing is the difference between the offer price and the first day of trading, scaled by the offer price.
Previous event is a dummy equal to '1' if a similar event has taken place in the six months prior and '0' otherwise.
The proxy for *Market sentiment* is the average three-month investment trust discount prior to the six-month period.

Table 17.6 (continued)

Notes:
GDP growth is the quarterly UK GDP growth in the quarter prior to the six-month period.
The dummy variable for *Market listing* takes the value of '1' if listed on the Main market and '0' otherwise.
Positive coefficients imply that increases in the variable are associated with higher probability of an event.
The statistics reported in brackets are the Z statistics.
The pseudo-R^2 is the log-likelihood of the maximum likelihood minus the log-likelihood when only the constant is included.
***, **, and * indicate statistical significance at a 1%, 5%, and 10% level, respectively.

timing in post-IPO corporate activity is offered by the positive and significant coefficients of market sentiment, as measured by the average investment trusts' discount for cash acquisitions, SEOs and even divestitures. An additional perspective on the strategic motivation behind acquisitions and SEOs is offered by their respective positive and negative coefficients for GDP growth. They indicate that acquisitions are a direct response to an expanding economy while SEOs are more likely to be launched in response to capital requirements, either for acquisitions or capital expenditure, at times of sluggish economic growth.

Consistent with the pattern of follow-on events shown in Table 17.4, the logit results also point to a strong serial pattern of follow-on corporate events by companies which have carried out recent IPOs. The positive and significant coefficients of a recent acquisition, SEO or divestiture suggest a recurring pattern in such transactions that are likely to be indicative of a long-term plan for future growth; such a pattern also provides further support to the market feedback hypothesis through closer monitoring and reductions in potential information asymmetries. Intintoli et al. (2011) find that firms that issue SEOs within the first year of their IPO are able to offer shares at a smaller discount as institutional demand is significantly higher for follow-on SEOs.

Finally, in line with Hovakimian and Hutton (2010a), we find that the likelihood of cash acquisitions increases with size as larger firms have better access to both debt and equity markets due to their greater transparency and lower risk. Larger firms are also more likely to hold more extensive cash reserves and are in a better position to fund their acquisitions by cash; stock acquisitions, on the other hand, are not affected by size. Rather surprisingly, we find that leverage is only related to divestitures but not to the decision to pursue acquisitions or SEOs; divestitures are also more likely among firms listed on the Main market.

We also investigate the likelihood of each of the events occurring in each of the three post-IPO years separately. Further unreported results suggest that the positive and significant coefficient of underpricing for stock and hybrid acquisitions is entirely due to the acquisitions which take place in the first 12 months post-IPO; such corporate events in the second and third years are not related to first-day performance. Also, the positive coefficient of market growth, found in the overall three-year results, is predominantly driven by the acquisitions which take place in the second year only. Otherwise, the annual logit regressions show remarkable persistence for all types of corporate event for each of the three years following an IPO.

6 AFTERMARKET PERFORMANCE

To assess the potential relationship between follow-on corporate activities and the long-term performance of IPO firms, we estimate BHARs for the sample as a whole, by the market of listing (Main versus AIM) and a number of strategies reflecting the volume of corporate events of any type during the three-year period after flotation. Table 17.7 reports BHARs for the whole sample of IPO companies from January 1995 to March 2008 calculated until the earlier of either the IPO's third anniversary or the delisting date; the latest date for returns was April 2011. We report results for the first six months and then at 12-month intervals, excluding first-day returns, using two alternative benchmarks: (1) the FTSE All-Share Index for Main and FTSE small-cap for AIM and (2) the 10 FTSE sector indices. The number of IPOs included in the calculation of BHARs declines with the month of seasoning. Panel A reports equal- and value-weighted BHARs for all IPOs, while panels B and C show separate results for the Main and AIM market, respectively. We also report performance results for all IPO firms and three alternative strategies reflecting their follow-on corporate activities, that is, no events, at least one event, and at least two events during the three-year period after the listing; event(s) refers to a single or a combination of any of the three types of corporate activity examined in this chapter.

The results for the entire sample of IPOs in Table 17.7 (panels A and B) are broadly consistent with the pattern of previous US and UK studies. The equally-weighted 36-month BHARs, both FTA- and industry-adjusted, are negative and statistically significant, confirming once again the long established pattern of long-term average underperformance, while the equivalent positive but non-significant value-weighted returns suggest that firm size plays some role in long-run performance. Follow-on corporate activity, however, emerges as the decisive discriminating factor for long-term performance. The average equally-weighted 36-month return for all IPOs without any follow-on activity drops to −33.80 percent in comparison to the average of −12.80 percent; on the other hand, the equivalent FTA-adjusted returns for IPO companies with at least one or two corporate events are not statistically significant from zero. A broadly similar pattern is also evident for value-weighted FTA- and industry-adjusted returns.

Panels B and C provide further detail on the issues of firm size and listing market by examining the 36-month performance of IPOs on the Main (panel B) and AIM (panel C) markets separately. While, for example, the average equally- and value-weighted 36-month BHARs for firms on the Main market are not statistically different from zero, IPO firms on AIM significantly underperform both the relevant market and industry benchmarks by 16.47 percent and 34.72 percent respectively during the same time window; the value-weighted returns are also very similar. At the same time, however, it is worth noting some of the performance differences across firms depending on the basis of their follow-on corporate activities. We find, for example, that the industry-adjusted BHARs for IPO companies with one or two follow-on events on the Main market are positive and significant. Moreover, in contrast to the negative and significant equal and value BHARs for IPO firms without any follow-on events on AIM, the equivalent performance of active firms (two or more events) is not statistically different from zero.

In Panels A and B of Table 17.8, we present the Fama and French (1993) three-factor model results based on monthly returns. The intercept of the time series regressions provides an estimate of the risk-adjusted performance of each of the three groups of IPO

Table 17.7 Buy-and-hold abnormal returns by volume of activity

Panel A: All IPOs

Equal-weighted

Month	All IPOs	FTA-adjusted No event	At least 1	At least 2	Month	All IPOs	Industry-adjusted No event	At least 1	At least 2
6	1.20	−5.85	0.72	1.75	6	−1.98	−4.92	−0.76	0.49
	(−0.60)	(−0.84)	(0.46)	(0.93)		(−0.97)	(−0.74)	(−0.43)	(0.27)
12	−9.19***	−21.32***	−4.24*	−1.71	12	−11.84***	−22.44***	−7.51***	−4.55*
	(−4.42)	(−6.45)	(1.74)	(0.64)		(−5.55)	(−6.81)	(−2.99)	(−1.74)
24	−17.34***	−35.36***	−10.55***	−6.73	24	−24.80***	−44.83***	−17.25***	−11.54**
	(4.42)	(−4.79)	(2.43)	(−1.27)		(−5.89)	(−6.58)	(−3.71)	(−2.12)
36	−12.80**	−33.80***	−5.16	−5.57	36	−26.52***	−50.54***	−17.78***	−15.98*
	(2.31)	(−3.98)	(−0.81)	(0.75)		(−3.78)	(−5.92)	(2.43)	(−1.86)

Value-weighted

Month	All IPOs	FTA-adjusted No event	At least 1	At least 2	Month	All IPOs	Industry-adjusted No event	At least 1	At least 2
6	5.57	−1.15	6.66	13.05**	6	6.63	−0.90	7.38**	13.08**
	(1.16)	(0.01)	(1.21)	(2.16)		(1.41)	(−0.28)	(1.40)	(2.20)
12	−7.05*	−23.71***	−4.82	−2.71	12	−4.52	−19.21***	−2.56	−0.63
	(−1.75)	(−6.05)	(−1.07)	(−0.53)		(−1.27)	(−5.16)	(−0.65)	(−0.13)
24	−1.57	−26.21***	1.51	−6.38	24	0.97	−21.11***	3.84	9.22
	(−0.15)	(−6.82)	(0.23)	(0.73)		(0.19)	(−6.88)	(0.58)	(1.21)
36	0.45	−19.93***	2.76	4.90	36	0.82	−19.80***	3.15	5.24
	(0.15)	(−3.42)	(0.40)	(0.58)		(0.17)	(−3.13)	(0.43)	(0.60)

Table 17.7 (continued)

Panel B: Main

Equal-weighted

Month	All IPOs	FTA-adjusted			Industry-adjusted		
		No event	At least 1	At least 2	No event	At least 1	At least 2
6	2.83	−9.29*	6.59**	8.29***	−9.29*	5.99**	7.95***
	(1.06)	(1.88)	(2.19)	(2.50)	(−1.88)	(2.02)	(2.35)
12	−4.85	−24.20***	1.26	3.61	−24.20***	1.12	3.35
	(−1.18)	(−3.16)	(0.30)	(0.71)	(−3.16)	(0.28)	(0.69)
24	5.07	−17.16	11.06	17.18*	−17.16	14.71*	20.69***
	(0.70)	(−1.44)	(1.28)	(1.79)	(−1.44)	(1.87)	(2.46)
36	3.13	−17.96	8.93	10.00	−17.96	14.64*	16.14**
	(0.47)	(−1.58)	(1.09)	(1.14)	(−1.58)	(1.94)	(2.04)

Value-weighted

Month	All IPOs	FTA-adjusted			Industry-adjusted		
		No event	At least 1	At least 2	No event	At least 1	At least 2
6	8.43	−1.19	9.15	14.16**	−1.19	9.68*	14.10**
	(1.54)	(0.22)	(1.55)	(2.16)	(0.22)	(1.69)	(2.19)
12	−5.73	−26.91***	−3.54	−3.06	−26.91***	−1.64	0.75
	(−1.26)	(−4.77)	(−0.72)	(−0.55)	(−4.77)	(−0.37)	(0.14)
24	1.56	−21.22***	3.82	7.21	−21.22***	6.33	10.72
	(0.23)	(−3.59)	(0.47)	(0.76)	(3.59)	(0.85)	(1.30)
36	3.10	−14.23*	4.65	5.60	−14.23*	5.84	7.08
	(0.44)	(−1.68)	(0.58)	(0.61)	(−1.68)	(0.69)	(0.74)

Panel C: AIM

Equal-weighted

		FTA-adjusted					Industry-adjusted		
Month	All IPOs	No event	At least 1	At least 2	Month	All IPOs	No event	At least 1	At least 2
6	−2.09	−5.25	−0.71	−0.07	6	−3.33	−5.44	−2.39	−0.07
	(−0.86)	(−0.68)	(0.35)	(−0.01)		(−1.29)	(−0.70)	(−1.17)	(−0.01)
12	−10.16***	−20.81***	−5.58*	−3.19	12	−13.88***	−23.81***	−9.61***	−3.19
	(−4.23)	(−5.74)	(−1.95)	(−1.05)		(−5.47)	(−6.34)	(−3.19)	(−1.05)
24	−22.39***	−38.40***	−15.94***	−13.52***	24	−32.56***	−50.77***	−25.22***	−13.52***
	(−5.34)	(−4.23)	(3.39)	(−2.35)		(−6.92)	(−6.01)	(−4.80)	(−2.35)
36	−16.47***	−36.63***	−8.69	−10.08	36	−34.72***	−57.53***	−25.91***	−10.08
	(2.38)	(−3.62)	(−1.11)	(−1.06)		(−3.54)	(−5.47)	(−2.59)	(−1.06)

Value-weighted

		FTA-adjusted					Industry-adjusted		
Month	All IPOs	No event	At least 1	At least 2	Month	All IPOs	No event	At least 1	At least 2
6	−11.16**	−6.20	−12.97*	0.51	6	−9.61**	−6.30	−10.82*	0.51
	(−2.00)	(−1.62)	(−1.67)	(0.11)		(−2.11)	(−1.50)	(−1.72)	(0.11)
12	−15.27***	−16.70***	−14.75*	1.63	12	−12.37***	−19.67***	−9.70***	1.63
	(−2.56)	(−2.88)	(−1.71)	(0.35)		(−4.30)	(−3.64)	(2.32)	(1.35)
24	−22.77***	−38.23***	−17.52***	−4.25*	24	−24.13***	−46.16***	−16.64***	−4.25
	(−5.73)	(−10.08)	(−2.90)	(−0.57)		(5.16)	(−12.32)	(−3.04)	(−0.57)
36	−18.65***	−34.06***	−13.79***	4.54	36	−27.48***	−50.15***	−20.33***	−4.54
	(−3.59)	(−4.26)	(−1.95)	(0.47)		(−4.42)	(−6.62)	(−2.86)	(−0.47)

Notes:
The total sample of 1504 IPOs during the period 1995–2008 was involved in a total of 2938 corporate events during the first 36 months of going public; this includes 1587 acquisitions, 915 SEOs and 436 divestitures.
For each IPO, the buy-and-hold returns are calculated by compounding daily returns up to the month of the IPO and from the on compounding monthly returns for 36 months.
Buy-and-hold returns (BHARs) in Panel A include IPOs both in the Main and AIM markets and are calculated using the FTSE-All Share index for IPO firms in the Main market and the FTSE Small-Cap index for their AIM counterparts; industry-adjusted BHARs are based on the FTSE 10 Group Industry Classification indices. Panels B and C show the equivalent BHARs for IPOs in the Main and AIM markets respectively.
Each of the three panels shows BHARs for all IPOs in the respective market(s) and separate estimates according to the number of corporate events for each IPO during the three years in the aftermarket; a corporate event could be an acquisition, an SEO or a divestiture.
***, **, and * indicate statistical significance at a 1%, 5%, and 10% level, respectively.

Table 17.8 Three-factor regressions on calendar-time monthly portfolio returns

	All	No event	At least 1 event	At least 2 events
Panel A: Equally-weighted				
Intercept	0.015	−0.002	0.023	0.007
	(1.15)	(−0.626)	(1.20)	(2.33)**
RMRF	1.917	1.186	2.214	1.392
	(3.05)***	(9.45)***	(2.49)***	(13.1)***
SMB	0.961	1.150	0.887	1.191
	(3.71)***	(5.12)***	(0.01)	(7.46)***
HML	−0.178	−0.115	−0.140	−0.614
	(−0.66)	(−0.75)	(−0.39)	(−4.02)***
Adjusted R^2	0.801	0.538	0.510	0.651
Panel B: Value-weighted				
Intercept	0.113	0.015	0.134	0.009**
	(1.03)	(1.13)	(1.03)	(1.98)
RMRF	6.616	1.274	7.672	1.540
	(1.28)	(6.72)***	(1.24)	(10.33)***
SMB	−1.107	1.251	−1.448	0.510
	(−0.57)	(1.89)**	(−0.62)	(2.44)**
HML	1.619	−0.231	1.968	−0.237
	(0.77)	(−1.07)	(0.78)	(−1.56)
Adjusted R^2	0.093	0.091	0.072	0.507

Notes:
The total sample of 1504 IPOs during the period January 1995 to March 2008 were involved in 2938 corporate during the first 36 months of going public; this includes 1587 acquisitions, 915 SEOs and 436 divestitures.
RMF is the market return on the FT All-Share Index minus the risk-free rate that is the UK one month Treasury bill rate.
SMB is the difference each month between the return of small and big firms.
HML is the difference each month between the return on a portfolio of high book-to-market stocks and the return on a portfolio of low book-to-market stocks.
The White heteroskedasticity robust t-statistics are reported in parenthesis.
***, **, and * indicate statistical significance at a 1%, 5%, and 10% level, respectively.

companies according to their follow-on corporate activity. Their positive and significant values for both equally- and value-weighted returns suggest that IPO firms with two follow-on events generate an average market-adjusted return of about 9 percent per annum.

Finally, to provide some further insights into the nature and drivers of aftermarket performance and their interaction with the pattern of follow-on corporate activity during the three years after flotation, Table 17.9 reports multivariate regression results using the 36-month equally-weighted buy-and-hold returns as the dependent variable. We relate aftermarket performance to a set of company-specific characteristics, such as market capitalization at the time of the offer, profitability in terms of EBITDA to total assets, and first-day returns. We also control for market sentiment, proxied by the discount on investment trusts, and the pattern of corporate event activity in terms of the timing, volume and composition of the follow-on acquisitions, SEOs and divestitures. More specifically, we differentiate between single events of any type and multiple events

Table 17.9 *Multivariate cross-sectional regressions for 36-month aftermarket performance*

	(1)	(2)	(3)	(4)
Market value	0.054**	0.056**	0.050***	0.045**
	(2.43)	(2.46)	(2.15)	(1.92)
EBITDA/TA	0.917***	0.931***	0.957***	0.935***
	(7.04)	(7.17)	(7.19)	(7.08)
Market sentiment	−6.476***	−6.310***	−6.79***	−6.850***
	(−5.80)	(−5.64)	(−6.10)	(6.16)
No corporate events within three years	−0.158**			
	(−1.96)			
At least one acquisition within the first six months		−0.291***		
		(−2.61)		
At least one SEO within the first six months		0.193*		
		(1.89)		
At least one divestiture within the first six months		0.111		
		(0.53)		
At least two acquisitions within three years			−0.078	
			(−0.85)	
At least two SEOs within three years			0.350***	
			(3.12)	
At least two divestitures within three years			0.099	
			(0.55)	
At least two cash acquisitions within three years				0.255*
				(1.78)
At least two stock acquisitions within three years				−0.543**
				(−1.98)
At least two hybrid acquisitions within three years				−0.042
				(−0.37)
At least two SEOs within three years				0.353***
				(3.20)
At least two divestitures within three years				0.103
				(0.58)
Intercept	−1.511***	−1.54***	−1.602***	−1.607***
	(−11.97)	(−12.31)	(−12.64)	(−12.65)
R^2 adjusted	0.091	0.095	0.096	0.099
No. of observations	1203	1203	1203	1203

Notes:
The dependent variable is the natural logarithm of the 36-month wealth relative using the FTSE All-Share index as the market benchmark.
The independent variables are the logarithm of Market Capitalization at the time of the IPO, *EBITDA/TA* is EBITDA scaled by total assets at the time of the IPO, the proxy for *Market Sentiment* is the average three-month investment trust discount at the time of the IPO.
We use a dummy equal to 1 and 0 otherwise to capture the different types of corporate events during the first year and within three years of the public listing.
The White heteroskedasticity robust *t*-statistics are reported in parenthesis.
***, **, and * indicate statistical significance at a 1%, 5%, and 10% level, respectively.

of the same type over the three-year time period and separate acquisitions according to their means of payment, that is, cash, stock, or hybrids.

Table 17.9 examines the relation between company-specific characteristics and 36-month performance using the logarithm of wealth relatives. As expected, in model (1), we find a positive and significant relation between both market capitalization and profitability with long-term aftermarket performance, which is consistent with a number of other studies suggesting that the long-term underperformance of IPO firms is predominantly due to small and immature firms that are probably too eager for a public listing. It is also worth noting that underperformance is a generic feature of smaller IPO companies rather than those just listed on AIM, as suggested by the results in Table 17.7. We also observe a negative and significant coefficient between market sentiment, in terms of investment trust discount, and 36-month performance; in other words, IPO firms floated in periods of positive market conditions clearly disappoint in the long term. Finally, the negative and significant coefficient for the no-event dummy suggests that IPO companies without any follow-on activities in terms of acquisitions, SEOs and divestitures underperform their active counterparts by the end of the three-year period.

Model (2) focuses on performance implications of early corporate activity. Consistent with the results of Brau et al. (2012), we find that IPO firms with at least one acquisition, of any type, within the first six months of listing perform significantly worse than average. On the other hand, in contrast to Levis (1995) and Jiang (2008), we find that there is a positive and significant relation between an SEO in the first six months of listing and long-run performance. At the same time, given the relatively limited divestiture activity at the early stages of public listing, it is not surprising that this type of activity is not related to long-term performance. Our results in model (3), however, suggest that the underperformance of IPO firms with early acquisitions is more likely to be related to the timing rather than the nature of such acquisitions. The negative but not significant coefficient for IPO firms with at least two acquisitions of any type during the three-year period indicates that the long-term performance of acquiring firms is not significantly worse than the average IPO. The coefficient for SEOs, however, remains positive and significant, confirming that IPO firms with at least two SEOs, with or without any other type of corporate event, perform better than their less active – in terms of raising equity capital – counterparts.

It is worth noting that in Table 17.4 we show that a considerable number of recent IPO firms involved in an SEO as their first event are very likely to follow it up with an acquisition. In other words, a sizeable proportion of the IPO firms raising additional equity capital are using at least part of the proceeds to pursue future cash acquisitions. Thus, the positive and significant coefficient for the 'at least two SEOs' dummy during the three-year period is likely to reflect the combined implications of SEOs and acquisitions on long-run performance. In some further unreported results, we also examine the performance of IPO firms involved in transactions of the same type only, but find no evidence of a relationship between such 'clean' patterns of activity and 36-month performance. In the case of divestitures, there is very little difference between the performance of combined and clean transactions as the divesting IPO firms in our sample are less likely to be engaged in other types of corporate event during the three-year period.

Our evidence so far appears inconsistent with a number of previous studies that report poor long-term performance for acquiring companies in general and recent IPO firms involved in subsequent acquisitions in particular. To shed some further light on this issue, model (4) replicates the analysis of model (3) but separates acquisitions by method of payment, that is, cash, stock, or hybrid. The results are quite revealing; while, for example, the coefficients for cash and hybrid acquisitions are non-significant, the coefficient for stock acquisitions is negative and significant suggesting that IPO firms that completed at least two such acquisitions, even if these were combined at some point with an SEO and/or divestiture, perform worse than other IPO companies. Thus, the apparent discrepancy of our results in model (3) with the evidence of Brau et al. (2012) for the US is likely to be related to the mix of cash and stock acquisitions in our respective samples. Our sample is broadly balanced between the two types of acquisition and thus the combined acquisitions dummy is not significant, whilst the negative relationship between performance and acquisitions in their sample is likely the result of a higher proportion of stock-based acquisitions in their sample. The method of payment may also account for the positive performance of European IPOs with subsequent acquisitions reported by Bessler and Zimmermann (2011).

Finally, it is important to note that our results are not directly comparable with any of the studies that focus on a single corporate event, that is, acquisitions or seasoned equity offerings. Our evidence suggests that it is the overall pattern and timing of the three types of corporate event that relate to aftermarket performance than any single type of event on its own. Such a pattern of follow-on corporate events provides a more representative view of a firm's ability to pursue successfully its long-term strategic plan for future growth.

7 CONCLUSIONS

Using a sample of 1504 IPOs listed in UK during the period January 1995 to March 2008, we track their follow-on corporate activities during the first three years of going public in terms of acquisitions, seasoned equity offerings and divestitures. We find that IPO firms become actively involved in a spree of acquisitions, funded either by cash, stock, or both, soon after their public listing and remain active over the whole three-year period in the aftermarket. In fact, about a quarter of the IPO companies made at least two acquisitions and one in 10 managed at least four such events during the same period; we also observe a broadly similar pattern for raising additional capital through SEOs. In contrast, the IPO firms' divestiture activity is mainly concentrated during the end of the three-year post-listing period. Moreover, the first type of corporate event often sets the pattern for the activities to follow. We also show that only 17 percent of the IPOs that survived the three-year period were not involved in any corporate activity after their public listing. The range and intensity of follow-on corporate events across a wide range of recent IPO firms provide strong support for the view that going public is part of a long-term strategy for growth through access to capital markets.

Our evidence suggests that all three types of corporate event are, to a certain extent, motivated by broadly similar considerations that relate to direct and indirect capital needs, recent price performance, market conditions, and the feedback received by key market participants. Cash acquisitions, for example, are likely to come early, funded by additional equity capital proceeds, and involve larger and more profitable firms. Stock acquisitions and SEOs, on the other hand, are linked to less profitable firms, strong market sentiment, significant underpricing at the time of flotation or recent rises in stock prices. Divestitures are also more likely among less profitable but larger firms following recent price declines.

We also provide evidence that the pattern and timing of subsequent corporate activity is related to IPO companies' long-term aftermarket performance. Firms with two or more corporate events during the first three years of going public outperform their passive counterparts by the end of the end of the three-year period after flotation. Such differences in performance, however, are not only linked to the type and intensity of post-IPO activity but to the timing and motivation of such corporate events as well.

In other words, our evidence suggests that the long-established pattern of aftermarket underperformance is not necessarily an inherent feature of newly listed firms. As in the case of any other publicly listed firm, their performance is related to their ability to pursue their strategic objectives for long-term growth; the implementation of this process is likely to include a combination of corporate events like acquisitions, SEOs and divestitures. Other recently listed firms, without a sustainable long term, choose to remain wholly inactive or bring to an abrupt end any further plans for corporate activity when their first attempt proves unsuccessful. We believe that this is a fruitful dimension for further research towards understanding the critical linkages between corporate activities and long-term performance of newly listed firms.

NOTES

1. See, for example, Levis (1993) for the UK and Chan et al. (2004) for China.
2. Newly listed firms, for example, with certain characteristics in terms of size (Ritter, 2011), underwriters' or venture capital sponsors' reputation (Chan et al., 2008; Krishnan et al., 2011)), privatizations (Choi et al., 2010), and PE backing (Brav and Gompers, 1997; Cao and Lerner, 2009; Levis, 2011) show positive aftermarket performance.
3. In a recent paper, Brau et al. (2012) examine the long-term performance of IPO companies involved in subsequent acquisitions, while Billett et al. (2011) investigate the implications of different issuing activities on long-term performance.
4. Schultz (2003) shows that underperformance by firms following equity offerings is very likely to be observed *ex post* in an efficient market and can be explained by a 'pseudo' market timing hypothesis. Thus, more firms may issue equity at higher stock prices even when the market is efficient and there is no timing ability.
5. Their sample includes IPOs from the UK, France, Germany and Italy. The UK component, however, is rather limited as it includes only 644 IPOs involved in 400 acquisitions. Our UK sample in this chapter during a shorter period (1996–2008) includes 1493 IPOs and 1 acquisition.
6. The number of divestitures is not included in the restriction due to unavailability.
7. When a firm in a portfolio is delisted from the database, the portfolio return for the next month is an equally-weighted average of the remaining firms in the portfolio. Thus, the proceeds of the delisted firm are equally allocated among the surviving members of the portfolio in each subsequent month.
8. Although the overwhelming majority of the IPO firms during this period (79.7 percent) were listed on AIM, they accounted for only 15.2 percent of the total amount raised. In other words, the average (median) amount raised by an IPO on the Main market is £233 million (£81 million) in comparison to an equivalent £11 million (£5 million) on AIM.
9. As the data on divestiture transactions is limited, Table 17.1 only shows values for IPOs, acquisitions, and SEOs.

REFERENCES

Baker, M., J.C. Stein and J. Wurgler (2003), 'When does the market matter? Stock prices and the investment of equity-dependent firms', *Quarterly Journal of Economics*, **118**, 969–1005.
Bancel, F. and U.R. Mittoo (2009), 'Why do European firms go public?', *European Financial Management*, **15** (4), 844–84.
Bessler, W. and J. Zimmermann (2011), 'Acquisition activities of initial public offerings in Europe, an analysis of exit and growth strategies', working paper, Justus-Liebig-University.
Billett, M.T., M.J. Flannery and J.A. Garfinkel (2011), 'Frequent issuers' influence on long-run post-issuance returns', *Journal of Financial Economics*, **99**, 349–64.
Brau, J. and S. Fawcett (2006), 'Initial public offerings: an analysis of theory and practice', *Journal of Finance*, **61**, 399–436.
Brau, J., C.B. Francis and N. Kohers (2003), 'The choice of IPO versus takeover', *Journal of Business*, **76** (4), 583–612.
Brau, J., R.B. Couch and N. Sutton (2012), 'The desire to acquire and IPO long-run underperformance', *Journal of Financial and Quantitative Analysis*, **47** (3), 493–510.
Brauer, M. and T. Stussi (2010), 'Performance implications of exit timing in industry divestiture waves', *Academy of Management Annual Meeting Proceedings*, Montreal, Academy of Management.
Brav, A. and P.A. Gompers (1997), 'Myth or reality? The long run underperformance of initial public offerings: evidence from venture capital and nonventure capital-backed companies', *Journal of Finance*, **52**, 1791–822.
Cao, J. and J. Lerner (2009), 'The performance of reverse leveraged buyouts', *Journal of Financial Economics*, **91**, 139–57.
Carow, K., R. Heron and T. Saxton (2004), 'Do early birds get the returns? An empirical investigation of early-mover advantages in acquisitions', *Strategic Management Journal*, **25**, 563–85.
Celikyurt, U., M. Sevilir and A. Shivdasani (2010), 'Going public to acquire? The acquisition motive in IPOs', *Journal of Financial Economics*, **96**, 345–63.
Chan, K., J.W. Cooney, J. Kim and A.K. Singh (2008), 'The IPO derby: are there consistent losers and winners on this track?', *Financial Management*, **37**, 45–79.
Chan, K., J.Wang and K.C.J. Wei (2004), 'Underpricing and long-term performance of IPOs in China', *Journal of Corporate Finance*, June, 409–30.
Choi, S.-D., I. Lee and W.L. Megginson (2010), 'Do privatization IPOs outperform in the long run?', *Financial Management*, **39**, 153–85.
Colak, G. and N. Tekatli (2010), 'Comovements in corporate waves', working paper, Florida State University.
Dranikoff, L., T. Koller and A. Schneider (2002), 'Divestiture: strategy's missing link', *Harvard Business Review*, **80**, 74–83.
Eckbo, B.E., R.M. Giammarino and R.L. Heinkel (1990), 'Asymmetric information and the medium of exchange in takeovers: theory and tests', *Review of Financial Studies*, **3**, 651–75.
Fama, E. and K. French (1993), 'Common risk factors in the returns of stocks and bonds', *Journal of Financial Economics*, **33**, 3–55.
Hollowell, B. (2009), 'The long-term performance of parent firms and their spin-offs', *The International Journal of Business and Finance Research*, **3**, 119–29.
Hovakimian, A. and I. Hutton (2010a), 'Merger-motivated IPOs', *Financial Management*, Winter, 1547–73.
Hovakimian, A. and I. Hutton (2010b), 'Market feedback and equity issuance: evidence from repeat equity issues', *Journal of Financial and Quantitative Analysis*, **45** (3), 739–62.
Howe, J.S. and S. Zhang (2010), 'SEO cycles', *The Financial Review*, **45**, 729–41.
Hsieh, J., E. Lyandres and A. Zhdanov (2011), 'A theory of merger-driven IPOs', *Journal of Financial and Quantitative Analysis*, **46** (5), 1367–405.
Intintoli, V.J., S.P. Jategaonkar and K.M. Kahle (2011), 'Why is SEO underpricing lower for recent IPO firms?', working paper, University of Arizona.
Iqbal, A., S. Espenlaub and N. Strong (2006), 'The long-run performance of UK rights issues', *Frontiers in Finance and Economics*, **3** (2), 18–54.
Jegadeesh, N., M. Weinsten and I. Welch (1993), 'An empirical investigation of IPO returns and subsequent equity offerings', *Journal of Financial Economics*, **34**, 153–75.
Jelic, R., B. Saadouni and M. Wright (2005), 'Performance of private to public MBOs: the role of venture capital', *Journal of Business Finance & Accounting*, **32**, 643–8.
Jiang, Y. (2008), 'Do firms time seasoned equity offerings? Evidence from SEOs issued shortly after IPOs', working paper, University of Iowa.
Kim, W. and M.S. Weisbach (2008), 'Motivations for public equity offers: an international perspective', *Journal of Financial Economics*, **87**, 281–307.

King, D., R. Slotegraaf and I. Kesner (2008), 'Performance implications of firm resource interactions in the acquisition of R&D-intensive firms', *Organization Science*, **19**, 327–40.

Klein, A. and J. Rosenfeld (2010), 'The long-run performance of sponsored and conventional spin-offs', *Financial Management*, **39**, 227–47.

Krishnan, C.N.V., V.I. Ivanov, R. Masulis and A. Singh (2011), 'Venture capital reputation, post-IPO performance, and corporate governance', *Journal of Financial and Quantitative Analysis*, **46**, 1295–333.

Lee, D.D. and R. Madhavan (2010), 'Divestiture and firm performance: a meta-analysis', *Journal of Management*, **36** (6), 1345–71.

Levis, M. (1993), 'The long-run performance of initial public offerings: the UK experience 1980–1988', *Financial Management*, **22** (1), 28–41.

Levis, M. (1995), 'Seasoned equity offerings and the short- and long-run performance of initial public offerings in the UK', *European Financial Management*, **1** (2), 125–46.

Levis, M. (2011), 'The performance of private equity backed IPOs', *Financial Management*, Spring, 253–77.

Loughran, T. and J.R. Ritter (1995), 'The new issues puzzle', *Journal of Finance*, **50**, 23–51.

Loughran, T. and A. Vijh (1997), 'Do long-term shareholders benefit from corporate acquisitions?', *Journal of Finance*, **52** (5), 1765–90.

Lowry, M. (2003), 'Why does IPO volume fluctuate so much?', *Journal of Financial Economics*, **67**, 3–40.

Lowry, M. and S.W. Schwert (2002), 'IPO market cycles: bubbles or sequential learning?', *Journal of Finance*, **57**, 1171–200.

Lyon, J.D., B.M. Barber and C.L. Tsai (1999), 'Improved methods for tests of long-run abnormal stock returns', *Journal of Finance*, **54**, 165–201.

Maksimovic, V., G. Phillips and L. Yang (2010), 'Public and private merger waves', working paper, University of Maryland.

Mikkelson, W.H., M.M. Patch and K. Shah (1997), 'Ownership and operating performance of companies that go public', *Journal of Financial Economics*, **44**, 281–307.

Rau, P.R. and A. Stouraitis (2011), 'Patterns in the timing of corporate event waves', *Journal of Financial and Quantitative Analysis*, **46** (1), 209–46.

Rau, P.R. and T. Vermaelen (1998), 'Glamour value and post-acquisition performance of acquiring firms', *Journal of Financial Economics*, **49**, 223–53.

Rhodes-Kropf, M., D. Robinson and S. Viswanathan (2005), 'Valuation waves and merger activity: the empirical evidence', *Journal of Financial Economics*, **77**, 561–603.

Ritter, J.R. (1991), 'The long-run performance of initial public offerings', *Journal of Finance*, **46**, 3–27.

Ritter, J.R. (2011), 'Equilibrium in the initial public offering market', *Annual Review of Financial Economics*, **3**, 347–74.

Schultz, P. (2003), 'Pseudo market timing and the long-run underperformance of IPOs', *Journal of Finance*, **58**, 483–517.

Shleifer, A. and R.W. Vishny (2003), 'Stock market driven acquisitions', *Journal of Financial Economics*, **70**, 295–311.

Spiess, D.K. and J. Affleck-Graves (1995), 'Underperformance in long-run stock returns following seasoned equity offerings', *Journal of Financial Economics*, **38**, 243–67.

Vismara, S., S. Paleari and J.R. Ritter (2012), 'Europe's second markets for small companies', *European Financial Management*, **18**, 352–88.

Welch, I. (1989), 'Seasoned offerings, imitation costs, and the underpricing of initial public offerings', *Journal of Finance*, **44**, 421–49.

Wiggenhorn, J., K.C. Gleason and J. Madura (2007), 'Going public to pursue acquisitions', *Quarterly Review of Economics and Finance*, **47**, 331–51.

18 Private equity, RLBOs and IPO performance
Jerry Cao

1 PRIVATE EQUITY, REVERSE LBOS AND IPO MARKET

This research is motivated by the unprecedented activity of private equity since the 1980s. The market not only witnessed records set for the amounts of aggregate fundraising or leveraged buyout (LBO) investment activity but also records size of the individual buyout funds raised or individual LBO transactions undertaken. Private equity (PE) investments have a profound economic impact in spurring entrepreneurship and restructuring in many industries worldwide. At the same time, the rapid growth and globalization of the PE industry started to worry policy makers by raising demands for increased regulation and disclosure of PE investment and the restructuring process.

One important and noticeable development of PE activity in the initial public offering (IPO) market is the reverse leveraged buyouts (RLBOs). Those are the IPOs of firms that have previously been bought out by professional later-stage private equity investors. For instance, in 2005, approximately 53 percent of IPOs in the US were backed by private equity investors and in 2006; 42 percent were RLBOs. Following Jensen (1986), there is a common recognition that PE investors are purported to create value in restructuring LBOs and that sponsors often take LBOs public once the restructuring process is complete. In practice, some critics assert that buyout sponsors create no value in LBOs but, rather, buy low and sell high by timing the market without enhancing operating efficiency. For example, in a recent C-suite survey[1] of chief executives, chief financial officers, and chief operating officers, the participants were primarily concerned about private equity's role in public corporations. The concern is whether buyout sponsors are 'merely financial engineers who go in there, lever debt up, cut costs and pump the thing out (exit) some time later'. Such public scrutiny has been surrounding the phenomenon of RLBOs. Some critics argue that, in fact, buyout sponsors create no value in the LBO restructuring process. They claim that rather than use the restructuring to achieve value-enhancing operating improvements, buyout sponsors simply exploit favorable market conditions and time the market (by buying low and selling high).

In the IPO literature, the general conclusion is that market conditions are the most important factor in a firm's decision to go public. Pastor and Veronesi (2005) propose 'optimal IPO timing' by suggesting that entrepreneurs tend to wait for more favourable market conditions before going public. Similarly, IPO timing applies to private-to-public transactions since buyout sponsors can react to IPO market conditions deciding when to list LBOs publicly. Initial public offering timing would have significant value implications, particularly for immature LBOs. If IPO timing leads buyout sponsors to pull capital out of LBOs prior to realizing operating efficiencies, doing so is likely to negatively impact restructuring efforts, resulting in poor operating performance or even financial distress post-IPO. Cao and Lerner (2009) provide (weak) evidence that, indeed, those LBOs that are hastily listed, or flipped, underperform other RLBOs or the market.

Their paper, however, does not examine the relationship between buyout sponsors' restructuring process and IPO market conditions.

In this chapter, I conduct two main analyses. In the first analysis, I examine two hypotheses regarding IPO timing of buyout sponsor in listing LBOs and timing impact on restructuring process and firm performance. The performance timing hypothesis posits that sponsors behave opportunistically by listing LBOs at the peak of pre-IPO cash flow or operating performance, and the market timing hypothesis posits that buyout sponsors tend to shorten the LBO restructuring process under more favorable external conditions for new issuance. In the second analysis, I examine whether IPO timing affects buyout sponsor's monitoring and exit strategies in post-IPO years.

Under the performance timing hypothesis, buyout sponsors take advantage of some temporary improvement in operating performance that leads to high equity valuations. In general, the IPO literature (for example, Jain and Kini, 1994) finds that new IPOs experience declines in operating performance post-issuance. Studies by Degeorge and Zeckhauser (1993) and Holthausen and Larcker (1996) document similar patterns of performance deterioration for RLBOs. Degeorge and Zeckhauser (1993) suggest that performance timing may explain such declines, with insiders listing LBOs when they see a temporary improvement in operating performance. Chou et al. (2006), who document increases in discretionary accruals prior to the listings, alternatively suggest that earnings management may explain such declines. These early findings on RLBOs, however, often depend on a small sample of RLBOs from the 1980s to the early 1990s, and they ignore IPO market conditions in their analysis. The recent development[2] of the private equity industry calls for more thorough examination of RLBOs' operating performance. I empirically test the above hypothesis by examining whether the operating performance of RLBOs deteriorates after going public.

Under the market timing hypothesis, in contrast, buyout sponsors bring LBOs to the public to take advantage of a favorable IPO market. During hot IPO issuance periods, buyout sponsors can earn greater proceeds by selling more LBO equity even when the restructuring process has not been completed (that is, operating efficiencies have not been fully realized). Hence, external market conditions can generate perverse incentives for sponsors to seek quick cash returns from selling immature LBOs, or to even pursue so-called 'quick flips', whereby sponsors avail themselves of rare but profitable opportunities to exit soon after acquiring the LBO. When LBOs succumb to such practices, sponsors are likely to spend less time on the restructuring process. Leveraged buyout duration, a proxy for LBO restructuring efforts, is therefore expected to be negatively related to favorable IPO market conditions and market returns. As a result, IPO timing is expected to result in a decline in RLBO performance. To test these predictions, I relate declines of RLBO performance post IPO to market conditions in multivariate analysis.

The empirical evidence from the above analysis rejects the performance timing hypothesis but supports the market timing hypothesis. Specifically, RLBOs show no declines in operating performance. The results provide empirical support for Pastor et al. (2009) who suggest that due to IPO timing, firm profitability declines after the IPO and that this decline is larger for firms with more volatile profitability and firms with less uncertain average profitability. The evidence suggests that RLBOs, firms with low profitability volatility and uncertainty, show no declines in profitability. I find that buyout sponsors appear to shorten LBO duration when market conditions are more favorable for new IPOs. Shortening duration leads to worse long-run performance and a greater probability of bankruptcy. Interestingly, the findings also provide support for Schultz's (2003) pseudo market timing, according to which buyout sponsors do not take advantage of mispricing by selling overpriced equity, but rather use favorable external IPO market conditions to expedite their exit of LBOs.

Next, I examine whether buyout sponsors maintain a post-issuance presence in RLBO companies following their IPO. The decision to maintain a presence post-IPO is important. First, given buyout sponsors specialize in monitoring (Gertner and Kaplan, 1996), a continued presence post-IPO suggests that buyout sponsors complete more of the restructuring process (that is, realize more operating efficiency gains). In addition, because the lockup provisions of new issuances[3] help align the interests of insiders with those of public investors (Field and Hanka, 2001; Aggarwal et al., 2002), and because RLBO lockup provisions are no different from those of other IPOs,[4] the interests of RLBO buyout sponsors are expected to be further in line with those of public investors. These arguments imply that IPO timing in going-public decision is not equivalent to buyout sponsors exiting quickly or cashing out. Indeed, many RLBOs use their IPO proceeds to reduce or retire debt that is approaching maturity, a potential benefit for bond investors in RLBO firms because going public strengthens the company's balance sheet.

Note that buyout sponsors are not subject to selling restrictions once their IPO lockup provisions expire. They may, however, choose exit strategies (both when and how to exit) to time the market. Hence, to address the question of whether market conditions and reputation concern affect buyout sponsor's exit post-IPO, this analysis follows Zingales (1995) and examines buyout sponsors' post-issuance exit strategies across market conditions and sponsor's characteristics. The findings suggest that sponsors' exit choices can be explained by firm cash flows, the sponsor's reputation, market conditions, and firm ownership structure. For example, buyout sponsors are more likely to maintain a post-IPO presence in RLBO companies when they can obtain greater cash flows from doing so or when market conditions are less favorable. Further, consistent with their control rights, reputable buyout sponsors are more inclined to exit by facilitating a post-IPO takeover when their ownership share is greater.

This research contributes to the literature along several dimensions. First, it sheds light on the factors that influence buyout sponsors' restructuring processes and exit strategies. Second, unlike earlier studies, this chapter employs a comprehensive sample of 594 RLBOs from 1981 to 2006. This expansion of the dataset is important because it captures the structural development of the private equity industry over the past two decades. Moreover, the large sample spans both hot and cold IPO waves, thereby enabling investigation of buyout sponsors' market timing. In sum, this chapter offers new evidence that buyout sponsors are able to take advantage of favorable IPO market conditions in private-to-public transactions.[5]

The remainder of the chapter is organized as follows. Section 2 provides a background discussion and a review of the related literature. Section 3 discusses the sample and outlines the chapter's empirical methods. Section 4 presents the empirical results on performance timing and market timing, and section 5 presents the empirical results on buyout sponsors' exit strategies in post-IPO years. Section 6 concludes.

2 BACKGROUND AND LITERATURE REVIEW

Reverse leveraged buyouts differ from other IPOs or IPOs backed by venture capitalists in two respects. First, being sponsored by private equity investors, RLBO companies usually have a highly leveraged capital structure; and second, their buyout sponsors, having concentrated ownership, are active and often controlling owners that play an intensive monitoring role. These buyout sponsors typically acquire public or private companies through their LBO funds[6] and subsequently spend time and effort restructuring the LBOs. Once the restructuring process is complete, they sell equity in the LBOs to the public through IPOs. In RLBOs specifically, the buyout sponsors' final compensation is dependent on the so-called carried interest.[7] This compensation structure gives sponsors incentives to extract maximum profits from their investments within a certain horizon. Since private equity investors exist to generate returns for their investors or limited partners, the faster they can do so, the better. Nonetheless, because buyout sponsors' interests as they stand ready to cash out are not necessarily aligned with those of outside public shareholders, there is concern that the delivery of quick profits in LBOs sacrifices public shareholder interests, particularly in RLBOs with very little restructuring effort.

Indeed, Cao and Lerner (2009) show that this conflict of interest is especially relevant in quick flips, portfolio companies flipped to public investors within a very short period after their LBOs (defined by the authors as less than one year from LBO to IPO).[8] Quick flips have thus been subject to recent scrutiny because public investors doubt that buyout sponsors have time to make enough improvements in operation or governance. To illustrate this problem, Figure 18.1 shows the operating performance of RLBO firms that are quick flips versus those that are not. Whereas the median of quick flip earnings before interest, tax, depreciation and amortization (EBITDA)/sales increases before the IPOs and decreases in post-IPO years, other RLBOs show no decline in EBITDA/sales. This peculiar pattern not only implies the propping up of performance in quick flips com-

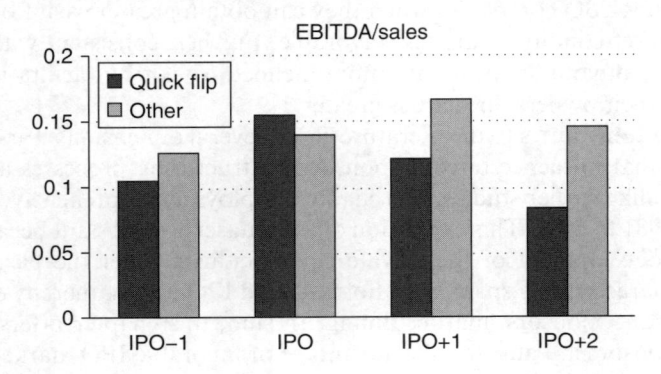

Notes:
Using the median value of EBITDA/sales for the years IPO-1, IPO, IPO+1, and IPO+2, this figure shows the operating performance of all RLBOs in the sample (1981–2006), including the 70 quick flips and the other RLBO companies.
Annual accounting data are taken from COMPUSTAT.

Figure 18.1 Operating performance of quick flips and other RLBOs around IPOs

pared to other RLBOs but reflects the doubt about whether buyout sponsors add any value in quick flips and whether they face perverse incentives to flip certain firms quickly.

General scrutiny of RLBOs stems from the potential moral hazard as, based on insider knowledge, buyout sponsors push problematic LBO firms public before hidden problems can unfold, thereby transferring the expected bankruptcy risk and loss to public investors. In fact, approximately 10 percent of the RLBO sample was delisted after going public, with most going bankrupt by filing Chapter 11 or Chapter 7. Hence, this analysis links the probability of post-IPO delisting to LBO duration to identify whether buyout sponsors push immature LBOs public because of the greater susceptibility to bankruptcy risk.

The interplay among buyout sponsors' incentives and corporate decisions is a critical issue for both researchers and investors, and the debate about buyout sponsors' controversial role, especially in PE-backed IPOs, is ongoing. Such controversy is clearly illustrated by the case of Warner Bros Music, bought in March 2004 for $2.6 billion by a group led by Thomas H. Lee Partners and Edgar Bronfman Jr and taken public 14 months later. Along the way, the sponsors had Warner Bros Music pay them dividends worth more than $1 billion. When Warner went public, analysts and investors said they expected the private equity firms to sell their stakes to lock in their gains. However, after the offering, these firms continued to control a majority stake worth about $2 billion. In fact, Warner Bros Music rejected a buyout offer from EMI, another large music publisher, and as a defensive strategy even made a counterbid. This case raises several important questions: why did the sponsors of Warner Bros Music reject the takeover offer for quick cash? In what sense should buyout sponsors maintain an active role in RLBO companies post IPO? How can the reputation of private equity investor groups mitigate the conflict of interest between buyout sponsors and outside investors?[9]

Several additional studies are highly relevant to this analysis. First, in an early study, Muscarella and Vetsuypens (1990) argue that stock market listing is an exit mechanism for professional pre-IPO investors such as buyout sponsors. More recent work by Brau et al. (2003) on the choice of private firms to either go public or sell to a publicly traded buyer finds that these companies favor the IPO route over a takeover when the firm size is large and the industry market-to-book ratio is low. Benninga et al. (2005), however, link the decision to go public to the possibility of sequential privatization (buyouts after IPOs). After linking these dynamic decisions to underlying cash flows, they suggest that entrepreneurs make tradeoffs between the benefits of keeping firms private and the value added of going public. One difficulty in such research is determining exactly when buyout sponsors exit from RLBOs. For instance, KKR spent approximately three years post-LBO holding Safeway as a portfolio company, but ultimately took more than 10 years to sell its stake in Safeway following the IPO. Therefore, like Giot and Schwienbacher (2007), this analysis focuses on sponsor's post-IPO presence in or exit from venture capital (VC)-backed IPOs.

Initial public offerings tend to cluster during hot periods. The literature suggests that this phenomenon can be explained in part by high cash flows (Benninga et al., 2005), industry effects (Ritter, 1984; Jain and Kini, 2006), and high underpricing (Lowry and Schwert, 2002). Alti (2005) further relates IPO clustering to market timing arguing that high offer-price realizations have positive spillover effects that attract subsequent IPOs. Ritter (1991) finds that IPO performance frequently involves long-run investment underperformance. In IPOs and seasoned equity offerings (SEOs) Loughran and

Ritter (1995) attribute long-run poor performance to temporary market mispricing; that is, new issuing firms take advantage of new equity overvaluation. However, Jain and Kini's (1994) study on post-issue operating performance finds that, although IPOs generally exhibit a decline in operating performance, IPOs with concentrated entrepreneurial ownership demonstrate relatively superior performance among issuing firms. Earlier research by Degeorge and Zeckhauser (1993) suggests that RLBO firms differ from IPOs: they are not only larger than the average IPO but often use IPO proceeds to reduce debt. Nonetheless, Holthausen and Larcker (1996) find that RLBO companies in the 1980s showed better operating performance post-IPO than the industry average, although their operating performance decreased as ownership concentration (of management and other insiders) decreased.

3 DATA AND EMPIRICAL METHODS

3.1 Sample Description

In this analysis, two criteria define an RLBO transaction. First, an IPO must have previously received LBO financing sponsored by a buyout group, and second, the LBO investment must be characterized by immense use of leverage. Buyout firms/funds that engage primarily in buyout investment activities were identified from Thomson's VentureXpert and Standard and Poors' Capital IQ. The sample excludes investments by buyout organizations that more closely resemble venture capital. The RLBO transactions were identified using two types of sources. The first included the Securities Data Company's (SDC) Corporate New Issues database, which flags IPOs with an identifier indicating a previous leveraged buyout, and LBO databases that indicate whether any transaction subsequently went public. These searches produced a sample of 229 RLBOs for the period from 1981 through the middle of 1998. The second set of sources included Dealogic and Capital IQ, both of which report IPOs backed by financial sponsors, as well as a search of news stories on Factiva using the same criteria. These sources generated an additional 297 RLBOs[10] to produce a final sample of 594 RLBOs from 1981 to 2006.[11] Companies were excluded based on the following criteria: offer sizes below $5 million, offer prices below $5.00 per share, unit trust, closed-end funds, American Depository Receipts (ADRs), and IPOs not listed on Center for Research in Security Prices (CRSP) within six months of issuing. Real estate investment trusts (REITs) are included because they make up a fair number of the sample.

The IPO underwriter reputation data, measured by an amended version of Carter and Manaster (1990), was obtained from Jay Ritter's website,[12] and the LBO information on buyout sponsors from the Factiva press search. Ownership data and board information at the time of the IPO were collected from the IPO prospectuses, while post-IPO board information and ownership data were taken from proxy filing statements on the Securities and Exchange Commission (SEC's) EDGAR website. Because of data availability issues that reduce the sample size, the analysis of post-IPO sponsor exit strategies requires a three-year window for ownership data. The regressions thus report the actual observations used in the multivariate analysis. The accounting data for RLBOs were obtained from COMPUSTAT, which measures accounting variables at the end of the

Table 18.1   Industry distribution of RLBOs

	RLBOs Frequency (%)	Other IPOs Frequency (%)
Manufacturing	44.16	33.63
Personal/business service	13.76	21.98
Retail	11.68	5.46
Healthcare	3.52	3.02
Restaurant/hotel	3.52	2.47
Radio/TV/telecom	3.04	2.97
Transportation	3.04	2.78
Wholesale	3.04	3.39
Natural resource	2.88	2.81
Insurance	2.24	3.44
Construction	1.44	1.30
Telecommunications	1.28	1.01
Other industry	6.40	15.74

Notes:
Using the first two digits of the SIC codes and based on IPO data from the SDC new issues file, this table reports the industry distribution of the 594 RLBOs in the sample (1981 to 2006).
This sample excludes RLBOs and other IPOs with an offer size below $5 million, a price below $5.00 per share, unit offers, closed-end funds, and ADRs, as well as IPOs not listed on the CRSP within six months of issuance.

calendar or fiscal year. Return, price, and delisting information were taken from the CRSP Monthly Stock database.

Table 18.1 presents the industry distribution of RLBOs and all other IPOs, the majority of which, in both cases, are concentrated in the manufacturing industry. The personal business industry accounts for the second largest concentration and retail for the third.

Table 18.2 lists the top 20 active RLBO sponsors and reports each sponsor's total number of RLBOs, average RLBO size, and average money left on the table (defined as the multiplication of underpricing and offer size). Many buyout sponsors are repeat players in IPO markets, with KKR topping the list as sponsor of 24 RLBOs. At the bottom of the list is Lehman Brothers with eight RLBOs.

Table 18.3 summarizes the yearly distribution of RLBOs, the average LBO duration each year, and the subsequent delisting numbers or post-IPO takeover (being acquired) activities. Reverse leveraged buyout distribution is highly correlated with the buyout cycles in a lagged fashion. For 1992, when many LBOs acquired in the late 1980s began returning to the public market, there are a staggering 63 offerings. The first LBO wave also gave rise to the first RLBO wave: 14 and 22 RLBOs for 1986 and 1987, respectively. However, after the collapse of the junk bond/LBO markets, RLBO activities dried up, with only four RLBOs in 1988 and three in 1989.

For the private years between LBO and IPO, RLBO companies exhibited great heterogeneity: some remained private for only a short period of time (for example, less than a year), while others stayed private for up to 10 years. Reverse leveraged buyout firms on average remained private[13] for 3.75 years, with a median duration of 2.83 years. Among all RLBOs, 70 deals (11.8 percent of the total sample) were quick flips, mostly

Table 18.2 Distribution of RLBOs according to sponsor

	Deal number	Average gross proceeds (in millions US$)	Money left on the table (in millions US$)
KKR	24	213.96	15.51
Warburg Pincus	17	112.45	9.59
GTCR Golder Rauner	16	140.49	11.50
Morgan Stanley Private Equity	16	179.64	17.01
Welsh, Carson, Anderson & Stowe	16	114.87	10.94
Bain Capital	14	199.54	7.68
Thomas H. Lee Partners	12	233.32	30.28
Hicks, Muse, Tate & Furst	11	284.12	22.56
Kelso & Company	11	128.92	6.45
Citicorp Venture Capital	10	111.08	9.52
Texas Pacific Group	10	224.74	79.09
Apollo Group	9	223.91	14.14
Blackstone Group	9	402.17	14.93
DLJ Merchant Banking Partners	9	115.44	25.39
Forstmann Little & Co.	9	253.94	25.15
Leonard Green & Partners	9	148.44	6.62
Madison Dearborn Partners	9	144.81	34.40
Merrill Lynch	9	69.03	4.67
Goldman Sachs	8	178.33	127.44
Lehman Brothers	8	120.66	23.41

Notes:
This table reports the distribution of the 594 RLBOs (1981–2006) in the full sample arranged by their 20 most active sponsors, together with the number of deals backed by each leading buyout sponsor, average first-day return, gross proceeds, and money left on the table.
IPO data, such as first-day return, offer size, and offer price, were obtained from the SDC new issues file. The sample excludes IPOs with an offer size below $5 million, a price below $5.00 per share, unit offers, closed-end funds, and ADRs, as well as IPOs not listed on the CRSP within six months of issuance.

taking place in 1987 and the late 1990s in hot LBO and IPO periods. A total of 61 firms subsequently delisted, and 199 firms (one third of the sample) were acquired within five years of going public. This proportion is similar to that for all listed firms acquired in takeovers.

3.2 Empirical Methods

Under the performance timing hypothesis, RLBO companies will exhibit drastic performance deterioration after going public. Therefore, the analysis of firm operating performance employs the EBITDA/sales and return on assets (ROA) (net income/asset) measures used in earlier studies to identify the general patterns of RLBO operating performance both around their IPOs and in post-IPO years. More specifically, based on industry and industry and performance-matched companies[14] as benchmarks, it reports the operating performance of both the whole sample and subsamples such as quick flips, as well as RLBO financial performance adjusted by the market in post-IPO years.

Table 18.3 Descriptive summary of RLBOs

Year	RLBOs	LBO duration	RLBOs' total market cap (millions US$)	Quick flips	Post-IPO delisting (non-merger)	Post-IPO mergers
1981	1	3.83	280.72	0	0	0
1982	0	0.00	0.00	0	0	0
1983	2	5.17	1097.44	0	1	3
1984	3	2.83	150.78	0	1	2
1985	7	2.04	324.65	2	1	4
1986	14	3.17	1588.53	2	1	8
1987	22	1.96	4873.18	7	2	14
1988	4	1.33	402.50	0	0	2
1989	3	6.19	672.57	0	1	1
1990	9	4.07	1595.88	0	8	5
1991	33	3.90	9440.54	1	6	13
1992	63	3.74	19086.25	2	8	32
1993	45	3.76	13792.68	5	5	24
1994	25	5.14	7440.84	1	2	11
1995	25	4.47	6787.93	3	6	12
1996	37	5.13	9920.52	3	7	12
1997	38	3.36	17212.91	10	4	14
1998	25	1.39	20652.57	8	2	9
1999	36	3.38	27562.33	3	3	8
2000	31	3.17	35356.69	6	1	7
2001	28	3.10	22406.83	2	0	4
2002	25	6.74	16122.71	0	0	6
2003	15	2.54	12238.37	2	0	4
2004	38	3.76	16884.25	4	1	1
2005	38	3.94	24846.82	6	0	3
2006	27	5.44	26423.05	3	0	0
Total	594	3.75	297161.54	70	60	199

Notes:
This table reports the year-number distribution of 594 RLBOs in the sample (1981–2006), the LBO duration (years between LBO and RLBO), RLBO total market capitalization (first day or earliest available after IPO) for each year, number of quick flips, and total number of post-IPO delisting and mergers.
Data on price, delisting, and merger were obtained from the CRSP.

The multivariate analysis regresses RLBO performance on variables of interest like LBO duration and the sponsor's reputation proxy, with the cross-section regression specified as follows:

$$Performance = \alpha_0 + \alpha_1 \, LBO \, duration + \alpha_2 \, Reputation + \alpha_3 \, Controls + \varepsilon \quad (18.1)$$

The performance measures include change in operating performance (measured by EBITDA/sales two years after IPO minus EBIDTA/sales in the year of the IPO) and stock performance (measured by buy-and-hold three-year return adjusted by the market). The other independent variables include the logarithm of firm size, changes in leverage (debt to asset ratio), a quick flip dummy, changes in industry performance, and the IPO market condition. As suggested by Holthausen and Larcker (1996), the change in industry operating performance is used to control the mean reversion in accounting measure. Consistent with Alti (2005), the IPO market condition is proxied by two variables – aggregate numbers of issuances or average underpricing of all IPOs in the previous three months, and IPO underpricing is measured as the first-day return (closing price at the IPO deflated by offer price). Following Cao and Lerner (2009), buyout sponsor reputation is measured as the capital they have historically managed and their vintage age.

Under the market timing hypothesis, favorable external market conditions affect LBO duration because buyout sponsors are more likely to take the LBO public quickly (hence, RLBO) to take advantage of the hotter issuance market for new IPOs. This assumption leads to two empirical predictions: a negative relationship between LBO duration and IPO market activities, and a greater likelihood of quick flips in hotter markets. Buyout sponsor reputation may also be important. For example, the reputation effect may align sponsors' interests with those of the public, encouraging more reputable sponsors to spend more time restructuring and improving LBOs before taking them public. Accordingly, the multivariate regression also assesses the determinants of LBO duration using the following OLS specification:

$$Log(LBO\ duration) = \alpha_0 + \alpha_1\ Market\ conditions + \alpha_2\ Reputation + \alpha_3\ Controls + \varepsilon, \quad (18.2)$$

where the dependent variable is the number of years that a firm stays private from LBO to RLBO. The explanatory variables include IPO market condition, industry Q, sponsor reputation, firm size, operating performance, leverage, and company EBITDA/sales.

Sponsor decisions about the length of LBO restructuring, however, are not homogeneous across RLBOs. Therefore, any analysis of the effect of duration on performance must take into account this self-selection issue, especially for quick flips. To control for this problem, I investigate the likelihood of a quick flip and its effects on subsequent firm performance using Heckman's selection regressions, a two-step estimation procedure:

$$\text{Step 1: Probit } (Quick\ flip) = \alpha_0 + \alpha_1\ IPO\ condition + \alpha_3 \cdot Controls + \varepsilon$$
$$\text{Step 1: } Performance = \alpha_0 + \alpha_1 \cdot Quick\ flip\ \alpha_2 \cdot Controls + \alpha_3 \cdot Lambda + \varepsilon \quad (18.3)$$

The first step is a probit regression in which the dependent variable is a dummy equal to 1 when the RLBO is classified as a quick flip (an LBO duration of less than one year[15]), 0 otherwise. The identifying instruments on the right-hand side include the industry dummy, IPO market condition, buyout sponsor reputation,[16] the relative size of LBO firms to their buyout sponsors' capital, and RLBO firm's prior operating performance. The inclusion of relative size captures the economic significance of a given RLBO to GP capital under management. For example, sponsors may be more likely to flip a relatively smaller firm. The second-step regression includes *lambda*, the inverse Mills ratio imputed from the first-step probit regression, as an additional control variable for selection bias. The dependent variable in the second stage is either a long-run performance measure of EBITDA of sales or a delisting dummy (measured within the three post-IPO years).

Because buyout sponsors are subject to lockup restrictions, however, an RLBO is not equivalent to a quick, complete sponsor exit. Moreover, as major active investors, sponsors may have to choose to continue ownership and monitoring during post-IPO periods. I therefore compile a descriptive summary of the ownership structure and board share of sponsors in RLBOs before and after IPOs. Since buyout sponsor's full exit is not fully observable in a long horizon, the analysis of buyout sponsor presence post IPO uses the Cox proportional hazard duration approach adopted by Giot and Schwienbacher (2007) in their analysis of venture capitalist's exits from VC-backed IPOs. The Cox regression for survival analysis is specified as follows:

$$h(t|x) = h(t) * exp(\alpha_1 \cdot x_1 + \alpha_2 \cdot x_2 + \ldots + \alpha_N \cdot x_N) \qquad x = x_1, x_2, \ldots, x_N \quad (18.4)$$

In this regression, the dependent variable is a survival (no full exit) dummy set to 0 if the sponsor's ownership is positive in year t after the IPO and 1 if the ownership drops to zero in year t. Because the cut-off point is a three-year post-IPO window, the parameter t takes the values 0, 1, 2, and 3. The explanatory variables include EBITDA/sales, stock monthly excess return over the market, Tobin's Q, and sponsor reputation. Tobin's Q, which measures a firm's growth opportunity (Kaplan and Zingales, 1997), is the ratio of the market value[17] of assets divided by their book value.

Buyout sponsors can choose at least two common mechanisms for a post-IPO exit: takeovers (RLBO acquisition by third parties) and gradual distribution of shares (to public investors and limited partners). The analysis of these exiting choices employs both binomial and multinomial probit regressions:

$$Exit\ dummy = \Phi\ (\alpha + \beta\ Cash\ flow + \delta\ Ownership + \Psi\ Reputation + \gamma\ Controls + \varepsilon). \quad (18.5)$$

In the binomial probit regression, the exit dummy takes the value of 1 (0 otherwise) if the sponsor fully exits via either takeover or gradual share distribution (i.e., ownership drops to zero). In the multinomial probit regression, the exit dummy is set to 1 if a full exit takes the form of a takeover (acquisition), 2 if a gradual distribution (ownership drops to zero), and 0 otherwise. Here, Φ is a cumulative probability function for normal distribution. Again, the cut-off point is three years post IPO. The explanatory variables of interest are EBITDA/sales, Tobin's Q, industry Q, ownership structure, LBO duration, and sponsor reputation. The control variables are firm size and leverage.

4 EMPIRICAL RESULTS

4.1 Univariate Analysis of Performance Timing

The univariate analysis tests the performance timing hypothesis that firms experience performance deterioration after their IPOs. Table 18.4 summarizes the key financial ratios and operating performance (both unadjusted and adjusted) of RLBO firms from year IPO-1 to year IPO+2. Panel A reports the sample mean of book asset, employees, EBITDA/sales, sales growth rate, debt/asset, long-term debt/total debt, and other credit conditions.

Table 18.4 RLBO firm characteristics, leverage, and performance

Panel A: RLBO characteristics

	IPO−1	IPO	IPO+1	IPO+2
Assets ($ million)	799.69	835.82	904.66	968.32
Employees (million)	4.21	4.75	5.29	6.00
Market to book ratio, Q	–	2.27	2.05	1.82
Sales growth rate (%)	28.21	54.89	27.57	18.12
ROA (net income/asset) (%)	0.33	2.63	3.58	1.51
EBITDA/sales (%)	13.20	16.25	15.72	12.79
CAPEX/sales (%)	19.87	17.91	13.95	11.34
Total debt/assets (%)	56.55	35.82	33.48	33.14
Debt equity ratio	4.72	2.66	2.42	1.58
Interest coverage	5.31	6.27	11.96	12.13
Subordinated debt/long-term debt (%)	27.38	19.15	16.87	14.98
Convertible debt and preferred stock/long-term debt (%)	91.91	46.85	2.21	3.93
Debt maturing in 2 years/long-term debt (%)	14.06	16.25	15.73	15.03
Debt maturing in 4 years/long-term debt (%)	11.96	10.51	15.69	13.96
Credit rating (percentage of investment grade) (%)	7.06	8.77	11.28	14.73
Observations	481	496	436	374

Panel B: Industry benchmark-adjusted operating performance (based on first three SIC digits)

		IPO−1	IPO	IPO+1	IPO+2
Full sample: ROA (net income/asset) (%)	-mean	−3.48***	−0.60	1.52**	−0.43
	-median	−2.58***	1.23	1.57*	0.98
EBITDA/sales (%)	-mean	−1.89**	4.27***	3.42***	3.67***
	-median	−3.42***	2.73**	2.98**	3.35***
Quick flips: ROA (net income/asset) (%)	-mean	−2.69**	−1.07*	−0.38	−3.80*
	-median	−1.76*	−0.53	−0.96	−2.54**
EBITDA/sales (%)	-mean	−7.27***	2.39**	0.97	−0.34
	-median	−5.58***	1.23	1.09	−1.82*

Panel C: Industry (first 2 SIC digits) and performance (matching EBITDA/sales at year IPO−1) benchmark-adjusted operating performance

		IPO−1	IPO	IPO+1	IPO+2
Full sample: ROA (net income/asset) (%)	-mean	0.09	2.13***	4.19***	3.68***
	-median	0.14	1.77**	2.23**	2.59***
EBITDA/sales (%)	-mean	0.38	5.28***	4.87***	5.13***
	-median	0.29	6.21***	5.85***	5.52***
Quick flips: ROA (net income/asset) (%)	-mean	0.13	1.65	0.84	−2.31**
	-median	0.11	0.92	−0.26	−1.97*
EBITDA/sales (%)	-mean	0.25	2.58**	1.72*	0.91
	-median	0.27	1.86	1.35	0.96

Table 18.4 (continued)

Panel D: Stock performance (buy-and-hold return)

		12 months after IPO	24 months after IPO	36 months after IPO
Full sample: Raw monthly stock return (%)	-mean	20.10***	33.73***	43.35***
	-median	13.06***	18.75***	17.32***
Market-adjusted monthly stock return	-mean	9.54***	11.35***	13.73**
	-median	3.25*	−5.58	−11.63
Quick flips: Raw monthly stock return (%)	-mean	18.70***	25.08***	32.03***
	-median	−1.64	14.29	16.65
Market-adjusted monthly stock return	-mean	6.77	6.82	4.88
	-median	−9.89	−12.15	−14.52*

Notes:
This table lists the key characteristics (mainly financial leverage) and operating/financial performance of the 594 RLBOs in the sample (1981 to 2006) and reports cross-sectional sample means for the years IPO−1, IPO, IPO+1, and IPO+2.
The performance measures include ROA, EBITDA/sales, sales growth, and EBIT/sales.
The leverage measures include total debt/asset, debt equity ratio, interest coverage (defined as EBITDA/interest expense), subordinated debt/long-term debt, convertible debt and preferred stock/long-term debt, debt maturing in two and four years/long-term debt, and the percentage of credit rating as investment grade.
Panel B reports the industry benchmark-adjusted performance for RLBOs in the full sample and for quick flips in the subsample. Panel C reports RLBO performance adjusted by the industry and performance benchmark (at year IPO−1), and panel D reports stock performance for both the full sample and the quick flip subsample.
The mean and median significance were tested using *t*-statistics and Wilcoxon *z*-statistics.
*, **, and *** indicate the 10%, 5%, and 1% significance level, respectively.

As the table shows, the debt ratio (total debt/book assets) peaks at one year before the IPO; the RLBO firms' assets and employees gradually increase around the IPO; and the ratio of convertible debt and preferred stock/long-term debt decreases substantially after the IPO, suggesting that a large portion of equity-linked (convertible) debt) is either converted into common stock or retired. The unadjusted operating performance in panel A, however, shows no consistent pattern of performance deterioration: ROA (net income/assets) gradually increases and peaks at IPO+1, while EBITDA/sales remain fairly stable around IPOs. Like that of other firms, RLBO firms' sales growth rate reaches its peak level in the first year of the IPO and gradually deteriorates afterwards.

Panels B and C report benchmark-adjusted RLBO performance, with EBITDA/sales and ROA adjusted by the industry mean or median or by the industry and performance benchmark (matched EBITDA/sales or ROA at year IPO−1), respectively. Neither measure of benchmark-adjusted operating performance exhibits any post-IPO deterioration. On the contrary, consistent with Degeorge and Zeckhauser (1993), RLBOs show persistently superior operating performance in post-IPO years: EBITDA/sales or ROA outperforms the relative benchmarks by a range from 1 percent to 5 percent. Such performance persistence suggests that buyout sponsors on average maintain superior RLBO operating performance; hence, the performance timing hypothesis can be rejected. In the special RLBO subsample of quick flips, however, there is a strong pattern of performance deterioration: both EBITDA/sales and ROA jump just before the IPO but decrease drastically after it. Given that this evidence is robust for both mean and median, the performance timing hypothesis is rejected for the full RLBO sample but supported for the quick flip subsample.

Panel D reports RLBO stock performance, specifically the one-year, two-year, and three-year buy-and-hold return post IPO, both unadjusted and adjusted by market (the value-weighted CRSP return). The results are consistent with Cao and Lerner (2009): RLBOs in general outperform or at least do not underperform the market. Quick flips, however, exhibit worse performance than other RLBOs and do underperform the market – their median market-adjusted buy-and-hold return is (weakly) negative and significant.

Table 18.5 reports the results of the cross-sectional regression of change in operating performance (EBITDA/sales) from the year of the IPO to year IPO+2, as well as the stock performance (the three-year buy-and-hold return over market). The explanatory variables in the OLS regression include LBO duration/a quick flip dummy, an IPO market condition proxy, sponsor reputation, and other firm characteristics. LBO duration is positively and significantly associated with performance change: firms remaining private one additional year show almost a 1 percent improvement in change in EBITDA/sales after the IPO. The evidence also suggests more performance deterioration in firms with shorter LBO duration: the quick flip dummy is negatively and significantly associated with a change in operating performance after going public.

Overall, the evidence in Table 18.5 suggests that LBO duration is a good proxy for sponsors' LBO restructuring efforts. Moreover, the change in performance is negatively related to the IPO market condition, indicating that performance timing must be specific to market condition: RLBOs issued under more favorable IPO market conditions are more likely to experience greater deterioration in operating performance. These results are robust to other measures of performance such as net income/assets.

4.2 Multivariate Analysis of Market Timing

Capital market conditions affect sponsor decisions of RLBO or staying private with more restructuring. Hence, the market timing hypothesis suggests that sponsors will shorten LBO duration and be more likely to take (immature) LBOs public given the advantage of a favorable IPO market. The results of the OLS regression to analyze LBO duration are given in Table 18.6, in which the dependent variable of LBO duration (the logarithm of one-plus years as a private LBO) is regressed on the IPO market condition proxy, sponsor reputation, firm operating performance, firm size (sales), and other firm characteristics.

As the table shows, LBO duration is positively associated with sales, suggesting that larger LBOs may require more effort and hence more time for improvement. Initial public offering market condition does affect LBO duration: the number of years as an LBO decreases with the aggregate IPO underpricing (a proxy for IPO market condition) during the previous three months. The general industry valuation is also important: not only is the industry Tobin's Q negatively associated with LBO duration, but both regression coefficients are significant at either the 5 percent or 10 percent level. This evidence supports the market timing hypothesis: buyout sponsors sell portfolio companies more

Table 18.5 Multivariate analysis of post-IPO RLBO performance

	ΔEBITDA/sales from IPO to IPO+2 1	ΔEBITDA/sales from IPO to IPO+2 2	36 months market-adjusted buy-and-hold return after IPO 3	36 months market-adjusted buy-and-hold return after IPO 4
Constant	0.056	0.071	−0.061	−0.206
	(0.19)	(0.28)	(0.15)	(0.28)
Log(LBO duration)	0.032*		−0.004	
	(1.80)		(0.31)	
Quick flip dummy	−0.023	−0.037*		−0.144
	(0.91)	(1.98)		(0.69)
Total debt/assets	−0.081**	−0.094**	−0.144	−0.171
	(2.52)	(2.21)	(0.61)	(0.72)
Log(assets)	−0.003	0.002	−0.173*	−0.215*
	(0.37)	(0.64)	(1.86)	(1.85)
Change in industry EBITDA/sales	0.238	0.307	0.009	0.011
	(1.47)	(1.19)	(0.24)	(0.09)
Log(buyout sponsor capital)	0.002	0.004	0.147*	0.148*
	(0.20)	(0.59)	(1.79)	(1.73)
IPO market average underpricing in previous 3 months	−0.325**		−0.521**	
	(2.21)		(2.09)	
Log(IPO numbers in previous 3 months)		−0.042		−0.063
		(0.77)		(0.38)
Year fixed effects	Yes	Yes	Yes	Yes
Adjusted R^2	0.04	0.07	0.13	0.15
Number of observations	290	290	290	290

Notes:
This table reports the results of the OLS regressions on the performance of the 594 RLBOs between 1981 and 2006.
The regression is specified as follows: Performance = α_0 + α_1 LBO duration + α_2 Reputation + α_3 Controls + ε. Columns 2 and 3 report the change in EBITDA/sales from IPO to IPO+2; columns 4 and 5 list the buy-and-hold stock return adjusted by the value-weighted market benchmark.
The independent variables include LBO duration, quick flip dummy, debt ratio (total debt/asset), logarithm of firm assets, industry change in EBITDA, sponsor capital raised, and average IPO underpricing/aggregate number of new IPOs in the previous three months.
The regressions also control the year fixed effects.
The cross-sectional heteroscedastically robust *t*-statistics are reported in parentheses.
*, **, and *** indicate the 10%, 5%, and 1% significance level, respectively.

quickly to public investors when general IPO market conditions are more favorable or industry valuation of firm assets is higher.

4.3 Market Timing and Performance of Quick Flips

The extreme case of shortened duration is the quick flip, an option that must be deliberately chosen by buyout sponsors based on information about portfolio characteristics,

Table 18.6 Multivariate analysis of LBO duration

	(1)	(2)	(3)	(4)	(5)
Constant	−0.023	−0.31	−0.28	−0.47	−0.51
	(0.78)	(0.95)	(0.86))	(1.12)	(1.33)
Log(sales)	0.073**	0.075***	0.077**	0.068**	0.075**
	(2.40)	(2.73)	(2.43)	(2.26)	(2.43)
Total debt/assets	0.092	−0.053	−0.029	−0.038	−0.031
	(0.77)	(0.49)	(0.23)	(0.32)	(0.25)
EBITDA/sales	0.880***	0.877***	0.688*	0.734**	0.687*
	(2.69)	(2.68)	(1.98)	(2.06)	(1.87)
Tobin's Q	−0.023	−0.023	−0.024	−0.025	−0.023
	(0.63)	(0.92)	(0.94)	(0.97)	(0.92)
IPO market average underpricing in previous 3 months	−0.296***	−0.307**	−0.401**	−0.419**	−0.403**
	(2.75)	(2.53)	(2.27)	(2.64)	(2.46)
Log(IPO numbers in previous 3 months)		0.024	0.028	0.033	0.028
		(0.49)	(0.53)	(0.64)	(0.51)
Log(buyout firm capital)			−0.021		−0.019
			(0.59)		(0.75)
Log(buyout firm vintage age)				−0.026	−0.007
				(0.56)	(0.34)
Industry Q					−0.053*
					(1.98)
Industry effects	Yes	Yes	Yes	Yes	Yes
LBO year effects	Yes	Yes	Yes	Yes	Yes
Adjusted R^2	0.07	0.08	0.07	0.06	0.08
Number of observations	343	343	290	290	290

Notes:
This table gives the results for the OLS regressions of buyout sponsors' LBO duration for the 594 RLBOs (1981–2006).
The OLS regressions are specified as follows: $Log(LBO\ duration) = \alpha_0 + \alpha_1$ Market conditions $+ \alpha_2$ Reputation$+ \alpha_3$ Controls $+ \varepsilon$.
The dependent variable is the logarithm of LBO duration (years of being private between LBO and RLBO). The explanatory variables to proxy market conditions include average IPO underpricing in the past three months, logarithm of the total number of IPOs in the previous three months, and industry Tobin's Q; the explanatory variables to proxy PE group reputation include logarithm of buyout sponsor capital raised and/or vintage age.
The control variables are logarithm of sales, debt ratio (total debt/assets), EBITDA/sales, and Tobin's Q, all measured at the year of IPO.
The cross-sectional heteroscedastically robust *t*-statistics are reported in parentheses.
*, **, and *** indicate the 10%, 5%, and 1% significance level, respectively.

firm quality, or market conditions. As outlined previously, the multivariate analysis controls for such selection decisions using Heckman's two-step procedure with lambda as a control: in the first-step probit regression on the quick flip decision, the dependent variable is set to 1 for quick flip, 0 for other RLBOs; in the second-step regression, the dependent variable is long-run RLBO performance (either EBITDA/sales or the delisting dummy).

As Table 18.7 shows, the relative size of RLBO firms (firm asset relative to sponsor

Table 18.7 Decision on quick flips and its effect on performance

	First step selection	Second-step regression		
	Quick flips	Industry adjusted EBITDA/sales	Delisting dummy	36 months buy-and-hold return after IPO
Constant		0.041	0.137	−0.179
		(1.19)	(0.98)	(0.49)
Quick flip dummy		−0.056*	0.467*	−0.072
		(1.87)	(1.72)	(1.45)
Dummy for IPO debt reduction		0.023	0.192	0.033
		(0.620)	(0.81)	(0.28)
Log(underwriter rank)		0.047	0.266	−0.011
		(1.07)	(0.20)	(0.23)
IPO underpricing		−0.063***	0.185	−0.465*
		(3.22)	(0.64)	(1.69)
Buyout sponsor ownership before IPO		−0.021	−0.081	−0.735**
		(0.49)	(0.17)	(2.21)
Log(sales) at IPO year		−0.012	−0.032*	−0.090*
		(0.35)	(1.69)	(1.78)
Firm assets before IPO/buyout sponsor size	−0.221*			
	(1.61)			
Log(buyout sponsor capital)	−0.003			
	(0.97)			
EBITDA/sales prior to IPO	0.072*			
	(1.73)			
Log(assets prior to IPO)	−0.004			
	(0.92)			
Log(total IPO numbers in previous 3 months)	0.162*			
	(1.55)			
IPO market average underpricing in previous 3 months	0.518			
	(0.98)			
Lambda		−0.625***	−0.611	−0.352
		(4.38)	(0.38)	(0.96)
R^2	0.06	0.18	0.23	0.08
Number of observations	272	272	272	272

Notes:
This table presents the results of the regressions of long-run performance on quick flip using Heckman's selection approach.
Estimations are based on the following: First step: Probit (Quick Flip) = $\alpha_0 + \alpha_1 \cdot$ Control variables + ε; Second step: Performance = $\alpha_0 + \alpha_1$ Quick flip + α_2 Control variables + α_3 lambda + ε.
Column 2 gives the first-step probit regression results for quick flips; columns 3, 4, and 5 present the second-step OLS regression. The OLS regression in column 3 uses EBITDA/sales; the probit regression in column 4 uses a delisting dummy, and the OLS regression in column 5 uses the buy-and-hold return.
EBITDA/sales are calculated as the average of the years IPO, IPO+1, and IPO+2, measured at the end of the year and adjusted by industry median.
The delisting dummy is set to 1 if a firm is delisted from the market within a three-year window post-IPO.
The buy-and-hold return is measured three years following IPO and adjusted by the value-weighted market benchmark.
Lambda is the inverse Mills ratio calculated from the first-step selection regression.
The heteroscedastically robust *t*-statistics are reported in parentheses.
*, **, and *** indicate the 10%, 5%, and 1% significance level, respectively.

392 *Handbook of research on IPOs*

size, measured by total historical capital under management) is negatively associated with the likelihood of quick flip, suggesting that this choice is more likely for relatively smaller LBOs. The likelihood of quick flip is also positively associated with the aggregate number of IPOs in the past three months and hotter IPO issuance periods. The coefficient of EBITDA/sales is positive and significant, possibly because firms having stable operating performance do not have to stay private for long or that, consistent with the evidence in Tables 18.5 and 18.6, quick flips experience more operating performance deterioration because sponsors are more likely to flip firms that are experiencing a performance peak (performance timing). Such quick flip markups in EBIDTA/sales before IPOs and subsequent performance drops are also illustrated in Figure 18.1.

In the second-stage Heckman analysis, quick flip dummy is significantly and negatively associated with long-run operating performance (average EBITDA/sales in the three years following the IPO). In contrast, the dummy is significantly and positively related to the likelihood of a firm being delisted within five years after the IPO. The evidence also reveals that, once the selection bias is controlled for, the long-run performance of quick flips is significantly worse than that of other RLBOs. This finding further supports the role of operating performance timing in the quick flips that tend to occur in the hotter IPO period. Moreover, sponsors' opportunistic timing decisions for immature LBOs lead to value destruction; that is, quick flips exhibit poorer performance in the long run.

5 EMPIRICAL RESULTS FOR SPONSOR EXIT

5.1 Analysis of Sponsors' Post-IPO Presence

As shown in Table 18.8, which reports the ownership structure of RLBOs around IPOs and in post-IPO years, buyout sponsors[18] on average hold approximately 60 percent of equity ownership prior to IPOs, but their ownership level decreases to 40 percent immediately after the IPO. This decrease is partly due to share dilution and partly to IPO stock sales. Moreover, as indicated by the summary statistics of sponsor ownership levels and percentage of board directors affiliated with buyout groups post IPO (panels B and C), buyout sponsors continue holding significant equity stakes in the long term. Specifically, their ownership decreases from about 32 percent to 24 percent from year IPO+1 to year IPO+3. Likewise, sponsors retain a significant board share: the percentage of buyout-affiliated directors decreases from 32 percent in year IPO+1 to 25 percent in year IPO+3.

In addition, since LBO funds have a limited lifecycle, sponsors have a greater impetus to exit from RLBO companies that have been held for a longer time. Hence, the analysis of sponsor decisions on post-IPO presence employs the Cox proportional duration approach (a survival model) to control for this unobserved liquidity demand. The results for the Cox proportional hazard regressions, specified in Equation (18.3), are presented in Table 18.9.

Whereas the coefficient of EBITDA/sales is negative and significant, the coefficient of Tobin's Q is significant and positive, suggesting that buyout sponsor's post-IPO

Table 18.8 Ownership structure of RLBOs and sponsors' post-IPO presence

Panel A: Whole sample

	Mean	Median	SD	Min	Max
Percentage of shares sold at IPO by buyout sponsors	6.35	0.00	18.23	−31.04	100
Buyout ownership before IPO	60.19	60.05	24.79	9.14	100
Insider ownership before IPO	54.18	59.60	35.41	0.00	100
Insider ownership immediately after IPO	34.68	37.85	26.55	0.00	96.6
LBO years (between LBO and RLBO)	3.75	2.83	2.82	0.25	17.5
Buyout firm capital ($ million)	4408.12	1794	6937.66	2.8	38990
Buyout firm vintage years	16.22	15	9.28	0.00	58

Panel B: Subsample from 1995–2005

Buyout group ownership					
IPO year	39.77	39.65	20.10	1.70	84.08
IPO +1 year	32.36	30.82	20.94	0.00	79.80
IPO +2 year	26.91	23.40	21.57	0.00	77.10
IPO +3 year	23.95	21.05	21.81	0.00	76.20
Board share of leading buyout group (%)					
IPO year	38.35	37.50	19.07	0.00	88.90
IPO +1 year	32.05	30.00	17.31	0.00	87.50
IPO +2 year	28.14	25.00	16.67	0.00	77.78
IPO +3 year	25.26	25.00	15.74	0.00	70.00

Notes:
Panel A reports the summary statistics for the full sample of 594 RLBO firms (1981–2006) on the following characteristics: percentage of shares sold by buyout firm at IPO, buyout firm ownership before and after IPO, insider (management and directors) ownership before and after IPO, LBO holding years (years after LBO and before RLBO), buyout firm capital (total capital raised from the firm's inception to the year before RLBO), and buyout firm vintage age (the difference in years between the firm's founding and the RLBO). Panel B reports the ownership and board share of sponsors for a subsample of RLBOs between 1995, when SEC filings of proxy statements became available, and 2005.

presence/retention of stakes, which is more likely in RLBO companies with better stock performance, increases cash flow but decreases equity valuation. However, general market conditions like industry valuation or stock market performance have a weak impact on post-IPO duration: the coefficient of the industry Q is positive and significant, but the coefficient of the market returns (S&P 500) is positive but insignificant.

Overall, the evidence from this analysis suggests that sponsors retain their post-IPO presence in firms with more cash flow but are more likely to reduce duration or sell stakes when firms have higher stock valuation. These findings provide new empirical evidence for Zingales' (1995) conclusions: incumbent buyout sponsors continue their presence post IPO to extract cash flow benefits but are more likely to cash out quickly (shorten their duration of post-IPO presence) when firms receive higher external valuations.

Table 18.9 Duration of sponsor's post-IPO exits

	1	2	3
Industry-adjusted EBITDA/sales	−3.378***	−3.662***	−3.661***
	(2.73)	(2.96)	(2.89)
Log(assets)	−0.006	−0.009	−0.008
	(0.16)	(0.38)	(0.23)
Total debt/assets	−0.229	−0.292	−0.276
	(0.34)	(0.44)	(0.42)
Tobin's Q	0.126***	0.122***	0.117***
	(6.22)	(5.13)	(3.68)
Excess stock monthly return over market	−0.901**	−0.105**	−0.101**
	(2.27)	(2.23)	(2.00)
Log(IPO numbers in previous three months)	0.382		
	(0.82)		
Average underpricing in previous three months		0.024	
		(0.44)	
Industry Q			0.058**
			(2.38)
Market return (S&P 500)			0.237
			(1.24)
Log(buyout firm capital)	0.019		0.021
	(0.39)		(0.86)
Log(1+buyout firm vintage age)		0.003	0.002
		(0.61)	(0.53)
Log likelihood	−1254.81	−1347.21	−1429.24
P-value, joint test	0.00	0.00	0.00
Number of observations	736	736	736

Notes:
This table shows the regression results for buyout sponsor duration post-IPO (from RLBO to final exit). The Cox proportional duration regression is specified as follows: $h(t|x) = h(t) * exp(\alpha_1 \cdot x_1 + \alpha_2 \cdot x_2 + \ldots + \alpha_N \cdot x_N)$ $x = x_1, x_2, \ldots, x_N$. The dependent variable is the survival variable measuring duration of sponsor's presence post-IPO up to their full exit. The independent variables include EBITDA/sales (industry adjusted), logarithm of asset, debt ratio (debt/asset), Tobin's Q, stock performance (excess monthly stock return over value-weighted market), total number and average underpricing of all IPOs in the past three months, industry Q, market return (S&P 500 index), and buyout sponsor reputation (capital raised/vintage age).
The heteroscedastically robust t-statistics are reported in parentheses.
*, **, and *** indicate the 10%, 5%, and 1% significance level, respectively.

5.2 Determinants of the Exiting Mechanism

Because sponsors may find it easier to exit and cash out when they can sell RLBO companies to a third party through takeover, the mechanism of exit matters for post-IPO duration. Table 18.10 outlines buyout sponsor choices between exit via a facilitating takeover (being acquired) and exit through gradual share distribution (to limited partners or public investors in SEOs until ownership drops to zero) as they relate to firm fundamentals, market conditions, and sponsor reputation.

Columns 2 and 3 report the probit analysis results for a sponsor's post-IPO exit via

Table 18.10 Determination of sponsor's post-IPO exit choices

	Probit Y = 1 if exit via takeover 0 otherwise		Probit Y = 1 if exit via gradual distribution, 0 otherwise		Multinomial probit Y = 1 if exit via takeover 2 if gradual sale 0 otherwise	
Constant	−2.658	−1.232	−0.952	−0.505	−1.349	−2.928
	(0.89)	(1.92)	(0.91)	(0.73)	(2.38)	(2.07)
Log(LBO holding	−0.444*	−0.167	0.776*	0.832	−0.412*	0.905
years)	(1.62)	(1.01)	(1.58)	(1.54)	(2.11)	(1.37)
EBITDA/sales at IPO	−0.713*	−1.448**	−0.707	−0.709	−0.103*	−0.880
year	(1.64)	(2.23)	(0.40)	(0.42)	(1.84)	(0.62)
Tobin's Q at IPO year	−0.142	−0.029	0.104*	0.162*	−0.020	0.131*
	(1.33)	(1.03)	(1.69)	(1.80)	(0.26)	(1.67)
Debt/assets at IPO	0.303	0.347	−1.412	−1.552	0.214	−1.587
year	(0.72)	(1.02)	(1.07)	(0.98)	(0.50)	(1.13)
Log(sales) at IPO	0.061	0.072	−0.195	−0.204	0.212**	−0.235
year	(0.80)	(1.16)	(0.45)	(0.65)	(2.44)	(0.45)
Industry Q		−0.033		0.257**	−0.017	0.306*
		(0.64)		(2.09)	(0.35)	(1.99)
Log(buyout firm	0.256***	0.190***	−0.062	−0.108	0.394***	0.006
capital)	(4.35)	(3.38)	(1.35)	(1.25)	(4.37)	(0.26)
Buyout sponsor		1.212**		−0.376**		
ownership after IPO		(2.50)		(2.38)		
Pseudo R^2	0.07	0.09	0.08	0.16		
Number of observations	272	198	272	198	272	

Notes:
This table gives the results for the regressions of buyout sponsors' full exit decisions on cash flow and other firm characteristics for the 594 RLBOs (1981–2006).
The probit regressions are specified as follows: *Exit dummy* = $\alpha_0 + \alpha_1 \cdot$ *Cash flow* + $\alpha_2 \cdot$ *Control variables* + ε.
In columns 2 and 3, the dependent dummy equals 1 if the sponsors exited via takeover post-IPO, 0 otherwise; in columns 4 and 5, it equals 1 if they exited via gradual distribution, 0 otherwise. In columns 6 and 7, the analysis uses a multinomial probit regression in which the dependent dummy equals 1 if the exit was via takeover, 2 if via gradual distribution, and 0 otherwise.
The independent variables include LBO duration, EBITDA/sales, Tobin's Q, debt ratio, sales, industry Q, and buyout reputation (capital raised/vintage age).
The control variables include logarithm of assets and total-term debt/assets.
The heteroscedastically robust *t*-statistics are reported in parentheses.
*, **, and *** indicate the 10%, 5%, and 1% significance level, respectively.

a facilitating takeover based on a dummy dependent variable set to 1 if RLBO firms are acquired within three years after going public, 0 otherwise. Columns 4 and 5 report the probit analysis results for sponsor exit via gradual distribution of shares, with the dependent variable set to 1 if sponsor ownership drops to zero without takeover (in which case, sponsors typically distribute shares to investors), 0 otherwise. In both cases, the sponsor's choice of exit decreases cash flow measures like EBITDA/sales, suggesting that sponsors retain a longer post-IPO presence when they can extract more cash flow. Thus, the probability of exit via takeover/share distribution increases/decreases with sponsor ownership. The evidence also suggests that sponsors extract more control benefit by exiting via facilitating takeover and are more reluctant to distribute all shares when ownership is highly concentrated.

Columns 6 and 7, which present the multinomial probit analysis of the two exit alternatives, show that the probability of a sponsor's exit via distributions increases with Tobin's Q, although Q is unrelated to the probability of exit via takeovers. The evidence also suggests that, among various exit choices, sponsors are more likely to choose exit via share distribution when companies have higher valuations. In addition, the coefficient of buyout sponsor reputation is significant for sponsor exit via facilitating takeover, suggesting that more reputable sponsors are more likely to choose exit via takeover than exit via share distribution. Sponsors are also more likely to choose exit via takeover when RLBOs are larger and their duration is longer. Overall, the evidence in Table 18.10 is consistent with a rational exit choice by buyout sponsors seeking to maximize both cash flow and control benefits.

5.3 Operating Performance around Sponsor's Full Exit

Because of the sponsor monitoring role, if the presence of buyout sponsors helps to improve RLBO operating performance, their full exit, possibly associated with performance deterioration, should result in an absence of monitoring. The analysis thus includes an empirical examination of RLBO operating performance around the year of the sponsors' full exit. Table 18.11 reports such performance adjusted by benchmarks and compares the operating performance one year before the exit with that one year after.

The operating performance measures like ROA and EBITDA/sales exhibit a weak pattern of deterioration following buyout sponsors' full post-IPO exit from RLBOs, and the evidence of performance drop is also fairly weak since the mean difference is either marginally significant or insignificant. This weakness may result from a selection issue: buyout sponsors are more likely to exit quickly if their ownership is less concentrated. This weak evidence does suggest, however, that the presence of buyout sponsors helps to improve operating efficiency.

6 CONCLUSIONS

Using a comprehensive sample of RLBOs between 1980 and 2006, this analysis examines the IPO timing of buyout sponsors in listing LBOs publicly and the impact of such IPO timing on firm performance and exit strategy post IPO. In contrast to earlier findings (for example, Degeorge and Zeckhauser, 1993), the results indicate that RLBO companies experience no significant deterioration in operating performance in post-IPO years. One explanation may be that their earlier study uses a small sample of RLBOs in the 1980s. Correspondingly, the findings of this present study suggest that performance timing and declines in performance are common in the quick flips that were typical in the early sample period.

I find evidence that buyout sponsor's LBO restructuring duration is affected by IPO timing: when facing favorable IPO conditions or high industry valuations, buyout spon-

Table 18.11 *Operating performance change around sponsors' full exit*

Panel A: Industry (first three SIC digits) benchmark

	1 year before exit (64 RLBOs)		Year of exit (64 RLBOs)		1 year after exit (64 RLBOs)		P-value, difference between −1 and +1 of exit year	
	Mean	Median	Mean	Median	Mean	Median	Mean	Median
ROA (net income/assets) (%)	2.22**	1.75*	2.09*	1.38	1.67	0.87	0.16	0.22
EBITDA/sales (%)	6.19***	5.83***	5.77**	5.04***	4.28**	4.19***	0.23	0.38

Panel B: Industry (first two SIC digits) and performance (matching EBITDA/sales at IPO−1 year) benchmark

	1 year before exit (64 RLBOs)		Year of exit (64 RLBOs)		1 year after exit (64 RLBOs)		P-value, difference between −1 and +1 of exit year	
	Mean	Median	Mean	Median	Mean	Median	Mean	Median
ROA (net income/assets) (%)	3.49***	2.24**	2.97***	2.08**	2.11**	1.43	0.10	0.13
EBITDA/sales (%)	5.41***	3.95***	4.82***	3.60***	3.21**	2.69**	0.09	0.11

Notes:
This table reports the summary statistics for RLBO operating performance around the year of the sponsors' final exit post IPO.
Of the 594 RLBOs between 1981 and 2006, 64 had sponsors that have fully exited.
The cross-sectional mean and median of the operating performance are reported for the following years: one year prior to exit, the year of exit, and one year following exit.
The performance measures, ROA and EBITDA/sales, are adjusted by industry benchmarks in panel A, and by industry and performance benchmarks (matching performance at two years before exit) in panel B.
The mean and median significance were tested using t-statistics and Wilcoxon z-statistics.
*, **, and *** indicate the 10%, 5%, and 1% significance level, respectively.

sors tend to shorten the time to restructuring LBOs privately. As a consequence of such IPO timing, RLBOs with shorter duration experience more deterioration in operating performance following their IPOs. Most particularly, buyout sponsors (quickly) flip LBOs to time both operating performance and market conditions. Hence, compared to other RLBOs, quick flips experience worse operating performance and greater probability of bankruptcy post IPO. However, RLBOs as a whole do not exhibit greater declines in operating performance or poorer stock performance than comparable firms. This evidence also provides empirical support for Pastor et al. (2009) in that new listed firms with low profitability volatility and uncertainty such as RLBOs show no declines in profitability.

Initial public offering timing drives RLBO decision but does not affect sponsor's exit post-IPO, while lockup provisions and concern for reputation help align buyout sponsor incentives to public investors. I find that sponsors sell few IPO shares and maintain a significant long-run post-IPO presence and that they make decisions about their post-IPO presence based on company fundamentals and market conditions. Across RLBOs, sponsors choose to maintain a longer presence in firms with higher cash flows and are more likely to exit RLBOs via facilitating takeover when their ownership is greater but via share distribution when the RLBO valuation is higher. Nonetheless, more reputable buyout sponsors are more likely to facilitate takeovers.

Overall, the combined provide empirical support for 'pseudo market timing' proposed by Schultz (2003) as well as 'optimal IPO timing' suggested by Pastor and Veronesi (2005), that is, buyout sponsors take advantage of favorable IPO market conditions for new LBO listings but not to sell overpriced equity. Buyout sponsor's IPO timing has important value implications for investors: listing immature LBOs destroys value and lead to financial distress, while sponsor's reputation partially mitigates this problem. Moreover, buyout sponsor's IPO timing does not necessarily lead to quick cash out, since in general they retain an active long-run presence post IPO and play important monitoring role.

NOTES

1. C-suite is a Canadian survey of executives at public companies on issues such as business and the economy.
2. The buyout industry today is far larger than it was during the years when it enjoyed its greatest returns. For instance, fundraising by US buyout funds was six times greater in 1998 than in 1987, and by 2005 it was nine times the 1987 level.
3. IPOs generally feature lockup agreements that prohibit corporate insiders from selling shares before a certain date, which may range from one month to several years after the IPO.
4. The RLBO lockup provisions in the sample averaged 186 days, not significantly different from those of other IPOs in the same industry. This result is not reported but is available upon request
5. Kaplan and Stromberg (2008) find that in private-to-public transactions, private equity investors may take advantage of market mispricing between the debt and equity markets.
6. Because LBO funds are often contracted to last for a limited life cycle, usually 10–12 years, buyout sponsors have increasing liquidity demands to exit from LBO companies as funds approach maturity.
7. Carried interest is the right to receive a specified share (20 percent to 25 percent) of the profits ultimately earned by an investment fund over some previously agreed upon benchmark return. Because general partner carries depend on the general cash return of a given investment, general partners have incentives to monitor and realize final cash returns.
8. Although this analysis employs different duration measures (less than one and a half years or two years), the empirical findings throughout the paper remain unchanged.
9. There is also a potential conflict of interest between debt holders and equity holders in LBOs and RLBOs.
10. There are overlaps between data from Dealogic/Capital IQ and the SDC's VentureXpert.
11. To ensure the quality of the final sample, the criteria and procedure follow Cao and Lerner (2009), who discuss the complications of identifying RLBO transactions.
12. http://bear.cba.ufl.edu/ritter
13. However, Kaplan and Stromberg's (2008) study of LBO longevity globally, including all exits including RLBOs and trade sales of portfolio companies, indicates a much longer holding period.
14. Barber and Lyon (1997) propose that an industry and performance benchmark is more robust to accounting measure reversals.
15. When, as a robustness check, I define quick flips using an alternative duration of two years, the results hold.
16. In the case of VC-backed IPOs, Gompers (1996) proposes a grandstanding hypothesis in which young venture capitalists take very young portfolio companies public to garner publicity for the next fund raising.

17. The market value of assets is their book value plus the market value of common equity less the sum of the book value of common equity (item 60) and balance sheet deferred taxes (item 74).
18. Both sponsor-managed capital and sponsor vintage years show large cross-sectional variation. The largest buyout sponsor has about $39 billion of capital raised, whereas the smallest sponsor has less than $5 million. Vintage age, however, does not distinguish between nonexistent and still existent private equity firms.

REFERENCES

Aggarwal, R., L. Krigman and K. Womack (2002), 'Strategic IPO underpricing, information momentum, and lockup expiration selling', *Journal of Financial Economics*, **66**, 5–137.
Alti, A. (2005), 'IPO market timing', *Review of Financial Studies*, **18**, 1105–38.
Barber, B. and J. Lyon (1997), 'Detecting long-run abnormal stock returns: the empirical power and specification of test statistics', *Journal of Financial Economics*, **43**, 341–72.
Benninga, S., M. Helmantel and O. Sarig (2005), 'The timing of initial public offerings', *Journal of Financial Economics*, **75**, 115–32.
Brau, J. C., B. Francis and N. Kohers (2003), 'The choice of IPO versus takeover', *Journal of Business*, **76**, 583–612.
Cao, J.X. and J. Lerner (2009), 'The performance of reverse leveraged buyouts', *Journal of Financial Economics*, **91**, 139–57.
Carter, R. and S. Manaster (1990), 'Initial public offerings and underwriter reputation', *Journal of Finance*, **45**, 1045–67.
Chou, D., M. Gombola and F. Liu (2006), 'Earnings management and stock performance of reverse leveraged buyouts', *Journal of Financial and Quantitative Analysis*, **41**, 407–37.
Degeorge, F. and R. Zeckhauser (1993), 'The reverse LBO decision and firm performance: theory and evidence', *Journal of Finance*, **48**, 1323–48.
Field, L.C. and G. Hanka (2001), 'The expiration of IPO share lock-ups', *Journal of Finance*, **56**, 471–500.
Holthausen, R.W. and D.F. Larcker (1996), 'The financial performance of reverse leveraged buyouts', *Journal of Financial Economics*, **42**, 293–332.
Gertner R. and S.N. Kaplan (1996), 'The value maximizing board', working paper, NBER.
Giot, P. and A. Schwienbacher (2007), 'IPO, trade sales and liquidations: modeling venture capital exits using survival analysis', *Journal of Bank and Finance*, **31**, 679–702.
Gompers, P. (1996), 'Grandstanding in the venture capital industry', *Journal of Financial Economics*, **42**, 133–56.
Jain. B. and O. Kini (1994), 'The post-issue operating performance of IPO firms', *Journal of Finance*, **49**, 1699–726.
Jain, B. and O. Kini (2006), 'Industry clustering of initial public offerings', *Managerial and Decision Economics*, **27**, 1–20.
Jensen C.M. (1986), 'Agency costs of free cash flow, corporate finance, and takeovers', *American Economics Review*, **76**, 323–9.
Kaplan, S.N. and P. Stromberg (2008), 'Leveraged buyouts and private equity', working paper, NBER.
Kaplan, S.N. and L. Zingales (1997), 'Do investment-cash flow sensitivities provide useful measures of financing constraints?', *Quarterly Journal of Economics*, **112**, 169–216.
Loughran, T. and J.R. Ritter (1995), 'The new issues puzzle', *Journal of Finance*, **50**, 23–51.
Lowry, M. and G.W. Schwert (2002), 'IPO market cycles: bubbles or sequential learning?', *Journal of Finance*, **57**, 1171–200.
Muscarella, C.J. and M.R. Vetsuypens (1990), 'Efficiency and organizational structure: a study of reverse LBOs', *Journal of Finance*, **45**, 1389–413.
Pastor, L. and P. Veronesi (2005), 'Rational IPO waves', *Journal of Finance*, **60**, 1713–57.
Pastor, L., L. Taylor and P. Veronesi (2009), 'Entrepreneurial learning, the IPO decision, and the post-IPO drop in firm profitability', *Review of Financial Studies*, **22**, 3005–46.
Ritter, J.R. (1984), 'The hot issue market of 1980', *Journal of Business*, **57**, 215–40.
Ritter, J.R. (1991), 'The long-run performance of initial public offerings', *Journal of Finance*, **46**, 3–27.
Schultz, P. (2003), 'Pseudo market timing and the long-run underperformance of IPOs', *Journal of Finance*, **58**, 483–517.
Zingales, L. (1995), 'Insider ownership and the decision to go public', *Review of Economic Studies*, **62**, 425–48.

19 The impact of venture capital/private equity investment on the performance of IPOs in Australia
Sian Owen and Jo-Ann Suchard

1 INTRODUCTION

The success of the venture capital (VC) and private equity (PE) sector is regarded as important for economic growth and innovation. Both theoretical and empirical research in the US and Europe is consistent with the proposition that VC/PE funds add value to their portfolio companies (Gompers and Lerner, 1999, 2001; Lerner, 1999, 2002a, 2002b; Kortum and Lerner, 2000; Hege et al., 2003; Gompers et al., 2005).

Venture capital/private equity investors are also frequent participants in the capital markets as a method of exiting from their investments (Lerner, 1994). Empirical observations suggest that they choose the exit channel strategically and build up reputation primarily through successful initial public offerings (IPOs) (Gompers, 1996). Venture capital/private equity investors tend to hold significant ownership and board positions (Barry et al., 1990), and continue to be involved in the firm after going public (Megginson and Weiss, 1991) and thus may provide access to capital even in the post-IPO period. Finally, VC/PE investors tend to put effective management structures in place, which assist in superior long run performance (Brav and Gompers, 1997).

Venture capital/private equity markets are influenced by many factors including a country's legal and institutional structure, liquidity and stock market performance, investor sophistication and ability to provide value-added assistance to entrepreneurial firms. Recent studies have demonstrated international differences in financial contracts, syndication, and exits (Barry et al., 1990; Megginson and Weiss, 1991; Cumming and MacIntosh, 2003; Das et al., 2003).

Australia is a VC/PE market that has received little attention in the academic literature. It has a legal and institutional structure similar to most common law countries where VC/PE markets have been the subject of much study (including Canada, the UK and the US), but is a relatively younger market. Investment in Australia VC/PE funds has increased 348 percent in the last decade (Australian Bureau of Statistics, 2010), yet accounts for only 0.58 percent of gross domestic product (GDP) compared to 1.8 percent of GDP in more mature markets such as the US (Probitas Partners, 2009). Australia only accounts for 1 percent of the global VC/PE market but is a significant part of the fastest growing region, representing around 14 percent of regional funds (Probitas Partners, 2009).

A significant difference between the Australian venture market and the US venture market is in the overall level of pension commitments. Australia's pension fund investment has been more conservative in nature and the proportion of investments in VC/PE has been below that of pension funds in the US. The Australian pension industry in total invests approximately 2–3 percent of their assets in VC/PE, compared with US evidence that suggests that 5–10 percent is the norm (Gompers and Lerner, 1998). The comparative dearth of pension fund investment in VC/PE in Australia is comparable to other developing VC/PE markets around the world (Jeng and Wells, 2000). Historically, the growth in pension fund commitments has been hampered by Australian tax law and fund structure, but changes since 2002 have removed some of these barriers. For example, historically VC/PE funds have been typically formed as closed end unit trusts rather than as limited partnerships as in other markets.

Although the Australian VC/PE market is a smaller, younger market, empirical evidence suggests that it has some characteristics which are similar to more developed markets. First, Fleming (2004) finds that similar to international evidence in Cumming and MacIntosh (2003) and Giot and Schwienbacher (2007), Australian venture capitalists tend to take the best investments to market to generate a reputation for quality investing and thus generate higher returns from IPOs than from other exit strategies. Second, Suchard (2009) finds that similar to more mature VC/PE markets, Australian VC/PE managers improve governance in portfolio firms by using their networks to recruit specialist independent directors. However, in contrast to international evidence, da Silva Rosa et al. (2003) do not find a difference in underpricing or long term performance for a small sample of VC-backed and non-VC backed IPOs.

The aim of this chapter is to investigate the impact of VC/PE backing of the performance of Australian IPOs. There is little publicly available information about the performance of Australian VC/PE funds and thus a focus on IPOs provides an avenue to examine the impact of VC/PE investors on portfolio firms. We consider both the stock market and operating performance of VC/PE backed versus non-VC/PE backed IPOs in the Australian market. This study is one of a few large-scale, non-US studies of the impact of VC/PE investment on IPO stock and operating performance.[1] The sample of IPOs differs from US samples as it is relatively widely spread across industries whereas US long-term IPO studies usually report a strong bias towards the high-technology sector (Jain and Kini, 1995).

In addition, we examine the impact on performance of the stage of investment by the VC/PE manager, that is, early stage investment (VC backing) versus later stage investment (PE backing). We also analyze the impact of the continuing investment in the firm by VC/PE investors after listing and consider the impact of VC/PE characteristics on IPO performance.

The results suggest that VC/PE-backed IPOs have worse stock performance (market and industry adjusted) than non-VC/PE backed IPOs in the first year of listing and that it is the sub-sample of VC-backed IPOs (rather than PE-backed IPOs) that underperform. However, both non-VC/PE and VC/PE-backed IPOs have similar performance after three years. Similarly, there is a significant decline in operating performance for all IPOs, except for PE-backed IPOs whose performance increases over three years.

These results hold after controlling for firm characteristics in the cross-sectional regressions. Venture capital/private equity involvement has a negative impact on the stock performance of firms in the first year of listing, but the impact dissipates over two and three years post-listing. Firms that listed during the hot market of the late 1990s and firms with higher leverage before the IPO have poorer long-term performance.

Thus, although most VC/PE investors retain some ownership in the firm post-listing, VC/PE backing does not have a sustained impact on the long-term stock or operating performance of Australian IPOs. Thus, the results find little support for the certification hypothesis in the Australian market. These results are in contrast to US and UK markets, and may be driven by less experienced managers operating in a relatively smaller and earlier stage VC/PE market. The remainder of the chapter is organized as follows: the next section reviews the evidence on the role of VC/PE investors in IPOs; section 2 describes the data and methodology; section 3 discusses the empirical results; and section 4 concludes the chapter.

2 THEORY AND EVIDENCE

It is well documented that the IPO process is characterized by information asymmetry, where insiders of an issuing firm possess superior information relative to outside investors. To avoid market breakdown resulting from the information asymmetry, third-party certification is introduced to ensure the success of an IPO. The certification hypothesis (Barry et al., 1990; Megginson and Weiss, 1991; Lerner, 1994), suggests that the certification role can be better performed by VC/PE managers. They actively monitor the firm, often hold board seats and have a longer and closer working relationship with the management team compared to other financial intermediaries. Further, the VC/PE manager's reputational concerns can control possible false certification. Gompers (1996) demonstrates that reputational concerns affect the decisions VC/PE managers make when they take firms public. Venture capital/private equity managers may tarnish their reputation and ability to bring firms public in the future, if they become associated with failures in the public market. Thus, VC/PE managers may be less willing to hype a stock or overprice it.

In addition, Brav and Gompers (1997) suggest that VC/PE investors have an impact on firms after listing. Venture capitalists stay on the board of directors long after the IPO and may continue to provide access to capital that non-VC backed firms lack. The VC/PE investor may put management structures in place that help the firm perform better in the long run. Venture capital/private equity investors may also affect who holds the firm's shares after an IPO. Venture capital/private equity investors have relationships with investment banks and may be able to entice more and higher-quality analysts to follow their firms, thus lowering potential asymmetric information between the firm and investors. Similarly, as institutional investors are the primary source of capital for VC/PE funds, institutions may be more willing to hold equity in firms that have been taken public by VC/PE managers with whom they have invested. The greater availability of information and the higher institutional shareholding may make VC/PE-backed firms prices less susceptible to investor sentiment.

In contrast, the grandstanding hypothesis first introduced by Gompers (1996), proposes that particularly younger VC/PE managers tend to encourage IPOs at earlier stages in order to establish a reputation for future fund-raising purposes. Thus, their portfolio companies may go public prematurely and end up performing poorly. The inexperience of young VC/PE managers, and thus less value-added support, may further contribute to the poor performance of their IPOs.

Thus, the certification hypothesis predicts that VC/PE-backed firms will have better performance than non-VC/PE backed firms but that this difference will decrease gradually over time as firms age and VC firms withdraw. In contrast, the grandstanding model predicts that VC/PE-backed firms will have worse performance than non-VC/PE backed firms, and this difference will increase as firms age and potential risks are realised.

In addition, Bruton et al. (2010) argue that it is problematic to believe that the VC/PE investors would be extensively involved in the monitoring of the firm. Lockup arrangements are associated with VC/PE investors to ensure that they remain involved in the firm after its IPO. However, the lockup period has a clear short and finite time horizon (Arthurs et al. 2009). The VC/PE investor is motivated to exit the investment in order to redeploy its assets elsewhere, to distribute assets to limited partner investors, and to establish an exit track record in order to raise further funds (Gompers, 1996; Brav and Gompers, 2003). Active monitoring by VC/PE investors may increase their opportunity costs after the listing of their portfolio firms, potentially limiting their efforts to redeploy assets to new investments. Thus, Bruton et al. (2010) argue that active monitoring by the VC/PE investor of their post-IPO firm would seem to be limited, which suggests that ongoing VC/PE ownership will not lead to greater post-IPO performance.

The empirical evidence shows that the presence of VC/PE investors in the ownership structure of US firms going public has been associated with improved long-term stock performance (Jain and Kini, 1995, Brav and Gompers, 1997, Doukas and Gonenc, 2005, and Krishnan et al., 2011, for VC-backed IPOs; Cao and Lerner, 2009, for PE-backed IPOs). The superior performance by VC-backed IPOs is often attributed to the establishment of better management teams and corporate governance structures that help firms perform better in the long run. Krishnan et al. (2011) provide further support for this view by showing that VC firms with better reputations invest in a portfolio of companies with better long-run post-IPO performance.

However, the international evidence on long-term market performance is mixed. In Japan and Israel, studies do not find significant long-term differences in the market performance of VC-backed IPO versus non-VC backed IPOs (Hamao et al., 2000, for Japan; Ber and Yafeh, 2004, for Israel). However, in the UK, PE-backed IPOs outperform non-PE backed IPOs (von Drathen and Faleiro, 2007; Levis, 2011) and in Germany, both VC- and PE-backed IPOs outperform non-VC/PE backed IPOs (von Drathen, 2007). Previous Australian research has focused on a small sample of VC-backed IPOs that listed in the 1990s and has not found a significant difference in long term performance.[2]

Many researchers have also documented a long-run decline in companies' post-IPO operating performance (see, for example, Jain and Kini, 1994, 1995, Mikkelson et al., 1997, in the US; Pagano et al., 1998, Meles, 2011, in Italy; Khurshed et al., 2003, Coakley et al., 2007, in the UK; Wang et al., 2003, in Singapore; Cai and Wei, 1997, Kutsuna et al., 2002, in Japan). Among these, only four specifically examine the role of venture capitalists but with contrasting results. Jain and Kini (1995) find that US VC-backed IPOs exhibit superior operating performance compared to non-VC backed IPOs, while Wang et al. (2003) find the post-IPO operating performance of VC-backed firms in Singapore is inferior. In contrast, Coakley et al. (2007) find similar operating performance for a UK sample and Meles (2011) for an Italian sample of mainly PE-backed IPOs.

We examine the impact of VC/PE backing on the long-term stock and operating performance of 471 Australian IPOs from December 1994 to July 2005 (71 VC/PE-backed and 400 non-VC/PE backed IPOs). In addition, we examine the impact on performance of the stage of investment by the VC/PE manager, that is, early-stage investment (VC backing) versus later-stage investment (PE backing). We also analyze the impact of the continuing investment in the firm by VC/PE investors after listing. The majority of Australian VC/PE investors do not fully divest their holdings at IPO, similar to US IPOs. However, Australian VC/PE investors tend to hold a smaller percentage of the listed firm immediately after listing, than US investors but comparable to other less mature markets. This may be due to the two-year mandatory escrow period that was in place for VC/PE investors prior to March 2002. In contrast, the US market has a usual lockup period of 180 days (Gompers and Lerner, 1998; Field and Hanka, 2001) and the mean lockup period was a little over one year for UK and French firms in Bruton et al. (2010). Finally, we consider the impact of VC/PE reputation on IPO performance.

3 DATA AND METHODOLOGY

The sample covers the period December 1994 to July 2005 and consists of 471 Australian, 400 non-VC/PE backed IPOs and 71 VC/PE-backed IPOs. The sample was truncated at July 2005 in order to calculate performance over three years after listing for all the IPOs in the sample and to exclude the impact of the global financial crisis (GFC) on returns which may downwardly bias the results. The VC/PE-backed firms are identified from the data provided by the Australian Venture Capital and Private Equity Association (AVCAL) and additional VC/PE-backed firms are identified by shareholder information in prospectuses obtained from the Connect4 database and FinAnalysis. The distinction between VC and PE backers is based on information provided by AVCAL and the websites of the fund management firms. Funds are classified as VC if they provide seed and early-stage investing.

We estimate stock price performance using both buy-and-hold and calendar time returns. Buy-and-hold returns are measured in excess of the buy-and-hold returns for the stock market index (All ordinaries). In addition, we examine stock price performance on an industry adjusted basis using the relevant industry index (Global Industry Classification Standard – GICS).[3] The buy-and-hold return is determined for a one-year (12-month), two-year (24-month) and three-year (36-month) holding period, beginning with the closing price at the end of the first month after the IPO. If a firm delists, it is then excluded from the analysis after the month of delisting. Stock price and market index data is obtained from Datastream and industry indices are obtained from the Securities Industry Research Centre of Asia Pacific (SIRCA).

Event time results may be misleading about the pervasiveness of underperformance. Barber and Lyon (1997) show that such long-term performance tests often suffer from potential biases arising from the non-standard distribution of long-run returns. Thus, we calculate calendar time portfolios by calculating the return for a portfolio strategy that invests in recent IPOs relative to an explicit asset-pricing model in calendar time. We use the Fama-French three-factor model where the benchmark returns for the portfolios, based on size and book-to-market, are calculated using data from Datastream.

Accounting performance is measured as the change in operating cash flow over total assets as this measure is less vulnerable to manipulation than other measures of accounting performance (Clementi, 2004). We measure operating performance of IPOs from the fiscal year of the IPO until three years post-IPO using the median change, in line with the existing literature (Jain and Kini, 1994; Mikkelson et al., 1997; Loughran and Ritter, 1997). We report a raw median as well as an industry adjusted median in which the industry adjustment is based on the yearly median operating performance of all firms in the same industry sector as the IPO firm. We measure operating performance as the operating cash flow divided by the average total assets in the previous two years. The accounting data is collected from FinAnalysis and IPO prospectuses on Connect4.

In order to assess the impact of VC/PE backing on long-term performance, we use a number of control variables in the cross sectional regressions. Ordinary least squares (OLS) regression is used to estimate the models and t-statistics are calculated using White's (1980) adjustment for heteroskedasticity.

3.1 Firm Characteristics

To control for differences in IPO demand or IPO firm quality, we include firm size from Brav and Gompers (1997) and Loughran and Ritter (2004), book to market from Brav and Gompers (1997) and firm age. Firm size (Firm) is measured by multiplying offer price by the total number of post-IPO shares, book to market ratio (BTM) is calculated as the post-issue (pro forma) book value of equity divided by the first-day's market value of equity and firm age (Age) is measured as the difference between the IPO year and the founding year as given in the IPO prospectus. Ritter (1991) suggests that older firms have greater experience and resources than their younger counterparts which may influence performance. In addition, debt in the firm may limit managerial discretion and mitigate potential agency conflicts, thus improving performance. The level of pre-IPO debt (Debt) is calculated as the ratio of interest-bearing debt over total assets, using audited pre-issue balance sheet figures.

3.2 Ownership Characteristics

Bruton et al. (2010) argue that concentrated ownership leads to a reduction of coordination costs related to multiple types of private and public equity investors in the IPO firm and creates incentive alignment between these investors. The concentration of ownership in the firm is measured as the total percentage of share ownership of the top 20 shareholders (Top20) and the total percentage of share ownership held by substantial shareholders (Block).

In addition, Filatotchev and Bishop (2002) and Sanders and Boivie (2004) suggest that IPO firms usually use diverse information to signal their value. Governance structures can serve as useful screening and sorting criteria that affect investors' valuation of the IPO firm. Thus, board independence (Indep) is measured as the percentage of the board that are independent (outside) directors at IPO.

3.3 IPO Characteristics

Carter et al. (1998) argue that larger offers are typically made by more established and financially stronger IPO issuers. The size of the issue (Issue) is calculated as the number of shares issued to the public multiplied by the offer price. The level of first-day returns can signal firm quality (Welch, 1989) or investor over-optimism (Ritter, 1991). The degree of underpricing (Underpricing) is calculated as the closing price on first day of listing minus the offer price and then divided by the offer price.

In addition underwriters can certify the quality of the firm. Underwritten is a dummy variable that equals one if the IPO is underwritten and zero otherwise. Retained ownership signals the founders' belief in the value of the firm to minority investors (Field and Hanka, 2001; Brav and Gompers, 2003) and thus should be positively related to performance. Retained ownership (Retown) is measured as the number of shares held by pre-IPO shareholders dividend by the number of shares on issue after the IPO. Ljungqvist et al. (2006) find that IPOs underperform in bubble markets due to the existence of sentiment investors driving prices beyond their fair value. Hotmkt is a dummy variable equal to one if the IPO occurred during the period 1998–2000 and zero otherwise.

4 RESULTS

4.1 Descriptive Statistics

The sample consists of 471 Australian IPOs listed between December 1994 and July 2005. The VC/PE backed IPOs comprise 15 percent of the total sample, of which 8.5 percent are VC backed and 6.5 percent PE backed, compared to 34 percent for US IPOs in Baker and Gompers (2003). The yearly distribution of IPOs is shown in Figure 19.1.

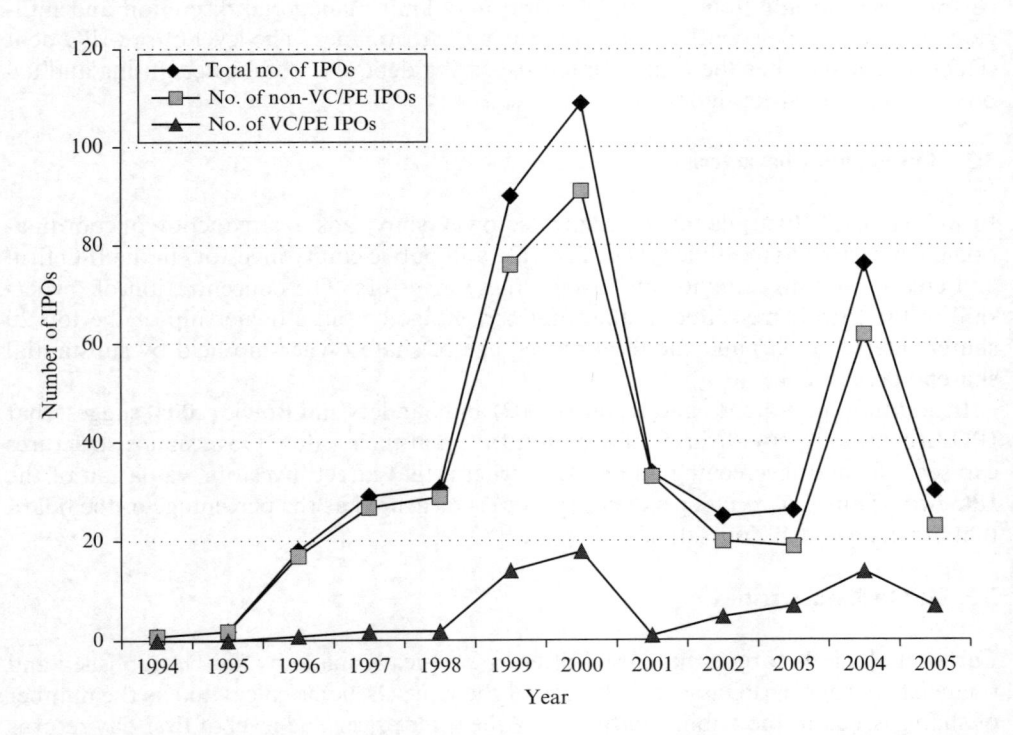

Figure 19.1 Number of IPOs per year of Australian VC/PE and non-VC/PE backed IPOs

A large proportion of IPOs (42 percent) in the sample period listed in the 1999–2000 period while the second largest group of listings occurred in 2004 (16 percent). A similar pattern holds for both VC/PE-backed and non-VC/PE backed IPOs where 45 percent of VC/PE-backed and 49 percent of non-VC/PE backed IPOs listed in the 1998–2000 hot market.

Approximately one-quarter (26 percent) of IPOs in the sample delisted during the sample period, the majority (72 percent) due to acquisitions or mergers. Venture capital/private equity backed firms had similar delisting rates to non-VC/PE backed firms over the sample period (24 percent versus 26 percent) but had lower failure rates (5 percent versus 30 percent). Over the three year performance period, VC/PE-backed firms had a lower rate of delisting than non-VC/PE backed firms (10 percent versus 37 percent) and all were due to acquisitions or mergers compared to two-thirds of the delisted non-VC/PE backed firms.

Further, Australian IPO firms are relatively young and small as the average (median) age and size prior to the IPO is 10 (5) years and $99 million ($30 million). Australian IPOs are closely held with the top 20 shareholders owning 70 percent of the firm, on average. In terms of underwriting, 81 percent of firms are underwritten, with 42 percent underwritten by a top underwriter. Retained ownership is 63 percent on average, suggesting that most of the original owners maintain a substantial holding in the firm after listing. Finally, four industries make up a significant amount of the sample, technology (21 percent), consumer discretionary firms (19.5 percent), health sector firms (18.5 percent) and telecommunications (7.2 percent). The industry grouping across the non-VC/PE backed and VC/PE backed firms is similar.

Venture capital/private equity investors own on average, 33.79 percent of the VC/PE backed firm before it lists on the stock exchange. Most VC/PE investors retain their stake in the firm (28.75 percent of VC/PE investors divest their holdings at the time of the IPO), and the average ownership after listing is 12.68 percent of the firm.

Table 19.1 examines the differences in firm, ownership and IPO characteristics between companies backed by VC/PE and those not backed by VC/PE.

Venture capital/private equity and non-VC/PE backed firms have similar firm characteristics. The similar age and size of VC/PE and non-VC/PE backed firms is consistent with prior Australian evidence in da Silva Rosa et al. (2003). The results suggest that Australian venture capitalists do not take firms public at an earlier stage than non-VC/PE backed firms. This result does not support the grandstanding hypothesis and is in contrast to US evidence (Megginson and Weiss, 1991; Gompers and Lerner, 2000; Lee and Wahal, 2004; Krishnan et al., 2011). Further, the size results are not consistent with UK evidence in Coakley et al. (2007) and Levis (2011). Coakley et al. (2007) find that VC/PE-backed IPOs are significantly larger in size and have higher debt levels than non-VC/PE backed IPOs. However, the difference in the results may be driven by the higher percentage of buyouts in the UK sample that usually are large, highly cash generative businesses involving relatively high levels of debt. Further, Levis (2011) finds that PE-backed IPOs are larger than non-VC/PE backed IPOs but VC-backed IPOs are smaller than non-VC/PE backed IPOs.

There are, however, differences in the ownership structure of Australian IPOs. Venture capital/private equity-backed firms are more widely held with VC/PE-backed firms having blockholders owning less of the firm than non-VC/PE backed firms.

Table 19.1 Mean characteristics of VC/PE-backed and non-VC/PE backed IPOs

	Non-VC/PE backed	VC/PE-backed	T-stat
A. Firm characteristics:			
Age	10.48	13.37	1.16
BTM	0.46	0.45	0.31
Debt	0.65	0.84	0.97
Firm	89.18	163.33	−1.59
B. Ownership			
Block	51.24	44.60	3.29[a]
Top20	70.34	66.08	0.30
C. IPO characteristics			
Issue	28.37	56.03	−1.99[b]
Underpricing	27.49	25.47	0.20
Ret own	64.34	55.86	2.71[a]

Notes:
Differences in the mean characteristics of 71 Australian VC/PE-backed and 400 non-VC/PE backed IPOs between 1994 and 2005.
Age is the difference between the IPO year and the founding year in the IPO prospectus; BTM is the book-to-market ratio calculated as the post-issue (pro forma) book value of equity divided by the first-day's market value of equity; Debt is the level of pre-IPO debt, calculated as the ratio of interest-bearing debt over total assets, using audited pre-issue balance sheet figures; Firm is the number of shares on issue post IPO multiplied by the offer price; Block is the total percentage share ownership of the substantial shareholders; Top20 is the total percentage share ownership of the top 20 shareholders; Issue is the number of shares issued to the public multiplied by the offer price; Underpricing is the closing price on first day of listing-offer price/offer price; Ret own is the number of shares of pre IPO shareholders/number of shares on issue post IPO.
[a] Significant at the 1% level.
[b] Significant at the 5% level.
[c] Significant at the 10% level.

Venture capital/private equity-backed IPOs issue a significantly larger amount of capital and they have a lower percentage of the firm retained by the original shareholders. The retained ownership results are consistent with US results (Megginson and Weiss, 1991; Habib and Ljungqvist, 2001).

Less than a third (29 percent) of VC/PE investors completely divested their holdings at the time of the IPO by selling their shares to the public in the IPO or through a share buyback that uses the IPO proceeds. Venture capital/private equity investors own on average 33 percent of the firm pre-IPO and 12 percent post-IPO. The post-IPO VC/PE ownership is similar to Singaporean firms (Wang et al., 2003), but lower than US and UK firms (Megginson and Weiss, 1991; Levis, 2011). Further, a significantly higher percentage of VC/PE-backed IPOs are underwritten compared to non-VC/PE backed IPOs (92 percent versus 79 percent).

4.2 Performance

The market- and industry-adjusted stock price performance over three years post listing, is shown in panel A of Table 19.2 for the whole IPO sample, non-VC/PE and VC/PE sub-samples. The entire sample of IPOs underperforms the market over two years but

Table 19.2 Buy-and-hold returns over three years post-listing

Panel A. Buy-and-hold returns

	1 year N	1 year Mean	2 year N	2 year Mean	3 year N	3 year Mean
All IPOs						
Market-adjusted returns	465	−4.17	464	−11.20[b]	443	−0.13
Industry-adjusted returns		−1.55		−6.87		4.04
Non-VC/PE IPOs						
Market-adjusted returns	394	−1.39	393	−10.53[c]	375	2.88
Industry-adjusted returns		−1.48		−5.76		7.50
VC/PE IPOs						
Market-adjusted returns	71	−19.64[b]	71	−14.90	68	−16.78
Industry-adjusted returns		−18.31[a]		−13.04		−14.96
VC IPOs						
Market-adjusted returns	40	−20.82[b]	40	−27.10	39	−26.73
Industry-adjusted returns		−20.26[b]		−22.22		−26.31
PE IPOs						
Market-adjusted returns	31	−18.12	31	0.84	29	−3.40
Industry-adjusted returns		−15.80[c]		−0.69		1.44

Panel B. Differences in means and medians over three years post listing

	1 year Mean	2 year Mean	3 year Mean
Non-VC/PE IPOs vs VC/PE IPOs			
Market-adjusted returns	18.25[a]	4.36	19.36
Industry-adjusted returns	16.83[b]	7.28	22.46
Non-VC/PE IPOs vs PE IPOs			
Market-adjusted returns	16.76	−11.73	−11.37
Industry-adjusted returns	14.32	−5.06	6.05
Non-VC/PE IPOs vs VC IPOs			
Market-adjusted returns	18.25[b]	16.65	29.61
Industry-adjusted returns	16.83[b]	16.46	33.81
PE IPOs vs VC IPOs			
Market-adjusted returns	2.27	29.88	27.76
Industry-adjusted returns	4.46	21.52	27.75

Notes:
Buy-and-hold returns over three years post listing for 40 Australian VC-backed, 31 Australian PE-backed and 400 non-VC/PE backed IPOs between 1994 and 2005.
The buy-and-hold returns are calculated from the end of the first month to the end of 12 months (one year), 24 months (two years) and 36 months (three years).
The return on the market and industry index over the same period is subtracted from the raw buy-and-hold return to calculate the adjusted return.
[a] Significant at the 1% level.
[b] Significant at the 5% level.
[c] Significant at the 10% level.

410 *Handbook of research on IPOs*

Table 19.3 Three-factor regressions on three-year calendar time portfolio returns

	All			VC/PE backed			Non-VC/PE backed		
	1 year	2 year	3 year	1 year	2 year	3 year	1 year	2 year	3 year
RMRF	1.248	1.153	1.115	1.605	1.753	1.502	1.197	1.064	1.057
	(10.91)[a]	(12.13)[a]	(13.68)[a]	(8.21)[a]	(9.23)[a]	(9.21)[a]	(10.34)[a]	(11.44)[a]	(12.98)[a]
SMB	−0.223	−0.211	−0.237	−0.373	−0.566	−0.416	−0.207	−0.161	−0.210
	(−1.56)	(−1.74)	(−2.31)[b]	(−1.61)	(−2.44)[b]	(−2.10)[b]	(−1.42)	(−1.34)	(−2.04)[b]
HML	0.196	−0.059	−0.096	0.102	0.087	−0.032	0.214	−0.073	−0.101
	(1.25)	(−0.46)	(−0.89)	(0.40)	(0.36)	(−0.16)	(1.34)	(−0.58)	(−0.92)
Alpha	−0.013	−0.013	−0.011	−0.021	−0.018	−0.014	−0.012	−0.013	−0.011
	(−2.89)[a]	(−3.42)[a]	(−3.63)[a]	(−2.85)[a]	(−2.42)[b]	(−2.35)[b]	(−2.61)[a]	(−3.36)[a]	(−3.52)[a]

Notes:
Three-factor Fama–French regressions on three-year calendar time portfolio returns for 71 Australian VC/PE-backed and 400 non-VC/PE backed IPOs between 1994 and 2005.
Equal- and value-weighted IPO portfolios are formed monthly.
T-statistics are reported in parentheses.
RMRF is the return on the All Ordinaries Index less the Risk free rate.
The Risk free rate is proxied by the three month treasury bill rate; HML is the difference each month between the return on a portfolio of high book-to-market stocks and the return on a portfolio of low book-to-market stocks; SMB is the difference each month between the return on small- and large-capitalization firms.
[a] Significant at the 1% level.
[b] Significant at the 5% level.
[c] Significant at the 10% level.

is insignificantly different from zero over one and three years. However, the sub-sample of VC/PE-backed IPOs significantly underperforms the market only after one year. The one-year underperformance occurs for VC-backed IPOs and not PE-backed IPOs, which have similar performance to the market.[4]

The results in panel B suggest that VC/PE-backed IPOs perform worse than non-VC/PE backed IPOs on a market-adjusted basis over the first year of listing but the difference is insignificant thereafter. This relatively poorer performance of the VC/PE-backed IPOs is driven by the sub-sample of VC-backed IPOs. Finally, the market-adjusted returns of VC-backed IPOs are not significantly different from the returns of PE-backed IPOs.[5]

In terms of the average industry adjusted result, we find that IPOs as a whole and the sub-sample of non-VC/PE backed IPOs both have similar performance to the industry index over the three-year period post-listing. In contrast, both VC- and PE-backed IPOs significantly underperform the industry index in the first year of listing. In panel B, similar to the market adjusted returns, the combined sample of VC/PE-backed IPOs perform worse than non-VC/PE backed IPOs only over the first year of listing, which is driven by VC-backed IPOs rather than PE-backed IPOs. These industry adjusted results are consistent with international evidence (Hamao et al., 2000; Ber and Yafeh, 2004) but inconsistent with US evidence.

Table 19.3 reports stock performance estimated on a calendar time basis using the Fama–French three-factor model. For all IPOs, the Fama–French three-factor model has a significant alpha of −0.013 to −0.011 percent per month over each of the post-listing years. The alphas are significantly negative for both VC/PE and non-VC/PE backed IPOs in all three years post-listing, demonstrating underperformance which is similar to US results in Brav and Gompers (1997).

We further investigate the impact of VC/PE manager characteristics on stock performance in section 4.3.

We examine the operating performance of IPOs by analyzing the changes in accounting returns over the three-year sample post-listing and report the results in Table 19.4. Panel A compares the differences in the medians of VC/PE-backed IPOs, non-VC/PE backed IPOs and VC- and PE-backed IPOs separately, while panel B reports the differences in the performance measures.

There is a significant decrease in raw median operating performance over three years for all IPOs. The decrease in performance seems to be driven by the non-VC/PE backed IPOs.[6] On an industry-adjusted basis, the entire sample has a significant decrease in operating performance over the first two years post-listing and over the first year for non-VC/PE backed IPOs. In contrast, VC/PE-backed and VC-backed IPOs do not have a significant change in industry-adjusted operating performance over three years. However, PE-backed firms demonstrate a significant increase on operating performance over three years.

Panel B shows that there are no significant differences in operating performance non-VC/PE backed and VC/PE-backed or VC-backed IPOs. However, PE-backed IPOs have better operating performance than VC-backed IPOs (raw and industry adjusted) and non-VC/PE backed IPOs (only industry adjusted) over three years post-listing. The VC-backed IPO results are similar to Coakley et al. (2007) and Wang et al. (2003) who do not find a difference in performance for UK and Singapore VC- and non-VC backed IPOs, but are in contrast to Jain and Kini (1995) who find that US VC-backed IPOs have better accounting performance. Thus the results generally do not support the certification hypothesis. However, later-stage (private equity) managers seem to improve operating performance. We further investigate the impact of VC/PE manager characteristics on operating performance in section 4.3.

4.3 The Determinants of IPO Performance

We run a number of cross-sectional regressions to estimate the impact of VC/PE backing on long-term IPO performance. The dependent variable in Table 19.5 is the buy-and-hold return.[7] The dependent variable in Table 19.6 is operating performance measured as the change in operating cash flows from the fiscal year of the IPO up to three years after the IPO. Table 19.7 presents results for the sub-sample of VC/PE-backed IPOs using both stock and operating performance.

We use two proxies for venture capital involvement to test the VC certification hypothesis which implies a positive relationship between these variables and IPO performance. Venture capital/private equity backed is a dummy for venture capital/private equity involvement that equals 1 if the IPO was VC/PE backed and zero otherwise. Venture capital/private equity holdings after the IPO (Vcpost) is derived following Lerner (1994) and Megginson and Weiss (1991). The control variables are as described previously.[8]

The results suggest that VC/PE involvement has an impact on the first-year stock performance of IPOs. The dummy variable VC/PE backed is significant in the first year

Table 19.4 Post issuing operating performance over three years post listing

Panel A. Post-issuing operating performance

	% change	0 to +1	0 to +2	0 to +3
		\multicolumn{3}{c}{Years relative to completion of IPO}		
All IPOs	Number	448	426	406
	Median	−3.31[a]	−2.17[a]	−0.93[b]
	Industry adjusted median	−2.19[a]	−1.09[b]	−0.14
Non-VC/PE IPOs	Number	380	360	342
	Median	−3.34[a]	−2.34[b]	−1.18
	Industry adjusted median	−2.43[a]	−1.27	−0.68
VC/PE IPOs	Number	68	66	64
	Median	−3.17[c]	0.16	1.52
	Industry adjusted median	−1.33	2.78	2.78
VC IPOs	Number	39	37	38
	Median	−4.42[c]	−2.88	−4.76
	Industry adjusted median	−2.89	−2.88	−1.95
PE IPOs	Number	29	29	26
	Median	−1.62	2.52	3.42[a]
	Industry adjusted median	−0.35	3.21	5.55[a]

Panel B. Differences in median post-issuing performance

	0 to +1	0 to +2	0 to +3
	\multicolumn{3}{c}{Years relative to completion of IPO}		
Non-VC/PE IPOs vs VC/PE IPOs			
Median difference	−0.17	−2.50	−2.70
Industry-adjusted median difference	−1.10	−4.05	−3.46
Non-VC/PE IPOs vs VC IPOs			
Median difference	1.08	0.54	3.58
Industry-adjusted median difference	0.46	1.61	1.27
Non-VC/PE IPOs vs PE IPOs			
Median difference	−1.72	−4.86	−4.60
Industry-adjusted median difference	−2.08	−4.48	−6.23[b]
PE IPOs vs VC IPOs			
Median difference	2.80	5.40	8.18[b]
Industry-adjusted median difference	2.54	6.09	7.50[a]

Notes:
Post issuing operating performance over three years post-listing for 40 Australian VC-backed, 31 PE-backed and 400 non-VC/PE backed IPOs between 1994 and 2005.
Performance in panel A is measured as the median change in operating cash flow over average total assets in measurement and previous year.
The significance tests for the change rates in panel B are based on the Wilcoxon signed rank test and test that change rates are different from zero.
[a] Significant at the 1% level.
[b] Significant at the 5% level.
[c] Significant at the 10% level.

Table 19.5 *Regressions of explanatory variables on buy-and-hold market-adjusted returns*

	1 year Model 1	1 year Model 2	2 year Model 1	2 year Model 2	3 year Model 1	3 year Model 2
Constant	0.17	0.37	1.10	1.25	1.46	1.65
	(0.25)	(0.53)	(1.11)	(1.233)	(0.83)	(0.93)
Age	−0.01	−0.01	−0.01	−0.02	−0.03	−0.03
	(0.76)	(0.89)	(0.71)	(0.54)	(0.69)	(0.63)
Underpricing	−0.03	−0.04	−0.15	−0.14	−0.16	−0.16
	(−0.53)	(−0.55)	(−2.33)[b]	(−2.24)[b]	(−1.67)[c]	(−1.66)[c]
BTM	−0.14	−0.17	−0.06	−0.03	0.14	0.20
	(−1.06)	(−1.17)	(−0.39)	(−0.20)	(0.42)	(0.55)
Debt	−0.120	−0.20	−0.14	−0.18	−0.19	−0.27
	(−1.80)[c]	(−3.20)[a]	(−2.59)[a]	(−2.97)[b]	(−2.12)[b]	(−2.51)[b]
Issue	−0.01	−0.01	−0.05	−0.06	−0.08	−0.09
	(−0.09)	(−0.33)	(−0.87)	(−1.05)	(−0.82)	(−0.97)
Underwritten	−0.04	−0.04	−0.20	−0.20	0.20	0.22
	(−0.28)	(−0.22)	(−1.22)	(−1.16)	(0.55)	(0.59)
Top20	0.61	0.59	0.44	0.47	0.61	0.63
	(2.10)[b]	(1.99)[b]	(1.56)	(1.59)	(1.44)	(1.47)
Block	−0.07	−0.08	0.27	0.29	0.04	0.09
	(−0.12)	(−0.23)	(0.82)	(0.88)	(0.06)	(0.15)
Hotmkt	−0.23	−0.23	−0.52	−0.50	−0.48	−0.46
	(−1.91)[c]	(−1.89)[c]	(−3.89)[c]	(−3.70)[a]	(−2.16)[b]	(−2.04)[b]
VC/PEBacked	−0.18		0.03		−0.16	
	(−2.14)[b]		(0.21)		(−0.80)	
VCown		−0.01		0.01		0.01
		(−0.78)		(1.37)		(0.10)
Indep	−0.30	−0.26	−0.42	−0.41	−0.26	−0.21
	(−1.00)	(−0.86)	(−1.48)	(−1.41)	(−0.42)	(−0.34)
Industry effects	Yes	Yes	Yes	Yes	Yes	Yes
R square	0.02	0.02	0.06	0.07	0.01	0.010

Notes:
Regressions of explanatory variables on buy-and-hold market-adjusted stock returns over three years post-listing for 71 Australian VC/PE-backed and 400 non-VC/PE backed IPOs between 1994 and 2005.
The buy-and-hold returns are calculated from the end of the first month to the end of 12 months (one year), 35 months (two years) and 36 months (three years).
The return on the market index over the same period is subtracted from the raw buy-and-hold return to calculate the adjusted return.
Age is the log of the number of years between the incorporation of the firm and listing; *Underpricing* is the (closing price of first day of listing − offer price)/offer price; *BTM* is the book-to-market ratio at IPO calculated as book value of assets/(number of shares on issue * closing price on first day of listing); *Debt* is debt/total assets; Issue is the log (number of shares issued to the public * issue price); *Underwritten* is a dummy variable equal to 1 if the IPO is underwritten; *Top20* is the percentage shareholding of the top20 shareholders post IPO; *Block* is the total percentage share ownership of the substantial shareholders; *Hotmkt* is a dummy variable equal to 1 if the firm listed between 1998 and 2000; *VC/PEbacked* is a dummy variable equal to 1 if the firm has VC/PE investors before listing; *Vcown* is the percentage shareholding of the VC/PE investor after the IPO; *Indep* is the percentage of the board that are independent (outside) directors.
[a] Significant at the 1% level.
[b] Significant at the 5% level.
[c] Significant at the 10% level.

Table 19.6 *Regressions of explanatory variables on operating performance*

	\multicolumn{6}{c}{Years relative to completion of IPO}
	\multicolumn{2}{c}{0 to +1}	\multicolumn{2}{c}{0 to +2}	\multicolumn{2}{c}{0 to +3}
	Model 1	Model 2	Model 1	Model 2	Model 1	Model 2
Constant	−69.46	−69.44	−154.17	−145.54	−222.02	−213.90
	(−1.93)[c]	(−1.88)[c]	(−2.09)[b]	(−1.99)[b]	(−0.32)	(−0.31)
Age	0.73	−0.10	2.83	2.55	−7.01	−6.94
	(0.44)	(−0.06)	(1.27)	(1.09)	(−0.25)	(−0.24)
Underpricing	−0.01	−0.07	−5.63	−6.15	13.40	13.38
	(−0.01)	(−0.03)	(−0.81)	(−0.88)	(0.93)	(0.93)
BTM	−6.66	−4.83	−3.01	−8.24	294.14	307.14
	(−0.75)	(−0.56)	(−0.21)	(−0.58)	(1.40)	(1.40)
Debt	−0.18	−0.51	−4.87	−5.19	40.15	37.98
	(−0.10)	(−0.29)	(−0.62)	(−0.64)	(1.28)	(1.27)
Issue	3.37	3.15	9.05	8.72	−17.49	−19.34
	(2.02)[b]	(1.84)[c]	(1.91)[c]	(1.93)[c]	(−0.46)	(−0.49)
Underwritten	2.39	4.84	19.69	20.22	94.82	103.80
	(0.42)	(0.93)	(1.71)[c]	(1.67)[c]	(0.57)	(0.61)
Top20	11.54	17.29	−9.45	−6.12	357.74	368.16
	(0.64)	(0.98)	(−0.34)	(−0.22)	(1.45)	(1.45)
Block	−3.00	−4.11	1.34	−1.22	39.44	40.13
	(−0.33)	(−0.45)	(0.06)	(−0.06)	(0.13)	(0.13)
Hotmkt	−1.89	−2.78	8.95	7.55	39.16	43.82
	(−0.39)	(−0.58)	(0.88)	(0.74)	(0.66)	(0.68)
VC/PEBacked	−6.85		−3.64		−53.46	
	(−1.02)		(−0.26)		(−1.05)	
VCown		−0.25		−0.99		−1.70
		(−0.65)		(−0.80)		(−0.98)
Indep	−4.30	−0.24	−2.15	−1.46	320.76	328.30
	(−0.31)	(−0.02)	(−0.08)	(−0.06)	(1.20)	(1.19)
Industry effects	Yes	Yes	Yes	Yes	Yes	Yes
R square	0.02	0.02	0.04	0.04	0.02	0.02

Notes:
Regressions of explanatory variables on operating performance over three years post listing for 71 Australian VC/PE-backed and 400 non-VC/PE backed IPOs between 1994 and 2005.
Age is the log of the number of years between the incorporation of the firm and listing; *Underpricing* is the (closing price of first day of listing − offer price)/offer price; *BTM* is the book-to-market ratio at IPO calculated as book value of assets/(number of shares on issue * closing price on first day of listing); *Debt* is debt/total assets; *Issue* is the log (number of shares issued to the public * issue price); *Underwritten* is a dummy variable equal to 1 if the IPO is underwritten; *Top20* is the percentage shareholding of the top20 shareholders post IPO; *Block* is the total percentage share ownership of the substantial shareholders; *Hotmkt* is a dummy variable equal to 1 if the firm listed between 1998 and 2000; *VC/PEbacked* is a dummy variable equal to 1 if the firm has VC/PE investors before listing; *Vcown* is the percentage shareholding of the VC/PE investor after the IPO; *Indep* is the percentage of the board that are independent (outside) directors.
[a] Significant at the 1% level.
[b] Significant at the 5% level.
[c] Significant at the 10% level.

Table 19.7 Regressions of explanatory variables on stock and accounting performance

	Year 1 Market	Year 1 OCF	Year 2 Market	Year 2 OCF	Year 3 Market	Year 3 OCF
Constant	−3.15[c]	−435.50	−1.84	−1354.67	−2.70	88.94
	(−1.78)	(−1.99)[b]	(−0.50)	(−1.19)	(−0.48)	(0.24)
Age	0.01	50.06	−0.03	−22.08	0.13	−1.62
	(0.04)	(0.60)	−(0.16)	(−0.80)	(0.45)	(−0.22)
Underpricing	0.01	−15.97	−0.09	49.51	−0.72	−51.10
	(0.05)	(−0.57)	(−0.19)	(0.69)	(−0.82)	(−1.03)
BTM	0.23	49.14	−0.35	148.62	−1.64	3.37
	(0.66)	(1.02)	(−0.47)	(0.99)	(−0.99)	(0.05)
Debt	−0.38	0.79	−0.85	−31.86	−1.10	−2.63
	(−3.07)[a]	(0.15)	(−2.37)[b]	(−1.01)	(−1.93)[c]	(−0.31)
Issue	0.14	19.31	0.11	68.55	0.14	−3.18
	(1.67)	(2.05)[b]	(0.53)	(1.18)	(0.51)	(−0.18)
Underwritten	0.13	12.12	0.22	115.48	0.79	−18.74
	(0.43)	(0.52)	(0.36)	(1.06)	(0.86)	(−0.38)
Top20	1.13	80.35	0.37	116.40	−0.87	33.22
	(2.36)[b]	(0.89)	(0.37)	(0.68)	(−0.66)	(0.43)
Block	−0.03	60.49	0.85	34.83	2.96	−34.59
	−(0.06)	(1.15)	(0.78)	(0.30)	(1.69)	(−0.50)
Hotmkt	−0.05	20.42	−0.42	91.87	−0.26	−5.21
	(−0.34)	(0.70)	(−1.13)	(0.89)	(−0.45)	(−0.19)
VCown	0.01	0.40	0.01	0.75	0.01	−1.70
	(0.28)	(0.59)	(1.11)	(0.40)	(0.62)	(−1.06)
Indep	0.47	8.11	0.50	14.54	2.35	−49.11
	(0.86)	(0.24)	(0.50)	(0.13)	(1.68)	(−0.87)
Fund size	0.01	0.00	0.01	0.04	0.01	−0.00
	(1.03)	(0.04)	(2.02)[c]	(0.99)	(0.36)	(−0.36)
Norounds	−0.10	−4.60	−0.00	11.86	−0.06	7.35
	(−1.99)[c]	(−0.67)	(−0.73)	(0.64)	(−0.38)	(1.02)
Industry effects	Yes	Yes	Yes	Yes	Yes	Yes
R square	0.49	0.38	0.39	0.39	0.34	0.30

Notes:
Regressions of explanatory variables on stock returns and accounting performance over three years post-listing for 71 Australian VC/PE-backed IPOs between 1994 and 2005.
Performance is measured as the median change in operating cash flow over average total assets in measurement and previous year.
Age is the log of the number of years between the incorporation of the firm and listing; *Underpricing* is the (closing price of first day of listing − offer price)/offer price; *BTM* is the book-to-market ratio at IPO calculated as book value of assets/(number of shares on issue * closing price on first day of listing); *Debt* is debt/total assets; *Issue* is the log (number of shares issued to the public * issue price); *Underwritten* is a dummy variable equal to 1 if the IPO is underwritten; *Top20* is the percentage shareholding of the top20 shareholders post IPO; *Block* is the total percentage share ownership of the substantial shareholders; *Hotmkt* is a dummy variable equal to 1 if the firm listed between 1998 and 2000; *Vcown* is the percentage shareholding of the VC/PE investor after the IPO; *Indep* is the percentage of the board that are independent (outside) directors; *Fundsize* is the capital under management at the time of the IPO; *Norounds* is the number of rounds of financing provided by VC/PE investors before the IPO.
[a] Significant at the 1% level.
[b] Significant at the 5% level.
[c] Significant at the 10% level.

but has an insignificant impact on longer-term performance. Firms that are more closely held have better performance in the first year, suggesting that they initially benefit from the monitoring of concentrated shareholders. The hot market dummy is significantly negative in all years, which implies, consistent with prior research, that firms who listed during 1998–2000 have poorer long-term performance. Finally, leverage has a negative impact on performance as firms with higher leverage before the IPO perform worse across all three years.

Table 19.6 presents the operating performance results. Venture capital/private equity backing or ownership does not have an impact on performance here, which is in contrast to UK and French firms where conflicting results are found, a negative relationship in Bruton et al (2010) and a positive relationship in Coakley et al (2007). There is a significant positive relationship between issue size and performance across both models for one and two years after listing, implying that smaller issues have poorer operating performance than larger issues, which is consistent with Jain and Kini (1995). Further, underwritten issues have better two-year operating performance than non-underwritten issues across both models, suggesting the benefit of certification of the quality of the issue by underwriters. The insignificance of the underpricing variable is consistent with Jain and Kini (1994) and Khurshed et al. (2003) for US IPOs.

Finally we examine VC/PE-backed IPOs separately in Table 19.7 and include two additional variables to capture fund characteristics. We use fund size as a proxy for venture capital reputation and the number of rounds of investment by a VC/PE investor in the firm. Fund size is measured as the capital under management at the time of the IPO, as reported by Thompson Venture Expert, and number of rounds is measured as the number of rounds of financing provided by VC/PE investors before the IPO. There is a negative relationship between leverage and stock performance across all years consistent with the full sample results. Venture capital/private equity investor characteristics have marginal impact of firm performance. No other variables are consistently significant across the three years.

5 CONCLUSION

This chapter presents an analysis of the long-term performance of Australian venture capital and private equity backed initial public offerings. We examine stock price and operating performance over three years for 71 VC/PE-backed IPOs and 400 non-VC/PE backed IPOs between December 1994 and June 2005. We use both buy-and-hold returns (market and industry adjusted) and calendar risk-adjusted returns to estimate stock price performance. In addition, we examine the impact on performance of the stage of investment by the VC/PE manager, that is, early-stage investment (VC backing) versus later-stage investment (PE backing). We also analyze the impact of the continuing investment in the firm by VC/PE investors after listing and consider the impact of VC/PE characteristics on IPO performance.

The Australian VC/PE market has differing characteristics to the US market. It has a legal and institutional structure similar to most common law countries where VC/PE markets have been the subject of much study (including Canada, the UK and the US), but is a relatively younger market. Investment in the Australian VC/PE sector accounts for a much smaller percentage of GDP and pension funds invest a substantially lower percentage of their assets in VC/PE compared to the US.

In contrast to the US, Australian VCs do not take firms public at an earlier stage than non-VC/PE backed firms which is in contrast to the grandstanding hypothesis. Australian VC/PE investors retain some or all of their stake in the firm, with less than a third fully exiting at the time of listing.

We find that, on average, Australian IPOs underperform the market index over two years post-listing but have similar performance after three years. However, there is no significant difference in the market-adjusted stock performance of VC/PE-backed and non-VC/PE backed IPOs, except in the first year of listing where VC-backed IPOs perform worse than non-VC/PE backed IPOs. However, when performance is measured on an industry-adjusted basis, IPOs as a whole and non-VC/PE backed IPOs have similar performance to the industry index over the three-year period post-listing. In contrast, VC- and PE-backed IPOs underperform the industry index in the first year of listing.

Similarly, there is a significant decline in operating performance for all IPOs, over three years and over one and two years on an industry-adjusted basis. The operating performance is similar for non-VC/PE backed IPOs and VC/PE-backed IPOs. In contrast, PE-backed IPOs have better cash flow performance than VC-backed IPOs over three years. The operating results are similar to the results found for the UK market but in contrast to the US and Singapore.

The cross-sectional results suggest that VC/PE involvement has a negative impact on the stock performance of firms in the first year of listing, but that the impact dissipates over two and three years post-listing. Firms that listed during the hot market of the late 1990s and firms with higher leverage before the IPO have poorer long-term performance.

We examine VC/PE-backed IPOs separately and find a similar negative impact of leverage as in the whole sample. Venture capital/private equity characteristics have marginal impact on performance (which may be driven by the limitations of the small sample). In terms of operating performance, VC/PE backing or ownership does not have an impact on performance over three years post-listing. Smaller issues have poorer operating performance than larger issues, which is consistent with the US IPOs reported in Jain and Kini (1995).

Thus, although most VC/PE investors retain some ownership in the firm post-listing, VC/PE backing does not have a sustained impact on the long-term stock or operating performance of Australian IPOs. Thus the results find little support for the certification hypothesis in the Australian market. These results are in contrast to US and UK markets and may be driven by less experienced managers operating in a relatively smaller and earlier-stage VC/PE market.

NOTES

1. Large scale is defined as a sample of approximately 500 IPOs. See Coakley et al. (2007) and Levis (2011) for UK firms, for other large-scale studies.
2. Da Silva Rosa et al. (2003) use 38 VC-backed and 295 non-VC backed Australian IPOs from 1991 to 1999.
3. For firms listed prior to the introduction of GICS, the old industry code at the time of listing was matched to the relevant Australian Stock Exchange (ASX) industry index.

4. We use both the standard and the skewness adjusted t-statistic and get similar results.
5. The median PE backed IPO performs better than the median VC-backed IPO over two years, although both underperform the market.
6. Non-VC/PE backed IPOs have a significant negative change in raw median operating performance over two years, while VC/PE-backed IPOs and VC-backed IPOs only have a marginally significant negative change over one year post-listing.
7. Market-adjusted return results are presented alone as industry-adjusted returns provide consistent results. We also use wealth relatives which provide similar results.
8. Industry dummies are also included for IPOs in the telecommunications, utilities, consumer discretionary, healthcare, and information technology industries. These terms are not reported, for reasons of brevity.

REFERENCES

Arthurs, J., L. Busenitz, R. Hoskisson and R. Johnson (2009), 'Signaling and initial public offerings: the use and impact of the lockup period', *Journal of Business Venturing*, **24**, 360–72.
Australian Bureau of Statistics (2010), 'Venture capital and later stage private equity survey'.
Baker, M. and P. Gompers (2003), 'The determinants of board structure at the initial public offering', *Journal of Law and Economics*, **46**, 569–98.
Barber, B. and J. Lyon (1997), 'Detecting long-run abnormal stock returns: the empirical power and specification of test statistics', *Journal of Financial Economics*, **43**, 341–72.
Barry, C.B., C.J. Muscarella, J.W. Peavy III and M.R. Vetsuypens (1990), 'The role of venture capitalists in the creation of public companies: evidence from the going public process', *Journal of Financial Economics*, **27**, 447–71.
Ber, H. and Y.Yafeh (2004), 'Can venture capital funds pick winners? Evidence from pre-IPO survival rates and post-IPO performance', CEPR Discussion Paper No. 4672.
Brav, A. and P.A. Gompers (1997), 'Myth or reality? The long-run under-performance of initial public offerings: evidence from venture and nonventure capital-backed companies', *Journal of Finance*, **52**, 1791–821.
Brav A. and P.A. Gompers (2003), 'The role of lock-ups in initial public offerings', *Review of Financial Studies*, **16**, 1–29.
Bruton, G., I. Filatotchev, S. Chahine and M. Wright (2010), 'Governance, ownership structure, and performance of IPO firms: the impact of different types of private equity investors and institutional environments', *Strategic Management Journal*, **31**, 491–509.
Cai, J. and C.J. Wei (1997), 'The investment and operating performance of Japanese initial public offerings', *Pacific-Basin Finance Journal*, **5**, 389–417.
Cao, J. and J. Lerner (2009), 'The performance of reverse leveraged buyouts', *Journal of Financial Economics*, **91**, 39–157.
Carter, R., F. Dark and A. Singh (1998), 'Underwriter reputation, initial returns, and the long-run performance of IPO stocks', *Journal of Finance*, **53**, 285–311.
Clementi, G. (2004), 'IPOs and the growth of firms', working paper, NYU Stern.
Coakley, J., L. Hadass and A. Wood (2007), 'Post-IPO operating performance, venture capital and the bubble years', *Journal of Business Finance and Accounting*, **34**, 1423–46.
Cumming, D. and J.G. MacIntosh (2003), 'A cross-country comparison of full and partial venture capital exits', *Journal of Banking and Finance*, **27**, 511–48.
Da Silva Rosa, R., G. Velayuthen and T. Walter (2003), 'The sharemarket performance of Australian venture capital-backed and non-venture capital-backed IPOs', *Pacific-Basin Finance Journal*, **11**, 197–218.
Das, S., M. Jagannathan and A. Sarin (2003), 'Private equity returns: an empirical examination of the exit of venture-backed companies', *Journal of Investment Management*, **1**, 152–77.
Doukas, J. and H. Gonenc (2005), 'Long-term performance of new equity issuers, venture capital and reputation of investment bankers', *Economic Notes*, **34**, 1–34.
Field, L. and G. Hanka (2001), 'The expiration of IPO share lockups', *Journal of Finance*, **56**, 471–500.
Filatotchev, I. and K. Bishop (2002), 'Board composition, share ownership, and underpricing of U.K. IPO firms', *Strategic Management Journal*, **23**, 941–55.
Fleming, G. (2004), 'Exit strategies venture capital: Australian evidence', *Venture Capital: An International Journal of Entrepreneurial Finance*, **6**, 23–45.
Giot, P. and A. Schwienbacher (2007), 'IPOs, trade sales and liquidations: modelling venture capital exits using survival analysis', *Journal of Banking and Finance*, **31**, 679–702.
Gompers, P. (1996), 'Grandstanding in the venture capital industry', *Journal of Financial Economics*, **42**, 133–56.

Gompers, P. and J. Lerner (1998), 'Venture capital distributions: short-run and long-run reactions', *Journal of Finance*, **53**, 2161–83.
Gompers, P. and J. Lerner (1999), *The Venture Capital Cycle*, Cambridge, MA: MIT Press.
Gompers, P. and J. Lerner (2000), 'Money chasing deals? The impact of fund inflows on the valuation of private equity investments', *Journal of Financial Economics*, **55**, 281–325.
Gompers, P. and J. Lerner (2001), *The Money of Invention: How Venture Capital Creates New Wealth*. Cambridge, MA: Harvard Business School Press.
Gompers, P., J. Lerner and D. Scharfstein (2005), 'Entrepreneurial spawning: public corporations and the genesis of new ventures, 1986–1999', *Journal of Finance*, **60**, 577–614.
Habib, M. and A. Ljungqvist (2001), 'Underpricing and entrepreneurial wealth losses in IPOs: theory and evidence', *Review of Financial Studies*, **14**, 433–58.
Hamao, Y., F. Packer and J.R. Ritter (2000), 'Institutional affiliation and the role of venture capital: evidence from initial public offerings in Japan', *Pacific-Basin Finance Journal*, **8**, 529–58.
Hege, U., F. Palomino and A. Schwienbacher (2003), 'Determinants of venture capital performance: Europe and the United States', working paper, HEC School of Management, Tilburg University and University of Namur.
Jain, B. and O. Kini (1994), 'The post-issue operating performance of IPO firms', *Journal of Finance*, **49**, 1699–726.
Jain, B. and O. Kini (1995), 'Venture capitalist participation and the post-issue operating performance of IPO firms', *Managerial and Decision Economics*, **16**, 593–606.
Jeng, L. and P. Wells (2000), 'The determinants of venture capital fundraising: evidence across countries', *Journal of Corporate Finance*, **6**, 241–89.
Khurshed, A., S. Paleari and S. Vismara (2003), 'The operating performance of initial public offerings: the UK experience', working paper, University of Manchester.
Kortum, S. and J. Lerner (2000), 'Assessing the contribution of venture capital to innovation', *RAND Journal of Economics*, **31**, 647–92.
Krishnan, C., R. Masulis, V. Ivanov and A. Singh (2011), 'Venture capital reputation and post-IPO performance', *Journal of Financial and Quantitative Analysis*, **46**, 1295–333.
Kutsuna, K., H. Okamura and M. Cowling (2002), 'Ownership structure pre- and post-IPOs and the operating performance of JASDAQ companies', *Pacific-Basin Finance Journal*, **10**, 163–81.
Lee, P. and S. Wahal (2004), 'Grandstanding, certification and the underpricing of venture backed IPOs', *Journal of Financial Economics*, **73**, 375–407.
Lerner, J. (1994), 'The syndication of venture capital investments', *Financial Management*, **23**, 16–27.
Lerner, J. (1999), 'The government as a venture capitalist: the long-run effects of the SBIR program', *Journal of Business*, **2**, 285–318.
Lerner, J. (2002a), 'Boom and bust in the venture capital industry and the impact on innovation', *Federal Reserve Bank of Atlanta Economic Review*, **87**, 25–39.
Lerner, J. (2002b), 'When bureaucrats meet entrepreneurs: the design of effective 'Public Venture Capital' programmes', *Economic Journal*, **112**, 73–84.
Levis, M. (2011), 'The performance of private equity-backed IPOs', *Financial Management*, Spring, 253–77.
Ljungqvist, A., F. Marston and W. Wilhelm (2006), 'Competing for securities underwriting mandates: banking relationships and analyst recommendations', *Journal of Finance*, **61**, 301–40.
Loughran, T. and J.R. Ritter (1997), 'The operating performance of firms conducting seasoned equity offerings', *Journal of Finance*, **52**, 1823–50.
Loughran, T. and J.R. Ritter (2004), 'Why has IPO underpricing changed over time?', *Financial Management*, **33**, 5–37.
Megginson, W.L. and K. Weiss (1991), 'Venture capitalist certification in initial public offerings', *Journal of Finance*, **46**, 879–903.
Meles, A. (2011), 'Do private equity investors create value for Italian initial public offerings?', *International Review of Finance*, **11**, 391–416.
Mikkelson, W., M. Partch and K. Shah (1997), 'Ownership and operating performance of companies that go public', *Journal of Financial Economics*, **44**, 281–307.
Pagano, M., F. Panetta and L. Zingales (1998), 'Why do companies go public? An empirical analysis', *Journal of Finance*, **53**, 27–64.
Probitas Partners (2009), 'The Asian private equity market in the global crisis', industry research report.
Ritter, J.R. (1991), 'The long-run performance of initial public offerings', *Journal of Finance*, **46**, 3–28.
Sanders, W. and S. Boivie (2004), 'Sorting things out: valuation of new firms in uncertain markets', *Strategic Management Journal*, **25**, 167–86.
Suchard, J. (2009), 'The impact of venture capital backing on the corporate governance of Australian initial public offerings', *Journal of Banking and Finance*, **33**, 765–74.
Von Drathen, C (2007), 'The performance of private equity-backed initial public offerings in Germany', working paper, London Business School.

Von Drathen, C. and F. Faleiro (2007), 'The performance of leveraged buyout-backed initial public offerings in the UK', working paper, London Business School.
Wang, C., K. Wang and Q. Lu (2003), 'Effects of venture capitalists' participation in listed companies', *Journal of Banking and Finance*, **27**, 2015–34.
Welch, I. (1989), 'Seasoned offerings, imitation costs, and the underpricing of initial public offerings', *Journal of Finance*, **44**, 421–49.
White, H. (1980), 'A heteroskedasticity-consistent covariance matrix estimator and a direct test for heteroskedasticity', *Econometrica: Journal of the Econometric Society*, **48**, 817–38.

20 Development in financial markets and the performance of German IPOs
Dimitrios Gounopoulos and Johannes Hoebelt

1 INTRODUCTION

Initial public offerings (IPOs) are part of various controversy discussions in finance, which document mainly three aspects regarding IPO performance. First, the global phenomenon that IPOs tend to be priced at a discount (underpricing). Second, listings of IPOs vary significantly dependent upon certain periods (hot issue markets). Third, it is well documented that IPOs appear to have poor long-term performance.

These conclusions were developed in a large body of empirical studies, which have been carried out subsequently in the past. Initially, Ibbotson and Jaffe (1975) presented empirical evidence on underpricing and connected it with the existence of hot and cold issue markets influencing the magnitude of the underpricing. Further, similar pattern were documented by Ritter (1984) analysing the 1980 US-hot issue market and Loughran et al. (1994) at international level, showing that this has not been a single event. On the other hand, Ritter (1991) and Thomadakis et al. (2012) concluded that IPOs underperform in the long-term, which was also connected to the timing of the IPO. Moreover, Loughran and Ritter (1995) confirmed this result by providing similar evidence on IPO long-term performance.

In order to explain these findings, many attempts were followed, with focus on different aspects regarding information asymmetry. For instance, Baron and Holmström (1980) and Baron (1982) argued that the agency problem between issuer and underwriter could cause a moral hazard situation. Rock (1986) documented that underpricing is driven by the 'winner's curse' based on uninformed investors and Beatty and Ritter (1986) further discussed 'ex ante uncertainty' about the intrinsic value of the firm as a main determinant. Later on, Allen and Faulhaber (1989), Welch (1989) and Grinblatt and Hwang (1989) established the signalling theory, which states that good companies signal their commitment through underpricing. Simultaneously, Benveniste and Spindt (1989) determined the book-building procedure as a main factor.

German IPO market has been intensively investigated in the past. Underpricing was first recognized by Wasserfallen and Wittleder (1994), Schuster (1996) and Ljungqvist (1997) who also documented poor IPO long-term performance. Ljungqvist (1997), especially, explored the variation of results depending upon main or parallel market listings and revealed German specifications. Therefore, later studies focused on specific aspects of the German market such as benchmark sensitivity (Sapusek, 2000), market segmentation (Hunger, 2003), future finance decisions (Bessler and Thies, 2007), accounting standards and ownership structure (Elston and Yang, 2010), share repurchases (Bessler et al., 2014). On the other hand, Pryshchepa and Stehle (2011) found out that these studies must be compared carefully because they all document different magnitudes of short- and long-term IPO performance. They explain the differences between the studies with the sample construction, the observed period and the chosen benchmark, which shows that German IPOs may not be poor investments depending upon these factors.

This study aims to contribute in two aspects, which affected the German stock markets, and consequently German IPOs. On the one side, the mandatory International Financial Reporting Standards (IFRS) adoption for listed companies in the European Union was introduced in 2005.[1] Unlike the voluntarily adoption of IFRS, which have not been proven to increase comparability among European financial statements (Elston and Yang, (2010), the mandatory adoption ensures accounting quality on another level. The German financial reporting system, especially, with the introduction of IFRS and German Accounting Law Modernization Act (Bilanzrechtsmodernisierungsgesetz – BilMoG) has changed over recent years. On the other hand, the Lehman Brothers bankruptcy and afterwards the 'state debt crunch' named as the 'recent financial market crisis' has been responsible for ongoing uncertainty on the financial markets worldwide. The number of IPOs has dropped significantly (Gao et al., 2011) in its aftermath and has driven many discussions among financial economists. Although the German stock market has been relatively stable during this time, Germany faces the uncertainty of the future regarding the vulnerable countries in the European Union (EU), which may be a burden for German IPOs as well.

Therefore based on these theories and the recent financial developments, this study addresses a number of questions regarding IFRS adoption and financial market crisis. First, to what extent has the recent financial market crisis influenced IPOs on the Frankfurt Stock Exchange? Second, does the mandatory IFRS adoption reduce information asymmetry and thus the level of underpricing in Germany? Third, how do German IPOs perform in the long term before and after IFRS adoption? Finally, how do German IPOs perform compared to distinct benchmarks such as the Deutsche Aktienindex (DAX) or the Composite Deutscher Aktieni IndeX (CDAX)?

In order to explore these questions, this chapter employs a sample of 606 German companies, issued between 1992 and 2012. During this period, there have been many changes on the German market, but the mandatory adoption of IFRS and the recent financial crisis are two specific amendments, with international effect and hence should be investigated. The long-term performance in this study is analysed by using a buy-and-hold abnormal Return (BHAR) approach applied by, for instance, Bessler and Thies (2007) and Pryshchepa and Stehle (2011). Moreover, this chapter applies the basic capital asset pricing model (CAPM), the Fama and French (1993) three-factors model and is extended with the momentum FF4F-type model as proposed by Carhart (1997).

This chapter provides several contributions to the existing literature. Initially, the chapter explores the latest developments in the financial markets through researching mandatory adoption of IFRS by German IPOs. Second, this is the first international study that explores in-depth the recent debt financial crises in the context of IPOs. Third, this is the first German study that investigates long-term returns through Fama and French's (1993, 1996 extended) value-weighted three-factors model. Fourth, the chapter provides additional evidence on the performance into the long term of German IPOs in 'hot' and 'cold' market periods. Fifth, an extended sample from 1992 to 2012 gives new insights into the performance of German IPOs. Owing to the wide range of variables, further evidence may be taken from the confirmation or contradiction of previous researches. For instance, according to the results, older companies have a better long-term IPO performance than younger ones, which is consistent with Ritter (1991). However, in the shortterm older companies have a lower underpricing than younger ones. This result contradicts the signalling model according to which better companies signal their quality through a higher underpricing. Furthermore, a stricter transparency standard is not associated with a lower underpricing, which is consistent with Hunger (2003).

The results show that mandatory IFRS adoption reduces IPO underpricing. Initial public offerings following IFRS adoption are associated with better performance in the end of first year of trading. Further, as a result of the recent financial market crisis the findings reveal a sharp reduction of underpricing, while investors buying shares during the IPO process enjoy good long-term returns. Any firm that would like to leave 'money on the table' should select a book-building mechanism.

The remainder of this chapter is organized as follows. Section 2 covers the relevant literature and reviews the most important explanations of short- and long-term performance. Section 3 formulates the hypothesis and explains the research design used in this study, while section 4 presents the data and scrutinizes the methodology. Section 5 analyses the descriptive results of IPOs and section 6 presents findings of the regression results. Concluding remarks and further areas of investigation are given in section 7.

2 EMPIRICAL STUDIES ON INITIAL PERFORMANCE OF INITIAL PUBLIC OFFERINGS

In Germany, securities can be traded in seven different stock exchanges, which are Frankfurt, Berlin, Hamburg, Stuttgart, Hanover, Dusseldorf and Munich. It is possible for an IPO to be listed simultaneously in more than one stock exchange, but the Frankfurt Stock Exchange (FSE), including the electronic trading platform XETRA, has about 92 per cent of the market share measured in total turnover (Deutsche Börse Group (2009). Owing to its importance, the following section comprises only regulations and segments from the FSE. These arrangements changed frequently over time and in order to understand, to categorize and to compare previous evidence in the German market, it is essential to know past and current regulations.

2.1 Institutional Arrangements in the Frankfurt Stock Exchange

Usually, there is a greater investor's demand for information based on legal regulations, when a company goes public. In order to ensure this legal consistency and transparency, either the domestic legislator (which is the EU in Europe) or the stock exchange, enact legislation for equity markets. Therefore as in Figure 20.A1 in the appendix to this chapter, the FSE mainly distinguishes between the EU-regulated market (Regulated Market) and the exchange regulated Market (Open Market), which provide legal regulations for the different transparency levels (Prime Standard, General Standard and Entry Standard).

Since November 2007, the Regulated Market is the combination of the two prior subdivisions Official Market (Amtlicher Markt) and Regulated Market (Geregelter Markt).[2]

Companies listed in this segment have to fulfil the highest EU-accepted law regulations.[3] For instance, the company must have issued 10 000 or more shares, which are publicly held by more than 25 per cent. In addition, the company must have been operating for at least three years and must provide an admission prospectus about the last three years, which comprises information about cash flow, income and assets. Furthermore, the company has to fulfil transparency requirements such as annual reports under IFRS or US generally accepted accounting principles (GAAP) and ad-hoc disclosures depending upon the chosen standard. The difference between both standards is that the Prime Standard is slightly stricter than the General Standard because it requires for instance quarterly reporting in German and English.

On the other hand, smaller companies, which would like to gain from the advantages of the stock exchange, but are unable to fulfil all the requirements of the Regulated Market, may alternatively list in the Entry Standard of the Open Market. This segment is the consequence from the repositioning of the Regulated Unofficial Market (Ungeregelter Freiverkehr) in October 2005 and is also divided into two subdivisions called First Quotation Board (FQB) and Second Quotation Board (SQB). The FQB comprises companies, which went initially public in the Open Market, while the SQB includes companies, which were initially listed on another international stock exchange. The Open Market is regulated by public law and thus less strict than an organized market under German Securities Trading Act. Therefore, investors should know that less and lower-quality information might be provided (Deutsche Börse Group, 2011).

Further, during the period 1997 to 2003, the Neuer Markt was a very popular market segment, where overall about 76 per cent of the IPOs were placed. The Neuer Markt was run on the FSE and was intended to be a segment for young, innovative and high growth companies, which were mostly financed by venture capital or private equity. The listing requirements were almost the same and even a bit stricter than those for the former Official Market (Deutsche Börse Group, 2000; Hunger, 2003).

2.2 Recent Impacts on the German Equity Market

2.2.1 Adoption of IFRS in Germany
In the last decade in Europe, especially, there have been controversy discussions about accounting quality and in particular which accounting system ensures the best quality from a stakeholder prospective. The general aim was to introduce harmonization in company's accounting practice and responding the high-quality accounting need (Van Tendeloo and Vanstraelen, 2005). This has led, first, to an adoption of the IFRS[4] in Germany for public listed companies on an optional basis in 1998 and, eventually, to a mandatory adoption since 2005 (Elston and Yang, 2010).

Germany GAAP accounting quality Many studies have been carried out in order to evaluate the accounting quality in different countries, which usually concentrate on differences between the country's law system and how it affects the accounting system (Ball et al., 2000). According to this research, Germany is a country which has a civil law system and, consequently, concentrated corporate ownership and a low minority investor protection (La Porta et al., 2000). The German GAAP are mainly organized in order to protect the debt-holders of a company. This is because the debt-holders do not have any legal rights to participate in the business, but may bear most of the costs if a company goes bankrupt by losing their capital completely (Jensen and Meckling, 1976). Therefore, the German financial statement's main functions are the documentation, information and distributable profit evaluation, which ensure accounting quality for the debt-holders together with the Grundsätze ordnungsgemäßer Buchführung (Principals of Orderly Bookkeeping) (GoB). Additional standards are the principle of prudence, which means that non-realized profits are not allowed to be reported (realization principle), but non-realized losses and risks must be included (imparity principle).[5]

International Financial Reporting Standards accounting quality The IFRS accounting quality is mainly driven by the principles in the conceptual framework. These state the main purpose of financial reporting, which is providing financial information that ensures decision usefulness for investors, lenders and other creditors (OB2). In order to meet this objective there are laid down two fundamental qualitative characteristics, which are relevance (QC6-10) and faithful representation (QC12-16). According to QC6-10 information is relevant if it is 'capable of making a difference in the decisions' of the user. This is ensured if the information has at least one of both, predictive or confirmatory value. On the other hand, QC12-16 state that perfect faithful represented data 'would be complete, neutral and free from error'. Moreover QC17 to QC18 explain that there is a trade-off between both mentioned fundamental qualitative characteristics because neither a reliable but irrelevant nor an unreliable but relevant information is useful. Therefore, the most efficient and effective way to apply these principles is to identify and rank useful and relevant information and determine faithful availability of the most relevant one.

Comparison between German GAAP and IFRS Owing to the widely historical accounting policy, German GAAP has internationally been acknowledged as conservative. On the other hand, it has also been recognized as a system, which enables managers to smooth earnings due to many accounting options.[6] However, since the BilMoG was introduced in 2009, many of the internationally criticized accounting options were removed or changed. For instance, the regulation of s. 249 Abs. 1 Satz 3, Abs. 2 HGB a. F regarding provisions for expenses (Aufwandsrückstellungen) no longer exists. Furthermore, the option for extraordinary depreciations if a non-current asset is temporarily reduced in value, has been changed to a prohibition. Further, if the option for an extraordinary depreciation is no longer valid, the current value has to, rather than might, be reinstated up to maximum the original value.[7]

On the other hand, one of the most important concepts in order to achieve the IFRS goals is fair-value accounting, which has become part of many standards and seems to be favoured by the International Accounting Standard Board (IASB) over historical cost accounting (Zimmermann and Werner, 2006). In several standards the fair value is defined as 'the amount for which an asset could be exchanged, or a liability settled, between knowledgeable, willing parties in an arm's length transaction' (for example, IAS 32.11) and may be used for measurement at or after recognition. Since the BilMoG, even in German GAAP the fair value has been introduced.[8] However, German GAAP and IFRS continue to differ in many aspects, which are mainly driven by the conflict of historic cost accounting (German GAAP) and fair-value approach (IFRS). A few major differences in measurement are listed in Table 20.A1.

Mandatory versus. voluntary IFRS adoption In Germany, IFRS adoption is mandatory for consolidated and unconsolidated financial statements, if the company is publicly listed on a stock exchange. Further, smaller private companies are allowed to report according to IFRS for unconsolidated statements on a voluntary basis as well. However in any case, German GAAP statements must also be provided for tax and dividend estimation reasons (Nobes and Parker, 2010).

Initially, there are distinct opinions among the international literature, whether mandatory or voluntary IFRS adoption leads to better or worse accounting quality. On the one hand, Horton et al. (2013) found in an international study testing more than 120 countries, that mandatory IFRS adoption led to an increase in the forecast accuracy and hence in an improvement of accounting quality. On the other hand, Soderstrom and Sun (2007) argued that generally (1) the standard quality, (2) the country's law and political system and (3) the reporting incentives are the main three factors, which drive the results. In Germany's case, Van Tendeloo and Vanstraelen (2005) and Paananen and Lin (2008) do not find any significant differences in accounting quality, neither for voluntary nor for mandatory IFRS adoption. Additionally, Elston and Yang (2010) cannot confirm that voluntary IFRS adoption decreases information asymmetry and thus reduces underpricing.

2.2.2 Financial market crisis

The recent financial crisis started in 2007 in the USA with the bubble of mortgage-backed securities. It was enhanced with the Lehman Brothers bankruptcy in September 2008 and the Eurozone debt crises which is still ongoing. Those three financial events deeply influenced the global financial markets and affected stock market returns and the global listings of IPOs (Liu and Ritter, 2010). German banks, which have a universal status (combination of commercial and investment bank), did not issue or securitize, but invested in subprime loans. As a consequence, even the relatively stable German banking system struggled and some of the banks requested the government's help, owing to large amounts of write-downs (Dietrich and Vollmer, 2012).

Owing to the different economies in the European Monetary Union (EMU), the European Central Bank (ECB) was unable to provide a specific monetary policy for all member states in order to stimulate the European economy. The crisis revealed that the benefits of an EMU are relatively stable over time (low transaction costs, no currency risk), whereas the costs vary in a timely manner (sovereign debt problems). Consequently, the ECB systematically attempted to prevent a resignation of vulnerable countries by increased lending and reduced interest rates as a respond to increased sovereign debt risk in these countries during the crisis (Eichler and Hielscher, 2012).

There have also been problems with the European accounting system. During the financial market crisis, fair-value accounting has been criticized. The so called Mark to market is significantly dependent upon the markets and only works smoothly if the markets do. However, when active markets burst and asset prices rely on fire-sales prices, markets might no longer be a reliable source. Furthermore, if markets appear to be inactive, the fair values have to be measured by using specific models, which are significantly dependent upon subjective estimates and assumptions by the management. Therefore, there is a potential for a lack of objectivity and reliability due to serious implementation problems (Zimmermann and Werner, 2006). On the other hand, historical cost accounting is much more consistent but also does not provide investors with significant price changes.

2.3 Long- and Short-term Evidence of IPO Performance in International Developed Markets

In one of the first German studies on IPOs, Wasserfallen and Wittleder (1994) provided evidence for underpricing in Germany using a sample of 92 IPOs that went public during the period from 1961 to 1987. They found that the share prices were signified by an average initial excess return of 17.6 per cent, but did not recover in the long run. Consistent with Ibbotson and Jaffe (1975), they also distinguish between hot and cold markets and come to the same conclusion, that is, a cold issue market might be a beneficial factor for the issuing company. Later, Ljungqvist (1997) questioned and commented on Wasserfallen and Wittleder (1994) with an expanded sample size of 189 companies which went public between 1970 and 1993. Ljungqvist measured underpricing at 10.57 per cent, which is lower than Wasserfallen and Wittleder (1994), and found significant positive relations between underpricing and (1) stock market, (2) maintaining insider ownership and (3) inverse of real gross proceeds. The main difference between both studies was the methodology, which included different risk proxies. For instance, Ljungqvist (1997) considered analysing separately the IPO underpricing and long-term performance of companies from the Ungeregelter Freiverkehr and other segments. He argued that the lower underpricing of the other segments (9.2 per cent compared with the 17.6 per cent of Wasserfallen and Wittleder (1994) could be explained by the higher competition in the underwriter's markets, which consequently lowers underpricing. Furthermore, Ljungqvist (1997) confirmed Wasserfallen and Wittleder (1994) by stating a poor long-term underperformance of −19.85 per cent of German IPOs alongside the broad market index.

These findings in Germany contradict the signalling model according to which underpricing increases with the quality of the firm.[9] However, in Germany the IPOs on the segments with lower transparency requirements (Open Market or former Ungeregelter Freiverkehr) comprise greater underpricing than high-quality segments (Regulated Market or former Amtlicher Markt or Geregelter Markt). Moreover, Hunger (2003) analysed the different German market segments[10] regarding information asymmetry by comparing the transparency requirements, and tested on this basis whether Rock's (1986) and Beatty and Ritter's (1986) hypotheses can be applied. Findings indicate that both hypotheses are rejected because the Neuer Markt – with the highest requirements mitigating the information asymmetry – despite the expectation for the lowest underpricing, had the highest with 53.64 per cent. However, Hunger (2003) compared this result with the similar situation of the US hot issue market of the early 1980s, discussed in Ritter (1984), where high underpricing was measured for the kind of companies included in the Neuer Markt. Additionally, Oehler at al. (2005), argued that in specific periods, investor sentiment could be the dominating underpricing factor rather than *ex ante uncertainty*, which is another explanation for the rejection of Beatty and Ritter's (1986) theory.

Elston and Yang (2010) attempted in their study to explain the German underpricing behaviour with factors such as concentrated ownership, accounting standards, universal banking system, venture capital markets and share allocation system. Initially, they find that ownership structure of German companies is relatively concentrated, which is a result of the civil law system and leads to lower minority shareholder protection.[11] However, a small number of strong shareholders (insiders) are able to monitor the management more efficiently and mitigate agency costs. Therefore, they hypothesize that this situation lowers the IPO underpricing effect as well. Second, since 2005 the IFRS have become mandatory for publicly listed companies, which leads the accounting principles towards convergence worldwide. Thus, IFRS increases international comparability and transparency for investors, mitigates information asymmetry and eventually reduces IPO underpricing. Third, and similar to Bessler and Kurth (2007), they report that Germany has a universal banking system, which legally compels banks to hold multiple positions at the same time. For instance, banks may act as creditor as well as underwriter for the same listing company, which mitigates the agency problem and IPO alleviate underpricing due to close communication between both counterparts. Fourth, Elston and Yang (2010) observed, especially for the Neuer Markt regarding venture capital, that about 40 per cent of the companies were venture capitalist (VC) backed. If this circumstance has a positive influence on the firm's value and information asymmetry among the investors, they argue that venture capital could mitigate underpricing. Interestingly, Elston and Yang (2010) did not find any significant relationship between IPO underpricing and the variables ownership, venture capital, accounting standards and banking system. Therefore, they concluded that the hypotheses might not be accurate, which could be a joint hypothesis problem. Contrarily, Bessler and Kurth (2007) observed significant agency problems that a company faces when a universal bank participates as a venture capitalist.

On the other hand, several studies have been focused on the long-term IPO performance. For instance, Sapusek (2000) analysed benchmark sensitivity of 142 IPOs between 1983 and 1992 and attributed the differences in the results to the respective benchmark chosen. Later, Bessler and Thies (2007) also stated that the most important factors, which influence the determination of an IPO performance is the methodology used calculating abnormal returns and in turn comparing these with an appropriate benchmark. Therefore, they use a broader approach in order to provide empirical evidence on IPO long-term performance and tested various factors which might explain why a company outperforms or underperforms the benchmark (positive or negative buy-and-hold abnormal returns – BHAR): (1) benchmark selection, (2) market condition ('hot' or 'cold'), (3) subsequent equity issue, (4) capital raised through the IPO, (5) size of company and (6) magnitude of underpricing. The results of Bessler and Thies (2007) mainly confirmed similar conclusions of prior studies, such as importance of benchmark selection or timing of an IPO. For instance, the German IPOs between 1991 and 1995 underperformed the portfolio by −55 per cent mainly due to Germany's cold economy, which is another indication for the existence of distinct market conditions. They especially highlight that the IPO could influence forthcoming share issues, too.

Furthermore, the literature attempted to explain the poor long-term performance with the investor's enthusiasm about company's future chances in the beginning of an IPO, which seems to convert into more realistic opinions over time. Pryshechepa and Stehle (2011) argued that poor long-term performance does not apply to all German market segments. They conclude that IPOs on the Amtlicher Markt are not performing significantly worse than other non-IPOs' shares and therefore contradict the overall view that IPOs are mostly poor investments in the long term. These results come mainly from studies, which combine different segments and include shares with a dominating market capitalization such as Neuer Markt or Ungeregelter Freiverkehr.

3 FORMULATION OF HYPOTHESES-DETERMINANTS RELATED TO RECENT FINANCIAL DEVELOPMENT

We hypothesize that German IPOs' performance is a combination of regulatory interventions, unforeseen market conditions and quality of listed firms when companies decide to go public. Few prior academic studies have documented the relationship between IPOs performance and latest development in the financial context. Characteristics such as listing board classification, age of the firm by the time it goes public, size, underwriters' reputations, hot IPO period, given ownership, time lag between the IPO announcement and the first day of trading, and industry classification, among others, could have further effects on performance, as the literature has already documented.

Horton et al. (2013) document that IFRS adoption has completely improved the quality of information intermediation in capital markets, increasing both information quality and accounting comparability. Since the IPO underpricing phenomenon can be, in part, attributed to information asymmetry in the capital markets, we contend that a fair and trustworthy evaluation of firms making use of IFRS to prepare its accounts, can alleviate the information asymmetry during the IPO process, and thus reduce IPO underpricing. Our first testable hypothesis is:

Hypothesis 1: Firms going public making use of IFR standards are underpriced significantly less than firms with German GAAP.

Next, we examine the effects of recent debt financial crises in the Eurozone on IPO underpricing. According to the information asymmetry explanation of IPO underpricing, it is the value uncertainty that affects underpricing, thus its level, which has reached phenomenal heights, is expected to cause an upturn in the level of underpricing. Further, as it is anticipated to be a considerably lower price in the immediate aftermarket, the stock prices are expected to rise in the long term and offer good returns to long-term investors.

Hypothesis 2: Debt financial crises will affect the invested capital on IPOs and thus reduce the level of underpricing. This capital will return in the markets in the long term (that is, following termination of the crisis) and will cause an increase in the stock price.

4 DATA AND METHODOLOGY

4.1 Data

The study provides new evidence on German IPOs and focuses on new issues in the German Regulated Market and the Open Market between 1992 and 2012. Data on the IPOs' date, offering price, the first-day closing price and general index historical prices were collected direct from the Frankfurt Stock Exchange. Data collection derives from three different sources: (1) FSE from 1997 to 2012, (2) Bloomberg for 1996 and (3) Schuster (1996) from 1992 to 1995. Additional data, regarding the independent variables such as equity and benchmark prices, were gathered from Datastream, Dealogic and Bloomberg.

In total 1704 new listings took place during this period. However this study had to exclude a number of firms in order to ensure consistency throughout the different data sources. On the one hand, the FSE divides the raw data into several categories such as New Issues (NI), Listing/Introduction (LI), Private Placement (PP), Dual Listing (DL) and Transfer (TR). Since the purpose of this study is to analyse a company's first listing, the 1026 mainly Open Market (87 per cent) cases of cross-listings (LI, DL), listings for specific investors (PP) and changes from one to another segment (TR) have been excluded. Bloomberg and Schuster (1996) do not provide this kind of differentiation; therefore it is assumed that these numbers were counted as new listings. These periods have been double-checked with Vismara et al. (2012), which are mainly constituent. This reduces the sample to 678 IPOs.

On the other hand, unavailability of sufficient data led to exclusion of 72 IPOs. In fact, 191 IPOs (18 per cent) have been delisted from the FSE for different reasons such as change of legal form, bankruptcy or mergers and acquisitions (M&A). Fortunately, data for most of the delisted companies were still available. However, accessibility especially regarding equity prices was fading the more time passed since the IPO. Consequently, the final sample for this study comprises 606 IPOs between 1992 and 2012.

4.2 Methodology

The adjusted return for issue i is defined as the raw return less the corresponding market return for the same time period used for raw return calculation:

$$AR_{it} = (R_{it}) - (R_{mt})$$

where R_{it} is the IPO return i at time t and R_{mt} is the market portfolio return at time t.

The average adjusted return on a portfolio of n stocks for event month t is the equally weighted arithmetic average of the adjusted returns:

$$AR_{it} = \frac{1}{n}\sum_{i=1}^{n} ar_{it} \qquad (20.1)$$

The abnormal IPO return for a certain period is defined as the cumulative abnormal return over a time period from the offer date, that is:

$$CAR_T = \sum_{t=0}^{T} AR_{it} \qquad (20.2)$$

To calculate the abnormal return $a_{i,t}$ the first benchmark we use is the standard capital asset pricing model (CAPM) which uses beta to describe the returns of the portfolio. The second is the Fama and French (1993) three-factors model which in comparison to CAPM uses two additional variables, 'small minus big market capitalization' and 'high (book to market ratio) minus low'. The third benchmark is another multi-index model where the factors are those specified by Carhart (1997), who extends the Fama and French model for momentum phenomena.

Model 1: CAPM

$$R_{it} - R_{ft} = a_{it} + \beta_i (R_{mt} - R_{ft}) + e_{it} \qquad (20.3)$$

where R_{it} is the monthly return for each security, R_{mt} is the return on the German market in event month t as measured by the return on the DAX and CDAX, R_{ft} is the treasury bill (T-bill) return in event month t, and β_i is the CAPM beta of company i.

Fama and French (1993) show that when the standard three-factor model (without the momentum factor in Equation (20.5) is estimated in randomly chosen sample firms with small size and low book-to-market ratio, the null hypothesis of zero abnormal performance is over-rejected. In section 2, we showed that the majority of our sample consists of small and growth firms, thus this potential problem can be particularly severe. Mitchell and Stafford (2000) also raise the possibility that the intercept under the null hypothesis may be biased under the standard calendar-time approach.

Model 2: Fama and French (1996) three-factors model (FF3F)

$$(R_{pt} - R_{ft}) = a_p + \beta_p (R_{mt} - R_{ft}) + \gamma_p SMB_t + \delta_p HML_t + e_{pt} \qquad (20.4)$$

The portfolio excess returns are regressed on to the four factors as introduced by Carhart (1997).

Model 3: Carhart (1997) four-factors model
This is an extension of the Fama–French model, containing an additional momentum factor (FF4F):

$$(R_{pt} - R_{ft}) = a_p + \beta_p (R_{mt} - R_{ft}) + \gamma_p SMB_t + \delta_p HML_t + \varepsilon_p UMD_t + e_{pt} \qquad (20.5)$$

where R_{pt} is the calendar-time portfolio return, R_{ft} (risk-free return rate) is the return of 1-month Treasury Bill, $(R_{mt} - R_{ft})$ is the return on the value-weighted portfolio, SMB_t stands for 'small (market capitalization) minus big' during month t, HML_t is the return differential of 'high (book-to-price ratio) minus low' value-weighted portfolios firms in a month, and UMD_t is the difference between returns of portfolios of high-and-low momentum stocks.

We estimate a series of multiple-regression models, using BHAR as dependent variables for a period up to three years after going public see Table 20.A3 in the appendix. The regression model is as follows:

$$(BHAR) \text{ or } (MAIR) \text{ or } (ERY1D1) \text{ or } (ERY1M1) = a + \beta_1 (1 + LnAGE) + \beta_2 \text{Log}(SIZE) + \beta_3 (UND) + \beta_4 (HC) + \beta_5 (FC) + \beta_6 (IND) + \beta_7 (REG) + \beta_8 (MAR) + \beta_9 (GO) + \beta_{10} (IFRS) + \beta_{11} (TLAG) + \beta_{12} (GEO) + \beta_{13} (POP) + \beta_{14} (CIRE) + \beta_{15} (BB) + \varepsilon_i \qquad (20.6)$$

5 DESCRIPTIVE STATISTICS

First, Table 20.2 summarizes and highlights important aspects such as adjusted and unadjusted average returns for the whole sample and the sub-samples before and after IFRS adoption and before and during the financial crisis. The initial return (percentage) demonstrates that German IPOs over the past 21 years were generally underpriced, which decreases sharply in the period after IFRS adoption (8.37 per cent) and during the financial crisis (2.07 per cent). This might be a first indicator that IFRS and the financial crisis mitigated underpricing. However, one should be careful in interpreting these results because the hot periods on the German market with the Neuer Markt samples dominate the later ones significantly. Judged by the amount of IPOs issued after 2005, the German market has been relatively cold, compared with the periods before 2005 (see Table 20.1, panel A). In addition to Table 20.2's summarized statistics sorted by sub-samples, Table 20.3 presents the variables and the respective sub-sample attributable. This will be more important during the analysis, where the significance of the variables will be explained.

Moreover, Table 20.4 demonstrates the average BHARs for all 606 sample IPOs issued between 1992 and July 2012. Panel A presents the unadjusted initial returns, which were calculated based on the offer price, on the first day closing price and the first month closing price. Further, panels B and C show the adjusted BHARs, which were measured by taking the respective prices of both issuing company and benchmark (DAX and CDAX) at the same point in time (that is, the last day of the offer period, first trading day and first month). Results indicate, consistent with earlier international findings Ibbotson and Jaffe (1975), Ritter (1991), Loughran et al. (1994) and, more recently, Thomadakis et al. (2012), that German IPOs were signified by an average underpricing of 29.10 per cent.

In the long-term arena, the one-year adjusted returns (based the first day closing price) for CDAX (19.37 per cent) and DAX (15.20 per cent) are positive, whereas the respective two- and three year adjusted returns are increasingly negative (CDAX: −19.13 per cent and −25.17 per cent; DAX: −23.33 per cent and −27.97 per cent). This result indicates that German IPOs were generally driven by a first optimism year, which decreased drastically within the second and third year of trading. Moreover, the same impression may be taken from Table 20.5, which shows the average monthly-adjusted returns (ARt) and the cumulative adjusted returns (CARt) for 36 months after the IPO. Following 16 months of trading the IPOs underperform consistently on average.

Tables 20.6 and 20.7 demonstrate the BHARs in the short- and long-term according to

Table 20.1 Descriptive statistics of the German IPOs

Panel A: Number of new issues in Germany from 1992 to 2012

Year	All German IPOs*	– Other than NI*	= New Listings (NI)*	NI (%) of total
2012	15	8	7	1.03
2011	218	203	15	2.21
2010	177	161	16	2.36
2009	56	53	3	0.44
2008	188	185	3	0.44
2007	212	168	44	6.49
2006	193	120	73	10.77
2005	58	40	18	2.65
2004	10	5	5	0.74
2003	1	1	0	0.00
2002	7	1	6	0.88
2001	27	7	20	2.95
2000	174	20	154	22.71
1999	193	27	166	24.48
1998	79	14	65	9.59
1997	38	13	25	3.69
1996	13	0	13	1.92
1995	20	0	20	2.95
1994	10	0	10	1.47
1993	7	0	7	1.03
1992	8	0	8	1.18
Total	1704	1026	678	100.00

Panel B: Construction of final sample of German IPOs from 1992 to 2012

Year	NI	All delisted	Legal form	Bankruptcy	M&A	Other	Total excluded	= Final sample
2003–2012	184	15	0	0	0	3	3	181
1998–2002	411	145	5	16	17	12	50	361
1992–1997	83	31	3	4	9	3	19	64
Total	678	191	8	20	26	18	72	606

Notes:
The table presents details of the German IPOs and control samples.
Panel A provides the number of listed IPOs in every calendar year this study covers.
*FSE divides the issue type into the following categories: New Issue (NI), Listing/Introduction (LI), Private Placement (PP), Dual Listing (DL) and Transfer (TR).
Panel B shows the sample construction and determines the reason for the exclusion of 72 IPOs. These were excluded due to unavailability of data which was caused by change of legal form, bankruptcy, Mergers & Acquisitions (M&A) and other reasons.

the sub-samples, which reveal similar results with high underpricing and poor long-term performance before and after IFRS adoption and before and during the financial crisis. The average underpricing, drops significantly from 37.58 per cent before to 8.37 per cent after IFRS adoption. The two- and three-years DAX-adjusted average returns based on

Table 20.2 Summary statistics for German IPOs between 1992 and 2012

Panel A:

	A – IPOs all sample	B – IPOs before IFRS adoption	C – IPOs after IFRS adoption	D – IPOs during financial crisis	E – IPOs before financial crisis
Offer price (EUR)	28.70	33.41	17.20	12.90	29.79
Initial return (IR %)	29.10	37.58	8.37	2.07	30.96
Market adjusted initial return (ARit % – CDAX)	43.62	57.43	9.88	2.89	46.42
Total capital gained (€ million)	155 653	161 853	140 507	114 612	158 477
Proportion (%) of sold ownership	34.53	34.92	33.57	32.90	34.64
Proportion (%) of IPOs in Regulated Market	81.52	92.33	55.11	64.10	82.72
Proportion (%) of IPOs from industrial sector	20.46	14.19	35.80	20.51	20.46
Proportion (%) of IPOs from financial sector	12.05	8.14	21.59	20.51	11.46
Proportion (%) of IPOs from software sector	21.45	26.51	9.09	7.69	22.40
Age (years) of the issuing company on the first trading day	23.31	22.48	25.33	42.92	21.96
Proportion (%) of IPOs with reputable underwriters	48.02	51.40	39.77	25.64	49.56
Time lag between offer and first trading day	15.77	10.84	27.46	32.42	14.63
Proportion of IPOs in a hot market	59.41	52.56	76.14	0.00	63.49
Issuer city distance (miles) from FSE	328.82	246.03	531.08	1388.59	255.92
Issuer city population	739 533	696 926	845 147	759 022	738 496

Notes:
Panel A: summary statistics of German IPOs all samples.
Panel B: summary statistics of German IPOs before IFRS adoption – 430 IPOs.
Panel C: Summary statistics of German IPOs after IFRS adoption – 176 IPOs.
Panel D: Summary statistics of German IPOs during financial crisis – 39 IPOs.
Panel E: Summary statistics of German IPOs before financial crisis – 567 IPOs.

Table 20.3 Sub-sample analysis for Germany IPOs between 1992 and 2012

VARIABLE		Total		Before IFRS		After IFRS		Before crisis		During crisis	
		No.	(%)	No.	(%)	No.	(%)	No.	(%)	No.	(%)
1) REG	Reg. Market	494	81.52	397	65.51	97	16.01	469	77.39	25	4.13
	Open Market	112	18.48	33	5.45	79	13.04	98	16.17	14	2.31
2) AGE	Old (10 years up)	290	47.85	196	32.34	94	15.51	273	45.05	17	2.81
	Young (0–9 years)	316	52.15	234	38.61	82	13.53	294	48.51	22	3.63
3) SIZE	Big (100m-up)	167	27.56	122	20.13	45	7.43	155	25.58	12	1.98
	Small (up to 99m)	439	72.44	308	50.83	131	21.62	412	67.99	27	4.46
4) GO	Low (41%–up)	466	76.90	340	56.11	126	20.79	439	72.44	27	4.46
	High (up to 40%)	140	23.10	90	14.85	50	8.25	128	21.12	12	1.98
5) UND	Reputable	291	48.02	221	36.47	70	11.55	281	46.37	10	1.65
	Unreputable	315	51.98	209	34.49	106	17.49	286	47.19	29	4.79
6) H/C	Hot	360	59.41	226	37.29	134	22.11	360	59.41	0	0.00
	Cold	246	40.59	204	33.66	42	6.93	207	34.16	39	6.44
7) IND	Industrial	124	20.46	61	10.07	63	10.40	116	19.14	8	1.32
	Non-industrial	482	79.54	369	60.89	113	18.65	451	74.42	31	5.12
8) GEO	Close (up to 199)	281	46.37	206	33.99	75	12.38	266	43.89	15	2.48
	Away (200-up)	325	53.63	224	36.96	101	16.67	301	49.67	24	3.96

Notes: This table presents the IPOs grouped into sub-samples according to the eight variables, which are discussed in this chapter: 1) Listing board classification, 2) Age of the company, 3) Size of the issue, 4) Sold ownership, 5) Underwirter reputation, 6) Market condition, 7) Industry classification and 8) Issuer city distance. It shows the proportion (%) and number (No.) of the IPOs sorted according to the variable before and after IFRS and before and during the recent financial crisis.

Table 20.4 Buy-and-hold adjusted returns for German IPOs between 1992 and 2012

Panel A: Buy-and-hold unadjusted returns

Return of	Number of IPOs	Mean return (%)	Median (%)	Minimum return (%)	Maximum return (%)	Standard deviation (%)
I) Unadjusted buy-and-hold returns based on the offer price					
1st day	606	29.10	4.30	−65.08	557.69	64.14
1st months	606	30.69	2.25	−68.25	516.87	78.66
12 months	598	36.87	−13.10	−99.17	2478.13	193.28
24 months	577	−29.95	−59.57	−99.67	825.11	97.24
36 months	562	−51.72	−77.66	−100.00	438.24	67.58
II) Unadjusted buy-and-hold returns based on the first day closing price					
1st months	606	0.06	−3.02	−50.00	146.54	24.79
12 months	598	9.35	−21.41	−99.07	1937.04	149.65
24 months	576	−41.59	−67.71	−99.91	550.94	73.29
36 months	558	−57.18	−79.70	−99.98	313.52	57.45
III) Unadjusted buy-and-hold returns based on the first months closing price					
12 months	598	7.96	−19.75	−98.72	1312.16	129.32
24 months	576	−40.09	−64.89	−99.92	554.02	75.68
36 months	558	−55.67	−79.54	−99.99	305.62	59.63

Panel B: Buy-and-hold adjusted returns based on CDAX

Return of	Number of IPOs	Mean return (%)	Median (%)	Minimum return (%)	Maximum return (%)	Standard deviation (%)
I) Excess or adjusted buy-and-hold returns based on the offer price					
1st day	606	43.62	23.39	−58.47	569.38	66.44
1st months	601	45.19	20.23	−72.32	535.08	80.45
12 months	598	48.78	0.43	−110.36	2464.28	191.30
24 months	575	−5.88	−33.09	−119.95	819.88	94.53
36 months	561	−18.41	−36.86	−101.33	422.74	63.06
II) Excess or adjusted buy-and-hold returns based on the first day closing price					
1st months	601	12.62	7.70	−62.13	155.98	32.53
12 months	598	19.37	−14.80	−110.57	1920.63	148.15
24 months	575	−19.13	−41.41	−122.70	555.50	72.17
36 months	561	−25.17	−39.82	−103.96	327.04	53.49
III) Excess or adjusted buy-and-hold returns based on the first months closing price					
12 months	598	2.10	−22.83	−124.32	1302.48	122.05
24 months	574	−35.59	−48.55	−148.56	557.47	69.17
36 months	558	−42.31	−47.02	−185.58	320.27	52.74

Panel C: Buy-and-hold adjusted returns based on the DAX

Return of	Number of IPOs	Mean return (%)	Median (%)	Minimum return (%)	Maximum return (%)	Standard deviation (%)
I) Excess or adjusted buy-and-hold returns based on the offer price					
1st day	606	40.95	20.87	−58.07	570.59	66.43
1st months	601	42.30	17.67	−72.29	531.36	80.37
12 months	598	44.76	−4.30	−108.50	2456.76	191.15
24 months	575	−9.94	−35.75	−119.25	811.41	94.88
36 months	561	−21.12	−38.65	−101.35	416.62	63.13

Table 20.4 (continued)

Panel C: Buy-and-hold adjusted returns based on the DAX						
Return of	Number of IPOs	Mean return (%)	Median (%)	Minimum return (%)	Maximum return (%)	Standard deviation (%)
II) Excess or adjusted buy-and-hold returns based on the first day closing price							
1st months	601	9.61	3.92	−68.73	155.66	33.47
12 months	598	15.20	−19.41	−111.12	1912.86	148.23
24 months	575	−23.33	−44.83	−122.05	555.32	73.01
36 months	561	−27.97	−41.11	−104.04	325.19	53.87
III) Excess or adjusted buy-and-hold returns based on the first months closing price							
12 months	598	0.44	−23.53	−123.56	1301.89	121.86
24 months	574	−38.46	−49.20	−147.78	556.19	69.47
36 months	558	−44.77	−46.93	−218.93	317.62	54.16

Notes:
This table covers all 606 IPO samples in Germany.
The buy-and-hold unadjusted returns in panel A are based on the (I) offer price, (II) first day closing price and (III) first month closing price.
The buy-and-hold adjusted returns in panel A and B are calculated as the difference between IPO and benchmark unadjusted returns for the same time period.
The benchmark taken for panel B is CDAX and DAX for panel C.
The aspects in order to present the returns are in percentages: mean, median, minimum, maximum and standard deviation.
The number of IPOs varies due to unavailability of prices of recent IPOs younger than three years.

the first-day closing price (panel D) become worse following IFRS adoption compared with before.

According to these results it seems that mandatory IFRS adoption assist in order to mitigate underpricing but did not maintain the good development in the long run. On the other hand, only a limited amount of information may be taken from Table 20.7 because of the small sample size for the period during the financial crisis. However, it seems that cold periods mitigate underpricing.

Discussed results clearly indicate that German IPOs have high underpricing and poor long-term performance, a similar pattern to international IPOs. However, owing to the German market and its specifications, one needs to be careful in analysing the results. Therefore, Table 20.8 provide also descriptive statistics for short- and long-term performance, which are sorted according to certain variable criteria such as AGE, MAR, GEO and SIZE.

5.1 Short-term Performance

Table 20.8 shows the short-term average initial returns sorted by certain variables. Literature, backed by results based on previous studies such as by Ljungqvist (1997), Hunger (2003) and Bessler and Thies (2007) do not support signalling models of Allen and Faulhaber (1989), Welch (1989) and Grinblatt and Hwang (1989). This study by

Table 20.5   Abnormal returns for IPOs between 1992 to 2012

Month	No. of firms trading	ARt (%)	CARt (%)	ARt (%)	CARt (%)
1	601	12.62	12.62	9.61	9.61
2	599	2.30	14.93	2.03	11.64
3	599	5.18	20.11	5.17	16.81
4	599	4.75	24.86	4.59	21.40
5	599	6.73	31.59	6.55	27.95
6	599	−1.76	29.83	−1.94	26.01
7	599	−1.18	28.65	−1.36	24.65
8	598	0.80	29.45	0.59	25.24
9	598	−0.62	28.83	−0.64	24.60
10	598	−4.38	24.46	−4.36	20.24
11	598	−2.24	22.22	−2.24	17.99
12	598	−2.85	19.37	−2.79	15.20
13	593	−3.79	15.58	−4.10	11.10
14	592	−7.30	8.28	−7.26	3.84
15	590	0.54	8.82	0.64	4.48
16	588	−5.97	2.85	−6.11	−1.63
17	587	−2.18	0.67	−2.21	−3.84
18	585	−2.66	−1.99	−2.85	−6.69
19	583	−0.35	−2.35	−0.25	−6.94
20	579	1.43	−0.91	1.31	−5.63
21	577	−3.22	−4.13	−3.21	−8.84
22	577	−13.61	−17.74	−13.36	−22.21
23	577	−0.33	−18.07	−0.09	−22.29
24	575	−1.06	−19.13	−1.04	−23.33
25	574	−1.00	−20.13	−1.02	−24.35
26	573	−1.80	−21.94	−1.61	−25.96
27	572	−0.96	−22.90	−0.65	−26.61
28	567	−0.15	−23.05	−0.04	−26.64
29	566	−0.78	−23.83	−0.80	−27.44
30	565	−0.68	−24.51	−0.71	−28.15
31	565	0.23	−24.28	0.34	−27.81
32	564	−1.03	−25.31	−0.94	−28.75
33	564	−0.73	−26.05	−0.57	−29.32
34	562	0.04	−26.00	0.16	−29.16
35	561	0.28	−25.72	0.51	−28.65
36	561	0.55	−25.17	0.68	−27.97

Note: This table presents the average adjusted returns (ARt) in % and the cumulative average returns (CARt) in % for 36 months after going public and excluding the initial return. These returns are shown based on the two benchmarks CDAX and DAX.

using the AGE variable provides further insights to the IPO puzzle, which is quite contradictory itself. As expected, the variable AGE demonstrates in panel A that younger companies have a higher average initial return than older, indicating that younger companies have a higher underpricing than older, more established companies (see panel A).

This further contradicts the signalling model because older companies are those with

Table 20.6 Buy-and-hold adjusted returns for IPOs before and after IFRS adoption

Panel A: Unadjusted buy-and-hold returns based on the offer price

Return of	Total sample		Before IFRS		After IFRS	
	Number of IPOs	Mean return (%)	Number of IPOs	Mean return (%)	Number of IPOs	Mean return (%)
1st day	606	29.10	430	37.58	176	8.37
1st months	606	30.69	430	40.57	176	5.87
12 months	598	36.87	430	49.97	168	2.95
24 months	577	−29.95	428	−31.48	149	−25.47
36 months	562	−51.72	423	−55.60	139	−39.90

Panel B: Unadjusted buy-and-hold returns based on the first-day closing price

Return of	Total sample		Before IFRS		After IFRS	
	Number of IPOs	Mean return (%)	Number of IPOs	Mean return (%)	Number of IPOs	Mean return (%)
1st months	606	0.06	430	1.15	176	−2.70
12 months	598	9.35	430	15.92	168	−7.65
24 months	576	−41.59	427	−45.12	149	−31.23
36 months	558	−57.18	420	−61.31	138	−44.62

Panel C: Unadjusted buy-and-hold returns based on the first-month closing price

Return of	Total sample		Before IFRS		After IFRS	
	Number of IPOs	Mean return (%)	Number of IPOs	Mean return (%)	Number of IPOs	Mean return (%)
12 months	598	7.96	430	13.21	168	−5.64
24 months	576	−40.09	427	−43.82	149	−29.17
36 months	558	−55.67	420	−59.92	138	−42.75

Panel D: Excess or DAX-adjusted buy-and-hold returns based on the offer price

Return of	Total sample		Before IFRS		After IFRS	
	Number of IPOs	Mean return (%)	Number of IPOs	Mean return (%)	Number of IPOs	Mean return (%)
1st day	606	40.95	430	53.32	176	10.73
1st months	601	42.30	430	56.24	171	7.25
12 months	598	44.76	430	63.05	168	−2.06
24 months	575	−9.94	428	−8.10	147	−15.30
36 months	561	−21.12	423	−19.84	138	−25.02

Panel E: Excess or DAX-adjusted buy-and-hold returns based on the first-day closing price

Return of	Total sample		Before IFRS		After IFRS	
	Number of IPOs	Mean return (%)	Number of IPOs	Mean return (%)	Number of IPOs	Mean return (%)
1st months	601	9.61	430	14.87	171	−3.61
12 months	598	15.20	430	26.99	168	−14.97

Table 20.6 (continued)

Panel E: Excess or DAX-adjusted buy-and-hold returns based on the first-day closing price

Return of	Total sample		Before IFRS		After IFRS	
	Number of IPOs	Mean return (%)	Number of IPOs	Mean return (%)	Number of IPOs	Mean return (%)
24 months	575	−23.33	428	−23.42	147	−23.09
36 months	561	−27.97	423	−26.61	138	−32.15

Panel F: Excess or DAX-adjusted buy-and-hold returns based on first-month closing price

Return of	Total sample		Before IFRS		After IFRS	
	Number of IPOs	Mean return (%)	Number of IPOs	Mean return (%)	Number of IPOs	Mean return (%)
12 months	598	0.44	430	6.32	168	−14.60
24 months	574	−38.46	427	−43.00	147	−25.28
36 months	558	−44.77	420	−49.17	138	−31.37

Notes: This table is made the same way as Table 20.4. However, this table takes into consideration the unadjusted and DAX-adjusted returns based on the offer price, the first day closing price and the first month closing price before and after IFRS adoption.

more secured future and higher cash flow predictions and thus should be able to afford a higher level of underpricing. Moving forward, Regulated Market in general have a higher underpricing (31.03 per cent) than the Open Market (20.97 per cent). This result, however, might be consistent with the signalling model because the Regulated Market and its stricter transparency requirements are generally a stronger commitment and therefore reveal quality to the market (see panel B).

Another aspect regarding the MAR variable is that it might be consistent with Hunger (2003), who analysed the German market divided into market segmentation and argued that a higher degree of transparency is expected to lower information asymmetry and thus underpricing. In this sense, it might be possible to draw a line to the winner's curse of Rock (1986) and the *ex ante* uncertainty of Beatty and Ritter (1986). Thus, the earlier presented results regarding underpricing of Regulated Markets (31.03 per cent) and Open Markets (20.97 per cent) might lead to a contradicting conclusion of these theories. But if one has a closer look in the results, as it is shown in panel B, the Neuer Markt presents an abnormal high underpricing with an initial return of 48.02 per cent, compared with other high quality segments such as General Standard (10.40 per cent) and Prime Standard (21.95 per cent). Therefore, a more demanding transparency level such as Neuer Markt does not necessarily mean that the information asymmetry and hence underpricing is mitigated through a higher degree of disclosure requirements.

However, Hunger (2003) points out that the companies listed in the Neuer Markt were young and innovative, comparable with the hot issue market of 1980 in Ritter (1984) and therefore a special case. On the other hand, Rock (1986) composed his model by separat-

Table 20.7 Buy-and-hold adjusted returns before and during financial crisis

Panel A: Unadjusted buy-and-hold returns based on the offer price

Return of	Total sample		Before crisis		During crisis	
	Number of IPOs	Mean return (%)	Number of IPOs	Mean return (%)	Number of IPOs	Mean return (%)
1st day	606	29.10	567	30.96	39	2.07
1st months	606	30.69	567	32.71	39	−2.91
12 months	598	36.87	567	39.18	31	−8.29
24 months	577	−29.95	565	−30.46	12	1.90
36 months	562	−51.72	560	−51.84	2	−18.18

Panel B: Unadjusted buy-and-hold returns based on the first day closing price

Return of	Total sample		Before crisis		During crisis	
	Number of IPOs	Mean return (%)	Number of IPOs	Mean return (%)	Number of IPOs	Mean return (%)
1st months	606	0.06	567	0.33	39	−4.47
12 months	598	9.35	567	10.37	31	−10.50
24 months	576	−41.59	564	−42.21	12	−2.34
36 months	558	−57.18	556	−57.30	2	−25.50

Panel C: Unadjusted buy-and-hold returns based on the first month closing price

Return of	Total sample		Before crisis		During crisis	
	Number of IPOs	Mean return (%)	Number of IPOs	Mean return (%)	Number of IPOs	Mean return (%)
12 months	598	7.96	567	8.67	31	−5.94
24 months	576	−40.09	564	−40.79	12	4.00
36 months	558	−55.67	556	−55.89	2	5.79

Panel D: Excess or adjusted buy-and-hold returns based on the offer price and DAX

Return of	Total sample		Before crisis		During crisis	
	Number of IPOs	Mean return (%)	Number of IPOs	Mean return (%)	Number of IPOs	Mean return (%)
1st day	606	40.95	567	43.64	39	1.85
1st months	601	42.30	567	45.05	34	−3.50
12 months	598	44.76	567	47.61	31	−7.26
24 months	575	−9.94	565	−9.98	10	−8.06
36 months	561	−21.12	559	−21.12	2	−18.99

Panel E: Excess or DAX-adjusted buy-and-hold returns based on first day closing price

Return of	Total sample		Before crisis		During crisis	
	Number of IPOs	Mean return (%)	Number of IPOs	Mean return (%)	Number of IPOs	Mean return (%)
1st months	601	9.61	567	10.63	34	−7.40
12 months	598	15.20	567	16.67	31	−11.64

Table 20.7 (continued)

Panel E: Excess or DAX-adjusted buy-and-hold returns based on first day closing price

Return of	Total sample		Before crisis		During crisis	
	Number of IPOs	Mean return (%)	Number of IPOs	Mean return (%)	Number of IPOs	Mean return (%)
24 months	575	−23.33	565	−23.49	10	−14.30
36 months	561	−27.97	559	−27.97	2	−28.65

Panel F: Excess or DAX-adjusted buy-and-hold returns based on first month closing price

Return of	Total sample		Before crisis		During crisis	
	Number of IPOs	Mean return (%)	Number of IPOs	Mean return (%)	Number of IPOs	Mean return (%)
12 months	598	0.44	567	0.73	31	−4.93
24 months	574	−38.46	564	−38.82	10	−18.30
36 months	558	−44.77	556	−44.85	2	−23.50

Note: This table is made such as Table 20.4. However, it takes into consideration the unadjusted and DAX-BHARs based on the offer, the first day closing and the first month closing price before and during the financial crisis.

ing the investors into groups of absolutely informed and absolutely uninformed. Hunger (2003) argued that these assumptions might not be applicable to smaller or slight distinctions in transparency. Moreover, it could be that the disclosure requirements do not enable investors to form a closer opinion about a company and therefore fail to mitigate information asymmetry. Nevertheless, even if it is not possible to distinguish between different market segments, there is a strong relationship between market segments and underwriting.

A unique contribution to the literature is the 'GEO' variable. The hypothesis expects to have lower underpricing the closer companies are located to the stock exchange. However, the results show that the initial return of companies up to 400 miles away from the stock exchange do not differ and vary between 28.28 per cent and 33.22 per cent, while companies situated 400 miles up have only an average initial return 10.14 per cent (see panel C).

Furthermore, the SIZE variable shows that bigger issues are signified with a lower underpricing. Specifically panel D demonstrates that middle-sized IPOs (that is, €100 and €300 million) have the higher underpricing rate, while very large issues have lower initial returns. This result confirms Ritter (1991), who said that smaller issues have higher underpricing. On the other hand, if size is connected with quality, the results indicate that middle-sized companies need to signal their expected future cash flows in order to attract potential investors. An explanation for this behaviour could be the lack of recognizability by middle-sized companies. Therefore, they need to signal their quality, unlike large companies, which already have recognition and their value is well known.

Table 20.8 Short-term performance processed certain variable criteria

Panel A: Variable AGE				
Age in years	No. of IPOs	Mean – IR	MAIR (CDAX)	MAIR (DAX)
0–1	53	30.40	40.54	37.67
2–4	88	30.29	40.46	36.93
5–9	149	30.41	43.24	40.68
10–19	143	36.35	49.09	45.71
20–up	173	20.98	41.97	40.30

Panel B: Variable MAR					
Market segment	No. of IPOs	Prob. %	Mean – IR	MAIR (CDAX)	MAIR (DAX)
Regulated Market	494	81.52	31.03	47.02	43.79
Open Market	112	18.48	20.97	28.97	28.74
Transparency level	No. of IPOs	Prob. %	Mean – IR	MAIR (CDAX)	MAIR (DAX)
Prime Standard	133	21.95	5.94	18.36	18.38
General Standard	63	10.40	4.11	42.96	42.47
Entry Standard	84	13.86	14.26	19.18	20.06
NeuerMarkt	291	48.02	50.55	62.85	57.60
SMAX	23	3.80	17.98	32.70	27.91
N/D	12	1.98	21.98	52.78	50.58

Panel C: Variable GEO				
Issuer city distance from stock exchange (miles)	No. of IPOs	Mean – IR	MAIR (CDAX)	MAIR (DAX)
0–99	93	32.31	48.57	45.85
100–199	188	28.28	43.72	41.07
200–299	168	33.22	48.01	45.37
300–399	117	28.42	41.55	38.93
400–up	40	10.14	19.25	16.35

Panel D: Variable SIZE				
Capital gained (€)	No. of IPOs	Mean – IR	MAIR (CDAX)	MAIR (DAX)
500 000–9 999 999	69	13.10	22.05	21.76
10 000 000–24 999 999	109	6.27	23.14	20.60
25 000 000–49 999 999	147	22.94	41.83	38.60
50 000 000–99 999 999	114	37.23	51.94	49.00
100 000 000–199 999 999	82	61.78	74.76	71.28
200 000 000–299 999 999	27	62.09	69.64	66.70
300 000 000–499 999 999	23	41.28	49.29	47.35
500 000 000–up	35	21.09	33.57	30.69

Notes:
This table presents the unadjusted and DAX and CDAX-benchmark-adjusted initial returns based on the offer price.
The variables are shown as follows: panel A: AGE, panel B: LBC, panel C: CITY, panel D: SIZE.

5.2 Long-term Performance

Table 20.9 demonstrates how DAX and CDAX-adjusted BHARs vary according to the specific variable analysed. Initially, panel A shows that older companies perform much better than the younger ones in the second and third year of trading. In the first year of trading the results are biased and must be interpreted carefully because of the Neuer Markt, which comprises most of the younger companies. These results are consistent with Ritter (1991) who presented much better performance of older and established companies than younger and innovative ones.

Secondly, the MAR variable turns out to be as predicted. According to panel B, the IPOs in the Regulated Market perform better than the IPOs listed in the Open Market. In the first year of trading, issues from the Regulated Market generate higher returns on average compared with the benchmarks CDAX and CAX (25.66 per cent and 20.74 per cent respectively), which then turns into clearly negative adjusted returns in the second (−17.54 per cent and −22.15 per cent) and third (−23.39 per cent and −26.27 per cent) year. This is consistent with the conclusion of Bessler and Thies (2007), that in the first year the optimism between the investors is high, and decreases over time. However, the result may be market driven because the Neuer Markt has the greatest changes from year one (32.84 per cent) to year two (−35.91 per cent) and three (−37.69 per cent).

Specifically these innovative and young companies operate well in the first year of trading but they were not able to confirm these good results in the subsequent years. Therefore, many investors were disappointed by the performance and lose their interests in the second and third year of trading. Further, consistent with Pryshchepa and Stehle (2011) the Prime Standard and General Standard, which comprise the more established quality firms, only slightly underperform the CDAX and the DAX in the third year, while overperforming the benchmarks in the first and second year. This provides support in the conclusion by Pryshchepa and Stehle (2011) that IPOs belonging in the top market segments[12] of the German markets are generally a good investment. Furthermore, this distinct consideration of the segments reveals that companies from the Open Market (Entry Standard) are generally 'poor' investments with an underperformance of −17.91 per cent, −26.38 per cent and −32.88 per cent in the first, second and third year respectively. This indicates that IPOs quality improve to the companies that went public during 1970 and 1993 in this segment, which were signified by a three-year BHAR of 144.63 per cent (Ljungqvist, 1997).

Thirdly, the long-term performance of IPOs related to GEO variable is consistent with the hypothesis. According to panel C the closer the headquarter to the stock exchange the better is the long-term performance. Especially for companies located more than 400 miles away, they perform worse than companies sited less than 400 miles away. This result clearly indicates that there is a link between company's location and performance.

As in the short term, the long-term analysis also does not provide clearly consistency with the SIZE hypothesis. According to panel D very large issues do only perform better in the second and third year, where they outperform the benchmarks. This is neither consistent with Ritter (1991) who found bigger issues performing better than smaller issues in the long run, nor with Bessler and Thies (2007). Latter found smaller companies performing better than bigger companies because they would use the gained capital more efficiently.

Table 20.9 Long-term performance processed certain variable criteria

Panel A: Variable AGE

Age in years	No. of IPOs	CDAX adjusted Mean 1y	Mean 2y	Mean 3y	DAX adjusted Mean 1y	Mean 2y	Mean 3y
0–1	53	−13.42	−40.92	−37.86	−17.57	−44.76	−40.47
2–4	88	−7.29	−39.44	−36.27	−12.43	−43.57	−38.42
5–9	149	43.10	−19.68	−24.76	38.76	−23.83	−27.35
10–19	143	19.19	−19.63	−29.83	14.28	−24.28	−32.67
20–up	173	22.11	−1.12	−12.11	19.18	−5.14	−15.48

Panel B: Variable MAR

Market segment	No. of IPOs	CDAX adjusted Mean 1y	Mean 2y	Mean 3y	DAX adjusted Mean 1y	Mean 2y	Mean 3y
Regulated Market	494	25.66	−17.54	−23.39	20.74	−22.15	−26.27
Open Market	112	−8.63	−26.01	−33.51	−9.50	−28.41	−35.96

Transparency level	No. of IPOs	Mean 1y	Mean 2y	Mean 3y	Mean 1y	Mean 2y	Mean 3y
Prime Standard	133	9.21	6.64	−0.66	8.91	4.87	−3.26
General Standard	63	20.32	7.22	−4.83	19.54	5.69	−7.04
Entry Standard	84	−17.91	−26.38	−32.88	−17.10	−27.26	−34.89
Neuer Markt	291	32.84	−35.91	−37.69	25.12	−42.16	−40.73
SMAX	23	25.95	−3.83	−22.33	18.86	−10.60	−25.22
N/D	12	35.02	17.16	−15.96	30.05	9.52	−22.69

Table 20.9 (continued)

Panel C: Variable GEO

Issuer city distance from stock exchange (miles)	No. of IPOs	CDAX adjusted			DAX adjusted		
		Mean 1y	Mean 2y	Mean 3y	Mean 1y	Mean 2y	Mean 3y
0–99	93	14.61	−17.18	−24.92	10.25	−21.80	−27.97
100–199	188	13.43	−9.42	−16.29	9.56	−13.27	−19.06
200–299	168	41.79	−20.15	−26.21	37.66	−24.35	−28.87
300–399	117	10.84	−29.80	−35.88	6.70	−33.80	−38.64
400–up	40	−14.37	−37.72	−35.34	−19.73	−43.54	−38.65

Panel D: Variable SIZE

Capital gained (€)	No. of IPOs	CDAX adjusted			DAX adjusted		
		Mean 1y	Mean 2y	Mean 3y	Mean 1y	Mean 2y	Mean 3y
500 000 – 9 999 999	69	−21.85	−36.15	−36.85	−22.15	−37.41	−38.57
10 000 000 – 24 999 999	109	24.63	−13.11	−22.26	21.34	−16.69	−24.74
25 000 000 – 49 999 999	147	52.16	−17.56	−25.32	46.96	−22.67	−28.77
50 000 000 – 99 999 999	114	8.58	−28.42	−32.29	3.63	−33.17	−35.31
100 000 000 – 199 999 999	82	17.13	−18.24	−22.61	11.50	−23.72	−25.80
200 000 000 – 299 999 999	27	3.75	−17.29	−30.38	−1.05	−21.70	−32.75
300 000 000 – 499 999 999	23	5.94	−10.57	−17.79	2.55	−14.30	−20.20
500 000 000 – up	35	2.28	7.99	4.59	−1.26	5.05	2.61

Panel E: Variable *IND*

	IPOs by sector	Proportion (%)	Issuer city (away)	Population	IR %	Long-term performance (3y BHAR)	
						CDAX	DAX
Industrial	124	20.46	334.52	498 972	20.40	−26.74	−29.56
Financial services	73	12.05	315.78	970 934	17.03	−26.69	−29.21
Software	130	21.45	270.62	839 718	49.84	−39.74	−42.75
Buildings	10	1.65	150.14	529 082	9.19	35.98	37.76
Consumer stocks	33	5.45	611.67	571 684	6.37	8.21	5.41
Media	49	8.09	215.86	891 741	55.46	−40.38	−43.53
Pharma and healthcare	42	6.93	327.37	1 037 997	24.16	−15.32	−17.79
Retailers	23	3.80	199.44	450 179	23.46	−18.93	−21.49
Technology	50	8.25	380.87	617 322	35.16	−25.02	−28.23
Telecommunication	23	3.80	217.57	760 020	41.06	−10.80	−14.02
Others	49	8.09	318.29	728 455	3.81	−7.46	−10.31
Total	606	100.00					

Notes:
This table shows the DAX and CDAX-benchmark-adjusted returns based on the first day of trading of the first, second and third year of trading. The long-term performance is based on the first-day closing price and therefore without underpricing.
The variables are presented as follows: panel A: AGE, panel B: LBC, panel C: CITY, panel D: SIZE, panel E: IND.

Further, panel E classifies the sample by industry and shows the distance and the population of the issuer city, the underpricing and the DAX and CDAX-adjusted three-years BHAR according to this classification. As can be seen, the majority of companies belong to software (21.45 per cent), financial services (12.05 per cent) and industrial (20.46 per cent) sectors. On the other hand, the magnitude of underpricing varies enormously between the industries. Media (55.46 per cent), software (49.84 per cent) and telecommunication (41.06 per cent) have the highest initial returns, whereas companies from industrial (20.40 per cent) and financial services (17.03 per cent) sectors have lower underpricing. The range of underwriting is consistent with findings by Ritter (1991) who reported similar variation. However, the outcome is opposite from the expected, that is, industrial companies would have higher underpricing compared with non-industrial companies. The reason for this result is the majority of the companies were initially listed in the Neuer Markt. Thus, the high proportion of the Neuer Markt segment (media 73 per cent, software: 82 per cent and telecommunication 65 per cent), dominates the results. Further, companies from financial services have an information advantage compared with the other industries and hence generate more money through the IPO. Further, banks and insurances as they have good contacts with institutional investors are in a better negotiable position. Thus, those companies may not signal their quality, which might be another aspect of the signalling model.

Table 20.10 reports the time series estimates of the CAPM, Fama and French three-factor model and the amended with the momentum factor Fama and French four-factor model. In all cases in 24 and 36 months the intercept term is negative, with abnormal returns for the 36 months portfolio of −5.3 per cent per month under the CAPM, −5.2 per cent per month for the FF3F and −5.5 per cent per month under the FF4F model. Furthermore, all cases are signified by a statistically significant underperformance per month. Market effects are significant from FF3F for the 12 months portfolio and the FF4F for the 24 months portfolio size effect is strongly significant in both FF3F and FF4F at 12 and 24 month portfolios. The book-to-market value (BMV) effect is significantly different from zero for the 12-month portfolio in the FF4F model and 24-month portfolio in the FF4F model but not for the 36-month portfolio. The implication of the results in Table 20.10 is that much of underperformance in tables occurs because a large proportion of sample firms went public in periods (such as 1998 and in the following years 1999–2000) which were subsequently associated with highly negative abnormal returns.

6 EMPIRICAL ANALYSIS

6.1 Discussion of Results

In the estimation of the cross-sectional regression, we use BHARs, which are computed on closing prices after the first day and first month of trading. In Table 20.11, regressions (1, 2) show the results on the short-term period using IR/MAIR as dependent variables while regressions (3, 4) do further explore the MAIR using a sample of IPOs that were listed during the recent financial crises. We continue by exploring the long term returns

Table 20.10 Calendar-time regression for alternative benchmark models

	CAPM	FF3F	FF4F
Panel A: 12-month portfolio			
Alpha	0.028	0.058	0.060
t-stat	(0.65)	(1.27)	(1.19)
Beta	0.070	0.053	0.054
t-stat	(1.71)	(3.14)	(1.24)
Gamma		0.126	0.129
t-stat		(−2.26)	(2.73)
Delta		−0.086	−0.092
t-stat		(1.27)	(−2.15)
Epsilon			−0.012
t-stat			(−0.09)
AdjR^2	0.098	0.064	0.054
Panel B: 24-month portfolio			
Alpha	−0.040	−0.039	−0.027
t-stat	(−13.742)	(−4.52)	(−4.61)
Beta	0.058	0.036	0.009
t-stat	(1.410)	(−0.66)	(−2.87)
Gamma		0.003	−0.018
t-stat		(−2.46)	(−0.93)
Delta		−0.067	−0.018
t-stat		(−4.52)	(−1.14)
Epsilon			0.026
t-stat			(1.19)
AdjR^2	0.12	0.19	0.21
Panel C: 36-month portfolio			
Alpha	−0.053	−0.053	−0.055
t-stat	(−22.894)	(−22.337)	(−22.372)
Beta	0.019	0.015	0.004
t-stat	(0.464)	(0.349)	(0.086)
Gamma		0.023	−0.051
t-stat		(−0.533)	(−1.149)
Delta		0.005	0.060
t-stat		(−0.106)	(1.133)
Epsilon			0.128
t-stat			(2.445)
AdjR^2	0.091	0.083	0.074

Notes:
This table reports the regression for alternative benchmark models.
Time-series models are the capital asset pricing model. Fama and French three-factors model and the Carhart (1997) extension of Fama and French (1993) FF4F model.
Figures in brackets are the t statistics.
The regressions in each case are estimated using monthly observations. with the dependent variable being either the return on a 12-, 24-, or the 36-month portfolio of IPOs minus the risk-free rate and the independent variables being the benchmark factors.
Beta is the sensitivity of the excess returns on the company to the excess return in the market; gamma is the sensitivity of the excess returns on the company to the 'small firms premium', and as SML for FF4F; delta is the sensitivity to the HML factor in the FF4F models; epsilon is the sensitivity to the momentum factor in the FF4F model.
In the case of the FF4F model, the dependent variable $(R_{pt} - R_{ft})$ is the excess return on an equally weighted (τ = 12, 24 or 36 months) portfolio of IPOs that were issued up to month t; alpha is the intercept term.

Table 20.11 Magnitude of underpricing

Variables	(1) IR	(2) MAIR	(3) MAIR	(4) Recent fin. crises	(5) MAIR in IFRS period
Constant	−125.4***	−125.0***	−120.1***	8.419	−10.75
	(0.0001)	(0.0001)	(0.0079)	(0.484)	(0.690)
AGE	−1.675*	−1.462		−7.815	1.644
	(0.096)	(0.527)		(0.330)	(0.402)
SIZE	11.72***	11.66***	11.05***	6.971	1.572
	(0.0001)	(0.0001)	(0.0003)	(0.296)	(0.315)
UND	−5.181	−5.111		0.599	9.562
	(0.373)	(0.380)		(0.846)	(0.366)
H/C	11.93*	11.46*	10.20**		3.945
	(0.065)	(0.076)	(0.045)		(0.658)
FC	16.458**	13.52*		12.58*	2.334
	(0.015)	(0.064)		(0.092)	(0.779)
IND	−0.359	−0.367		−0.921	13.06
	(0.946)	(0.945)		(0.813)	(0.185)
REG	17.64***	17.58***	17.93***	1.956	8.095
	(0.005)	(0.005)	(0.005)	(0.738)	(0.193)
MAR	−37.02***	−36.89***	−37.71***		
	(0.0006)	(0.0008)	(0.0009)		
GO	−0.289***	−0.284***	−0.306***	0.0333	−0.126
	(0.003)	(0.0045)	(0.002)	(0.671)	(0.236)
IFRS	10.41*	10.57*	9.043**		
	(0.091)	(0.087)	(0.043)		
TLAG	−0.0699	−0.0723	−0.0753	0.0452	−0.0177
	(0.185)	(0.168)	(0.141)	(0.141)	(0.710)
BB	−27.31**	−27.07**	−27.39**	−17.553*	−30.27*
	(0.043)	(0.046)	(0.032)	(0.092)	(0.076)
Observations	596	596	596	42	176
Adj R^2	0.144	0.143	0.147	0.105	0.124

Notes:
This table presents the magnitude of underpricing (based on the unadjusted and adjusted initial returns) on the first trading day.
IR – measures the unadjusted returns at the end of the first day of trading.
MAIR – returns to investors in the end of first day of trading adjusted with the returns of the market.
AGE – age of the firm starting from the year of its establishment until the year it goes public.
SIZE – the logarithm of the total market capitalization of an IPO.
UND – underwriters' reputation: '1' for reputable underwriters and '0' for non-reputable.
H/C – IPOs listed in the hot period get the value '1' and IPOs listed in the cold period get the value '0'.
FC – financial crises: '1' IPOs listed before the recent financial crises and '0' for IPOs listed after the recent financial crises.
IND – '1' IPOs defined as industrial, that is, chemical, industrial (pure), Manufacturing, Metals, Minerals and Shipyards and '0' for all other.
REG – Regulated Market: '1' for IPOs listed in regulated markets and '0' for other markets.
MAR – market classification: we insert the value '1' if an IPO is listed in Main Market and '0' if listed in the Parallel or New Markets.
GO – given ownership measured by the total number of shares sold in proportion to the number of shares outstanding at the point in time of the IPO.

Table 20.11 (continued)

Notes:
IFRS – takes into consideration companies listed before and after IFRS. IPOs issued before IFRS '1' and IPOs listed after IFRS '0' adoption.
TLAG – period between IPO announcement (the date of prospectus) and first day of trading.
BB – book-building mechanism: IPOs listed with bookbuilding '1' and IPOs issued with another method '0'.
***   Significance at the 1 per cent level.
**   Significance at the 5 per cent level.
*   Significance at the 10 per cent level.
T-statistics are robust for heteroscedasticity using the Newey-West HAC Standard Errors and Covariance process.

using one, two and three-year BHARs and FF4F-CARs. The results can be seen in Tables 20.12 and 20.13.

The coefficient for AGE_i is negative and statistically significant for IR, indicating that IPOs with a short operating history before going public are highly associated with short-term initial returns/underpricing. The result turns exactly the opposite in the long-term, when FF4F-CARs is employed and consistent with Ritter (1991), older IPOs experience better returns in a period up to three years after going public.

The firm size, a proxy for *ex ante* uncertainty, is measured by the capital raised during the offering. To be consistent with Miller's (1977) prediction (that is, a negative relationship between the long-run performance and uncertainty), regressions should yield positive coefficients for Log(Size) because the *ex ante* uncertainty is inversely related to a firm's size. Our findings using BHAR as a dependent variable strongly reveal that large IPOs offer significantly better short and long-term adjusted returns in a period up to three years. The last result aligns with previous studies (Keloharju, 1993; Goergen et al., 2007), which predict better long-term performance for large IPOs.

Further, a factor that proves to affect the newly listed firms' is hot/cold market conditions during the listing period. In the short term, we do not find any association between market conditions and returns. In the long term, the findings show that 'hot' IPOs have significantly better returns. A positive sign indicates that IPO issuers should be very careful with the timing of the listing, and they should decide to go public only when bullish periods are prevailing in the market. The findings hold in every period in the long term and signal that buying in 'hot' market conditions can prove a good investment decision for the future.

The coefficient for market conditions measured by 'hot' and 'cold' market, indicate that IPOs listed on the Frankfurt Stock Exchange with a reputable underwriter will immediately reward their investors with positive returns. The results reveal exactly the opposite in the long term as there is a negative determinant in two regressions out of four (one and three years). The finding suggests the possibility that reputable underwriters foster high aftermarket prices in the short run (that is, in the first month of trading), producing more pronounced subsequent negative returns.

Market classification has traditionally been one of the most researched variables in the literature. Results on the German case show that IPOs listed in the parallel or new market experience high level of underpricing. Results swap in the long run and confirms the positive returns taken for the IPOs listed in the main market of the stock exchange.

Table 20.12 Results of multiple regressions using three-year BHARs

Variables	(1) Y1D1	(2) Y2D1	(3) Y3D1	(4) Y1M1	(5) Y2M1	(6) Y3M1
Constant	−44.17	−125.3***	−131.6**	−5.159	−115.3***	−89.03
	(0.287)	(0.002)	(0.026)	(0.905)	(0.003)	(0.284)
AGE	3.652	6.606***	1.682	3.964	6.314**	1.817
	(0.167)	(0.005)	(0.464)	(0.185)	(0.014)	(0.467)
SIZE	1.638	3.250	5.087***	0.503	3.646*	4.755***
	(0.464)	(0.122)	(0.003)	(0.820)	(0.052)	(0.009)
UND	3.757	−2.781	−3.755	−5.531	−3.935	−6.120
	(0.613)	(0.664)	(0.413)	(0.538)	(0.511)	(0.205)
H/C	41.75***	−23.43***	−26.26***	50.68***	−15.63**	−23.64***
	(1.07e−06)	(0.001)	(3.94e−08)	(1.36e−06)	(0.0126)	(2.67e−06)
FC	−48.44***	23.41	53.32	−57.98***	8.939	11.39
	(0.0001)	(0.254)	(0.327)	(2.77e−05)	(0.673)	(0.885)
IND	6.540	2.602	−5.327	0.762	2.019	−5.265
	(0.476)	(0.714)	(0.325)	(0.927)	(0.773)	(0.343)
REG	−2.440	−0.133	−2.726	−11.09	0.0773	−3.389
	(0.805)	(0.989)	(0.696)	(0.212)	(0.993)	(0.642)
MAR	−4.693	17.53**	−4.064	−7.556	17.70**	−0.743
	(0.615)	(0.029)	(0.522)	(0.467)	(0.0172)	(0.914)
GO	0.0717	0.196	−0.0349	−0.0598	0.147	−0.00550
	(0.637)	(0.326)	(0.822)	(0.741)	(0.404)	(0.971)
IFRS	28.39***	−17.93*	−36.72***	30.55***	−16.63*	−34.38***
	(0.005)	(0.098)	(3.40e−05)	(0.002)	(0.095)	(0.001)
TLAG	−0.0631	−0.0746	−0.0728	−0.0593	−0.0930	−0.0836
	(0.507)	(0.279)	(0.189)	(0.507)	(0.169)	(0.138)
BB	−3.698	3.570	−8.039	−2.630	1.347	−5.555
	(0.736)	(0.811)	(0.594)	(0.805)	(0.923)	(0.702)
Obs.	604	564	548	587	564	548
AdjR^2	0148	0.161	0.181	0.145	0.154	0.182

Notes:
This table reports the results of multiple regressions using one-, two- and three-year BHAR. Multivariate regression analysis of cross-sectional variation in long-run market index-adjusted (excess) returns subsequent to listing for 606 German initial public offers of ordinary equity made between January 1992 and June 2012, calculated on the basis of an investment in each issue purchased at the closing price of the first day or first month, for a holding period of one-, two- and three years for various explanatory variables, with related t-statistics in parentheses.
Y3D1 – adjusted returns for market effect from first-day price to three years after going public.
Y3M1 – adjusted returns for market effect from first-month price to three years after going public.
AGE – age of the firm starting from the year of its establishment until the year it goes public.
SIZE – the logarithm of the total market capitalization of an IPO.
UND – underwriters' reputation: '1' for reputable underwriters and '0' for non-reputable.
H/C – IPOs listed in the hot period get the value '1' and IPOs listed in the cold period get the value '0'.
FC – financial crises: '1' IPOs listed before the recent financial crises and '0' for IPOs listed after the recent financial crises.
IND – '1' IPOs defined as industrial, that is, chemical, industrial (pure), manufacturing, metals, minerals and shipyards and '0' for all other.
REG – Regulated Market: '1' for IPOs listed in regulated markets and '0' for other markets.
MAR – market classification: we insert the value '1' if an IPO is listed in Main Market and '0' if listed in the Parallel or New Markets.

Table 20.12 (continued)

Notes:
GO – given ownership measured by the total number of shares sold in proportion to the number of shares outstanding at the point in time of the IPO.
IFRS – takes into consideration companies listed before and after IFRS. IPOs issued before IFRS '1' and IPOs listed after IFRS adoption '0'.
TLAG – period between IPO announcement (the date of prospectus) and first day of trading.
BB – book-building mechanism: IPOs listed with bookbuilding '1' and IPOs issued with another method '0'.
***   Significance at the 1 per cent level.
**   Significance at the 5 per cent level.
*   Significance at the 10 per cent level.
T-statistics are robust for heteroscedasticity using the Newey-West HAC Standard Errors and Covariance process.

The result is consistent with Ljungqvist et al. (2003) and Schlag and Wodrich (2004), who report that IPOs traded in the primary market yield significantly high returns in the long run, whereas those that are listed in the secondary market tend to underperform their market benchmarks by more negative results.

An interesting finding of this study relates to the 'time lag' variable, the period between the IPO announcement and the first day of trading period. In the long term, once FF4F is employed as a metric for the performance of new listed firms, IPOs with a short waiting period reward their investors with better returns. Further listing with a book-building mechanism appear to have a significant effect in the performance of IPOs. Specifically, those firms which choose to go public with book-building leave 'less money on the table' compared with the IPOs which choose an alternative method. There is no further effect in the long term as the information is all absorbed in the immediate aftermarket period.

6.2   Adoption of IFRS

Towards our effort to explore recent financial development we examine the relationship between the performance of German IPOs and the adoption of IFRS. Table 20.11 shows strong significance as IFRS adoption significantly reduce the level of underpricing in the short term. On the other hand, during the German GAAP period, when all previous German studies took place, underpricing has been at higher level. The results continue to be exciting in the long term. Sub-sample analysis into one, two and three years making use of market or market-size BMV and momentum effects reveal a very interesting picture.

The coefficient in one year (that is, adjustment for market effect) is positive and highly statistically significant (at the 1 per cent level) for the IFRS sub-sample. The magnitude of the coefficient suggests that adoption of IFRS is associated with better long-term returns in a period up to a year, *ceteris paribus*. In contrast, the effect disappears in the second year after listing, and alternates in the third year as IPOs switching to IFRS offer poor returns to their loyal investors. Robustness check reveal that the results hold no matter if we calculate from the end of first day or first month of trading.

Table 20.13 present the results for the long-term analysis adjusted for market-size

Table 20.13 Results of multiple regressions using one-, two- and three-year FF4F-CARs

Variables	(1) FF4F1Y1D	(2) FF4F2Y1D	(3) FF4Y3Y1D	(4) FF4F1Y1M	(5) FF4F2Y1M	(6) FF4Y3Y1M
Constant	11.26	−144.1***	−105.1***	9.507	−143.9***	−103.0***
	(0.830)	(0.0002)	(0.002)	(0.855)	(0.0004)	(0.005)
AGE	2.482	6.384***	4.118**	2.029	6.101**	3.849*
	(0.517)	(0.004)	(0.0447)	(0.587)	(0.012)	(0.082)
SIZE	−0.517	4.238**	2.538	−0.355	4.193*	2.370
	(0.853)	(0.045)	(0.215)	(0.899)	(0.053)	(0.268)
UND	1.263	1.566	1.916	−3.797	−1.396	−0.532
	(0.898)	(0.801)	(0.690)	(0.691)	(0.826)	(0.915)
H/C	85.79***	20.79***	−4.762	85.92***	23.61***	−3.652
	(0.002)	(0.001)	(0.355)	(0.0001)	(0.0005)	(0.498)
FC	−81.33***	−46.46***	−35.74***	−82.67***	−48.94***	−36.95***
	(0.0078)	(0.0004)	(0.0004)	(0.0003)	(0.0005)	(0.008)
IND	2.758	3.468	−3.057	−0.803	2.614	−3.652
	(0.772)	(0.607)	(0.538)	(0.927)	(0.706)	(0.481)
REG	−10.81	4.912	−0.196	−11.72	6.195	−0.0288
	(0.344)	(0.587)	(0.977)	(0.228)	(0.518)	(0.997)
MAR	−7.048	41.26***	47.37***	−0.651	44.69***	50.66***
	(0.513)	(0.0001)	(0.0006)	(0.951)	(0.0001)	(0.0007)
GO	−0.0767	0.188	0.0354	−0.0577	0.190	0.0399
	(0.710)	(0.300)	(0.830)	(0.760)	(0.273)	(0.804)
IFRS	45.38***	23.29**	12.24	46.50***	26.89**	14.86
	(0.0006)	(0.022)	(0.175)	(0.0002)	(0.0111)	(0.119)
TLAG	−0.134	−0.177***	−0.0659	−0.172**	−0.190***	−0.0782*
	(0.179)	(0.003)	(0.173)	(0.0446)	(0.00137)	(0.0957)
BB	−4.038	−0.584	−1.367	−2.946	0.228	−0.0179
	(0.726)	(0.960)	(0.912)	(0.790)	(0.985)	(0.999)
Obs.	593	593	593	593	593	593
AdjR^2	0.106	0.118	0.180	0.108	0.120	0.178

Notes:
This table reports the results of multiple regressions using one-, two- and three-year FF4F-CARs. Multivariate regression analysis of cross-sectional variation in long-run market index-adjusted (excess) returns – CARs for the Fama and French (FF) four-factor model $R_{pt}-R_{ft} = \alpha_i + \beta_i(R_{mt}-R_{ft}) + \gamma_i SMB_t + \delta_i HML_t + \varepsilon_i UMD_t + \varepsilon_{pt}$ subsequent to listing for 606 German initial public offers of ordinary equity made between January 1992 and June 2012, calculated on the basis of an investment in each issue purchased at the closing price of the first day or first month, for a holding period of one-, two- and three years for various explanatory variables with related *t*-statistics in parentheses.
FF4F3Y1D – adjusted returns for market, size, BMV and momentum effect from first-day price to three years after going public.
FF4F3Y1M – adjusted returns for market, size, BMV and momentum effect from first-month price to three years after going public.
AGE – age of the firm starting from the year of its establishment until the year it goes public.
SIZE – the logarithm of the total market capitalization of an IPO.
UND – underwriters' reputation: '1' for reputable underwriters and '0' for non-reputable.
H/C – IPOs listed in the hot period get the value '1' and IPOs listed in the cold period get the value '0'.
FC – financial crises: '1' IPOs listed before the recent financial crises and '0' for IPOs listed after the recent financial crises.

Table 20.13 (continued)

Notes:
IND – '1' IPOs defined as industrial, that is, chemical, industrial (pure), manufacturing, metals, minerals and shipyards and '0' for all other.
REG – Regulated Market: '1' for IPOs listed in regulated markets and '0' for other markets.
MAR – market classification: we insert the value '1' if an IPO is listed in Main Market and '0' if listed in the Parallel or New Markets.
GO – given ownership measured by the total number of shares sold in proportion to the number of shares outstanding at the point in time of the IPO.
IFRS – takes into consideration companies listed before and after IFRS adoption.
IPOs issued before IFRS '1' and IPOs listed after IFRS '0'.
TLAG – period between IPO announcement (the date of prospectus) and first day of trading.
BB – book-building mechanism: IPOs listed with bookbuilding '1' and IPOs issued with another method '0'.
***   Significance at the 1 per cent level.
**   Significance at the 5 per cent level.
*   Significance at the 10 per cent level.
T-statistics are robust for heteroscedasticity using the Newey-West HAC Standard Errors and Covariance process.

BMV and momentum effects. The most interesting outcome concern the change of the coefficient in a three year period as it turns positive but statistically insignificant. Further, in addition to one year after listing, IPO going public with IFRS continue to offer good returns to their investors in a period covering at least two years.

6.3 Financial Crises Effect

The recent financial crisis is not like anything that has been explored over the past decades. It has deep characteristics which makes it unique, an outcome of countries' wrong financial strategies for decades and it will be here long term (that is, at least four years), as French President Francois Holland recently declared. It is therefore interesting to examine whether such a crisis is associated with opportunities for risk premium investors.

Short-term findings reveal that firms listed before the financial crises are positively related with good returns to their investors. Crises brought a turnaround and returns were dramatically reduced. Strangely, in the long-term arena, IPOs with a listing during the financial crisis appear to provide spectacular returns to investors in any time framework. A logical explanation can be the low starting point, those IPOs have either in terms of offer price or as a price at the end of the first-day of trading.

Table 20.11 presents the results on the effects of the financial crisis to the performance of IPOs using a model (4) dedicated to this period. The dependent variable here is a binary variable taking the value of one for IPOs which have gone public during the recent financial crisis and zero for IPOs which were listed prior to the crisis. Based on those, the time lag between offer price announcement and listing appears to be positively related to underpricing, indicating that IPOs which show a reluctance to start trading are penalized with a large amount of money left on the table. Uncertainty, which is highly related to crises periods, forced low-quality IPOs to delay their listing and revealed high-quality firms.

7 CONCLUSION

Initial public offerings in Germany have been part of many discussions and research studies. Unlike previous evidence, this chapter attempts to provide evidence on an expanded sample of German IPOs listed between 1992 and 2012 covering two major amendments on the financial market: IFRS adoption and the recent financial crisis. The purpose has been to provide insights on the performance of IPOs within this context and, in particular, to exlore if severe underpricing phenomenon can be mitigated through IFRS and if new standards can lead to a better IPO performance in the long run.

Results indicate that IFRS adoption has reduced underpricing in Germany and has significantly affected its long-term performance. This clearly shows the advantage of preparing IFRS accounts which might be an incentive for private companies to use IFRS voluntarily. Similarly, firms that have gone public during the recent financial crisis offered significantly less initial returns to their aftermarket investors. Findings reveal initial returns of 48.02 per cent for IPOs from the Neuer Market with General Standard at 10.40 per cent and Prime Standard 21.95 per cent. This result indicates that stricter transparency measures do not necessarily mitigate underpricing. Further, going public with a book-building mechanism is worth it as it alleviates underpricing phenomenon.

In response to the questions raised in the introduction, the findings of this chapter imply that: (1) the recent financial market crisis has a strong influence on IPOs behaviour on the Frankfurt Stock Exchange; (2) the mandatory IFRS adoption reduced information asymmetry and thus the level of underpricing in Germany; and (3) the performance of German IPOs in the long term before and after IFRS adoption depends on the benchmarks we employ. Once we adjust only for market effect, IPOs going public during German Generally Accepted Accounting Principles (AGAAP) perform better for up to a year but underperform compared with IFRS-listed companies in two and three years' time. Switching to the more sophisticated FF4F model, AGAAP-listed firms perform better up to 24 months. Overall, this chapter sheds more light on the long-standing puzzle of IPO behaviour in financial crises – an important corporate finance issue.

NOTES

1. In fact, the International Accounting Standards Board (IASB) publishes these accounting principles, which then have to be enacted into law by the European Parliament. In September 2002 the Regulation (EC) No.1606/2002 were passed and designated the application of IFRS from 1 January 2005.
2. In order to prevent confusion, this study will always state the English term for the segments (Regulated and Open Markets) and the transparency level (Prime, General and Entry Standards). However, if earlier studies differentiate between the segments, this will be marked using the original German term (Amtlicher Markt, Geregelter Markt, Ungeregelter Freiverkehr and Neuer Markt).
3. In fact, these are the German Security Trade Act (Wertpapierhandelsgesetz – WpHG), the German Stock Exchange Act (Börsengesetz – BörsG), the German Securities Prospectus Act (Wertpapierprospektgesetz – WpPG) as well as the Stock Exchange Admission Regulation and the Exchange Rules.
4. Since the International Accounting Standards (IAS) have been renamed to International Financial Reporting Standards (IFRS), this study uses the last name throughout for simplicity.
5. Please refer to s. 238 Abs. 1239 Abs 2–4 and 252 Abs. 1 Nr. 4 HGB.
6. Compare for instance, Ball et al. (2000), Van Tendeloo and Vanstraelen (2005) and Nobes and Parker (2010).
7. Please compare ss. 253 Abs. 3 Satz 4 and 253 Abs. 5 HGB n. F.
8. This is based on s. 340e Abs. 3 s. 1 HGB n. F., which regulates the reporting of financial instruments for banks.

9. See also Bessler and Thies (2007).
10. At this point time four segments existed on the German market: Amtlicher Markt, Geregelter Markt, Ungeregelter Freiverkehr and Neuer Markt.
11. See also, for instance, La Porta et al. (2000) and Franks et al. (2009) for further information.
12. Pryshchepa and Stehle (2011) analysed the Amtlicher Markt as the top market segment, while this study refers to Prime and General Standard. This is just a necessary adoption due to changes in the German market segment regulations.

REFERENCES

Allen, F. and G. Faulhaber (1989), 'Signaling by underpricing in the IPO market', *Journal of Financial Economics*, **23**, 303–23.
Ball, R., S.P. Kothari and A. Robin (2000), 'The effect of international institutional factors on properties of accounting earnings', *Journal of Accounting and Economics*, **29**, 1–51.
Baron, D. (1982), 'A model of the demand for investment banking advising and distribution services for new issues', *Journal of Finance*, **37**, 955–76.
Baron, D. and B. Holmström (1980), 'The investment banking contract for new issues under asymmetric information: delegation and the incentive', *Journal of Finance*, **35**, 1115–38.
Beatty, R. and J.R. Ritter (1986), 'Investment banking, reputation, and the underpricing of initial public offerings', *Journal of Financial Economics*, **15**, 213–32.
Benveniste, L. and P.A. Spindt (1989), 'How investment bankers determine the offer price and allocate new issues', *Journal of Financial Economics*, **24**, 343–61.
Bessler, W. and A. Kurth (2007), 'Agency problems and the performance of venture-backed ipos in Germany: exit strategies, lock-up periods, and bank ownership', *European Journal of Finance*, **13**, 29–63.
Bessler, W. and S. Thies (2007), 'The long-run performance of initial public offerings in Germany', *Managerial Finance*, **33**, 420–41.
Bessler, W., W. Drobetz and M. Seim (2014), 'Share repurchases of initial public offerings: Motives, valuation effects, and the impact of market regulation', *European Journal of Finance*, forthcoming.
Carhart, M. (1997), 'On persistence in mutual fund performance', *Journal of Finance*, **52**, 57–82.
Deutsche Börse Group (2000), Rules and regulations Neuer Markt, Frankfurt: Frankfurt Stock Exchange.
Deutsche Börse Group (2009), *Factbook 2009*, Frankfurt: Frankfurt Stock Exchange.
Deutsche Börse Group (2011), *Deutsche Börse Listing Guide*, Frankfurt: Frankfurt Stock Exchange.
Dietrich, D. and U. Vollmer (2012), 'Are universal banks bad for financial stability? Germany during the world financial crisis', *Quarterly Review of Economics and Finance*, **52** (2), 123–34.
Eichler, S. and K. Hielscher (2012), 'Does the ecb act as a lender of last resort during the subprime lending crisis? Evidence from monetary policy reaction models', *Journal of International Money and Finance*, **31**, 552–68.
Elston, J.A. and J.J. Yang (2010), 'Venture capital, ownership structure, accounting standards and IPO underpricing: evidence from Germany', *Journal of Economics and Business*, **62**, 517–36.
Fama, E. and K. French (1993), 'Common risk factors in the returns on bonds and stocks', *Journal of Financial Economics*, **33**, 3–56.
Fama, E. and K. French (1996), 'Multifactor explanations of asset pricing anomalies', *Journal of Finance*, **51**, 55–84.
Gao, X., J.R. Ritter and Z. Zhu (2011), 'Where have all the IPOS gone?', Working Paper, Warrington Business School.
Goergen, M., A. Khurshed and R. Mudambi (2007), 'The long run performance of IPOS: can it be predicted', *Managerial Finance*, **33**, 401–19.
Grinblatt, M. and C. Hwang (1989), 'Signaling and the price of new issue', *Journal of Finance*, **44**, 47–58.
Horton, J., G. Serafeim and I. Serafeim (2013), 'Does mandatory IFRS adoption improve the information environment', *Contemporary Accounting Research*, **30**, 388–423.
Hunger, A. (2003), 'Market segmentation and IPO-underpricing: the German experience', working paper, Ludwig-Maximilians-Universität München, February.
Ibbotson, R. and J. Jaffe (1975), 'Hot issue markets', *Journal of Finance*, **30**, 1027–42.
Jensen, M. and W. Meckling (1976), 'Theory of the firm: managerial behaviours agency costs and ownership structure', *Journal of Financial Economics*, **3**, 305–60.
Keloharju, M. (1993), 'The winner's curse, legal liability, and the long-run price performance of initial public offerings in Finland', *Journal of Financial Economics*, **34**, 251–77.
La Porta, R., F. Lopez-de-Silanes, A. Shleifer and R. Vishny (2000), 'Investor protection and corporate governance', *Journal of Financial Economics*, **58**, 3–27.

Liu, X. and J.R. Ritter (2010), 'The economic consequences of IPO spinning', *Review of Financial Studies*, **23**, 2024–59.
Ljungqvist, A. (1997), 'Pricing initial public offerings: further evidence from Germany', *European Economic Review*, **41**, 1309–20.
Ljungqvist, A., T. Jenkinson and W. Wilhelm (2003), 'Global integration in primary equity markets: the role of U.S. banks and U.S. investors', *Review of Financial Studies*, **16**, 63–99.
Loughran, T. and J.R. Ritter (1995), 'The new issues puzzle', *Journal of Finance*, **50**, 23–51.
Loughran, T., J.R. Ritter and K. Rydqvist (1994), 'Initial public offerings: international insights', *Pacific-Basin Finance Journal*, **2**, 165–99. (An update is available on Jay Ritter's website.)
Miller, R. (1977), 'Risk, uncertainty and divergence of opinions', *Journal of Finance*, **32**, 1151–68.
Mitchell, M.L. and E. Stafford (2000), 'Managerial decisions and long-run stock price performance', *Journal of Business*, **73**, 287–320.
Nobes, C. and R. Parker (2010), *Comparative International Accounting*, 11th edn, London: Financial Times/Prentice Hall.
Oehler, A., M. Rummer and P. Smith (2005), 'IPO pricing and the relative importance of investor sentiment – evidence from Germany', working paper, University of Bamberg.
Paananen, M. and H. Lin (2008), 'The development of accounting quality of IAS and IFRS over time: the case of Germany', working paper, University of Portland.
Pryshchepa, O. and R. Stehle (2011), 'Long-run stock performance of German initial public offerings: survey and update', working paper, University of Lancaster.
Ritter, J.R. (1984), 'The hot issue market of 1980', *Journal of Business*, **57**, 215–40.
Ritter, J.R. (1991), 'The long performance of initial public offerings', *Journal of Finance*, **46**, 3–28.
Rock, K. (1986), 'Why new issues are underpriced', *Journal of Financial Economics*, **15**, 187–212.
Sapusek, A. (2000), 'Benchmark-sensitivity of IPO long-run performance: an empirical study for Germany', *Schmalenbach Business Review*, **52**, 374–405.
Schlag, C. and A. Wodrich (2004), 'Has there always been underpricing and long-run underperformance? IPOs in Germany before World War I', working paper, Johann Wolfgang Goethe-University Frankfurt.
Schuster, J. (1996), 'Underpricing and crises – IPO performance in Germany', Discussion Paper 252, Financial Markets Group, London School or Economics.
Soderstrom, N. and K. Sun (2007), 'IFRS adoption and accounting quality: a review', *European Accounting Review*, **16**, 675–702.
Stehle, R., O. Ehrhardt and R. Przyborowsky (2000), 'Long-run stock performance of German initial public offerings and seasoned equity issues', *European Financial Management*, **6** (2), 173–96.
Thomadakis, S., D. Gounopoulos and C. Nounis (2012), 'Long term performance of Greek IPOS', *European Financial Management*, **18**, 117–41.
Thomadakis, S., D. Gounopoulos, C. Nounis and A. Merikas (2012), 'Price cap effect in the performance of Greek IPOs', Working Paper, University of Surrey.
Van Tendeloo, B. and A. Vanstraelen (2005), 'Earnings management and German GAAP versus IFRS', *European Accounting Review*, **14**, 155–80.
Vismara, S., S. Paleari and J.R. Ritter (2012), 'Europe's second markets for small companies', *European Financial Management*, **18**, 352–88.
Wasserfallen, W. and C. Wittleder (1994), 'Pricing initial public offerings evidence from Germany', *European Economic Review*, **38**, 1505–17.
Welch, I. (1989), 'Seasoned offerings, limitations costs and the underpricing of initial public offerings', *Journal of Finance*, **44**, 421–49.
Zimmermann, J. and Werner, J. (2006), 'Fair value accounting under IAS/IFRS: concepts, reasons, criticisms', in G.N. Gregoriou and M. Gaber (eds), *International Accounting Standards, Regulations and Financial Reporting*, London: Elsevier.

APPENDIX

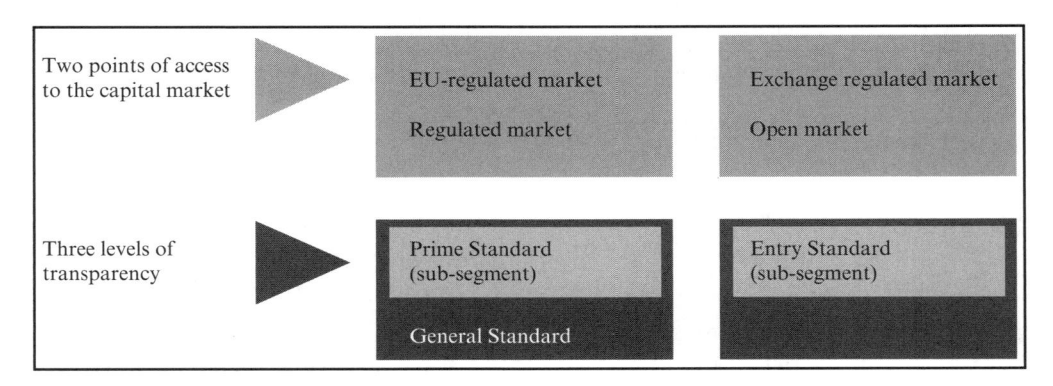

Source: Deutsche Börse Group (2012).

Figure 20.A1 Market segments and transparency levels of the FSE

Table 20.A1 Some important differences between German GAAP and IFRS

Topic	German GAAP	IFRS
1. Fixed assets	HCA or lower (s. 253 Abs. 1, 3, 5 HGB)	First, at cost (IAS 16.15) and later at 'Cost model' or 'Revaluation model' for all investments (IAS 16.29)
2. Goodwill (G)	Original G: Prohibition, derivative G: HCA or lower (s. 246 Abs. 1 Satz 4 HGB)	First, at cost (IAS 38.21) and later at 'Cost model' or 'Revaluation model' for all investments (IAS 38.72)
3. Financial instruments	HCA or lower (s. 253 Abs. 1, 3-5 HGB) (except banks)	First, at fair value (IAS 39.43) and later at amortized costs or fair value (derivatives, IAS 39.47)
4. Investment property	HCA or lower (s. 253 Abs. 1, 3, 5 HGB)	First, at cost (IAS 40.20) and later at 'Cost model' or 'Revaluation model' for all investments (IAS 40.30)

Table 20.A2   Empirical evidence on German IPOs

Panel A: Empirical evidence on underpricing for German IPOs

Journal article	Sample period	No. of IPOs	Underpricing (IR)	Market segment
Wasserfallen & Wittleder (1994)	1961–1987	92	17.60	All
Schuster (1996)	1988–95	126	8.83	All
Ljungqvist (1997)	1970–93	189	10.57	All
	1970–93	180	9.22	All but Ungeregelter Freiverkehr
	1970–93	9	37.48	Ungeregelter Freiverkehr
Hunger (2003)	1997–2001	387	21.9	All
	1997–2001	69	9.31	Official Trading
	1997–2001	41	9.62	Regulated Market
	1997–2001	21	30.27	Unofficial Regulated Market
	1997–2001	256	26.57	Neuer Markt
Elston and Yang (2010)	1996–2001	320	52.15	All
	1996–2001	131	35.81	VC-backed
	1996–2001	189	63.48	Non-VC-backed

Panel B: Empirical evidence on long-term performance for German IPOs

Journal article	Sample period	No. of IPOs	Long-term perf.*	Market segment	Adjustment (long run)
Schuster (1996)	1988–95	126	−14.13	All	FAZ index (CAR)
Ljungqvist (1997)	1970–93	189	19.85	All	DAFOX (BHAR)
	1970–93	180	−12.11	All but Ungeregelter Freiverkehr	DAFOX (BHAR)
	1970–1993	9	−143.63	Ungeregelter Freiverkehr	DAFOX (BHAR)
Sapusek (2000)	1983–93	142	−20.03	All	Matching firms (BHAR)
	1983–93	142	−10.48	All	DAFOX (BHAR)
	1983–93	142	1.66	All	DAX (BHAR)
Stehle et al. (2000)	1960–92	187	−6.61	All	Size portfolio (BHAR)
	1960–92	187	1.54	All	Market portfolio (BHAR)
Bessler and Thies (2007)	1977–95	218	−12.7	All	DAX (BHAR)
Pryshchepa and Stehle (2011)	1960–2004	170	−8.34	Amtlicher Markt	CDAX (BHAR)
	1960–2004	170	−7.15	Amtlicher Markt	Size portfolio (BHAR)

Note: *36-month BHAR without IR.

Table 20.A3 Variables definitions

Variable name in abbreviation	Variable definition
Panel A: Measures of abnormal returns	
IR	Measures the returns at the end of the first day of trading
MAIR	Returns to investors in the end of first day of trading adjusted with the returns of the market. Adjusted initial returns (RIR) are adjusted for market changes taking into account the Frankfurt Stock Exchange General Index (DAX) between the offer price closing date and the end of first day of trading
Y3D1	Adjusted returns for market effect from first-day price to three years after going public
Y3M1	Adjusted returns for market effect from first-month price to three years after going public
FF4F1Y1D	Adjusted returns from first day price to first year after going public
FF4F2Y1D	Adjusted returns from first day price to two years after going public
FF4Y3Y1D	Adjusted returns from first day price to three years after going public
FF4F1Y1M	Adjusted returns from the end of first month of trading to first year after going public
FF4F2Y1M	Adjusted returns from the end of first month of trading to two years after going public
FF4Y3Y1M	Adjusted returns from the end of first month of trading to three years after going public
Panel B: Definition of Accounting Standards	
GAAP	German Generally Accepted Accounting Principles (DGAAP) refer to the standard framework of guidelines for financial accounting used in Germany, generally known as accounting standards. GAAP includes the standards, conventions, and rules accountants follow in recording and summarizing, and in the preparation of financial statements
IFRS	International Financial Reporting Standards (IFRS) are principles-based standards, interpretations and the framework adopted by the International Accounting Standards Board. In order to be approved for use in the Netherlands, standards must be endorsed by the Accounting Regulatory Committee (ARC), which is advised by a group of accounting experts known as the European Financial Reporting Advisory Group
Panel C: IPOs characteristics	
AGE	Age of the firm starting from the year of its establishment until the year it goes public
SIZE	Market capitalization measured by log of the total number of outstanding shares after the IPO multiplied by price per share
UND	Dummy variable: '1' for reputable underwriters, '0' otherwise
H/C	IPO listed in hot periods '1' and IPOs listed during cold periods gets '0'
FC	Dummy variable: '1' for before financial crisis, '0' for during financial crisis
IND	This research defined as 'industrial' IPOs those firms which belong to chemical, industrial (pure), manufacturing, metals, minerals & shipyards sub-sectors and attached to them a value of one. Those not industrial are mainly conglomerate, real estate/property, transportation, tourism/hotels etc. and get the value of zero

Table 20.A3 (continued)

Variable name in abbreviation	Variable definition
Panel C: IPOs characteristics	
REG	Dummy variable: '1' for Regulated Market and '0' for other markets
MAR	Dummy variable: '1' if an IPO is listed in Main Market and '0' if listed in Parallel or New Market
GO	Given ownership measured by the total number of shares sold in proportion to the number of shares outstanding at the point in time of the IPO
IFRS	Takes into consideration companies listed before and after IFRS. IPOs issued before IFRS '1' and IPOs listed after IFRS '0'
TLAG	Period between IPO announcement (the date of prospectus) and first day of trading
BB	Dummy variable: IPOs listed with bookbuilding '1' and IPOs issued with another method '0'

Note: *Adjusted returns for market, size, BMV and momentum effect.

PART VI

SPECIAL TYPES OF IPOS

21 The IPO as an exit strategy for venture capitalists: regional lessons from Canada with international comparisons
Douglas Cumming and Sofia Johan

1 INTRODUCTION

The quantity and quality of innovation capital is essential for the success of the development of knowledge-based growth firms in the twenty-first century (Audretsch, 2007a, 2007b). In this regard, government bodies around the world provide much needed support to entrepreneurs and innovators in their capital raising efforts (see, for example, Cumming, 2007 World Bank, 2004) to facilitate the healthy growth of knowledge-based economies. This support comes in the form of indirect government intervention with tax subsidies and other entrepreneur-friendly regulation (for example, lenient bankruptcy laws and lax securities laws), as well as direct government programs to provide capital for entrepreneurs. One rationale for this support is that there is a perception of the existence of a capital gap for entrepreneurs, since the risks to financing early stage high-technology firms is very pronounced and the rewards not sufficient to entice enough investors. A second rationale is that there are returns to society for having innovation and entrepreneurship. Since the private returns do not account for the social returns, there is an insufficient supply of capital for innovation and entrepreneurship.

It is, unfortunately, difficult to ascertain whether there is in fact a capital gap in financing entrepreneurs. Not all entrepreneurs who apply for capital should be funded, as not all projects are positive net present value projects. And it is these entrepreneurs who mainly complain of a capital gap. There is some evidence, however, that entrepreneurs are typically able to obtain the capital that they need, albeit not in the form they always want (Cosh et al., 2009). Some types of capital are more suited to fast-growing businesses, and certain investors mainly provide value-added assistance to their investees to facilitate the growth of the entrepreneurial firm and bring the investment to fruition.

Venture capital (VC) finance is viewed as being among the more important types of capital for entrepreneurs, if not the most important. Entrepreneurs benefit not only from the financial investment, but more significantly from having access to value-added VC investors with coaching and training ability (for example, financial, strategic, marketing, legal, administrative and human resource advice), and investors with an ability to connect entrepreneurs to others that afford strategic alliances to help the entrepreneurial firm grow and prosper. Small high-technology firms contribute disproportionately to innovation and economic growth (Kortum and Lerner, 2000), and VCs are a primary source of capital for innovative high-technology start-up firms (Gompers and Lerner, 1999). For example, during the 1983–92 period, while venture capital investee firms averaged less than 3 percent of corporate research and development, they were nevertheless responsible for more than 8 percent of industrial innovation in the US (Kortum and Lerner, 2000). Similarly, Cumming and Li (2013) find that an increase in the rate of change in VC deals per population by 1 percent gives rise to a 2.1 percent increase in the rate of change in new start-ups per population in the US (see also Samila and Sorenson, 2011, for consistent estimates). Samila and Sorenson (2011) further show that a doubling in the number of firms funded by VC also results in a 0.22 percent to 1.24 percent expansion in the number of jobs, and a 0.48 percent to 3.78 percent increase in aggregate income. Overall, therefore, empirical evidence is highly consistent with the notion that VC is important for both innovation and entrepreneurship. The reason is that nascent entrepreneurs are likely to recognize the need for capital in the future and therefore are more likely to establish firms in regions that increase their odds of obtaining that funding from value added investors. Further, VCs are value-added investors, and these investors and their investee firms encourage others to engage in entrepreneurship through a demonstration effect and by training future start-up firm founders.

In this chapter, we examine the importance of exits for VCs, with particular reference to IPO exits. Because VCs invest in early stage companies without cash flows to pay interest on debt or dividends on equity, VCs invest for reasons of capital gains. Hence, the exit event is arguably the most important event for a VC. Prior work has established that VCs structure their deals and investment activity primarily with regard to expected exit outcomes (Cumming, 2008; Cumming and Johan, 2008a, 2013). Exit outcomes typically can come to fruition anywhere from two to seven years after initial investment.

In this chapter, we present worldwide VC investment, exit and initial public offering (IPO) data up to 2010. Also, we focus on investment activity at the local level with reference to data from Canada and the US. We provide statistics which highlight how differences in investment and IPO exit patterns are important for regional prosperity, with particular reference to Canada and Ontario. We consider the VC market in Ontario, Canada, and abroad, drawing on extensive data from the Thompson Financial SDC VentureXpert database. We consider the amount and structure of VC investment in Ontario and the sources of capital, as well as exits from investments. Comparisons are made in reference to economic conditions in the different jurisdictions. We identify empirical proxies for value-added provided by VCs in different regions that have been well established in the literature as leading to business innovation and commercialization. These proxies include, for example, staging frequency, syndication, and portfolio sizes.

This chapter is organized as follows. Section 2 provides a review of the literature on capital gaps in entrepreneurial finance and the importance of IPOs, with reference to the Canadian institutional setting. Section 3 provides an analysis of the Thompson Financial SDC database, and discusses governmental programs in other jurisdictions. Section 4 discusses the 2008 financial crisis and future opportunities for jurisdictions outside the US. Concluding remarks and policy lessons are summarized in section 5.

2 EARLY-STAGE RISK CAPITAL: LESSONS FROM CANADA

This section briefly discussed two unique institutional features about Canada pertinent to VC and IPOs that are somewhat distinct from other countries: low listing standards and retail VC funds.

First, a very unique and notable feature of entrepreneurial finance in Canada is the fact that firms can go public at a very young age and with little or no capital, revenues or income. Further, while there is disclosure in an IPO, firms in Canada can opt out of disclosure by entering the public market at a pre-revenue stage with minimal disclosure via reverse mergers (RMs). Initial public offerings and RMs are equally common in Canada (Carpentier et al., 2012). The junior capital market in Canada, the TSX-V, markets itself as being in competition with private VC and encourages firms not to seek capital from private investors but rather to list very early on in their life cycle (Johan, 2010). Unfortunately, the returns to IPOs in Canada are very low and much lower than that reported from other countries without such low listing standards. The returns to RMs are even worse. The low listing standards in Canada also have detrimental implications for the value of firms that go public. Carpentier et al. (2010) show that IPOs are valued at least 30 percent lower in Canada than in the US, even after one matches for the quality of the issues in terms of size, revenues, profitability, liquidity, and other things. The low listing standards, therefore, facilitate access to capital but raise the cost of capital in Canada and lower the returns to entrepreneurship and discourage entrepreneurial activity in Canada. As a related matter, fragmented securities regulation has been argued to have given rise to a higher cost of capital in Canada, which is to the detriment of firms trying to raise finance, including privately held firms.[1]

Second, Canada has a large proportion of VC funds with a unique structure. Most VC funds around the world are organized as limited partnerships (Cumming and Johan, 2006, 2009). Institutional investors are the limited partners and VC fund managers are the general partners. Partnerships typically are set up to last for 10 years with an option to continue for two or three years if investments are not yet wound up and brought to fruition. Without institutional investor participation in limited partnerships, VC industries would flounder. Limited partnerships are widely recognized as being the superior form of organization for VCs given their autonomous structure and decision-making in the hands of fund managers (general partners), the flexibility in structuring limited partnership contracts (cash flow and control rights) to meet the needs of the fund, respond to market conditions and mitigate any potential for opportunistic behavior (Gompers and Lerner, 1999; Cumming and Johan, 2013).

Canada has comparatively lower levels of limited partnership VC funds, and instead has a large proportion of government subsidized labour-sponsored venture capital corporations (LSVCCs), which are essentially tax-subsidized mutual funds that invest in private firms. Contributors to LSVCCs are individuals, not institutional investors as in the case of limited partnership VC funds. Individuals have tax incentives to invest: for someone with annual income over $100000, the after-tax cost of a $5000 investment is $1180, which generates a 323.73 percent rate of return for the investor in the year of investment, assuming the fund does not lose the money (Cumming and MacIntosh, 2007, table 21.1). Investors are subject to a hold period that has typically been eight years, after which they can sell their investment. Labour-sponsored venture capital corporations get the tax benefit in exchange for agreeing to statutory covenants, including but not limited to time limits to reinvest contributed capital and not taking majority stakes or controlling interests in the companies in which they invest (Cumming and MacIntosh, 2007). There is evidence that Canadian institutional investors invest half as much in VC relative to US institutional investors (Chemla, 2004). Anecdotal evidence is consistent with the view that Canadian institutional investors do not invest in Canada due to the poor historic returns in VC. Reasons for such poor returns in Canada, include the dominant presence of LSVCCs, the low listing standards on stock exchanges, and the dearth of talented VCs in Canada. We discuss these issues below, alongside the presentation of the data.

3 EMPIRICAL EVIDENCE ON VC INVESTMENTS AND EXITS IN CANADA AND WORLDWIDE

The richest data on venture capital investments in Canada and around the world is from Thompson Financial SDC VentureXpert.[2] This dataset comprises information on VC and related deal types for 136 countries around the world. The figures and tables in this section provide select information in the data that highlight salient features on the VC market in Ontario and Canada relative to other jurisdictions. We concentrate on funds that focus on seed, early and expansion stage VC investments (definitions of investment stages and other items are provided in Table 21.1), and the investee firms at

Table 21.1 Definitions of terms

Variable name	Definition
Seed	Financing provided to research, assess and develop an initial concept before a business has reached the start-up phase, or financing provided to companies firms for product development and initial marketing. Companies' firms may be in the process of being set up or may have been in business for a short time, but have not sold their product commercially
Early	Financing to companies' firms that have completed the product development stage and require further funds to initiate commercial manufacturing and sales. They will not yet be generating a profit
Expansion	Financing provided for the growth and expansion of a company firm which is breaking even or trading profitably. Capital may be used to finance increased production capacity, market or product development, and/or to provide additional working capital
Late	Financing provided to a company in the mezzanine stage or just prior to a company going public
Buyout	Management buyout – Financing provided to enable current operating management and investors to acquire an existing product line or business Management buyin – Financing provided to enable a manager or group of managers from outside the company firm to buy-in to the company firm with the support of private equity investors
Other stage	Other stages include: Refinancing bank debt – To reduce a company's firm's level of gearing Bridge Financing – Financing made available to a company firm in the period of transition from being privately owned to being publicly quoted

Table 21.1 (continued)

Variable name	Definition
	Secondary purchase/replacement capital – Purchase of existing shares in a company firm from another private equity investment organization or from another shareholder or shareholders Rescue/turnaround – Financing made available to an existing business firm which has experienced trading difficulties (firm is not earning its cost of capital (WACC)), with a view to re-establishing prosperity
Round amount estimated	The estimated amount of investment in an investment round
Round amount disclosed	The actual disclosed amount of investment in an investment round
Number of rounds per company	The number of staged investment rounds that the company had received until exit or 25 June 2010
Number of companies in which fund invested	The number of companies financed by the venture capital fund
Number of executives in fund	The number of executives making investment decisions in the venture capital fund
Number of syndicated funds invested	The number of investors that financed the same investee company
Portfolio size per manager	The number of companies in which the fund invested divided by the number of executives in the fund
Went public	A dummy variable equal to 1 if the company went public on or before at 25 June 2010
In registration	A dummy variable equal to 1 if the company was in registration to go public on or before at 25 June 2010
LBO	A dummy variable equal to 1 if the company was sold as an LBO on or before at 25 June 2010
Merger	A dummy variable equal to 1 if the company was sold in a merger on or before at 25 June 2010
Acquisition	A dummy variable equal to 1 if the company was sold as an acquisition on or before at 25 June 2010
Pending acquisition	A dummy variable equal to 1 if the company was pending acquisition on or before at 25 June 2010
Active	A dummy variable equal to 1 if the company was still an active investment on or before at 25 June 2010
Private company (non-PE)	A dummy variable equal to 1 if the company was sold as a private company (e.g., entrepreneur repurchased shares) or before at 25 June 2010
Bankruptcy – Chapter 11	A dummy variable equal to 1 if the company was in Chapter 11 bankruptcy on or before at 25 June 2010
Bankruptcy – Chapter 7	A dummy variable equal to 1 if the company was in Chapter 7 bankruptcy on or before at 25 June 2010
Defunct	A dummy variable equal to 1 if the company was defunct on or before at 25 June
Other exit	A dummy variable equal to 1 if the company had some other exit outcome on or before at 25 June 2010

470 *Handbook of research on IPOs*

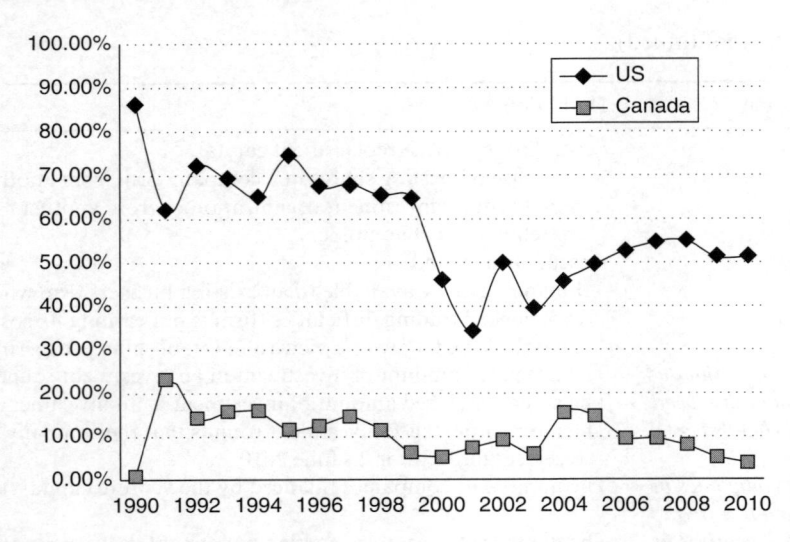

Note: This figure presents the number of first round (new) investments in seed, early and expansion stage investments in Canada and the US as a percentage of total world wide investments in first round seed, early and expansion stage investments. 1 January 1990–25 June 2010.

Source: Thompson SDC VentureXpert.

Figure 21.1 Investments in Canada and the US relative to the world

these development stages. We focus on the time period 1 January 1990 to 25 June 2010 to provide current evidence as well as historical trends.

Relative to the rest of the world, Canada's share of new (first round) seed, early and expansion stage VC investment has been declining from 2004 to 2010 from 15.5 percent of the total number of deals worldwide in 2004 to 3.9 percent of the total number of deals worldwide in 2010 (Figure 20.1). The only year where more than 20 percent of new seed, early and expansion deals were done in Canada was 1991. Over 85 percent of new seed, early and expansion deals were carried out in the US in 1990, but from 2005–10 only a little more than 50 percent of deals were carried out in the US. In 2001 only 34 percent of seed-, early- and expansion-stage VC investments were in the US (Figure 21.1). In 2010, there were more new investments in seed, early and expansion stage deals in France, the UK, China, Israel, and Germany (Figure 21.2), and Canada's share relative to these countries has steadily declined since 2004 (Figure 21.2). Similar patterns are observed for dollar amounts invested in seed-, early- and expansion-stage investments in Canada relative to other countries (Figure 21.3).

Fundraising patterns in Ontario, Quebec, British Columbia, Massachusetts and California are presented in terms of the numbers of funds in Figures 21.4 and 21.5, and in terms of the US dollar amounts per gross domestic product (GDP) in Figures 21.6 and 21.7. The data are presented for any type of fund that has a mandate to invest in seed, early and/or expansion stage investments. Ontario experienced a rise in the number of funds trying to raise capital, particularly in 2009 (Figures 21.4 and 21.5). However, the US dollar amounts raised in Ontario are low relative to the other jurisdictions.[3]

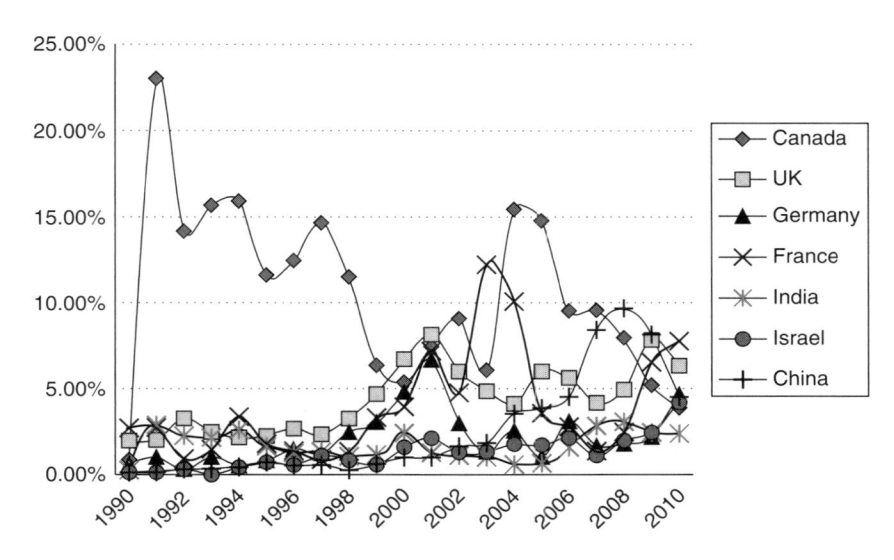

The IPO as an exit strategy for venture capitalists 471

Note: This figure presents the number of first round (new) investments in seed, early and expansion stage investments in Canada, the UK, Germany, France, India, Israel and China as a percentage of total world wide investments in first round seed, early and expansion stage investments, 1 January 1990–25 June 2010.

Source: Thompson SDC VentureXpert.

Figure 21.2   Investments in Canada and other countries relative to the world

Figure 21.7 shows that over the 2000 to 2008 period, there was 12.8 times the amount of new capital commitments to newly established funds focused on investment in seed, early and expansion stage entrepreneurial ventures in Massachusetts on a per GDP basis than there was in Ontario.[4] (The comparable comparison is 8.9 times for California to Ontario on a per GDP basis.) It would have required an additional US$37.5 billion of new capital committed to seed, early and expansion stage capital for Ontario to be at the level of VC per GDP that is comparable to that which has been enjoyed by Massachusetts-based funds over the period 2000 to 2008. These fundraising statistics indicate there has been a huge dearth of VC funds in Ontario focused on seed, early and expansion stage companies.

The numbers of new first-round investments in seed, early and expansion stage firms are presented in Figures 21.8 and 21.9 for Ontario, Quebec, British Columbia and California. There have been substantially more new investments in California, followed by Massachusetts, Quebec and Ontario and British Columbia. The differences in fundraising in Figure 21.7 are more pronounced than the differences in new investments in Figure 21.9 between Massachusetts and Ontario. The reason, as highlighted below, is that there are a large number of US fund investments into Canada.

The US dollar amounts invested per GDP in all new first-round and follow-on seed, early and expansion stage investments (from any type of fund) in 2004–08 are presented in Figure 21.10 for all of the Canadian provinces as well as Massachusetts and California. The data show enormous differences across the regions. Between 2004 and 2008, amounts invested averaged 1 percent of GDP in Massachusetts, 0.98 percent of

472 *Handbook of research on IPOs*

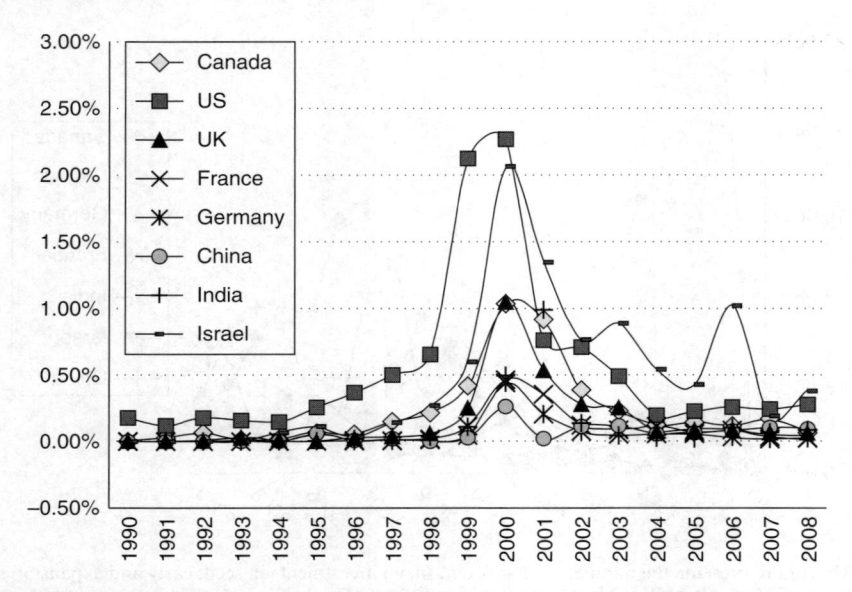

Note: This figure presents the amounts invested in seed, early and expansion stage investments for all investment rounds in Canada, the United States, the United Kingdom, France, Germany, China, India and Israel as a percentage of GDP, 1 January 1990–31 December 2008.

Source: Thompson SDC VentureXpert and World Bank.

Figure 21.3 Dollar amounts of venture capital investment per GDP by country

GDP in California, 0.20 percent of GDP in British Columbia, and 0.15 percent of GDP in Quebec and Ontario. In other words, even accounting for cross-border investment, there is a shortfall in Ontario relative to Massachusetts by 650 percent on a US dollar per capita basis.

Figures 21.11, 21.12, 21.13 and 21.14 show the percentage of new first-round investments taken at different stages of firm development in Ontario, Quebec, Massachusetts and California, respectively. In Ontario and Quebec there has been a relative decline in seed, early and expansion stage investment relative to buyout and late/other investment stages since 1990 (albeit in 2010 the most number of new investments have been at the expansion stage). The pictures are quite different in Massachusetts and California, which show most new investment activity is at the seed and early stages. In other words, Massachusetts and California have a vastly greater focus on initiating investments in nascent firms compared to Ontario and Quebec. The number of investments in seed, early and expansion stages versus other staged is highlighted in Ontario versus other provinces in Figure 21.15, which shows a relative decline in Ontario compared to the rest of Canada since Ontario's peak in 1992. (Note, however, that seed, early and expansion stage investments are typically staged with much greater frequency. Hence, when one considers follow-on investments in the same firm, the data show more activity in early and expansion stages in Ontario, as illustrated in Figure 21.16.)

Figures 21.17 and 21.18 show investment activity in seed, early and expansion stages in different cities in Ontario (Figure 21.17) and the rest of Canada (Figure 21.18). Within

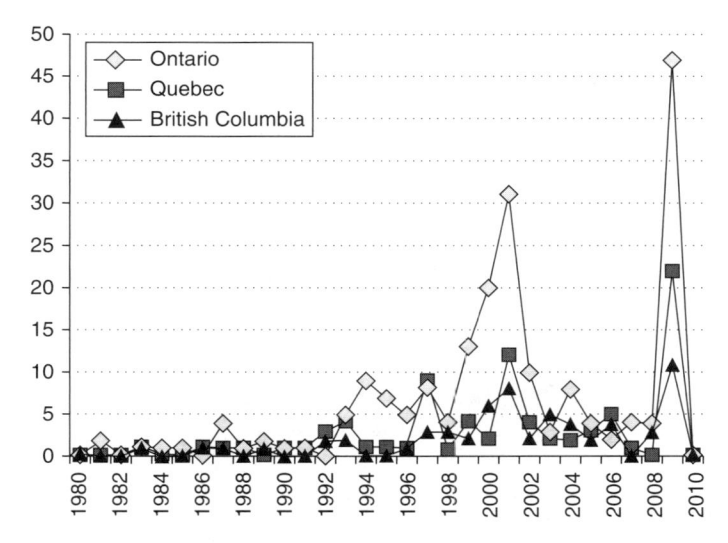

The IPO as an exit strategy for venture capitalists 473

Note: This figure shows the number of new funds focused in seed, early and expansion investments (for any type of fund).

Source: All available venture capital transactions from Thompson Financial VentureXpert, 1 January 1990–25 June 2010; Thompson Financial SDC.

Figure 21.4 Canadian comparisons of VC fundraising in numbers

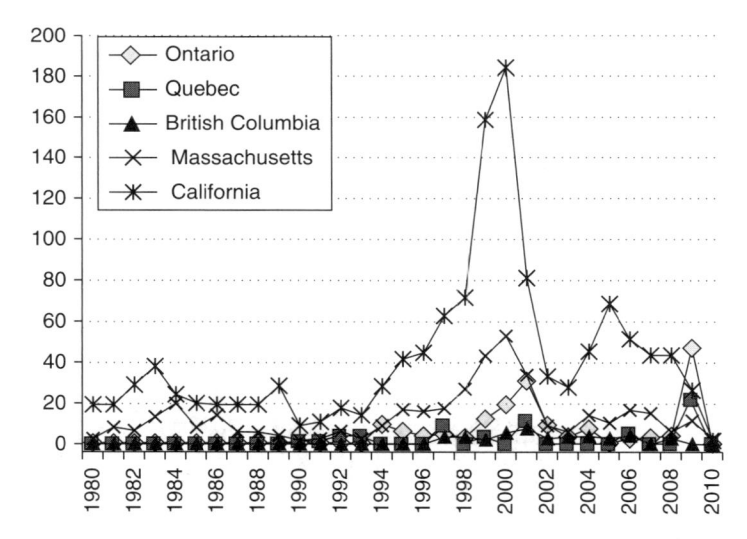

Note: This figure shows the number of new funds focused in seed, early and expansion investments (for any type of fund).

Source: All available venture capital transactions from Thompson Financial VentureXpert, 1 January 1990–25 June 2010; Thompson Financial SDC.

Figure 21.5 Canadian and US comparisons of VC fundraising in numbers

474 *Handbook of research on IPOs*

Note: This figure shows the dollar amounts of new funds raised per GDP focused in seed, early and expansion investments (for any type of fund).

Source: All available venture capital transactions from Thompson Financial VentureXpert, 1 January 1990–25 June 2010.

Figure 21.6   Canadian comparisons of VC fundraising in dollars

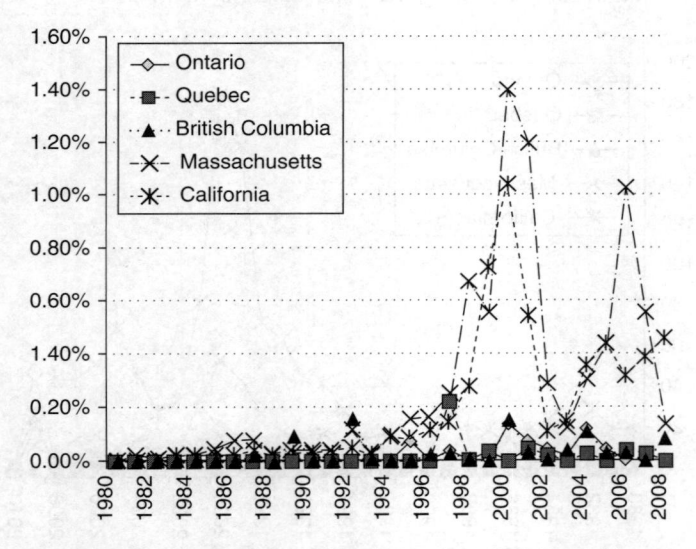

Note: This figure shows the dollar amounts of new funds raised per GDP focused in seed, early and expansion investments (for any type of fund).

Source: All available venture capital transactions from Thompson Financial VentureXpert, 1 January 1990–25 June 2010.

Figure 21.7   Canadian and US Comparisons of VC fundraising in dollars

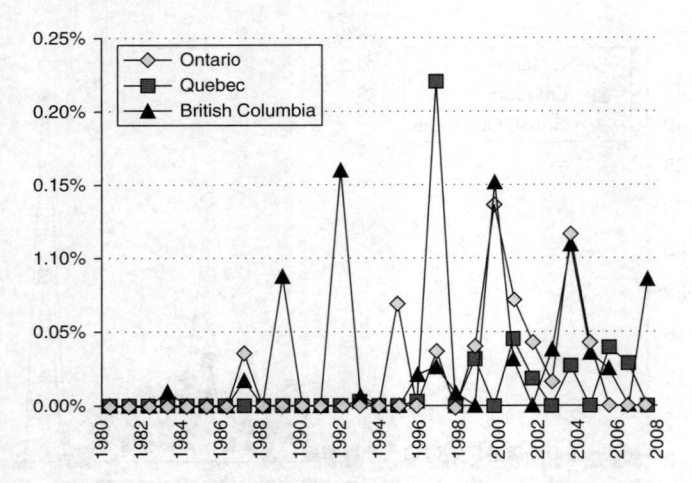

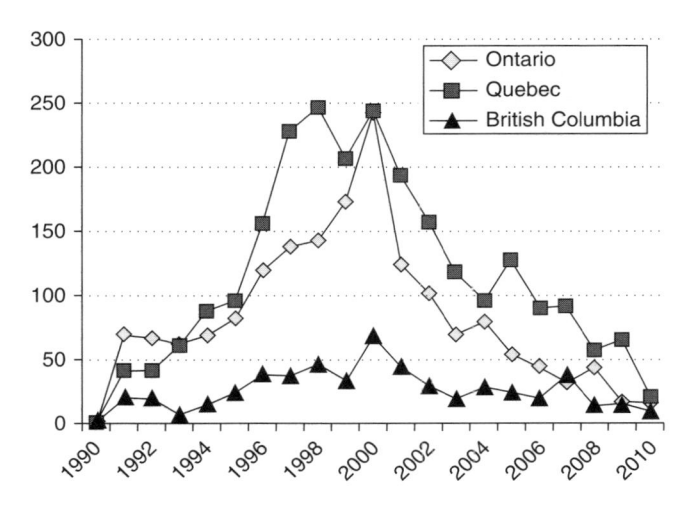

The IPO as an exit strategy for venture capitalists 475

Note: This figure summarizes the total number first round investments in seed, early and expansion stage investments by all types of investors for all industries in select Canadian provinces, January 1990–June 2010.

Source: Data from Thompson Financial SDC VentureXpert.

Figure 21.8   First-round investments in Canada by province

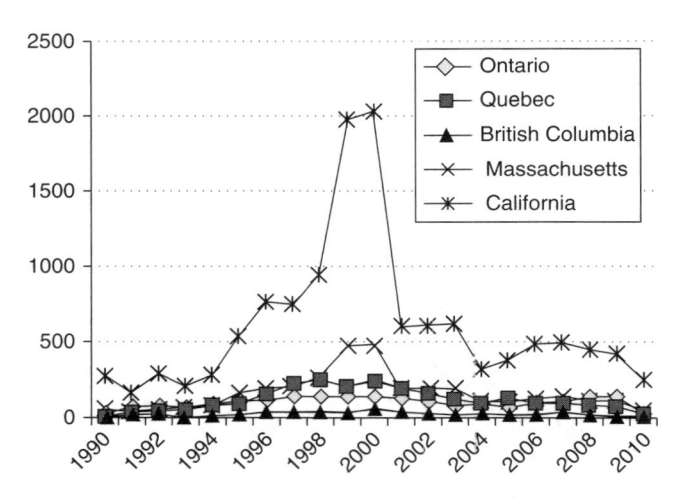

Note: This figure summarizes the total number first round investments in seed, early and expansion stage investments by all types of investors for all industries in select US states and Canadian provinces, January 1990–June 2010.

Source: Data from Thompson Financial SDC VentureXpert.

Figure 21.9   First-round investments in US and in Canada by province or state

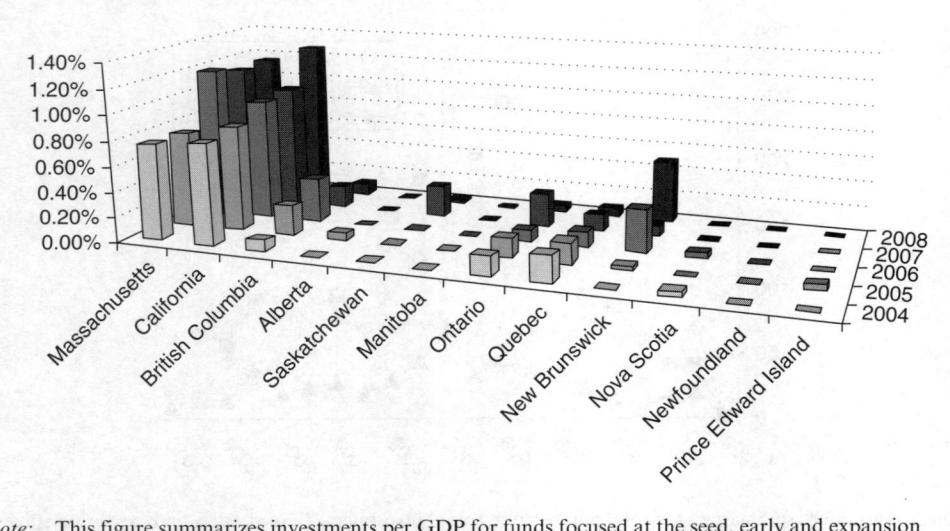

476 *Handbook of research on IPOs*

Note: This figure summarizes investments per GDP for funds focused at the seed, early and expansion stage investments relative to GDP by all types of investors for all industries in select US states and Canadian provinces, January 2004–December 2008.

Source: Data from Thompson Financial SDC VentureXpert.

Figure 21.10 *Investments for funds in Canada by Province, 2004–08*

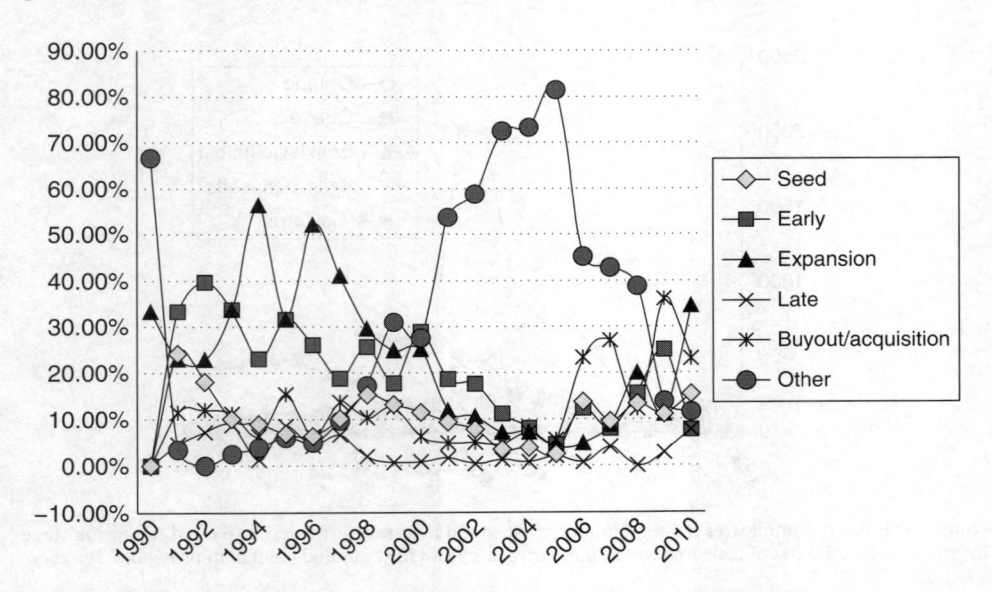

Note: This figure summarizes the percentage of investments in terms of the first investment rounds made by all types of venture capital and private equity backed companies in Ontario for all industries, January 1990–June 2010.

Source: Data from Thompson Financial SDC VentureXpert.

Figure 21.11 *First investment rounds in Ontario by stage of development*

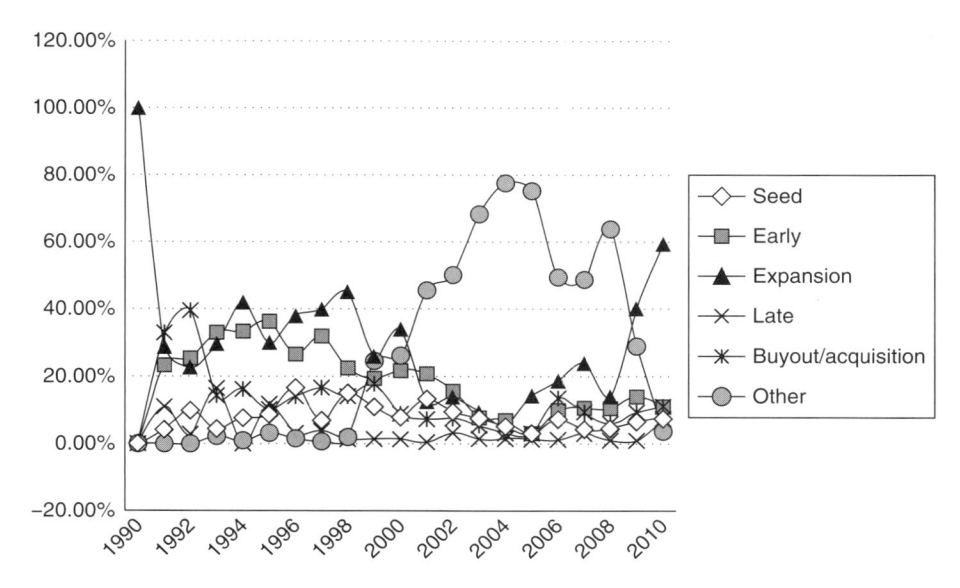

The IPO as an exit strategy for venture capitalists 477

Note: This figure summarizes the percentage of investments in terms of the first investment rounds made by all types of venture capital and private equity backed companies in Quebec for all industries, January 1990–June 2010.

Source: Data from Thompson Financial SDC VentureXpert.

Figure 21.12 First investment rounds in Quebec by stage of development

Ontario, most investment activity takes place in Toronto (593 new investments), followed by Ottawa (257), Mississauga (126), Markham (86), Waterloo (61), Burlington (36), Hamilton (17), and Kitchener (16) (Figure 21.17). Comparing across Canada since 1990, Montreal has had 746 new first-round investments, followed by Toronto (593), Vancouver (314), Ottawa (257), Calgary (184), Winnipeg (99), Quebec City (97) and Edmonton (81) (Figure 21.18).

Table 21.2 presents the data on seed, early and expansion investments by industry in the Canadian provinces as well as California and Massachusetts over the 1990–2010 period. In Ontario, most investment activity is in software (20.77 percent of new investments), followed by Internet (12.67 percent), and communications (11.68 percent). In Quebec the highest percentage is in consumer related (14.00 percent), followed by computer software (12.84 percent), and industrial/energy (11.35 percent). In British Columbia the highest percentage is in computer software (17.72 percent), Internet specific (12.61 percent), and semiconductor/electricity (10.05 percent). In Massachusetts the highest percentage is computer software (24.33 percent), followed by Internet specific (15.97 percent), health (11.68 percent) and biotechnology (10.75 percent). In California the highest percentage is in Internet specific (21.86 percent), followed by computer software (19.24 percent) and communications (11.02 percent).

Table 21.3 presents investment and exits statistics by country for average amounts invested per round (both estimated by Thompson Financial and actually disclosed by the funds), number of financing rounds, portfolio size (number of firms financed) per fund

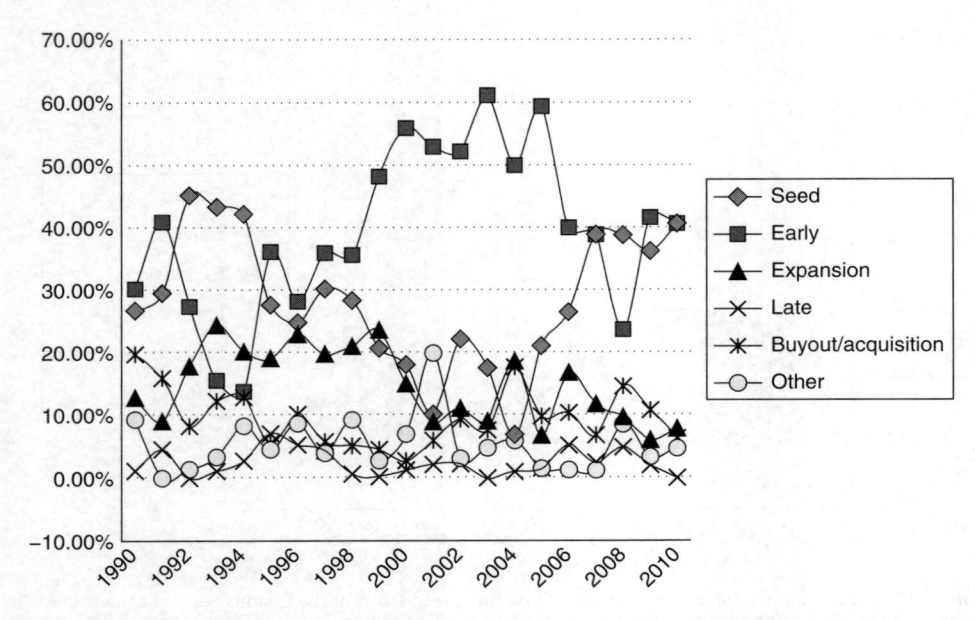

Note: This figure summarizes the percentage of investments in terms of the first investment rounds made by all types of venture capital and private equity backed companies in Massachusetts for all industries, January 1990–June 2010.

Source: Data from Thompson Financial SDC VentureXpert.

Figure 21.13 First investment rounds in Massachusetts by stage of development

manager, and the status of the firms financed (as at June 2010) for seed, early and expansion stage investments. There are some striking differences across countries. Investment amounts are typically smaller in Canada (US$2.558 million disclosed) relative to the US (US$9.787 million disclosed) and other countries, and there are more financing rounds in Canada than the US (3.48 compared to 2.86 on average). The number of firms financed per fund manager is much larger in Canada (27.76) than the US (6.58) and all other countries. There is theoretical work and empirical evidence that shows funds with larger portfolios (numbers of firms financed) per manager tend to put less effort into monitoring and advising their investee firms (Kanniainen and Keuschnigg, 2003, 2004; Keuschnigg, 2004; Cumming, 2006), and hence returns are significantly lower for such investments (Cumming and Walz, 2010). Further, it is noteworthy that there is less syndication on average in Canada (2.98 funds per investee firms) relative to the US (4.17 funds per investee firm). Syndication is often useful as it enables better screening and more value-added advice to the investee firm, thereby enhancing exit outcomes and investment returns (Cumming and Walz, 2010). The data show Canada has a lower rate of firms going public (6.47 percent) than all other countries except Germany (also 6.47 percent), and significantly lagging that of the US (11.26 percent) and the other countries indicated in Table 21.3. Overall, these data suggest that there is a problem with the number of VC fund managers and the quality of VC in Canada relative to other countries.

Tables 21.4–21.6 present similar investment and exit statistics as in Table 21.3, but

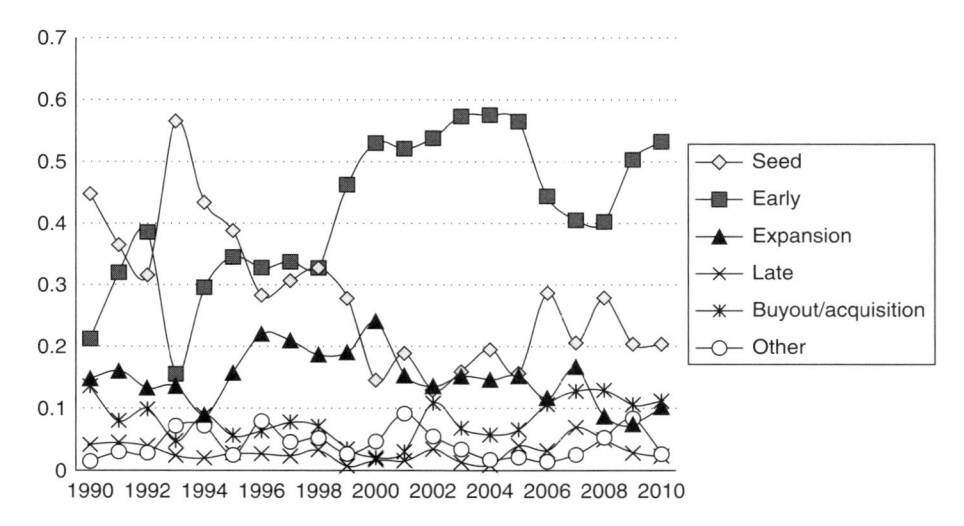

Note: This figure summarizes the percentage of investments in terms of the first investment rounds made by all types of venture capital and private equity backed companies in California for all industries, January 1990–June 2010.

Source: Data from Thompson Financial SDC VentureXpert.

Figure 21.14 First investment rounds in California by stage of development

for different provinces and states (Table 21.4), and different cities (Tables 21.5 and 21.6). From Table 21.4, it is noteworthy that Quebec shows a lower rate of IPO exits (4.86 percent), less syndication (2.54 funds per investee firm), larger portfolio sizes per manager (42.55 investee firms per manager) and smaller average investment amounts (US$1.505 million disclosed). Ontario has an IPO exit rate of 6.23 percent, syndication of 3.28 funds per investee firm, portfolio sizes per manager of 18.36 and average disclosed investment amounts of US$3.833 million. Massachusetts has an IPO exit rate of 11.42 percent, syndication of 4.51 funds per investee firm, portfolio sizes per manager of 6.37 and average disclosed investment amounts of US$9.089 million. California has an IPO exit rate of 11.93 percent, syndication of 4.50 funds per investee firm, portfolio sizes per manager of 7.08 and average disclosed investment amounts of US$10.554 million.

Regarding portfolio sizes per manager in Canada and Ontario specifically, two items are noteworthy. First, portfolio sizes are smaller for Ontario based funds than international funds that invest in Ontario. For Ontario based funds that invest in Ontario, average portfolio size is 10.49 companies per manager. The smaller portfolio size per manager for Ontario funds in Ontario means that local investors provide more monitoring and advice to their investees (see also Cumming, 2006). Similarly, portfolio sizes for funds that invest locally in Massachusetts and California are likewise smaller (for investments and investors in the same province, it is 5.78 in Massachusetts and 6.43 on average in California). Local investors are more active investors in their companies. Portfolio sizes of funds that invest in Ontario and Canadian companies are on average much larger because most investments are made by funds that are not local.

Second, median portfolio sizes are lower than average portfolio sizes. Median portfolio

480 *Handbook of research on IPOs*

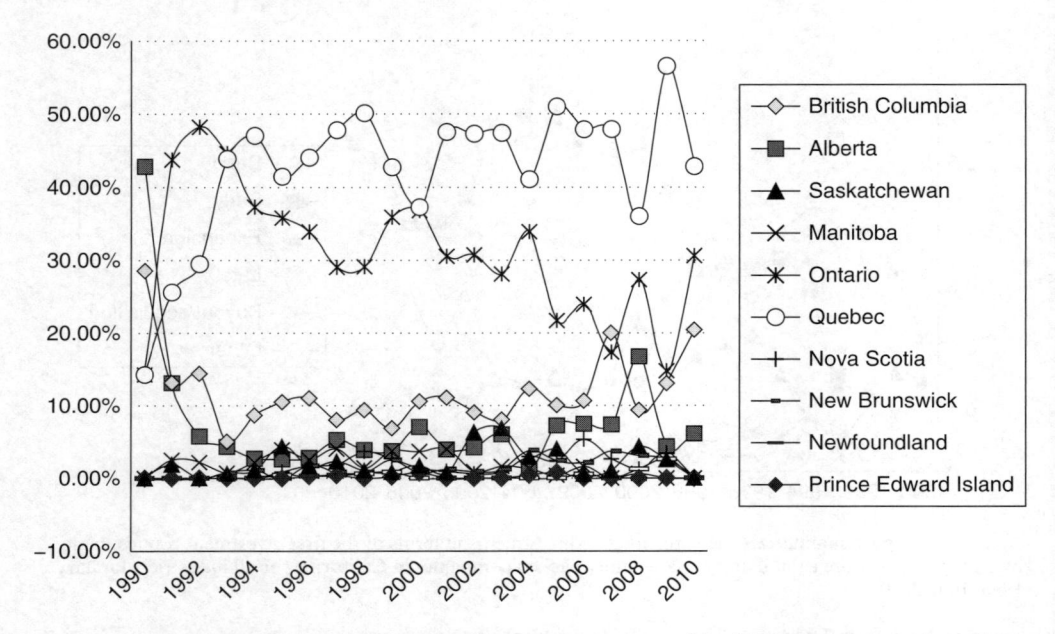

Note: This figure summarizes the percentage of investments in terms of the first investment rounds made in seed, early and expansion stage investments by all types of investors in Canada for all industries, January 1990–June 2010.

Source: Data from Thompson Financial SDC VentureXpert.

Figure 21.15 First round investments in Canada by province

size per manager for Ontario funds that invest in Ontario is 3.83. Averages are skewed in the sense that some funds invest in many companies per manager. Median portfolio size of Massachusetts (California) based funds that invest in Massachusetts (California) companies is 2.51 (2.81). Hence, there is still an implied difference of more value added in leading jurisdictions such as Massachusetts and California as funds that have smaller portfolios per manager provide more advice and have better returns and better performing entrepreneurial companies in their portfolio (Cumming and Walz, 2010).

A possible implication from the portfolio size statistics is that government efforts to attract foreign investors to invest in Ontario is not as effective as getting foreign funds to *establish* offices in Ontario and be proximate to their investee firms and add more value and provide active monitoring of their investee firms. Moreover, syndication frequency is not very different between US cross-border investment and domestic Canadian investment. Table 21.7 shows that 43.87 percent of investment rounds from US investors into Canada have just one investor (non-syndicated), while 48.89 percent of domestic investments had just one investor. Anecdotally (based on meetings with VCs in July 2010), and based on extant evidence (Gompers and Lerner, 1999; Cumming and Johan, 2009), the lead investor in VC deals do substantially more than non-lead syndicated VCs, and VCs have found syndication to be particularly troublesome in recent years due to increased negotiation costs, costs of delay and disagreement with investment decisions. Ontario

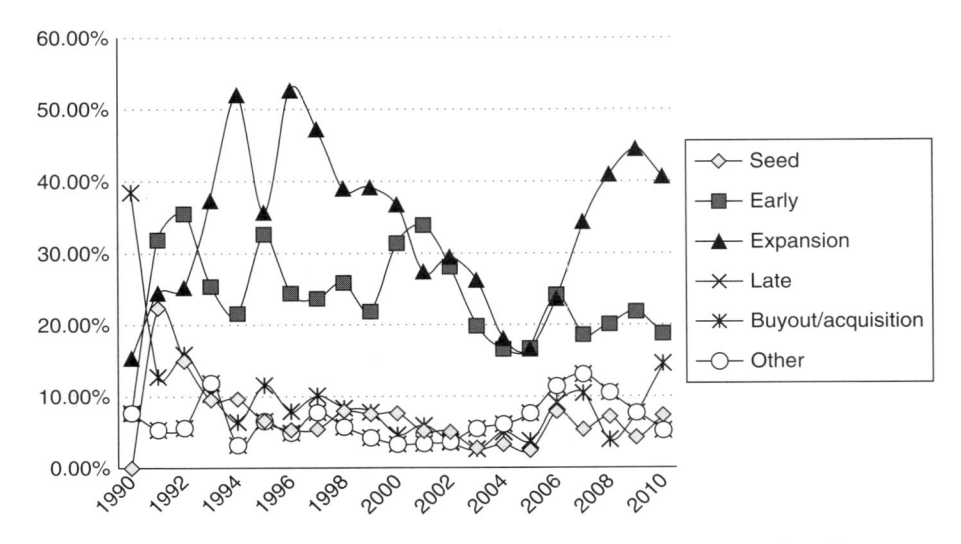

The IPO as an exit strategy for venture capitalists 481

Note: This figure summarizes the percentage of investments in terms of the total number of investment rounds made by all types of venture capital and private equity backed companies in Ontario for all industries, January 1990–June 2010.

Source: Data from Thompson Financial SDC VentureXpert.

Figure 21.16 All investment rounds in Ontario by stage of development

should not hope for foreign syndication opportunities to help bolster local investment levels because foreign syndicated investors give rise to increased costs; moreover, the portfolio size statistics show that foreign investors add much less value to the investee firms.

From Table 21.5, it is noteworthy that there are large differences in the IPO exit rate by city. The highest percentage of exits as IPOs comes from Waterloo (19.75 percent), Calgary (17.12 percent) and Mississauga (14.22 percent), while the lowest percentages are from Toronto (5.95 percent), Montreal (4.67 percent) and Ottawa (4.02 percent). Similarly, evidence from Massachusetts and California show a much higher percentage of IPO exits not from San Francisco and Boston but rather from Silicon Valley and Route 128 (Table 21.6).

Figures 21.19, 21.20 and 21.21 shows the broader picture of IPO exit success from different countries. Around the world in 2010 there have been scant VC backed IPOs in recent years (Figure 21.19). The share of IPOs coming from the US has been in sharp decline since 1995 (Figure 21.20), which is attributable to the rise of non-US VC markets as well as the increasing costs of going public in the US since Sarbanes–Oxley legislation in June 2002. Canada's share of the IPO market in terms of numbers of VC backed IPOs has been fairly strong relative to the UK, France, Israel, India and Germany in the past couple of years (Figure 21.21), but significantly lagging China (Figure 21.20). Put differently, the number of VC-backed IPOs are scant around the world (Figure 21.19) and things are no worse in Canada than most other countries.

Why is Canada's VC market so different from other countries? The best explanation,

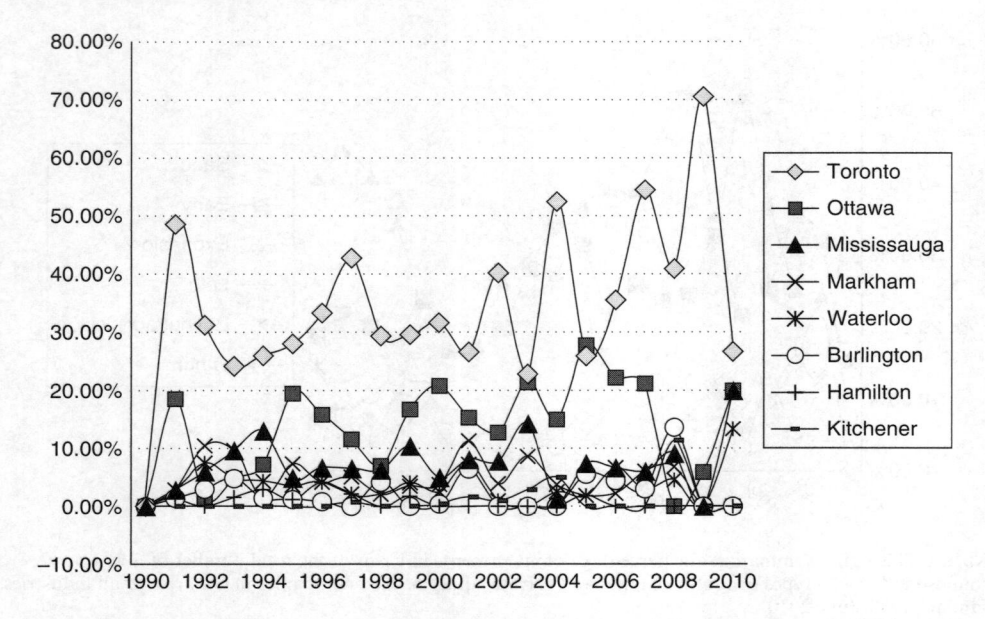

Note: This figure summarizes the percentage of investments in terms of the first investment rounds made in seed, early and expansion stage investments by all types of investors in Ontario for all industries, January 1990–June 2010.

Source: Data from Thompson Financial SDC VentureXpert.

Figure 21.17   First-round investments in Ontario by city

as argued by Cumming and MacIntosh (2006, 2007), is perhaps associated with the introduction of labour-sponsored venture capital corporations (LSVCCs) in the different provinces in the 1980s and 1990s (for example, Quebec in 1983; British Columbia in 1989; Ontario in 1992). As discussed further in section 6, LSVCCs are tax-subsidized mutual funds that invest in private equity. Cumming and MacIntosh (2006) argue and present empirical evidence consistent with the view that the tax subsides provided to LSVCCs crowd out private VC investment. That is, the presence of the tax subsidies discourages institutional investors from contributing capital to fund managers in Canada. The LSVCC tax subsidies enable them to raise large amounts of capital cheaply (Figure 21.22), and they have done so despite serious underperformance (Figure 21.23). Since 2002, LSVCCs have comprised more than 50 percent of capital under management in Canada (Figure 21.22), and their economic rates of return have lagged behind 30-day risk free t-bills. They also have inefficient statutory governance structures that exacerbate agency problems and limit the value-added that fund managers can provide to their investee firms (Cumming and MacIntosh, 2006, 2007). The underperformance of LSVCCs is highlighted in reference to the TSX and relative to US VC returns in Figure 21.20. Since LSVCCs raise capital from tax subsidies, they are less accountable to their investors, and as such have attracted significant capital (Figure 21.22) despite underperformance.

The tax incentives toward LSVCCs have led to massive capital accumulation among

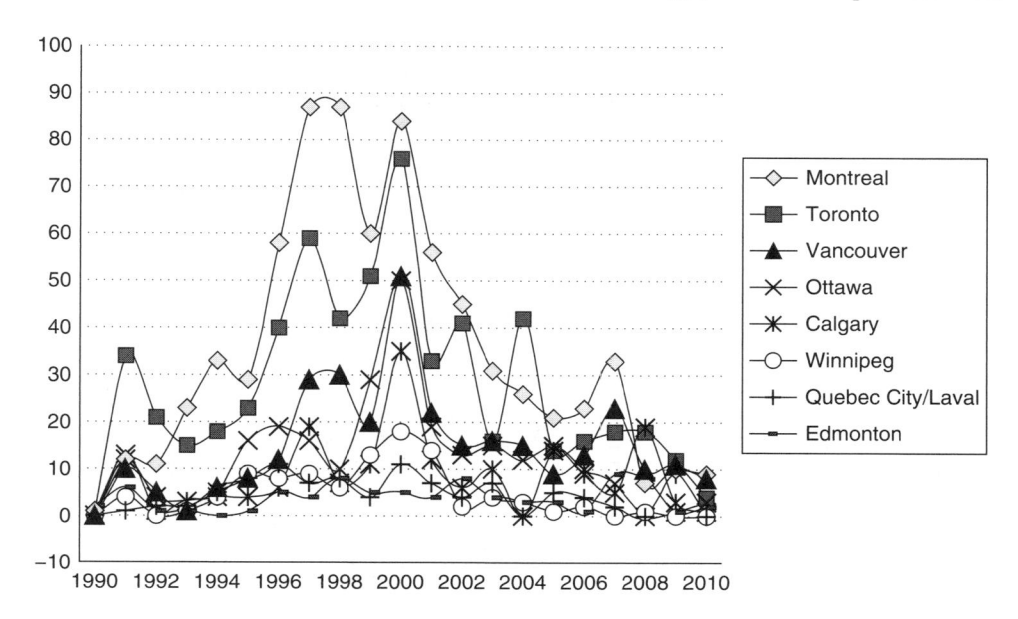

The IPO as an exit strategy for venture capitalists 483

Note: This figure summarizes the number of investments in terms of the first investment rounds made in seed, early and expansion stage investments by all types of investors for all industries, January 1990–June 2010.

Source: Data from Thompson Financial SDC VentureXpert.

Figure 21.18 First-round investments in seed, early stage and expansion stages by city

LSVCCs, and since the turn of the century they control more than half of VC that is under management in Canada (Figure 21.22). Many LSVCCs have in fact received so much capital that they have had extended periods where they refuse additional capital contributions, in view of the fact that they have time limits to reinvest contributions into entrepreneurial firms (failing which they pay a fine to the government or risk revocation of their licence to operate a LSVCC). This is surprising, since fund managers get paid in part based on the amount of capital received. As well, LSVCCs' management expense ratios (MER) are very high, with the average MER in 2006 being in excess of 4 percent (Cumming and MacIntosh, 2007). According to http://www.globefunds.com in 2009, the average MER of LSVCCs was in excess of 5 percent. A typical active mutual fund in the US has MERs around 1.5 percent and in Canada a little over 2 percent (Ruckman, 2003).

Non-tax economic returns to LSVCCs have been extraordinarily low. Labour-sponsored venture capital corporations returns have even lagged risk-free 30-day t-bills, with the sole exception of the peak of the Internet bubble in late 1999 and early 2000 (Figure 21.23). Further, examining individual fund returns, there is not one LSVCC that does well (or at least as well as the market). All LSVCC funds have returns that are substantially underperforming any comparable benchmark (Cumming and MacIntosh, 2007). Reasons for this underperformance include excessive capital under management relative to the number of managers (Cumming and MacIntosh, 2007), lack of control and ability of effect change in investees due to minority stakes (Cumming and MacIntosh,

Table 21.2 Industry breakdowns of seed, early and expansion investment in Canada

	British Columbia	Alberta	Saskatchewan	Manitoba	Ontario	Quebec	New Brunswick	Nova Scotia	Newfoundland	Prince Edward Island	Massachusetts	California
Agriculture/forestry/fisheries	3.07%	2.33%	36.29%	6.98%	1.18%	3.30%	0.00%	2.02%	0.00%	0.00%	0.06%	0.10%
Biotechnology	9.71%	7.64%	6.45%	6.20%	5.73%	8.05%	2.53%	9.09%	0.00%	0.00%	10.75%	6.21%
Business serv.	4.60%	5.98%	3.23%	13.18%	6.85%	9.25%	5.06%	3.03%	0.00%	0.00%	1.20%	1.46%
Communications	7.84%	3.32%	0.81%	0.00%	11.68%	5.53%	6.33%	7.07%	5.88%	0.00%	9.57%	11.02%
Computer hardware	5.11%	2.33%	0.00%	1.55%	3.76%	2.77%	3.80%	5.05%	0.00%	16.67%	7.35%	9.40%
Computer other	0.00%	0.00%	0.00%	0.00%	0.00%	0.04%	0.00%	0.00%	0.00%	0.00%	0.25%	0.20%
Computer software	17.72%	18.94%	2.42%	6.98%	20.77%	12.84%	29.11%	23.23%	47.06%	16.67%	24.33%	19.24%
Construction	0.17%	1.99%	0.00%	0.78%	0.95%	3.59%	1.27%	4.04%	0.00%	0.00%	0.08%	0.12%
Consumer related	5.79%	5.65%	10.48%	28.68%	7.80%	14.00%	12.66%	11.11%	17.65%	33.33%	3.05%	4.01%
Financial services	1.53%	1.99%	1.61%	5.43%	3.82%	1.32%	2.53%	1.01%	0.00%	0.00%	0.83%	0.92%
Industrial/energy	8.18%	22.26%	19.35%	5.43%	7.64%	11.35%	12.66%	4.04%	11.76%	0.00%	6.56%	3.13%
Internet specific	12.61%	13.62%	4.03%	3.88%	12.69%	4.83%	7.59%	12.12%	0.00%	25.00%	15.97%	21.86%
Manufacturing	3.24%	1.99%	7.26%	6.98%	1.63%	6.52%	7.59%	1.01%	11.76%	8.33%	0.58%	0.55%
Medical/health	9.37%	5.32%	4.03%	9.30%	5.50%	7.43%	2.53%	12.12%	0.00%	0.00%	11.68%	10.57%
Other	0.00%	1.00%	0.00%	0.00%	0.11%	0.21%	1.27%	0.00%	0.00%	0.00%	0.19%	0.30%
Semiconductor/electricity	10.05%	2.33%	0.00%	1.55%	8.76%	6.15%	5.06%	5.05%	5.88%	0.00%	7.24%	10.50%
Transportation	0.34%	2.66%	4.03%	3.10%	0.95%	2.23%	0.00%	0.00%	0.00%	0.00%	0.23%	0.40%
Utilities	0.68%	0.66%	0.00%	0.00%	0.17%	0.58%	0.00%	0.00%	0.00%	0.00%	0.08%	0.02%
Total number of observations	587	301	124	129	1781	2422	79	99	17	12	4846	16703

Notes:
This table summarizes the percentage of seed, early and expansion first round (new) investments in Canada and select US states.
Sample period: 1 January 1990–25 June 2010.

Source: Thompson Financial VentureXpert.

484

Table 21.3 Investment and exit statistics by country

	Canada	US	India	China	France	Germany	Australia	UK	Israel
Round amount estimated (US$000)	$2017	$3808	$4295	$4136	$1717	$2075	$1380	$2925	$1738
Round amount disclosed (US$000)	$2558	$9787	$7875	$13606	$5299	$6992	$3175	$7699	$798
Number of rounds per company	3.48	2.86	1.65	1.62	2.12	1.87	2.51	2.22	1.97
Number of companies in which fund invested	107.17	52.59	53.46	56.03	32.53	46.88	16.08	58.73	46.47
Number of executives in fund	10.11	17.04	24.80	23.46	22.19	31.52	8.59	36.56	18.46
Number of syndicated funds invested	2.98	4.17	1.78	2.82	3.19	2.81	1.88	2.81	3.47
Portfolio size per manager	27.76	6.58	2.95	7.06	3.17	6.39	4.12	2.74	3.75
Went public	6.47%	11.26%	14.09%	10.52%	10.58%	6.47%	11.33%	7.44%	9.00%
In registration	0.00%	0.38%	0.42%	0.97%	0.21%	0.00%	0.27%	0.09%	1.43%
LBO	0.26%	0.68%	1.04%	0.30%	2.55%	2.31%	2.01%	2.62%	0.08%
Merger	0.50%	1.55%	0.83%	0.36%	1.47%	2.68%	1.27%	2.26%	3.08%
Acquisition	22.86%	27.51%	6.04%	3.59%	15.76%	15.05%	19.18%	19.99%	14.03%
Pending acquisition	0.45%	0.20%	0.28%	0.30%	0.07%	0.14%	0.07%	0.55%	0.23%
Active	62.25%	38.82%	73.00%	82.13%	57.41%	59.25%	54.53%	60.10%	66.32%
Private company (non-PE)	0.05%	0.00%	0.07%	0.00%	0.00%	0.00%	0.00%	0.00%	0.00%
Bankruptcy – Chapter 11	0.10%	0.91%	0.00%	0.00%	0.05%	0.88%	0.13%	0.53%	0.00%
Bankruptcy – Chapter 7	0.03%	0.64%	0.07%	0.00%	0.73%	0.64%	1.34%	0.17%	0.30%
Defunct	6.97%	17.90%	4.16%	1.82%	11.13%	12.41%	9.66%	6.15%	5.55%
Other exit	0.07%	0.15%	0.00%	0.00%	0.05%	0.17%	0.20%	0.10%	0.00%
Number of observations	10918	89168	1441	1645	4358	2950	1491	5834	1333

Notes:
This table summarizes investment and exit data for seed, early and expansions investments by country.
Sample period: 1 January 1990–25 June 2010.

Source: Thompson Financial SDC VentureXpert.

Table 21.4 Investment and exit statistics by Canadian provinces and select US states

	British Columbia	Alberta	Saskatchewan	Manitoba	Ontario	Quebec	New Brunswick	Nova Scotia	Newfoundland	Prince Edward Island	Massachusetts	California
Round amount estimated (US$000)	$2728	$1465	$1259	$2728	$3031	$1199	$1268	$593	$770	$252	$3848	$4055
Round amount disclosed (US$000)	$3452	$2224	$1371	$3452	$3833	$1505	$1891	$636	$879	$252	$9089	$10554
Number of rounds per company	3.53	3.20	3.35	3.53	3.47	3.50	3.25	2.47	3.48	1.43	2.92	2.95
Number of companies in which fund invested	79.43	56.10	77.22	79.43	70.02	161.30	71.96	76.57	48.58	209.29	53.60	59.58
Number of executives in fund	15.29	8.68	10.52	15.29	11.33	7.38	12.83	9.62	9.15	14.29	18.84	17.60
Number of syndicated funds invested	4.06	2.85	2.57	4.06	3.28	2.54	2.43	2.00	2.52	1.29	4.51	4.50
Portfolio size per manager	16.43	21.10	21.00	16.43	18.36	42.55	14.19	15.17	21.44	11.64	6.37	7.08

Went public	10.45%	13.07%	3.27%	10.45%	6.23%	4.86%	2.56%	0.55%	0.00%	0.00%	11.42%	11.93%
In registration	0.00%	0.00%	0.00%	0.00%	0.00%	0.00%	0.00%	0.00%	0.00%	0.00%	0.23%	0.44%
LBO	0.77%	0.22%	0.00%	0.77%	0.16%	0.21%	0.00%	0.00%	0.00%	0.00%	0.29%	0.31%
Merger	0.00%	1.09%	0.00%	0.00%	0.22%	0.96%	0.00%	0.00%	0.00%	0.00%	1.44%	1.33%
Acquisition	31.10%	18.52%	3.92%	31.10%	33.23%	14.59%	4.49%	9.84%	0.00%	0.00%	31.62%	28.52%
Pending acquisition	0.00%	0.65%	0.00%	0.00%	0.22%	0.87%	0.00%	0.00%	0.00%	0.00%	0.10%	0.33%
Active	48.52%	64.27%	69.28%	48.52%	52.83%	71.42%	85.26%	85.79%	100.00%	85.71%	37.11%	38.54%
Private company (non-PE)	0.00%	0.00%	0.00%	0.00%	0.11%	0.02%	0.00%	0.00%	0.00%	0.00%	0.00%	0.01%
Bankruptcy – Chapter 11	0.00%	0.00%	0.00%	0.00%	0.30%	0.00%	0.00%	0.00%	0.00%	0.00%	0.82%	0.87%
Bankruptcy – Chapter 7	0.00%	0.00%	0.00%	0.00%	0.00%	0.07%	0.00%	0.00%	0.00%	0.00%	1.00%	0.52%
Defunct	8.71%	2.18%	23.53%	8.71%	6.67%	7.02%	7.69%	3.83%	0.00%	14.29%	15.89%	17.11%
Other exit	0.45%	0.00%	0.00%	0.45%	0.03%	0.00%	0.00%	0.00%	0.00%	0.00%	0.07%	0.08%
Number of observations	1550	459	153	1550	3689	4387	156	183	33	7	10565	37263

Notes:
This table summarizes investment and exit data for seed, early and expansions investments by select US states.
Sample period: 1 January 1990–25 June 2010.

Source: Thompson Financial SDC VentureXpert.

Table 21.5 Investment and exit statistics by select Canadian cities

	Toronto	Ottawa	Mississauga	Markham	Waterloo	Montreal	Calgary	Edmonton	Winnipeg	Vancouver
Round amount estimated (US$000)	$3017	$4266	$1538	$1746	$2279	$1786	$1467	$1436	$254	$3687
Round amount disclosed (US$000)	$4426	$5033	$1874	$2479	$2706	$2160	$2297	$2323	$290	$4515
Number of rounds per company	3.51	4.16	2.71	3.51	2.80	3.74	2.37	3.16	4.01	3.51
Number of companies in which fund invested	59.28	74.02	74.62	89.07	74.21	151.74	58.98	50.75	50.94	74.09
Number of executives in fund	12.45	11.89	9.08	11.21	8.32	8.47	9.34	8.69	8.31	15.13
Number of syndicated funds invested	2.95	4.24	2.37	3.60	2.94	2.89	2.55	3.39	1.35	4.26
Portfolio size per manager	15.67	17.34	24.99	23.45	26.21	37.53	24.22	15.89	16.12	15.97
Went public	5.95%	4.02%	14.22%	7.77%	19.75%	4.67%	17.12%	6.74%	13.48%	9.33%
In registration	0.00%	0.00%	0.00%	0.00%	0.00%	0.00%	0.00%	0.00%	0.00%	0.00%
LBO	0.52%	0.00%	0.00%	0.00%	0.00%	0.00%	0.45%	0.00%	0.00%	1.33%
Merger	0.00%	0.00%	1.96%	0.00%	0.00%	1.58%	0.00%	2.81%	0.00%	0.00%
Acquisition	32.72%	29.75%	49.51%	39.38%	41.98%	17.92%	22.07%	20.22%	13.48%	34.42%
Pending acquisition	0.61%	0.00%	0.00%	0.00%	0.00%	2.22%	1.35%	0.00%	0.00%	0.00%
Active	53.11%	57.65%	32.84%	48.19%	35.19%	68.01%	59.01%	66.85%	70.43%	48.97%
Private company (non-PE)	0.09%	0.00%	0.98%	0.00%	0.00%	0.00%	0.00%	0.00%	0.00%	0.00%
Bankruptcy – Chapter 11	0.00%	0.00%	0.00%	0.00%	0.00%	0.00%	0.00%	0.00%	0.00%	0.00%
Bankruptcy – Chapter 7	0.00%	0.00%	0.00%	0.00%	0.00%	0.18%	0.00%	0.00%	0.00%	0.00%
Defunct	7.00%	8.58%	0.49%	4.66%	3.09%	5.43%	0.00%	3.37%	2.61%	5.94%
Other exit	0.00%	0.00%	0.00%	0.00%	0.00%	0.00%	0.00%	0.00%	0.00%	0.00%
Number of observations	1143	921	204	193	162	1713	222	178	230	825

Notes:
This table summarizes investment and exit data for seed, early and expansions investments by select Canadian cities.
Sample period: 1 January 1990–25 June 2010.

Source: Thompson Financial SDC VentureXpert.

Table 21.6 Investment and exit statistics by select Canadian and US cities

	Toronto	Ottawa	Boston	San Francisco	San Diego	Emeryville	Palo Alto	Canton (Boston)	Milton (Route 128)	Waltham (Route 128)	Lexington (Route 128)
Round amount estimated (US$000)	$3017	$4266	$2308	$3237	$3934	$2576	$4567	$4139	$1841	$4186	$6165
Round amount disclosed (US$000)	$4426	$5033	$7373	$10131	$9610	$10181	$11687	$6905	$2411	$9050	$11364
Number of rounds per company	3.51	4.16	2.50	2.59	3.22	3.88	2.59	3.79	2.00	2.58	2.69
Number of companies in which fund invested	59.28	74.02	49.15	63.42	44.87	66.91	60.11	23.92	18.80	58.97	54.88
Number of executives in fund	12.45	11.89	19.39	16.44	15.54	19.28	17.71	8.08	8.60	19.63	20.94
Number of syndicated funds invested	2.95	4.24	3.29	4.04	4.87	3.90	4.18	4.60	2.10	4.35	4.91
Portfolio size per manager	15.67	17.34	5.84	7.51	6.22	8.72	6.49	11.60	3.59	6.11	6.45
Went public	5.95%	4.02%	5.22%	4.12%	11.82%	9.01%	11.15%	24.53%	15.00%	10.57%	6.59%
In registration	0.00%	0.00%	0.12%	0.03%	1.63%	9.88%	0.00%	0.00%	0.00%	1.57%	0.00%
LBO	0.52%	0.00%	0.00%	0.03%	0.04%	0.00%	0.00%	0.00%	15.00%	0.00%	0.00%
Merger	0.00%	0.00%	0.73%	0.99%	1.14%	0.00%	1.57%	0.00%	0.00%	1.14%	0.88%
Acquisition	32.72%	29.75%	23.82%	24.34%	30.21%	27.33%	23.65%	45.28%	5.00%	29.43%	39.56%
Pending acquisition	0.61%	0.00%	0.00%	0.21%	0.00%	0.00%	0.00%	0.00%	0.00%	0.00%	0.00%
Active	53.11%	57.65%	49.57%	45.18%	39.13%	42.73%	48.43%	28.30%	45.00%	35.57%	33.63%
Private company (non-PE)	0.09%	0.00%	0.00%	0.00%	0.00%	0.00%	0.00%	0.00%	0.00%	0.00%	0.00%
Bankruptcy – Chapter 11	0.00%	0.00%	0.97%	0.88%	0.76%	0.00%	0.00%	1.89%	0.00%	5.14%	0.00%
Bankruptcy – Chapter 7	0.00%	0.00%	2.07%	0.80%	0.38%	0.00%	0.00%	0.00%	0.00%	0.86%	0.00%
Defunct	7.00%	8.58%	17.50%	23.33%	14.89%	11.05%	15.19%	0.00%	20.00%	15.71%	19.34%
Other exit	0.00%	0.00%	0.00%	0.08%	0.00%	0.00%	0.00%	0.00%	0.00%	0.00%	0.00%
Number of observations	1143	921	823	3738	2632	344	1336	53	20	700	455

Notes:
This table summarizes investment and exit data for seed, early and expansions investments by select Canadian and US cities.
Sample period: 1 January 1990–25 June 2010.

Source: Thompson Financial SDC VentureXpert.

490　*Handbook of research on IPOs*

Table 21.7 Syndication of US versus Canada investments

Round number of investors	US funds investing in Canadian entrepreneurs			Canadian funds investing in Canadian entrepreneurs		
	Frequency	Percent	Cumulative frequency	Frequency	Percent	Cumulative frequency
1	1223	43.87	43.87	1320	48.89	48.89
2	863	30.95	74.82	690	25.56	74.44
3	345	12.37	87.2	346	12.81	87.26
4	191	6.85	94.05	215	7.96	95.22
5	87	3.12	97.17	80	2.96	98.19
6	35	1.26	98.42	32	1.19	99.37
7	12	0.43	98.85	2	0.07	99.44
8	8	0.29	99.14	14	0.52	99.96
10	9	0.32	99.46	1	0.04	100.00
15	15	0.54	100	0	0	100.00
Total	2788	100.00		2700	100.00	

Notes:
This table summarizes the number of investors (syndicated partners) of US cross border investments in Canadian companies versus Canadian domestic investments.
Round number of investors of '1' means the investment was not syndicated.
Frequency refers to the number of investments.

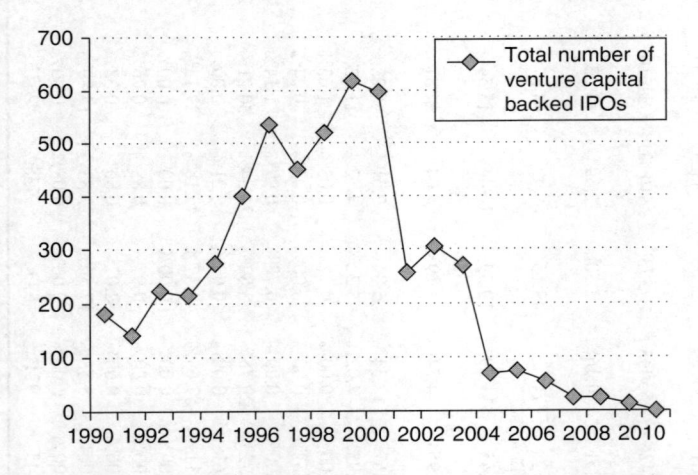

Note: This table presents the number of IPO exits from first round (new) investments in seed, early and expansion stage investments from all countries in the Thompson SDC VentureXpert database, 1 January 1990–25 June 2010.

Figure 21.19 IPO exits from seed, early and expansion stage investment worldwide

2006, 2007), excessive numbers of investee firms per fund manager (Cumming, 2006, shows that LSVCC portfolio size per manager is over twice that of private funds, which means that value-added provided is diminished; see also Kanniainen and Keuschnigg, 2003, 2004; Keuschnigg, 2004), and minimal time spent screening investments due to

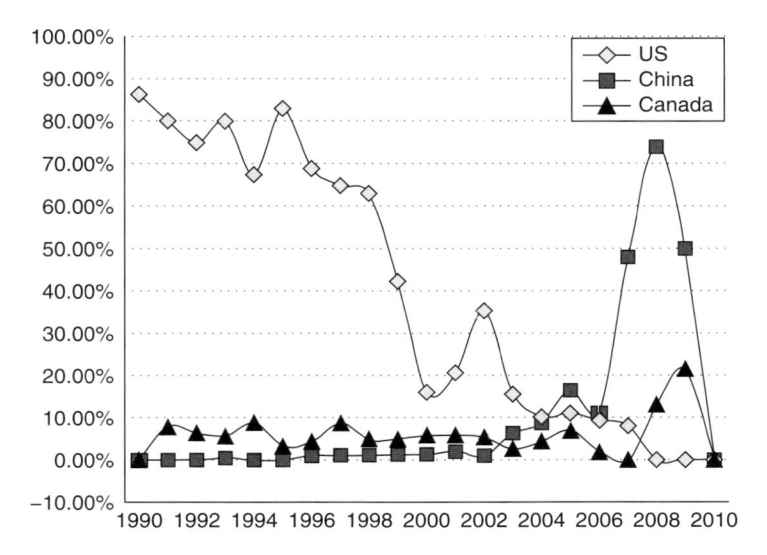

The IPO as an exit strategy for venture capitalists 491

Note: This table presents the number of IPO exits from first round (new) investments in seed, early and expansion stage investments in Canada, China and the US as a percentage of total world wide IPO exits from first round seed, early and expansion stage investments, 1 January 1990–25 June 2010.

Source: Thompson SDC VentureXpert.

Figure 21.20   IPO exits in Canada, China and the US relative to the world

time limits to reinvest capital (Cumming and MacIntosh, 2003, 2007). When one examines specific investments made by LSVCCs and compares to non-LSVCCs in Canada, one sees that LSVCC-backed firms are less likely to be sold as IPOs and acquisitions and more likely to be sold as secondary sales and buybacks (Cumming and Johan, 2008b), and those latter exits are appropriate for the poorer performing investee firms (Cumming and MacIntosh, 2003). Further, LSVCCs are more likely to exit sooner than that which would otherwise be optimal for the investee firm (Cumming and Johan, 2009, 2013), which negatively contributes to the development of the investee firm (Cumming and MacIntosh, 2003).

Figures 21.22 and 21.23 highlight the misallocation of capital in the Canadian VC market. With negligible rates of return (see also Cumming and MacIntosh, 2007) and weaker exit results than private investors (Cumming and Johan, 2008b), LSVCCs attracted the most capital (Figure 21.22). They also compete with private funds for deal flow. Labour-sponsored venture capital corporations had accumulated so much capital from investors that only cared about their tax incentives without regard to economic rates of return that LSVCC fund managers could overpay for any investment and outbid private investors. Private investors are responsible to institutional investors that do care about rates of return. We would expect private investment to be replaced ('crowded out') by LSVCCs. In fact, if institutional investors are risk averse, then they might overestimate the growth in LSVCCs from one year to the next, and crowding out might in fact exceed 100 percent so that the presence of LSVCCs actually reduces the overall supply of VC relative to what it otherwise would have been but for the presence

492 *Handbook of research on IPOs*

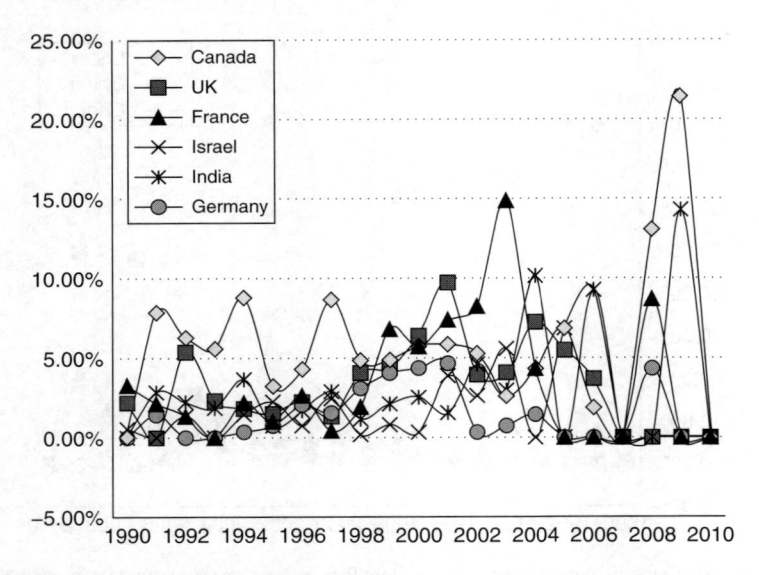

Note: This figure presents the number of IPO exits from first round (new) investments in seed, early and expansion stage investments in Canada, the UK, France, Israel, India and Germany as a percentage of total world wide IPO exits from first round seed, early and expansion stage investments, 1 January 1990–25 June 2010.

Source: Thompson SDC VentureXpert.

Figure 21.21   IPO exits in Canada and other countries relative to the world

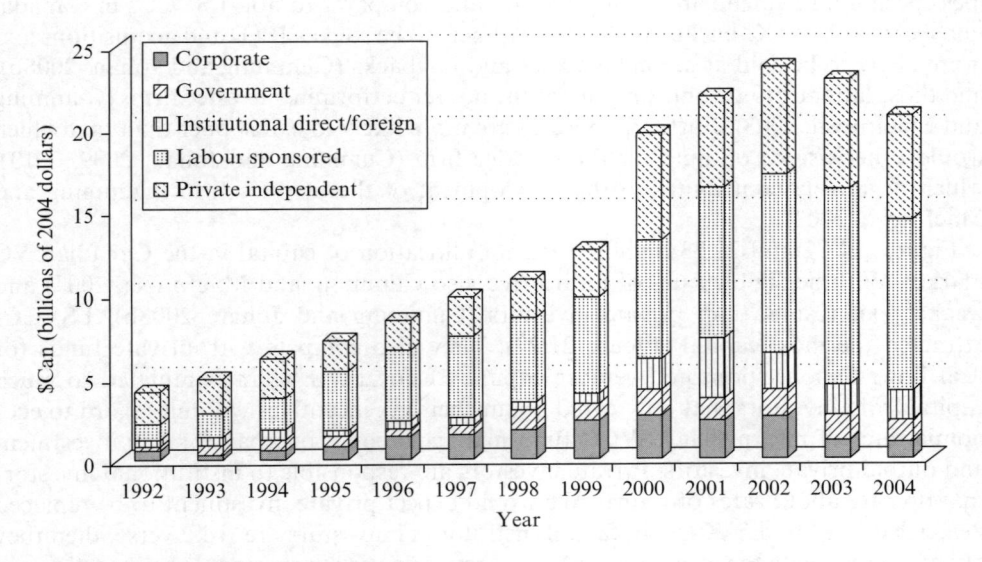

Source: Cumming and MacIntosh (2006).

Figure 21.22   Growth of different forms of venture capital in Canada, 1992–2004

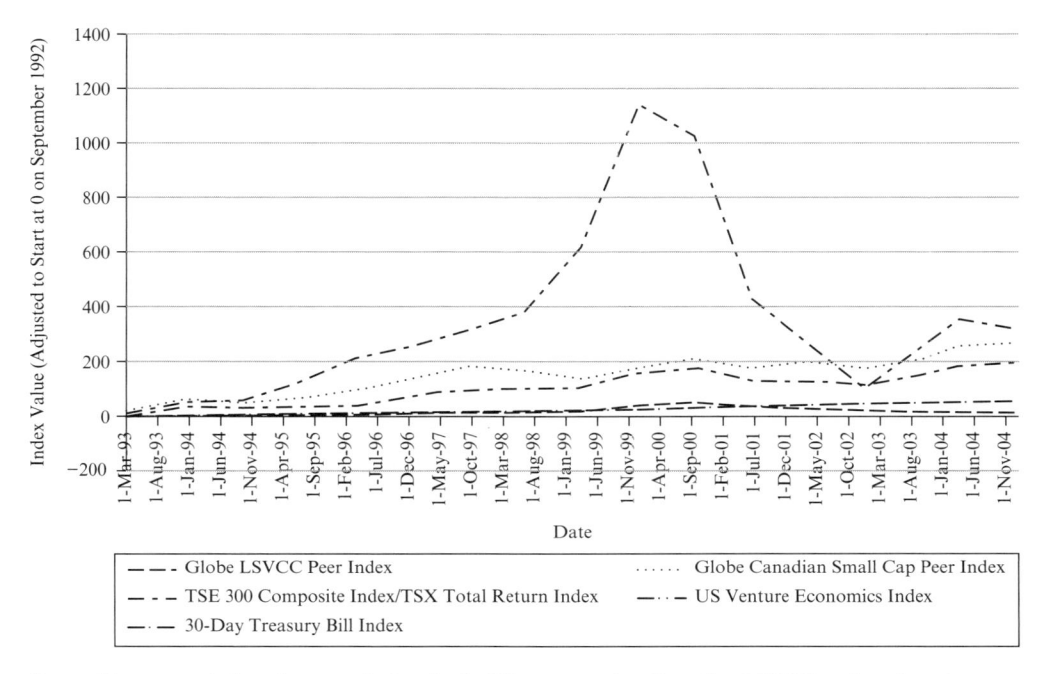

The IPO as an exit strategy for venture capitalists 493

Note: Venture capital performance indices in the US, compared to Canadian LSVCCs, selected stock indices and 30-day t-bills, 1993–2005.

Source: Cumming and MacIntosh (2007).

Figure 21.23   Venture capital performance indices

of LSVCCs. The empirical evidence in Cumming and MacIntosh (2006) is highly consistent with not merely 100 percent crowding out, but rather more than 100 percent crowding out.

Empirical evidence from LSVCC and non-LSVCC transactions shows that LSVCCs have inferior exit outcomes (Cumming and MacIntosh, 2003; Cumming and Johan, 2008b), inefficient investment duration (Cumming and MacIntosh, 2003; Cumming and Johan, 2009, 2010), excessively large numbers of investments per fund manager (Cumming, 2006), and LSVCC-backed companies have less research and development (R&D) and generate fewer patents (Brander et al., 2008). Further, fund-level data indicate that all LSVCC funds underperform all benchmarks, and older LSVCCs have not achieved better performance than newer LSVCCs (Cumming and MacIntosh, 2007). There is evidence that the only entrepreneurs that care that the Government of Ontario is phasing out the LSVCC tax credit are entrepreneurs currently supported by LSVCCs (Cumming and Johan, 2010, 2013), while entrepreneurs not affiliated with LSVCCs did not mind at all that the LSVCC tax credit was phased out in 2011. Overall, the evidence overwhelmingly supports the view that the Government of Ontario should not support LSVCCs. Labour-sponsored venture capital corporations' tax credits are expensive; LSVCCs crowd out private investors and reduce the overall amount of VC in Ontario, generate little in the way of economic returns and real outcomes,

494 *Handbook of research on IPOs*

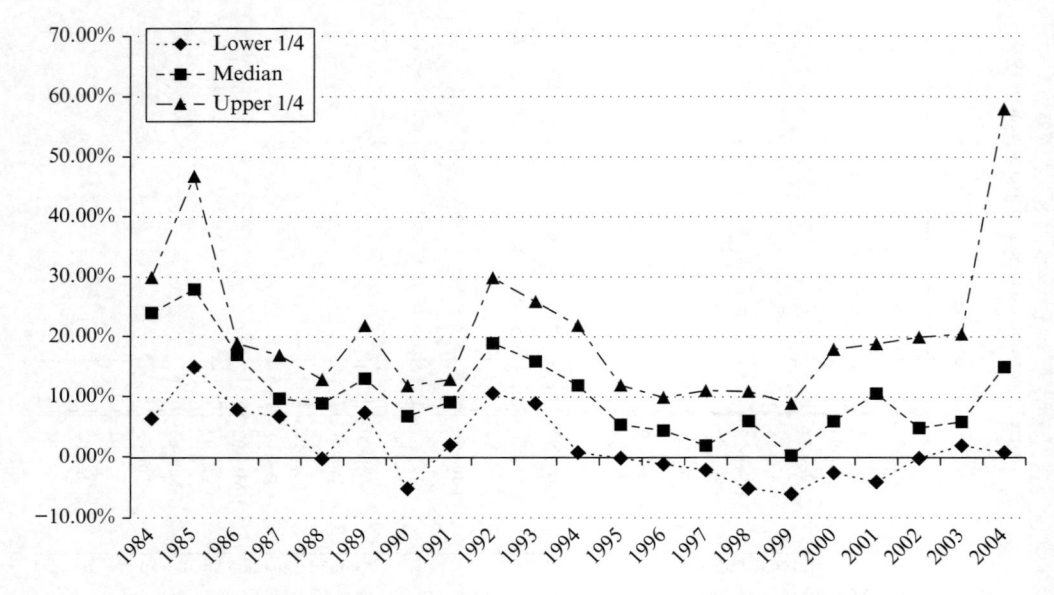

Note: This figure shows US performance persistence in private equity limited partnerships by vintage year.

Source: Kaplan (2007).

Figure 21.24 Performance persistence in private equity

and hence not only lower the quantity of VC but also lower the quality of VC in Ontario.

In the US, there are substantial differences in performance across different funds, and these performance differences show remarkable persistence over time (Figure 21.24). Top quartile funds in one year are much more likely to be top quartile funds in the next year, due to the superior ability of fund managers to add value to their investee firms, and their ability to attract better investee firms (Kaplan and Schoar, 2005). Unfortunately, returns to VC have been very low and persistently low due to the dominant presence of LSVCCs (Figures 21.22 and 21.23), and resemble the bottom quartile funds in the US presented in Figure 21.24.

The Thompson Financial SDC data show that prior to 1990, private Canadian VC funds invested more often in US entrepreneurial firms than Canadian entrepreneurial firms (Figure 21.25). In connection with the dearth of VC funds in Canada and dearth of private limited partnership funds (Figures 21.5 and 21.7), it is important to note that most Canadian VC investment at the seed, early and expansion stage involve US-based VC funds (Figure 21.26). Even accounting for all types of investors, including government investors and LSVCCs in Canada, there has been a greater presence of US investors in Canada than Canadian investors (Figure 21.27), but US investors, at the same time, invest only a small fraction of their investments in Canada (Figure 21.28). Foreign investment patterns are not uncommon in other parts of the world, as highlighted in Figure 21.29.

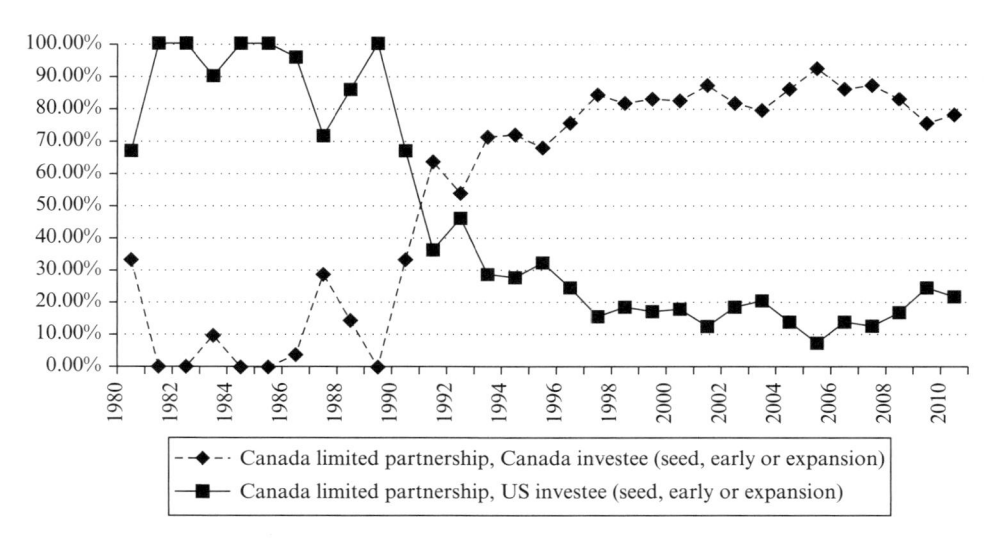

The IPO as an exit strategy for venture capitalists 495

Note: This figure shows cross-border private fund investments into Canadian and US investees in terms of percentages of the total numbers of investments each year in seed, early stage and expansion stage investee companies.

Source: All available venture capital transactions from Thompson Financial VentureXpert, 1 January 1990–25 June 2010.

Figure 21.25   Canadian limited partnership cross-border investment into the US

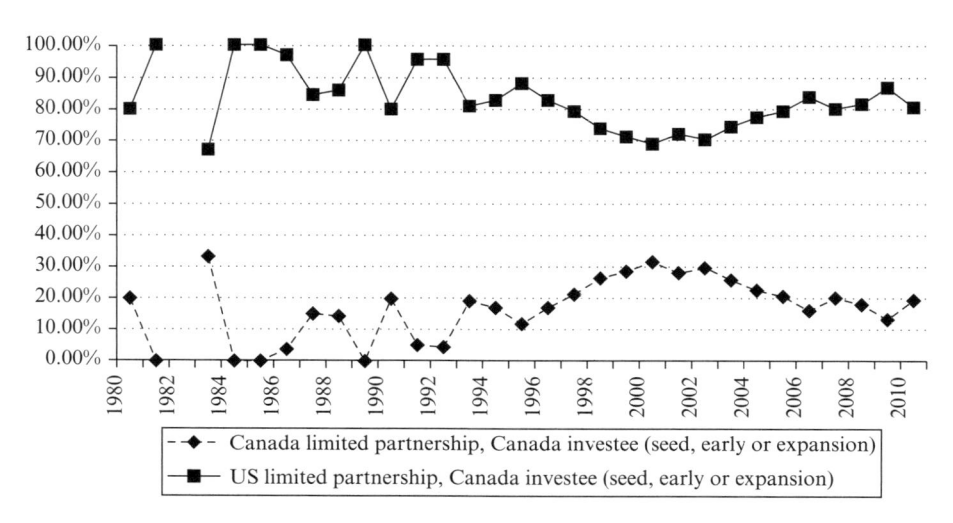

Note: This figure shows private fund investments into Canadian investees in terms of percentages of the total numbers of investments in Canada each year in seed, early stage and expansion stage investee companies.

Source: All available venture capital transactions from Thompson Financial VentureXpert, 1 January 1990–25 June 2010; Thompson Financial SDC.

Figure 21.26   Canadian and US limited partnership investment in Canada

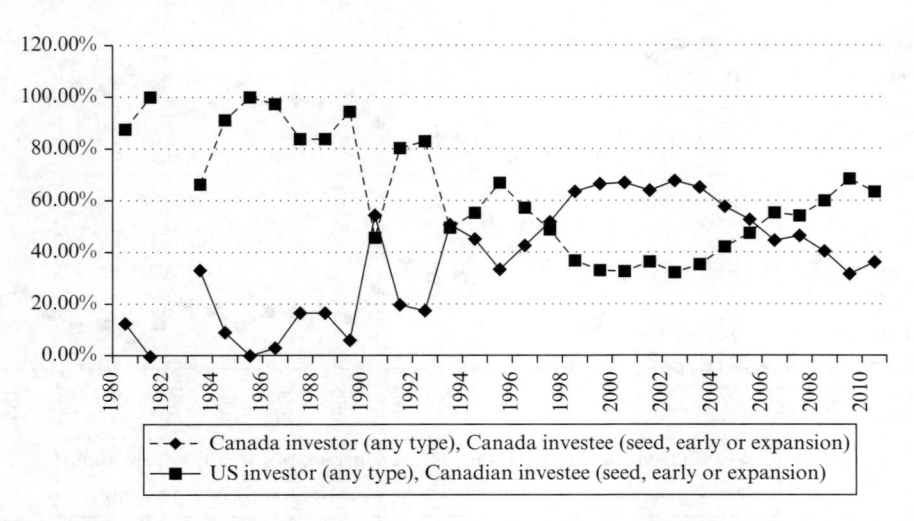

Note: This figure shows investments from any type of fund into Canadian investees in terms of percentages of the total numbers of investments in Canada each year in seed, early stage and expansion stage investee companies.

Source: All available venture capital transactions from Thompson Financial VentureXpert, 1 January 1990–25 June 2010; Thompson Financial SDC.

Figure 21.27 Investments from any type of fund into Canadian investees

4 2008 FINANCIAL CRISIS AND FUTURE OPPORTUNITIES

Indubitably, during the crisis, VC activity slowed down. In Block et al. (2012), the authors found that the crisis led to a decrease in the number of funding rounds. This decrease occurred within all industries and is larger for first rounds than for later rounds. The authors observed that VC funds were more reluctant to provide first-round investments toward 'new' start-up firms during the crisis than during the pre-crisis period, especially in the biotechnology, internet, and medical/health care industries. Within these industries, the percentage decrease in first-round investments was approximately four times larger than the decrease in later-round investments.

The slowdown of VC activity due to the crisis has been found to be more severe in the US than elsewhere. Block et al. (2012) not only show that the decrease in the number of funding rounds per month is more pronounced within than outside the US, but also that the difference is particularly strong for first-round investments in nearly all industries in the US. This difference in US versus non-US investments is confirmed with the Thompson SDC presented in Figure 21.30.

In addition to weakening in fundraising and weakening of performance, VCs are finding it increasingly difficult to exit from their investments. Looking at Figure 21.31, it is clear that not only have the number of IPO exits for VC funds in the US drastically declined since 2002, and this drop has been more severe in the US than outside the US. It has been much more difficult to take a company public in the US since 2002, and the number of VC-backed IPOs in 2008 and 2009 were actually higher in Canada than the

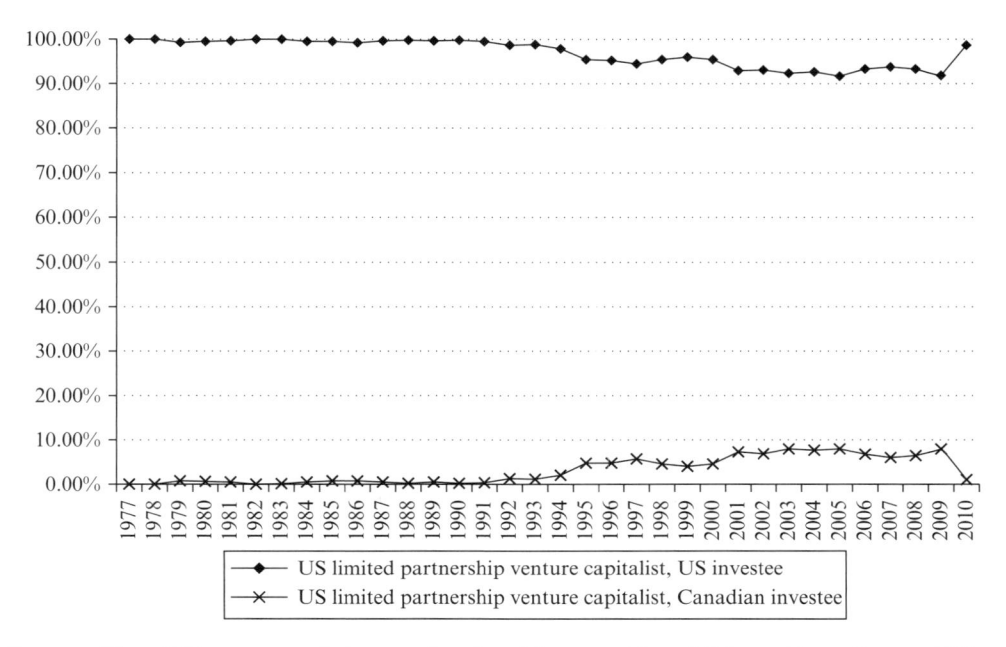

The IPO as an exit strategy for venture capitalists 497

Source: All available venture capital transactions from Thompson Financial VentureXpert, January 1977–March 2010.

Figure 21.28 US limited partnership cross-border investment into Canada

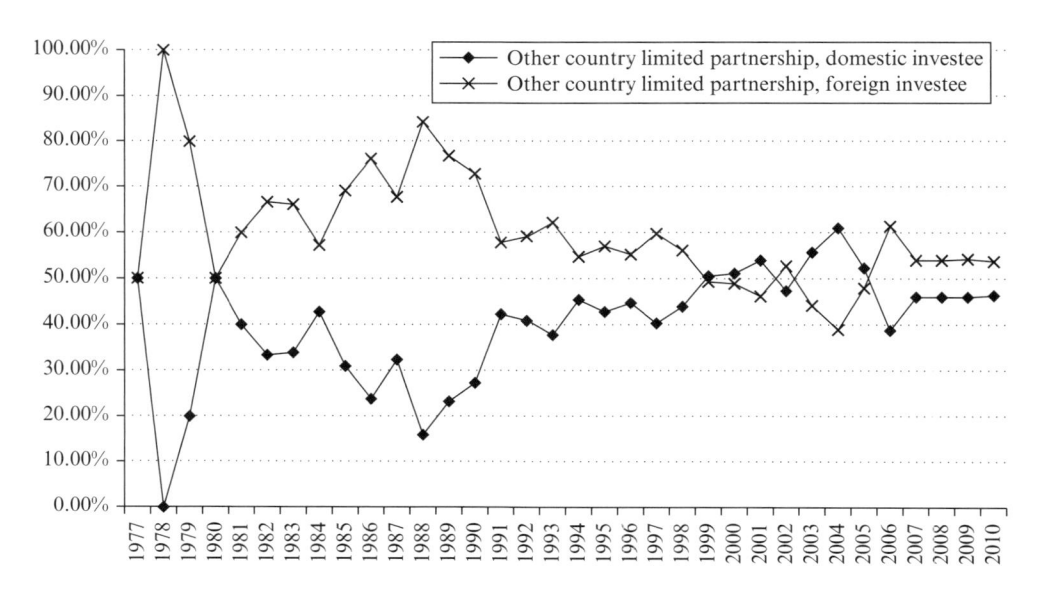

Source: All available venture capital transactions from Thompson Financial VentureXpert, January 1977–March 2010.

Figure 21.29 VC investments in domestic versus cross-border entrepreneurial firms

498 *Handbook of research on IPOs*

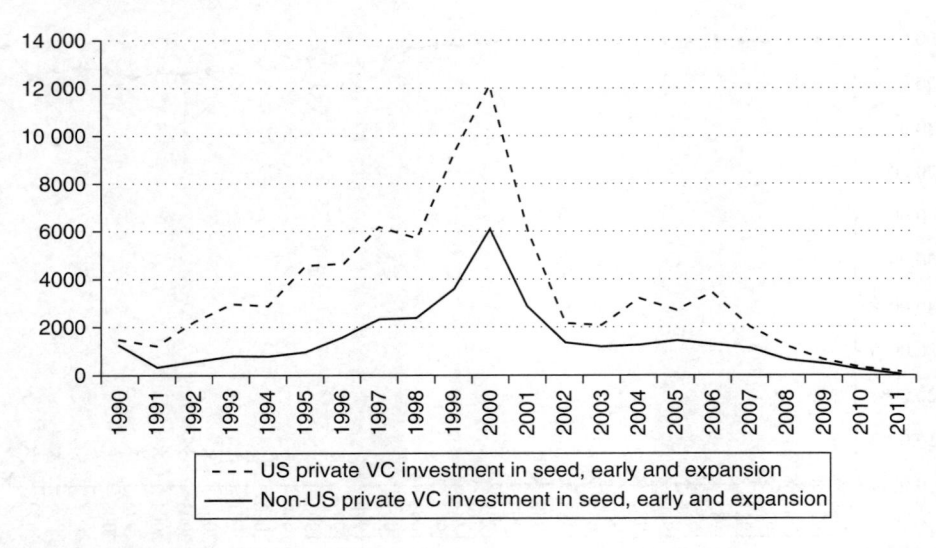

Source: Thompson SDC.

Figure 21.30 US versus non-US venture capital investment by fund vintage year

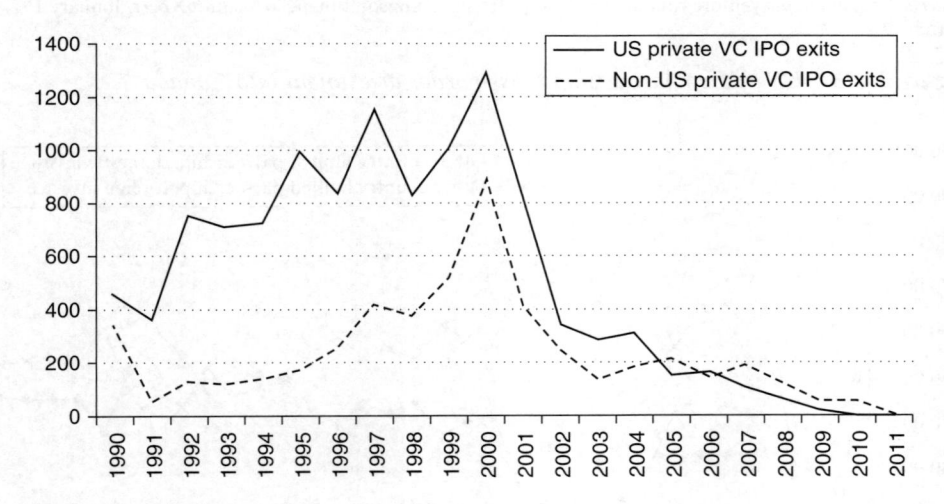

Source: Thompson SDC.

Figure 21.31 US versus non-US venture capital IPO exits by fund vintage year

US. Initial public offering exits are central to the VC investment process (Black and Gilson, 1998; Gompers and Lerner, 1999; Cumming and MacIntosh, 2003). These statistics suggest that there is significant reason to expect a growing interest from VCs in Canada and Ontario from the US and other countries in future years.

This decline in IPOs may not necessarily be attributed to the crisis, as the numbers have been declining since the bursting of the technology bubble and even more so after the introduction of the Sarbanes–Oxley Act as firms found the more onerous operational and disclosure requirements too costly to implement. It is essentially too expensive for nascent firms to seek listing and as such it is taking longer for these companies to go public. As these firms take longer to initiate an IPO, VCs are unable to provide their fund investors with the sought after profits by the time the fund life ends, traditionally 10 years from fund establishment. It may be the case that the traditional life of a fund has to be extended to 15 years, and while this may deter fund investors who do not wish to be locked into an investment for that duration, the extension will enable VCs to dedicate both the financial and value-added resources to ensure that their investee firms are more than ready to initiate an IPO (see also Metrick and Yasuda, 2010).

In addition to increased difficulties to exit from their investments through IPOs, and particularly since the global financial crisis, there has been a growing market in secondary private fund interests whereby fund investors transfer their limited partner interests to secondaries. The market for secondaries represents an important way for many investors to achieve liquidity, particularly since most funds are closed ended at the end of their 10-year lifespan and do not offer early redemption rights. Most of these secondaries to date have been buyout fund portfolios, often held by banks, although there is increasing interest in VC by secondaries. For the secondaries in the buyout market, it has been reported that sellers routinely achieve 90 percent of a portfolio's net asset value. With a growing secondaries market, it is possible that more investors may re-evaluate their view of VC and even when new fund structures with increased lifespans are introduced, such investments may still be attractive to potential fund investors. And for the sake of nascent companies, it is crucial that VCs remain an attractive investment class.

5 CONCLUDING REMARKS

In this chapter we reviewed data from Thompson Financial SDC that highlighted some interesting patterns about VC investments and IPO exits in Canada, with comparisons to other jurisdictions around the world. It is hoped that the highlighted patterns may stimulate future research efforts, with the use of data from other countries. It is worth highlighting three key statistics from the data presented herein. First, note that from 2000 to 2008, there was 12.8 times the amount of new capital commitments to newly established funds focused on investment in seed, early and expansion stage entrepreneurial ventures in Massachusetts on a per GDP basis than there was in Ontario. In other words, during 2000–08, it would have required an additional US$37.5 billion of new capital committed to seed, early and expansion stage capital for Ontario to be at the level of VC per GDP comparable to that enjoyed by Massachusetts-based funds. Hence, any government support would have to result in a pronounced multiplier effect. Future research may focus on what indirect government intervention with tax subsidies and other entrepreneur-friendly regulation (for example, lenient bankruptcy laws and lax securities laws), as well as direct government programs would provide such results.

Second, note that much of the VC investment in Canada at the seed, early and expansion stages of development is carried out by US-based VCs. In fact, in recent years, a majority of the investment in Canada is carried out by US-based VCs. For the subset of private VC funds in Canada and the US, a substantial majority of the investment is carried out at the seed, early and expansion stages of investment. Over the past 30 years, while the percentages fluctuate, roughly 70–90 percent of all seed, early and expansion stage deals financed by private limited partnerships in Canada involve US VCs, compared to 10–30 percent that are Canadian-based private VC funds investing in Canada. Future research analyzing the complementary roles of local and foreign investors in stimulating local innovation and entrepreneurship may be needed.

Third, we reviewed evidence consistent with the view that there is a problem with the quality of VC investment in Ontario. The rate of firms going public, typically viewed as being the best exit outcome for VC-backed firms, is lower in Canada than comparable nations (roughly 6 percent in Canada compared to 11 percent in the US and 9 percent in Israel). Further, the average VC investor in Canada finances a very large number of projects per manager, to such a degree that one wonders how they can possibly have time to add significant value-added advice, monitoring and governance to their investee firms. The average portfolio size (number of investee firms) per manager investor in Canada is roughly four times as large as that for comparable nations, which implies all else being equal to the value-added provided by a typical Canadian investor is a quarter of that provided by a US investor. In view of the related evidence in points one and two immediately above, these statistics on IPO exit outcomes and portfolio size per manager imply there is a shortage of skilled VCs in Canada, just as there is equally a shortage of VC talent in other jurisdictions.

These statistics, among others reviewed in this chapter, suggest there is a problem with both the quantity and quality of VC in Ontario and Canada. The number of firms financed, the amount of financing relative to GDP, and the funds raised from local VCs is substantially less than that in leading jurisdictions such as Massachusetts. Also, there is a problem with the quality of VC in Ontario. There are relatively few fund managers financing too many projects, such that portfolio sizes per manager are much larger than in other regions and countries. As a result, performance suffers in Ontario and Canada, as evidenced by the comparative dearth in VC-backed IPOs in Canada relative to other countries over the past 20 years.

The data presented herein showed that most investment activity at the seed, early and expansion stage level in Canada is a result of US investors. The costs of going public in the US, however, are extremely high and, as such, exit opportunities from VC in the US have been declining since 2002. International VC activity outside the US has picked up significantly in recent years. Canada could be well positioned to attract international capital, and would be well placed to encourage top-tier funds to locate to Ontario, but more research is warranted to identify the best methods to achieve this.

NOTES

1. See, for example, http://www2.parl.gc.ca/Content/LOP/ResearchPublications/prb0838-e.htm (accessed Sept. 2012).
2. http://thomsonreuters.com/ (accessed Sept. 2012).
3. The data presented in Figures 21.6 and 21.7 stop in 2008, not 2010, as GDP figures per province and state for 2009 and 2010 are not yet confirmed as at July 2010.
4. This statistic does not include generalist funds or late-staged focus funds, but rather only those funds with

a mandate to invest in seed, early or expansion stage entrepreneurial firms. Also, this statistic does not include follow-on fundraising by labour-sponsored venture capital corporations (LSVCCs) in Ontario. Unlike private VC funds that obtain capital commitments at the start of the life of the limited partnership, LSVCCs raise capital each year. The Province of Ontario announced the phase-out of tax subsidies to LSVCCs in 2005, and this phase out is effective for 2011 (see, for example, Cumming and Johan, 2010).

REFERENCES

Audretsch, D.B. (2007a), 'Entrepreneurship capital and economic growth', *Oxford Review of Economic Policy*, **23**, 63–78.
Audretsch, D.B. (2007b), *The Entrepreneurial Society*, Oxford: Oxford University Press.
Black, B.S. and R.J. Gilson (1998), 'Venture capital and the structure of capital markets: banks versus stock markets', *Journal of Financial Economics*, **47**, 243–77.
Block, J., G. De Vries and P. Sandner (2012), 'Venture capital and the financial crisis: an empirical study across industries and countries,' in D. Cumming (ed.), *Oxford Handbook of Venture Capital*, Oxford: Oxford University Press, ch. 2.
Brander, J.A., E. Egan and T. Hellmann (2008), 'Government sponsored versus private venture capital: Canadian evidence', in J. Lerner and A. Schoar (eds), *International Differences in Entrepreneurship*, Chicago, IL: University of Chicago Press, ch. 10.
Carpentier, C., D. Cumming and J.M. Suret (2010), 'The valuation effect of listing requirements: an analysis of venture capital-backed IPOs', working paper, Laval University and York University.
Carpentier, C., D. Cumming and J.M. Suret (2012), 'The value of capital market regulation: IPOs versus reverse mergers', *Journal of Empirical Legal Studies*, **9**, 56–91.
Chemla, G. (2004), 'Pension fund investment in private equity and venture capital in the U.S. and Canada', *Journal of Private Equity*, **7**, 64–8.
Cosh, A., D. Cumming and A. Hughes (2009), 'Outside entrepreneurial capital', *Economic Journal*, **119**, 1494–533.
Cumming, D. (2006), 'The determinants of venture capital portfolio size: empirical evidence', *Journal of Business*, **79**, 1083–126.
Cumming, D. (2007), 'Government policy towards entrepreneurial finance: innovation investment funds', *Journal of Business Venturing*, **22**, 193–235.
Cumming, D. (2008), 'Contracts and exits in venture capital finance', *Review of Financial Studies*, **21**, 1947–82.
Cumming, D. and S.A. Johan (2006), 'Is it the law or the lawyers? Investment covenants around the world', *European Financial Management*, **12**, 553–74.
Cumming, D. and S. Johan (2008a), 'Preplanned exit strategies in venture capital', *European Economic Review*, **52**, 1209–51.
Cumming, D. and S.A. Johan (2008b) 'Information asymmetries, agency costs and venture capital exit outcomes, venture capital: an international', *Journal of Entrepreneurial Finance*, **10**, 197–231.
Cumming, D. and S.A. Johan (2010), 'Phasing out and inefficient venture capital tax credit', *Journal of Industry, Competition and Trade*, **10**, 227–52.
Cumming, D. and S.A. Johan (2013), *Venture Capital and Private Equity Contracting*, 2nd edn, Oxford: Elsevier.
Cumming, D. and D. Li (2013), 'Public policy and business creation in the United States', *Journal of Corporate Finance*, forthcoming.
Cumming, D. and J. MacIntosh (2003), 'Venture capital exits in Canada and the United States', *University of Toronto Law Journal*, **53**, 101–200.
Cumming, D. and J. MacIntosh (2006), 'Crowding out private equity: Canadian evidence', *Journal of Business Venturing*, **21**, 569–609.
Cumming, D. and J. MacIntosh (2007), 'Mutual funds that invest in private equity? An analysis of labour sponsored investment funds', *Cambridge Journal of Economics*, **31**, 445–87.
Cumming, D. and U. Walz (2010), 'Private equity returns and disclosure around the world', *Journal of International Business Studies*, **41**, 727–54.
Gompers, P.A. and J. Lerner (1999), *The Venture Capital Cycle*, Cambridge, MA: MIT Press.
Johan, S. (2010), 'Listing standards as a signal of IPO preparedness and quality', *International Review of Law and Economics*, **30**, 128–44.
Kanniainen, V. and C. Keuschnigg (2003), 'The optimal portfolio of start-up firms in venture capital finance', *Journal of Corporate Finance*, **9**, 521–34.

Kanniainen, V. and C. Keuschnigg (2004), 'Start-up investment with scarce venture capital support', CESifo Working Paper No. 439, *Journal of Banking and Finance*, **28**, 1935–59.
Kaplan, S. (2007), 'Private equity: past, present and future', paper presented at the American Enterprise Institute, Washington, DC, November.
Kaplan, S. and S. Schoar (2005), 'Private equity returns: returns, persistence and capital flows', *Journal of Finance*, **60**, 1791–823.
Keuschnigg, C. (2004), 'Taxation of a venture capitalist with a portfolio of firms', *Oxford Economic Papers*, **56**, 285–306.
Kortum, S. and J. Lerner (2000), 'Assessing the contribution of venture capital to innovation', *RAND Journal of Economics*, **31**, 674–92.
Metrick, A. and A. Yasuda (2010), 'The economics of private equity funds', *Review of Financial Studies*, **23**, 2303–41.
Ruckman, K. (2003), 'Expense ratios of North American mutual funds', *Canadian Journal of Economics*, **36**, 192–223.
Samila, S. and O. Sorenson (2011), 'Venture capital, entrepreneurship, and regional economic growth', *Review of Economics and Statistics*, **93**, 338–49.
World Bank (2004), *World Bank Group Support for Small Business*, Washington, DC: World Bank.

22 Choice between alternative routes to go public: backdoor listing versus IPO

Philip Brown, Andrew Ferguson and Peter Lam

1 INTRODUCTION

Going public is the dream of many owners of private companies and it constitutes a major event in the life cycle of the firm. Listing has its advantages, among them being (1) an enhanced company reputation and profile, (2) access to an organized share market when raising additional capital, (3) a lower cost of capital, (4) liquidity for owners who wish to cash out, and (5) the ability to use shares to pay for future acquisitions. However going public is also costly. The out-of-pocket costs of an initial public offering (hereafter IPO) typically involve fees paid to investment banks, accountants, auditors, lawyers, other experts (such as geologists in the case of a mining company), underwriters and brokers. The IPO firm must also pay for the prospectus, stock exchange listing fees and numerous compliance costs. Other costs are less obvious, such as initial underpricing, the time spent by senior management to prepare the company for public listing, and the ongoing costs of meeting more stringent disclosure and regulatory requirements.

Traditionally going public via an IPO has been the predominant path for a private firm to obtain listing status on a stock exchange, although alternative routes for going public are available. Two alternatives are a reverse takeover (hereafter RTO; or a reverse merger, hereafter RM), and a sell-out to a publicly listed firm. These two alternatives are similar in that they both involve a publicly listed company taking over a privately owned firm. The major difference between the two lies in the ultimate control of the combined entity. In RTOs (or RMs), the private firm's shareholders acquire control whereas in the case of sell-outs the public firm's shareholders retain control. Because of the unique features of RTO (or RM) transactions, going public through this path is commonly known as backdoor listing (hereafter BDL).

A BDL deal is a complex inter-corporate transaction by which an unlisted privately held firm achieves listing status through the corporate shell of a publicly listed company. Normally the deal is structured as a takeover of the private firm by the public company, but in essence the vendors of the private firm obtain control of the enlarged public shell (hence the name reverse takeover). From the listed company's point of view, a BDL represents a major corporate restructuring which typically involves a change of name, business activities, board of directors, and management. From the private firm's perspective, a BDL can be seen as an alternative route to go public.

Backdoor listings occur on numerous stock exchanges around the globe. They are popular in Australia as there has been no shortage in the supply of listed shell companies on the Australian Securities Exchange (hereafter ASX). The ASX has been dominated by the mining sector, with many small exploration companies being listed. Given their high business risk and the cyclical nature of the mining sector, it is not unusual for a fair proportion of these firms to become financially distressed as a result of their failure to find a worthwhile deposit and their funds drying up. These distressed firms then serve as ideal targets for a backdoor listing.

In Australia, there is no formal regulation of BDL transactions as such. However, the ASX may impose re-admission requirements – requiring the merged entity to satisfy the initial listing requirements again as if it were applying for a new listing – when it holds the view that the RTO or RM transaction constitutes a significant change in either the nature or scale of the activities of the listed shell company. The initial listing requirements include fulfilling the 'profit test' or 'asset test',[1] meeting the shareholder spread requirement,[2] and lodgement of a prospectus.

Despite their prevalence, BDLs are under-researched in the academic literature. To illustrate, a BDL is often touted as a cheaper, easier and faster way to go public. Yet evidence to support this claim is sparse and largely anecdotal. Whether a BDL in fact brings all of the benefits commonly believed remains an open question. We provide evidence addressing that question. Another question we address is how private firms choose between the front door (that is, an IPO) and the backdoor when they do decide to go public.

2 PRIOR LITERATURE

There are some recent studies that do examine the decisions of private firms to go public through alternative routes. Most rely on evidence from the US and Canadian markets. For example, Gleason et al. (2005) and Gleason et al. (2008) examine reverse takeovers as an alternative to an IPO. They find RTO firms are generally smaller, younger and less profitable than their IPO counterparts. Reverse takeover firms also tend to have lower balance sheet liquidity and higher leverage (Gleason et al., 2008). Reverse merger firms tend to exhibit higher information asymmetry as a result of no prospectus requirement (Floros and Shastri, 2009; Carpentier et al., 2012), they have a lower tendency for insider shareholders to cash out, and they rely heavily on PIPE (private investments in public equity) investors for financing (Floros and Shastri, 2009).

Sjostrom (2008) argues that RMs and IPOs (in the US) are not directly comparable as the two primary benefits of going public, capital raising and liquidity, are largely absent for RM firms. Australian BDL firms are different in that disclosure by way of a prospectus and concurrent capital raisings are found in the large majority of cases (about 80 per cent of our sample). Thus Australian BDL firms are closer substitutes for IPOs than RM firms in the US or Canada. The Australian setting thereby provides a 'cleaner' setting when it comes to examining the choice between an IPO and a BDL.

Earlier studies have analysed outright sell-out to a public firm as an alternative to an IPO. Brau et al. (2003) find the IPO route is preferred by a firm operating in a highly concentrated market, with higher levels of insider ownership and assets but lower leverage and liquidity. An IPO is more likely when the three-month T-bill rate is higher. In a related setting, Poulsen and Stegemoller (2008) find a private firm taking the IPO path tends to have higher pre-transaction insider ownership and higher growth, with more investments and R&D expenditures, than a firm that chooses an outright sell-out to a public firm. As mentioned earlier, a sell-out is similar to an RTO (or BDL) in the sense that both involve the acquisition of the private firm by a public firm. The differentiating feature is that in a sell-out, even though the private firm's vendors may end up holding blocks of shares in the merged entity, no change of control takes place. That is, the shareholders of the public firm retain control of the enlarged entity after the acquisition. In the case of a BDL, the vendors of the private company gain control.

Listing by introduction is another alternative path to going public. By this process, private firms obtain listing status in exactly the same way as an IPO but without the concurrent offering of any primary or secondary shares. Derrien and Kecskes (2007) examine listings by introduction that are followed by an equity issue in the aftermarket. They argue trading in the aftermarket helps reduce the valuation uncertainty of these firms, which in turn lowers the degree of underpricing when shares are offered in the second stage. For a hand-collected sample of firms listed by introduction in the UK, they find initial returns are 10 to 30 per cent lower than for comparable IPOs. They also find evidence these firms engage in market timing, both when they list and when they issue shares at a later date. To the extent that BDL transactions represent an alternative for the backdoored firm to gain exchange listing status plus an option to issue more shares later, they resemble the two-stage strategy of listing by introduction.

3 DATA AND METHOD

3.1 BDL Sample

Backdoor listing typically comprises a sequence of structured inter-company events whereby a private firm achieves listing status. It does this by undertaking a reverse takeover of a publicly listed 'shell' (that is, a firm whose shares are listed on the stock exchange but otherwise are worth little). In Australia, reverse takeover transactions are normally structured as an acquisition by the public firm of all of the shares in the private firm, so that the latter becomes a wholly owned subsidiary of the former. The deal can also be structured as an acquisition of assets and business operations from the private firm's vendors. The public firm pays for the acquisition by issuing a large quantity of new shares with voting rights in the company. The shares issued to the vendors of the private firm may be supplemented by other forms of consideration, such as cash, stock options, convertible notes, and earn-outs (for example, performance shares). At the conclusion of the reverse takeover transaction, the vendors obtain effective control of the now combined public–private entity. The private firm becomes part of an enlarged group, which is publicly listed. The private firm's business and assets typically become the dominant focus of the merged entity.

From the above discussion, it is evident that change of control is the critical aspect of a reverse takeover transaction. Jensen and Ruback (1983, p. 5) define corporate control as 'the rights to determine the management of corporate resources'. In other words, control can be regarded as the ability to set the future strategic direction of a company or change the way its assets are deployed. The change of control generally can be effected through the following means: (1) ownership control, that is, controls more than 50 per cent of the voting shares, (2) board control, that is, controls more than half the seats on the board of directors, and (3) management control, that is, controls or occupies the position of chief executive officer (CEO) or managing director. For publicly listed companies, because of the dispersion of ownership, a majority shareholding (that is, more than 50 per cent) may not be necessary to gain effective control. In fact a much lower threshold (20 per cent) of ownership has been set as triggering the takeover provisions in the Australian Corporations Act.

We operationalize change of control as follows. If vendors of the private firm collectively control 50 per cent or more of the voting rights of the enlarged (former shell) company through share ownership, a change of control is deemed to have occurred. Alternatively if the 50 per cent shareholding threshold is not reached, then a change of control is deemed to have occurred if the private firm's vendors (1) collectively become the largest blockholder of shares in the merged company, and (2) either control more than half the seats on the board of directors or occupy the position of CEO or managing director.

Since information on BDLs on the ASX is not readily available, these transactions have to be painstakingly identified from various sources. Although no official definition of backdoor listing or reverse takeover exists in Australia, the media has used these terms to report news of corporate transactions of a similar vein. Consequently, media search was our primary source of information for BDL transactions. The following steps were followed to identify through Factiva a preliminary sample of BDL transactions.

1. A search of the Factiva database located 1604 media articles that contain the keywords (1) 'ASX' and (2) 'backdoor listing' or 'reverse takeover' or 'reverse merger' or 'change of activities', for the years 1992–2007.[3]
2. Through careful reading of the media articles (to eliminate irrelevant and duplicate cases), 296 potential BDL cases were identified.
3. The details of each deal were studied to ascertain whether it met the definition of a BDL transaction.
4. A history of name changes, including former names and dates of change, for each of the potential firms was then reconstructed, from information available on DatAnalysis (available through Aspect/Huntley) and www.delisted.com.au. The date of a name change is useful as the public firm typically changed its name after a BDL transaction to reflect a break with the past and the identity of the principal asset that was acquired through the BDL. Further, the date of the name change provides a reasonable guide to the timing of the BDL transaction.
5. Using the Signal G platform (available through Aspect Financial), corporate announcements and disclosures made by each firm about the transaction were read to confirm it was a BDL.
6. Once a potential case was confirmed as a BDL transaction, all relevant corporate announcements and documents about the proposed acquisition were acquired. They included any notice of suspension of trading on the ASX, notice of a general meeting of shareholders, any information memorandum or independent expert's report to shareholders, the results of any general meeting of shareholders, any prospectus or pre-quotation disclosures, and any notice of reinstatement to the ASX's official list.
7. Steps (5) and (6) were repeated for all 296 potential cases.
8. At the end of the process, a total of 183 cases meeting the operational definition of a BDL transaction had been identified.

Table 22.1   Sample identification of backdoor listing transactions completed on ASX

Preliminary cases through Factiva media search	296
Cases not meeting BDL definition	113
Confirmed BDL cases from media	183
Preliminary cases from Zephyr, Bureau van Dijk	46
Cases not meeting BDL definition	29
Confirmed BDL cases from Zephyr	17
All confirmed BDL cases (183 + 17)	200
Of which: Industrial firms	175
Financial firms	25

At a later stage of the data collection process, a second source of BDL cases became available to us in the form of Bureau van Dijk's Zephyr database on mergers and acquisitions. A search through Zephyr yielded 46 deals classified as reverse takeovers of ASX-listed firms over the period 1999–2007.[4] Further research into these firms using detailed company announcements resulted in the identification of 17 more cases, and a total of 200 BDLs spanning the period from January 1992 to December 2007. They comprise 173 ASX-listed entities, of which 148 were involved in one BDL transaction, 23 were involved in two, and two were involved in three BDL transactions. Table 22.1 summarizes our sampling procedure.

3.2   Matching IPO Sample

To examine the issue of why private firms choose to go public through the backdoor rather than the front door, a sample of IPO firms is also needed. Conceivably the choice is driven by macroeconomic forces. For instance, casual and anecdotal evidence indicates BDL transactions cluster by time and industry.[5] In addition there is evidence (Gleason et al., 2008; Adjei et al., 2008; Floros and Shastri, 2009; Capentier and Suret, 2012) that firms opting for the backdoor route are relatively small. An appealing question to consider is, after controlling for these three factors (timing, industry and firm size), what are the important determinants of the route choice of firms that do go public? Thus the IPO sample was matched with the BDL sample according to when the BDL occurred (based on the listing year), the BDL firm's industry (two-digit GICS sector),[6] and its size (total assets of the combined firms at listing).[7]

An initial sample of IPO firms was obtained from the Connect-4 database (for the years 1994–2007) and from SDC Platinum (for the years 1992–93). This sample was supplemented by IPO data made available by Gerry Gallery for the time period 1994–2007. After elimination of duplicates and IPOs where no data was available, the final sample contains 1660 IPOs that went public during the period 1992–2007. This compares with a total of 200 firms in the BDL sample over the same time period.

Matches were found as follows. For each firm in the BDL sample, an IPO firm which went public in the same year, belonged to the same GICS sector and had similar total assets was chosen. However given the fact that the number of IPOs on the ASX in some years within the sampling period is small, it can be difficult to identify an IPO firm that operates in the same industry sector and is sufficiently similar in size. To circumvent this difficulty, the definition of industry sector was broadened by collapsing the 10 GICS sectors into three broad categories, namely, extractives, industrials and financials, when an IPO firm of similar size could not be found within the conventional GICS sector.

3.3 Choice Model

By pooling both the BDL and the matched IPO samples together, the propensity of a private firm to choose to go public through the backdoor (rather than via an IPO) can be estimated using a logit regression framework. In this setting, the dependent variable is an indicator variable that takes a value of '1' if the firm goes public through the backdoor (BDL) and '0' if it is an IPO. Two groups of explanatory variables are employed, relating to the characteristics of the firm and the transaction. Several variables, relating to the financial characteristics of firms, are thought to impact the route decision of going public transactions. These include balance sheet liquidity, financial leverage, development stage, and profitability.

Upon listing, IPO firms may, relative to their BDL counterparts, exhibit a higher level of liquidity since they might have raised substantial proceeds from the public offering of their shares. In addition Gleason et al. (2008) report RTO firms have lower liquidity than IPOs. Although a case can be made for BDL firms exhibiting a higher level of liquidity if the shell company they have been backed into is essentially a 'cash box', the fact that many shell companies show signs of financial distress makes this scenario less plausible. Therefore a negative relation between balance sheet liquidity and the probability of a BDL is expected. Balance sheet liquidity (LIQ) is proxied by the ratio of cash and cash equivalents to total assets.

Gleason et al. (2008) find RTO firms are more highly levered than their matched IPO counterparts. It is also possible that BDL firms could become burdened by debt when they assume the liabilities of the shell companies. Thus a positive relation is predicted between financial leverage and the likelihood the firm chooses a BDL. Financial leverage (LEV) is proxied by the balance sheet ratio of total debt to total assets.

Compared to a sample of penny-stock IPOs, RM firms tend to be smaller and still in the development stage (Floros and Shastri, 2009). If private firms going public through the backdoor are younger and less developed than their IPO counterparts, their sales revenue is likely to be lower relative to their asset base. Thus we proxy a firm's development stage by its asset turnover ratio (ATO); that is, its ratio of sales to total assets, with a higher ATO indicating a more developed firm. Firms in an early development stage are inherently more risky because their business models and operations are not proven. Consequently a negative relation is predicted between the firm's ATO metric and the likelihood it chooses a BDL.

Backdoor-listing firms are likely to be less profitable than matched IPO firms at the time of going public. An initial listing requirement of the ASX is that firms meet either the 'profit test' or the 'asset test' before they can be admitted to the official list. Where a firm chooses the IPO route but does not meet the profit test, it is likely to be subject to pre-screening by any underwriter and will come under close scrutiny during the public offering process. In comparison, not all BDL firms have to fulfil the re-admission requirements and only a subset of them raised equity capital concurrently with the BDL transaction. On these grounds we may expect BDL firms to be less profitable than IPO firms. We proxy profitability by return on assets (ROA), measured as the ratio of earnings before interest and tax to total assets, and predict that firms with a lower ROA are more likely to choose the backdoor route.

Initial public offering transactions are known to involve a lengthy and complicated process, which can require the concerted efforts of a number of professional service providers and regulators. In contrast, BDLs are promoted by practitioners as a simpler and faster way to achieve listing status. Floros and Shastri (2009) report the median duration for their RM transactions is 51 days, compared with 83 days for IPO firms. Following Floros and Shastri (2009), we measure the duration of a transaction (DURN) by the time elapsed (in days) from the first announcement date to the completion date of the transaction for a BDL, and from the prospectus lodgement date to the first day of trading on the ASX for an IPO. For a BDL transaction, the completion date is defined as the date the merged entity is re-admitted to trading on the ASX (if re-admission requirements are imposed) or the date following shareholder approval of the transaction (if re-admission is not required). On the basis of the common belief among professionals and US evidence, a negative relation is predicted between the transaction's duration and the likelihood it is a BDL.

A going-public transaction may be accompanied by a cashing-out by the original owners of the private firm. In an IPO transaction, the original owners may choose to sell down their stake in the going-public firm by offering some of their shares as part of the public offering. However this may be construed by the market as a negative signal (overvaluation). For a BDL transaction, cashing-out may occur during the reverse takeover process when part of the consideration paid by the shell company to the private firm's shareholders is in the form of cash. Accepting the RTO consideration partially in cash reduces the proportional ownership of the private firm's shareholders in the merged entity. To the extent that reduced ownership would not adversely affect the exercise of effective control by the private firm's owners, it is plausible that cashing-out activities would take place. Cashing-out using a RTO transaction has the added advantage of avoiding some of the potentially negative signal (over-valuation) attached to a sell-down by insiders, since accepting part of the consideration in the form of cash is common in takeovers. However it may be argued that cashing-out by owners is more likely when the firm is more highly developed and more profitable. Thus it could also be expected that BDL transactions are associated with less cashing-out by insiders (that is, a negative relation). To capture the effect of cashing-out on the going-public route decision, we employ a dummy variable (CASH_OUT), which takes a value of '1' if the original shareholders sell down part of their shareholding in the firm during the going public transaction and '0' otherwise. Whether cashing-out is more common among BDL or IPO transactions is an empirical question.

Retained ownership (RET_OWN) is the percentage stake that private firm owners hold in the listed entity at the time of listing. Floros and Shastri (2009) find the change in insider ownership is smaller in RM than IPO firms. However the change in insider ownership is affected by both cashing-out and equity dilution resulting from the going-public process. For IPO firms, dilution occurs when shares are sold to the public as part of the listing process. For BDL firms, dilution can occur twice – once during the RTO, which typically results in the shell company's shareholders owning an interest in the merged entity, and possibly a second time where the backdoored firm raises additional capital concurrently with the BDL. As section 4 shows, almost 80 per cent of our BDL firms were involved in a concurrent capital raising. Thus it is conceivable that the original shareholders of BDL firms would end up with a lower level of retained ownership in the listed entity than their IPO counterparts. On these grounds a negative relation is expected between retained ownership and the probability of a BDL transaction.

It is well documented in the literature that shareholders of IPO firms have suffered losses due to underpricing, which represents a significant cost of going public. Proponents of alternative ways of going public argue that this cost can be reduced or avoided by a BDL. There is some evidence consistent with this view. For example, Gleason et al. (2008) show that RTO firms in the US have a mean (median) first trading day return of 7.88 (2.12) per cent, as compared to 23.05 (9.15) per cent for a control sample of IPO firms. To examine this possibility in Australia, the first-day return (DAY1_RET) for both the BDL and IPO samples is constructed, following Gleason et al. (2008). For firms with no concurrent capital raising, the metric is measured as the change in closing share price on the first full trading day after completion (either the day after shareholder approval or re-admission to ASX) relative to the price the day before. For transactions that also involved concurrent capital raisings, first-day return is calculated as the change in price at the close of the first trading day relative to the offer price. Since all IPO firms involved an offering of shares prior to listing, their first-day return is calculated in the same way as the capital-raising BDL firms. It is expected that BDL firms would have a lower first-day return (less underpricing) than the IPO firms.

Given the higher level of publicity and extensive marketing campaigns associated with IPO issues, it is likely that IPOs raise relatively more capital during the going-public transaction. Moreover, since not all BDL transactions involve raising additional capital, it is generally expected that BDL firms as a group would raise less capital than the IPO firms. To test this prediction, the natural logarithm of proceeds raised (PRCDS) during the going-public transaction is included as an explanatory variable in the logit model. In addition, since the size of the proceeds raised may be affected by whether an underwriter is present, an underwriter dummy variable (UNDERWTR), which takes the value of '1' if the issue is underwritten and '0' otherwise, is included as an additional explanatory variable. An underwriter is expected to be more frequently involved in IPO transactions than in BDL transactions that also raise capital.

Besides the above firm-specific and deal-specific factors, two additional variables are included to control for bias that may be introduced as a result of imperfect matching of the BDL and IPO samples. The first variable controls for cross-sectional differences in size and is proxied by the natural logarithm of total assets (ASSETS), obtained from the first post-listing balance sheet. The second variable controls for high-tech companies. It is proxied by an indicator variable (TECH) which takes a value of '1' if the private firm is engaged in biotechnology, internet, information technology, telecommunications or related businesses and '0' otherwise.

In summary, the cross-sectional model for the propensity of private firms to use a BDL transaction (rather than an IPO) to go public is specified as follows:

$$\begin{aligned}Pr(BDL_i) = {} & \beta_0 + \beta_1 Ln(ASSETS)_i + \beta_2 TECH_i + \beta_3 LIQ_i + \beta_4 LEV_i + \beta_5 ATO_i \\ & + \beta_6 ROA_i + \beta_7 Ln(DURN)_i + \beta_8 RET\_OWN_i + \beta_9 DAY1\_RET_i \\ & + \beta_{10} Ln(PRCDS)_i + \beta_{11} UNDERWTR_i + \varepsilon_i\end{aligned}$$

The coefficients of the explanatory variables are estimated in a logit regression framework using a pooled sample of BDL and matched IPO firms. The dependent variable is an indicator variable (BDL = '1'; IPO = '0'). The results are reported in section 4.4.

3.4 Data

Accounting variables are sourced from the first set of financial statements post-listing, obtained from Aspect/Huntley's FinAnalysis database. Where financial statement data is missing from FinAnalysis, equivalent information is obtained from company annual reports. Information on the gross proceeds raised and the underwriter, if any, is taken from the prospectus and verified by referring to Aspect/Huntley's DatAnalysis and company announcements through the Signal G/Image Signal platform. Daily share price data for computing the first-day return of the BDL and IPO firms is obtained from the Core Research Database compiled by the Securities Industry Research Centre of Asia-Pacific (SIRCA).

Ideally for the choice model to have predictive power, all firm-specific accounting variables would be based on the pre-transaction (that is, *ex ante*) financial statements of the private firms. However pre-transaction financial data for the private firms in the BDL sample is not usually available. In most cases, only selected balance sheet items are provided and no data at all from the income statement. The situation for the IPO sample is better but still less than ideal. This is particularly true for IPO firms that went public by meeting the assets test of the listing requirements: these IPO firms tend to have a short operating history. Any requirement that pre-listing financial data of the private firms be available would greatly restrict the number of observations that can be used to estimate the choice model. As an alternative, data for accounting-related variables from the first set of financial statements after going public is used to fit the logit model.[8] This set of financial data is not ideal because it will include operating results from the reconstruction date until the end of the financial year along with the proceeds raised from going public. So for a robustness check, the natural logarithm of any proceeds raised is included as an additional control variable in some models.

In the univariate and multivariate analysis that follows, only non-financial companies are included in the final sample. Financial firms typically have distinctive operating characteristics compared with firms in other industries and the structure of their financial statements and the information they disclose are different as well. Pooling financial and industrial firms together would render the results difficult to interpret. The exclusion of financial firms results in the final sample comprising 175 BDL firms and 175 IPO firms matched on year, industry, and size.

A preliminary check of the summary statistics for the BDL sample firms indicated that three ratios (LEV, ATO, and ROA) had extreme values, resulting in their respective pairwise correlations being close to unity. Further investigation revealed these extreme correlations were driven by one outlying firm, which had a total asset value of a mere (AUD) $10 801 (approximately GBP 7000). When this outlier is deleted from the sample,

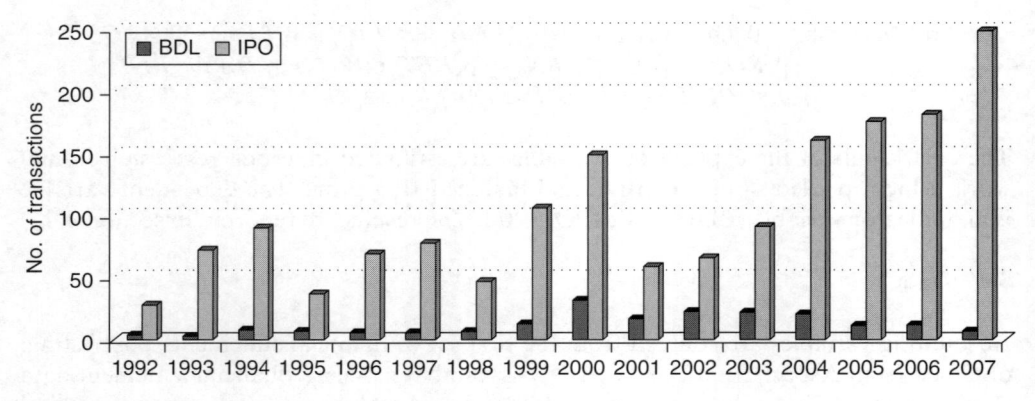

Figure 22.1   BDL versus IPO activity on ASX: 1992–2007

the summary statistics and the pairwise correlations of the three ratios become more in line with the corresponding measures for the matched IPO firms. Therefore the final sample to be used in the detailed analysis comprises 174 BDL firms together with their matched IPO counterparts.

4   RESULTS

4.1   Descriptive Statistics

Figure 22.1 plots the distribution of all 200 BDL transactions identified as occurring on the ASX over the period 1992–2007, together with the distribution of IPO transactions for comparison. The figure reveals a generally quiet epoch of BDL activity in the first half of the sampling period but more activity in the second half, with a clear break in 1999. Less than 10 BDL transactions were completed each year from 1992 to 1998, the lowest number being three in 1993 and the highest being eight in 1994. Starting in 1999, backdoor listing activity increased on the ASX. The number of transactions almost doubled from seven in 1998 to 13 in 1999; it peaked at 32 cases in 2000, before dropping to 17 in 2001. The number then remained at a relatively high level (more than 20) in each of the years 2002–04. Towards the end of the sampling period BDLs appear to have lost favour, with on average one transaction per month in 2005 and 2006. During the last year (2007), the number of transactions dropped back to seven, which is similar to pre-1999 levels. Overall the 1992–98 sub-period includes 41 BDL cases (20.5 per cent of the total) while the 1999–07 sub-period includes 159 (79.5 per cent).

Australian IPO activity has also gone through periods of relatively hot and cold markets, with troughs observed in 1992, 1995, 1998 and 2001, and peaks in 1994, 1997, 2000 and 2007. Another noticeable trend is that the number of IPOs increased substantially towards the end of the sample period, with a spike in 2007 when there were 249 IPOs in that year alone.[9]

For comparison, Table 22.2 tabulates the number of BDL and IPO transactions, and their sum, across the sample period. On a yearly basis, BDLs ranged from a low of 2.7

Table 22.2 Number of BDL and IPO transactions by year on ASX

Year	BDL (1)	IPO (2)	Total (3)	BDL as % of total (4)
1992	4	28	32	12.5
1993	3	72	75	4.0
1994	8	90	98	8.2
1995	7	37	44	15.9
1996	6	69	75	8.0
1997	6	78	84	7.1
1998	7	47	54	13.0
1999	13	106	119	10.9
2000	32	149	181	17.7
2001	17	59	76	22.4
2002	23	66	89	25.8
2003	22	91	113	19.5
2004	21	161	182	11.5
2005	12	176	188	6.4
2006	12	182	194	6.2
2007	7	249	256	2.7
All years	200	1660	1860	10.8

per cent (in 2007) to a peak of 25.8 per cent (in 2002). For the overall sample period, BDL transactions constituted 10.8 per cent of all going-public transactions on the ASX.

Figure 22.2 plots the distribution of going-public transactions across industry sectors. Based on the two-digit GICS classification, IPO firms seem to be more heavily represented in the materials (GICS15) and financials (GICS40) sectors, whereas BDL firms are more prevalent in health care (GICS35) and information technology (GICS45). This seems consistent with the view that BDL transactions are more popular among higher-risk technology firms.

Table 22.3 reports the summary statistics of selected characteristics of the 174 non-financial BDL transactions together with the matched IPO sample. The BDL sample has mean (median) total assets of $92.2 ($16.7) million, compared to $59.9 ($17.3) million for the matched IPO firms. Despite the apparently large disparity in mean values, the difference is not significant (two-sample t-statistic = −0.942, p-value = 0.3469). A non-parametric Wilcoxon rank-sum test shows the medians are not significantly different at conventional levels either (z = −0.116, p-value = 0.9075). Thus the two samples are reasonably well matched on the firms' post-listing sizes.

Table 22.3 reveals that the BDL sample is more dominated by technology firms than its IPO counterparts. This can be seen from the larger values for the mean of the TECH dummy variable in the BDL sample. The difference between the two samples is strongly significant (p-value <0.01, two-tailed). On average, 56.3 per cent of the firms in the BDL sample are engaged in a technology-related business while 41.4 per cent of the matched IPO firms are technology-related. This is the case despite the two samples being matched by industry.

In terms of financial characteristics, there is some evidence that firms in the BDL

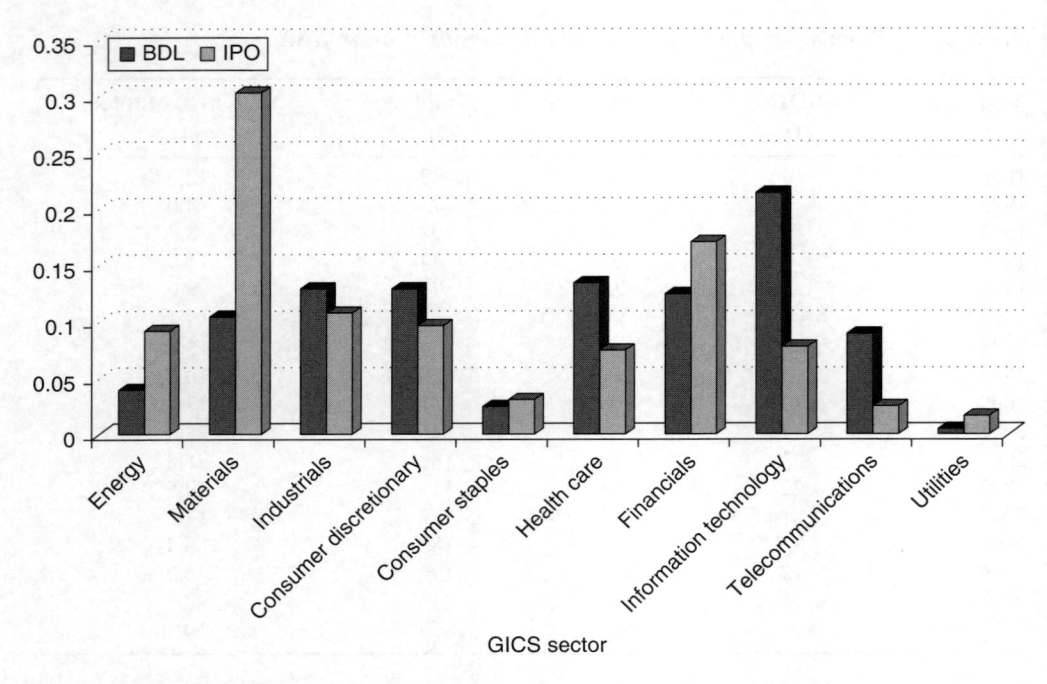

Figure 22.2 Distribution of BDL and IPO firms on ASX by GICS sector: 1992–2007

sample have a lower level of balance sheet liquidity, a smaller asset turnover ratio, and a lower (more negative) level of profitability, as measured by the return on assets ratio, than their IPO counterparts. The difference in median values between the two samples is strongly significant (p-value <0.01, two-tailed) for all three financial ratios. As for financial leverage, both the mean and the median values of the BDL firms are smaller than the corresponding values for the IPO firms, although the differences are not statistically significant.

Contrary to common belief, BDL transactions take longer than IPO transactions to complete. Measured from the first announcement date until the completion date, it takes a mean (median) duration of 162.9 (130.5) days for a BDL transaction to be concluded. For the matched IPO sample, Table 22.3 shows that the mean (median) duration, measured from the prospectus lodgement date until the first date of trading, is 54.5 (50) days. The difference between the two samples is highly significant for both the mean and the median values (p-value <0.0001, two-tailed).

Backdoor-listing firms tend to have a lower level of retained ownership than IPO firms and the results are statistically significant at the 0.0001 level (two-tailed). The mean (median) value for the BDL and IPO samples is 52.3 (52.8) and 61.3 (64.9) per cent, respectively. The lower level of retained ownership for BDL firms could be explained by the fact that, by design, original shareholders of the shell companies almost invariably hold an equity stake in the post-BDL merged entity. In addition the merged BDL firms may need to issue shares either to meet the ASX's shareholder spread requirement or to raise fresh equity capital. This would lead to further dilution of retained ownership.

Table 22.3 Descriptive statistics of BDL sample and size-matched IPO control sample

	\multicolumn{3}{c	}{BDL sample}	\multicolumn{3}{c	}{Size-matched IPO sample}	\multicolumn{2}{c	}{2-sample t-test}	\multicolumn{2}{c	}{Wilcoxon rank-sum test}
	N	Mean	Median	N	Mean	Median	t-stat	p-value	z-stat	p-value
ASSETS ($m)	174	92.20	16.70	174	59.90	17.30	−0.942	0.3469	−0.116	0.9075
TECH	174	0.563	1	174	0.414	0	−2.812	0.0052	−2.784	0.0054
LIQ	174	0.212	0.131	174	0.328	0.214	4.074	0.0001	3.170	0.0015
LEV	174	0.291	0.196	174	0.328	0.272	0.912	0.3626	0.983	0.3258
ATO	174	0.391	0.063	174	0.820	0.372	3.552	0.0004	3.610	0.0003
ROA	174	−0.239	−0.101	174	−0.154	−0.014	1.088	0.2772	4.625	0.0000
DURN (days)	174	162.9	130.5	174	54.5	50	−12.511	0.0000	−13.102	0.0000
RET_OWN	174	0.523	0.528	174	0.613	0.649	3.986	0.0001	4.552	0.0000
CASH_OUT	174	0.287	0	174	0.149	0	−3.149	0.0018	−3.109	0.0019
DAY1_RET	174	0.244	0.050	174	0.244	0.105	−0.001	0.9993	2.338	0.0194
PRCDS ($m)	137	7.54	4.08	137	26.20	8.66	2.269	0.0240	6.661	0.0000
UNDERWTR	137	0.314	0	137	0.644	1	6.092	0.0000	5.766	0.0000

Notes:
Table 22.3 reports descriptive statistics of selected firm and deal characteristics for the BDL sample and an IPO control sample. IPO control firms are matched on year of going public, GICS industry sector and size (post-listing total assets) with the backdoor-listed treatment firms.
ASSETS is post-listing total assets.
TECH is an indicator variable that equals 1 if the private firm is a high-tech business and 0 otherwise.
LIQ is a measure of balance sheet liquidity, calculated as the ratio of cash and cash equivalents to total assets.
LEV is the ratio of total debt to total assets.
ATO, calculated as the ratio of sales to total assets, is used to proxy for the firm's development stage.
ROA is return on assets, calculated as the ratio of earnings before interest and tax to total assets. DURN is duration in days between the first announcement date and the completion date for a BDL transaction and between the prospectus lodgement date and the listing date for an IPO.
RET_OWN is the percentage shareholding that private firm shareholders retain in the listed entity at the time of going public.
CASH_OUT is an indicator variable that equals 1 if private firm's shareholders sell down their holding during the going public transaction and 0 otherwise.
DAY1_RET is first trading day return, calculated as the change in closing share price on the first full trading day post-transaction from the day prior (for BDL firms with no concurrent capital raising) or from the offer price (for both capital raising BDL and IPO firms). PRCDS is the proceeds raised during the going-public transaction. UNDERWTR is an indicator variable that equals 1 if an underwriter is used and 0 otherwise.
The t-stat/z-stat tests the difference in mean/median between the BDL and IPO control sample.

515

Backdoor-listing transactions involve more frequent cashing-out by owners of the private firms than the matched IPO transactions. On average, 28.7 per cent of the BDL transactions involved cash as part of the overall consideration paid by the shell companies. In contrast, only 14.9 per cent of the IPOs involved the sale of existing shares by their original shareholders. The difference between the two samples is again significant. The greater prevalence of cashing-out associated with BDL transactions may help explain the lower level of ownership retained by the private firms' owners.

Table 22.3 reveals that BDL firms and their matched IPO counterparts have similar mean first-day returns (about 24 per cent). However the latter tend to have a larger median value (10.5 per cent) than the former (5 per cent) and the difference is statistically significant (p-value <0.05, two-tailed). The inconsistent result between the mean and median values indicates the computed first-day return for the BDL sample is more right-skewed compared to the IPO sample.

A prospectus was required by the ASX in 137 (78.7 per cent) of the 174 BDL cases. This is in stark contrast to the evidence for the North American markets and has implications for the information environment of BDL firms. Not all BDL transactions involve concurrent capital raisings. As Table 22.3 shows, 137 BDL firms (out of a total of 174) undertook concurrent capital raisings during the going-public transaction, whereas all IPO firms undertook a public offer and raised equity capital. In terms of the size of the proceeds, BDL firms tend to raise less capital, with a mean (median) value of $7.54 ($4.08) million, compared to $26.20 ($8.66) million for the IPO sample, and the difference is significant at the 0.05 (0.0001) level. The lower level of balance sheet liquidity observed for BDL firms reflects the fact that not all BDL transactions concurrently raised capital and the proceeds were generally smaller.

Of the 137 BDL transactions that did raise capital concurrently, 31.4 per cent engaged the services of an underwriter. This compares with 64.4 per cent for the IPO sample. Not surprisingly the difference between the two samples for the UNDERWTR variable is highly significant for both the mean and the median values (p-value <0.0001, two-tailed). It is, however, important to note that not all BDL-related capital raisings are necessarily public offers. Private placements of shares, which typically would not involve the use of underwriters, are common among BDL firms. This would contribute to the less frequent appointment of an underwriter in BDL-related capital raisings.

4.2 Duration of Transaction

Evidence presented in Table 22.3 indicates a much longer duration for BDL transactions than for similar IPO transactions. Since this result is inconsistent with the findings of Floros and Shastri (2009) and contrary to common belief, further examination is warranted. Table 22.4 reports the duration (in days) of BDL transactions across various subsamples. For all 174 firms in the sample, the mean (median) duration is 162.9 (130.5) days. For transactions that did not require re-admission by the ASX, the mean (median) duration is 97.4 (87) days whereas it is 180.6 (143) days when re-admission was required. The mean (median) duration is 154.0 (128) days for firms that did not raise any equity capital and 184.2 (153) days when capital was raised in the process. Based on capital-raising type, transactions involving public offers do not seem to be of longer duration,

Table 22.4 Duration of BDL and IPO transactions

	N	Mean	Median	SD	Min	Max
BDL transactions:						
Full sample	174	162.9	130.5	112.6	7	677
No re-admission	37	97.4	87	74.9	7	450
Re-admission	137	180.6	143	114.7	41	677
Re-admission & no raisings	16	154.0	128	67.3	56	281
Re-admission & all raisings	121	184.2	153	119.3	41	677
Re-admission & public offers	100	185.2	153	121.7	41	677
IPO transactions:						
Lodgement to listing	174	54.5	50	19.9	23	154
Kick-off to listing	174	96.5	92	19.9	65	196

Notes:
Table 22.4 reports the duration of the two types of going-public transaction.
For BDLs, duration is measured as the number of days elapsed between the first announcement date and the completion date of the transaction, where completion date is taken as the date following shareholders' approval of the transaction (if no re-admission requirement is imposed by ASX) or the date the merged entity is re-admitted to trading (if re-admission requirement is imposed by ASX).
For IPOs, duration is measured from either the prospectus lodgement date or the date of the kick-off meeting with the investment bank/underwriter until the listing date.

with a mean (median) value of 185.2 (153) days, which is similar to the corresponding measure for the overall capital-raising subsample.

Based on their industry experience, Kuo and Humphrey (2002) provide an indicative timetable for a typical backdoor listing transaction on the ASX. Their timetable starts with the appointment of advisors and ends with the re-listing of the backdoor firm on the ASX, but excludes any concurrent capital raising. Their experience suggests an indicative duration of 12 weeks (or 84 days). This compares with a median of 130.5 days for all the firms in the BDL sample and 143 days for cases in which re-admission is required. For cases with no capital raising, the median duration of 128 days is still much longer than Kuo and Humphrey (2002) indicate. Their indicative duration of 84 days is comparable to that of the no re-admission subsample, which has a median duration of 87 days. Note that the longest task in Kuo and Humphrey's indicative timetable is the drafting of the prospectus, which takes up to five weeks (35 days) to complete.

For the IPO sample, transaction duration is measured as the number of days between the date of lodgement of the prospectus and the listing date. For all IPO firms in the matching sample, the mean (median) duration is 54.5 (50) days. The above results indicate private firms take significantly longer to complete a BDL transaction than an IPO. This is still the case even if no re-admission requirement is imposed by the ASX on the backdoor firm.

The way the transaction duration is measured may understate the time it takes to complete the IPO process, which typically starts not from the date of the prospectus lodgement but from the date of the kick-off meeting between the IPO firm and the investment bank/underwriter, or even earlier. Floros and Shastri (2009) show, for the US IPO market for penny stocks, the median duration between the first registration of the prospectus and the offer date is around 83 days, and between the kick-off meeting and the offer date it is around 125 days. In other words, the average time between the kick-off meeting and the registration of prospectus is of the order of 42 days. This 42-day period is consistent with the indicative timetable of Kuo and Humphrey (2002), who suggest five weeks for prospectus drafting and another week or so for lodgement with the regulator, the Australian Securities and Investments Commission.

For a robustness check, this extra duration of 42 days, representing the average time between the kick-off meeting and the registration of the prospectus, is added to the original duration measure. Results from Table 22.4 show that this new duration measure for IPOs has a mean (median) of 96.5 (92) days, which is still significantly shorter than the duration measure for the BDL firms (p-value <0.0001, two-tailed).

Of course one can argue that the IPO process starts earlier than the kick-off meeting. Private firms may have spent years preparing themselves for the IPO. However the same argument also applies to backdoored private firms. The difficulty is that no objective measure is available to address this problem.

4.3 First-day Return

Similar to transaction duration, the first-day return metric for the BDL sample is computed differently across the sample, depending on whether the firm also undertakes a concurrent capital raising. The first-day return metric for the BDL firms is tabulated in Table 22.5 for different subsamples according to the transaction's attributes. There is a significant difference between BDL and IPO firms in the no re-admissions and/or no capital raisings subsamples. For the majority of firms which require re-admission or undertake a concurrent capital raising, there is no significant difference in first-day return. Thus BDL and IPO firms experience a similar level of underpricing when going public.

4.4 Logit Analysis

Table 22.6 reports the results from the logit regression analysis. Four sets of results are presented, corresponding to (1) the full sample, (2) the re-admissions subsample, (3) the re-admissions and capital raisings subsample, and (4) the re-admissions and public offers subsample, with the BDL firms in each subsample increasingly resembling their IPO counterparts. It can be argued that BDL firms in the fourth category are essentially de facto IPOs, since they have to re-meet the ASX's initial listing requirements and they concurrently raise capital through a public offer. Since not all BDL firms involve concurrent capital raisings, the two factors relating to the proceeds raised and the use of an underwriter are included only for the two subsamples where additional equity capital is involved.

Columns 1 and 2 of Table 22.6 present the results estimated for the full sample of BDL and IPO firms. The coefficient for the natural logarithm of total assets is negative but not statistically significant, reaffirming that the BDL and IPO samples are well matched on size. The coefficient for the TECH dummy variable is positive and highly significant (at the 0.01 level), indicating high-technology firms are more likely to go public through the backdoor (the same result was found in the univariate analysis). As for their financial characteristics, BDL firms tend to have a lower level of balance sheet liquidity. They are

Table 22.5 First-day returns between BDL and IPO firms across subsamples

	N	BDL firms Mean	BDL firms Median	Size-matched IPO firms Mean	Size-matched IPO firms Median	t-stat (p-value)	z-stat (p-value)
Full sample	174	0.244	0.050	0.244	0.105	−0.001 (0.9993)	2.338 (0.0194)
Re-admissions	137	0.299	0.075	0.220	0.100	−0.973 (0.3314)	1.204 (0.2286)
Capital raisings	137	0.256	0.075	0.238	0.110	−0.249 (0.8037)	1.054 (0.2921)
Re-admissions & raisings	121	0.285	0.083	0.227	0.120	−0.761 (0.4473)	0.686 (0.4930)
Re-admissions & public offers	100	0.241	0.078	0.207	0.100	−0.405 (0.6858)	0.784 (0.4331)
No re-admissions	37	0.040	0.017	0.333	0.110	2.444 (0.0170)	3.129 (0.0018)
No capital raisings	37	0.199	0.000	0.265	0.100	0.349 (0.7279)	3.411 (0.0006)
No re-admissions & no raisings	21	0.045	0.014	0.342	0.150	2.139 (0.0386)	3.115 (0.0018)

Notes:
Table 22.5 reports first-day returns for both BDL and matched IPO firms.
First-day return is calculated as the change in closing share price on the first full trading day post-transaction from the day prior (for BDL firms with no concurrent capital raising) or from the offer price (for both capital raising BDL and IPO firms).

more likely to be in the development stage (as reflected by the lower level of asset turnover) and to be less profitable. However no significant result is found for leverage.

Turning to transaction-specific factors, BDL transactions generally take longer to complete (DURN) and result in the private firm's owners having a lower level of retained ownership (RET_OWN). They are also more likely to be associated with the private firm's owners cashing out (CASH_OUT) part of their stake in the business. The coefficients estimated for these three factors are all strongly significant. No significant result can be established for the first-day return as a differentiating factor. The logit regression results are similar for the re-admissions only BDL subsample (together with their matched IPOs). As columns 3 and 4 show, except for the ROA factor, the same results hold for the significant factors identified for the full sample of firms.

Apart from slight differences in the significance of the coefficients estimated, the results for the two capital raising subsamples are similar to each other. As expected, Ln(PRCDS) and UNDERWTR load negatively, implying IPO firms raise more capital and are more likely to have used an underwriter to do so. When these two factors are excluded from the model, the results (columns 5 and 7) are broadly consistent with those found for the full and re-admissions samples. However after controlling for the two capital raising variables (columns 6 and 8), two noticeable changes emerge. The size proxy is positive and significant while the liquidity factor (LIQ) loses significance. Recall

Table 22.6 Choice between backdoor listing and initial public offering

	Predicted Sign	Full sample (1)	Full sample (2)	Re-admissions (3)	Re-admissions (4)	Re-admissions & capital raisings All offer types (5)	Re-admissions & capital raisings All offer types (6)	Re-admissions & capital raisings Public offers (7)	Re-admissions & capital raisings Public offers (8)
CONSTANT		2.007 (1.06)	−5.122* (−1.93)	2.887 (1.17)	−12.317*** (−3.03)	−11.778** (−2.54)	−5.570 (−0.91)	−13.029** (−2.35)	−3.452 (−0.48)
Ln(ASSETS)	−	−0.078 (−0.73)	−0.010 (−0.08)	−0.117 (−0.83)	−0.019 (−0.11)	0.019 (0.09)	1.824*** (3.97)	0.072 (0.29)	1.477*** (3.02)
TECH	+	0.790*** (3.14)	0.935*** (3.40)	0.870*** (3.08)	1.027*** (3.01)	1.334*** (3.38)	1.242** (2.51)	1.075*** (2.54)	1.039** (2.04)
LIQ	−	−2.975*** (−5.36)	−2.451*** (−4.13)	−3.161*** (−5.13)	−2.341*** (−3.29)	−3.144*** (−3.85)	−0.595 (−0.57)	−3.233*** (−3.56)	−1.132 (−0.98)
LEV	+	0.210 (0.40)	0.491 (0.96)	−0.663 (−1.07)	−1.047 (−1.45)	−1.386* (−1.71)	−0.576 (−0.42)	−1.601* (−1.78)	−0.992 (−0.71)
ATO	−	−0.783*** (−3.95)	−0.732*** (−3.61)	−0.735*** (−3.12)	−0.652** (−2.36)	−0.888** (−2.27)	−1.237** (−2.18)	−0.807* (−1.93)	−0.960* (−1.66)
ROA	−	−0.419* (−1.71)	−0.434* (−1.70)	−0.401 (−1.51)	−0.389 (−1.36)	−0.939** (−2.15)	−1.835*** (−2.88)	−0.965** (−2.15)	−1.661*** (−2.66)
Ln(DURN)	−		1.381*** (4.59)		2.912*** (5.75)	2.874*** (5.29)	2.937*** (4.79)	3.023*** (4.89)	2.740*** (4.27)

CASH_OUT	–	0.973***		1.450***		2.010***	1.334**	1.811**
		(2.85)		(3.09)		(2.66)	(2.29)	(2.24)
RET_OWN	–	−1.790***		−1.383*	1.335**	−6.956***	−3.060***	−6.390***
		(−2.96)		(−1.87)	(2.54)	(−5.29)	(−3.06)	(−4.53)
DAY1_RET	–	−0.030		0.281	−2.871***	0.043	0.051	0.069
		(−0.15)		(0.97)	(−3.31)	(0.10)	(0.14)	(0.15)
Ln(PRCDS)	–				0.158	−2.206***		−1.918***
					(0.47)	(−5.10)		(−4.30)
UNDERWTR	–					−1.522***		−1.254**
						(−3.07)		(−2.47)
No. of observations	348	348	274	274	242	242	200	200
Log likelihood	−210.21	−185.96	−163.26	−125.26	−99.32	−67.32	−82.07	−60.11
LR Chi-squared	62.01	110.50	53.33	129.31	136.84	200.84	113.12	157.04
Pseudo R^2	0.1285	0.2291	0.1404	0.3404	0.4079	0.5987	0.4080	0.5664
Correctly classified	0.6839	0.7414	0.7044	0.8139	0.8374	0.8884	0.8200	0.8650

Notes:
Table 22.6 reports the results from a logit regression of the choice of a **BDL** or **IPO** transaction on a set of firm and deal characteristics as potential determinants. The dependent variable is set to 1 for **BDLs** and 0 for **IPOs**. For a description of the individual explanatory variables, refer to the notes in Table 22.3. Z-statistics are reported in parentheses.
*, ** and *** indicates significance at the 10%, 5% and 1% level, respectively.

that the BDL and IPO sample firms are matched on post-listing total assets, which include any proceeds raised during their going-public transaction. To the extent that IPO firms raised more proceeds during their public offering than their BDL counterparts (as indicated by the negative coefficient for proceeds), these results can be taken to imply that the latter group is actually larger (in terms of total assets) than the former group on a pre-money basis. After controlling for the amount of capital raised, the LIQ factor is insignificant. In other words, on a pre-money basis, IPO firms are not necessarily more liquid than their BDL counterparts. There is also some weak evidence (significant at the 0.1 level) that IPO firms tend to be more highly levered than their capital-raising BDL counterparts. However the results are insignificant when proceeds from capital raisings are controlled for.

Overall the logit regression models perform reasonably well in differentiating firms between backdoor and front-door listing. The pseudo R^2 ranges from 0.23 for the full sample to 0.60 for the re-admissions and capital raisings subsample, with the corresponding percentage of firms correctly classified being 74 per cent and 89 per cent, respectively.

To gauge the economic significance of each explanatory factor, its marginal effect is evaluated as follows. Using the coefficients estimated from the logit regression models, the probability of the 'typical' private firm using the backdoor route is first evaluated by setting each individual factor equal to its respective (pooled) median value. This is the base case scenario. Where a particular factor is measured as a continuous variable, its marginal effect is gauged by computing the change in probability resulting from a one standard deviation decrease from the pooled median value of the factor, while holding all other variables constant at their median values. Where a particular factor is an indicator variable, its marginal effect is evaluated by the effect of a discrete change in its value: from zero to one if the median is zero, and from one to zero if the median is one. This procedure is repeated for each factor in the logit models and the results are tabulated in Table 22.7.

For the full sample of firms, the most significant determinant of firms opting for the backdoor path is CASH_OUT. Controlling for other factors, its effect on the marginal probability of a BDL (as opposed to an IPO) is 0.24. This is followed closely by TECH (0.23) and ATO (0.21). The results are similar but stronger for the re-admissions subsample. Again BDL transactions are more likely to involve cashing-out activities (0.34) and high-technology firms (0.25). However, instead of ATO, transaction duration comes up as the third most significant factor. A one standard deviation decrease in Ln(DURN) would result in the probability of a BDL transaction dropping by 0.24. Other significant determinants of BDLs include UNDERWTR and Ln(DURN) for the 'all offer types' subsample and Ln(PRCDS) and CASH_OUT for the 'public offers only' subsample.

The size factor reveals its significance only in the two re-admissions and capital raisings subsamples. After controlling for the amount of proceeds raised, a one standard deviation decrease in Ln(ASSETS) corresponds with a marginal probability of −0.46 and −0.31 for the 'all offer types' and 'public offers only' subsamples, respectively. While the size difference suggests BDL firms are larger on a pre-money basis, this result could be artifactual since BDL and IPO firms are matched according to their post-transaction assets.

Table 22.7 Marginal effect of individual factors on the likelihood of BDL over IPO

	Full sample	Re-admissions	Re-admissions & all offer types	Re-admissions & public offers
Ln(ASSETS)	0.0030	0.0052	−0.4561	−0.3082
TECH	0.2288	0.2513	−0.2881	0.2453
LIQ	0.1650	0.1612	0.0308	0.0790
LEV	−0.0441	0.0906	0.0392	0.0990
ATO	0.2062	0.1893	0.1860	0.2681
ROA	0.0775	0.0730	0.1752	0.2994
Ln(DURN)	−0.1567	−0.2430	−0.3420	−0.2836
RET_OWN	0.0954	0.0710	0.1817	0.2931
CASH_OUT	0.2376	0.3450	0.2130	0.3753
DAY1_RET	0.0046	−0.0426	−0.0050	−0.0100
Ln(PRCDS)			0.2483	0.4905
UNDERWTR			−0.3561	−0.2673

Notes:
Table 22.7 reports the marginal effect of individual factors on the likelihood of a private firm choosing the backdoor route to go public as opposed to an IPO.
The probability of an 'average' private firm choosing the backdoor route is first evaluated by using the coefficients estimated from the logit model and setting each factor to its respective pooled median value. The marginal effect of a particular factor is then gauged by computing the change in probability resulting from a one standard deviation change (decrease) in the value of the factor from its pooled median, while holding all other factors constant at their median value (the marginal effect of an indicator variable is evaluated by a change in value from zero to one or from one to zero, depending on its median value).

5 ROBUSTNESS TESTS

One concern regarding the matched sample approach is that if BDL firms are in fact typically smaller, then matching the IPO firms with the BDL firms on size would render the matched IPO sample not representative of the overall population. This may limit the extent to which the above results can be generalized.

5.1 Checks Based on IPO Size Deciles

To address the above concern, all 1660 IPO firms are sorted into 10 size deciles according to their post-listing total assets (converted to 2007 constant dollars). The sample of BDL firms is then assigned to these size deciles according to their post-transaction total assets (also converted to 2007 constant dollars). If the claim that BDL firms are smaller firms compared to their IPO counterparts is valid, then BDL firms should be clustered in the left tail of the size deciles.

Figure 22.3 plots the distribution of the percentage of BDL firms across the IPO size deciles, with decile 1 representing the smallest and decile 10 the largest. As is evident from the plot, BDL firms are well represented across all 10 deciles. Instead of being skewed to the left (smaller size), the BDL sample demonstrates a typical bell-shaped distribution, with a higher density observed across the mid-range (4, 5, 6, 7 and 8) size

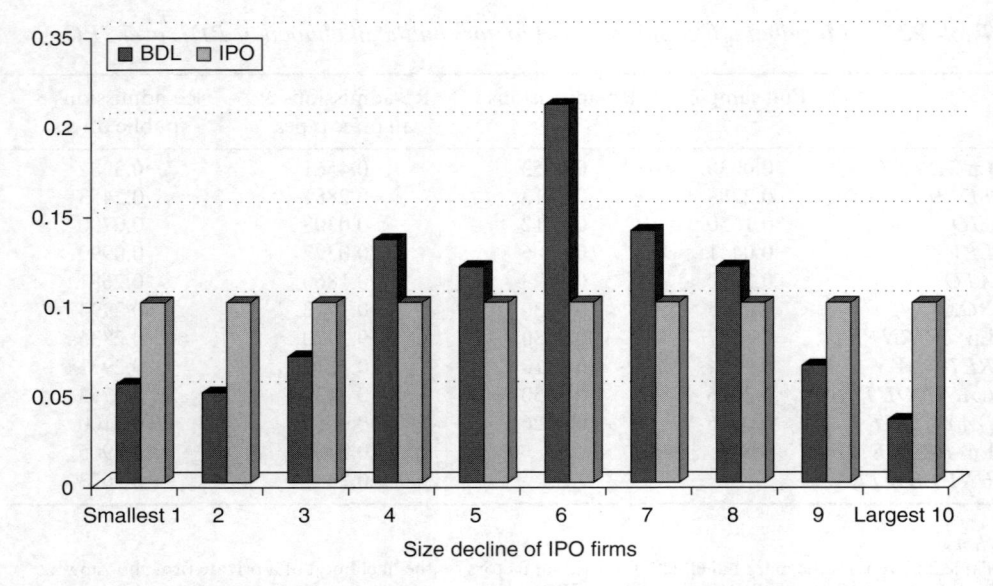

Figure 22.3 Distribution of BDL firms across IPO size deciles on ASX: 1992–2007

deciles and lower density observed in both tails. This evidence suggests that the results based on the size-matched IPO sample are not particularly biased towards smaller firms.

5.2 IPO Control Sample Randomized on Size

To further ascertain the sensitivity of the choice model results, we construct a second sample of IPO firms matched with the BDL firms on year and industry, but not size. The same choice model is then re-estimated using this new set of IPO firms.

Table 22.8 reports the summary statistics for the non-size matched IPO sample. Randomization on size yields a sample of IPOs that are, on average, larger in total assets. The mean (median) size of the IPO firms is $101 ($20.5) million. This compares with a mean (median) value of $92.2 ($16.7) million for the BDL sample and $59.9 ($17.3) million for the size-matched IPO sample.

Other than size, the only other noticeable difference from the size-matched sample is that the proportion of IPO transactions involving cashing-out activities by private firm owners has increased substantially to 26 per cent, which contrasts with 15 per cent for the size-matched sample and 29 per cent for the BDL sample. This set of combined results seems to suggest that original shareholders of larger IPO firms are more likely to sell down their stakes during the public offering process, relative to smaller IPO firms. However, controlling for size, owners of backdoored private firms are still more likely to partially cash out their holdings.

Table 22.9 reports the results from the logit regression analysis. Overall the results are broadly consistent with the previous results found for the size-matched IPO sample, with a few notable exceptions. The negative coefficient estimated for ATO and ROA

Table 22.8 Descriptive statistics of BDL sample and non-size matched IPO control sample

	BDL sample			Non-size matched IPO sample			2-sample t-test		Wilcoxon rank-sum test	
	N	Mean	Median	N	Mean	Median	t-stat	p-value	z-stat	p-value
ASSETS ($m)	174	92.20	16.70	174	101.00	20.50	0.224	0.8229	0.945	0.3445
TECH	174	0.563	1	174	0.460	0	−1.935	0.0538	−1.928	0.0539
LIQ	174	0.212	0.131	174	0.335	0.241	4.304	0.0000	3.396	0.0007
LEV	174	0.291	0.196	174	0.296	0.237	0.134	0.8932	0.504	0.6142
ATO	174	0.391	0.063	174	0.776	0.358	3.225	0.0014	2.947	0.0032
ROA	174	−0.239	−0.101	174	−0.083	0.007	2.075	0.0387	5.767	0.0000
DURN (days)	174	162.9	130.5	174	57.5	50	−11.917	0.0000	−12.780	0.0000
RET_OWN	174	0.523	0.528	174	0.595	0.628	3.221	0.0014	3.894	0.0001
CASH_OUT	174	0.287	0	174	0.259	0	−0.600	0.5488	−0.601	0.5480
DAY1_RET	174	0.244	0.050	174	0.235	0.100	−0.117	0.9069	1.753	0.0797
PRCDS ($m)	137	7.54	4.08	174	41.30	10.50	3.210	0.0015	7.454	0.0000
UNDERWTR	137	0.314	0	174	0.621	1	5.625	0.0000	5.366	0.0000

Notes:
Table 22.8 reports descriptive statistics of selected firm and deal characteristics for the BDL sample and an IPO control sample. IPO control firms are matched on year of going public and GICS industry sector only, but not size, with the backdoor-listed treatment firms.
ASSETS is post-listing total assets.
TECH is an indicator variable that equals 1 if the private firm is a high-technology business and 0 otherwise.
LIQ is a measure of balance sheet liquidity, calculated as the ratio of cash and cash equivalents to total assets.
LEV is the ratio of total debt to total assets.
ATO, calculated as the ratio of sales to total assets, is used to proxy for the development stage of firms.
ROA is return on assets, calculated as the ratio of earnings before interest and tax to total assets.
DURN is duration in days between the first announcement date and the completion date for BDL transactions and between the prospectus lodgement date and the listing date for IPOs.
RET_OWN is the percentage shareholding that private firm shareholders retain in the listed entity at the time of going public.
CASH_OUT is an indicator variable that equals 1 if private firm shareholders sell down their shareholding during the going public transaction and 0 otherwise.
DAY1_RET is first trading day return, calculated as the change in closing share price on the first full trading day post-transaction from the day prior (for BDL firms with no concurrent capital raising) or from the offer price (for both capital raising BDL and IPO firms).
PRCDS is the proceeds raised during the going-public transaction.
UNDERWTR is an indicator variable that equals 1 if an underwriter is used and 0 otherwise.
The t-stat/z-stat tests the difference in mean/median between the BDL and IPO control sample.

Table 22.9 Choice between backdoor listing and initial public offering (non-size matched IPO control sample)

	Predicted sign	Full sample		Re-admissions		All offer types		Public offers	
		(1)	(2)	(3)	(4)	(5)	(6)	(7)	(8)
CONSTANT		4.310**	−1.795	5.543**	−6.948**	−8.780**	−2.898	−13.142***	−5.708
		(2.33)	(−0.71)	(2.40)	(−1.96)	(−2.17)	(−0.55)	(−2.64)	(−0.91)
Ln(ASSETS)	−	−0.220**	−0.155	−0.267**	−0.128	0.043	1.728***	0.1889	1.381***
		(−2.07)	(−1.33)	(−2.03)	(−0.84)	(0.24)	(4.35)	(0.90)	(3.45)
TECH	+	0.637**	0.776***	0.645***	0.815**	1.276***	1.429***	1.034**	1.225**
		(2.49)	(2.84)	(2.22)	(2.46)	(3.22)	(2.93)	(2.34)	(2.36)
LIQ	−	−3.172***	−2.790***	−3.679***	−2.917***	−3.591***	−1.812*	−3.671***	−2.435**
		(−5.65)	(−4.79)	(−5.72)	(−4.18)	(−4.54)	(−1.84)	(−4.19)	(−2.26)
LEV	+	1.426*	1.608**	0.481	0.212	0.404	−0.170	−0.361	−0.536
		(1.92)	(2.06)	(0.53)	(0.20)	(0.31)	(−0.11)	(−0.25)	(−0.32)
ATO	−	−1.042***	−1.005***	−1.034***	−0.915***	−1.380***	−1.293***	−1.197***	−1.145**
		(−4.72)	(−4.35)	(−3.92)	(−3.03)	(−3.41)	(−2.70)	(−2.80)	(−2.28)
ROA	−	−0.839***	−0.777**	−0.870**	−0.771*	−1.955***	−3.076***	−2.039***	−2.713***
		(−2.67)	(−2.49)	(−2.18)	(−1.86)	(−3.43)	(−4.20)	(−3.40)	(−3.62)
Ln(DURN)	−		1.174***		2.263***	2.230***	2.397***	2.748***	2.628***
			(4.12)		(5.30)	(4.80)	(4.59)	(4.70)	(4.29)

CASH_OUT	—				0.370	0.233
					(0.69)	(0.35)
RET_OWN	—	0.282	0.195	0.159	0.156	
		(0.88)	(0.48)	(0.34)	(0.25)	
		−1.574**	−1.846**	−3.553***	−7.971***	−4.105***	−7.673***
		(−2.52)	(−2.41)	(−3.84)	(−5.40)	(−3.66)	(−4.69)
DAY1_RET	—	0.153	0.245	0.235	−0.022	0.595	0.276
		(0.84)	(1.23)	(0.99)	(−0.07)	(1.19)	(0.52)
Ln(PRCDS)	—				−2.089***		−1.589***
					(−5.24)		(−3.94)
UNDERWTR	—				−0.465		−0.751
					(−0.94)		(−1.37)
No. of observations	348	348	274	274	242	242	200	200
Log likelihood	−203.58	−188.65	−154.84	−130.63	−99.32	−71.18	−77.95	−60.52
LR Chi-sq	75.27	105.13	70.16	118.58	136.85	193.13	121.36	156.21
Pseudo R^2	0.1560	0.2179	0.1847	0.3122	0.4079	0.5757	0.4377	0.5634
Correctly classified	0.7040	0.7126	0.7336	0.7956	0.8099	0.8760	0.8300	0.8750

Notes:
Table 22.9 reports the results from logit regression of the choice of a BDL or IPO transaction on a set of firm and deal characteristics as potential determinants. The dependent variable is set to 1 for BDLs and 0 for IPOs.
For a description of the individual explanatory variables, refer to the notes in Table 22.3.
Z-statistics are reported in parentheses.
*, ** and *** indicates significance at the 10%, 5% and 1% level, respectively.

appears to be stronger and more significant across the various subsamples than before. In addition the coefficient for the LIQ factor remains negative and significant even after controlling for the size of the proceeds raised. Taken together, these results imply that IPO firms are more highly developed, more profitable, and financially stronger. Consistent with the univariate results in Table 22.8, no significant coefficient is found for the CASH_OUT variable in the multivariate framework. The UNDERWTR variable is also insignificant after controlling for other factors.

6 CONCLUSION

Private firms can go public by ways other than an IPO. A backdoor listing is another popular and viable way. We examine BDL transactions in the Australian market, developing an empirical model of the factors that potentially influence the choice between an IPO and a BDL.

Critics have argued that IPOs in North America cannot be directly compared with reverse takeovers or reverse mergers which are a form of BDL, because BDLs typically do not require a prospectus and do not raise any capital during the process. By exploiting the unique institutional features of Australian backdoor listing transactions, including a stock exchange re-admissions requirement, prospectus disclosures and concurrent capital raisings, we provide results that afford a more meaningful comparison between the two alternative routes of going public.

Based on the existing literature and the special features of the Australian capital market, a set of firm-specific characteristics and deal-related factors is identified as potential determinants of the decision on which path to follow. A choice model is then estimated using a unique, hand-collected sample of BDL and matched IPO transactions in a logit regression framework. Overall results show that BDL firms are not necessarily smaller than IPO firms in terms of size (as proxied by post-listing total assets). After controlling for the amount of proceeds raised during the going-public transaction, there is evidence that BDL firms are in fact larger than their IPO counterparts. This could result from the fact that the total assets of the backdoor-listed firm are the combined assets of the shell company and the private firm. If only the size of the pre-transaction private firms is compared, the conclusion could be different.

In terms of firm characteristics, a BDL transaction is more likely to be associated with a private firm engaged in a high-technology business. In addition BDL firms tend to be at an earlier stage of development, less profitable, and less liquid than their matched IPO counterparts.

Contrary to popular belief, Australian BDLs take longer to complete than IPOs, a result that holds across BDL subsamples. The implication is that going public through the backdoor may not be easier and faster than a front-door listing via an IPO.

In terms of deal design, BDL transactions are associated with more cashing-out activity by private firm owners, who also have a lower retained ownership in the listed entity at the time of listing. This result contradicts the notion that owners of more developed firms (that is, IPO firms) are more likely to sell down their stake and cash-out than insiders of firms that are still developing.

When BDL firms that are subject to the re-admission requirement and conduct a concurrent capital raising are examined separately, their matched IPO firms tend to raise more capital. So it is not surprising that IPO firms are more likely to engage the services of an underwriter.

Finally no significant difference in the degree of underpricing (first-day return) between BDLs and IPOs can be established across the subsamples. This result casts doubt on the claim that backdoor listing helps to avoid or minimize any losses from underpricing suffered by shareholders of IPO firms when going public.

NOTES

1. The 'profit test' requires an entity to have an aggregated profit of at least (AUD) $1 million from the last three financial years, of which the profit from the latest 12 months before applying for admission must exceed $400,000. The 'assets test' requires the entity to have net tangible assets of at least $2 million after deducting any costs of fundraising or a market capitalization of at least $10 million at the time of admission.
2. The shareholder spread requirement stipulates an entity should have (1) at least 500 holders each with a marketable parcel (with a value of at least $2000) of the main class of securities or (2) at least 400 holders with a marketable parcel of securities and persons who are not related parties must hold at least 25 per cent of securities to be quoted.
3. Due to various limitations, both the availability and reliability of the archival data tend to decline the further back in time it goes. Thus a sampling period from January 1992 to December 2007 was chosen to capture all BDL transactions which were completed within this 16-year time period. The year 1992 was when the Second Board Markets in all states were closed and witnessed a flurry of companies in those markets transferred their listing to the ASX. As many of these firms were smaller and weaker, they served potentially as prime targets for backdoor listings. Thus 1992 is a good starting point for the current study. The end of 2007 is the latest feasible time when the data was collected.
4. The Zephyr database on reverse takeovers for ASX-listed firms begins in 1999 and the coverage is relatively limited.
5. The most noticeable episode is the backdoor listing of internet firms using mining companies as shells during the dotcom era of 1999–2000.
6. The Global Industry Classification Standard (GICS) was jointly developed by Standard & Poor's and Morgan Stanley Capital International. The system classifies firms into 10 broad (two-digit) industry sectors: Energy (GICS10), Materials (GICS15), Industrials (GICS20), Consumer discretionary (GICS25), Consumer staples (GICS30), Health care (GICS35), Financials (GICS40), Information technology (GICS45), Telecommunication services (GICS50) and Utilities (GICS55).
7. Ideally the pre-listing total assets of the private firms would have been used for matching. The fact that not all private firms opting for the backdoor route disclosed their pre-listing total assets means this approach is not feasible. See also the discussion on data in section 3.4.
8. One may argue that using data from the post-listing financial statements in estimating the logit model introduces a look-ahead bias that limits the usefulness of the choice model. In practice insiders of the private firms would normally have reasonable expectations of the firm's post-listing financial profile, which would be factored into their decision process when choosing the route to go public.
9. Increased IPO activity over the period 2004–07 was largely driven by the mining boom. The percentage of mining IPOs surged from roughly 29 per cent in 2004 to nearly 48 per cent in 2007. If firms from the energy sector are also included, the percentage jumps to more than 63 per cent in 2007.

REFERENCES

Adjei, F., K. Cyree and M. Walker (2008), 'The determinants and survival of reverse mergers vs. IPOs', *Journal of Economics and Finance*, **32**, 176–94.
Brau, J., B. Francis and N. Kohers (2003), 'The choice of IPO versus takeover: empirical evidence', *Journal of Business*, **76**, 583–612.
Carpentier, C. and J.-M. Suret (2012), 'Entrepreneurial equity financing and securities regulation: an empirical analysis', *International Small Business Journal*, **30**, 41–64.

Carpentier, C., D. Cumming and J.-M. Suret (2012), 'The value of capital market regulation: IPOs versus reverse mergers', *Journal of Empirical Legal Studies*, **9**, 56–91.
Derrien, F. and A. Kecskes (2007), 'The initial public offering of listed firms', *Journal of Finance*, **62**, 447–79.
Floros, I. and K. Shastri (2009), 'A comparison of penny stock initial public offerings and reverse mergers as alternative mechanisms for going public', available at: http://ssrn.com/abstract=1460979 (accessed 10 Aug. 2011).
Gleason, K., R. Jain and L. Rosenthal (2008), 'Alternatives for going public: evidence from reverse takeovers, self-underwritten IPOs, and traditional IPOs', *Financial Decisions*, **20**, 1–24.
Gleason, K., L. Rosenthal and R. Wiggins III (2005), 'Backing into being public: an exploratory analysis of reverse takeovers', *Journal of Corporate Finance*, **12**, 54–79.
Jensen, M. and R. Ruback (1983), 'The market for corporate control: the scientific evidence', *Journal of Financial Economics*, **11**, 5–50.
Kuo, R. and N. Humphrey (2002), 'The growing acceptance of backdoor listings', *JASSA*, issue 4 (Summer), 28–32 & 40.
Poulsen, A. and M. Stegemoller (2008), 'Moving from private to public ownership: selling out to public firms versus initial public offerings', *Financial Management*, **37**, 81–101.
Sjostrom, W. (2008), 'The truth about reverse mergers', *Entrepreneurial Business Law Journal*, **2**, 743–59.

23 An empirical analysis of cross-listing decisions in share-issue privatizations: evidence from developed and developing countries
Juliet D'Souza, William L. Megginson and Robert Nash[1]

1 INTRODUCTION

Privatization, the sale of previously state-owned enterprises (SOEs) to private investors, has transformed financial markets around the world. An economic and political event as profound as privatization raises many important questions, such as why governments privatize, how they privatize, and where (in which markets) governments choose to sell shares. As summarized in Megginson and Netter (2001) and Estrin et al. (2009), financial economists have thoroughly examined the 'why' question (Megginson et al., 1994; Dewenter and Malatesta, 1997; Boubakri and Cosset, 1998) and the 'how' question (Boycko et al., 1996; Jones et al., 1999; Megginson et al., 2004). On the other hand, the 'where' question has received less attention.

In this chapter we identify factors that affect a government's decision regarding where to privatize. We specifically examine the firm-level and institution-level factors that may affect why some share-issue privatizations (SIPs) are conducted entirely on domestic equity markets while others involve cross-listings, whereby all or part of the offering is done on a foreign equity market. We focus on cross-listing decisions by privatizing governments because of the significance of these share offerings. Boutchkova and Megginson (2000) and Bortolotti and Faccio (2009) report that SIPs are the largest and most important equity offerings in almost all national markets. Furthermore, Bortolotti et al. (2002) note that, of the world's 21 largest equity offerings (all privatizations), 15 of these SIPs involved listing shares on more than one exchange. Thus, since they frequently involve cross-listings, an understanding of SIPs is critical to understanding cross-listing in general. In fact in his seminal survey of the cross-listing literature, Karolyi (1998) chooses firms involved in privatizations (Telefonos de Chile, Huaneng Power and Deutsche Telekom) as his three examples of reasons for cross-listing. To develop a better knowledge of these substantial stock offerings, we examine factors driving the cross-listing decisions in share-issue privatizations.

The rise in the level of global competition between stock exchanges has also amplified the importance of choice of markets for SIPs. Zingales (2007), Ernst and Young (2007), Doidge et al. (2007, 2009a, 2010), and Fernandes et al. (2010) describe how globalization of capital markets has intensified the efforts of the world's exchanges to attract the largest capital flows. To better understand how exchanges compete, we need to more closely consider how privatizing governments make decisions regarding their cross-listing location choice.

We examine cross-listing decisions in 822 privatizing share offerings from 78 countries during 1985–2007. The data indicate that both firm-level and institution-level factors significantly impact these actions. Of the firm-level characteristics, we find that offering size, industry and product market significantly shape the privatizing government's cross-listing choices. Furthermore institutions also matter. Our analysis reveals that cross-listings are more likely in developed economies and in deeper capital markets. Surprisingly, we find that the protection of shareholder rights, commonly recognized as an important factor in cross-listing by private firms, generally plays no significant role in the decision to cross-list in privatizations. Finally, we identify that the factors determining cross-listing decisions vary significantly between developed and developing nations.

The remainder of this chapter is organized as follows. Section 2 identifies potential determinants of cross-listing decisions and section 3 describes firm-level factors which may impact these cross-listing choices. Section 4 specifies institution-level factors which may affect cross-listings, while section 5 describes our data and methodology. In section 6 we present our results. Section 7 concludes.

2 DETERMINANTS OF CROSS-LISTING DECISIONS

As described by Karolyi (2006) and Lel and Miller (2008), the extant literature documents that firms may cross-list securities to gain liquidity and avoid cross-border barriers to investment, to obtain access to deeper pools of capital, to enhance the firm's visibility and bolster name and product recognition and to build credibility by bonding to markets that ensure stronger shareholder protection. La Porta et al. (1997, 1998) contend that firms in countries that provide weaker legal protection for minority shareholders find it difficult to raise money in their own country. To improve credibility and create opportunities for future capital acquisition, these firms may choose to cross-list in markets where shareholder rights are more strongly protected. Based on the work of Coffee (2002) and Stulz (1999), this bonding hypothesis contends that firms wishing to signal a higher level of protection for minority shareholders may do so by issuing securities in capital markets providing stronger legal rights to minority shareholders. For example, firms listing shares on the US exchanges generally must adhere to stricter disclosure standards relative to listings on other exchanges of most other countries.

Bonding may be especially advantageous for firms that have larger growth opportunities and thus have greater need for continuous access to capital. Doidge et al. (2004) show that companies cross-listing in the US had significantly higher growth options than non-cross-listed firms from the same country. Furthermore, Doidge et al. (2004) suggest that a US cross-listing reduces the extent to which controlling shareholders engage in expropriation and thereby increases the firm's ability to take advantage of investment opportunities. La Porta et al. (1999) contend that the costs of extracting private benefits of control increase with the need for outside funds. The private benefits of control are generally less valuable in firms with larger growth opportunities and greater needs to access external capital markets. Accordingly, growth opportunities are more highly valued for firms that choose to cross-list in the US, particularly those from countries with poorer protection of investor rights.

Reese and Weisbach (2002) further note that firms with a large demand for equity capital have incentives to cross-list in the US as a way to bond themselves to protect minority shareholders. Reese and Weisbach (2002) find a significant increase in both the number and value of equity offerings following a cross-listing. Also after initial cross-listings in the US, companies from weak-protection countries are more likely to raise additional capital through a subsequent equity offering. Firms from strong-protection countries are less likely to do follow-on equity offerings (Reese and Weisbach, 2002). These findings are consistent with the bonding arguments.

Karolyi (1998) summarizes articles showing that stock prices increase in the home market at the announcement of cross-listing. Foerster and Karolyi (2000) investigate the long-run return performance of non-US firms that cross-list in the US market. The authors find firms issuing equity by Rule 144A private placement underperform, especially issues from countries with weaker accounting standards. This is also consistent with the bonding hypothesis in that Rule 144A offerings do not require as extensive disclosure as do public US offerings.

Next, we identify specific firm-level and institution-level factors that may affect the privatizing government's actions regarding cross-listings.

3   FIRM-LEVEL FACTORS AFFECTING CROSS-LISTING DECISIONS

In this section we describe firm-level characteristics which may impact the actions of privatizing governments when making cross-listing decisions.

3.1   Industry Factors

The industry of the privatizing firm may affect the state's cross-listing choices. First, certain exchanges have the reputation and infrastructure to better handle listings from specific industries. Pagano et al. (2002) and Blass and Yafeh (2001) argue that US exchanges are better suited for listings by high-technology firms. These authors argue that high-technology firms gravitate towards New York because the prevalence of knowledgeable analysts and investors contributes to a more efficient flow of information and a deeper understanding of the nuances of the industry. While US exchanges (especially the National Association of Securities Dealers Automated Quotations – NASDAQ) are better known as a listing destination for high-technology firms, Pagano et al. (2002) note that the European markets appear to attract cross-listings by more mature companies.

Furthermore, Pagano et al. (2002) and Saudagaran (1988) document a 'follow the leader' effect whereby firms are compelled to cross-list in the same markets as their competitors. This industry clustering facilitates comparisons between peers and allows for a better assessment of risk and relative valuation. Providing evidence of this effect, Pagano et al. (2002) find that a firm's cross-listing decision is positively related to the number of companies in the same industry that are already listed on a specific exchange. To test how industry may affect SIP cross-listing decisions, our empirical analysis includes industry-specific indicator variables.

3.2 Product Market

Sarkissian and Schill (2004) and Kang and Stulz (1997) find that firms that produce tradable goods – products that can be sold in foreign markets – are more likely to cross-list. This is because tradable goods such as industrial and consumer products are more commonly known by foreign investors. As proposed by Merton (1987), the 'investor recognition' hypothesis holds that investors are more likely to purchase shares of companies that are better known in that country.[2] Therefore, firms selling tradable goods in a specific country should find that market more receptive to an equity offering because investors are more likely to already be familiar with the firm. Furthermore, the publicity and visibility that emanates from the firm's listing and subsequent trading will boost marketing efforts and provide a form of 'free' advertising (Saudagaran and Biddle, 1995; Fanto and Karmel, 1997). In our subsequent empirical analysis, we follow the methodology of Sarkissian and Schill (2004) to identify the firms that produce tradable goods. We designate these firms with an indicator variable.

3.3 Firm Size

Pagano et al. (2002), Reese and Weisbach (2002) and Bailey et al. (2006) show that larger firms are more likely to cross-list. First, a larger firm will be able to more easily bear the substantial fixed costs associated with a multinational listing. Second, a bigger firm will typically be raising a greater amount of capital per offering. Especially for firms located in countries where access to capital is limited, the home exchange may not have the absorptive capacity to solely handle the offering. As documented by Boutchkova and Megginson (2000), many privatizing share offerings are huge, so cross-listing may be required to avoid overwhelming the local market. Accordingly, we expect a positive relation between a SIP's offering size and the probability of cross-listing. Our proxy for firm size is the dollar amount of each equity offering.

4 INSTITUTION-LEVEL FACTORS AFFECTING CROSS-LISTING DECISIONS

In addition to firm-level characteristics, we also expect institution-level factors to impact cross-listing decisions. Doidge et al. (2007), Boehmer et al. (2005) and D'Souza et al. (2005) find that institutional factors, such as legal protection for minority investors and the country's level of economic and financial development, explain more of the cross-country variance in financial policies than do firm-specific characteristics. In the following sections, we identify institution-level factors and present expectations regarding how each may affect SIP cross-listing decisions.

4.1 Economic Environment

Ball et al. (2000), Lang et al. (2003), Boehmer et al. (2005) and D'Souza et al. (2005) find there are substantial institutional differences between developing and developed markets. Furthermore, Bailey et al. (2006), Sarkissian and Schill (2004) and Foerster and Karolyi (1999) note that the impact of cross-listing appears to differ between firms from developed and developing markets. Because we expect the nation's economic environment to influence cross-listing decisions, we subsequently separate the data into two groups: Organisation for Economic Co-operation and Development (OECD – developed) and non-OECD (developing) countries. Much of our empirical analysis is to ascertain whether the factors affecting cross-listing decisions differ according to level of economic development.

4.2 Capital Market Development

Our study considers how cross-listings by governments in share-issue privatizations may differ from cross-listings by private firms. How the level of capital market development impacts cross-listing decisions is one area where these differences become more apparent. First, unlike private firms, governments may have a policy goal of seeking to enhance capital market development. Accordingly, the overall development of the privatizing country's capital market may affect a government's cross-listing decisions. Governments may use domestic offerings of SIPs to spur the growth of fledgling local financial markets. Megginson et al. (2004) note that privatizing with share offerings can jump-start stock market development and trigger increased economic growth and efficiency by triggering the kind of snowball effect predicted by Subrahmanyam and Titman (1999). That is, as new firms go public, the enhanced liquidity and efficiency encourage more firms to go public and the capital market experiences rapid growth. The benefits from SIPs' creation of large numbers of new, tradable securities should be especially pronounced in emerging or less-developed equity markets.

Alternatively, if the domestic equity market is relatively primitive, it may be difficult for share-issue privatizations to succeed, in part because it may be hard to find buyers for the frequently very large offerings. In this case, governments in countries where access to capital is limited may find that cross-listing is necessary to be able to place all of the shares in a large SIP. Thus, the relation between capital market development and cross-listing choice is ambiguous. Governments may wish to offer more shares domestically to spur the development of the local financial market, but large SIPs might not be efficient (or even possible) if the local capital market is less active.

In the following empirical analysis, we seek to clarify how local capital market conditions affect cross-listing decisions. Our proxy for capital market development is the Capital Access Index (from the Milken Institute). The Capital Access Index (CAI) measures the ease with which a firm may be able to raise capital within a country. The CAI specifically reflects the development of a country's equity market, bond market and banking system, as well as the availability of alternative sources of financing such as venture capital and foreign direct investment.

4.3 Legal and Accounting Environment

Firms face tradeoffs when making cross-listing decisions. Romano (1998) and Coffee (2002) describe the phenomenon of 'issuer choice'. That is, an issuing firm can choose its level of disclosure since the quality and rigor of accounting standards and legal protection vary by exchange. It is widely held that US markets have the most stringent disclosure requirements.[3] While the higher disclosure standards and stronger protection of shareholder rights provided by US exchanges may contribute to greater valuation and an enhanced ability to raise equity capital in follow-on offerings, these stricter institutional standards will also reduce the value of the private benefits of control. Therefore, when contemplating a cross-listing, a privatizing government must weigh the costs and benefits that may result from a change in legal and accounting environment.

Much recent literature (Pagano et al., 2002; Reese and Weisbach 2002; Lang et al., 2003; Doidge, et al., 2009b) emphasizes how the private benefits of control affect the issuer's cross-listing decision. If there are larger private benefits of control within a firm, such that the controlling blockholder can expropriate minority shareholders, the majority owners of those firms may seek to protect the private benefits and avoid listing on a high-disclosure exchange. Johnson et al. (2000) and Dyck and Zingales (2004) note that in some countries, particularly those with civil law systems, it is easier for controlling shareholders to exploit private benefits of control because of lower levels of legal protection and lower amounts of accounting transparency. This contributes to larger private benefits of control in these countries.

On the other hand, a listing in the US ensures stronger legal protection for minority shareholders. While potentially decreasing the private benefits of control, cross-listing in a market with strong legal and accounting standards provides greater credibility, which increases the firm's value and improves its ability to raise additional capital in subsequent offerings. Accordingly, Doidge et al. (2009b), Sarkissian and Schill (2004) and Reese and Weisbach (2002) suggest that firms from a weaker institutional environment have greater incentives to cross-list in a market that ensures stronger protection for investors. This is consistent with the bonding hypothesis.[4]

The prediction regarding how a country's legal and accounting environment affects the cross-listing decision is therefore unclear. As noted by Johnson et al. (2000), owners of firms operating in weaker investor-protection environments typically enjoy the greatest private benefits of control and these benefits might be reduced by a cross-listing. However, the 'bonding' hypothesis extols the advantages that these same firms may gain from cross-listings. In our empirical analysis, we seek to identify which effect dominates.

Following the preponderance of the extant literature, we measure legal environment with the Anti-Director Rights Index (ARI) as originally presented in La Porta et al. (1997). Since stockholders can exert influence through the voting mechanisms, these authors primarily evaluate shareholder rights by gauging the legal protection of voting procedures. They explicitly measure shareholder protection by forming an index based on whether or not certain legal mechanisms are in place to ensure shareholder rights. The ARI takes on a higher value as the legal protection of stockholder rights increases.

While the La Porta et al. (1997) Anti-Director Rights Index has been very widely used as a measure of legal environment, criticisms have been leveled by Pagano and Volpin (2005) and Spamann (2010) regarding conceptual ambiguities and coding mistakes. In response to these concerns and in an attempt to define corporate law with better precision, several authors have developed additional indicators of shareholder legal protection. To help confirm the robustness of our analysis, we also prepare models including alternative measures of legal environment. In various robustness tests, we include the Revised Anti-Director Index (Djankov et al., 2008), the Anti Self-Dealing Index (Djankov et al., 2008), the adjusted Anti-Director Rights Index (Spamann, 2010), and an indicator variable to distinguish nations with a common law legal tradition from those with a civil law system (La Porta et al., 1997).

We also examine the relation between a country's level of accounting standards and the privatizing government's decision to cross-list. Our measures of accounting standards are also from La Porta et al. (1997). Higher values of these accounting scores reflect stricter levels of required disclosure within a country. In our robustness analysis, we also include alternative indicators of each country's disclosure environment.

5 DATA AND METHODOLOGY

Our empirical analysis focuses on whether or not the privatizing government chooses to cross-list, defined as conducting all or part of the share-issue privatization on a stock market other than that of its home country. We specifically seek to understand the firm-level and institution-level factors that affect these cross-listing decisions.

Data on share-issue privatizations are from the Securities Data Corporation (SDC) – Thomson One Banker database. Transaction-specific data provide details regarding the issuer (firm name, country, industry) and the offering (amount, terms, markets). We verify and supplement with data from other sources, such as Privatization Barometer, Privatization International and the World Bank Privatization database. Our data are from 1985–2007 and cover 822 SIPs from 78 countries. Sources for the firm-level and institution-level factors include the *Emerging Stock Markets Factbook*, *International Financial Statistics*, *International Country Risk Guide (PRS Group)*, databases from the World Bank and others, and various academic papers.

6 EMPIRICAL RESULTS

6.1 Univariate Results

Our primary variable of interest is whether a privatizing share offering is cross-listed. Table 23.1 provides issue details for each of the countries in the sample. The 822 share-issue privatizations spanned 78 countries and raised almost $1 trillion. Approximately 35 percent of the privatizing issues have been cross-listed in more than one market. Of the cross-listings, almost 50 percent of the cross-listed issues have taken place in the US market. The UK stock markets are the next most likely destination for cross-listings, attracting 27 percent of all cross-listings. Consistent with the bonding hypothesis, these two most likely locations for cross-listings are stock markets that provide for the most stringent protection of shareholder rights. These two countries also host large and active stock markets.

Table 23.2 provides issue details of SIP cross-listing activity arrayed according to offering size (panel A) and industry (panel B). Panel A documents a strong relation between offering size and cross-listing frequency. The smallest issues (that is, less than $500 million) are the least likely to be cross-listed. As offering size increases, the likelihood of cross-listing generally increases. Furthermore, the larger SIPs are increasingly more likely to involve a cross-listing on the US markets. These patterns are as expected

Table 23.1 Summary details of share-issue privatizations: 1985–2007

Country	Issue size ($ million)	No. of issues	% cross-listed	% cross-listed in US	% cross-listed in UK	% cross-listed in other countries
Argentina	689	7	100	86	14	0
Australia	4217	11	64	86	0	14
Austria	279	29	31	56	56	33
Bahrain	124	3	33	0	0	100
Belgium	394	2	50	0	0	100
Brazil	2236	5	80	75	0	25
Canada	542	11	64	86	0	14
China	185	56	18	80	30	0
Croatia	724	2	100	0	100	0
Czech Rep	76	2	0	0	0	0
Denmark	697	5	20	100	100	0
Dominican Rep	127	2	0	0	0	0
Egypt	48	49	8	75	75	0
Estonia	221	1	100	0	100	0
Finland	493	23	57	54	62	0
France	1921	40	60	63	17	54
Gabon	12	1	0	0	0	0
Georgia	130	1	0	0	0	0
Germany	2473	18	28	80	20	80
Ghana	488	1	100	100	100	0
Greece	551	29	48	79	64	21
Hong Kong	1201	6	17	100	0	0
Hungary	146	26	46	42	83	58
Iceland	53	1	0	0	0	0
India	355	8	38	67	67	0
Indonesia	395	20	15	100	0	0
Ireland	1184	4	75	33	100	0
Israel	122	26	12	33	100	0
Italy	2261	46	50	74	43	4
Ivory Coast	21	1	0	0	0	0
Japan	13109	8	63	100	60	0
Jordan	174	2	0	0	0	0
Kenya	13	6	0	0	0	0
Kuwait	180	7	14	0	0	100
Latvia	43	3	33	0	100	0
Lithuania	180	1	100	0	100	0
Luxembourg	77	1	100	100	100	100
Malaysia	314	8	25	50	0	50
Mexico	1244	3	100	100	0	0
Mongolia	0.2	2	0	0	0	0
Morocco	156	14	14	100	50	50
Netherlands	1146	12	50	100	17	17
New Zealand	245	2	100	0	0	50
Nigeria	31	19	0	0	0	0

Table 23.1 (continued)

Country	Issue size ($ million)	No. of issues	% cross-listed	% cross-listed in US	% cross-listed in UK	% cross-listed in other countries
Norway	708	12	67	50	50	0
Oman	392	2	0	0	0	0
Pakistan	169	7	14	100	0	0
Papua New Guinea	235	1	100	0	0	0
Peru	469	3	100	100	33	0
Philippines	117	6	33	0	0	100
Poland	146	57	14	38	63	38
Portugal	538	37	41	73	40	20
Qatar	681	2	0	0	0	0
Romania	0.6	4	0	0	0	0
Russian Fed	337	4	50	50	100	0
Saudi Arabia	4079	1	0	0	0	0
Senegal	60	2	0	0	0	0
Singapore	373	10	10	100	0	0
Slovak Rep	113	1	0	0	0	0
Slovenia	448	1	100	100	0	0
South Africa	332	4	25	100	0	0
South Korea	634	18	33	100	33	0
Spain	1373	24	67	100	50	13
Sri Lanka	20	5	0	0	0	0
St Lucia	20	1	0	0	0	0
Sweden	1656	11	45	80	40	0
Switzerland	2649	5	40	50	0	50
Taiwan	445	22	9	100	50	0
Tanzania	9.31	4	0	0	0	0
Thailand	130	9	11	100	0	0
Tunisia	3.6	2	0	0	0	0
Turkey	447	9	67	50	33	33
Uganda	1.18	1	0	0	0	0
United Arab Emirates	298	2	0	0	0	0
United Kingdom	3372	19	42	100		50
United States	1793	4	75		0	0
Zambia	2.2	3	0	0	0	0
Zimbabwe	28	5	0	0	0	0

Notes:
This table presents issue details for each country in our sample of share-issue privatizations (SIPs).
Data regarding share-issue privatizations are from the Securities Data Corporation (SDC) – Thomson One Database and include 822 privatizing share offerings from 78 countries during 1985–2007.
A share-issue privatization is cross-listed if the privatizing government conducts all or part of the share offering on a stock market other than that of the home country.

Table 23.2 Summary statistics of cross-listing details based on size and industry

Panel A: Cross-listing issue details based on issue size

Issue size	No. of issues	No. cross-listed	% cross-listed	% cross-listed in US	% cross-listed in UK	% cross-listed in other countries
Less than $500 million	580	114	20	55	47	24
$500 million – $1.0 billion	71	37	52	73	41	19
$1.0 billion – $1.5 billion	55	40	73	80	43	18
$1.5 billion – $2.0 billion	21	19	90	84	26	26
Greater than $2.0 billion	84	64	76	88	36	19

Panel B: Cross-listing issue details based on industry

Industry	Issue size ($ mil)	No. of issues	% cross-listed	% cross-listed in US	% cross-listed in UK	% cross-listed in other countries
Telecom & communications	3019	112	65	81	44	16
Utilities	1275	71	45	75	34	16
Manufacturing	699	415	27	71	36	26
Airline and transport	684	45	29	77	23	38
Financials	392	179	25	47	62	18

Notes:
This table presents univariate statistics of the issue details for our sample of privatizing share-offerings.
In this table, we partition the data based on industry affiliation and on issue size.
Panel A presents issue details based on issue size (US$ in millions) while Panel B presents issue details based on industry.
Telecoms include firms in the telecommunications, radio and broadcasting industry.
Utilities include firms in the electric, gas, and water industry.
Manufacturing includes firms in manufacturing, mining and the petroleum industry.
Airline and transport include firms in the airline, airport, railways and transport industry.
Financial includes firms in the banking and insurance industry.
Issue details are missing for 11 firms.

since larger share offerings may require cross-listing to access deeper pools of capital, with the deepest pool being the US equity market.

Additionally, Table 23.2 (panel B) presents results regarding the association between industry and SIP cross-listing decisions. The data indicate that privatizations of telecom firms are the most likely to be cross-listed and the most likely to be cross-listed on the US markets. This greater prevalence of cross-listings by telecoms on the US market is consistent with the industry clustering described by Pagano et al. (2002). Also, telecom SIPs are the largest offerings (average size of $3.0 billion) and may require cross-listing in the deeper equity markets in order to access the immense amounts of capital raised in these privatizations. Utilities SIPs are also very large offerings (average size of $1.3 billion). However, especially when compared to the other very large offerings by the telecoms, utilities SIPs are less likely to be cross-listed. Therefore, factors other than size may be at work in shaping the cross-listing propensity of SIPs from different industries.

Table 23.3 provides summary statistics of SIP cross-listing activity based on legal

An empirical analysis of cross-listing decisions in share-issue privatizations 541

Table 23.3 *Summary of cross-listing issues based on legal origin of privatizing country*

Panel A: Cross-listing issue details based on legal origin

Legal system of issuer	Issue size ($ million)	No. of issues	% cross-listed	% cross-listed in US	% cross-listed in UK	% cross-listed in other countries
Common law	895	178	26	74	35	20
Civil law	889	641	36	70	43	22

Panel B: Cross-listing issue details based on the Anti-Director Rights Index

Anti-Director Rights Index (ARI) of issuer	Issue size ($ million)	No. of issues	% cross-listed	% cross-listed in US	% cross-listed in UK	% cross-listed in other countries
Anti-Director: 0	2128	51	53	74	37	7
Anti-Director: 1	1258	59	36	76	48	38
Anti-Director: 2	733	288	39	74	39	21
Anti-Director: 3	1174	134	22	67	50	7
Anti-Director: 4	1810	73	49	81	22	25

Notes:
This table presents issue details for our sample of share-issue privatizations (SIPs) based on the legal environment within each country.
Panel A arrays the sample according to type of legal system.
We classify an offering as common law (civil law) if the privatization is conducted by a government from a country with a legal system based on common law (civil law).
Panel B provides issue details for subsamples assigned according to the privatizing country's Anti-Director Rights Index (ARI).
As specified by La Porta et al. (1997), higher values of the Anti-Director Rights Index indicate stronger legal protection for minority shareholders.

environment. These data reveal that firms from weaker-protection legal environments choose to cross-list as a means to 'bond' or commit to stricter legal rights for investors. Specifically, La Porta et al. (1997, 1998) document that investors receive the weakest legal protection in civil law countries and the strongest legal protection in common law countries. Therefore, in panel A, we partition the sample according to the legal system of the privatizing government: common law versus civil law. The data indicate a much greater propensity for cross-listings of SIPs of firms based in civil law systems than in common law systems. The higher proportion of cross-listings by firms from civil law environments (36 percent of these SIPs involve cross-listing versus 26 percent of SIPs from common law countries) is consistent with the bonding hypothesis.

Table 23.3 (panel B) presents preliminary univariate results for cross-listing differences between subsamples based on values of each country's Anti-Director Rights Index. Firms in countries with the weakest shareholder protection (an ARI of 0) seem to cross-list more frequently than firms in countries providing relatively stronger shareholder protection (higher values of the ARI). The greater prevalence of cross-listings by firms from countries with the weakest shareholder protection (53 percent cross-listings if the ARI is 0) is consistent with the bonding hypothesis. However, panel B also offers

Table 23.4 Effect of legal environment on cross-listing frequency and issue size

Panel A: Frequency of cross-listing					Panel B: Issue size			
Variable	Mean rank	Sample size	KW test Chi-squared statistics	Variable	Mean rank	Sample size	KW test Chi-squared statistics
ARI = 0	60.6	51	3.31	ARI = 0	63.1	51	5.39
ARI = 1	51.1	59	0.07*	ARI = 1	48.9	59	0.02**
ARI = 0	189.7	51	3.34	ARI = 0	225.5	51	20.2
ARI = 2	166.5	288	0.07*	ARI = 2	158.9	286	0.00***
ARI = 0	113.5	51	16.09	ARI = 0	125.3	51	29.18
ARI = 3	85.2	134	0.00***	ARI = 3	78.3	131	0.00***
ARI = 0	63.8	51	0.16	ARI = 0	69.8	51	3.62
ARI = 4	61.6	73	0.69	ARI = 4	57.4	73	0.06*
ARI = 1	168.8	59	0.27	ARI = 1	195	59	3.47
ARI = 2	175.1	288	0.60	ARI = 2	168.5	286	0.06*
ARI = 1	105.8	59	3.66	ARI = 1	116.1	59	12.02
ARI = 3	93.1	134	0.06*	ARI = 3	86.2	131	0.00***
ARI = 1	61.5	59	2.59	ARI = 1	65.3	59	0.11
ARI = 4	70.5	73	0.11	ARI = 4	67.5	73	0.74
ARI = 2	222.8	288	11.56	ARI = 2	217.9	286	4.96
ARI = 3	93.1	134	0.00***	ARI = 3	189.6	131	0.02**
ARI = 2	177.3	288	2.43	ARI = 2	173.9	286	4.895
ARI = 4	195.5	73	0.12	ARI = 4	204	73	0.03**
ARI = 3	94.2	134	15.8	ARI = 3	92.3	131	10.88
ARI = 4	122	73	0.00***	ARI = 4	120.8	73	0.00***

Notes:
This table presents analysis of subsamples based on the anti-director rights index (ARI) for each firm's country.
We specifically test for significant differences in the likelihood of cross-listing (panel A) and in the issue size (panel B) between the groups in each subsample.
The table presents the mean rank for each subsample and the Kruskal-Wallis statistic for tests of significant differences between subsamples.
*** denotes significance at the 1% level; ** denotes significance at the 5% level, and * denotes significance at the 10 % level.

evidence inconsistent with the bonding hypothesis. Panel B indicates that firms in countries with an ARI of 4 (which indicates the highest level of shareholder protection) cross-list more frequently than firms in countries with lower levels of shareholder protection (an ARI of 1, 2 or 3). *Ceteris paribus*, the bonding hypothesis predicts a lower likelihood of cross-listing by SIPs from countries that already provide strong protection of shareholder rights. Since we observe the opposite effect (with an ARI of 4), we further explore this finding in our subsequent empirical analysis.

In Table 23.4 (panel A), we examine how protection of shareholder rights affects cross-listing decisions of privatizing governments. As also suggested by the results from Table 23.3, the data show that firms in countries with an ARI of 0 (low protection) cross-list significantly more than firms in countries with an ARI of 1, 2 and 3 (higher protection). Again, this is consistent with the bonding hypothesis. Perhaps the most intriguing result is that the data indicate no significant difference in the frequency of cross-listing of SIPs from countries with an ARI of 0 (lowest legal protection) and those with an ARI of 4 (strongest legal protection).

The lack of a significant difference in cross-listing frequency between the weak protection countries and the strong protection countries lead us to conduct a deeper examination of the sample. We note some important characteristics about these two segments of our data. Of the SIPs from countries with an ARI of 0, Italian cross-listings dominate the subsample (85 percent of the cross-listed issues from countries with an ARI of 0). The Italian SIPs are very large, with an average size of $2.3 billion. Of the SIPs from countries with an ARI of 4, British and Australian offerings (41 percent of issues with an ARI of 4) drive the results. These SIPs from the UK and Australia are also very large with an average issue size of $3.7 billion. In Table 23.4 (panel B), we test for significant differences in the issue size of each sample based on the Anti-Director Rights Index. Specifically, the issue sizes originating from countries with an ARI of 0 and with an ARI of 4 are significantly greater than the other groups. Since issue size should have a positive impact on cross-listing activity, it may be that the effect of issue size may play the larger role in deciding to cross-list or not. That is, the apparently anomalous result that we note – no significant difference in the cross-listing frequency between high-protection and low-protection countries – may be driven by the impact of issue size.

6.2 Multivariate Results – Full Sample

Table 23.5 presents findings from our initial multivariate analysis. We first focus on results using the full sample of share-issue privatizations. The dependent variable is based on privatizing equity offerings as reported by SDC-Thomson One Banker. Our dependent variable takes a value of 1 if the respective transaction involves a cross-listing. Accordingly, our analysis uses logit regressions. The independent variables represent firm-level and institution-level factors expected to affect the cross-listing decision.

Model 1 focuses on the relation between offering size and the cross-listing decision. We choose this initial functional form because the sheer size of many SIPs is the factor that is typically most closely analyzed by capital market observers. For the total sample, the data indicate a positive, significant relation between the offering size and the likelihood of cross-listing. One reason that this result is expected is that many share-issue privatizations are huge transactions and may need to be spread across multiple markets.

Model 2 expands the number of independent variables to explore the impact of a wider array of firm-level and institution-level factors. As in model 1, we find that larger offerings are significantly more likely to be cross-listed. Additionally, model 2 indicates that the industry and product market effects are highly significant. Building upon the results of Blass and Yafeh (2001), we document that the governments privatizing high-technology firms more frequently cross-list the offerings.[5] While Blass and Yafeh (2001) focused on IPOs of private companies, our study examines only privatizations. Nevertheless, regardless of the ownership structure (private or state owners), it appears that high-technology firms are well suited for cross-listings. This cross-listing may occur because of the clustering of analysts and peer firms on certain markets (such as in the US equity markets). The data further indicate that privatizing

Table 23.5 Regressions testing for factors affecting cross-listing decisions in share-issue privatizations

Independent variables	Model 1	Model 2	Model 3	Model 4	Model 5
Constant	−1.07	−2.25	−2.245	2.01	1.68
	(0.091)***	(0.453)***	(0.453)***	(1.534)	(1.527)
Issue size	0.001	0.001	0.001	0.001	0.001
	(0.000)***	(0.000)***	(0.000)***	(0.000)***	(0.000)***
Tradable goods		0.38	0.51	0.61	0.68
		(0.211)*	(0.216)**	(0.246)**	(0.249)***
High-technology industry		1.09		1.25	
		(0.258)***		(0.313)***	
Telecommunication industry			1.19		1.08
			(0.292)***		(0.340)***
Anti-Director Rights Index		0.11	0.11	0.15	0.14
		(0.101)	(0.101)	(0.118)	(0.118)
Accounting standards		0.00	0.00	0.02	0.02
		(0.008)	(0.008)	(0.011)	(0.011)
Capital access				−1.19	−1.10
				(0.417)***	(0.413)***
OECD nation		1.34	1.31	1.40	1.36
		(0.265)***	(0.263)***	(0.372)***	(0.370)***
Sample size	811	557	557	401	401

Notes:
This table presents results from logistic regressions designed to identify factors affecting a government's decision to conduct cross-listings during share-issue privatizations.
The dependent variable for each model is an indicator (1 if the offering involves a cross-listing, 0 otherwise). The independent variables are: *issue size* (US$ of offering), *Tradable goods* (indicator variable of 1 if firm produces tradable goods; as defined by Sarkissian and Schill (2004)), *High-tech industry* (indicator variable of 1 if firm is from a high-technology industry; as defined by Pagano et al., 2002), *Telecommunication industry* (indicator variable of 1 if firm is a telecom), *Anti-Director Rights Index* (higher values indicate greater protection), *Accounting standards* (higher values indicate stricter accounting standards), *Capital access* (higher values indicate greater access to capital; as defined by the Milken Institute) and *OECD nation* (indicator variable of 1 if nation is an OECD member at time of offering).
First row presents the coefficients; second row provides the standard error.
*** denotes significance at the 1% level; ** denotes significance at the 5% level, and * denotes significance at the 10% level.

firms that produce tradable goods – essentially physical products that can be sold on foreign markets – are significantly more likely to cross-list. Again, this is consistent with our hypothesis because tradable goods should be more recognizable by consumers in foreign markets. Thus, there is a greater chance that the firm will be known in the foreign country. Furthermore, the listing and subsequent trading of the stock will provide an advertising benefit by generating publicity for the firm and its products in the overseas markets.

In addition to identifying the impact of these firm-level variables, model 2 specifies how institutional factors may affect the SIP cross-listing decision. First, the country's level of economic development is a significant determinant of cross-listing activity. Model 2 indicates that privatizations from OECD countries are significantly more likely to involve cross-listings. This is as expected since SIPs from OECD countries are typically larger than those from developing countries.

For the full sample, the results in Table 23.5 suggest that the other institutional variables have no significant effect. It is potentially insightful to note the insignificant impact of the legal variables. To be consistent with the preponderance of the prior literature, we measure the legal environment with the Anti-Director Rights Index of La Porta et al. (1997, 1998). Updates and adjustments to these data have been developed by Djankov et al. (2008) and by Spamann (2010). Using these alternative measures of legal environment in our empirical models yields results similar to those we document in Table 23.5. We also obtain similar results when we include measures of the effectiveness of law enforcement, such as the Rule of Law Index from La Porta et al. (1998). Therefore, regardless of how measured, legal environment has no significant impact on cross-listing decisions in our broad sample of share-issue privatizations. The bonding hypothesis predicts that privatizing governments from weaker legal systems should be more likely to cross-list. While the univariate results provide some preliminary evidence consistent with the 'bonding' hypothesis, the multivariate analysis reveals no relation between legal environment and cross-listing activity.

Model 3 (Table 23.5) presents results that are virtually identical to model 2. The only difference in the specification is that the industry variable in model 3 focuses on whether or not the firm is a telecommunication (indicator variable of 1 if a telecommunication firm, 0 otherwise). Consistent with our expectations, this variable is positive and significantly related to the likelihood of cross-listing. As with the result for the high-technology indicator variable in model 2, this finding may be driven by an industry clustering effect. Also, as documented by D'Souza and Megginson (1999) and in panel B of Table 23.2, telecommunication offerings are also very large; all models indicate that the larger SIPs typically involve cross-listings.

Models 4 and 5 include a measure of each country's level of capital market development. The full-sample regressions reveal that the degree of capital market development is also significantly associated with the likelihood of cross-listings by privatizing governments. If the infrastructure of the country's financial market is such that there is limited access to capital, the SIP is more likely to be cross-listed. This negative relation between capital market development and cross-listing should be most prevalent when the share offerings are large, as is the case with most SIPs. Finally in models 4 and 5, the results for all other institutional and firm-specific variables are identical to those in each of the other specifications.

6.3 Multivariate Results – Developed versus Developing Countries

Since the data from Table 23.5 indicate that the level of economic development significantly affects the cross-listing decisions of privatizing governments, we next form subsamples composed of firms from OECD (developed) countries and firms from non-OECD (developing) countries. We test to determine how factors affecting cross-listing decisions may vary based on the country's level of economic development. Table 23.6 provides these results.

For the OECD countries (Table 23.6, panel A), the first columns indicate that the government's cross-listing choices are most significantly impacted by firm-level factors. The

Table 23.6 Regressions testing for factors affecting cross-listing decisions in share-issue privatizations – subsamples based on country's level of economic development

Panel A		OECD nations			
Independent variables	Model 1	Model 2	Model 3	Model 4	Model 5
Constant	−0.56	−1.13	−1.17	1.74	1.47
	(0.113)***	(0.597)*	(0.597)**	(1.783)	(1.773)
Issue size	0.001	0.001	0.001	0.001	0.0011
	(0.000)***	(0.000)***	(0.000)***	(0.000)***	(0.000)***
Tradable goods		0.59	0.67	0.61	0.71
		(0.250)**	(0.252)***	(0.263)**	(0.266)***
High-technology industry		1.27 (0.313)***		1.31 (0.341)***	
Telecommunication industry			1.19 (0.333)***		1.18 (0.368)***
Anti-Director Rights Index		0.02 (0.104)	0.02 (0.104)	0.10 (0.120)	0.09 (0.119)
Accounting standards		0.017 (0.010)	0.01 (0.010)	0.015 (0.012)	0.02 (0.011)
Capital access				−0.78 (0.454)*	−0.72 (0.450)
Sample size	469	378	378	335	335
Panel B		Non-OECD nations			
Independent variables	Model 1	Model 2	Model 3	Model 4	Model 5
Constant	−1.90	−3.01	−3.08	10.97	9.76
	(0.171)***	(0.908)***	(0.921)***	(4.958)**	(4.830)**
Issue size	0.00	0.001	0.001	0.000	0.000
	(0.001)***	(0.000)***	(0.000)***	(0.001)	(0.001)
Tradable goods		−0.48	−0.31	1.01	0.77
		(0.487)	(0.503)	(0.836)	(0.811)
High-technology industry		0.61 (0.531)		1.64 (0.986)*	
Telecommunication industry			0.928 (0.631)		0.76 (1.038)
Anti-Director Rights Index		1.16 (0.423)***	1.17 (0.425)***	1.32 (1.270)	0.92 (1.221)
Accounting standards		−0.04 (0.017)**	−0.04 (0.017)**	0.17 (0.110)	0.16 (0.107)
Capital access				−6.19 (2.661)**	−5.46 (2.559)**
Sample size	340	179	179	66	66

Notes:
This table presents results from logistic regressions designed to identify factors affecting a government's decision to conduct cross-listings during share-issue privatizations.
Panel A presents results for OECD nations (developed economies).
Panel B presents results for non-OECD (developing economies).
The dependent variable for each model is an indicator (1 if the offering involves a cross-listing, 0 otherwise).

Table 23.6 (continued)

Notes:
The independent variables are: *Issue size* (US$ of offering), *Tradable goods* (indicator variable of 1 if firm produces tradable goods; as defined by Sarkissian and Schill (2004)), *High-technology industry* (indicator variable of 1 if firm is from a high-technology industry; as defined by Pagano et al., 2002), *Telecommunication industry* (indicator variable of 1 if firm is a telecom), *Anti-Director Rights Index* (higher values indicate greater legal protection), *Accounting standards* (higher values indicate stricter accounting standards) and *Capital access* (higher values indicate greater access to capital; as defined by the Milken Institute).
First row presents the coefficients; second row provides the standard error.
*** denotes significance at the 1% level; ** denotes significance at the 5% level, and * denotes significance at the 10% level.

firm's size, industry and product market appear to be primary determinants of whether a SIP is cross-listed. As expected, the size of the offering is positively related to the likelihood of cross-listing. Also, in every instance that we test, the firm's industry and product market are significant determinants of cross-listing by OECD governments. OECD-country SIPs from telecommunication and high-technology industries are significantly more likely to cross-list as are firms that produce tradable goods. Each of these industry and product market results is consistent with our earlier hypotheses. Furthermore, OECD firms from countries with limited capital market activity – as proxied by the country's capital access index – are significantly more likely to cross-list privatizing share offerings. This is as expected since privatizing governments may cross-list the large SIPs in order to access a deeper pool of capital or to spread the offering over multiple markets. Panel A also confirms that the protection of shareholder rights plays no significant role in the cross-listing decisions. This is again inconsistent with the bonding hypothesis.

The data tell a different story for the non-OECD sample (Table 23.6, panel B). Unlike for developed countries, firm-specific factors are not the primary determinants of cross-listing decisions in the non-OECD nations. With the exception of offering size, the firm-specific variables are generally not significant in the non-OECD sample. Institutional factors are instead more frequently significant determinants of cross-listing decisions.

In the developing nation sample, the country's accounting standards and legal environment are both significantly associated with SIP cross-listings. Neither of these institutional factors is significant in our analysis of firms from developed economies. Specifically, the data indicate that non-OECD firms from weaker accounting environments are significantly more likely to cross-list. This provides support for the findings of Bailey et al. (2006) who contend that the information enhancement from a cross-listing is more pronounced for firms domiciled in poor disclosure environments (such as those in many developing countries). Also, the benefits of cross-listing may be greater for privatizing firms from poor-disclosure economies since those markets are more likely to be neglected by analysts and the media. Alexander et al. (1988), Chaplinsky and Ramchand (2000), Baker et al. (2002), Lang et al. (2003) and Zingales (2007) argue that a cross-listing will enhance visibility and promote analyst and media coverage.

The level of capital market development (capital access) is another institutional variable which significantly impacts the cross-listing decisions in non-OECD SIPs. In panel B, models 4 and 5 show that firms in the non-OECD nations with less active capital markets are significantly more likely to cross-list. The significance level of this variable is higher in the non-OECD sample than in the OECD sample. A stronger proclivity to cross-list may be expected in SIPs from non-OECD nations since access to capital may be relatively more constrained in many developing economies. Panel B also reveals a greater likelihood of cross-listing by non-OECD firms from nations providing stronger protection of shareholder rights. The bonding hypothesis predicts the opposite relation.

Table 23.6 shows that the factors affecting SIP cross-listing decisions may differ based on the country's level of economic development. In developed nations, firm-level factors most significantly affect SIP cross-listings. However, in developing nations, institutional factors are the primary determinants of SIP cross-listings. Evidence that institutional factors are more influential in the developing nations is consistent with the World Bank (2002) report that emphasizes the importance of institution-building in emerging economies. Furthermore, Boubakri et al. (2005) and D'Souza et al. (2005) identify a similar pattern when considering the determinants of performance improvements in newly privatized firms. These studies find that institutional factors matter more in developing nations, while firm-level factors are more important in developed nations.

7 SUMMARY AND CONCLUSIONS

We examine the determinants of cross-listing decisions by privatizing governments. Our empirical analysis investigates how both firm-level and institution-level factors affect cross-listing choices in share-issue privatizations. The data indicate that the offering's size is significantly positively related to cross-listing. We expect this relation since a larger offering may require a cross-listing in order to access a deeper pool of capital. Additionally, the industry and the product market of the privatizing firm significantly affect the cross-listing decisions. Privatizing firms are more likely to cross-list if they are high-technology, in the telecommunication sector, or produce tradable goods that are sold on foreign markets. Institution-level characteristics also affect cross-listing decisions. We find that the sophistication of the nation's financial infrastructure significantly affects cross-listing decisions. Cross-listings are significantly more likely in nations with lower degrees of capital market development. The data also indicate that the nation's level of economic development is a very important determinant of SIP cross-listings. The likelihood of cross-listing is significantly higher in privatizations from developed countries.

We further investigate how the factors affecting SIP cross-listing decisions vary based on the country's level of economic development. We separate the data into subsamples of privatizing offerings from OECD (developed) economies and non-OECD (developing) economies and find several significant differences in the factors affecting cross-listing decisions across the two samples. While larger SIPs in both subsamples are significantly more likely to be cross-listed, firm-level factors generally appear to be the more important determinants of cross-listings in developed countries. For example, OECD nation privatizations in the telecommunication and in the high-technology industries are significantly more likely to cross-list. Additionally, companies from OECD nations that produce tradable goods are more likely to cross-list. These firm-level factors are never significant when considering the cross-listing decisions of SIPs from non-OECD countries.

Our study identifies that institutional factors are generally much more critical determinants of cross-listing activity in the SIPs from developing economies. Institutional variables such as accounting standards and legal environment are only significant when considering non-OECD SIPs. Our findings that institutional infrastructure most significantly affects cross-listing decisions in the developing nations is consistent with the World Bank (2002) conclusions regarding the importance of institutional development in emerging economies.

The results from our comparison of OECD versus non-OECD subsamples are especially important since the most widely cited empirical study of SIP cross-listing (Bortolotti et al., 2002) focuses entirely on privatizations in OECD countries. By considering privatizations from nations of all levels of economic development (and thus various degrees of institutional development), our analysis allows us to identify significant differences in the determinants of cross-listing decisions across countries.

NOTES

1. We thank Ginka Borisova and Veljko Fotak for research assistance with this project. We also benefited from comments offered by Jay Cai, Lal Chugh, Chitru Fernando, Edith Ginglinger, Ciarán mac an Bhaird, Pradeep Yadav, an anonymous referee, seminar participants at the University of South Carolina, and participants at the 2008 Global Conference on Business and Finance (Costa Rica), the 2008 FMA Europe Conference (Prague, Czech Republic), the 2009 Eastern Finance Association annual meeting, the 2009 INFINITI Conference (Dublin, Ireland), the 2010 World Finance Conference (Portugal) and the 2010 Southern Finance Association annual meeting.
2. Chaplinsky and Ramchand (2000) and Kang and Stulz (1997) provide empirical evidence that supports the investor recognition hypothesis.
3. For examples, see Stulz (1999), Coffee (2002) and Reese and Weisbach (2002).
4. For empirical evidence in support of the bonding hypothesis, see Miller (1999), Errunza and Miller (2000), Baker et al. (2002), Lang et al. (2003), Lel and Miller (2008) and Fernandes, et al. (2010).
5. In their study of capital acquisition decisions by private firms, Blass and Yafeh (2001) similarly found that high-technology firms are more likely to cross-list in New York (NASDAQ).

REFERENCES

Alexander, G., C. Eun and S. Janakiramanan (1988), 'International listings and stock returns: Some empirical evidence', *Journal of Financial and Quantitative Analysis*, **23**, 135–51.
Bailey, W., A. Karolyi, C. Salva (2006), 'The economic consequences of increased disclosures: evidence from international cross-listings', *Journal of Financial Economics*, **81**, 175–213.
Baker, H.K., J. Nofsinger, D. Weaver (2002), 'International cross-listing and visibility', *Journal of Financial and Quantitative Analysis*, **37**, 495–521.
Ball, R., S. Kothari, A. Robin (2000), 'The effect of international institutional factors of properties of accounting earnings', *Journal of Accounting and Economics*, **29**, 1–51.
Blass, A. and Y. Yafeh (2001), 'Vagabond shoes longing to stray: why foreign firms list in the United States', *Journal of Banking and Finance*, **25**, 555–72.
Boehmer, E., R. Nash and J. Netter (2005), 'Bank privatizations in developing and developed countries: cross-sectional evidence on the impact of economic and political factors', *Journal of Banking and Finance*, **29**, 1981–2013.
Bortolotti, B. and M. Faccio (2009), 'Government control of privatized firms', *Review of Financial Studies*, **22**, 2907–39.
Bortolotti, B., M. Fantini and C. Scarpa (2002), 'Why do governments privatize abroad?', *International Review of Finance*, **3**, 131–61.
Boubakri, N. and J. Cosset (1998) 'The financial and operating performance of newly privatized firms: evidence from developing countries', *Journal of Finance*, **53**, 1081–110.

Boubakri, N., J. Cosset and O. Guedmani (2005), 'Liberalization, corporate governance, and the performance of newly-privatized firms', *Journal of Corporate Finance*, **11**, 767–90.

Boutchkova, M. and W.L. Megginson (2000), 'The impact of privatization on capital market development and individual share ownership', *Financial Management*, **29**, 31–76.

Boycko, M., A. Shleifer and R. Vishny (1996), 'A theory of privatization', *Economic Journal*, **106**, 309–19.

Chaplinsky, S. and L. Ramchand (2000), 'The impact of global equity offerings', *Journal of Finance*, **55**, 2767–89.

Coffee, J. (2002), 'Competition among securities markets: a path dependent perspective', working paper, Columbia University.

Dewenter, K. and P.H. Malatesta (1997), 'Public offerings of state-owned and privately-owned enterprises: an international comparison', *Journal of Finance*, **52**, 1659–79.

Djankov, S., R. La Porta, F. Lopez-de-Silanes and A. Shleifer (2008), 'The law and economics of self-dealing', *Journal of Financial Economics*, **88**, 430–65.

Doidge, C., A. Karolyi and R. Stulz (2004), 'Why are foreign firms listed in the U.S. worth more?', *Journal of Financial Economics*, **71**, 205–38.

Doidge, C., A. Karolyi and R. Stulz (2007), 'Why do countries matter so much for corporate governance?', *Journal of Financial Economics*, **86**, 1–39.

Doidge, C., A. Karolyi and R. Stulz (2009a), 'Has New York become less competitive in global markets? Evaluating foreign listing choices over time', *Journal of Financial Economics*, **91**, 253–77.

Doidge, C., A. Karolyi and R. Stulz (2010), 'Why do foreign firms leave U.S. equity markets?', *Journal of Finance*, **65**, 1507–53.

Doidge, C., A. Karolyi, K. Lins, D. Miller and R. Stulz (2009b), 'Private benefits of control, ownership, and the cross-listing decision', *Journal of Finance*, **64**, 425–66.

D'Souza, J. and W. Megginson (1999), 'The financial and operating performance of privatized firms during the 1990s', *Journal of Finance*, **54**, 1397–438.

D'Souza, J., W. Megginson and R. Nash (2005), 'Effect of institutional and firm-specific characteristics on post-privatization performance: evidence from developed countries', *Journal of Corporate Finance*, **11**, 747–66.

Dyck, A. and L. Zingales (2004), 'Private benefits of control: an international comparison', *Journal of Finance*, **59**, 537–600.

Ernst and Young (2007), 'Accelerating growth – Global IPO trends 2006', available at: www.ipocongress.ru/download/guide/article/ipo_trends.pdf (accessed 15 May 2013).

Errunza, V. and D. Miller (2000), 'Market segmentation and the cost of capital in international equity markets', *Journal of Financial and Quantitative Analysis*, **35**, 577–600.

Estrin, S., J. Hanousek, E. Kocenda and J. Svejnar (2009), 'The effects of privatization and ownership in transition economies', *Journal of Economic Literature*, **47**, 699–728.

Fanto, J. and R. Karmel (1997), 'A report on the attitudes of foreign companies regarding a U.S. listing', *Stanford Journal of Law, Business, and Finance*, **3**, 51–83.

Fernandes, N., U. Lel and D. Miller (2010), 'Escape from New York: the market impact of loosening disclosure requirements', *Journal of Financial Economics*, **95**, 129–47.

Foerster, S. and A. Karolyi (1999), 'The effects of market segmentation and investor recognition on asset prices: evidence from foreign stocks listing in the United States', *Journal of Finance*, **54**, 981–1013.

Foerster, S. and A. Karolyi (2000), 'The long-run performance of global equity offerings', *Journal of Financial and Quantitative Analysis*, **35**, 499–528.

Johnson, S., R. La Porta, F. Lopez-de-Silanes and A. Shleifer (2000), 'Tunneling', *American Economic Review*, **90**, 22–7.

Jones, S., W. Megginson, R. Nash and J. Netter (1999), 'Share issue privatizations as financial means to political and economic ends', *Journal of Financial Economics*, **53**, 217–53.

Kang, J. and R. Stulz (1997), 'Why is there a home bias? An analysis of foreign portfolio equity ownership in Japan', *Journal of Financial Economics*, **46**, 3–28.

Karolyi, A. (1998), 'Why do companies list shares abroad? A survey of the evidence and its managerial implications', *Financial Markets, Institutions, and Instruments*, **7**, 1–60.

Karolyi, A. (2006), 'The world of cross-listings and the cross-listings of the world: challenging conventional wisdom', *Review of Finance*, **10** (1), 99–152.

La Porta, R., F. Lopez-de-Silanes and A. Shleifer (1999), 'Corporate ownership around the world', *Journal of Finance*, **54**, 471–517.

La Porta, R., F. Lopez-de-Silanes, A. Shleifer and R. Vishny (1997), 'Legal determinants of external finance', *Journal of Finance*, **52**, 1131–50.

La Porta, R., F. Lopez-de-Silanes, A. Shleifer and R. Vishny (1998), 'Law and finance', *Journal of Political Economy*, **106**, 1113–50.

Lang, M., K. Lins and D. Miller (2003), 'ADRs, analysts, and accuracy: does cross-listing in the United States

improve a firm's information environment and increase market value?', *Journal of Accounting Research*, **41**, 317–45.
Lel, Uger and Darius Miller (2008), 'International cross-listing, firm performance, and top management turnover: a test of the bonding hypothesis', *Journal of Finance*, **63**, 1897–937.
Megginson, W. and J. Netter (2001), 'From state to market: a survey of empirical studies on privatization', *Journal of Economic Literature*, **39**, 321–89.
Megginson, W., R. Nash and M. Randenborgh (1994), 'The financial and operating performance of newly privatized firms: an international empirical analysis', *Journal of Finance*, **49**, 403–52.
Megginson, W., R. Nash, J. Netter and A. Poulsen (2004), 'The choice of public versus private markets: evidence from privatizations', *Journal of Finance*, **59**, 2835–70.
Merton, R. (1987), 'A simple model of capital market equilibrium with incomplete information', *Journal of Finance*, **42**, 483–510.
Miller, D. (1999), 'The market reaction to international cross-listings: evidence from depositary receipts', *Journal of Financial Economics*, **51**, 103–23.
Pagano, M. and P. Volpin (2005), 'The political economy of corporate governance', *American Economic Review*, **95**, 1005–30.
Pagano, M., A. Roell and J. Zechner (2002), 'The geography of equity listing: why do companies list abroad?', *Journal of Finance*, **57**, 2651–94.
Reese, W. and M. Weisbach (2002), 'Protection of minority shareholder interests, cross-listings in the United States, and subsequent equity offerings', *Journal of Financial Economics*, **66**, 65–104.
Romano, R. (1998), 'Empowering investors: a market approach to securities regulation', *Yale Law Journal*, **107**, 2359–430.
Sarkissian, S. and M. Schill (2004), 'The overseas listing decision: new evidence of proximity preference', *Review of Financial Studies*, **17**, 769–810.
Saudagaran, S. (1988), 'An empirical study of selected factors influencing the decision to list on foreign stock exchanges', *Journal of International Business Studies*, **19**, 101–27.
Saudagaran, S. and G. Biddle (1995), 'Foreign listing location: a study of MNCs and stock exchanges in eight countries', *Journal of International Business Studies*, **26**, 319–42.
Spamann, H. (2010), 'The "Antidirector Rights Index" revisited', *Review of Financial Studies*, **23**, 467–86.
Stulz, R. (1999), 'Globalization, corporate finance, and the cost of capital', *Journal of Applied Corporate Finance*, **26**, 3–28.
Subrahmanyam, A. and S. Titman (1998), 'The going public decision and the development of financial markets', *Journal of Finance*, **54**, 1045–82.
World Bank (2002), *Building Institutions for Markets*, New York: Oxford University Press.
Zingales, L. (2007), 'Is the U.S. capital market losing its competitive edge?', working paper, University of Chicago.

24 How bank health affects the capital structure and performance of IPO firms: evidence from the Japanese financial crisis in the 1990s
Kazuo Yamada[1]

1 INTRODUCTION

The effect of the propagation of liquidity shocks through the bank–firm lending relationship is one of the central topics in banking research. For example, it is known that a negative shock on the banks leads to increases in the interest rate to their client firms (Kang and Stulz, 2000) that may have a negative impact on the investment activities and subsequent performance of the lender (Gibson, 1995). However, little is known about whether the bank's health affects the behavior of lending firms who have a close relationship with the unhealthy bank. If a firm and a bank have a close relationship and it is difficult for the firm to change to another bank, this gives the bank the advantage of being able to require a higher interest rate from the firm or of lending more to the firm.

Although in the short term the over-lending increases the revenue of the bank, in the long term, it may harm the source of the profit. The over-lending pushes up the cost of capital because of the increasing default cost and the fact that paying extra interest rates reduces the cash flow of the firm. Furthermore, the reduction of cash flow may cause firms to have insufficient equity capital after the IPOs and may lead to an increase in the cost of capital.

This chapter investigates whether the over-lending by poor-health banks leads to inefficient decision-making for their client firms, especially those trying to go public. Through the initial public offering (IPO) process, firms can raise significant amounts of new capital by issuing new shares. Furthermore, since going public is a lengthy process, it is plausible that these banks use their client firms as a source of revenue, even though that is a myopic decision. Thus, poor-health banks have an additional incentive to lend to their client firms, especially those intending to go public, and raise more proceeds than they need so that firms have to repay loans with interest after the listing. Thus, IPO firms may be encouraged to raise more proceeds than they plan to, or raise funds after their IPOs, to repay the over-lending by poor-health banks.

The purpose of this chapter is to examine whether over-lending by poor-health banks really occurs and how such over-lending affects the decision-making of the IPO firms. The empirical findings can be summarized as follows. First, we investigate whether the health condition of the bank affects the firm's pre-IPO leverage. The empirical findings suggest that IPO firms associated with banks with poor performance have higher leverage. This is evidence of over-lending by poor-health banks for pre-IPO firms.

Second, we explore how firms repay insufficient loans from poor-health banks and examine the correlation between the health of banks and their client firms' performance. We investigate two possible ways: by issuing more shares at the time of an IPO and by conducting seasoned equity offerings (SEOs) post-IPO. Over-lending by the bank increases the financial leverage of its client firm, leading to an increase in the default cost. In order to repay such insufficient loans, IPO firms may then increase proceeds by issuing more shares than they initially need. Alternatively, they may issue shares after the IPO to raise funds for repaying loans from poor-health banks. In this chapter, we find a strong relationship between a bank's health and the amount of the primary shares at the time of an IPO and the probability of an SEO within three years.

Finally, we investigate whether the over-lending and insufficient issuing equity from the poor-health bank affects the stock performance of IPO firms. The additional equity issues caused by over-lending from poor-health banks are not a positive net present value (NPV) project for firms. Moreover, over-lending may increase the default risk of a firm. Such firms may suffer a lower valuation in the stock market as a result. The empirical findings suggest that the aftermarket performance of IPOs associated with poor-health banks is worse than that of IPOs related with healthier banks. Using the buy-and-hold abnormal return as the measurement of long-term stock performance, we find that firms' stock returns are lower when their main bank's health is worse.

This chapter makes several contributions to the current debate about the banking sector's effect on real economy sectors. First, this chapter shows the negative side of a close firm–bank relationship; namely, the resulting over-lending and subsequent inefficient raising of capital. Empirical evidence in this chapter shows that the banking sector crash caused the misallocation of capital, which caused inefficient investment by the client firms. Furthermore, such capital misallocation worsened the stock performance of IPO firms.

This chapter also contributes to the debate on the implications of the financial crisis. Most researchers investigating the shock in the financial sectors argue for the propagation of the liquidity crunch. However, less is known about the path of the propagations. In this chapter, we investigate how the bank liquidity crunch affects the behavior of firms.

2 THE ROLE OF BANKS IN THE JAPANESE BANKING CRISIS AND THE INCREASE IN THE IPO MARKET IN THE LATE 1990S

2.1 Pros and Cons of the Firm–Bank Relationship

It is known that the firm–bank relationship benefits firms in some settings. Hoshi et al. (1991) show that firms with strong bank relationships have easier access to external financing than those with weak associations with banks. They conclude that the strong relationships decrease information asymmetry between the firms and the banks, which reduces the cost of capital.

However, it is also known that the firm–bank relationship has two disadvantages: the hold-up problem caused by asymmetric information and capital misallocation during banking sector shocks. The firm–bank relationship causes the hold-up problem (Rajan, 1992; von Thadden, 2004; Weinstein and Yafeh, 1998). Rajan (1992) assumes that the situation in which a firm has a relationship with only one primary bank and the bank knows information about the firm that other banks do not know causes the hold-up problem. If only one bank has the necessary information about a firm whose quality is good, the firm incurs additional costs in switching banks. Because other banks do not have the information, the firm is categorized as low quality when it offers to build a relationship, although its quality is actually high. Hence, these banks require a higher interest rate for the new lending contract. In such situations, a firm that has a relationship with a bank can secure an interest rate that is slightly lower than the uninformed banks can offer. Multiple bank relationships can mitigate a bank's information monopolies, leading to a reduction in interest rates. Using a Japanese dataset, Weinstein and Yafeh (1998) show that, although strong firm–bank relationships lead to increases in the availability of capital to borrowing firms, the cost of capital is high and the relationships do not lead to higher profitability or growth. These studies indicate that if only the main bank has the necessary information on the firm and others do not, it is difficult for firms to switch banks; hence, asymmetric information causes the hold-up problem.

It is also known that banking sector shocks negatively affect the real economy (Chava and Purnanandam, 2011; Fukuda and Koibuchi, 2007; Gibson, 1995; Hubbard et al., 2002; Ivashina and Scharfstein, 2010) and causes capital misallocation. Gibson (1995) studies the relationship between a bank's credit rating and its client firm's investment activity, and shows that if the main bank of a firm has the lowest credit rating, the firm's investment activity is lower. The shock in the banking sector also has a negative impact on the performance of client firms. Hubbard et al. (2002) shows that the lending rate from poor-health banks is higher than that from sound-health banks. Using a case study of the failure of two large Japanese banks, the Long-Term Credit Bank of Japan (LTCB) and the Nippon Credit Bank (NCB), Fukuda and Koibuchi (2007) observe the negative impact of the bankrupt of banks on the performance of their client firms. Furthermore, they show that the impact is deeper for small firms, which take more time to recover their profits. Chava and Purnanandam (2011) examine the effect of the Russian crisis in the autumn of 1998 on the US banking system and find that it worsened the performance of their borrowers.

Recent studies on the 2008 US financial shock indicate that banks seek alternative ways to raise equity capital. Ivashina and Scharfstein (2010) show that bank lending has decreased during the recent US financial crisis, but by only a small degree, as the banks seek other sources of capital. The same result is observed in Acharya et al. (2009), who show that banks try to find other funding sources such as private investors and government-funded capital injections. Hoshi and Kashyap (2004) assert that Japanese banks, in contrast, failed to seek alternative sources of gain in their lending contracts during the financial crisis.

2.2 Crisis in the Banking Sector and the IPO Market in the 1990s

Japan experienced a major financial crisis during the 1990s (Hoshi and Kashyap, 2001, 2004, 2010). The collapse of the land price boom in 1991 increased the number of non-performing loans by Japanese banks, since Japanese firms borrow using land as collateral. This shock in the banking sector culminated in a liquidity crisis in 1999. In November 1997, Sanyo Securities declared bankruptcy. In October and December of 1998, LTCB and NCB failed, respectively. As shown above, because of the shock in the financial sector, Japanese firms suffer lower productivity (Akiyoshi and Kobayashi, 2010; Gibson, 1995, 1997; Kang and Stulz, 2000) and capital misallocation (Peek and Rosengren, 2005).

During the same period, an IPO boom occurred in Japan. In 1995, the number of listing firms on the OTC exchange was 173, which was higher than in the previous years. This was more than in the previous 1989–90 land price boom. During the land price bubble period, the numbers of IPOs on the OTC were 71 and 90 in 1989 and 1990, respectively.

This is rather surprising, because it is known that the number of IPOs and the condition of the real economy are positively correlated. Lowry (2003) shows that aggregate IPO volume is positively correlated with macro factors, such as future gross domestic product (GDP) growth, investment growth or sales growth. Furthermore, it is well documented that equity issue volume and investor sentiment are positively correlated. Loughran and Ritter (1995) show that long-run performance following equity issue is negative and argue that firms tend to issue equity when their valuation is high. Furthermore, Baker and Wurgler (2002) show that high amounts of aggregate volume of equity issues, including both IPOs and SEOs, cause lower market returns. They argue that this low return is caused by firms capturing the market timing and issuing equity when their valuation is high.

Figure 24.1 shows the correlation between the Japanese stock market index and the number of IPOs. The Russell Nomura Total Market Index is used as the stock market index, because it includes all public firms and includes dividends. Both the stock market index and the number of IPOs bottomed out in 1992. After that, the level of the stock market index recovered to approximately half the level of 1989 (it was 659.85 in 1989 and

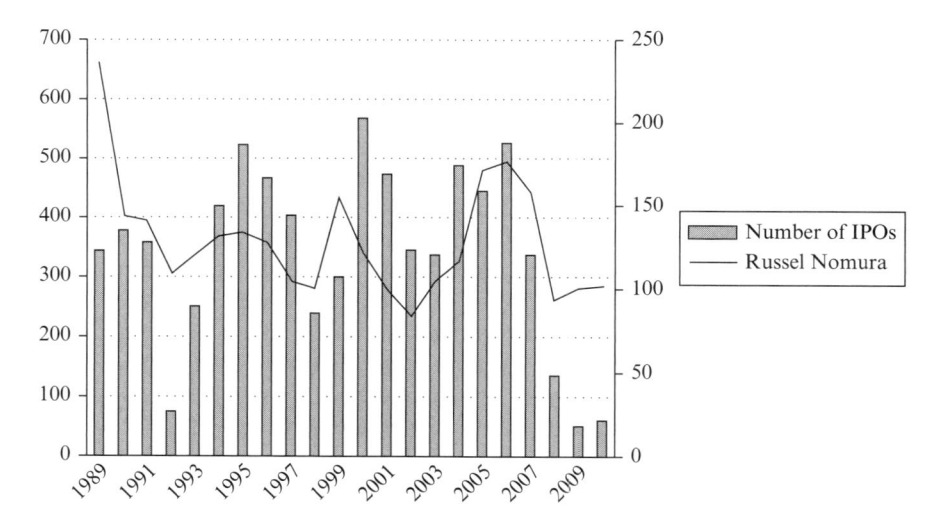

Note: This figure reports the number of IPOs per year and the stock market return. The grey bar chart reports the number of IPOs per year, and the black line plots the stock market return (Russel Nomura) on the last day of the year.

Figure 24.1 Number of IPOs and market index

374.7 in 1995). However, the number of IPOs in the second peak was larger than that in the first peak when Japan was in a bubble period.

There are several reasons for this increase in Japanese IPOs in the 1990s. The first is the deregulation of the IPO market. Before 1994, the number of IPOs was restricted to two or fewer firms per week to control the demand for IPO stocks. In April 1995, this limit was deregulated, and the number increased. In 1994, the number of IPOs in the OTC exchange was 114, which indicates that more than two firms were listed every week. The second reason is the deregulation of the OTC market: The Japan Securities Dealers Association announced the formation of a new market for new technology venture firms or research-based firms. This deregulation enables relatively financially weak firms to go public.

As we note, at the time of IPOs, firms can raise a sufficient amount of capital from the market. Banks in poor financial condition need additional revenue to maintain their capital adequacy ratios. In this chapter, we examine how banks use the IPO-intended firms to gain from them and how the bank's health affects the firm's investment activity and subsequent performance. If a bank knows when its client firm will go public, and the health of the bank is poor, the bank might lend more than the firm needs and gain by way of interest rates.

This over-lending to firms is not the optimal decision for the bank, in the long term, for the following reasons. In over-lending, firms must pay interest rates that will not increase the future cash flow of the firm. Furthermore, over-lending increases the financial leverage ratio, which in turn increases the probability of default and the cost of capital. Thus, considering the default cost, it is not optimal for the main bank to over-lend and increase the probability of default. However, if such banks have low performance and an incentive to pursue short-term benefit, they may over-lend to their client firms, especially those that would raise funds at an early date. Gibson (1995) shows that debt leverage is high if the health of the primary bank is poor.

As mentioned above, in the banking crisis period in Japan, the number of IPOs increased. It is natural for low-performing banks that take a short-sighted view to exploit these IPO firms to better maintain their operating performance. Thus, the first hypothesis is as follows. Healthy banks also have an incentive to gain from IPO firms. However, there are several reasons that healthy banks do not over-lend, or at least not to the degree seen with unhealthy banks. First, it is not optimal for banks to raise the risk of the firm, because income by interest rates is constant. Increasing the financial leverage leads to increasing risk. Banks with long-term relationships and constant earnings may lend reasonable amounts of money; on the other hand, banks with financial problems try to generate future cash flows and try to lend more than is needed. Second, it is not optimal for firms to borrow more than they need, because over-lending is not a project with positive NPV. Furthermore, the payment for paying interest rates would be an inefficient use of capital arising from investors, since it does not create positive NPV.

Hypothesis 1: The financial leverage of the IPO firms with unhealthy banks is higher than that of the IPO firms with healthy banks prior to IPO.

Next, because of the over-lending by unhealthy banks, those firms intend to raise more funds by increasing the IPO proceeds or SEOs after IPOs. We can now build the following hypotheses.

Hypothesis 2a: Firms with poor-health banks and high debt leverage raise more equity at the IPO.

Hypothesis 2b: Firms with poor-health banks and high debt leverage have a high probability of SEO.

If the loan is not what a firm intended and is more than it needs, the repayment may reduce the cost of capital of IPO firms. Then, such a firm's long-term stock performance would worsen.

Hypothesis 3: Firms with poor-health banks and high financial leverage have poorer long-term stock performance.

3 DATA AND METHODOLOGY

3.1 Sample and Data

The sample consists of firms completing an IPO in Japan between January 1996 and December 2005. The number of IPOs during this period was 1375. After excluding firms that belong to the financial sector, real-estate investment trusts (REITs), financial companies and second-time IPOs, the final sample used in this study consists of 1357 IPOs. The primary data sources for our sample are the *Kabushiki Joujou Hakusho* (*Factbook on New Listing Companies*), *Kabushiki Tentou Joujou Hakusho* (*Factbook on New Listing Companies in the OTC Market*), and *Kabushiki JASDAQ Joujou Hakusho* (*Factbook on New Listing Companies in JASDAQ*), all published by Pronexus (ex. Asia Shouken Insatsu) annually. We use financial data on IPO firms and banks from FinancialQUEST, provided by Nikkei Media Marketing. Bank lending data is obtained from the Corporate Borrowing by Financial Institutions Dataset provided by Nikkei Media Marketing.

We determine the main bank by using the following procedures. Initially, we use the Corporate Borrowing by Financial Institutions Dataset and regard the top lender as the main bank. Next, if the dataset is omitted, we use the *Japan Company Handbook* (*Kaisha Shikiho*), which is published by Toyo Keizai Sha, and regard the first bank among the principal bank list as the main bank. One problem of using these sources is that they both rely on post-IPO data. The Corporate Borrowing by Financial Institution Dataset is limited to listed firms; then we use them after they go public.

As a measurement of the health of main banks, we use the following three variables: *Main bank bad loan* ratio, *Main bank return on assets* (*ROA*), and *Main bank market/book* (*MB*) *ratio*. The *Main bank bad loan ratio* is defined as the amount of bad loan divided by the total outstanding loans. The *Main bank ROA* is the ROA of the main bank, where ROA is defined as the net income divided by total assets at the beginning of the period. The *Main bank MB ratio* is the market-to-book ratio of the main bank. Since the valuation by the stock market is used to define the MB ratio, it is thought to more accurately measure bank health. However, in the period used in this study, some banks went private, and thus, they could not be evaluated using the market-to-book ratio.

Table 24.1 Summary statistics of bank-related variables

Panel A

	No.of IPOs	Mean of bank health measurement		
		Bad loan ratio	ROA	MB ratio
1996	143	0.041	−0.003	2.473
1997	122	0.042	−0.001	2.954
1998	95	0.050	−0.007	2.283
1999	132	0.053	−0.004	1.916
2000	197	0.054	0.000	1.521
2001	157	0.060	−0.001	1.441
2002	123	0.081	−0.007	1.107
2003	126	0.069	−0.007	0.663
2004	167	0.050	−0.001	1.105
2005	95	0.036	0.000	1.851

Panel B

	Bad loan ratio	ROA	MB ratio
Bad loan ratio	1		
ROA	−0.369	1	
MB ratio	−0.292	0.064	1

Notes:
This table reports the summary statistics of bank-related variables.
In panel A, the number of observations per year and summary statistics of three measurements of bank health are reported.
Main bank bad loan ratio is defined as the total amount of bad loan divided by the total assets.
Main bank ROA is the main bank's ROA defined as net income divided by the total assets at the beginning of the period.
Main bank MB ratio is the market book ratio of the main bank.
In panel B, the correlation of the three bank measurements of bank health is reported.

Table 24.1 reports the summary statistics of the three variables regarding bank health. Panel A of Table 24.1 summarizes the number of observations and three bank health variables. The bank loan ratio was 4.1 percent in 1996 and approximately doubled to 8.1 percent in 2002. The average *Main bank ROA* was between −0.7 percent and 0 percent, indicating that in this period, most of the banks' net income was negative. The *Main bank MB ratio* was 2.47 in 1996 and decreased to 0.66 in 2003. In 2003, most banks had a market value lower than their book value. After this, in 2005, it recovered to 1.85. The number of IPOs increased, especially between 1998 and 2001. At the same time, the bad loan ratio increased, and the market-to-book ratio decreased, which indicates that although the operating performance of banks worsened, the number of IPOs increased in this period. In the other period, the number of IPOs and bank health do not necessarily positively correlate.

Panel B of Table 24.1 reports the correlation between the three variables. Since these three variables capture the different aspects of bank performance, they are not necessarily highly correlated. The absolute values of the correlations of the bad loan ratio of the

How bank health affects the capital structure and performance of IPO firms 559

bank with the other two variables are about 0.3. The ROA of the bank and the market-to-book ratio of the bank are not correlated, the correlation being only 0.06.

3.2 Empirical Models

To examine the hypotheses, we develop a number of empirical models. Initially, we investigate whether bank health affects financial leverage before IPOs. The empirical model is as follows:

$$Debt/total\ assets = \alpha + \beta_1 \times Main\ bank\ bad\ loan\ ratio + \beta_2 \times Main\ bank\ ROA + \beta_3 \times Main\ bank\ MB\ ratio + \Sigma\gamma \times Control\ variables + \Sigma\theta \times year + \varepsilon \quad (24.1)$$

Using this estimation model (Equation 24.1), we evaluate the effect of the health of the main bank on the debt leverage of the firms before going public. The dependent variable *Debt/total assets* is defined as the cumulative loan from all financial intermediates divided by the total assets pre-IPO. Ideally, we should use the loan from the main bank. However, the Corporate Borrowing by Financial Institutions Dataset, which is used to identify the main bank in this study, does not include the lending data before IPOs.[2] This data constraint prevents us from using the precise measurement of the amount of loans from main banks and may cause bias in our predictions. We predict that poor bank health negatively affects financial leverage. More specifically, the coefficient of *Main bank bad loan ratio* should be negative, while the coefficient of the other two variables, *Main bank ROA* and *Main bank MB* ratio, should be positive.

Next, we investigate whether bank health affects the number of primary shares at the time of IPO. The dependent variable *Primary share/share outstanding* is defined as the number of shares newly issued at IPO divided by the total number of shares before IPO. We hypothesize that as the bank deteriorates in health and over-lends to the IPO firms, the IPO firms must raise more proceeds than they need. Then, the portion of primary share would increase. The empirical model is as follows:

$$Primary\ share/share\ outstanding = \alpha + \beta_1 \times Main\ bank\ bad\ loan\ ratio + \beta_2 \times Main\ bank\ ROA + \beta_3 \times Main\ bank\ MB\ ratio + \Sigma\gamma \times Control\ variables + \Sigma\theta \times year + \varepsilon \quad (24.2)$$

The alternative way for IPO firms to cope with over-lending is to conduct SEOs after their IPOs. We also investigate the probability of SEOs after IPO within one or three years of IPOs being affected by bad bank health. The dependent variable is the binary variable that takes the value of 1 if the IPO firm issues equity one or three years after IPO and takes the value of 0 otherwise. We use the probit model and estimate as follows:

$$\Pr[SEO\ 1yr\ (or\ 3yr)] = \alpha + \beta_1 \times Main\ bank\ bad\ loan\ ratio + \beta_2 \times Main\ bank\ ROA + \beta_3 \times Main\ bank\ MB\ ratio + \Sigma\gamma \times Control\ variables + \Sigma\theta \times year + \varepsilon \quad (24.3)$$

Finally, we investigate whether over-lending by poor-health banks and unnecessary additional equity issues at the time of IPO or post-IPO affect the performance of IPO firms. These equity issues may decrease the cost of capital of IPO firms. Furthermore, repaying the over-lent loans does not contribute to a positive NPV. Such over-lending and subsequent extra equity issue worsen the stock performance of firms. Next, we investigate the effect of bank health on stock performance. The empirical model is as follows:

$$BHAR\ 1yr\ (or\ 3yr) = \alpha + \beta_1 \times Main\ bank\ bad\ loan\ ratio + \beta_2 \times Main\ bank\ ROA + \beta_3 \times Main\ bank\ MB\ ratio + \Sigma\gamma \times Control\ variables + \Sigma\theta \times year + \varepsilon \quad (24.4)$$

As a dependent variable, we use a one- or three-year buy-and-hold abnormal return. As a market index, we use TOPIX or the market index of the Tokyo Stock Exchange.

To control for the firm's fundamental characteristics, we use the following variables as control variables for each estimation: *ROA*, ln(*Total assets*), ln(*Tobin's Q*), *Intangible assets/total assets* and *Debt ratio pre-IPO*. The definitions of each variable are as follows. The firm's *ROA* is measured as the firm's operating income as a share of its total assets for the prior year. It is well known that small or younger firms suffer high degrees of asymmetric information. We include ln(*Total assets*) and ln(*Age*) as indicators of asymmetric information. The variable ln(*Total assets*) is the natural logarithm of the total assets, and ln(*Age*) is the natural logarithm of the number of years between the firm's establishment and its IPO. To control for potential investment activity, we include ln(*Tobin's Q*), which is the natural logarithm of Tobin's Q. To calculate the Tobin's Q, the first day's closing price is used to evaluate the market value of equity. Year dummies are also included to capture the macroeconomic effect. It is commonly known that the amount of intangible assets affects the capital structure. *Intangible assets/total assets* is used for controlling the firm's availability of debt and is defined as the amount of intangible assets divided by the amount of total assets.

Table 24.2 shows the summary statistics for each variable. The mean (median) of the bad loan ratio of the banks in this period is 5.4 (5.2) percent. The mean bank's ROA is negative, but the median bank ROA is positive, though both are near zero. Lastly, the mean of the main bank's market-to-book ratio is 0.674. This indicates that the market values of the banks in this period are lower than their book values. The mean (median) of the ROA is 0.06 (0.05). On average, it takes 15 years from a firm's establishment to its IPO. The median value of this time period is 22 years. The mean (median) of the total asset pre-IPO is 32 924 (6855) million yen. We can see that about 27 percent of the total assets are the loans from financial intermediaries, and the standard deviation of Debt/total assets is 22 percent, indicating that the amount of the total loan is highly dispersed.

3.3 Empirical Results

3.3.1 Bank health and financial leverage and equity issues

Table 24.3 reports the results of the multivariate estimates where *Debt/total assets* is used as the dependent variable. The coefficient of *Main bank bad loan ratio* is positive and statistically significant. This indicates that for firms whose banks' bad loan ratio is higher, the debt ratio before IPO is higher. Banks must clean up their bad loan from

Table 24.2 Summary statistics of the variables used in this empirical study

	N	Mean	Median	Std Dev.
Debt/total assets	1357	0.269	0.242	0.217
Main bank bad loan ratio	1357	0.054	0.052	0.023
Main bank ROA	1357	−0.003	0.001	0.009
Main bank MB ratio	1035	0.674	0.462	1.382
ROA	1357	0.065	0.049	0.068
Age	1357	22.207	19.000	15.904
Total Assets (million yen)	1357	32924	6855	217232
Tobin's Q	1357	5.514	1.956	16.364
Intangible assets/total assets	1357	0.022	0.006	0.048

Notes:
This table reports the summary statistics of the variables used in this empirical study.
Main bank bad loan ratio is defined as the amount of bad loan divided by the total outstanding loans.
Main bank ROA is the main bank's ROA defined as net income divided by the total assets at the beginning of the period.
Main bank MB ratio is the market book ratio of the main bank.
Because some banks went public in this period, the number of observations of *Main bank MB ratio* is lower than that for other variables.
ROA is the IPO firm's measure as the ratio of operating income to the total asset at pre-IPO.
Ln(*Age*) is the natural logarithm of the firm age at the time of IPOs.
Ln(*Total asset*) is the natural logarithm of the total asset.
Ln(*Tobin's Q*) is the natural logarithm of the Tobin's Q.
Intangible assets/total assets is defined as the amount of intangible assets divided by the amount of total assets.

their assets. IPO firms would be safer borrowers for such banks. Such IPO firms would be lent to in expectation of repayment with interest rates after their IPOs that would reduce the amount of bad loans. The coefficients of the other two variables, *Main bank ROA* and *Main bank MB ratio*, are negative, which indicates that banks with worse operating performance or banks with lower market value lend more to IPO firms. The coefficients are however not statistically significant at least at the 10 percent level. The coefficient of *Intangible assets/total assets* is negative and statistically significant at least at the 5 percent level. This indicates that firms with more intangible assets face difficulty in lending. Overall, we have found evidence of over-lending by unhealthy banks to pre-IPO firms.

Next, we investigate whether bank health affects the number of primary shares at the time of IPO (Table 24.4). To measure bank health, we use three variables: *Bad loan ratio*, *ROA* and *MB ratio*. The coefficient of *Main bank bad loan ratio* is positive and statistically significant, and that of *Main bank MB ratio* is negative and statistically significant. These indicate that the IPO firms whose main banks suffer a large bad loan ratio and lower valuation in the stock market raise more than the other firms at the time of IPO. The coefficients of *Debt ratio* are positive and statistically significant in two of three estimates. This indicates that firms with many more loans from the banks raise more proceeds at the time of IPOs. All of these results are consistent with our hypothesis. Firms with bad health and higher financial leverage increase the number of primary shares at the time of IPO.

Table 24.3 Relationship between the bank health and the debt leverage

Variables	(1)	(2)	(3)
		Debt/total assets	
Main bank bad loan ratio	0.651***		
	(2.91)		
Main bank ROA		−0.929	
		(−1.31)	
Main bank MB ratio			−0.005
			(−0.95)
ROA	−0.809***	−0.800***	−0.950***
	(−4.05)	(−4.04)	(−4.26)
ln(Age)	−0.046***	−0.045***	−0.061***
	(−4.83)	(−4.75)	(−5.60)
ln(Total assets)	0.035***	0.035***	0.033***
	(6.32)	(6.34)	(5.07)
ln(Tobin's Q)	−0.035***	−0.035***	−0.018
	(−3.05)	(−3.11)	(−1.25)
Intangible assets/total assets	−0.243**	−0.255**	−0.363***
	(−2.33)	(−2.44)	(−2.79)
Constant	0.158***	0.181***	0.275***
	(2.81)	(3.33)	(4.07)
Observations	1357	1357	1035
R-squared	0.189	0.187	0.151

Notes:
This table shows the relationship between the bank health and the debt leverage.
Dependent variable is the debt leverage before IPO that is defined as the total loan from all financial intermediations divided by the total assets.
Main bank bad loan ratio is defined as the amount of bad loan divided by the total outstanding loans.
Main bank ROA is the main bank's ROA that defined as net income divided by the total asset at initial of the period.
Main bank MB ratio is the market book ratio of main bank.
ROA is the IPO firm's ROA, which is measured as the ratio of operating income to total assets pre-IPO.
Ln(*Age*) is the natural logarithm of the firm age at the time of IPOs.
Ln(*Total asset*) is the natural logarithm of the total assets.
Ln(*Tobin's Q*) is the natural logarithm of the Tobin's Q.
Intangible assets/total assets is defined as the amount of intangible assets divided by the amount of total assets.
Year dummies are also included as independent variables but not reported.
The standard error, which is clustered by industry, is reported.
***, ** and * indicate statistical significance at the 1%, 5% and 10% level, respectively.

The coefficient of ROA for IPO firms is negative and statistically significant, indicating that firms with less profitability at the time of IPO raise more funds. Both ln(*Age*) and ln(*Total assets*) are negative and statistically significant. This means that younger or smaller firms raise more proceeds through IPOs. This may be because such firms simply need additional funds for investment.

We also investigate whether bank health affects the probability of SEOs. To raise funds for repaying loans, IPO firms may issue equity after their IPOs. To investigate

Table 24.4 Relationship between bank health and primary shares at the IPO

Variables	(1)	(2)	(3)
	\multicolumn{3}{c}{Primary share/share outstanding}		
Main bank bad loan ratio	17.986***		
	(2.98)		
Main bank ROA		−2.700	
		(−0.21)	
Main bank MB ratio			−0.220**
			(−2.21)
ROA	−10.765***	−10.315***	−14.375**
	(−3.73)	(−3.47)	(−2.22)
ln(Age)	−0.424*	−0.440*	−0.453**
	(−1.85)	(−1.89)	(−2.02)
ln(Total assets)	−0.669***	−0.695***	−0.676***
	(−4.07)	(−4.28)	(−3.30)
ln(Tobin's Q)	−0.187	−0.231	−0.108
	(−0.61)	(−0.78)	(−0.40)
Intangible assets/total assets	0.652	0.673	3.284
	(0.17)	(0.18)	(0.76)
Debt ratio	2.087***	2.137***	1.047
	(3.27)	(3.28)	(1.17)
Constant	18.871***	20.111***	20.633***
	(8.28)	(9.56)	(8.21)
Observations	1356	1356	1035
R-squared	0.055	0.049	0.055

Notes:
This table shows the relationship between bank health and the number of primary shares at the IPO.
The dependent variable is the *Primary share/share outstanding*, which is defined as the number of primary shares divided by the number of shares offered before IPOs.
Main bank bad loan ratio is defined as the amount of bad loan divided by the total outstanding loans.
Main bank ROA is the main bank's ROA defined as net income divided by the total assets at the beginning of the period.
Main bank MB ratio is the market book ratio of the main bank.
ROA is the IPO firm's ROA, which is measured as the ratio of operating income to total assets pre-IPO.
Ln(*Age*) is the natural logarithm of the firm age at the time of IPOs.
Ln(*Total asset*) is the natural logarithm of the total assets.
Ln(*Tobin's Q*) is the natural logarithm of the Tobin's Q.
Intangible assets/total assets is defined as the amount of intangible assets divided by the amount of total assets.
Year dummies are also included as independent variables but not reported.
The standard error, which is clustered by industry, is reported.
***, ** and * indicate statistical significance at the 1%, 5% and 10% level, respectively.

the possibility, we conduct the probit estimates and show the result in Table 24.5. The dependent variable takes the value of 1 if the IPO firm issues equity one (three) year(s) after its IPO. If banks with bad health over-lend to the IPO firms and they do not raise more funds at the time of IPO, these firms may raise funds after IPOs by issuing equity of SEOs. The dependent variable takes the value of 1 if the IPO firm issues equity within one year of IPO (columns 1 to 3) or within three years of IPO (columns 4 to 6).

Table 24.5 Relationship between bank health and the probability of SEO after IPOs

Variables	(1)	(2)	(3)	(4)	(5)	(6)
	\multicolumn{3}{c}{Pr(SEO 1yr)}		Pr(SEO 3yr)	
Main bank bad loan ratio	6.218***			4.991***		
	(2.82)			(3.12)		
Main bank ROA		−8.937**			−12.900***	
		(−2.15)			(−2.74)	
Main bank MB ratio			−0.144**			−0.007
			(−2.14)			(−0.24)
ROA	0.873	0.952	1.092	0.943	1.033	0.568
	(0.59)	(0.64)	(0.57)	(1.19)	(1.38)	(0.47)
ln(Age)	−0.352***	−0.351***	−0.370***	−0.241***	−0.248***	−0.310***
	(−3.68)	(−3.60)	(−3.55)	(−3.55)	(−3.60)	(−4.37)
ln(Total assets)	0.014	0.008	0.087	0.003	−0.002	0.004
	(0.24)	(0.14)	(1.40)	(0.07)	(−0.05)	(0.08)
ln(Tobin's Q)	0.104	0.085	0.180**	0.025	0.012	0.040
	(1.29)	(1.05)	(1.97)	(0.28)	(0.13)	(0.43)
Intangible assets/total assets	−3.152*	−3.321*	−3.796**	−0.381	−0.438	−0.235
	(−1.95)	(−1.93)	(−2.10)	(−0.49)	(−0.53)	(−0.27)
Debt ratio	1.162***	1.122***	0.922**	1.057***	1.045***	1.030***
	(3.25)	(3.19)	(2.02)	(5.28)	(5.24)	(3.78)
Constant	−1.828***	−1.423**	−1.949***	−0.664	−0.348	−0.174
	(−3.16)	(−2.47)	(−3.21)	(−1.32)	(−0.70)	(−0.39)
Observations	1357	1357	1035	1357	1357	1035
Pseudo R-squared	0.09	0.09	0.11	0.04	0.05	0.05

Notes:
This table shows the relationship between bank health and the probability of SEO after IPOs.
The dependent variable takes the value of 1 if the IPO firm issues equity within one (three) year(s) of their IPOs.
A probit estimate is used.
Main bank bad loan ratio is defined as the amount of bad loan divided by the total outstanding loans.
Main bank ROA is the main bank's ROA defined as net income divided by the total assets at the beginning of the period.
Main bank MB ratio is the market book ratio of the main bank.
ROA is the IPO firm's ROA, which is measured as the ratio of operating income to total assets pre-IPO.
Ln(*Age*) is the natural logarithm of the firm age at the time of IPOs.
Ln(*Total asset*) is the natural logarithm of the total asset.
Ln(*Tobin's Q*) is the natural logarithm of the Tobin's Q.
Intangible assets/total assets is defined as the amount of intangible assets divided by the amount of total assets.
Year dummies are also included as independent variables but not reported.
The standard error, which is clustered by industry, is reported.
***, ** and * indicate statistical significance at the 1%, 5% and 10% level, respectively.

The coefficient of the *Main bank bad loan ratio* is positive and statistically significant at the 1 percent level in each estimate. Furthermore, the coefficient of the *Main bank ROA* is negative and statistically significant at least at the 5 percent level. Lastly, the coefficient of the *Main bank MB ratio* is negative and statistically significant in column 3. Overall, these results indicate that firms with higher ratios of bad loans or lower operating per-

Table 24.6 Relationship between bank health and post-IPO long-term stock performance

Variables	(1)	(2)	(3)	(4)	(5)	(6)
	BHAR 1yr			BHAR 3yrs		
Main bank bad loan ratio	−0.524*** (−2.76)			−0.697** (−2.40)		
Main bank ROA		0.454 (0.72)			0.329 (0.60)	
Main bank MB ratio			0.004 (0.76)			0.005 (0.88)
ROA	−0.060 (−0.86)	−0.069 (−0.97)	−0.048 (−0.55)	−0.018 (−0.18)	−0.029 (−0.28)	−0.007 (−0.05)
ln(Age)	0.014** (2.22)	0.013** (2.04)	0.017** (2.25)	0.006 (0.59)	0.004 (0.44)	0.005 (0.47)
ln(Total assets)	0.005 (1.34)	0.005 (1.37)	0.008* (1.70)	0.014*** (2.85)	0.014*** (2.89)	0.020*** (3.57)
ln(Tobin's Q)	0.029*** (5.15)	0.029*** (5.02)	0.031*** (3.94)	0.037*** (4.86)	0.037*** (4.74)	0.032*** (2.85)
Intangible assets/ total asset	−0.131 (−1.22)	−0.122 (−1.11)	−0.091 (−0.85)	−0.095 (−0.67)	−0.085 (−0.61)	−0.060 (−0.35)
Debt ratio	0.008 (0.35)	0.006 (0.24)	−0.014 (−0.51)	0.059** (2.43)	0.056** (2.27)	0.037 (1.12)
Constant	−0.947*** (−25.33)	0.965*** (−25.74)	1.004*** (−22.87)	1.251*** (−27.39)	1.274*** (−26.94)	−1.339*** (−22.92)
Observations	1333	1333	1023	1288	1288	989
R-squared	0.638	0.636	0.647	0.733	0.732	0.739

Notes:
This table shows the relationship between bank health and post-IPO long-term stock performance.
The dependent variable is the one (three) year buy-and-hold abnormal return.
Main bank bad loan ratio is defined as the amount of bad loan divided by the total outstanding loans.
Main bank ROA is the main bank's ROA defined as net income divided by the total assets at the beginning of the period.
Main bank MB ratio is the market book ratio of the main bank.
ROA is the IPO firm's ROA, which is measured as the ratio of operating income to total assets pre-IPO.
Ln(*Age*) is the natural logarithm of the firm age at the time of IPOs.
Ln(*Total asset*) is the natural logarithm of the total assets.
Ln(*Tobin's Q*) is the natural logarithm of the Tobin's Q.
Intangible assets/total assets is defined as the amount of intangible assets divided by the amount of total assets.
Year dummies are also included as independent variables but not reported.
The standard error, which is clustered by industry, is reported.
***, ** and * indicate statistical significance at the 1%, 5% and 10% level, respectively.

formances or lower valuations from the stock market issue equity. The coefficients of *Debt ratio* are positive and statistically significant in all estimates.

Lastly, we investigate whether the insufficient issuing equity caused by the unhealthy banks affects the stock performance of IPO firms. The additional equity issues caused by over-lending from unhealthy banks do not produce additional value. In other words, repaying loans is not a positive NPV project for firms. Such firms may in fact suffer harm to their market valuation.

In Table 24.6, we investigate whether bank health affects post-IPO long-term stock returns. One- or three-year buy-and-hold abnormal returns are used as the dependent variables. The coefficient of *Main bank bad loan ratio* is negative and statistically significant in both specifications. This indicates that the stock returns of IPO firms with banks whose bad loan ratio is high perform worse. The other two bank-related variables also have positive coefficients, but these are not statistically significant. Overall, these results may be weak evidence that bank health affects a firm's post-IPO performance.

4 CONCLUSION

This chapter has investigated how bank health affects the capital structure of firms, especially those planning IPOs, and thus influences decision-making within IPO firms. Previous researchers have argued that the firm–bank relationship has disadvantages, including the hold-up problem and capital misallocation during banking sector crises. This chapter has demonstrated that poor-health banks lend more money to their client firms that intend to go public. We have also found that to resolve the over-lending, firms issue more shares than they need, or the probability of the subsequent SEO increases. Lastly, the empirical evidence has revealed that such insufficient capital raising at the time of IPO and pre-IPO reduces long-term stock performance.

Following the recent US banking shock, a number of studies have examined the impact on the productivity of the real sector. Empirical evidence in this chapter supports the theory that Japanese banks also try to seek alternative funding sources. This behavior is similar to that of US banks in the recent banking shock (Acharya et al., 2009; Ivashina and Scharfstein, 2010).

We believe that focusing on the IPO market does not reduce the generality of these findings. The initial public offering is a unique event for a firm; most firms undergo it only once. Banks, however, support a number of their clients in going public. In addition, because it is widely known when firms will go public, it is easy for banks to forecast how much funding their client firms will gain from IPOs.

NOTES

1. The author wishes to thank the participants of the 2011 AJBS annual conference.
2. We tried to find other data sources such as IPO prospectuses; however, no data sources were found that disclosed the loans and the names of banks that IPO firms borrow from before IPOs.

REFERENCES

Acharya, V., I. Gujral and H. Shin (2009), 'Dividends and bank capital in the financial crisis of 2007–2009', SSRN Discussion Paper Series 1362299.
Akiyoshi, F. and K. Kobayashi (2010), 'Banking crisis and productivity of borrowing firms: evidence from Japan', *Japan and the World Economy*, **22** (3), 141–50.
Baker, M. and J. Wurgler (2002), 'Market timing and capital structure', *Journal of Finance*, **57** (1), 1–32.

Bolton, P. and D. Scharfstein (1996), 'Optimal debt structure and the number of creditors', *Journal of Political Economy*, **104** (1), 1–25.
Chava, S. and A. Purnanandam (2011), 'The effect of banking crisis on bank-dependent borrowers', *Journal of Financial Economics*, **99** (1), 116–35.
Fukuda, S. and S. Koibuchi (2007), 'The impacts of "shock therapy" on large and small clients: experiences from two large bank failures in Japan', *Pacific-Basin Finance Journal*, **15** (5), 434–51.
Gibson, M. (1995), 'Can bank health affect investment? Evidence from Japan', *Journal of Business*, **68** (3), 281–308.
Gibson, M. (1997), 'More evidence on the link between bank health and investment in Japan', *Journal of the Japanese and International Economies*, **11** (3), 296–310.
Hoshi, T. and A. Kashyap (2001), 'The Japanese banking crisis: where did it come from and how will it end?', B.S. Bernanke and K.S. Rogoff (eds), *NBER Macroeconomics Annual*, Cambridge, MA: MIT Press, pp. 129–201.
Hoshi, T. and A. Kashyap (2004), 'Japan's financial crisis and economic stagnation', *Journal of Economic Perspectives*, **18** (1), 3–26.
Hoshi, T. and A. Kashyap (2010), 'Will the U.S. bank recapitalization succeed? Eight lessons from Japan', *Journal of Financial Economics*, **97** (3), 398–417.
Hoshi, T., A. Kashyap and D. Scharfstein (1991), 'Corporate structure, liquidity, and investment: evidence from Japanese industrial groups', *Quarterly Journal of Economics*, **106** (1), 33–60.
Hubbard, G., K. Kuttner and D. Palia (2002), 'Are there bank effects in borrowers' costs of funds? Evidence from a matched sample of borrowers and banks', *Journal of Business*, **75** (4), 559–81.
Ivashina, V. and D. Scharfstein (2010), 'Bank lending during the financial crisis of 2008', *Journal of Financial Economics*, **97** (3), 319–38.
Kang, J. and R. Stulz (2000), 'Do banking shocks affect borrowing firm performance? An analysis of the Japanese experience', *Journal of Business*, **73** (1), 1–23.
Loughran, T. and J.R. Ritter (1995), 'The new issues puzzle', *Journal of Finance*, **50** (1), 23–51.
Lowry, M. (2003), 'Why does IPO volume fluctuate so much?', *Journal of Financial Economics*, **67** (1), 3–40.
Peek, J. and E. Rosengren (2005), 'Unnatural selection: perverse incentives and the misallocation of credit in Japan', *American Economic Review*, **95** (4), 1144–66.
Rajan, R. (1992), 'Insiders and outsiders: the choice between informed and arm's-length debt', *Journal of Finance*, **47** (4), 1367–400.
Von Thadden, E. (2004), 'Asymmetric information, bank lending and implicit contracts: the winner's curse', *Finance Research Letters*, **1** (1), 11–23.
Weinstein, D. and Y. Yafeh (1998), 'On the costs of a bank-centered financial system: evidence from the changing main bank relations in Japan', *Journal of Finance*, **53** (2), 625–72.

Index

Abbreviations used in the index:

BDL – backdoor listing
LBO – leveraged buyout
M&As – mergers and acquisitions
PE – private equity
RLBO – reverse leveraged buyout
SEO – seasoned equity offering
VC – venture capital

abnormal returns
  around lockup expiry 278–81
  measurement 282–3, 303
  see also BHAR (buy-and-hold abnormal returns)
Abukari, K. 300
Acharya, V. 554
acquisition of entrepreneurial firms 186–9
acquisitions by IPOs 347–72
  likelihood 358–63
  and performance 364–71
  statistics 352–8
Acs, Z.J. 180
adverse selection 183–4
age of firm and IPO performance 438–40, 451
Aggarwal, R. 210, 259, 333
Aghion, P. 196
AIM (Alternative Investment Market) 25, 237–52
Alberta Stock Exchange 127
Alexander, G. 547
Allen, F. 103, 119, 421, 437
Almeida, H. 330
Alternative Investment Market (AIM) 25, 237–52
Alti, A. 77, 85, 87, 96, 379, 384
Amihud, Y. 60, 332
analyst coverage, and IPO performance 257–73
analyst recommendations and IPO duration 169–72
Ang, J. 59
Angel, J. 103, 104, 106
Anti-Director Rights Index (ARI) 143, 144, 536, 541–3, 545
Appadu, N. 299
asset market value 112
auctions 209–10
Audretsch, D.B. 180, 183, 186, 192, 193

Australia
  backdoor listings 503–4, 505–29
  venture capital and private equity IPOs 400–417
backdoor listing 503–29
Bae, K.-H. 330
Bailey, W. 534, 547
Baker, G.P. 185, 186
Baker, H.K. 58, 547
Baker, K. 102
Baker, M. 192, 234, 406, 555
Ball, E. 54
Ball, R. 534
Bancel, F. 58, 59, 60, 62–4, 69, 71
Banerjee, S. 87, 96
bank health
  and capital structure and performance of IPO firms 552–66
  and financial leverage pre-IPO 559, 560–61
  and primary shares 559, 561–2
  and probability of SEOs 562–5
  and stock performance 560, 565–6
Bankruptcy Law (Royal Decree 267/42), Italy 144, 145
banks 194–5
  Japanese banking crisis and IPO market 554–6
  relationship with firms 553–4
  see also bank health
Barber, B. 404
Baron, D. 421
Bascha, A. 197
Bayar, O. 54
Beatty, R. 312, 421, 427, 440
Benninga, S. 379
Benveniste, L.M. 77, 85, 95, 161, 210, 216, 219, 332, 421

Berle, A.A. 179
Bertoni, F. 210–11, 216
Bertrand, M. 330–31
Bessler, W. 299, 300, 321, 351, 371, 421, 422, 428, 437, 444
Beuselinck, C. 183
BHARs (buy-and-hold abnormal returns) 260–61, 303, 305–6, 313
  following corporate activities 364–71
  German IPOs 432
  orphan and non-orphan IPOs 262–72
BHR (buy-and-hold returns) 305, 307–8, 313
Bhushan, R. 259
Billett, M.T. 351, 372
Birley, S. 190
Bishop, K. 405
Bittelmeyer, C. 299
Björnali, E. 193
Black, B.S. 59, 197
Blass, A. 533, 543
Block, J. 496
boards of directors 191–3
Boehmer, B. 210
Boehmer, E. 534
Boivie, S. 405
Bolton, P. 196, 281
Bonardo, D. 188, 198, 299
bonding hypothesis 532, 536, 545
book-building 209
  and underpricing 332–3
  and underwriter reputation 161–6
Booth, J. 219
Boreiko, D. 210
Bornstein, P. 135, 137
Bortolotti, B. 531
Bottazzi, L. 197, 198
Boubaker, S. 259
Boubakri, N. 548
Bouis, R. 161, 162
Boutchkova, M. 531, 534
Bradley, D. 54, 59, 169, 257–8, 259, 271, 275, 278, 279
Bradshaw, M.T. 331
Brancato, C. 119
Brau, J.C. 54, 58, 59, 66–7, 67–8, 69, 101, 187, 275, 278, 279, 280, 347, 349, 350, 361, 370, 371, 372, 379, 504
Brav, A. 260, 275, 276, 278, 279, 280, 402, 405, 411
Brennan, M. 103, 104, 106, 333
Brunninge, O. 192
Bruton, G. 403, 405, 416
Burhop, C. 143
Burton, B. 69–71
business group ownership structure 329–31

Bustamante, M.C. 87, 96
buyout sponsors 377, 392–6

Canada
  IPO exits 477–9, 481
  junior IPO market 124–39
  VC investment 466–500
Canadian Venture Exchange (CDNX) 126
Cao, J.X. 375, 378, 384
capital asset pricing model (CAPM) 431
capital market development and cross-listing 535, 545
Capital Pool Company (CPC) program 125, 126–8, 134–8
capital recovery 35–54
Cardon, M.S. 190
Carhart, M. 422
Carhart four-factors model 431
Carpentier, C. 467
Carter, R. 219, 405
cashing-out, IPOs and RTOs 509, 516, 528
Celikyurt, U. 349, 354, 361
certification hypothesis 219, 402–3, 411
Chambers, D. 76, 149
Chang, S.J. 330
change of control in reverse takeover 505–6
Chaplinsky, S. 547, 549
Chava, S. 554
Chemmanur, T. 54, 58, 59, 62, 63, 222, 233, 259
Choe, H. 61
Chou, D. 376
civil-law countries, motivations for going public 69–71
Clarysse, B. 192
Cliff, M. 257, 259
Coakley, J. 403, 407, 416
Cochrane, J. 36, 40, 42
Coffee, J. 532, 535
Colaco, H.M.J. 159, 161
Colak, G. 61, 87, 350
Colombo, M. 188, 198
commission charged by underwriters 134
Companies Act and directors' trading 277–8
competition and corporate governance 185–90
Conroy, R. 118
control change in reverse takeover 505–6
Cornelli, F. 210, 234, 333
corporate events post-IPO 347–72
  likelihood 358–63
  and long-term performance 364–71
  statistics 352–8
corporate governance 179–200
  institutional mechanisms 190–99
  market mechanisms 185–90
  regulations 198–9

corruption and underpricing 335, 340
Corwin, S. 258, 259
cost of capital as motivation for IPO 60, 64, 66
costs of IPO 60–61, 64
CPC (Capital Pool Company) program 125, 126–8, 134–8
creditor rights index 143, 144
cross-listing in share-issue privatizations 531–49
Cumming, D. 137, 401, 466, 482, 493
Curley, A.J. 327, 332

D'Mello, R. 102
D'Souza, J. 534, 545, 548
Da Rin, M. 197
da Silva Rosa, R. 401, 407
Daily, C.M. 192
Dalton, D. 192
Das, S. 259
Davis, G.F. 331
De Luca, G. 149
De Meza, D. 196
DeAngelo, H. 60
DeAngelo, L. 60
debt as governance mechanism 195
Degeorge, F. 210, 376, 380
DeGraw, I. 67–8
delisting post-IPO 22–3
demand satisfaction ratio 213
Demirgüç-Kunt, A. 68
Demsetz, H. 200
Denis, D. 60, 257, 259
Derrien, F. 234, 505
DeTienne, D.R. 190
Dimson, E. 76, 149
directors' trading around lockup expiry 275–92
  impact on share price 280
  measurement 282
  regulations, UK 277–8
disclosure standards and cross-listing decisions 535–6
divestitures and IPO performance 347–72
Djankov, S. 145, 545
Doidge, C. 239, 531, 532, 534, 536
DPI Multiple 50
duration of transaction, see IPO duration
Dyck, A. 536

economic development level and cross-listing 545–8
economies of scope 11–34
Ellis, K. 259
Elston, J.A. 421, 426, 428
English-system countries, motivations for going public 69–71

entrepreneurial firms, corporate governance 179–200
ePals Corporation 125
Espenlaub, S. 143, 239, 275, 276, 277, 279–80
Estrin, S. 531
EU-regulated market, Frankfurt Stock Exchange 423–4, 440, 444
Europe
  IPO activity 11–34
  motivations for going public 62–4, 68–71
  second-tier markets 25–9, 124, 237–52
  securities regulation 13–14
  underwriters in second tier markets 240–42
exchange-regulated (unregulated) markets 240
  Open Market, Frankfurt Stock Exchange 423–4, 440, 444
exit mechanisms in corporate governance 190–91
exit rate
  Canada 481
  compared with M&A 35–9
  reasons for decline 38–9
exit returns, IPOs and M&As 39–48
exit strategies 189–90, 392–6
  as motivation for going public 59–60, 64

Faccio, M. 531
Facebook 275
Falkenstein, E. 102
Fama, E. 112, 186, 189, 260
Fama and French three factors model (FF3F) 262, 264, 265, 351–2, 364, 404, 410, 431, 448
family-owned groups and underpricing 328
Faulhaber, G. 421, 437
Fawcett, S.E. 58, 66–7, 101, 349, 361
Fernandes, N. 531
Fernando, C.S. 101, 102, 104, 161
Fidrmuc, J.P. 276
Field, L.C. 275, 276, 278–9, 280
Filatotchev, I. 405
file delay 220, 222
  and age of VC backer 231–2
  and offer delay 232–3
  and short-run performance 223–30
financial analyst coverage and IPO performance 257–73
financial analyst recommendations and IPO duration 169–72
financial crises
  and German equity market 426–7
  and German IPO performance 455
  and underpricing 429
  and VC activity 496–9

financial flexibility as motivation for going public 60, 62
financial leverage, effect of bank health 559, 560–61
financial structure, entrepreneurial and newly listed firms 194–8
financing hypothesis and likelihood of acquisition 358, 361
firm–bank relationship 553–4
firm size
  and cross-listing decisions 534
  and performance 19–20
  and profitability 19–20
  and second-tier markets 25–9
first-day return, see underpricing
Fleming, G. 401
Floros, I. 509, 516, 517
Foerster, S. 533, 534–5
foreign listings in European markets 15, 21–2; see also cross-listing
Francis, B. 300
Frankel, R. 106
Frankfurt Stock Exchange 423–4
Franks, J. 333
fraud
  and CPC program 135–7
  in entrepreneurial firms 182–3
French, K. 112, 164, 186, 260; see also Fama and French three-factors model
Fukuda, S. 554
Fulghieri, P. 58, 59, 62, 63
funding for growth as motivation for going public 58–9, 62

GAAP (generally accepted accounting principles) 424–5
  compared with IFRS 425–6
Gajewski, J.-F. 299
Gallagher, P. 102
Gamba, A. 60
Gao, X. 11, 13, 20, 33, 210, 239, 297, 319
geographic location and performance 442, 444
Gerakos, J. 239
Germany 421–56
  Frankfurt Stock Exchange 423–4
  IFRS adoption 424–6, 453–5
  impact of financial crisis 426–7, 455
  IPO performance 427–56
  long-term IPO performance 444–8
  short-term IPO performance 437–22
Gibson, M. 554, 556
Gilson, R.J. 59, 197
Giot, P. 379, 385, 401
Giudici, G. 210–11, 216

Gleason, K. 504, 508, 510
Goergen, M. 275, 299
Goldreich, D. 210, 333
Goldstein, M. 119, 312
Gompers, P. 102, 119, 192, 219, 220, 259, 260, 275, 276, 278, 279, 280, 300, 398, 402, 405, 406, 411
Gopalan, R. 330
governance, see corporate governance
Graham, J.R. 60
grandstanding 220, 233, 234, 300–301, 402–3
Granstrand, O. 187
green-shoe option 210
Gregory, A. 239
Gresse, C. 299
Grimpe, C. 188
Grinblatt, M. 421, 437
Gulbrandson, M. 193
Günay, H. 61, 87

Habib, M.A. 160
Hamza, O. 301
Hanka, G. 275, 276, 278–9, 280
Hanley, K.W. 209, 210, 332, 333
Hansen, C. 192
Hart, O. 179, 194
Harvey, C.R. 60
Hasan, I. 300
Hegde, S.P. 159, 161
Hellman, T. 184
Helwege, J. 76, 77, 85, 87, 88, 91, 95
Henkel, J. 188
Hermalin, B.E. 191
Hibara, N. 312
Hirschman, A.O. 190
Hoberg, G. 273
hold-up problems and firm–bank relationship 553–4
Holmström, B. 64, 421
Holthausen, R.W. 376, 380, 384
Hong, J. 330
Horton, J. 426, 429
Hoshi, T. 553, 554
hot markets 85–95
  industry concentration 88–91
  and performance 313
  proceeds raised 92–5
  and underpricing 312
Hovakimian, A. 349, 350, 355, 356, 361, 363
Howe, J.S. 350
Hsieh, J. 59
Hsu, S. 300
Hubbard, G. 554
Hughes, P. 103, 104, 106

Hulle, C. 60
Humphrey, N. 517, 518
Hunger, A. 421, 423, 427, 437, 440, 442
Hussinger, K. 188
Hutton, I. 349, 350, 355, 356, 361, 363
Huyghebaert, N. 60
Hwang, C. 421, 437

Ibbotson, R. 81, 332, 421, 427, 432
IFRS (International Financial Reporting Standards)
  accounting quality 425
  and German equity market 424–7
  and IPO performance, Germany 453–5
  and underpricing 429, 453
industry area and cross-listing 533, 540, 543–4, 545
industry distribution
  of CPC firms 137–8
  and hot markets 85, 88–91
  of RLBOs 381
information gathering by investors 103
initial public offerings (IPOs), *see* IPOs
initial returns and volume 81–3
innovation and venture capital finance 465–6
institution-level factors affecting cross-listing decisions 534–7, 544–5
institutional investors
  information gathering 103–4
  and IPO offer price 104, 111, 116–17
  share allocation 210, 211, 217
institutional ownership
  and IPO offer price 104, 111, 116–17
  and value of firm 116
International Financial Reporting Standards, *see* IFRS
investment, *see* venture capital
investor protection
  and IPO survival 142–3, 146–55
  Italy 143–5
IPOs
  characteristics 315–20, 405–6
  and venture capital 300–301, 465–500
IPO activity
  compared with M&As 35–7
  Europe 11–34
  reasons for decline 38–9
  US 13
  see also IPO waves
IPO duration (IPOD) 159–73
  and analyst recommendations 169–72
  compared with BDLs 509, 514, 516–18
  and price and share amendments 167–9
  and underwriters 160–62
IPO performance, *see* performance

IPO proceeds, *see* proceeds of IPOs
IPO scaling ratio 213
IPO timing 61, 64, 66–7, 375–7, 385–92
IPO waves
  Europe 295–323
  and follow-on corporate events 352–3
  and future VC activity 321–2
  and hot markets, UK 76–96
  and long-run performances 297, 304–10, 313–21
  and underpricing 297, 304–12
issue size and performance 442, 444
Italy
  allocation and pricing strategies 211–16
  investor protection 143–5
  investor protection and IPO survival 141–2, 146–55
  motivations for going public 71
Ivashina, V. 554

Jaffe, J. 81, 421, 427, 432
Jain, B. 259, 319, 380, 403, 411, 416, 417
James, C. 259
Japan
  bank health and IPO structure 556–66
  financial crisis and IPO market 554–6
Jegadeesh, N. 332, 350
Jenkinson, T. 210
Jensen, M.C. 61, 179, 181–2, 375, 505
Jiang, Y. 370
Jog, V. 300, 312
Johan, S.A. 137
Johnson, S. 536
Jones, H. 210
Jumpstart Our Business Startup (JOBS) Act 39
junior markets, *see* second-tier markets

Kadapakkam, P. 118
Kang, J. 534, 549
Kaplan, S. 298, 398
Karceski, J. 259
Karolyi, A. 531, 532, 533, 535
Kashyap, A. 554
Kecskes, A. 505
Kennedy, R.E. 185, 186
Khanna, T. 330
Khorana, A. 258
Khurshed, A. 416
Kim, E.H. 331
Kim, W. 59, 62
Kini, O. 259, 319, 380, 403, 411, 416, 417
Klein, A. 361
Koibuchi, S. 554
Kooli, M. 301

Krigman, L. 160–61, 257, 258
Krishnan, C. 403
Krishnan, K. 222, 233
Kuo, R. 517, 518
Kurth, A. 299, 428

La Porta, R. 68, 141, 143, 145, 146, 154, 329, 532, 536, 537, 541, 545
Labégorre, F. 259
labour-sponsored venture capital corporations (LSVCC) 467, 482–94
Lang, M. 259, 534, 547
Larcker, D.F. 376, 380, 384
large shareholders 193–4
lead–lag relationship between initial returns and volume 81–3
Lee, P. 220, 300
Leff, N.H. 329
legal environment
  and corporate governance 198–9
  and cross-listing decisions 535–7, 540–43, 545
Lehmann, E.E. 186, 188, 197
Lel, U. 196, 532
Lerner, J. 259, 298, 375, 378, 384, 411
Levis, M. 299, 320, 370, 407
Li, D. 466
Li, X. 235
Liang, N. 76, 77, 85, 87, 88, 91, 95
limited partnership venture capital funds 467
Lin, H. 426
Lintner, J. 57
liquidity, IPOs and RTOs 508
listing
  advantages and costs 503
  backdoor listing 503–29
  by introduction 505
  standards, Canada 467
Ljungqvist, A. 106, 160, 210, 234, 406, 421, 427, 437, 453
lockup agreements 275–6, 277, 279–80
lockup expiry and director trading 275–92
Logue, D.E. 332
Lombardo, S. 210
London Alternative Investment Market (AIM) 25, 237–52
long-term performance
  and analyst coverage 260–73
  and economies of scope hypothesis 14–15, 19–20
  following corporate activity 350–51, 364–71
  German IPOs 444–8
  and IPO waves 306–9, 313
  and underpricing 303–9
  and VC/PE backing 403

Loughran, T. 59, 164, 209, 257, 259, 312, 333, 334, 379–80, 405, 421, 432, 555
Loutskina, E. 259
Lowry, M. 61, 76, 81, 95, 299, 350, 555
LSVCC (labour-sponsored venture capital corporations) 467, 482–94
Lyandres, E. 59
Lyon, J. 261, 404

M&A, *see* mergers and acquisitions
MacIntosh, J. 124, 401, 482, 493
Majluf, N. 60
Maksimovic, V. 58, 61, 62, 68
manager portfolio sizes, Canada 479–81
Manaster, S. 219
Manigart, S. 183
Marchisio, G. 71
market capitalization, second market IPOs 246
market classification and IPO performance 451–3
market conditions
  and IPO performance 451
  and volume of IPO activity 83–5
  see also hot markets
market conditions hypothesis 11, 12
market feedback hypothesis 350
  and likelihood of acquisition 361
markets
  for corporate control in entrepreneurial firms 186–9
  for managers in entrepreneurial firms 189–90
  for secondaries 499
  see also second-tier markets
market grandstanding hypothesis 234
market mechanisms and corporate governance 185–90
market misevaluation hypothesis 349
market timing
  decisions 61, 64, 66–7, 375
  and performance of quick flips 389–92
  and RLBOs 388–9
market timing hypothesis
  and corporate events 361
  and hot markets 85
  and LBOs 376, 388
market-to-book ratios and IPO waves 318
market valuation of IPO firms 77–9, 108–9
  as motivation for going public 66
Masulis, R. 235, 334
Mathew, P. 312
Maug, E. 60
McInish, T. 118
Means, G.C. 179
Meckling, W.H. 61, 179, 181–2

Mediobanca 149
Megginson, W.L. 113, 219, 411, 531, 534, 535, 545
Meles, A. 403
Mello, A.S. 59, 333
Mendelson, H. 60
Meoli, M. 248, 299
mergers and acquisitions (M&A) activity 15, 22–3
  capital recovery 52–3
  returns compared with IPOs 35–54
mergers and acquisitions strategy as motivation for going public 59, 64, 66
Merton, R. 59, 102, 105, 534
Metrick, A. 102, 119, 320
Michaely, R. 332
Michel, J. 234
Miller, D. 532
Miller, E. 233
Miller, M.H. 60, 194
Minichilli, A. 192
Mitchell, M.L. 431
Mittoo, U.R. 58, 59, 60, 62–4, 69, 71
Model Code of the London Stock Exchange 278
Modigliani, F. 60, 194
'money left on the table' 327
moral hazard in entrepreneurial firms 182–3
Morck, R. 331
motivations for going public 57–72
  European firms 62–4
  Italian firms 71
  US firms 66–8
Muscarella, C. 102, 379
Myers, S. 60

Netter, J. 531
Neue Markt, Frankfurt Stock Exchange 424, 440, 444
Nomads (Nominated Advisors) 126, 237–8, 240–42, 248–52

O'Brien, P. 259
Oehler, A. 427
Ofek, E. 275, 278, 281
offer delay and file delay 232–3
offer price, *see* pricing
Open Markets, Frankfurt Stock Exchange 423–4, 440, 444
operating performance around sponsor's exit 396
optimal IPO timing 375, 398
orphan and non-orphan IPOs 257–73
overallotment option 216

over-lending by poor-health banks 552–3, 556–66
oversubscription ratio 211–13
overvaluation 233–4
ownership structure
  and analyst coverage 259, 266–7
  Australian IPOs, VC/PE backing 407–8
  and IPO pricing 327–41
  measurement 405
  post-IPO RLBOs 392–6

Paananen, M. 426
Pagano, M. 57, 60, 61, 71, 77, 83, 85, 95, 533, 534, 536, 540
Palepu, K. 330
Park, Y.S. 330
Parrino, R. 104
Parsons, J.E. 59, 333
passive control 190–91
Pastor, L. 375, 376, 398
Pástor, V. 76, 83, 87, 95
Patricof, Alan 39
pension commitments, Australian venture market 400–401
performance
  and analyst coverage 257–73
  and bank health 560, 565–6
  and follow-on corporate events 364–71
  Germany 427–56
  around lockup expiry 288–9
  and VC/PE investment 400–417
performance timing hypothesis 376, 382–4, 385–8
Pichler, P. 58, 61, 62
Pilcher, J.C. 57
Piotroski, J. 239
portfolio sizes, Canada 479–81
post-IPO period
  acquisitions, SEOs and divestitures 347–72
  M&A activity and delisting 22–3
  sponsor presence 377, 392–6
Poulsen, A. 54, 504
Powell, G. 102
price amendments and IPO duration 168, 169
pricing
  impact of directors' trading on share price 275, 278–80, 287–9
  and ownership structure 327–41
  price selection 101–18
  see also underpricing
primary shares, effect of bank health 559, 561
private equity investment 124
  crowded out by LSVCCs 491–3
  and IPO performance, Australia 400–417
  and reverse LBOs 375–7

privatization and cross-listing 531–49
proceeds of IPOs
  European second markets 131
  in hot markets 92–5
  TSX-V 128–32
  by underwriter type 133–4
product market and cross-listing decisions 534, 544
profitability
  and backdoor listing 508–9
  and economies of scope 14, 17–19
Pryshchepa, O. 421–2, 422, 429, 444
Pulliam, S. 333
Purnanandam, A. 233, 554
pyramidal layers and underpricing 328, 335, 337–40

quick flips 378–9, 389–92

Rabimov, S. 119
Rajan, R. 60, 68, 259, 553
Ramchand, L. 547, 549
Rasch, S. 124
Rau, P. 29, 299, 350
Ravasi, D. 71
Rees, W.P. 76
Reese, W. 532–3, 534, 536
Regulated Market, Frankfurt Stock Exchange 423–4, 440, 444
regulations
  Europe 13–14
  and IPO activity 239
  and IPO survival 142–3
  TSX-V and European second markets 126
  see also IFRS
regulatory overreach hypothesis 11
Reilly, F.K. 332
reputation
  as motivation for going public 66
  of underwriter, *see* underwriter reputation
research institutes as shareholders 197–8
retained ownership, IPOs and BDLs 509–10, 514
Reuer, J. 187
reverse leveraged buyouts (RLBOs) 375–98
  and IPO timing 375–7, 385–92
  sponsor presence post-IPO 377, 392–6
reverse takeover (RTO) 503–29
Richardson, M. 275, 278, 281
Riemer, D.S. 135
Ritter, J.R. 20, 59, 164, 207, 209, 210, 257, 259, 262, 299, 312, 313, 327, 332, 333, 347, 379, 380, 405, 421, 423, 427, 432, 440, 442, 444, 448, 451, 555
RLBOs, *see* reverse leveraged buyouts

Rocholl, J. 210
Rock, K. 216, 219, 421, 427, 440
Röell, A. 61
Romano, R. 535
Rosenfeld, J. 361
Royal Decree 262/42 (Civil Code), Italy 144
Royal Decree 267/42 (Bankruptcy Law), Italy 144, 145
Ruback, R. 505
Ryan, P. 67–8

Samila, S. 466
Sanders, W. 405
Sapusek, A. 421, 428
Sarbanes–Oxley Act (SOX) 11, 38–9
Sarkissan, S. 534, 536
Saudagaran, S. 533
Scharfstein, D. 554
Schill, M. 534, 536
Schlag, C. 453
Schultz, P. 102, 103, 258, 259, 372, 377, 398
Schumpeter, J. 185
Schuster, J. 421
Schwert, G.W. 61, 76, 81, 95, 350
Schwienbacher, A. 379, 385, 401
seasoned equity offerings (SEOs)
  and bank health 562–5
  and IPO performance 347–72
  likelihood 358–63
  volume of activity 355–6
second-tier markets
  Canada 124–39
  Europe 25–9, 240, 243–4
  underwriters, Europe 237–8, 239–52
secondaries market 499
securities regulation in Europe 13–14
Seim, M. 299–300
sell-out to publicly listed firm 503, 504–5
SEOs, *see* seasoned equity offerings
separation of ownership and control 181–2
Servaes, H. 259
Seyhun, H. 273
share allocation 207–17
share amendments and IPO duration 168–9
share-issue privatizations, cross-listing 531–49
share offering size and cross-listing 537–40, 543
share price, *see* pricing
shareholder rights and cross-listing 535–7, 540–43, 545
Shastri, K. 509, 516, 517
Shaw, W.H. 332
Shen, J.-C. 187
Sherman, A.E. 209, 210, 333
Shin, H.-H. 330

Shleifer, A. 181
short-term performance
　German IPOs 437–42
　impact of file delay 223–30
Sibilkov, V. 60
signaling theories of underpricing 332
Simon, C.J. 142
Sjolander, S. 187
Sjostrom, W. 504
small firms
　IPO activity decline 11–12, 17
　performance 19–20
　profitability 17–19
Smith, R. 219, 333
Soderstrom, N. 426
Sorenson, O. 466
SPACs (special purpose acquisition corporations) 125
Spamann, H. 536, 545
Spatt, C.S. 332
special purpose acquisition corporations (SPACs) 125
Spindt, P.A. 216, 219, 332, 421
sponsors
　buyout timing 375–7, 382–92
　post-IPO presence 377, 392–6
Srinivasan, S. 239
Srivastava, S. 332
Stafford, E. 431
Stanzel, M. 299
Stegemoller, M. 54, 504
Stehle, R. 421–2, 422, 429, 444
Stephan, P. 193
Stern, R.L. 135, 137
Stiglitz, J.E. 195
stock liquidity enhancement as motivation for going public 60
stock market index and IPOs, Japan 555–6
Stoll, H.R. 118, 327, 332
Stoughton, N.M. 333
Stouraitis, A. 299, 350
Stromberg, P. 398
Stulz, R. 532, 534, 549
Subrahmanyam, A. 535
Suchard, J. 401
Sun, K. 426
survey method 57
survival rates
　AIM companies 239
　Italian IPO firms 150–51
　and M&A activity 15
Swaminathan, B. 233

Tekatli, N. 350
Thies, S. 421, 422, 428, 437, 444

Thomadakis, S. 421, 432
time-series regressions on IPO activity 29–33
timing of IPO 61, 64, 66–7, 375–7, 385–92
Tirole, J. 64
Titman, S. 333, 535
Toronto Stock Exchange Venture Market (TSX-V) 124–34
tradable goods production and cross-listing decisions 534, 544
Triantis, A. 60
TSX-V (Toronto Stock Exchange Venture Market) 124–34
tunneling 330–31
TVPI Multiple 50
Tykvová, T. 299

Udell, G. 196
UK, *see* United Kingdom
underpricing 327, 332–3
　and analyst coverage 259
　BDLs and RTOs 516, 518
　Germany 427–8, 429, 432–42
　and IPO waves 306–9, 309–12
　and ownership structure 334–41
　reduction through BDL 510
　and underwriter characteristics 249
underwriter reputation 113
　and IPO duration 160–61
　and IPO offer price levels 117
　measurement 164
　and value of firm 116
underwriters
　characteristics 246–8
　efficiency 161–2, 166
　Europe 240–42
　European second markets 237–52
　and IPO allocations and pricing 210
　and IPO performance 249
　IPOs and BDLs 516, 529
　TSX-V IPOs 132–4
　and underpricing 249
　see also underwriter reputation
United Kingdom
　directors' trading around lockup expiry 281–92
　hot markets 85–95
　IPO market 76–96
　IPO waves 81–5
　lockup agreements 275–6, 277
United States
　IPO cycles 76
　IPO decline 13, 297
　lockup agreements 275–6
　motivations for going public 66–8, 68–9

VC investment in Canada 480–81, 494, 496–8, 499–500
universities as shareholders 197–8
unregulated (exchange-regulated) markets 240
US, *see* United States

value of firm 115–16
value-to-assets measure 112
Van Praag, C.M. 189
Van Tendeloo, B. 426
Vanstraelen, A. 426
venture capital 124, 298–9, 300–301, 465–6
　age of VC and file delay 231–2
　and analyst coverage 259, 265
　Australia 401–2, 404–17
　Canada 465–500
　capital recovery, IPO and M&A exits 35–54
　future activity 321–2
　investment timing and IPO pricing 219–34
　and IPO performance 402–4
　and IPO waves in Europe 295–323
venture capitalists and governance of entrepreneurial firms 196–7
Vermaelen, T. 59
Veronesi, P. 76, 83, 87, 95, 375, 398
Vetsuypens, M. 102, 379
Vijh, A.M. 59
Vishny, R.W. 181
Vismara, S. 12, 25, 33, 96, 124, 126, 129–31, 299, 430
voice 190
Volpin, P. 536
von Thadden, E.-L. 281

Wahal, S. 220, 300
Waltz, U. 197
Wang, C. 403
Wang, L. 312
Warner Bros Music 379
Wasserfallen, W. 421, 427
Webb, D. 196
Weinstein, D. 554
Weisbach, M.S. 59, 62, 191, 532–3, 534, 536
Weiss, A. 195
Weiss, K. 219, 411
Weiss, V.A. 113
Welch, I. 59, 207, 262, 327, 332, 333, 349, 421, 437
Weld, W. 118
Westhead, P. 190
Wilhelm, W.J. 210, 332, 333
Wittleder, C. 421, 427
Wodrich, A. 453
Wolfenzon, D. 330
Wood, R. 118
Wurgler, J. 555

Yafeh, Y. 533, 543, 554
Yang, J.J. 421, 426, 428
Yasuda, A. 320
Yeung, B. 331
Yung, C. 87

Zechner, J. 333
Zeckhauser, R. 376, 380
Zhang, S. 350
Zhdanov, A. 59
Zimmerman, J. 300, 351, 371
Zingales, L. 59, 68, 184, 377, 393, 531, 536, 547